FOUNDATIONS FOR
VISUAL
PROJECT ANALYSIS

FOUNDATIONS FOR VISUAL PROJECT ANALYSIS

edited by

RICHARD C. SMARDON
JAMES F. PALMER
JOHN P. FELLEMAN

assisted by

ROBERT MARSHALL,
Graphics Editor

JOANN BARONE,
Graphic Artist

A Wiley-Interscience Publication
JOHN WILEY & SONS
New York • Chichester • Brisbane • Toronto • Singapore

Copyright © 1986 by John Wiley & Sons, Inc.

All rights reserved. Published simultaneously in Canada.

Reproduction or translation of any part of this work beyond that permitted by Section 107 or 108 of the 1976 United States Copyright Act without the permission of the copyright owner is unlawful. Requests for permission or further information should be addressed to the Permissions Department, John Wiley & Sons, Inc.

Library of Congress Cataloging in Publication Data:

Main entry under title:
Foundations for visual project analysis.
  A Wiley-Interscience Publication.
  Bibliography: p.
  Includes indexes
  1. Landscape assessment. I. Smardon, Richard C.
II. Palmer, James F., 1950– . III. Felleman, John P.
GF90.F68 1986 712 85-22758
ISBN 0-471-88184-8

Printed in the United States of America

10 9 8 7 6 5 4 3 2 1

CONTRIBUTORS

MIGUEL AGUILO   Universidad Politecnia de Madrid, Escuela Tecnica Superior de Ingenieros de Montes, Catedra de Planificacion y Proyectos, Madrid, Spain

SANTIAGO G. ALONSO   Universidad Politecnia de Madrid, Escuela Tecnica Superior de Ingenieros de Montes, Catedra de Planificacion y Proyectos, Madrid, Spain

WILLIAM G. E. BLAIR   Jones and Jones, Seattle, Washington

RICHARD CHENOWETH   Department of Landscape Architecture, University of Wisconsin, Madison, Wisconsin

TONY COSTELLO   College of Architecture and Planning, Ball State University, Muncie, Indiana

PAUL H. GOBSTER   Department of Landscape Architecture, University of Wisconsin, Madison, Wisconsin

KATE GRINDE   Moscow, Idaho

HARRY EGGINK   College of Architecture and Planning, Ball State University, Muncie, Indiana

JAN JANSSENS   Department of Theoretical and Applied Physics, Lund Institute of Technology, Lund, Sweden

AL KOPF   Asheville Planning Department, Asheville, North Carolina

Rikard Küller Environmental Psychology Unit, Lund Institute of Technology, School of Architecture, Lund, Sweden

Andrej B. Pogačnik University Edvard Kardeljat Ljubljana, Ljubljana, Yugoslavia

Angel Ramos Universidad Politecnia de Madrid, Escuela Tecnica Superior de Ingenieros de Montes, Catedra de Planificacion y Proyectos, Madrid, Spain

Sally Schauman Landscape Architecture Program, College of Architecture and Urban Planning, University of Washington, Seattle, Washington

Stephen R. J. Sheppard Dames and Moore, San Francisco, California

Joseph Stevens Department of Psychology, University of Arizona, Tucson, Arizona

Joanne Vining Institute for Environmental Studies, University of Illinois, Urbana, Illinois

William C. Yeomans Consulting Landscape Architect, Hornby Island, British Columbia, Canada

Ervin H. Zube Landscape Architecture Program, School of Renewable Natural Resources, University of Arizona, Tucson, Arizona

FOREWORD

The foundations of visual project analysis lie within the aesthetics of the landscape. Concentrating on visual dimensions to the exclusion of our other perceptions is an attempt to simplify the complexities of aesthetics, and at the same time recognize that we are primarily visual animals. Dwelling on the visual also allows this particular book to serve its intended purpose of providing a practical means of predicting and controlling the impacts of change within our surroundings. It may also be timely to say that we know more about the visual landscape than we know of its aesthetics. Through visual investigation, we peck away at some of the dilemmas of aesthetics.

Considering the length of time we have been trifling with the American–European landscape, there has been a concurrent history of nature appreciation. Thoreau and Muir expressed some of this appreciation in the nineteenth century, helping to identify a segment of landscape aesthetics. Marsh also foresaw that we needed to conserve this heritage. In the twentieth century, ecologists Leopold and Dasmann continued the tradition of appreciation by discovering only how landscape values may emerge from ecological insight but that good land stewardship—the development of a land ethic—is essential to landscape conservation. The practice of landscape architecture before and during the present century has retained a principle of creating a sensitive relationship with the surrounding landscape, but that concept has not been widely expressed beyond the profession and its works.

By the time of the Lyndon Johnson administration, it appeared legitimate for the Federal government to be concerned with the quality of the landscape. There was earlier evidence of that concern, but it was obscure. The White House Conference on Natural Beauty seemed to be based on an innate feeling—shared by many—that the landscape's beauty and its state of health was important to the quality of life. During the mid-1960s, research was beginning on the visual landscape; it involved a surprisingly diverse group of disciplines in both academic institutions and design-planning-management agencies. The National Environmental Policy Act of 1969 (NEPA) followed, with a broad concern for landscape resources and their contribution to our aesthetic satisfaction. State enactments of environmental protection legislation helped spread an awareness of landscape values beyond the bounds of Federal jurisdictions. NEPA built in the requirement for public hearings, and the environmental thrust of the 1970s brought the voice of public participation into conservation issues. Also during the 1970s, the U.S. Forest Service's policy on visual landscape management came into being and was followed by somewhat similar policies adopted by the Bureau of Land Management. The Soil Conservation Service also developed a strategy for rural landscape conservation. The Federal land management policies, public support of landscape protection, and contemporary practice—both public and private—of the environmental design arts all contribute to a sympathetic atmosphere for the appearance of *Foundations for Visual Project Analysis*. The emergence of the concept that the landscape is a visual resource with aesthetic values has been built on a variably continuous but intermittent stream of historic insights, events, attitudes, legal acts, management policies, and research.

The present state of visual resources analysis and related landscape management methodology is that of a temporary plateau. The field is relatively well known, but it consists of rather disjointed parts and pieces. Management strategies now in place, as in National Forest lands, are subject to improvement from empirical applications and research.

Visual resources research is fragmented now and has been ever since its fairly recent beginnings. This condition reflects the many different disciplines that have had a hand in it; these include social scientists, economists, psychologists, geographers, geologists, hydrologists, engineers, landscape architects, environmental planners, foresters and others. With such a diversity of approaches, it is not surprising that there is as Jay Appleton notes, a "theoretical vacuum" surrounding the research endeavor. Modest financial support has fostered small projects and single disciplines, not multidisciplinary teams that would be desirable for coordinative results. A split has resulted from two different backgrounds and intents: professional design people seeking physical problem solutions and academics looking for basic knowledge about landscape values and peoples' perceptions. Visual resource management schemes have been based on assumptions made before research validations could be accomplished. Research does move at a slower pace than do design and management decisions. Fortunately, we are beginning to see the strengths of research, participation, and professional insight being brought together. This book is a significant contribution to the unification of those different strengths.

What can be said for the future needs of visual resource analysis? What does it need to become? Perhaps it is good to state that the landscape is a distressingly complex phenomenon and that research will slowly and painfully assemble seemingly simple answers. As an aesthetic conception, the landscape is a philosophical object, and yet design, planning, management, and use make pragmatic demands of it. Many attributes of the landscape can be quantitatively measured, which is desirable for analysis; at the same time much of visual analysis must be done qualitatively. It is ridiculous to expect that we will ever have wholly quantitative answers to landscape quality questions. There must also be room left for qualitative responses.

Foundations for Visual Project Analysis describes specific and detailed methods of landscape evaluation and conservation that will flesh out the broadly conceived ideas found in Ian McHarg's *Design with Nature* and Kevin Lynch's *Managing the Sense of a Region*. McHarg and Lynch agree in their integrative approaches, but they cover different levels of scale and detail. This book adds comprehensiveness, alternate methodologies, and different solutions to landscape problems that vary, for example, from the National Forest Landscape Management handbooks that are restricted to national forest policies. The authors of this book bring together concepts and methods that must otherwise be gleaned from numerous articles, emphemeral publications (symposia proceedings), and a relatively small number of hardback books. It should be a welcome reference to students and instructors of the environmental design field, landscape designers and planners, and resource managers in both private practice and public agencies.

R. BURTON LITTON, JR.

PREFACE

In the past decade, project scenic impact analysis has evolved from an academic research subject, to a topic mandated by environmental legislation, to a major daily activity engaged in by public and private offices throughout the United States and Europe. This rapid growth has created a significant information gap, both for practicing professionals with no formal training in the area and for students of the subject who need a comprehensive treatment.

This book is needed because there is no comprehensive resource on the market which addresses this specific subject matter in an intensive and all-encompassing way. The only other comparable books are conference proceedings. There are books and series of books which deal with environmental perception and research, but these do not deal specifically with assessment of the landscape as a visual resource nor are they written for design and planning practitioners. This book is written for design and planning practitioners as well as students concerned with visual resource analysis at the project review level of application. Specific professions and academic programs include landscape architecture, environmental planning, community planning, architecture, civil engineering, resource planning, and environmental impact assessment.

This particular book has four specific objectives:

1. The chapters are structured in a sequential fashion so that the student/reader will progress from elementary material to more complex material.

2. Visual analysis methodological considerations are treated across several environmental contexts, for example, wildland, rural, and urban, but the focus is primarily on the project review level of application.
3. A comprehensive array of landscape description and assessment conceptual approaches and methods are now combined in one book—a novel feature.
4. The last and most important objective of this book is to synthesize from key projects and highly qualified authors the best *practical* visual resource management methods and procedural guidance for students and professionals.

Many of the chapters are commissioned papers that have not appeared before. The editors have attempted to integrate the material as far as referencing one chapter to another. There is no unified approach to visual analysis, but rather a number of approaches with different directional underpinnings. What we have attempted to do is encourage contributing authors to develop decision rules that aid the reader in choosing which approach may be best depending on environmental and decision-making contexts.

In Part 1 we trace basic landscape values development—why we need to manage visual landscapes—and a history of legal consideration of landscape values—major court cases and laws, followed by an overview of the structure in the remainder of the book.

Part 2 is a concise basic primer on visual perception—the mechanics of vision, major findings about how we perceive the landscape, and a summary of the mechanics of visibility assessment—when we can see the landscape and when we can't, and why.

Part 3 presents basic methods and terminology for accurate description and analysis of wildlands, rural countrysides, and urban landscapes.

Part 4 builds directly on the previous section to summarize and show how to do landscape assessment and evaluation, various visual simulations, and visual impact assessments for both natural/rural and urban landscape contexts.

Part 5 is an international sampler to demonstrate that visual landscape analysis is being used on an international basis. Typical state-of-the-art case studies are presented.

Part 6 is a basic illustrated glossary of landscape analysis terminology, concepts, and methods to complement the text. This is followed by a reference section for the whole book.

The book is designed both as a basic textbook in visual project analysis and as a professional reference tool for landscape architects, architects, engineers, planners, and other environmental design professionals.

RICHARD C. SMARDON
JAMES F. PALMER
JOHN P. FELLEMAN

Syracuse, New York
February 1986

ACKNOWLEDGMENTS

This work would have not come about without the encouragement of our editor Bill Salo, who kept in touch with us all the way from our National Landscape Conference at Incline Village, Nevada, in 1979. We would also like to thank our contributors for the overall quality of their work and patience through rewrites. From the United States these individuals include Joseph Stevens, Joanne Vining, and Ervin Zube from the University of Arizona, Tucson; Richard Chenoweth and Paul Gobster from the University of Wisconsin, Madison; Sally Schauman from the University of Washington, Seattle; Stephen Sheppard from Dams and Moore, San Francisco; and William Blair from Jones and Jones, Seattle. Similar thanks go to our international contributors for the same reasons. These individuals include William Yeomans from Victoria, Canada; Andrej Pogačnik from the University Edvard Kardebat Ljubljana, Yugoslavia; Jan Janssens and Rikard Küller from the School of Architecture and the Lund Institute of Technology, Sweden; and Santiago Alonso, Miguel Aguilo, and Angel Ramos from the Universidad Politecnia of Madrid, Spain.

Special gratitude goes to Robert Marshall, who served as graphics editor for part of the production process, to Joanne Barone, the graphic artist who did most of the hand-drawn graphic work and was the major force in graphic coordination, and to Joanne Arany and Harley Kelly, who assisted with the graphic work. Special thanks also go to George Snyder, who did much of the photography and printing, and to Sarah Remon, who faithfully retyped many of the chapter manuscripts. The three editors take responsibility for any omissions, errors, or substantive changes that may have occurred during the technical editing process.

R.C.S.
J.F.P.
J.P.F.

CONTENTS

PART 1 INTRODUCTION

1 LANDSCAPE VALUES: HISTORY, CONCEPTS, AND APPLICATIONS   3
Ervin H. Zube

CONCEPTS OF LANDSCAPE AND LANDSCAPE BEAUTY	**4**
The Modern Concept of Landscape	5
The Beautiful, the Picturesque, and the Sublime	5
Picturesque and Sublime in America	7
Anti-Urbanism	8
Elites and Common Folks	8
The Shaping of American Landscape Values	9
NORMATIVE PUBLIC VALUES	**9**
Landscape Disposal	10
Landscape Preservation	10
Recreation Landscapes	11
Ameliorating Scenic Ills	12
Environmental Planning	13
Recapitulation	13

	IDENTIFYING LANDSCAPE VALUES	14
	Conferences and Symposia	15
	Critiques and Reviews	17
	DISCUSSION	18
2	**DECISION-MAKING MODEL FOR VISUAL RESOURCE MANAGEMENT AND PROJECT REVIEW**	**21**

Richard C. Smardon, John P. Felleman, and James F. Palmer

	THE LEGAL CONTEXT OF SCENIC PROJECT ANALYSIS	22
	Introduction	22
	Jurisdiction	22
	Regulatory Process	22
	Review of Major Legal Progressions and Trends	25
	APPROPRIATE CONTEXT FOR PROJECT REVIEW	26
	Project Geotemporal Scales	30
	Project Planning Context	30
	TOWARD AN AESTHETIC ANALYSIS DECISION-MAKING FRAMEWORK	30
	A Generic Process	30

PART 2   BASIC VISUAL PROCESS

3	**VISUAL PHYSIOLOGY**	**39**

John P. Felleman

	OVERVIEW	40
	ANATOMY	40
	Retina	42
	Retinal Processing	44
	Acuity and Contrast	45
	ANALYSIS IMPLICATIONS	46
4	**LANDSCAPE VISIBILITY**	**47**

John P. Felleman

	INTRODUCTION	48
	Decision Framework	48
	VISIBILITY PHYSICS	49
	Energy Sources	50

ATMOSPHERE	51
Distance Zones	53
LANDFORM	**54**
VIEWER ENVIRONMENT	**55**
SIGHTLINE SIMULATION	**56**
Field Simulations	56
Iconic Two-Dimensional	56
Three-Dimensional Iconic	57
Analog	57
Numeric-Digital	57
ENVIRONMENTAL DATA	**59**
Data Types	59
Sampling	60
Sensitivity	61
SUMMARY	**62**

5 ENVIRONMENTAL PERCEPTION 63

James F. Palmer

INTRODUCTION	64
ENVIRONMENTAL STRUCTURE	**65**
Medium	65
Substances	66
Surfaces	66
ENVIRONMENTAL MEANING	**67**
Layout	68
Events	68
Affordances	68
Ambient Optic Array	69
Perception	70
THEORIES OF PICTURE PERCEPTION	**71**
Conventions	71
Similarity	71
Elements of Light	72
Optic Information	72
PRINCIPLES OF PICTORAL DEPICTION	**73**
Stationary Monocular Perspective	73
Line Drawings	74
Motion Perspective and Motion Pictures	75
SUMMARY	**76**

PART 3 LANDSCAPE DESCRIPTION AND ANALYSIS

6 WILDLAND DESCRIPTION AND ANALYSIS — 81
Richard E. Chenoweth and Paul H. Gobster

INTRODUCTION	82
WILDLANDS DEFINED	82
WILDLANDS IN THE UNITED STATES	83
Legislation	83
Ownership	84
Distribution	85
Management	85
PURPOSES, METHODS OF CHOICE, AND CRITERIA FOR WILDLAND DESCRIPTION	86
Purposes	86
Choice of Methods	88
Historical and Popular Perspectives	88
Professionally Based versus Publicly Based Methods	90
Quantitative versus Nonquantitative Approaches	93
Verbal versus Visual Approaches	94
Sets of Available Criteria	100
Selecting a Procedure	100
CONCLUSION	101

7 COUNTRYSIDE LANDSCAPE VISUAL ASSESSMENT — 103
Sally Schauman

ASSESSMENT CONTEXT	104
CLIENT/USER	105
LANDSCAPE	106
EVALUATION	109
OVERALL PROCESS	113

8 URBAN VISUAL DESCRIPTION AND ANALYSIS — 115
Richard C. Smardon with Tony Costello and Harry Eggink

INTRODUCTION	116
DECISIONS/ACTIONS	117

DEVELOPMENT OF EXPERT APPROACH	118
PROFESSIONAL OR EXPERT RECORDING AND ANALYSIS TECHNIQUES	**122**
Process	122
Establishing Visual Control Points	122
Visual Elements	123
Analysis	123
Visibility	124
Light	125
Summary of Expert Approach	129
A SOCIAL SCIENCE APPROACH TO URBAN VISUAL ASSESSMENTS	**129**
Media of Presentation	130
Observers	131
Response Formats	133
Purpose of Environmental Display	133
COMBINING EXPERT AND SOCIAL SCIENCE APPROACHES	**133**
PROCEDURAL GUIDANCE FOR URBAN VISUAL STUDIES	**133**
NEW TECHNIQUES	**135**

PART 4   LANDSCAPE ASSESSMENT AND EVALUATION

9   REVIEW OF AGENCY METHODOLOGY FOR VISUAL PROJECT ANALYSIS   141

Richard C. Smardon

INTRODUCTION	**142**
Recent History of VRM System Development	142
REVIEW OF VRM METHODS FOR LANDSCAPE PLANNING	**145**
SCOPING THE VISUAL IMPACT ASSESSMENT	**151**
CEQ Regulations and Scoping	151
Scoping Visual Impacts	152
New York State's Environmental Quality Review Act: Visual Scoping Process	152
VISUAL EAF ADDENDUM	**154**
Federal Highway Scoping Questionnaire	155
Sample Scoping Questionnaire	156
HUD Threshold Approach	158

DETAILED VISUAL IMPACT ASSESSMENT	164
For Highway Projects	164
SUMMARY	166

10 THE ASSESSMENT OF LANDSCAPE QUALITY: MAJOR METHODOLOGICAL CONSIDERATIONS   167

Joanne Vining and Joseph J. Stevens

INTRODUCTION	168
ASSESSMENT METHODS	170
Surveys and Questionnaires	170
Perceptual Preference Assessment	174
Behavioral Measures	178
ASSESSMENT DESIGNS	179
Case Study	179
Experimental Designs	180
Correlation Methods	182
Quasi-experimental Designs	183
CRITERIA FOR EVALUATING ASSESSMENT METHODS	184
Reliability	184
Validity	184
Sampling	185
SUMMARY AND CONCLUSIONS	186

11 SIMULATING CHANGES IN THE LANDSCAPE   187

Stephen R. J. Sheppard

INTRODUCTION	188
THE ROLE OF SIMULATIONS IN VISUAL IMPACT ANALYSIS	188
SIMULATION RESEARCH AND INFORMATION SOURCES	189
Research	189
Technical Guides	190
Simulation Examples in Practice	190
THE PRINCIPLES OF SIMULATION	192
Representative Simulation	192
Accurate Simulation	192
Credible Simulation	193
Comprehensible Simulation	193
Bias-free Simulations	193

	A SELECTIVE CRITIQUE OF SIMULATION METHODS	194
	Selected Simulation Media	194
	General Simulation Techniques	195
	CONCLUSION	199

12 VISUAL IMPACT ASSESSMENT: CHANGES IN NATURAL AND RURAL ENVIRONMENT 201

William C. Yeomans

INTRODUCTION	202
The Demand for Rural and Wildland Areas: Trends in Public Use	202
The Meaning of Naturalness	202
Unique Qualities of Rural and Wildland Environments	203
VIA SYSTEMS APPLICATION	203
The U.S. Forest Service	203
The U.S. Bureau of Land Management	204
British Columbia	204
Private Practioners	204
Research in VIA Methodology	205
VIA APPLICATIONS: A RECOMMENDED FRAMEWORK	205
VIA Criteria: A Summary	205
A Model Format for VIA Procedures	206
Phase One: Landscape Description	206
Phase Two: Observer Characteristics	209
Phase Three: Line-of-Sight Determinations	210
Phase Four: Key Viewpoint Analysis Sensitivity Levels, and Scenic Assessment	212
Phase Five: Assess Impacting Activity/Land Use Characteristics	213
Phase Six: The Visual Impact Assessment and Mitigation Summary	216
Summary Statement	218
APPENDIX: DESIGN GUIDELINES	218
General Guidelines	220
Rehabilitation	222

13 VISUAL IMPACT ASSESSMENT IN URBAN ENVIRONMENTS 223

William G. E. Blair

INTRODUCTION	224
VISUAL IMPACT ASSESSMENT PROCESS	224

MAJOR ISSUES IN URBAN VISUAL IMPACT ASSESSMENT	224
LEGISLATIVE JUDICIAL, AND ADMINISTRATIVE UNDERPINNINGS	225
DEFINING THE VISUAL CHARACTERISTICS OF THE PROJECT	226
Structures	226
Site Improvements	227
Uses	228
DEFINING THE AFFECTED VISUAL ENVIRONMENT	229
Project Information	229
Existing Documentation	234
Field Observations	235
DETERMINING VISUAL IMPACTS	235
Viewing Conditions	236
Site and Environs	238
EVALUATION OF VISUAL IMPACTS	241
Criteria	241
Significance	243
MITIGATION MEASURES	243
Specific Measures	243

PART 5 INTERNATIONAL PERSPECTIVES

14 VISUAL-AESTHETIC COMPONENTS IN THE CYBERNETICS OF URBAN PLANNING 247

Andrej B. Pogačnik

INTRODUCTION	248
HISTORICAL BACKGROUND, GOALS, AND ISSUES	248
INFORMATION SOURCES	248
DESCRIPTION OF COLLECTED INFORMATION	250
SOME TECHNICAL ASPECTS OF THE VISUAL INFORMATION SYSTEM	251
ROLE OF THE COMPUTER	252
GENERAL USE OF THE VISUAL INFORMATION SYSTEM	252
PRACTICAL TESTING OF THE VISUAL MODEL: FUTURE LAND USE OPTIMIZATION	254

	HIGHWAY TEST	256
	USE OF THE VISUAL MODEL IN THE MASTER PLAN OF LJUBLJANA	257
	LOCATION CRITERIA ACCORDING TO VISUAL AESTHETICS	259
	ENVIRONMENTAL PREFERENCES AS PART OF THE VISUAL MODEL	261
	CONCLUSION	263
15	**UTILIZING AN ENVIRONMENTAL SIMULATION LABORATORY IN SWEDEN**	**265**

Jan Janssens and Rikard Küller

	THE DEVELOPMENT OF THE LUND SIMULATOR	266
	THE NEED FOR SYSTEMATIC EVALUATION	268
	COMPARING VARIOUS MODES OF REPRESENTATION	270
	THE SIMULATOR IN PRACTICE	271
	RECENT DEVELOPMENTS AND FUTURE PERSPECTIVES	273
16	**VISUAL IMPACT ASSESSMENT METHODOLOGY FOR INDUSTRIAL DEVELOPMENT SITE REVIEW IN SPAIN**	**277**

Santiago G. Alonso, Miguel Aguilo, and Angel Ramos

	INTRODUCTION	278
	VISUAL FRAGILITY	278
	Visual Fragility: Biophysical Factors	279
	Visual Fragility: Perceptual Factors	282
	Historic and Cultural Factors	282
	Accessibility	282
	VISIBILITY	283
	The Viewshed	283
	Susceptibility	295
	VISUAL QUALITY EVALUATION	295
	Landscape's Components	296
	Basic Visual Elements	297
	Visual Impact Assessment	297
	OPERATIVE PROCESS	299

ILLUSTRATED GLOSSARY	**307**
Kate Grinde and Al Kopf	
REFERENCES	**335**
AUTHOR INDEX	**355**
SUBJECT INDEX	**359**

PART 1

INTRODUCTION

The introductory section sets the cultural and institutional context for visual analysis in America and to a lesser extent other Western countries. Recognition that the landscape had scenic value, as well as resource values, did not simply appear as a new social fact with the passage of the National Environmental Policy Act (NEPA) in 1969. In the first chapter, Ervin H. Zube reviews the history of landscape values and their implications for our situation. He finds the birth of the modern image of landscapes as a source of human pleasure and satisfaction rising to challenge the crumbling medieval belief that nature was sinful and to be feared. The evolution of our current values are traced from these roots through two dominant themes: an appreciation of the beautiful, picturesque, and sublime, and a foundation of antiurbanism. These values can be seen in the five phases or movements of development in America's landscape policy: Disposal of public lands, preservation of the unique and beautiful, establishment of a recreation system, ameliorating scenic ills, and environmental planning. Finally, he reviews the major highlights where environmental professionals have explored ways to integrate these values into managing and assessing the landscape.

If the first chapter tries to encompass the cultural milieu that colors our landscape vision, then the second attempts to bring order and meaning to the contextual reality of governmental regulation and control that faces anyone concerned with project review. In this chapter, the editors review the underpinnings of the legal, regulatory, and judicial processes and principles relating to visual quality.

Examples are taken from the literature of visual studies conducted at a variety of scales: regional, corridor, citywide, and project sites. A review of nearly 100 environmental assessments in the decade after NEPA's passage indicates that substantial adverse visual impacts are recognized but little consideration is given to their mitigation. The final half of this chapter proposes a decision-making framework for conducting aesthetic resources analyses. While this process has sufficient detail to provide real guidance, it is flexible enough to be applied to analysis at any scale and broad enough to recognize impacts identified by public, professional, or institutional criteria. Many of the contributions in this volume can be usefully evaluated and better understood when placed in this decision-making context.

DEFINE RESOURCES	INVENTORY RESOURCES	ASSESS EFFECTS	APPRAISE EFFECTS
/////			

CHAPTER 1

LANDSCAPE VALUES: HISTORY, CONCEPTS, AND APPLICATIONS

Ervin H. Zube

The visual quality of the American landscape became a topic of increased concern during the decades of the 1960s and 1970s. The visual consequences of rapid and extensive growth and development in the post-World War II era were becoming ever more apparent. His concern was chronicled in books bearing provocative titles such as *Man-Made America: Chaos or Control?* (Tunnard and Pushkarev 1963), *God's Own Junkyard* (Blake 1964), and *The American Landscape: A Critical View* (Nairn 1965). National attention was focused on the issue of visual quality in 1965 when President Lyndon B. Johnson sponsored the White House Conference on Natural Beauty (1965).

Long-standing interests in the beauties of wild and rugged landscapes expanded to encompass less than wild places in rural America and on the fringe of metropolitan areas. While there were notable attempts to direct attention to the lack of aesthetic qualities in American cities, greatest attention was directed to nonurban landscapes. These were, and continue to be, the locations where large-scale environmental changes occur, including construction of new subdivisions, communities, dams, reservoirs, highways, airports, and recreation areas as well as timber harvests and surface mining. A substantial body of public policy promulgated at the national level set the stage for the conduct of visual landscape assessments, the preparation of environmental impact statements, and the use of simulation techniques to convey the visual consequences of alternative plans. These policies also served as significant stimuli for research in landscape aesthetics. Of considerable pragmatic importance to practitioners, and a challenge to researchers, was the development of systematic and objective methods for visual resource assessment.

This chapter is organized in three sections. the first presents a review of the evolution of the modern concept of landscape, of changing human-landscape relationships and changing concepts of landscape beauty. The second section considers the history of American public policy related to landscape. Policy shifts over time, usually the result of compromises among interested parties, are presented as reflecting normative public values. The final section discusses and categorizes concepts and approaches that have been offered by designers, planners, and scientists during the past two decades to identify, describe, and evaluate landscape values or scenic beauty and to incorporate such values information into landscape design, planning, and management decisions.

CONCEPTS OF LANDSCAPE AND LANDSCAPE BEAUTY

One of the first visual simulations of the consequences of alternative management decisions on the landscape was executed in Siena, Italy during the fourteenth century. Landscape simulation is currently an important technique for assessing the visual consequences of proposed landscape alterations (See Chapter 11). A very early example of a landscape simulation is found in the Sala della Pace of the Palazzo Publico in Siena. In the late 1330s Ambrogio Lorenzetti graphically portrayed the effects of good and bad administrative and managerial decisions on urban and rural landscapes.

Three walls of the Sala della Pace are covered by frescoes. Lorenzetti painted on facing walls the "effects of bad government in the town and country" and the "effects of good government in the town and country." Cole (1980) observes that "the citizen standing in the Sala della Pace would have been able to make a graphic comparison between two types of government simply by looking at the room's two long walls."

Each fresco consists of two parts, the town and the country. The good town shows handsome, orderly buildings and the bad town shows decaying, untended buildings. The good town is full of activity with animals and people, including 10 lovely young women dancing in a handsome piazza. The good country contains panoramic views to distant hills that are undoubtedly representative of the beautiful, gentle, humanized landscape of Tuscany, a countryside of rolling hills with hayfields, vineyards, animals, farm workers, and buildings. What remains of the bad government fresco suggests a somber and chaotic countryside lacking in signs of productivity or pastoral qualities.

Lorenzetti's frescoes also signal an awakening to landscape as an element in art to be considered in itself as a source of pleasure and human satisfaction rather than as incidental decoration or background to other pictorial content. Clark (1961) suggests that Ambrogio Lorenzetti together with his brother Pietro and Simone Martini (also

FIGURE 1.1. Ambrogio Lorenzetti, *The effects of good government in the town,* fourteenth century.

painters in Siena) and the poets Petrarch, Dante, and Boccaccio represent a sharp break with medieval tradition and introduce the modern concept of landscape. Martini and the Lorenzettis departed from the stylized, detailed depiction of elements of landscape as minor parts of pictorial compositions and treated landscapes as illusionistic, spatial compositions meriting attention unto themselves. Petrarch, Dante, and Boccaccio wrote of enjoying the pleasures of nature and the viewing of beautiful landscapes—a position that is in sharp contrast with earlier prevailing medieval beliefs about the sinfulness of earthly pleasures and the unknown dangers and fears associated with nature.

The Modern Concept of Landscape

The emergence of this modern concept of landscape as a source of pleasure and satisfaction was enhanced by subsequent developments in landscape painting and garden design. The evolution of gardens from places of utility for growing food and medicinal plants to places of beauty and enjoyment paralleled the emergence of landscape painting in the Middle Ages and into the Renaissance. Artists sought to capture the many moods of nature and to express her personality and the joy she provided. This occurred during a time when the western world was becoming increasingly secular.

Turner (1966) notes that landscape painting also paralleled the Renaissance development of city life and its attendant merchant class and monetary economy. The merchant class became patrons of secular art and sought the pleasures of nature in their country villas and gardens. Nature in the gardens, however, was carefully controlled and manipulated. It was not evocative of wild landscapes or surrounding rural landscapes. The

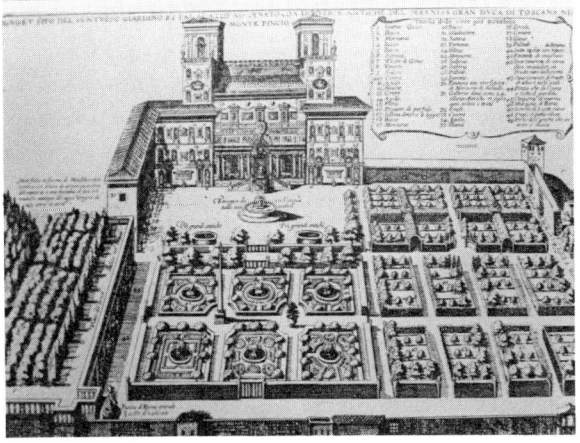

FIGURE 1.2. Geometric design of the sixteenth century Villa Medici, Rome.

garden was a carefully designed place of geometric, usually symmetrical, architectural forms into which plants and water were introduced under conditions of careful control. Nevertheless, the walls of the palazzos and loggias in the villas were frequently decorated with paintings and frescoes depicting wild nature and the surrounding countryside. This geometric approach to garden design prevailed for several centuries throughout Europe, although the scale of gardens varied immensely from the relatively modest walled garden of a fifteenth-century Italian villa to the grand scale of Versailles in seventeenth-century France.

The very word *landscape* wasn't introduced into the English language until the sixteenth century. It was a technical term, *landschap*, used in Dutch landscape paintings of beautiful scenery (Stilgoe, 1982; Punter, 1982). The English version of this word, *landskip*, later became transformed to *landscape*, the word we use today. The meaning of the word changed, however, after its introduction into England. Within a few decades it also meant vistas of rural countryside, hilltop panoramic views and large ornamental gardens as well as paintings of rural scenery.

The Beautiful, the Picturesque, and the Sublime

A profound change in garden design occurred in England during the eighteenth century. Stimulated by the idealized landscape paintings of late seventeenth-century artists Rosa, Poussin, and Claude, designers sought to recreate landscapes of bucolic beauty, landscapes of softened hills and valleys, with trees—singly and in clumps—in their natural forms, and buildings—alone or in groups—usually of classical design (Fleming and Gore, 1979). The geometry and symmetry of Renaissance and Baroque gardens were replaced with a kind of stylized nature that avoided straight lines and angles and embraced sweeping, serpentine curves. Nature was made soft, rounded, neat, and tidy.

This romantic view of nature was found not only in painting and gardens but also in poetry. Alexander Pope in his *Essay on Criticism* (1715) admonished young poets to

> First follow Nature, and your judgment frame
> By her just standard, which is still the same:
> Unerring Nature, still divinely bright,
> One clear, unchang'd and universal light,
> Life, force, and beauty, must to all impart,
> At once the source, and end, and test of Art.
> That Art is best which most resembles her,
> And still presides, yet never does appear.

Fleming and Gore (1979) suggest that these words were also applicable to landscape gardening of the time.

Humphrey Repton (1907), a highly successful eighteenth-century landscape gardener and practitioner of this "stylized nature" approach to design, devised a graphic means of making his designs meaningful to his clients. He wrote:

> *To make my designs intelligible, I found that a mere map was insufficient; as being no more capable of conveying an idea of the landscape than the ground-plan of a house does of its elevation.*

Where Ambrogio Lorenzetti in the fourteenth century painted frescoes of the effects of good and bad government, Repton devised another and more modest means of simulating the consequences of change. He prepared an illustration, frequently a watercolor sketch, of the place as it existed, with a fold-up sketch hinged at the bottom—usually about one-half page in height—that depicted the place as it would appear after his design had been executed. Thus Repton could show his client how a formal geometric garden could be modified to blend into the surrounding landscape or *park* as he called it by folding up

FIGURE 1.3. The effect of removing trees in the oblique view of an avenue at Longley Park and creating a veiw "infinitely more interesting than any row of trees..." (Repton, 1907, p. 26).

the hinged sketch to cover that portion that would be changed by his design.

There was a tendency during this period to judge landscapes in the same way as paintings, which led to use of the term *picturesque*. Picturesque landscapes demanded more contrast than that found in the landscape gardens of earlier practitioners of the art such as William Kent and Lancelot (Capability) Brown. The Reverend William Gilpin, regarded as the founder of the Picturesque School, decried the use of uniform green lawns with clumps and belts of trees as looking insipid in a picture. Capability Brown's gardens, in Gilpin's view, lacked the contrast with rugged materials and aspects and thus might be beautiful but not picturesque. The picturesque park surrounding a house and garden was one that was irregular in detail, rough and coarse in texture, intricate in pattern, and variegated in color and shading (O'Brien, 1981). Picturesque parks included fallen trees, rocky grottos, and gothic ruins. Sir Uvedale Price, an avowed advocate of the picturesque school of landscape gardening, also drew a distinction between the picturesque landscape and the sublime (O'Brien 1981; Allentuck 1974). The *sublime* he defined as including greatness of dimension and being founded on principles of awe and terror. Price suggested that landscape gardeners could create beautiful and picturesque landscapes, but they did not have the power to create sublime landscapes. These were created by a higher power.

Picturesque and Sublime in America

The English picturesque landscape and a fascination with wilderness or sublime landscapes were two dominant factors that influenced American landscape values in the nineteenth century and that continue to influence landscape values in the later decades of the twentieth century. Initially, wilderness was a foe to be conquered. it was the landscape from which settlers wrested sites for homes and farms in the seventeenth and eighteenth centuries; it was a vast unknown area that stretched far to the west from the thin band of widely separated settlements along the eastern seaboard. Conquering the wilderness was viewed as an essential task in the formation of a new and independent nation.

By the early nineteenth century, however, another view of wilderness was emerging, notably among a group of artists and writers. The painter George Catlin, in 1832, was among the very first to argue for setting aside a section of America's wilderness to be protected as a national park (Gatlin 1968). Writers such as James Fenimore Cooper eloquently described the beauties and rugged qualities of wilderness landscapes in his romantic novels (Nevius 1976). Other writers such as William Cullen Bryant and Henry David Thoreau extolled the virtues and beauty of America's natural landscapes. In a new country that lacked the artistic artifacts and cultural history of Europe, wild nature could be a symbol of national pride. It was one thing America had that was equal to or better than anything that could be found in Europe.

The landscape of the Hudson River Valley was such a symbol of national pride (Stilgoe 1982). The landscape was romanticized through associations with the Revolutionary War; it possessed geological features that contributed to its sublimity; and it had the intricacies of pattern associated with picturesque landscapes. The terms *sublime* and *picturesque* represented important concepts in the aesthetic evaluation of romanticized landscape in nineteenth-century America as well as in England. Contained by the sublime landscape of the highlands, a picturesque landscape was created in the lower levels of the valley. Land-

FIGURE 1.4. Hudson River Valley painting by John Frederick Kensett, *View near Cozzens Hotel, West Point 1863*. The New-York Historical Society, New York.

scape gardener Andrew Jackson Downing played a significant role in this landscape transformation through his application of the principles of picturesque gardening that had been brought to America from England (Downing 1869). The valley was also immortalized in the writings of Washington Irving and in the paintings and sketches of the Hudson River Valley School of Painting with which many of the great nineteenth-century landscape painters were associated including Albert Bierstadt, Frederick Church, Thomas Cole, Jasper F. Cropsey, Asher Durand, Martin Johnson Heade, and John F. Kensett.

Anti-Urbanism

Intellectuals such as Thomas Jefferson promoted the virtues of an agrarian society and, indirectly, the values of rural landscapes. In *Notes on the State of Virginia* he wrote, "Those who labor in the earth are the chosen people of god.... The mobs of great cities add just so much to the support of pure government, as sores do to the strength of the human body" (Jefferson, 1955). Morton and Lucia White (1962) suggest that there has been a consistent pattern of anti-urbanism among American intellectuals, from Jefferson and Thoreau to Louis Sullivan and Frank Lloyd Wright. They argue that many of the individuals who are responsible for our intellectual history are those who, like Jefferson, saw virtue in rural living and alienation in the city. Among these elites were also the advocates of wild nature. Whether one described the landscape as picturesque or sublime, or as a healthful place of escape from the city, the intellectual response in nineteenth- and twentieth-century America has represented a fairly consistent value orientation to nature and natural landscapes.

Frederick Law Olmsted, Sr. shared the belief about the value of nature. He embraced the English landscape park with its rural characteristics as a fitting form for American urban parks (Olmsted 1979). He believed in the curative power of such parks where urban residents suffering from illness could spend a few hours every day in "The Park."

It is also interesting to note that Olmsted and Vaux adopted a technique similar to that used by Repton a century earlier to depict the visual consequences of their design for Central Park (Beveridge and Schuyler 1983). A series of comparative sketches were prepared illustrating "Present Outlines" and the "Effect Proposed" for various areas throughout the park.

Elites and Common Folks

Whether the landscape values of the nineteenth-century intellectual elites were shared by the majority of the American population is a difficult question to address. Undoubtedly many of those who were better educated read works by Bryant, Cooper, Thoreau, and others. They may also have visited exhibits of landscape paintings at the New York National Academy of Design, Yale School of Fine Arts, or the Boston Athenaeum. Nevertheless, these individuals undoubtedly represented a modest percentage of the population. Furthermore, Stebbins (1980) indicates that in a number of the exhibitions, landscape paintings rarely accounted for more than 30 percent of the exhibited works, and frequently less.

Zube (1981) studied the diaries and journals of settlers and visitors in the southwest to identify what these individuals valued in the landscape and how their values differed from those of the intellectual elite. By the second half of the nineteenth century, the American West had been symbolized as wilderness, despoiled nature, and a garden. Concern was voiced about the destruction of natural landscapes: clearing of forests, digging of mines, and the building of towns and railroads. The ax and the plow were symbolic of this perceived despoliation of nature. There were, however, a number of writers who conveyed an image of the wilderness as transformed to a garden, from the sublime to the picturesque, and projected images of rural productivity and pastoral scenes as exemplified in Jefferson's idealized agrarian society. Zube concluded that early settlers in this wilderness area did share some of these images and values. The notable exception, however, was that they rarely perceived the cutting of timber, mining, or the building of towns as destroying nature. Most often these activities were viewed as improving the landscape, making it more hospitable, and realizing personal ambitions. They saw significant pragmatic, economic values in the landscape, as well as aesthetic values. This is an important difference from the perceptions of the intellectual elites.

The Shaping of American Landscape Values

In summary, the concept of landscape as a source of pleasure and satisfaction is, historically, relatively recent. Even more recent is the popular fascination with the beauty of wild nature. The eighteenth- and nineteenth-century English aesthetic concepts of sublime and picturesque landscapes originally associated with gardens and their surrounding "parks" and wild landscapes were adopted by American writers and painters early in the nineteenth century. The Hudson River Valley provided a center of attention for these intellectuals and also provided a setting for application of these aesthetic concepts. American values were shaped during the nineteenth century to look with favor on natural and rural landscapes and to look with disfavor on urban landscapes. Wild and rural landscapes were sources of pleasure and emotional satisfaction.

NORMATIVE PUBLIC VALUES

During the first 100 years of America's existence as a nation, public policies—normative public values—concerning land and landscape were shaped by a number of factors: a belief in an inexhaustible stock of landscape resources; a perceived need to settle the unsettled areas of the nation; and the need to tame and conquer nature—to transform the landscape from a savage wilderness into a bountiful garden (Smith 1970). Stories abound about the overharvesting and destruction of forests, abusive agricultural practices that destroyed soil fertility and induced erosion, and mining operations that paid no heed to site reclamation or the effects on the surrounding landscape. The use of the ax and the plow as symbols of landscape destruction was not without meaning. And the expressed concerns of literary and aesthetic elites for protection of sublime and

TABLE 1.1. Phases and Selected Events in Landscape Policy Development

LANDSCAPE
DISPOSAL.........1785, General Ordinance of 1785
                 1855, Military Bounty Act
                 1862, 1904, 1909, 1916, Homestead Acts
                 1864, Morrill Act
                 1873, Timber Culture Act
                 1877, Desert Land Act

LANDSCAPE
PRESERVATION.....1864, Yosemite State Park
                 1872, Yellowstone National Park
                 1885, Adirondack Forest Preserve
                 1906, Antiquities Act
                 1916, National Park Service Created
                 1964, Wilderness Act

RECREATION
LANDSCAPES.......$1920^{\pm}$, State Park Movement
                 1960, Multiple Use and Sustained Yield Act
                 1962, Outdoor Recreation Resources Review Committee Report
                 1965, Land and Water Conservation Fund Act
                 1968, Wild and Scenic Rivers Act
                 1968, National Recreation and Scenic Trails Act

AMELIORATE
SCENIC ILLS......1965, White House Conference on Natural Beauty
                 1965, Highway Beautification Act
                 1970, 1977, Clean Air Act Amendments
                 1977, Surface Mining Control and Reclamation Act

ENVIRONMENTAL
PLANNING.........1969, National Environmental Policy Act
                 1972, Coastal Zone Management Act
                 1974, Forest and Rangeland Renewable Resources Planning Act
                 1976, Federal Land Policy and Management Act
                 1976, National Forest Management Act

picturesque landscapes were slow in reaching the hearing of policy makers.

Table 1.1 indicates five phases in landscape policy during the past two centuries and lists exemplary events in each of the phases. Starting with the general disposal of public lands following the Revolutionary War, subsequent phases were: preservation of unique landscapes, the development of recreation landscapes, the amelioration of visual blight, and, finally, the integration of aesthetic landscape values into broad-based environmental planning.

Landscape Disposal

The General Ordinance of 1785 not only provided for the selling of public lands to the highest bidder, but also profoundly affected the visual image of a vast portion of America. The adoption of the grid system of public land survey established the pattern of much of rural America. The location of roads along section lines resulted in long straight stretches with nearly 90-degree curves. Farm fields were rectangular in shape regardless of topography and farm houses and barns were evenly spaced across the countryside according to the size of the farm and the grid.

A major thrust in land disposal occurred around the time of the Civil War with the signing of the first Homestead Act and the Morrill Act providing for state land grant universities. Nearly 300 million acres were disposed of under the several Homestead Acts and about 10 million acres under the Morrill Act. Land grants to railroads and individual states accounted for another 320 million acres. This major era of disposal ended around the turn of the century (Dana and Fairfax 1980). Overall, in excess of 1000 million acres of the public domain have been disposed under various laws since 1785.

Undoubtedly, there were many who saw land disposals as a way of transforming the wilderness into a garden. The Homestead, Timber Culture, and Desert Land Sales Acts were sympathetic to Jefferson's ideal of an agrarian society.

Landscape Preservation

It wasn't until 1865 that the landscape concerns first expressed in the Hudson River Valley were realized in formal public action at the national level when Congress ceded Yosemite Valley to the State of California for a state park. This action, as has frequently been noted, marked the start of the movement for preservation of unique and beautiful landscapes. George Catlin's call in 1832 for a national park to protect a section of America's wilderness wasn't realized, however, until 1874—40 years later—when Yellowstone National Park was established. Yellowstone was the first national park not only in the United States, but also in the world. It is important to remember, however, as Runte (1979) makes clear, that Congress had to be convinced that lands proposed for national parks contained no resources of economic value. If there were commercial timber stands, for example, they were purportedly too remote or difficult of access to be harvested economically. Aesthetics could not easily win out over economics in Congress.

The establishment of Yosemite State Park (it became a national park in 1890) and Yellowstone National Park also marked significant accomplishments in support of the spirit of cultural nationalism. These were outstanding landscapes—unique in the world—that Americans could point to with pride. They were truly sublime landscapes, superior to anything that existed in Europe.

In 1885 the New York State legislature established the Adirondack Forest Preserve, protecting from timber harvest a vast area in 14 counties and extending the concept of landscape preservation to the level of state grovernment. The action was motivated by concerns for aesthetic and recreational values and, of great importance, for protection of the watershed for purposes of water supply and flood control.

The Antiquities Act of 1906 provided the president with authority to establish national monuments and thus protect areas of historic and scientific interest. This Act enabled the president to preserve cultural landscapes and wildlife habitat areas by proclamation.

The establishment of additional national parks led in 1916 to the creation of the National Park Service, which was charged with responsibility to preserve the landscape and provide for the enjoyment of future generations.

The last major preservation policy to be enacted was the Wilderness Act of 1964. At long last, the aesthetic and spiritual values of sublime wilderness that had been espoused by a literary and artistic elite of more than a century earlier received official recognition. Implementation of the Wilderness Act over the two decades of its existence, however, has frequently been met with strong resistance from commodity resource interests including grazing, timber harvest, and mining. Economic and aesthetic interests still come in conflict when the issue of landscape preservation is raised.

Landscape preservation now encompasses more than aesthetic values. Cultural, biological, and geological values currently figure prominently in preservation programs, along with aesthetics. Furthermore, landscape preservation programs are active around the world. International leadership is provided by the United Nations World Heritage List (Development Forum 1980) and the UNESCO Biosphere Reserve (UNESCO 1973) designation under the Man and the Biosphere Program. The World Heritage list includes cultural and natural landscapes while biosphere reserves are limited to exemplary ecosystems. However, ecosystems are defined as including man—they are not limited to natural, undisturbed landscapes. World Heritage sites are to the world what national cultural and natural parks are to individual countries. They bespeak of internationally recognized aesthetic, historic, and cultural values. Biosphere reserves are also of international significance, representing global ecosystems. The primary value orientation, however, is neither aesthetic nor historic but rather scientific. They are landscapes that are protected as monitoring sites and may also contain rare and endangered species of plants and animals.

Recreation Landscapes

Railroads provided a primary means of access for affluent visitors to national parks in the late nineteenth and early twentieth centuries (Shankland 1970). Shortly thereafter, however, the availability of the automobile enabled more Americans to travel and become tourists. Cars rapidly replaced trains as the primary means of access to national parks (Belasco 1981), freeing travelers from the restrictions of railroad timetables and inflexible routings. The automobile reinforced the sense of cultural nationalism, enabling many Americans to see for themselves that the scenery of the United States was equal to or better than anything Europe could offer. The car also ushered in a major demand for outdoor recreation landscapes.

After the establishment of Yosemite State Park in 1865, the state park idea spread slowly and sporadically until the 1920s when a number of states, including California, Connecticut, Iowa, Michigan, Minnesota, New York, and Wisconsin, began developing state park systems. This movement was aided by the public works programs of the 1930s, notably the Civilian Conservation Corps (CCC) which established some 475 CCC camps in state parks around the country (Wirth 1980). Labor provided by the young men in these camps helped to build roads, trails, picnic and campgrounds and to install water and sewer systems.

If national parks were the crown jewels of the national landscape, many state parks were the crown jewels of the states. These parks, however, were frequently more extensively developed for active recreation than most national parks. Nevertheless, they reinforced the prevailing value orientation toward natural landscapes.

The next wave of interest in recreation landscapes followed World War II and was again stimulated by the automobile and the mobility it provided. The beauty of national forests made them major attractions for Americans seeking outdoor recreation opportunities. The Multiple Use and Sustained Yield Act of 1960 provided the U.S. Forest Service with legislative authority to manage national forests for outdoor recreation and wildlife and fish in addition to their traditional management responsibilities for range, timber, and watershed. As one Forest Service professional stated the case, researchers and managers were now challenged "to integrate timber production and aesthetics" (Shafer 1967).

The Outdoor Recreation Resources Review Commission (ORRRC) was established in 1958 to identify outdoor recreation wants and needs for the nation, determine recreation resources available, and determine the necessary policies and programs to meet the needs (ORRRC 1962). The Commission's report was issued in 1962. It contained a substantial list of recommendations, several of which resulted in important landscape legislation. Both the Wild and Scenic Rivers Act and the National Recreation and Scenic Trails Act of 1968 were outcomes of ORRRC findings about needs and resources. The automobile was found to provide the most popular recreational activity of all, driving for pleasure. Proposals to establish a national scenic highway system failed to gain congressional support, however.

A major boost in providing recreation landscapes was provided by the Land and Water Conservation Fund Act of 1965. This act contributed significantly to the growth of state and local park systems as well as to expansion of federal agency land holdings. States were required to have a statewide comprehensive outdoor recreation plan to qualify for available funds. This legislation marked a significant advance in landscape policy in that it added to the federal public landscape as well as to state and local public landscapes.

Ameliorating Scenic Ills

There was a growing awakening during the early 1960s that our landscape was becoming increasingly ugly and abused. This was particularly evident in and around major population centers, but was also visible in rural ares. This awakening was significant for several reasons: first, attention was directed to the ugly and degrading aspects of landscape rather than to the beautiful and satisfying; and second, primary attention was directed to the impact of humans on the landscape rather than to natural landscapes. It is of interest, nevertheless, that when President Johnson convened his White House Conference in 1965, a conference that addressed such issues as townscapes, water and water fronts, highway design, roadside control, landscape reclamation, undergrounding utilities, auto junk yards, and suburbia, it was called the White House Conference on Natural Beauty. There were sessions on parks and open spaces, scenic roads and parkways and the farm landscape, but the emphasis was on human-made landscapes. Implicit in the charge to the conferees was the notion that the beauty of our natural landscapes provided a yardstick for assessing the visual quality of the built environment and the impact of humans on the landscape. Furthermore, it was implied that in most cases these effects had not measured up to the natural landscape standard and that in many instances the result was a significant degradation of visual quality.

This concern with the decreasing visual quality of America was vividly expressed in the three books cited in the opening paragraph of this chapter: *Man-Made America: Chaos or Control* (Tunnard and Pushkarev 1963), *God's Own Junkyard* (Blake 1964), and *The American Landscape: A Critical View* (Nairn 1965). Authors of these books were not addressing problems of preserving sublime and picturesque landscapes. They were making statements, sometimes angry ones (Blake 1964) about what was wrong with the landscape—the man-made landscape—and what might be done about it (Tunnard and Bushkarev 1963; Nairn 1965). They were addressing the same issues as the White House Conference.

This antiugly movement gained additional support from the belief that there was greater consensus among the public about what was ugly than about what was beautiful (Kates 1966–67). The old adage "beauty is in the eye of the beholder" was accepted with little question. The White House Conference served as a model and stimulus for similar conferences at the state level across the country. In addition to focusing attention on the increasing ugliness of the landscape, the Conference presaged the environmental movement that followed a few years later.

The Highway Beautification Act of 1965 is perhaps most representative of the concern with decreasing visual quality and increasing ugliness. Billboards and junkyards were symbols of landscape neglect. In an automobile-oriented society they also confronted millions of Americans daily on their commutes to and from work. Elimination of billboards, screening of junkyards, and general enhancement of the landscape were viewed as important steps in restoring visual quality to the everyday landscape. Implementation of the Act, however, was very sporadic, with few states taking an aggressive position.

Another prominent eyesore on the landscape was the vast area of derelict surface mines. At the time of the Conference there were 3.2 million acres that had been surface mined in the country. Only one-third of that area had been reclaimed by either natural forces or human intervention. The Appalachian Regional Development Act included regulations on surface mining for that region of the country. It took another decade, however, until the Surface Mining Control and Reclamation Act of 1977 was passed and provided regulation for the strip mining of coal in all regions of the country.

Even national parks and wilderness areas, the nation's sublime landscapes, were susceptible of visual degradation. In 1977 Congress enacted amendments to the Clean Air Act that included designation of large national parks and wilderness areas as Class I areas in which little air quality deterioration would be allowed. Visibility values were recognized as an essential component of these landscapes.

Environmental Planning

On January 1, 1970 President Nixon signed the National Environmental Policy Act of 1969 (NEPA). This was a landmark piece of legislation. It recognized issues and themes that had been identified at the White House Conference in 1965 and in particular "the impact of man's activities on the interrelations of all components of the natural environment,...." It also required that all agencies of the federal government "identify and develop methods and procedures... which will insure that presently unquantified environmental amenities and values may be given appropriate consideration in decision making along with economic and technical considerations." The NEPA ushered in an era of interdisciplinary environmental planning in which visual values could be included in the planning and design decision-making process. It made evident the lack of valid and reliable methods and procedures for identifying visual values and visual impacts of proposed developments. Agencies were challenged to develop such methods and procedures to meet the requirements of the Act. And NEPA also served as a model for a number of states that adopted similar environmental policies and interdisciplinary planning objectives. Most important, however, is that the NEPA made it clear that visual values, the visual quality of the landscape, was not only of concern with reference to uniquely beautiful or ugly landscapes but to all landscapes that were affected by federal design, planning, or management activities. The implementation road for the NEPA was rocky and torturous, but as indicated later in this chapter and in following chapters, impressive progress was made.

The four other legislative acts listed under Environmental Planning in Table 1 are representative, with respect to visual or aesthetic values, of nearly all environmental legislation enacted during the 1970s. For example, the Coastal Zone Management Act (CZM) called for "giving full consideration to ecological, cultural, historic and aesthetic values as well as to needs for economic development." The intent of Congress is clearly stated and is responsive to the conditions set forth in the NEPA. The CZM provided for a cooperative federal-state approach to planning the landscape of the coastal zone. It provided a mechanism whereby the federal government encouraged states to undertake broad-based interdisciplinary environmental planning. The extent to which aesthetic values were addressed in the participating states, however, varied considerably—sometimes figuring prominently in plan development and sometimes being lightly glossed over.

The three other acts relate specifically to public lands. The Forest and Rangeland Renewable Resources Planning Act, the National Forest Management Act, and the Federal Land Policy and Management Act address planning and management policies on Forest Service and Bureau of Land Management lands. These acts also build upon the policies set forth in the NEPA and call for interdisciplinary planning teams and for consideration of a full array of resource values including aesthetics. Dana and Fairfax (1980) point out, however, that the question of priorities among values in decision making is not addressed in the two Forest Service Acts. For visual values this can be both good and bad. On the positive side it provides managers with flexibility to weight values differently in order to meet different needs in various parts of the forest. It also means that an *a priori* decision has not been made that visual values always come after timber, forage, and watershed values. On the negative side it could mean that aesthetic and other amenity values could systematically receive only token attention under commodity-oriented supervisors and managers, as was the case in a number of states under the CZM.

Recapitulation

Landscape policy has evolved significantly during the past two centuries with an ever increasing rate of change as it moved through the five phases from disposal through preservation and recreation to scenic ills and environmental planning. Conceptually this represents a broadened perspective on the values of landscape aesthetics. The expansion from preservation to recreation is recognition that attractive landscapes can be experienced physically and socially as well as visually, and that for many people the experiences are inextricably intertwined and mutually reinforcing.

The further expansion from preservation and recreation to the reclamation of scenic ills implicitly recognized a continuum of scenic values from the uniquely beautiful to the uniquely ugly. Furthermore, as the uniquely beautiful was assumed to provide psychological benefits of pleasure and satisfaction, it was assumed that the ugly provided psychological costs. In her opening comments at the White House Conference on Natural Beauty, Mrs. Lyndon B. Johnson voiced her belief that "one of the most pressing challenges for the individual is the depression and the tension resulting from existence in a world which is increasingly less pleasing to the eye. Our peace of mind, our emotions, our spirit—even our souls—are conditioned by what our eyes see" (White House Conference on Natural Beauty 1965).

The final phase in this evolution of policy, environmental planning, is obviously much broader than visual or aesthetic landscape issues. Its vital importance, however, is that it moved toward establishing a policy and administrative environment, at the national level and in a number of states, in which aesthetics are to be considered in environmental decision making "along with economic and technical considerations."

Each succeeding phase in this policy sequence provided landscape architects and others concerned with visual values with increasingly difficult tasks. During the first phase, visual values essentially were ignored. The national priorities appeared to be clear—conquer and settle the landscape. During the preservation phase, identification of the uniquely beautiful landscapes of the country was a relatively straightforward task. Getting action taken to preserve them was a very real challenge, however. The economics versus aesthetics argument surfaced early in this phase and has never disappeared. The recreation phase built upon the challenges of the preservation phase. Landscape analysis methods and procedures had to be developed to select attractive and physically suitable sites for recreation. And this frequently had to be part of a multiple-use planning activity. This phase also saw the rise of public interest in decisions made about landscape and resource allocations. Public participation was surfacing as an integral part of large-scale planning and design activities. Parallel with this development was a growing interest in gaining better understanding of public perceptions of landscape values and their consonance with decision makers' perceptions.

The fourth phase, addressing the amelioration of scenic ills by doing away with ugliness in the environment, was both an extension of the recreation phase and an introduction to the environmental planning phase. Public participation interests that emerged in the late 1950s and early 1960s continued to grow, confronting professionals with a broadened view of who the clients were. There was also a new set of design problems identified—designs to reclaim ugly and derelict landscape—and a challenge to devise strategies for minimizing the recurrence of such landscapes in the future.

The environmental planning phase saw public participation become institutionalized as a requirement in essentially all federal environmental legislation. It provided landscape architects with the challenge of interdisciplinary team work and it further challenged them and others interested in visual values with developing valid and reliable methods and procedures for assessing visual values and for incorporating them into interdisciplinary planning and decision making.

IDENTIFYING LANDSCAPE VALUES

Public policy, particularly since the early 1960s, has provided the major stimulus for development of better methods and procedures for assessing landscape values. During this period of time an impressive body of work has been undertaken in the United States and England by individuals from an array of disciplines. The breadth of work undertaken is a reflection of the breadth of the field. Ecologists, economists, foresters, geographers, landscape architects, planners, and psychologists have all contributed. There have been a number of state-of-the-art conferences and symposia, and, recently, a number of scholarly critiques and reviews of the literature that document developments in the field. Both the conferences and the literature reviews provide excellent windows on the approaches being taken to study landscape values and on the kinds of pragmatic and conceptual problems involved in landscape assessment.

Conferences and Symposia

In May, 1967 the Landscape Research Group in England organized a symposium on Methods of Landscape Analysis (Murray 1967). The introduction to the symposium identified four main groups of problems:

1. Techniques for measuring quickly, to a suitable degree of accuracy and detail, the physical characteristics of a landscape.
2. Techniques for measuring human reaction to environmental conditions.
3. Techniques for manipulating the very large quantities of data (some of it new in kind) thus made available.
4. Means of incorporating the results of this work into the design process.

The symposium addressed only the first group of problems. Primary attention was directed to methods that were systematic and objective. There was recognition that describing landscape attributes and characteristics is usually a highly subjective process and that for landscape data to have utility in planning and design decision making they should not be idiosyncratic to the individual but that the methods used should produce the same results if employed by several individuals.

A second conference was held at the University of Massachusetts in November, 1973 and was organized around three themes: values, perceptions, and resources (Zube et al. 1975). The first theme provided a humanistic perspective and traced landscape values historically and from the vantage point of several disciplines. In this context the concern was primarily with people and how they interact with and are affected by the landscape, rather than with the landscape per se. The second theme addressed both conceptual and applied questions in assessing perceptions of landscape quality. Among the questions addressed were what is or are: (1) the validity of various forms of landscape simulation; (2) the extent of agreement between experts and lay persons; (3) the characteristics of valued landscapes; and (4) the differences among (a) descriptive assessments which depict or measure attributes of specific landscape, (b) evaluative appraisals—relative landscape judgments employing an explicit or implicit standard of comparison, and (c) personal, subjective, preferential judgments. The third theme was approached through conceptual models and case studies demonstrating different approaches to landscape assessment. Unifying elements running through all of the models and cases were objectivity and systematic designs. None of the cases directly utilized data provided by perception studies. Most of the American examples, however, implicity reflected assumed values for sublime and picturesque landscapes.

Another conference was held at the State University of New York at Syracuse in 1975 and was oriented to a specific kind of landscape, the coastal zone (Harper and Warbach 1975). The conference consisted of three sessions that in part paralleled the Amherst meeting a year earlier: visual attitudes and perceptions; visual quality assessment methods; and visual quality planning on the coast. Running through each session was the consistent tie to coastal landscapes. The last session included both general strategies and methods and specific examples of coastal planning activities. The conference was timely and meshed well with the then-current planning activities carried on under the Coastal Zone Management Act mentioned earlier in this chapter.

In September 1976 the Landscape Research Group in England held another symposium, this one entitled "The Aesthetics of Landscape" (Appleton 1976). While this symposium also addressed applied issues, the primary emphasis was on a humanistic interpretation of landscape and the distinctions and similarities among disciplinary orientations including education, geography, history, landscape architecture, literature, and the visual arts. As is the case with many conferences and symposia, questions such as this are rarely answered and frequently lead to more questions. But they also open up discussions and suggest new concepts and approaches. Two particularly provocative questions were raised by artist-educator, Ewart Johns (1976):

1. Do our aesthetic values, especially as they relate to the environment, date from the nineteenth century or earlier and are they, in consequence, of little use to us now in our attempts to distinguish the "good" from the "bad" or the "better" from the "worse"?
2. How much do we perceive individual objects—especially those which are the product

of modern technology—as separate "items" and hence as intrusive elements in the general scene?

He was asking, in part, whether the eighteenth- and nineteenth-century values associated with picturesque and sublime landscapes prevailed and, if so, whether they stand in the way of our appreciating twentieth-century contributions. In partial answer to his own question he suggested that "the notion of total discontinuity between this and previous centuries" needed to be dispelled.

The most recent and certainly the largest conference was held at Incline Village, Nevada in 1979 and was organized under the aegis of the Forest Service, Soil Conservation Service, Bureau of Land Management and 12 additional institutional and agency cosponsors (Elsner and Smardon 1979). The overriding theme of the conference was on "applied techniques for analysis and management of the visual resource." These techniques were categorized as descriptive approaches, computer and quantitative approaches, and psychometric and social science approaches. Descriptive approaches derive primarily from the techniques of landscape architects and resource managers, but can also include historic and geographic landscape descriptions. Computer and quantitative approaches were developed initially for working with large landscapes that may be difficult of access and for which there are available quantitative and spatial geographic data such as slope, vegetation type, elevation, and percentage of tree cover. They provide descriptive information about variability in landscape characteristics and can identify at different viewing points, for example, which areas can be seen and which are hidden from view because of topographic configuration or vegetative cover. They also introduce new computer simulation techniques for assessing the effects of different planning, management, and design decisions, techniques that extend well beyond the original efforts of Lorenzetti and Repton for considering a wide array of alternatives. Psychometric and social science approaches use the human as the measuring instrument. They attempt to elicit descriptive, preferential, or evaluative judgments from observers and users of the landscape and to understand the quality and nature of human-landscape interactions.

These applied techniques were discussed within the context of a series of landscape design, planning, and management topics including: surface mining and reclamation, urbanization, highway development, recreational development, rural and agricultural development, utility corridors and power plant siting, timber management, water resource development, and coastal energy development. The parallel between these topics and those of the White House Conference on Natural Beauty held 14 years earlier is striking.

There are a number of inferences that can be drawn from the structure and content of these conferences and symposia. The first, and perhaps most obvious, is that the field of visual analysis has experienced continual development in England and the United States during the relatively short time span of less than 20 years. For example, attendance at the early conferences and symposia ranged from 75 to 100 with the exception of Amherst with an attendance of 200. Nearly 800 people attended the Incline Village conference where 74 papers were presented and 104 papers were included in the proceedings. Furthermore, a 1976 review of the broader field of environmental perception research (Craik and Zube 1976) concluded that more work had been done in the subareas of natural and recreation environments than any other subarea except the sonic environment. Other subareas included urban, residential and institutional environments, and the environmental media of air, water, and land.

Secondly, the field is certainly multidisciplinary and employs a wide array of study techniques and methods. While some techniques and methods have evolved over a long time period and others have been developed within the field, most have been adapted from the disciplines of landscape architecture, psychology, geography, and history.

Thirdly, the previously noted parallel between the topical content of the 1965 White House Conference on Natural Beauty and the 1979 Incline Village Conference, "Our Natural Landscape," suggests that the problem domain has not changed significantly during the intervening years.

And fourthly, the field has been responsive to changing policy emphases from recreation and multiple use to scenic rivers and trails, surface mine reclamation, highway design, forest management, and visual impact assessment. The NEPA also provided an important avenue for visual analysis to become integrated in a broad array of development and management proposals as part of the broader environmental impact assessment process.

Critiques and Reviews

Five scholarly critiques and reviews of the field were published in 1981 and 1982. Three were published in journals and two in monographs. The journals, indicating the disciplinary breadth of the field are *Landscape Planning* (Zube et al. 1982), *Journal of Environmental Psychology* (Porteus 1982) and *Progress in Human Geography* (Penning-Rowsell 1981). Both of the monographs, *Human Behavior and Environment* (Daniel and Vining 1982) and *Valued Environments* (Punter 1982) are multidisciplinary in authorship. A detailed comparative analysis of the contents of these reviews will not be presented here as it has been done elsewhere (Zube 1984). Of importance for this chapter are the converging conclusions that were reached independently in nearly all of the reviews.

Three of the reviews emphasized work that had a predominantly rural or wild landscape orientation (Zube et al. 1982; Penning-Rowsell 1981; Daniel and Vining, 1982), one took a broader view encompassing the entire landscape spectrum from urban to wild (Porteus 1982), and one concentrated on the urban landscape (Punter 1982). Each of the reviews identified a set of paradigms or models for purposes of categorizing the multiple approaches to visual analysis. While there was considerable agreement in the conceptualization of these models or paradigms, there was considerably less agreement on nomenclature. It should also be noted that the terminology for the process or activity being reviewed was equally disparate, ranging from landscape aesthetics and landscape perception to landscape quality, landscape value, and environmental aesthetics.

Table 1.2 illustrates the different terminology used to describe the various models or paradigms. Regardless of the terminology, however, there are three fairly consistent categorizations common across most reviews. They are indicated as

TABLE 1.2. Models/Paradigms in Landscape Assessment

	Professional A		Behavioral B		Humanistic C
Daniel and Vining (1982)	Ecological	Formal Aesthetic	Psychophysical	Psychological	Phenomenological
Penning-Rowsell (1981)	Intuitive Statistical Sophistication		Preference		
Porteous**	Planners		Experimentalists		Humanists
Punter (1982)	Landscape/Visual Quality		Landscape Perception		Landscape Interpretation
Zube, Sell and Taylor (1982)	Experts		Psychophysical	Cognitive	Experiential

*Adapted from (45)
**Porteous also includes an activist category made up of individuals with "immediate practical aims" relating to "issues of conservation, preservation and rehabilitation" of non-urban and urban landscapes.

professional, behavioral, and humanistic. The professional paradigm represents the work of designers, planners, and resource managers. It is based on formal principles of design and, in some instances, on beliefs about relationships between aesthetics and management—for example, the belief that a well-managed forest is a beautiful forest. The emphasis, however, is on the systematic use of the formal principles of design. The product is usually a description of the landscape in physical and aesthetic/design terms with assigned values on the basis of such descriptions.

The behavioral paradigm draws predominantly on the discipline of psychology. It differs from the professional paradigm in several significant ways. It uses the observer or participant in the landscape as the measuring instrument and the objective is to learn what the user's responses to the landscape are. There are two primary categories of responses that have been studied: (1) perceptions of beauty or visual quality, and (2) connotative meanings. Work frequently includes the development of predictive landscape dimensions which may be physical such as vegetation, topography, and water, or design and cognitive concepts such as mystery, complexity, and legibility. Statistical analysis relates ratings of beauty with variations in landscape dimensions and thus provides some understanding about how variations in the landscape—whether they be expressed as mystery and legibility or topography and vegetation—relate to variations in perceptions of beauty.

The humanistic paradigm draws on the traditions and methods of disciplines such as anthropology, cultural geography, history, and phenomenology. It attempts to understand the transactions between humans and landscape, personal experiences of landscape, and meanings of the everyday landscape. The products of humanistic studies vary with the disciplinary orientation but tend to be qualitative rather than quantitative. Where the behavioral paradigm yields group norms on perceptions of landscape beauty or connotative meanings, this paradigm yields detailed information about individuals and specific places. It does not lead to predictive equations but to descriptions of experiences.

These reviews lead to several general conclusions. Each paradigm has strengths and weaknesses and offers a unique contribution to the field. No individual paradigm as it currently exists is adequate to meet today's needs for landscape assessment. The professional paradigm has been most extensively employed and is dominant in the literature (Zube et al. 1982). However, several recent studies have raised important questions about the reliability of results produced under this paradigm (Craik and Feimer 1979; Feimer et al. 1979; Ross and Kopka 1983). In other words, there are important questions to be addressed about the agreement among assessments by different individuals when assessing the same landscape using the same methods and procedures. The efforts for objectivity in method and practice apparently have not as yet produced the required degree of reliability in field applications.

The behavioral paradigm provides the most rigorous approach to landscape assessment. Drawing heavily on psychological research designs and employing statistical analyses of data, questions of validity and reliability are answered within specified limits of confidence. Unless these data are related to landscape attributes or characteristics that the designer, planner, or manager can manipulate, however, they have limited utility in decision making. Also, in times of shrinking budgets, the costs for behavioral studies tend to exceed professional studies—even when landscape simulations are used in lieu of onsite assessments.

The humanistic paradigm provides the greatest depth of understanding about the meanings and experiences of landscapes. The methods employed, however, are frequently highly idiosyncratic and, when coupled with a focus on a limited number of individuals, they yield data that cannot readily be generalized to a larger population. Hence, direct utility is limited.

DISCUSSION

Johns (1976) questioned whether "our aesthetic values . . . date from the nineteenth century or earlier and are they, in consequence, of little use to us now . . .?" He was questioning values born in fourteenth century Italy, shaped in eighteenth- and nineteenth-century England, and adopted in nineteenth-century United States. If we accept public policy as normative public values, it appears that those values associated with sublime and picturesque landscapes are still operative, but it also appears that the landscape value spectrum has been extended beyond wild and rural landscapes to urbanizing and urban landscapes. Nevertheless, the body of work to date has emphasized the wild and rural.

In part this is probably attributable to the existence of public bureaus and agencies such as the Forest Service (FS), Bureau of Land Management (BLM), National Park Service (NPS), Soil Conservation Service (SCS), Army Corps of Engineers, and Department of Transportation which, under various policy mandates and specifically under NEPA, began to institutionalize the assessment of visual values and visual impacts as part of their planning and decision-making processes. There has been no equally effective institution addressing the urban environment as these in the rural and wild environment. Nor has there been an urban agency that has the direct management responsibility that the FS, BLM, and NPS have or the grass-roots organization in rural America that the SCS has. This is not to suggest that these bureaus and agencies have been consistently successful but rather that conditions existed that made it more likely for some kind of success in the rural and wild landscapes than in urban landscapes under the policies that were adopted and the political leadership through much of the 1960s and 1970s.

Better understanding of the attributes of wild and rural landscapes that people value might contribute to our understanding about how to improve urban landscapes. There may be principles of order, diversity, scale, coherence, and continuity that can be investigated and applied to urban problems. Greater emphasis on the humanistic paradigm could expand our knowledge of the symbolic and practical meanings that people associate with different landscapes and the relative priorities of values. Such qualitative information could be used to enrich the array of issues studied in the behavioral paradigm and provide the quantitative data desired by decision makers.

An important question now is whether the field has made great enough advances to survive the more restrictive conditions that prevail in the postenvironmental movement era? The available evidence suggests a tentative affirmative answer. Several methodological and theoretical advances could greatly enhance this cautious but positive outlook. The first has already been alluded to. It is the development of a firm understanding of the significant contribution of each paradigm to the field. While the professional paradigm has been criticized for lack of reliability, and validity is yet to be demonstrated, it is highly unlikely, because of costs and time, that every visual analysis project is going to employ behavioral paradigm methods and involve panels of users to assess values. What seems more plausible is that the behavioral paradigm will be followed when major or new types of projects or new subgroups of the public are involved. The professional paradigm will still provide the primary mode of analysis and evaluation. However, definite steps will have to be taken to increase reliability, to train professionals to be responsive to the identified values of various groups, and to provide quantitative data where required to be compatible with other contributions to the interdisciplinary planning process.

Finally, the field needs a conceptual framework or unifying theory that links the three paradigms and provides a means of assessing the cumulative contribution that two decades of study and application have made to the preservation and enhancement of the landscape and to the quality of life and well-being (Zube 1984). Such a framework or theory will both help us to better understand what has already been done and to more intelligently plan what needs to be done in the future in the areas of research, applications, and education.

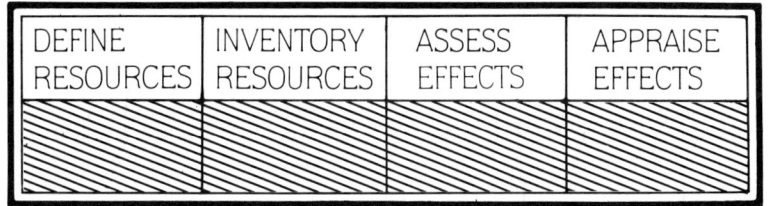

CHAPTER 2

DECISION-MAKING MODEL FOR VISUAL RESOURCE MANAGEMENT AND PROJECT REVIEW

Richard C. Smardon, John P. Felleman, and James F. Palmer

THE LEGAL CONTEXT OF SCENIC PROJECT ANALYSIS

Introduction

As seen from Chapter 1, the importance of scenic resources is deeply ingrained in cultural values. In traditional societies, the visual harmony between development and context was made possible through widely shared traditions and the resulting similarity of project types and forms extended over periods of time. This was commonly known as vernacular design. Such internal cohesiveness is often not possible in modern society. Technological advances have created projects and materials never seen before. The rapid growth of communications and transportation has led to potential development pressures on even the most remote locations, while escalating real estate markets make feasible the development within urbanized areas of previously impractical sites.

These forces have placed many of our culturally valued scenic resources in jeopardy. In modern society, imbalances between the public good and the free market are typically mediated through government control. Due to our federal system of government, such regulation can become quite complex. It is safe to say that the vast majority of project-related scenic analyses are conducted to satisfy some regulatory requirement. Therefore, the purpose of this chapter is to provide a typological framework to aid the analyst in understanding the legal determinants which these studies must satisfy.

Jurisdiction

The Constitution of the United States explicitly divides powers between the federal government and the states, with special powers being reserved for all citizens. Although aesthetics were not initially considered, their current legitimacy is grounded in the roots of the federal system.

The federal government can own and manage property. This is the basis for vast ownership, ranging from offshore lands and wilderness parks to penitentiaries and post offices. The federal government can regulate interstate commerce. This has led to controls on hydroelectric power, transportation, and telecommunications. The federal government is also responsible for national defense. Included are all military installations as well as nuclear energy facilities and interstate (national defense) highways.

State governments are also granted the right to own and manage property. In addition, they are granted the traditional "police powers"—the protection of health, safety, morals, and general welfare. These powers are applied on a statewide basis for the management of critical resource areas such as wetlands and scenic rivers. Other land use controls are delegated to local jurisdictions; these include, for example, zoning bylaws, subdivision regulations, and building codes.

Ratification of the Constitution was predicated on the addition of the first ten amendments, the Bill of Rights. Two significant rights are freedom of expression and just compensation for property taken for the common good. The former places limits on government's ability to control development form such as architectural style and color. The principle of taking includes both physical acquisition and regulatory control of viable economic use of the land.

In addition to explicit powers, governments have evolved a wide range of implicit powers during the past 200 years. These occurred in part due to the complexity of modern society, and in part because of the vast amounts of wealth that accumulated at state and national levels from increased tax revenues. These powers have led to government involvement in such diverse areas as housing and the arts. In addition to engaging in explicit areas of responsibility, units of government can enact broad legislative policies which control the manner in which all governmental activities will be implemented. Examples include freedom of information, public participation, and environmental quality. Thus a policy statement such as the National Environmental Policy Act (NEPA) affects practically all federal activities involving the land, air, or water.

Regulatory Process

The powers of government are generally divided among three branches: legislative, executive, and judicial. This separation of power is intended to provide a set of checks and balances.

The primary function of the legislative branch is to establish policy through creating laws. "A legislative body is at its best in determining the direction of a major policy.... It is ill suited for handling masses of detail, or for applying to shifting and continuing problems the ideas supplied

THE LEGAL CONTEXT OF SCENIC PROJECT ANALYSIS 23

by scientists or other professional advisors" (Davis 1971, 15). A classic example of this broad-brush approach to law making is the National Environmental Policy Act.

The executive branch is charged with implementing the law. Agencies and departments typically establish internal operating policies and procedures for management of government resources. The Visual Management System of the U.S. Forest Service (1974) is an example of such a procedure. Agencies promulgate rules and regulations for regulation of private activities and property. Regulations are commonly implemented through a permit process which articulates both procedural and substantive components. Procedure encompasses timetables, communications, information requirements, and fee schedules. Substance identifies the specific grounds on which the permit application decision will be based. Often in the case of new regulations an agency will develop a set of guidelines to direct the applicants' analyses. Conformance to guidelines is usually recommended but not required.

The actual test of a law's legitimacy is in the courts (See Table 2.1). In order to bring a case

TABLE 2.1. Major Court Cases and Hearings Involving Aesthetic Issues

Common Name	Legal Citation	Aesthetic Analysis/or Background Source
Old Man in the Mountain, New Hampshire Highway Project	Soc. for the Protec. of N. H. Forests v. Claude S. Brinegar. Civ. A Nos. 74-217, 394 F. Supp. 105 (1975).	C. Frey (1978) J. French (1975)
Scenic Hudson, New York; Proposed Pumped Storage Power Plant	354 F. 2d 608 (2nd Cir. 1965) Cert. denied 384 U.S. (1966)	Sive (1970a) Sive (1970b) Goodman (1972)
Mineral King, California; Proposed Ski Resort	Sierra Club v. Morton 92 S. Ct. 1361 405 U.S. 727 (1972)	Note (1970) Ferguson & Bryson (1972) Johnson (1974) Sax (1973)
Rainbow Bridge; Reservoir	Friends of the Earth v. Armstrong 485 F. 2d 1 (10th Cir. 1973)	Draper (1974) Thompson (1973)
Walton v. St. Clair Minnesota; Bounday Waters Canoe Area; Mining Activity	Walton v. St. Clair 313 F. Supp. 1312 (1970)	Ferguson & Haggard (1973) Haggard (1975)
East Meadow Creek; Colorado Timber Cutting Activity	Parker v. U.S. 448 F. 2d 793 (1971) Cert. denied 92 S. Ct. 1252 (1971)	Cutler (1972)
Overton Park, Tennessee; Highway Project	Citizens to Preserve Overton Park v. Volpe 401 U.S. 402 S. Ct. 814	Giorgio (1972)
Death Valley Monument, California; Proposed Mining Activity	Death Valley National Monument et al. v. The Dept. of the Interior. Civ. Act. No. 76-401 (D.N.D. Cal. filed Feb. 26, 1976).	Hamson and Ristau (1979)
Ice Age National Monument, Wisconsin; Proposed Power Line	Wisconsin Public Service Commission (PSCW) 1977. Hearing record of case 6680-CE-13 and Wisconsin; Public Service Comm. Findings of fact & order. Case 6680-CE-13.	Murray & Neiman (1979)

TABLE 2.1. (continued)

Common Name	Legal Citation	Aesthetic Analysis/or Background Source
Ogunquit, Maine; Dune Reconstruction	Ogunquit Village Corp. et al. v. R.M. Davis et al. C.A. 76-1426 (First Cir. April 26, 1977).	Schauman (1982).
Cross Lake, Louisiana I-220 Highway Bridge	Louisiana Environmental Society, Inc. and Mrs. Vernon B. Chase, Sr. v. Claude S. Brinegar; U.S. Dept. of Transportation and Dept. of Highways, State of Louisiana, Civ. A. No. 17, 233 U.S. Dist. Ct., Western District of Louisiana, April 9, 1981.	Atkins & Blair (1983).
Santa Barbara Oil Spill, California	County of Santa Barbara v. Hickel Civil No. 69-636 D.C. Cal., filed April 4, 1969.	Baldwin (1970)
Hells Canyon Dams. Washington, Idaho, Oregon. Proposed Dams and Reservoirs	Presiding Examiners Initial Decision on Remand, in Pacific Northwest Power Company, Project No. 2243 and Washington Public Power Supply System Project No. 2273, 1 E.L.R. 30017	Leopold (1969) Poland (1969)
Dept. of Ecology Private Shoreline Development	Dept. of Ecology et al. v. Pacesetter Construction Co.	Washington State Dept. of Ecology (1977)
McCormick Oseetah Lake New York; Private Shoreline Development	McCormick et al. v. Lawrence 83 Misc. 2d 64, 72 N.Y.S. 2d 156, 8 E.R.C. 1461 5 E.L.R. 20650, App. Div. 54 A.D., 2d 153, 387 N.Y.S. 2d 919, 6 E.L.R. 20795	Kanter (1980) Note (1975)
Miners Ridge Case Washington; Glacier Peak Wilderness; Proposed Mining		McCloskey (1967)
Grand Central Terminal; Proposed Highrise	Penn Central Transportation Co. et al. v. New York City et al. C.A.N.Y., No. 77-444, (June 26, 1978) ___U.S. ___.	11 E.R.C. 1801
Greene County Nuclear Power Plant		USNRC (1979)

before a court, a complainant must have legitimate standing. Parties directly involved in an administrative or regulatory matter, such as the agency or a project sponsor, typically have direct standing. In addition, many precedents have indicated that a broad range of third parties, such as national conservation groups, may have standing in situations that affect public resources.

Generally, judicial review follows two stages, procedural and substantive. In procedural review, issues such as timetables, notification, and documentation are examined. Nonconformance can lead to either a reversal of an administrative action or to an order to begin the administrative process anew.

If no procedural problems are found, then the courts may examine issues of substantive due process. These may include the extent and accuracy of the data utilized, the adequacy of analytical methods, and the incorporation of study findings in the ultimate management or regulatory decision. Courts tend to overthrow actions which are found to be arbitrary and capricious.

Obviously, the resolution of substantive questions is partially determined by the specificity of the administrative procedure or regulation. In general, three groupings of controls can be identified: *consideration, specification,* and *performance*. Some policies and regulations merely list aesthetics as one of many factors to be considered in a decision process. Professionals operating in this situation are provided little guidance in developing an analytical approach.

Specification standards can include data and design results. For example, the N.Y. Public Service Commission requires power line applications to include views from selected viewpoints (Kusler 1980). (Note that there is no specification of viewshed delineation method.) The Adirondack Park Agency protects scenic shorelines by prohibiting development closer than a specified distance. In this type of regulation, one or more of the resultant project's form parameters are given even though a project so many feet away may be highly visible and one a certain number of feet away may be hidden. The most sophisticated control approach is to establish performance standards and let the project sponsor substantiate conformance. The U.S. Forest Service's (1974) visual management classification system yields localized performance objectives. (See Chapter 9 for detailed review of the Forest Service's Visual Management System.)

Review of Major Legal Progressions and Trends

The evolution of the treatment of aesthetic values by the legal system can be summarized into a number of significant trends.

1. There is a shift in emphasis from (1) private action affecting private property (common nuisance) to (2) local public action regulating private property (zoning and architectural controls), to (3) public action taking private property (eminent domain), to (4) public action regulating public agency actions and public property (federal and state legislation) with some regulations and taking of common trust property (coastal zone, rivers, and so forth) (see Figure 2.1).

2. There is a gradual shift in the court's desire and ability to face issues involving environmental aesthetic values. This shift evolves from (1) not facing it, to (2) fictionalizing or masking aesthetics under other issues, to (3) facing up to the procedural right to address aesthetic injury in an antropocentric sense of the present human user.

3. Both these trends are occurring within the context of a highly erratic legal pendulum swinging from conservative to liberal decisions in linear time sequence. The liberal decisions are always labeled as maverick or the exception, but somehow are also signposts for

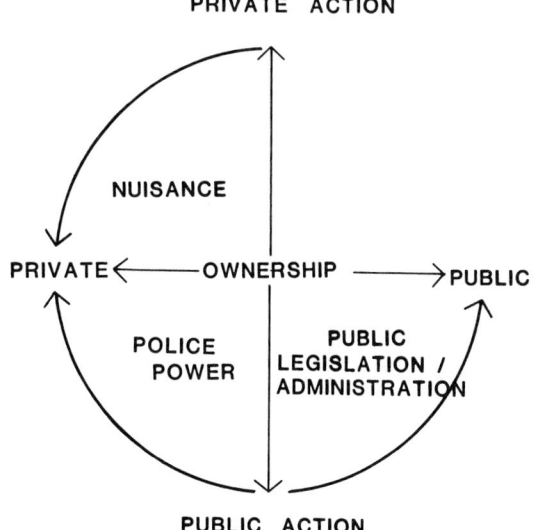

FIGURE 2.1. Shifts in legal emphasis.

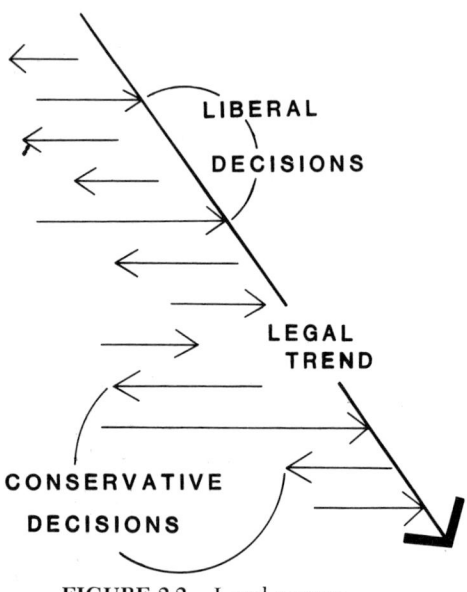

FIGURE 2.2. Legal process.

the overall general trend (see Figure 2.2 and Table 2.1).

APPROPRIATE CONTEXT FOR PROJECT REVIEW

Thus far, we have reviewed considerations of specificity of administrative procedure or regulation as well as major legal considerations affecting procedural and substantive review. Before a specific overall process is presented, a geotemporal scale reflected by actual visual studies and other considerations affecting amount of study detail will be reviewed.

Project Geotemporal Scales

In Table 2.2, some seven different geotemporal scales are indicated. The first two scales, national and subnational/regional scale are *large-scale areawide*. Aesthetic resource analyses are often initiated by federal or national agencies. These studies are usually engaged to surface visual resource values and issues over large geographic areas. Some examples include water resource reconnaissance studies for large drainage areas and areawide assessments for timber and range management (Litton and Tetlow 1978). Large-area assessments of a national scale such as the Countryside Commission of Scotland study (1979), a recent Australian study (Gerne, Sanderson, Faggetter, and Chessman 1979) as well as statewide studies in the United States for Vermont and Alaska have the purpose of classifying landscapes and identifying landscapes with high priority for preservation or special protection.

Regional scale landscape studies include landscape inventories and assessments for regional land use planning (see Fines 1968; Palmer 1973; Zube et al. 1974) for multiple resource planning for national forests; river basin planning (Jones and Jones 1975, 1973; Jackson et al. 1977) as well as shoreline and coastal planning (Chrisholm et al. 1974; Vineyard Open Land Foundation 1973). A special subcategory of coastal/shoreline studies are prescriptive design guidelines for compatible coastal development (Roy Mann Assoc. 1975).

At the town or citywide scale, a number of studies have included visual inventory and analysis for land use planning, urban renewal and urban design and image assessment. Most of these studies were done in the sixties and seventies in the United States under the Housing and Urban Development Administration 701 planning assistance program and were highly varied in quality and approach.

A particular kind of study which merges regional and site scales are linear or scenic corridor studies. These studies are usually for highway visual quality (Appleyard et al. 1964) or scenic rivers (Smardon et al. 1984). All of the previously mentioned studies were performed by private firms and government agencies to inventory, classify, analyze, and identify existing levels of landscape quality. This information can then be used for various planning actions. The remaining studies address specific project/activity decisions from regional to site scale. Many of these studies are generic impact assessments for linear and point phenomena location and general project planning. These generic visual impact studies include planning for forestry activity, national recreation area development, coal development programs over large areas, assessing generic impacts of power plants on river recreation, assessing generic corridor impacts of locating power transmission lines, assessing generic visual impacts of new liquid natural gas offloading facilities (Baird et al. 1979), and assessing potential impacts of implementing scenic river management policies (Steinitz et al. 1978).

In contrast to the studies illustrated above, we finally have site project scale studies which at-

TABLE 2.2. Matrix of Visual Resource Analyses: Scales, Decision Needs, Examples of Studies

SCALE	DECISION NEEDS/PROCESSES	SPECIFIC STUDIES
National Scale	• national landscape inventory/priority	Countryside Commission of Scotland (1979
Sub-National/ Regional Scale	• multiple river basin water resource planning studies	Litton and Tetlow (1978); Gerner Sanderson Faggetter Cheesman (1979)
Statewide Scale	• statewide landscape inventory for land use planning	Gordon and Shane (1978)
Regional Scale	• inventories and assessment for land use planning	Fines (1968); Zube et al. (1974)
	• for multiple resource planning for national forests	
	• river basin planning	Jones & Jones (1975, 1973); Jackson, Valesques and Harper (1977)
	• shoreline & coastal zone planning	Vineyard Open Land Foundation (1973); Chisholm et al. (1974); Roy Mann Assoc. (1975)
Town Scale Area Wide	• visual inventory & analyses for land use planning; urban renewal; urban design and image assessment	
Regional/Town Scale linear/corridor	• transportation and river planning	Appleyard, Lynch & Meyer (1964); Smardon et al. (1984)
Regional to Site	• generic impact assessment for linear and point phenomena, location and general project planning for: ◦ forestry activity	Kell (1979)
	• National recreation areas	
	• coal development	Tetlow & Sheppard (1977)
	• power plants	
	• power transmission lines	Blair et al. (1976)
	• LNG off-loading terminals	Baird et al. (1979)
	• scenic river management policies	Steinitz et al. (1978)
Site/Project Scale	• Detailed visual impact assessment of alternatives in environmental assessments or E.I.S.'s. Visual mitigation for: ◦ coal development ◦ quarry ◦ oil development ◦ oil pipeline/accessories ◦ power plants (nuclear refuse & coal)	Wirth Assoc. (1980); Fitzgerald (1979); Cairns, W.J. & Assoc. (1974); Architects Design Group (1978); Jones et al. (197); EDAW (1978); Petrich (1979 a & b)
	◦ windpower generators ◦ power lines ◦ dams & reservoirs	Wagstaff & Brady (1982); Sherer & Embree (1983); Dougal et al. (1973); Sydney (1970); Ady et al. (1979 a & b)
	◦ flood control alternatives ◦ coastal structures & dredging	Roy Mann Assoc. (1975); Smardon et al. (1980);
	◦ observatory ◦ ski area development	Univ. of Calif., Santa Cruz Angelo Johnson (1974)
	• Visual impact assessment & mitigation for: ◦ highways	Blair (1980); Kunit & Calhoun (1973);
	◦ urban development	Bosselman (1983); Stewart (1980); Erickson (1980); Smardon (1983);
	◦ port redevelopment ◦ industrial redevelopment	Blair et al. (1980, 1982); James, Johnson & Roy (1980)
	• Project management and evaluation, long-term mitigation for: ◦ highways	Colorado Dept. of Highways (1978); Hampe & Noe (1979);
	◦ forest harvesting ◦ waterfall management	Schwartz (1977); Int'l. Joint Commission (1975)

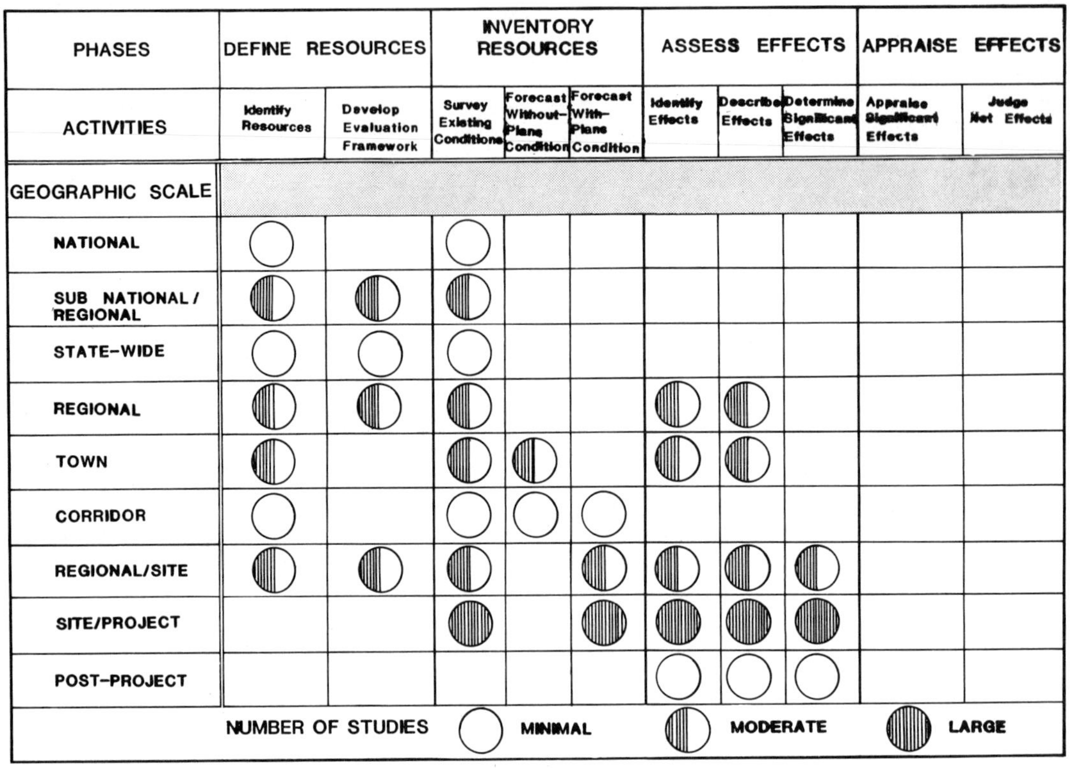

FIGURE 2.3. Phases/activities of aesthetic evaluation by geographic scale and frequency of studies.

tempt to assess the detailed visual impact of project alternatives in environmental assessments, environmental impact statements, or other similar studies which include visual impact mitigation. Most of the 30 sample projects that the authors had access to were done in the United States and the United Kingdom.

Project types for which detailed visual impact studies have been done include coal strip mine, hard rock quarry, oil and gas development, oil pipelines and pumping stations, nuclear, conventional fossil fueled power plants, and refuse burning power plants, windpower generators, electric power transmission lines, dams and reservoirs, flood control alternatives, coastal structures and dredging, mountain top observatory, ski area development, highway development, urban development, port redevelopment, and industrial redevelopment. Note that this is a limited sample of detailed visual impact assessment reports that appear in the literature and that are executed mainly by private firms. The broad range of project types which have had detailed visual impact reports is notable but does not include environmental assessments and environmental impact statements or reports that included visual resource analyses as part of the report along with other resource considerations.

A content analysis of 96 Environmental Impact

TABLE 2.3. Proportion of EISs by Federal Agency Considering Visual/Aesthetic Impacts as Derived from Water Resources Abstracts 1968–1977

Agency	Number of EISs
U. S. Department of the Army Corps of Engineers	77 (80%)
U.S. Department of Agricultue	
Forest Service	2
Soil Conservation Service	2
U.S. Department of Energy	
Federal Power Commission	3
Tennessee Valley Authority	1
U.S. Department of Interior	
Bureau of Land Management (OCS)	2
Bureau of Outdoor Recreation	1
Bureau of Reclamation	5
Environmental Protection Agency	2
Ohio River Basin Commission	1
Total	96

Statement (E.I.S.) abstracts from the Water Resources Abstracts from 1968 to 1977 was done to see the types of aesthetic impacts identified, whether alternatives were considered, and whether measures to minimize harm were considered. The basic results of this analysis can be seen in Tables 2.3 and 2.4. The majority of the EISs (80%) were done by the Corps of Engineers, which is not surprising since Water Resources Abstracts would key into water resource projects. Fifteen percent of the EISs claimed aesthetic enhancement of the environment, which is understandable for certain urban projects. Fifty-eight percent of the EISs were adverse aesthetic impacts. The degree of adversity generally increases as you read down Table 2.4. However, the vague and general terms used to describe visual impacts in most cases made judgement almost impossible in regard to severity of visual impact. The reader should note also that very few EISs considered visual quality alternatives or detailed measures to minimize harm. Note that the three major types of adverse visual impact encountered in these EISs were: (1) unnatural intrusion of man-made appearance or disfigurement or the general criterion of naturalness in relation to the context; (2) partial degradation, reduction, or impairment of the existing level of visual quality; and (3) the complete loss of the visual resource, whether it is a natural stream, marsh, stand of trees, and so forth.

What can be seen from this analysis and other reports (Andrews and Waits 1978) is that, procedurally, visual considerations as treated in EISs have rarely met the requirements as stated in NEPA and the CEQ (Council on Environmental Quality) guidelines. Subsequently, the treatment of visual and aesthetic considerations has often not advanced with a few notable exceptions in certain EISs and environmental assessments. The most notable exceptions in the advanced state-of-the-art in visual environmental assessment often utilize different forms of visual simulation in order to better understand the visual aesthetic impacts for professional analysis and to better communicate these visual impacts to affected publics.

TABLE 2.4. Treatment of Aesthetic Impacts

		Actual #	% of E.I.S.s Sampled
I.	Identification of Impacts		
	Enchancement of Aesthetics		
	Environment unspecified	1	
	Improved view	1	
	Improved aesthetic appeal/improvement in aesthetic conditions/ elimination of unsightliness/increase in recreational potential	12	15%
	Subtotal	14	15%
	Adverse Effects on Aesthetics		
	Adverse effects unspecified	2	
	Temporary/short term	6	
	Partial degradation/impairment	14	
	Unnatural intrusion/man-made appearance/disfigurement	15	
	Unsightliness	3	
	Scale incompatibility	1	
	Restriction of views	2	
	Complete loss of resource	10	
	Long-term irreversible effect	2	
	Unavoidable adverse effect	2	
	Subtotal	57	58%
II.	Consideration of visual alternatives/design treatments	4	
III.	Consideration of measures to minimize harm	8	
	Subtotal	12	13%

The final level of geotemporal scale involves management decisions that need to be made once the project is in place or the activity has started. This often involves monitoring of activity or construction while the project is being built or after construction is finished. Examples include studies conducted by the U.S. Park Service of vegetation management along national parkways (Hampe and Noe 1979), detailed visual mitigation documentation of mountain highway construction (Colorado Dept. of Highways 1978) and detailed evaluation of timber harvesting techniques (Schwarz 1977). One of the best-known studies was the study of alternatives to maintain the appearance of Niagara Falls by the Joint International Commission (1975).

Project Planning Context

As can be seen from all the previously described visual analyses, they are in response to three types of regulatory situations: (1) public land management and planning; (2) public projects involving private lands; and (3) public regulation of private projects (after Smardon and Felleman 1982). The overall process that follows within this book is applicable to all three regulatory situations. Also, as pointed out by Palmer (1983) in an overview article of the field of visual quality and visual impact assessment, we will be proposing methods for integrating visual assessments within four general stages of environmental decision making: (1) environmental inventory; (2) policy formation; (3) program planning or project design; and (4) postimpact evaluation. The overall emphasis will be clearly weighted toward stage three—project planning and design decisions.

Also, we need to place the implied process of this book within a general project design/planning process. Such a process should allow us to fit visual resource assessment in at various stages of decision making and allow for modification in the planning or design process as a result. Note that the following figures and description include detailed activities and steps for both preliminary or large-scale reconnaissance planning studies as well as more detailed preconstruction planning and design studies. This particular process provides suggestions as to the general phases and specific steps that are needed given the geotemporal scale of project.

TOWARD AN AESTHETIC ANALYSIS DECISION-MAKING FRAMEWORK

A Generic Process

To better integrate aesthetic resources into planning and decision-making processes affecting water resource development, a special subcommittee of the National Research Council was convened (See Coughlin et al. 1982). The committee's work resulted in a generalized procedure for aesthetic resources evaluation and was later incorporated in the Economic and Environmental Principles and Guidelines for Water and Related Land Resource Implementation Studies (U.S. Water Resources Council 1983). This procedure was interpreted and embellished enough to teach it to personnel from the U.S. Corps of Engineers as part of a short course on Aesthetic Resources: Identification, Analysis and Evaluation (Hawks, Felleman, Lambe, Palmer, and Smardon 1983). The basic structure of this framework is both comprehensive and sound enough to organize material presented in this chapter as well as the rest of the book. The following sections will present the generalized aesthetic evaluation procedure.

Before getting into the four main phases of the procedure, the authors would like to introduce the notion of Red Flag criteria, which are a way of noting immediate problems and opportunities which arise when a given project or study is proposed for a given site or study area. Problems as illustrated in Figure 2.4 are predominantly negative factors which may complicate project planning or positive factors in that they may provide mitigating opportunities.

After the Red Flag criteria are applied to identify problems and opportunities, we get into the four major phases as identified in Figure 2.5. They are: (1) defining aesthetic resources that are *significant* and likely to be affected by the project, and developing an evaluation framework; (2) inventorying aesthetic resources, which includes surveying existing conditions and forecasting with and without plan conditions; (3) assessing effects on the landscape from generic or detailed alternatives; and (4) appraising effects via public evaluation in terms of significance and overall effects after mitigation.

Each of the phases and steps will be described in more detail, utilizing Figure 2.6 as a guide.

PROBLEMS:

☐ Actual site of landscape painting, poetic subject, literary subject or artistic treatment in study area.
☐ Project can be seen or is near local, state or federal park, scenic route, historic site, marine or estuarine sanctuary, wilderness or primitive area, landmark, wild and scenic river, research preserve or similar designation.
☐ The study area is unofficially recognized (e.g. in tourist guidebooks, on local maps) as being particularly scenic or historic.
☐ The study area is used for passive recreation (e.g. sightseeing, bicycle riding, horseback riding, etc.)
☐ Tourism is a major keystone in the locality's or region's economy.
☐ The study area is easily accessible by a major population center.
☐ The type of project is typically highly visible and/or requires major changes in the existing landscape.

☐

☐

☐

OPPORTUNITIES:

☐ The dominant visual qualities of an area allow a sympathetic design form.
☐ The project area has low scenic quality and limited visibility.
☐ The project will increase access to views of high scenic quality.
☐ The project will create scenic easements, especially views to surface water.
☐ The project will improve the scenic quality of an area (e.g. urban waterfront renewal).

☐

☐

☐

☐

FIGURE 2.4. Red flag criteria.

PLANNING PROCESS:	AESTHETIC RESOURCE STUDY:
1. Specify Problems and Opportunities	Red Flag Criteria
2. Inventory and Forecast Resource Conditions	Phases of 1. Define resources 2. Inventory resources
3. Formulate Alternative Plans	Design Prototypes and Impact Mitigation Through Design!
4. Evaluate Effects	Phases of 3. Assess effects 4. Appraise effects
5. Compare Alternatives	Weight Aesthetic Criteria Against Other Appropriate Criteria
6. Select Plan	Implement Recommendations in Final Design, Construction, and Management Activities

FIGURE 2.5. Major steps in aesthetic quality planning.

PHASES:	ACTIVITIES:	FEASIBILITY STUDY LEVEL OF DETAIL		
		OR PRELIMINARY DETAIL OF RECONNAISANCE STUDY		AND REVISED DURING PRE-CONSTRUCTION PLANNING
DEFINE RESOURCES	IDENTIFY RESOURCES	Identify Resources based on Scoping Study that are: 1) Significant, and 2) Likely to be Affected		Identify the Viewshed of the Project Using the Prototype Design Form.
	DEVELOP EVALUATION FRAMEWORK	Define an Aesthetic Quality Evaluation Process Using the Aesthetic Evaluation Framework Matrix		Identify the Key Viewpoints within the Project Viewshed. (Create Visual Simulations for Use in Aesthetic Quality Evaluation.)
INVENTORY RESOURCES	SURVEY EXISTING CONDITIONS	Classify the Various Visual Landscape Types (Visual Resources)	Classify the Various Landscape Viewsheds (Management Units)	Classify and Evaluate the Existing Landscape within Each Visual Simulation.
		Rank the Landscape Types and Viewsheds, and Combine to Create a Composite Map of Selected Visual Characteristics		
	FORECAST WITHOUT-PLANS CONDITION	Forecast the Without-Plan Conditions for the Study Area to Revise the Composite Map.		Forecast Without-Plan Conditions for the Viewshed and Revise the Existing Landscape Evaluation.
	FORECAST WITH-PLAN CONDITION	If Alternative Project Sites Have **Not** Been Determined, Make Assumptions about the Potential Alternative Project Types.	If Alternative Project Sites Have Been Determined, Use the Generic Prototype of Each Project to Forecast With-Plan Conditions to Revise the Composite Map.	Forecast With-Plan Conditions for the Viewshed Using the Anticipated Project Design.
ASSESS EFFECTS	IDENTIFY EFFECTS	Identify Relevant Qualities of the Generic Prototype Design Form for Each Likely Alternative.	Identify Any Changes in Landscape Character or Landscape Views. (For Each Alternative)	Create a Visual Simulation of the Anticipated Project to Identify the Visual Impacts.
	DESCRIBE EFFECTS	Describe the Potential Effects of Each Generic Prototype within the Various Landscape Types and Viewsheds.	Describe Beneficial and Adverse Changes in the Landscape Character within Each Selected Viewshed.	Use the V.I.A. Rating Form to Describe the Visual Impacts of the Project.
	DETERMINE SIGNIFICANT EFFECTS	Rank Zones of the Composite Map with Respect to the Potential Effects of Each Generic Project Alternative.	Determine Which Changes of the Visual Landscape Are Significant Effects.	Determine which Visual Impacts Are Significant Effects and to What Degree.
APPRAISE EFFECTS	APPRAISE SIGNIFICANT EFFECTS	Recommend Sites for Each Project Type Based on the Ranked Zones of the Composite Map.	Explore Mitigation Measures for All Significant Adverse Effects.	Explore Design Alternatives for the Project and Other Mitigation Measures to Eliminate or Reduce the Significant Effects.
	JUDGE NET E.Q. EFFECTS	Select Sites for Further Study (Return to Forecast With-Plan Condition Activity in Next Column)	Select Recommended Project Alternative(s) and Location(s).	Select Recommended Design Form and Management Activities.

NOTE: This figure is an illustrative outline of the appropriate activities involved in a visual impact assessment study. The amount of detail and number of revisions for each activity will vary according to specific projects. In some cases, sonic and olfactory qualities of a project will require the appropriate complementary study.

FIGURE 2.6. Aesthetic environmental quality evaluation process.

A. **Define Resources:** This phase is performed to identify aesthetic or visual resources that should be evaluated.

1. IDENTIFY AESTHETIC RESOURCES: This is accomplished by reviewing existing information to identify aesthetic resources that are:
   a. Significant because of *institutional, public,* or *technical recognition;* and/or
   b. Likely to be affected by one or more of the alternative plans.

   Institutional, public and technically significant aesthetic resources can be defined as follows:

   Institutional recognition: The aesthetic attribute is ackknowledged in the laws, adopted plans, and other policy statements of public agencies or private groups.

   Public recognition: Some segment of the public recognizes the importance of an aesthetic attribute or resource.

   Technical recognition: The importance of the resource is based on scientific or technical knowledge or judgement of critical resource characteristics.

   Interrelated aesthetic resources having more than one aesthetic attribute should be considered, for example, a salt marsh yielding sound, smell, and visual sensations. As such, many aesthetic resources will be deemed significant by more than one criteria. At such a preliminary stage in the process, a determination of likelihood as to whether a significant aesthetic resource may be affected by a project is needed. Exhaustive documentation of cause and effect linkages are not needed. Future conditions may also change the types of aesthetic resources affected or create new ones.

2. DEVELOP EVALUATION FRAMEWORK: The appropriate attributes to be assessed should be arranged in the evaluation framework as shown in Figure 2.7. Note that such attributes are primarily visual but may include other senses. Although such attributes may be partially embodied in physical landscape attributes, the most appropriate aesthetic

Resource Subsystems	Attributes Major Indicators	Operational Indicators	Physical Geographic Units						Modifying Variables
			Landform	Water	Vegetation	Structures	Human Activity	Wildlife	
Visual Landscape Quality (90%)	Landscape Compatibility	Form Line Color Texture	(Examples) Basins Geology Gorges Knolls Peaks Valleys Pinnacles Towers Ridges Dunes Desert	(Examples) Creek Geyser Glacier Lake Pond Pool Rapid Reservoir River Spring Stream Swamp Wetland Waterfall	(Examples) Forest Grassland Plain Desert Wetlands	(Examples) Buildings Districts Features Products Objects Structures		(Examples) Individual & Groups of Species, Birds, Mammals Reptiles	Light Direction Movement Seasonal Changes Temporal Patterns Observer Position Observer Angle Distance Visual Acuity
	Scale Contrast								
	Spatial Dominance								
	Uniqueness/ Scarcity	Presence				Historic Landmarks	Festivals Cultural Activities	Rare and Endemic Species	
	Visibility	Viewshed							Distance Observer Position Movement
Sonic Quality	Uniqueness	Presence		Waterfall		Chimes Bells Whistles			Distance
	Pleasantness								
	Lack of Noise	Decibels							
Olfactory Taste Quality	Uniqueness	Presence					Baking and Food Processing		Wind Direction
	Lack of Noxious Smells								
Tactile Quality	Uniqueness	Presence				Pavement Pattern			
	Lack of Tactile Problems								

FIGURE 2.7. Aesthetic evaluation framework (example).

indicators relate to levels of enjoyment or pleasure experienced by people's exposure to the resource. For indicators of presence of aesthetic resources, one must rely on subjective judgement of either professionals in the appropriate fields or key persons. The unit of analysis, on the other hand, should be set by the resource professional.

B. **Inventory Resources:** An inventory process collects or develops information which is useful for assessing the effects of alternative plans and employs the evaluation framework to determine data useful for specific indicators as well as units of analysis.

1. SURVEY EXISTING CONDITIONS: This activity involves an inventory of existing landscape conditions utilizing inventory and classification systems for such phenomena as landform, land cover, and cultural landscape patterns.

2. FORECAST OF CONDITIONS WITHOUT PLANS: A forecast should be proposed of the most probable conditions of the future landscape at the appropriate time line. Of particular importance, for example, would be the possible creation of or loss of significant vistas or change in landscape quality due to vegetative growth and succession.

3. FORECASTS WITH ALTERNATIVE PLANS: Alternative plans could be described in a manner consistent with the chosen landscape classification system and scales used in steps B.1. and B.2. The condition of the landscape under each alternative plan should be described. Secondary effects of the proposed project, such as new land development that may be generated in connection with the project, should be included.

C. **Assess Effects:** This phase's purpose is to identify and describe effects of alternative plans on aesthetic resources.

1. IDENTIFY EFFECTS: The affected area from which the project is visible should be determined using visibility analysis; then significant places in the affected area should be identified based on indications of exposure, use, or other indications of culturally significant aesthetic values. Simultaneously, the potentially impacting activity should be analyzed in terms of identifying project characteristics which affect specific parts of the landscape such as fills affecting landform, vegetation cuts, or new structures or activities.

2. DESCRIBE EFFECTS: Significant visual effects can be described with respect to critical viewpoints in the affected area. Critical viewpoints can be based on such considerations as highly frequented viewpoints, culturally significant views, and representative views of landscapes. For each vista or viewing mode, a representation or simulation of the scene is needed with and without the project to describe potential effects. The potential effects also need to be traced back to the causal attributes of the project or activity.

3. DETERMINE SIGNIFICANT EFFECTS: This step includes the assessment of professional findings or public preferences concerning the aesthetic impacts of project alternatives. Public preferences and evaluative appraisals are needed to determine the degree of significance of potential effects on the landscape.

D. **Appraise Effects:** This phase is performed to identify the appropriate weight of significant effects on aesthetic resources, individually and collectively, for each alternative plan. This is the phase in which aesthetic resources are compared with other resources in terms of importance of effects, and decisions are made concerning the proposed project(s).

1. APPRAISE SIGNIFICANT EFFECTS: The significant effects of each alternative should be appraised. Such an analysis may lead to modifications or mitigation of effects if causal linkages are known through steps C.1. and C.2.

2. JUDGE OVERALL EFFECTS: Judgement of the overall effect on environmental quality of each alternative is the final step. The visual analyst represents the

visual resource in this process and advises the final decision maker or client.

The remainder of the chapters contain an index graphic at the beginning of the chapter. Within each graphic is indicated the basic steps in an overall aesthetic evaluation process that is addressed in that particular chapter, for example, define resource, inventory resources, assess effects, and appraise effects. It is hoped that this device will aid the reader in locating particular processes or methods that are needed.

PART 2

BASIC VISUAL PROCESSES

Throughout human history, people have struggled to understand their environment. The problem is not straightforward because our only direct means of experiencing contextual phenomena is through our senses. Thus, to know nature we must, in essence, know ourselves. The ancient Greeks posed the essential dialectic that still concerns us today: does "reality" preexist within our minds, thus relegating the external world to a collage of imperfect patterns, or is the external world "reality," which can be understood through logical investigation?

A modern version of this dialectic is contained in two conventional wisdoms relating to landscape scenery: "beauty is in the eye of the beholder," and "the eye is a camera." The former implies that sensory perception is highly situational and individualistic, by implication unpredictable, while the latter assumes a simple mechanistic cause and effect model.

Obviously, one means for resolution of the dialectic is to pose a synthesis. The underlying assumption of all scenery analysis is that populations share common bases in how they "see" and subsequently respond to various landscapes. The purpose of this section is to briefly provide the physical and psychological bases for a broad variety of scenic analysis methods. A communications model of visual perception provides a useful framework.

The model is clearly dynamic; more stimuli are available that can be processed. Therefore, our receptors require continuous focusing as we actively seek out useful information. In addition, responses are a product of the interaction of short- and long-term memory.

At second, related model will provide the structural basis for the organization of this section. This approach entails a hierarchial sequence of visual processing, (Utall 1981, 266). Chapter 3 addresses vision and the eye, including the physiology of the eye and the immediate signal processing which takes place in the adjacent neural network. Chapter 4 is an examination of visibility, descriptions of outdoor environments as generators, propagators, and absorbers-reflectors of electromagnetic energy in the visible spectrum. Chapter 5 covers basic concepts of perception and cognition. The central subjects include pattern identification and response generation. It should be noted that these higher levels of processing are not fully understood physiologically. Applied analysis must therefore rely heavily on methods of behavioral psychology.

| DEFINE RESOURCES | INVENTORY RESOURCES | ASSESS EFFECTS | APPRAISE EFFECTS |

CHAPTER 3

VISUAL PHYSIOLOGY

John P. Felleman

OVERVIEW

This chapter includes a summary of the physiology of vision. Emphasis is placed on those attributes which are directly related to the processing of outdoor landscape stimuli.

Human senses have evolved to efficiently extract selected types and classes of energy inputs from the surrounding environment. Our visual system is the most important sensor in terms of the quantity and complexity of environmental information processed. It responds to a narrow band of the electromagnetic spectrum as shown in Figure 3.1a.

Modern physics describes light utilizing two theories, waves and quantum mechanics. Since in the vast majority of outdoor environmental situations we have more than enough energy (quanta) to excite our retinal receptors, the discussion below will be limited to a treatment of light as a wave phenomenon.

We are continuously bathed in a sphere of direct and reflected incident light. The energy flows from the environment to the brain are depicted in Figure 3.1b. The position of the head and orientation of the eyes provides the primary mask to the spherical potential inputs. Eye muscles position the pupil and establish both lens thickness and the effective focal length to the retina. In the retina, photosensitive chemicals generate electrical responses which are transmitted through a variety of pathways to the vision centers of the brain. The signal is modified and selectively enhanced during the process.

ANATOMY

Our visual system evolved as an integral part of our entire anatomy and physiology. For pedestrian analyses, it is typically assumed that the average eye height is five feet above the ground. This becomes more detailed for auto drivers and passengers where the standard design height is 3.75 feet (note: this dimension is currently being studied due to the trend to smaller and lower cars).

As discussed in the Overview, the sensory systems are interrelated. The body's balance system, centered in the semicircular canals of the ear, gives us a continuous sense of the upright condition. This is reinforced visually by the frequently level position of the horizon in our field of view. Figure 3.2a shows the location of the horizon for typical standing views while Figure 3.2b shows a normal landscape horizon at approximately the two-thirds point of the picture plane.

The location of our eyes within the skull provides a unique geometrical configuration for the stimulus inputs. This is shown in Figure 3.3 (Levitt 1981, 208). Each eye has a field of vision of approximately 166 degrees (head stationary, eye moving). The skull position creates a central area of 124 degrees where the images overlap.

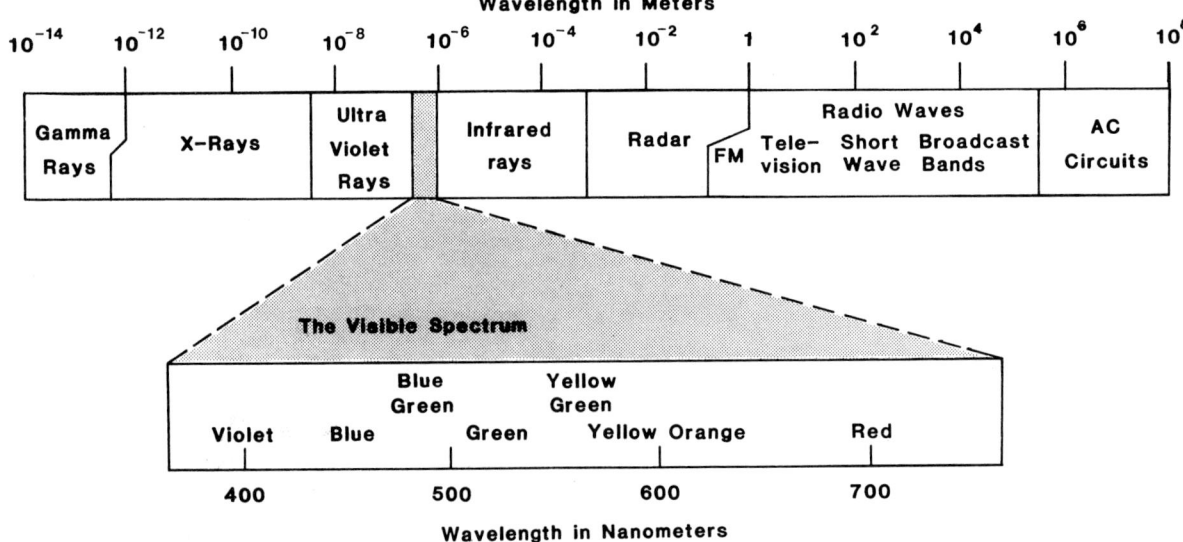

FIGURE 3.1a. Electromagnetic spectrum.

ANATOMY 41

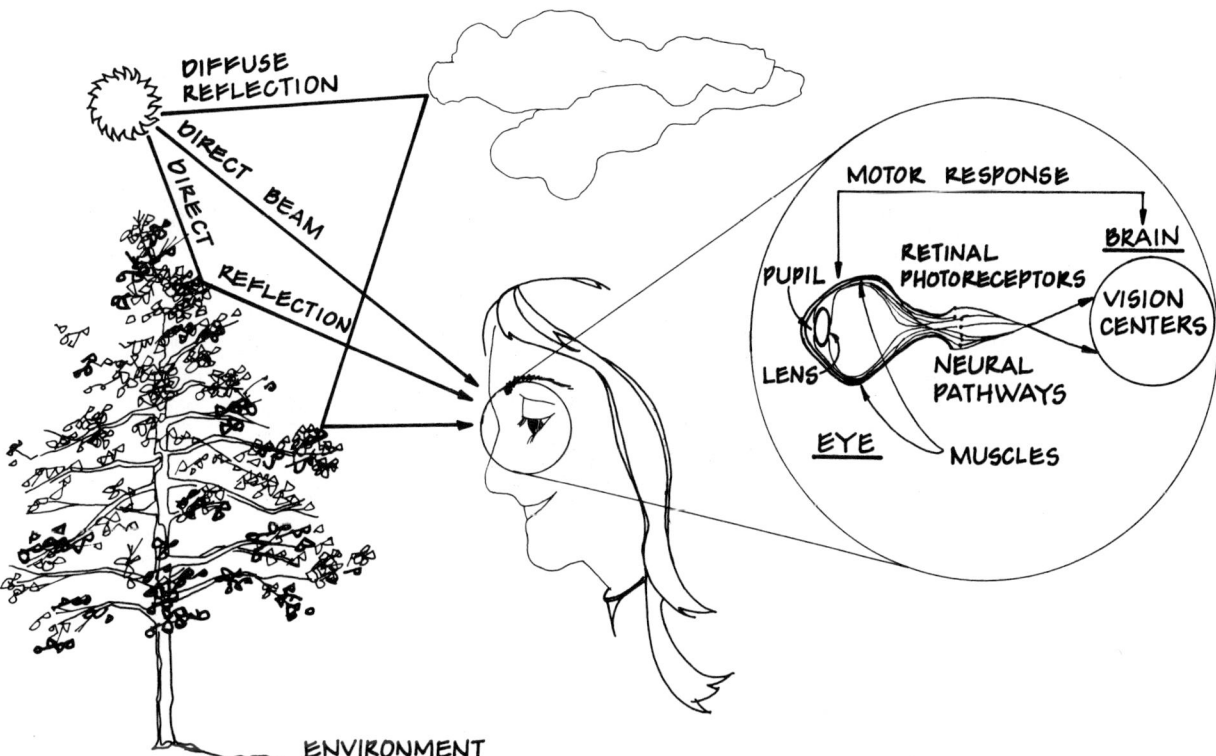

FIGURE 3.1b. Visual energy flows, *Source:* Gregory, R.L., 1978, *Eye and Brain, The Psychology of Seeing,* New York: McGraw-Hill, 85, 123.

This is called the binocular field. It is of particular importance due to the stereo nature of depth perception which occurs in this region. Within the binocular field is a narrow region of highest acuity, the foveal (macular) field.

On either side is a monocular field of 42 degrees, containing inputs from only one eye. These are commonly referred to as peripheral vision areas. The total resultant cone of vision is 208 degrees (Schiffman 1982, 193). A graphic comparison between these physiological angles and those incorporated by 35 mm camera lenses is depicted in Figure 3.4 (Ray, 1976, 71).

Of course, eyes, head, and body can all move. Under normal conditions, a viewer is continuously sampling a much broader portion of the environment even though at any one instant the new stimuli are limited to the angles described above. This sampling, which constructs a stable image of the immediate context in short-term memory, is the primary rationale for the use of panoramic views in much current simulation work.

The size of the pupil, like the iris in a camera, controls the amount of light which enters the eye.

The response is not entirely determined by the intensity of incident light. It has been shown that pupil size also relates to emotional and physical states.

There are two basic sets of eye muscle functions, accommodation, and pupil movement (Schiffman 1982, 193). Accommodation involves squeezing of the eye to change the focal length

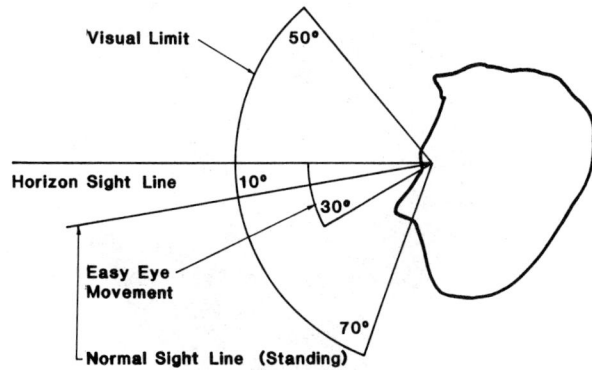

FIGURE 3.2a. Location of horizon-anatomy, *Source:* Diffrient, N. et al., 1980, *Humanscale: A Project of Henry Dreyfuss Associates.* Cambridge, MA: MIT Press.

42 VISUAL PHYSIOLOGY

(*note: dimension is based on tangent of angle).

FIGURE 3.2b. Location of horizon-view. *Source:* Diffrient, N. et al., 1980, *Humanscale: A Project of Henry Dreyfuss Associates,* Cambridge, MA: MIT Press.

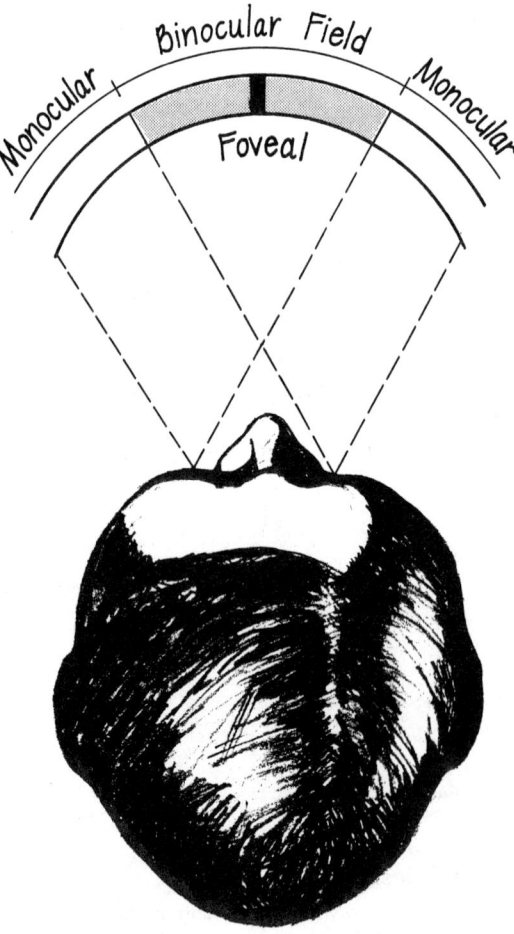

FIGURE 3.3. Field of vision.

between pupil and retina. If the amount of change required is beyond the eyes' limits, it is a simple matter to provide corrective lenses for nearsighted or farsighted conditions. Accommodation only occurs for close objects (approximately within 20 feet).

Pupillary movements provide two distinct functions. Large movements, either conscious or unconscious, provide a simple means of realigning the cone of vision to allow a different portion of light from the potential environmental field to contact the retinal receptors and subsequently be processed. Independent of these are continuous, involuntary saccide movements, which are short, rapid jumps that serve to enhance the retinal processes (such as photochemical restoration), but are typically not noticeable to the observer (Schiffman 1982, 228).

Retina

We have the ability to "see" throughout a tremendous range of light intensities (see Figure 3.5). This ability is due to the unique physiology of the retina. A simple way to understand the complexities of the retina is to recognize that humans have evolved two different environmental light sensory systems for daytime and night.

Historically, the vast majority of human environmental activities occurred during the day. In

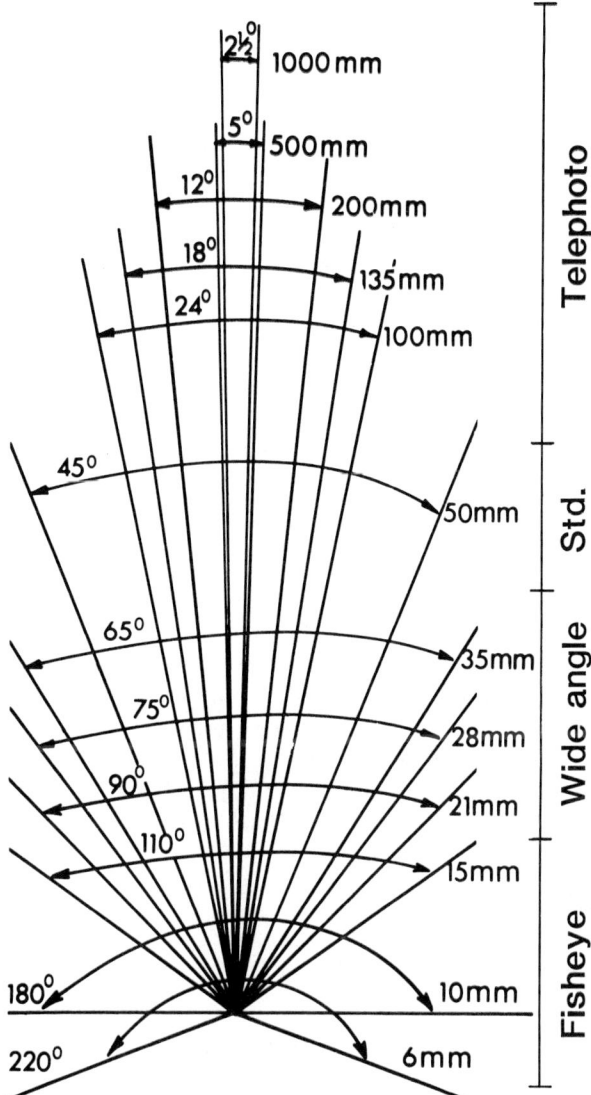

FIGURE 3.4. Angles of view for 35mm camera lenses. *Source:* Ray, S. 1976, *The Lens in Action*, Focal Press, Stoneham, MA: Butterworth, 71.

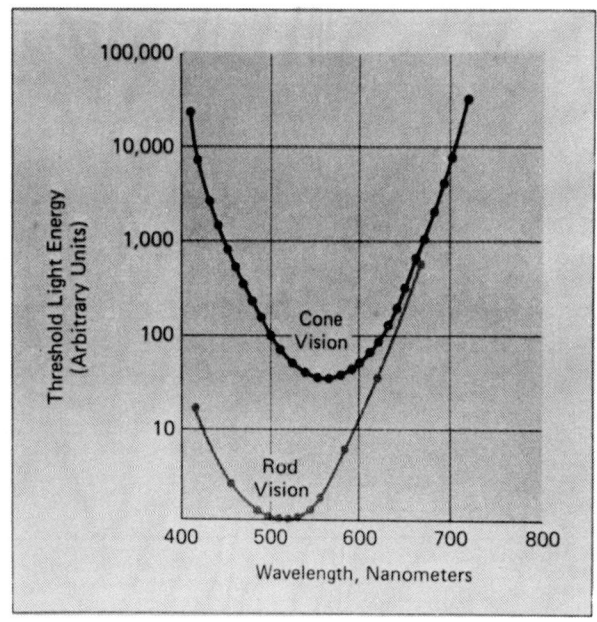

FIGURE 3.5. Vision light energy thresholds. *Source:* Grives, P.M. and K. Schlesinger, 1979, *An Introduction to Biological Psychology*, Dubuque, IO: William C. Brown.

this period, there is an abundance of incident light energy, and the behavioral need is to make a vast number of rapid, specific form and pattern distinctions at all distances. At night, humans historically have very limited outdoor activity patterns. Those visual decisions that had to be made probably tended to be gross form identification utilizing the limited natural energy of dusk or moonlight.

The retina contains two different types of light sensitive receptors: cones and rods. The names were based on their shapes. The former are often directly connected to a single nerve. This provides us with good resolution. However, it requires a relatively large amount of light energy in order to transmit a signal. Thus the cones are best suited to daytime vision. In contrast, many rods are typically connected to a nerve. This acts as an amplifier wherein collectively they can generate a signal in very low light conditions. The tradeoff comes in resolution since the cluster of rods covers a larger area of the retina than a single cone. Vision with cones is called photopic, and vision with rods is called scotopic.

These photoreceptors are not evenly distributed in the retina. Figure 3.6a (Scharf 1975, 80) shows that the least amount of both types are found at the edges. This explains the lack of clarity in our peripheral vision. The cones exhibit an extremely high concentration in one small central location, the fovea. This region subtends a visual cone of about six to eight degrees. This macular vision represents the area of greatest detail instantaneously available to the viewer (Levitt 1981, 210). The blind spot (that is, the absence of photoreceptors) occurs where the optic nerve connects to the retina.

A major difference between photopic and scotopic vision involves the perception of color. We have all experienced the gradual loss of landscape color during and after sunset. Individual cones

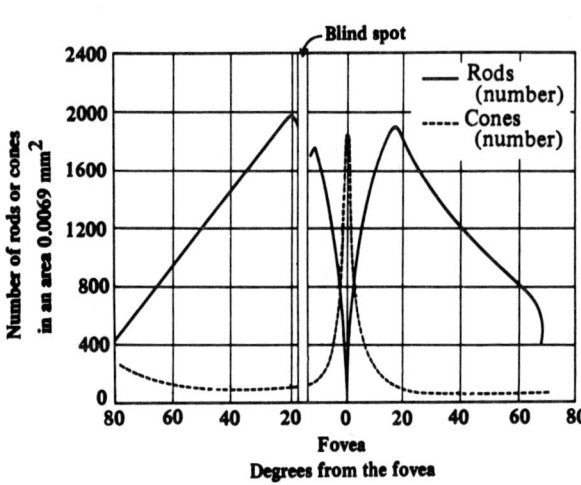

FIGURE 3.6a. Distribution of receptors in retina.

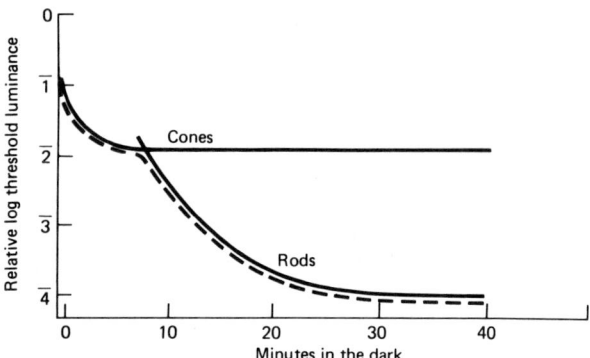

FIGURE 3.7. Dark adaption. *Source:* Kaufman, L., 1974, *Sight and Mind, An Introduction to Visual Perception*, New York: Oxford University Press, 83.

are sensitive to either blue-violet, green, or yellow-red wavelengths as shown in Figure 3.6b. As a result of subsequent processing, the cone-based photopic system allows us to differentiate the full spectrum of colors from combinations of these three signals, while the rod-based scotopic system is essentially limited to monochrome.

Modern color printing and the design of color television is based on the psychological integration of distinct red, green, blue stimuli. Even within the fovea, sensitivity to wavelength is not uniform. Highest sensitivity occurs around 560 nm (Ganz, in Scharf 1975, 219) which is yellow-green. This explains the use of yellow for safety-related equipment because it can be detected in the lowest light intensity conditions.

The switch from a bright to a dark environment is called dark adaptation; the reverse is light adaptation. These dramatic shifts in stimuli levels cannot be responded to instantaneously due to complex changes in retinal chemicals (Scarf 1975, 230). Pragmatically, "night blindness" and "glare" are of significant concern in projects such as highway safety and negative impacts of night-related land uses, like a shopping center adjacent to residences. The classic dark adaptation curve is shown in Figure 3.7 (Kaufman 1974, 83). It illustrates the time lag necessary for restoration of vision. Glare is a function of contrast and is discussed below.

Retinal Processing

In this discussion, we will distinguish between two wave characteristics of light: amplitude and wave length. The former deals with the amount of light intensity and is related to brightness. Wavelength, as seen previously (Fig. 3.1a), is the prime determinant of color.

As matter, the smallest unit of light is the photon. Although portions of the human eye are sensitive to even a few photons (Levitt 1981, 202), the photon is so small it is not practical to attempt to measure the numbers which are incident per unit area directly. Different systems of units have been established for describing intensity. Incident light which comes directly to a surface from a source is called illuminance and is measured in foot-candles. This unit is equivalent to the light reaching a one-foot square placed one foot from a standard candle.

Most of the scenery that we view in the landscape consists of light that has been reflected from

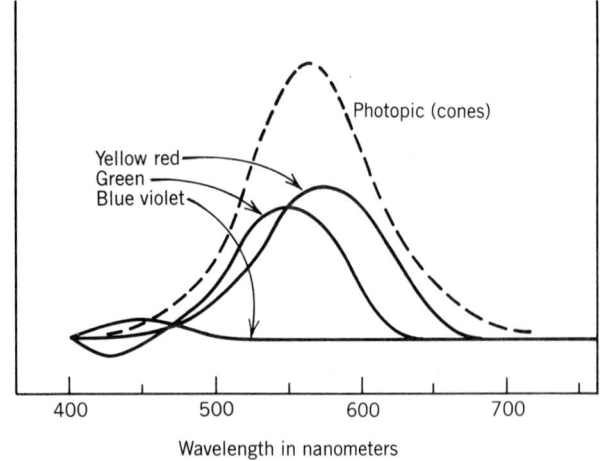

FIGURE 3.6b. Rod and cone sensitivity.

surfaces. Reflected intensity is called luminance and is measured in lamberts. A foot-lambert is the intensity reflected from a perfect reflector-diffuser surface receiving one foot-candle of radiation.

All of our sensory systems exhibit two similar characteristics: response to a finite range of stimuli and the ability to function over a vast range of energy levels. A fundamental psychophysics concept involves the "jnd," just noticeable difference. Fechner developed the fundamental formula: $*S = k*I/I$, where $*S$ is the perceived change in sensation, k is a constant, $*I$ is the change in stimulus intensity equal to the jnd, and I represents the environmental background intensity (Scharf 1975, 36). Although recent researchers have articulated more complex relationships, Fechner's approach is quite useful. As discussed below, concepts such as the brightness and contrast of an object are contextually based, rather than absolutely determined.

Acuity and Contrast

A central question in landscape visual studies is how far away and under what light conditions can we "see" existing or proposed objects? As described above, the great concentration of conical photoreceptors in the fovea allows us to ascertain fine-grained detail in the landscape. Vision scientists differentiate between a variety of acuity types including: detection, recognition, and resolution (Schiffman 1982, 224).

Visual angle is defined as the angle subtended by a target size s, at a distance d from the eye. therefore: tan (B/2) = s/2d (see Figure 3.8, Schiffman 1982, 255). Visual detection involves finding a target in a field. Physiologically we can detect, under ideal conditions, objects intercepting 0.5 seconds of arc. Recognition acuity involves identifying a target in a field. The familiar eye chart tests this phenomena. Under ideal conditions, we can perform this task for objects intercepting 30 seconds of arc.

A major question in all visibility studies is how large an influence zone must be studied for a proposed project. This is particularly critical because the size and cost of the analysis increases geometrically with distance. A number of factors are involved as discussed in Chapter 4, on visibility. The recognition threshold provides an absolute maximum. For example, a 50-foot high building, under ideal conditions, could be recognized at 65 miles! A cognition-related issue involves how much of an object must be seen in order for it to be identified.

Resolution acuity involves the ability to distinguish between discrete elements within a pattern. This relates directly to the use of surface texture in design. In magnitude, resolution acuity is similar to recognition, the threshold being approximately 30 seconds of arc (Schiffman 1982, 224).

In all of this discussion, the term *ideal conditions* has been used. As described, foveal vision can take place under a wide range of light intensity levels. The concept underlying acuity is contrast. Threshold contrast is defined as the minimum percentage difference of light intensity levels between an object and its background at which the object can be detected. In lab studies, this threshold is about two to three percent. Maximum contrast occurs when light and dark object backgrounds are juxtaposed. Most field conditions are far from ideal; thus the acuity threshold defined above should be modified in application.

The perception of contrast is more complicated physiologically than the simple one-to-one generation of nerve responses by foveal cones. We have evolved within our retinas a mechanism of lateral inhibition which acts to enhance contrast at the borders of objects. Figure 3.9 illustrates this

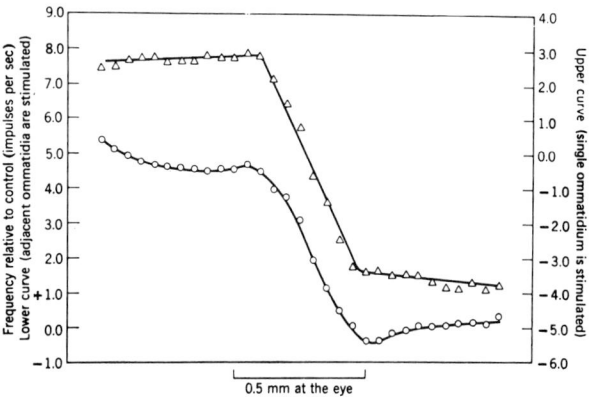

FIGURE 3.9. Lateral inhibition enhancing edge contrast. *Source:* Schiffman, H.R., 1976, *Sensation and Perception*, New York: Wiley, 261.

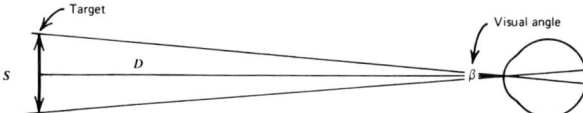

FIGURE 3.8. Visual angle. *Source:* Schiffman, H.R., 1976, *Sensation and Perception*. New York: Wiley, 225.

phenomenon (Schiffman 1982, 261). This process may be further accentuated by the saccide eye movements which tend to rapidly scan the edges of objects we are examining. Together, lateral inhibition and saccide movements play central roles in figure-ground perception discussed in Chapter 4.

Our ability to discern textural qualities is neither uniform nor linear. The optimum spacing for acuity occurs in the range of 20–30 minutes of arc. Spacing smaller or larger than this exhibits less contrast. This phenomenon can be utilized in all levels of design, from placing a set of objects in the landscape to determining the scale of architectural textures and surface details.

ANALYSIS IMPLICATIONS

The above discussion of the eye and retinal processing is necessarily general. The material has been selected to provide both a comprehensive framework and to relate directly to the design and conduct of scenery analyses. The following table contains some of the major applications:

TABLE 3.1. Vision and Analysis Topics

Vision Topic	Analysis Topic
Cone of Vision	Visibility: Simulation design
Balance	Importance of horizon
Pupil size	Viewer emotion
Pupil movement	Viewer attention to scene composition
Rods	Night, peripheral Vision
Cones	Day, foveal, color vision
Adaptation	Glare, safety
JND	Context relativity
Lateral inhibition	Figure ground, importance of horizon
Acuity	Detection, recognition
Contrast	Detection, recognition
Texture	Detection, recognition

CHAPTER 4

LANDSCAPE VISIBILITY

John P. Felleman

48 LANDSCAPE VISIBILITY

INTRODUCTION

Visibility analyses determine those portions of the landscape which can be seen and the content and composition of available views. As such, visibility studies play a central role in most scenic analyses. Sometimes visibility is an end in itself, such as the delineation of a scenic jurisdiction. Often, visibility results provide the basis for subsequent aesthetic judgments.

It is useful to consider landscape visibility as a subset of a more general environmental design and planning need—the prediction of physical performance. This need applies to a broad range of phenomena including wind, sound, runoff, and light. Figure 4.1 depicts a generic environmental performance prediction model. The components may be clustered in three general categories: input, analysis, and output. At a more specific level, five components will be addressed in this chapter: decision framework, phenomenon physics, data types and sampling, simulation, and sensitivity analysis.

Decision Framework

As discussed below, there are numerous methodological choices involved in conducting a visibility study. Therefore it is essential that a clear decision framework be established at the outset of a study in order to insure both adequacy of results and efficient use of resources. Major dimensions of such a framework include: authority base, output format, scenario probability, and accuracy requirements.

The authority basis for visibility studies is situationally variable. Unlike many other spatial environmental concerns, such as wetlands, floodplains, or airport noise zones, no general consensus or analytical visibility methods have emerged in the decade and a half of mandated impact studies. An authority spectrum ranges from regulatory specification to precedent to professional judgement. This spectrum can be arrayed in a matrix against the primary components: data, simulation, and sensitivity.

For example, a state utility commission may

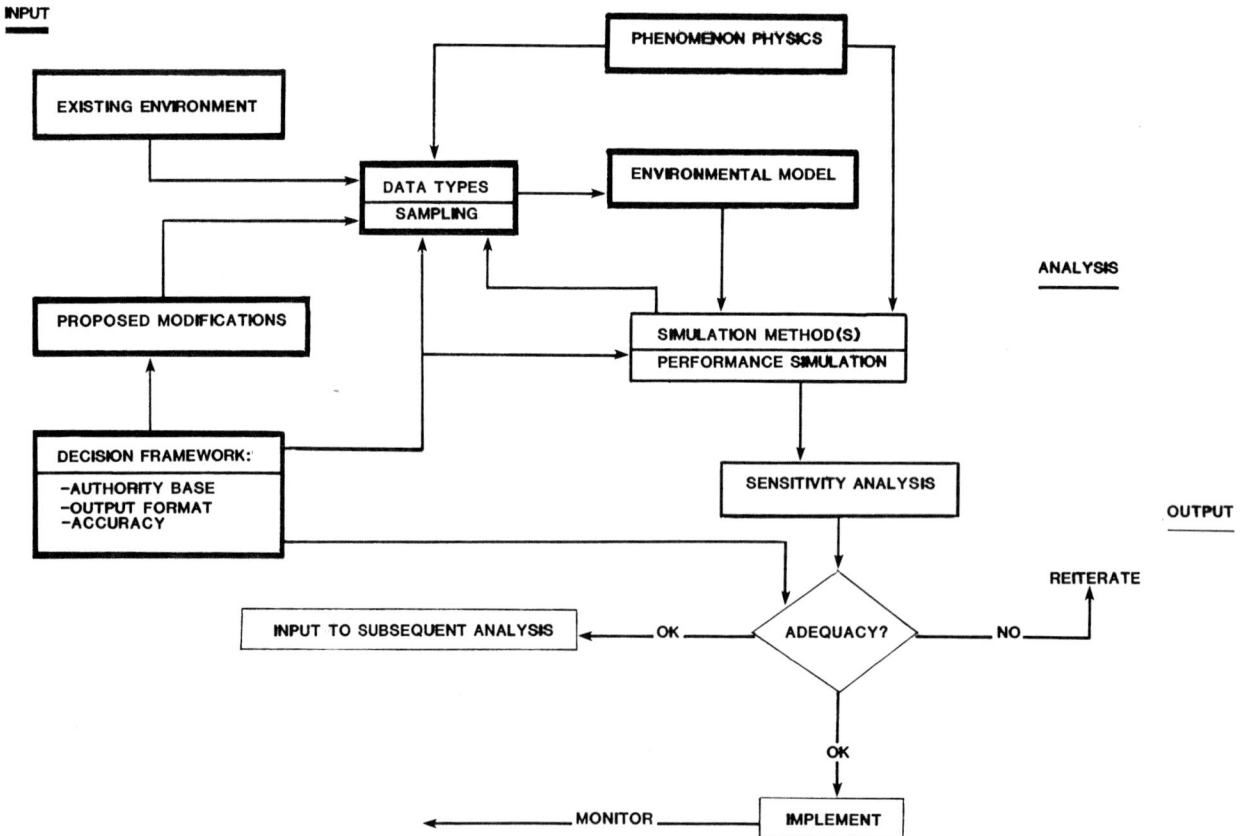

FIGURE 4.1. Generic environmental performance prediction model.

require that a power line application include visibility from all existing residences within one-half mile of the proposed alignment. Alternately, a federal agency procedure could dictate the use of an in-house digital routine in the evaluation of mining permits. Finally, a local zoning ordinance may contain the open-ended charge: scenic impact must be considered in all applications for a variance. The analyst has two basic options: research previous applications to establish a methodological precedent, or develop a custom approach.

The output format of a visibility study is crucial to its ultimate success. Although visibility involves four dimensions (three-dimensional space, and time), the vast majority of output communications involve two-dimensional formats. Basic two-dimensional formats are: planimetric viewshed maps (see Figure 4.2) and perspective scenes (see Figure 11.7f). Video modeling and computer graphic animations will increase the use of perspective views that vary over time, such as the simulation of views along a canoe trip.

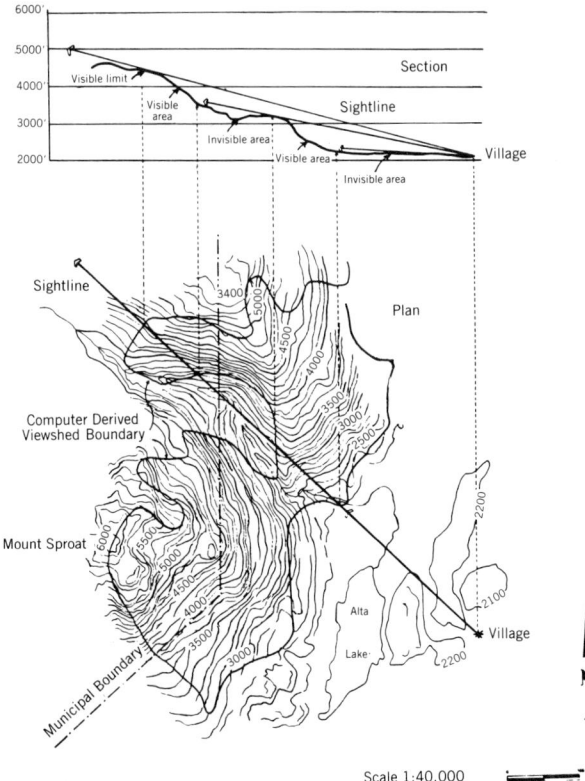

FIGURE 4.2. Viewshed map, *Source:* Ministry of Forests, British Columbia, 1981, Forest Landscape Handbook, Ministry of Forests, Province of British Columbia, Victoria, Canada, 70, map 3.

Key considerations in selecting output formats can be identified by examining the linkage arrows in Figure 4.1. The outputs must be capable of displaying the required environmental data. They need to be internally consistent with the selected simulation method. For example, if visibility is analyzed digitally, perspective outputs are typically in the form of line plots as shown in Figure 11.9. (Note: many viewshed programs only produce planimetric ouputs.) Finally, visibility outputs need to be consistent with subsequent scenic analyses. For example, a citizen photo preference survey would require photo simulations of proposed project views.

Performance predictions are necessarily based on the probability of a particular scenario's occurrence. All scenery analyses involve landscape views and compositions that will change over time due to climatic, ecological, geomorphic, or human influences.

Engineering studies commonly utilize one or more of four scenarios: average or typical; high (such as a 50-year flood; or thirtieth highest annual traffic hour); maximum expected during project life; and absolute maximum possible. Clarification of scenario is a prerequisite for construction of the environmental data model and the subsequent simulation.

Due to the lack of standardized methods, accuracy standards for most visibility work is currently nonexistent. Unquestionably, alternative methods produce different results (Felleman 1982). The issue of accuracy will become increasingly important in the near future. This is due to the clear trend for environmental litigation to move beyond issues of procedure to concerns of substance (Smardon 1984). Ideally, accuracy parameters are established at the project initiation.

VISIBILITY PHYSICS

Visibility involves the generation and propagation of environmental electromagnetic energy in the visible spectrum. A graphic model of this phenomena is shown in Figure 4.3. An energy source emits light into the environment. The light paths and spectral composition is modified by the atmosphere. The energy subsequently contacts landform and surface features which are essentially opaque. Different wavelengths are selectively absorbed and reflected. Viewer positions

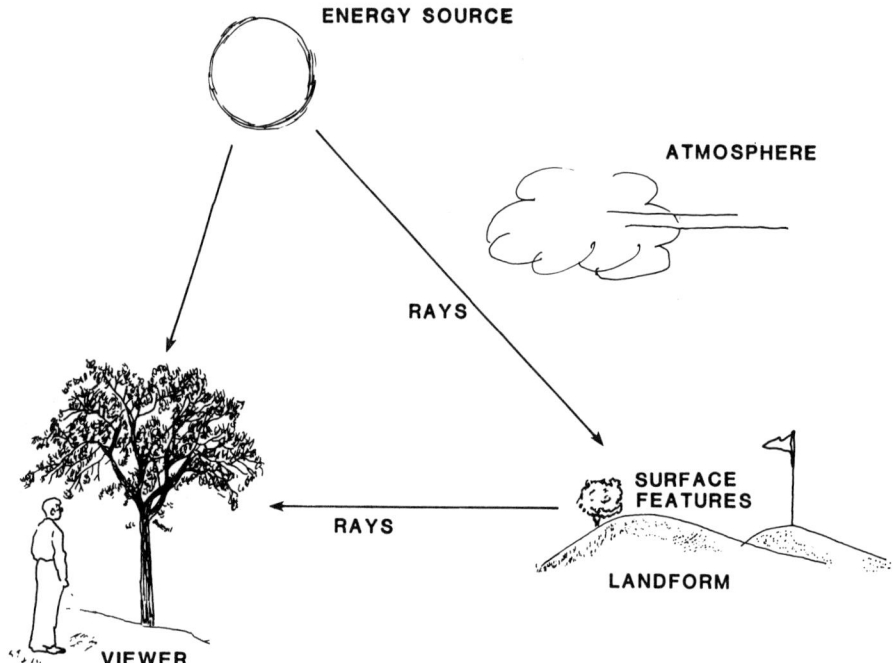

FIGURE 4.3. Visibility physics.

can occur throughout the landscape. Each contains localized features which block or filter light paths. The resultant visible landscape consists of the locus of all environmental surfaces which transmit light to the observer.

Energy Sources

Visibility analyses may involve a wide range of energy sources ranging from midday sunshine to night driving. Parameters of interest are energy type, spectrum, power, position, and directionality.

Sunlight is an incandescent source. All matter emits electromagnetic energy as a function of the fourth power of its absolute temperature. The wavelength of maximum emission is inversely related to surface temperature. Figure 4.4 depicts the spectral distribution which reaches the earth's surface (Rosenberg 1974, 24). Note that although direct sunlight contains all visible wavelengths, and thus appears white, it has more energy in the red portion of the spectrum. It is interesting to compare the "trough" in the yellow green portion (approximately 520), with the retinal sensitivity shown in Figure 3.5. The power of the solar source can be understood in the context of the brightness of illumination sources as shown in Figure 4.5.

The regularity of solar movements plays a significant role in all life on earth. Examples abound, including plant orientation, insect travel, and religious calendars. Figure 4.6 contains a common approach used by planners and designers to predict solar position (that is, horizontal azimuth and vertical altitude) at any time during the year for a particular latitude. These can be used to create accurate illumination/shadow configurations in simulations.

Artificial lighting uses a variety of energy

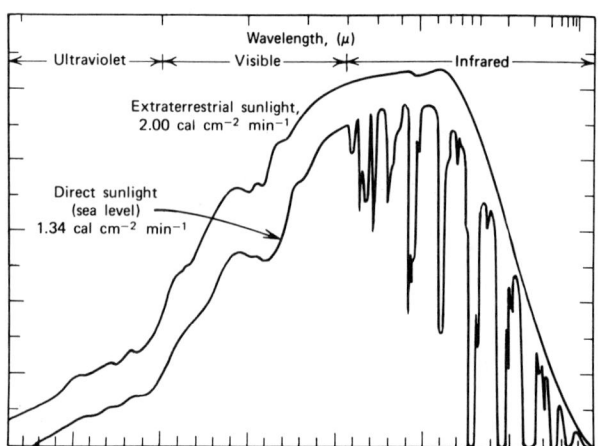

FIGURE 4.4. Solar spectrum at earth's surface. *Source:* Rosenberg, N., 1974, *The Biological Environment*, New York: Wiley, 24.

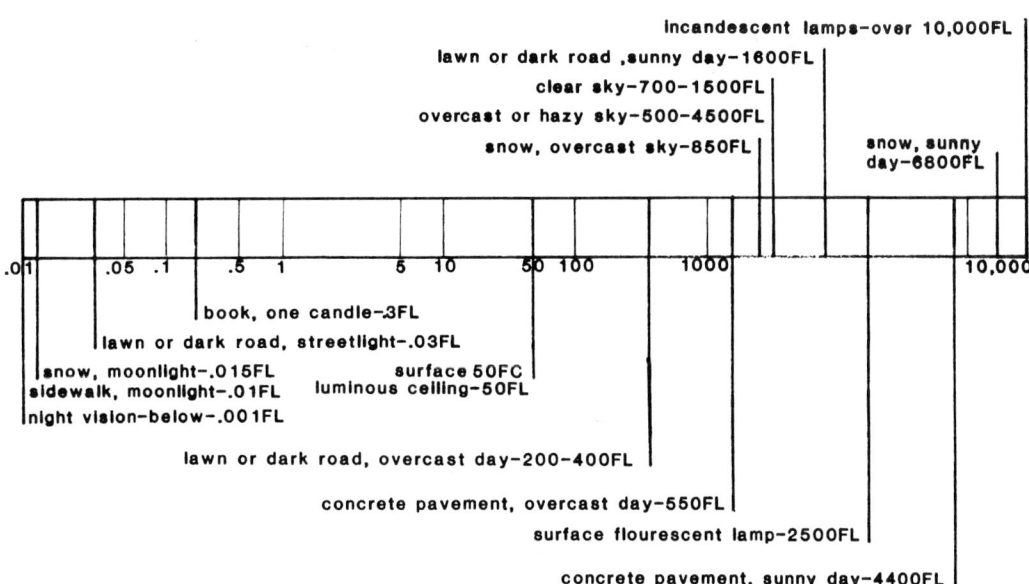

FIGURE 4.5. Commonly experienced brightness levels.

transforming means. Incandescent bulbs incorporate a heated filament which obeys the same basic temperature-related emission laws discussed above for the sun. Fluorescent lamps generate ultraviolet energy which activates a phospher coating that emits visible light. High intensity discharge lamps utilize the direct passage of an electric current through a pressurized gas.

Figure 4.7 shows the resultant color characteristics of a range of sources (Lam et al. 1980, 83).

Designers involved in night applications consider both horizontal and vertical source positions as well as directional spread. The latter is a function of fixture design, particularly the internal reflector and the lens.

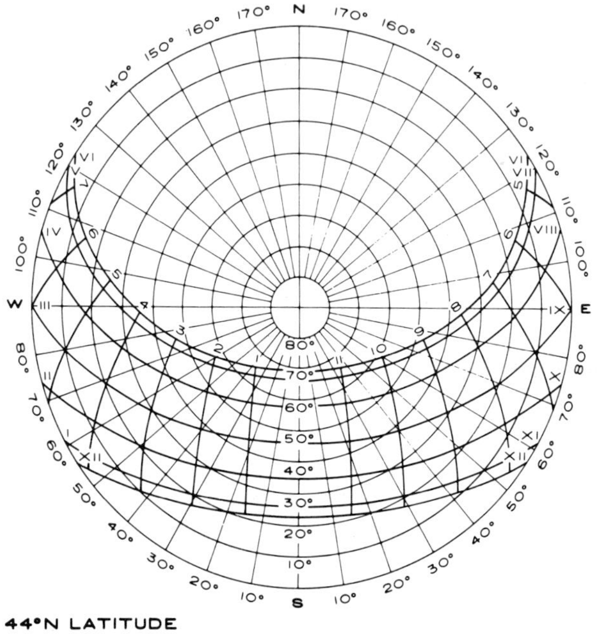

ATMOSPHERE

Light passing through the atmosphere exhibits all the classic characteristics of wave propagation including absorption, reflection, refraction, and diffraction (bending). The latter is not of prime importance in landscape scenes (except in the analysis of mirages).

We've all experienced blue skies, red sunsets, and foggy valleys. Obviously, the atmosphere is one of the key determinants of landscape visibility.

The atmosphere has major effects on both brightness contrast and color contrast. As depicted in Figure 4.8, landscape elements are seen in a context, typically against a landform backdrop or against the sky at the horizon. As reflected light passes from the element to the observer, two simultaneous processes take place: some of the light

FIGURE 4.6. Solar angles nomograph. *Source:* Ramsey, C.G. and Sleeper, H.R. eds., 1970, *Architectural Graphic Standards*, New York: Wiley, 71.

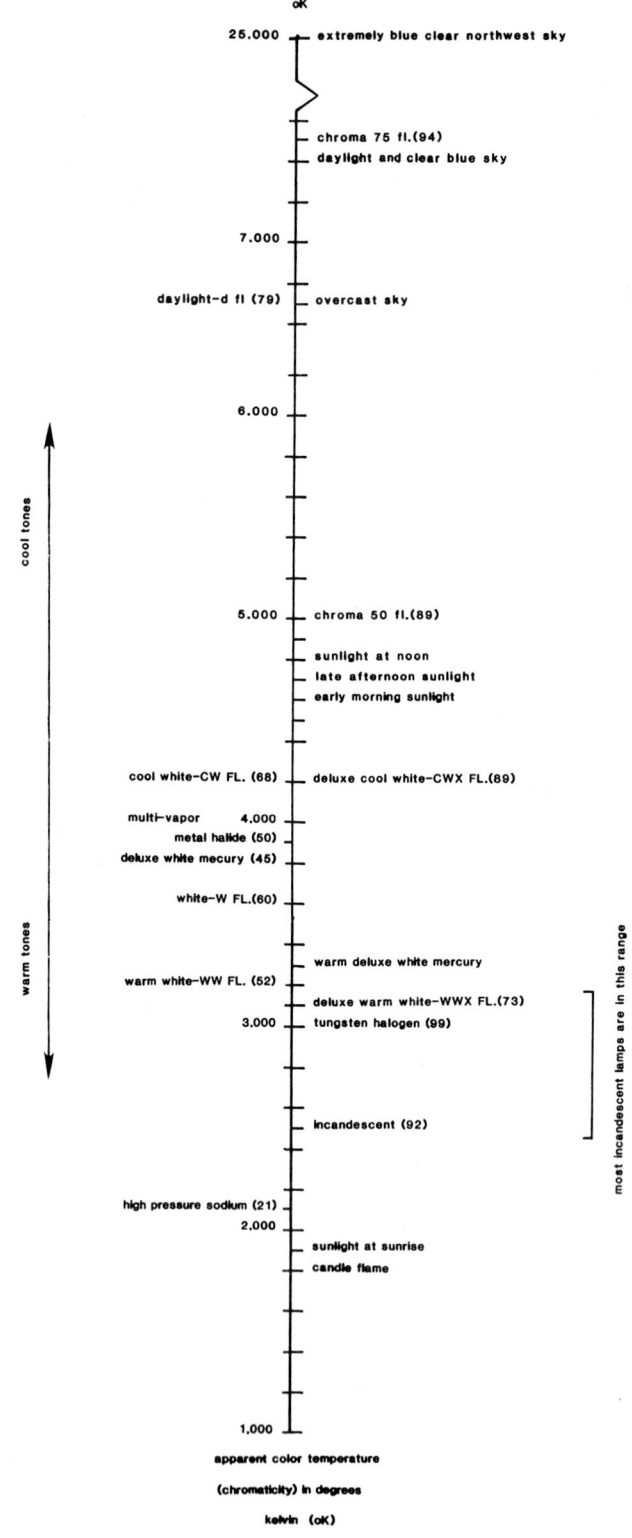

FIGURE 4.7. Color characteristics of light sources.

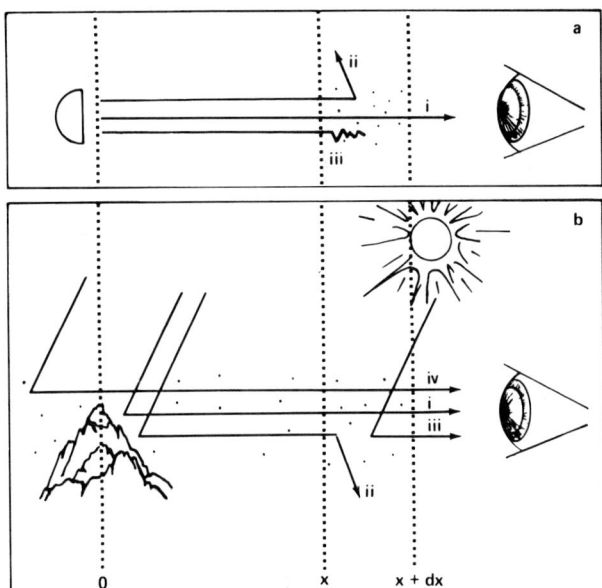

FIGURE 4.8. Atmospheric extinction. *Source:* USEPA, 1979, Protecting Visibility—An EPA Report to Congress, USEPA, Research Triangle Park, NC, fig. 2–9, 2–10.

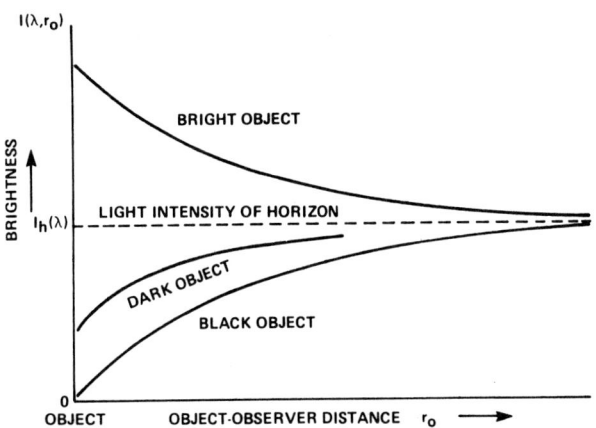

FIGURE 4.9. Atmospheric visibility. *Source:* USEPA, 1979, Protecting Visibility—An EPA Report to Congress, USEPA, Research Triangle Park, NC, fig. 2–10, 2–12.

is absorbed or reflected (scattered), and a fraction of the daylight which contacts the atmosphere along the sight-light path is scattered toward the observer.

Physically, a variety of interactions are taking place. Air molecules scatter light (Raleigh scatter), as an inverse function of the fourth power of the wavelength. Thus blue is most scattered and red least. Nitrogen dioxide also scatters blue and can give a brownish coloration against white backgrounds. The influence of atmospheric particles (aerosols) depends on the particle size and shape. Fine particles tend to scatter blue light while large particles such as water droplets scatter all wavelengths, giving clouds a white coloration. Some particles such as carbon absorb light, darkening the sky (E.P.A. 1979, Section 2.3).

An important historical question is how far we can see. This issue took on new significance with the advent of aviation. A simple, consistent approach was needed to quantify visual range. Standard horizontal visibility was defined as the distance at which a "large" black object could just be seen against the horizon. The term large is used because the size must be above the acuity threshold and could vary in size with distance in order to maintain visual angle. A black reference is used because, having no reflectance, it is unaffected by solar position. The result was: "... that distance for which the contrast transmitted the atmosphere is two percent" (Middleton 1952, 104)—two percent being the contrast level at which approximately 50 percent of the population can detect an object in a field.

A graphical depiction of atmospheric extinction is shown in Figure 4.9 (E.P.A. 1979, 2–12). As distance increases, the brightness of objects approaches that of the horizon. When the object's contrast reaches approximately two percent, it is at the visual range. It is important to note that since most objects are not black, the visual range for project studies may be significantly less than the airport-related statistic.

In addition to changes in brightness, an object's apparent color changes with distance as the red end of the spectrum is preferentially transmitted, and blue and white light is both scattered and added. Once subjective judgements, both visual range (Hoffman 1979) and color (MacAdam 1981) can now be quantitatively established by field instrumentation.

Since atmospheric conditions change continuously, visual range is a variable. Figure 4.10 contains a generalized visual range map for the continental United States (E.P.A. 1979, 1–18).

Distance Zones

The shape of the atmospheric extinction curves in Figure 4.9 are clearly continuous exponentials and not linear or step functions. However, many scenic analysis systems require visibility to be input as homogeneous zones rather than as a con-

54 LANDSCAPE VISIBILITY

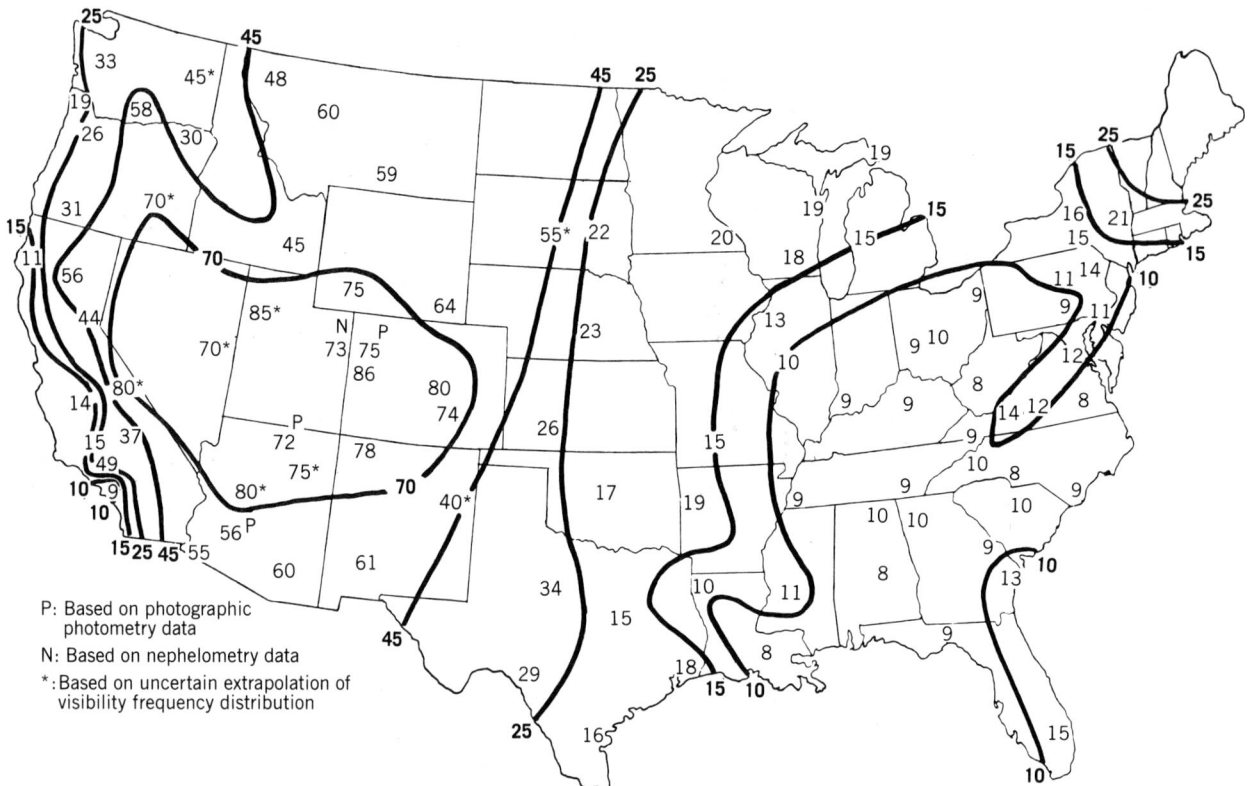

FIGURE 4.10. Visual range map. *Source:* USEPA, 1979, Protecting Visibility—An EPA Report to Congress, USEPA, Research Triangle Park, NC, fig. 1–11, 1–18.

tinuum. Such a system was popularized by the U.S. Forest Service as shown in Figure 4.11a. The basis for this approach was apparently field experience in the Western United States (Jones and Jones 1976, 84). Two other studies have generated somewhat different results as shown in Figure 4.11b and 4.11c (Jones and Jones 1976, 87; Felleman, 1982, 258), one in Idaho-Montana, the other in Central New York.

The phenomena is complex, involving atmospheric optics, local shapes and textures, physiology, and perception. The most immediate zone is the limit of focal accommodation, approximately 30 feet. Other ranges include a general limit for object steropsis of about 3000 feet due to the spacing between our eyes (Allen 1970, 51).

The foreground can be equated with the clear detection of surface textures and the fullest range of surface colors. Cognitively, in this zone, human scale plays a key role in judging spatial relationships.

Perceptually, the midground can be associated with visualizing complete surface features, such as tree stands and building clusters, and small landforms. This scale is a function of local surficial geology and development patterns. The midground plays the most significant role in understanding the seen landscape due to its integrative role in defining compositional content.

The background is dominated by the horizon. In many fine-textured or heavily vegetated landscapes, the background may be rarely seen. Typically, atmospheric effects reduce colors to blue-grays, while surface characteristics are lost. Analysts are recommended to establish distance zones on a case-by-case basis rather than adopting a single scale.

LANDFORM

The primary role of land and surface forms in spatial visibility is interposition. As shown in Figure 4.2, objects which intersect the paths of light rays block views to portions of the landscape. In order to fully analyze interposition, it would be necessary to comprehensively desribe all environmental surfaces in three dimensions.

VIEWER ENVIRONMENT

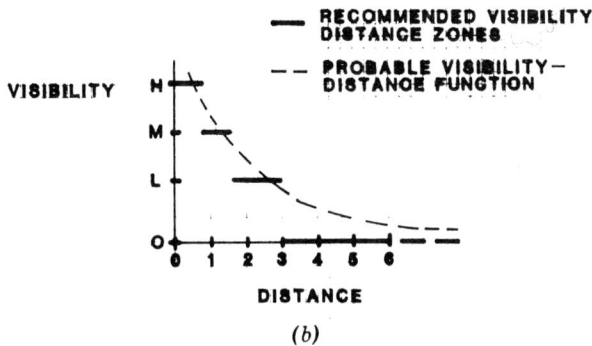

FIGURE 4.11a, b, and c. Distance zones. *Source:* USDA, Forest Service, 1974, vol. 2, chapt. 1, USDA Handbook No. 462, US Govt. Print. Off., Washington, DC: Jones and Jones, 1976; Fellman, 1982, 258.

Land and surface forms also play a significant role in scenery composition including form, color, shading, and texture.

VIEWER ENVIRONMENT

The physics of the viewer environment are generally similar to that of landform. Local objects, such as roadside trees or windows, limit light transmission by interposition.

Viewing analysis is frequently divided between stationary and moving viewers. The latter can be assumed to be moving along a defined path and are processing highly complex stimuli. The vast majority of controlled research on visibility in motion has been concerned with navigation safety, such as the optimal placement of roadway signs. A major product of this work has been the concept of an effective view cone which is smaller than the feasible field. Figure 4.12 (Hornbeck and Okerlund 1973, 115) is an example of such a cone. It should be noted that scenery viewing is not the same as safety, and that the driver and particularly the passengers may observe a broad swath of landscape.

A final important characteristic of the viewer environment is position. A typical scene has the horizon approximately two-thirds of the vertical height. As depicted in Figure 4.13, positions in relatively high (viewer superior) or low (viewer inferior) elevations provide compositions with significantly different horizon locations and potentially generate different viewer responses.

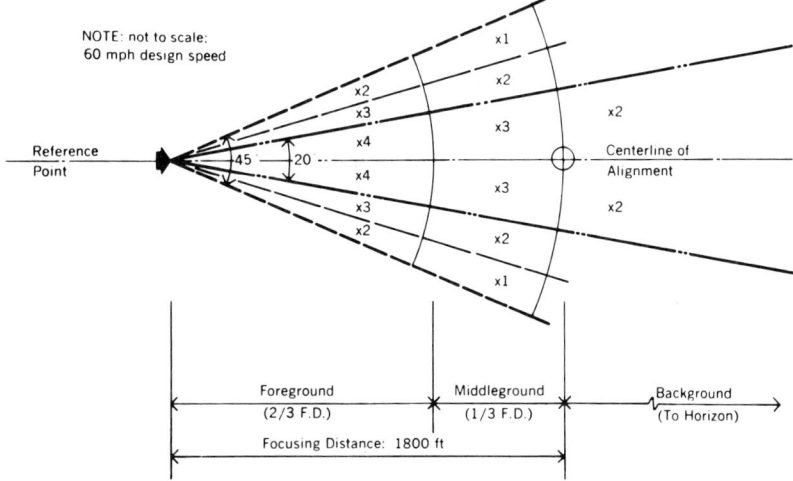

FIGURE 4.12. Effective view cone. *Source:* Hornbeck, P. and Okerlund, G.A., 1973, Visual Values for the Highway User, Washington, DC, U.S. Government Printing Office, 115.

56 LANDSCAPE VISIBILITY

FIGURE 4.13. Viewer position. *Source:* Litton, R.B., Jr., 1968, Forest Landscape Description and Inventories-a basis for land planning and design, USDA For. Serv. Res. Paper PSW-49, Pacific Southwest Forest and Range Exp. Stn., Berkeley, California, 5.

SIGHTLINE SIMULATION

Environmental simulation is used to analyze existing conditions and to investigate future proposals. Simulations are undertaken for all physical phenomena, such as noise and air pollution. A finite set of generic simulation processes have been developed by engineers and physical scientists, each having its own operational characteristics. Processes, discussed below, include field testing, two dimensional iconic, three dimensional iconic, digital/numeric, analog, and hybrid. All of these have been adopted for visibility studies. In all cases, sightlines from the viewer position to the environment are equated with light ray paths from the environment to the viewer. Except in views involving heated surfaces, which may cause mirages, or large bodies of water, these sightlines are assumed to be straight.

Field Simulations

The great strength of a field visibility simulation is the comprehensiveness of the environmental model (see Figure 4.3). Nothing is omitted. Drawing on the simple sightline concept, field studies may involve looking at the landscape from the proposed project, and/or looking from the landscape towards the project.

An example of the former is the study of a high stack to be constructed in rugged western landscapes. A helicopter could hover at the position of the stack top, with panoramic photos taken of the surrounding countryside. These photos may then be interpreted to delineate visible and hidden areas.

Views to the project are often more informative. These involve the placement of a target object such as a helium filled balloon in the project location. This approach has been successfully applied to the siting of communication towers in a sensitive suburban setting (Impact Consultants 1981). It also may be adapted to simulate patterns in the landscape, such as a proposed timber cut (U.S.F.S. 1974), or the water level created by a proposed dam.

The growing popularity of field simulations is indicated by its utilization by environmental agencies including New York's Adirondack Park Agency (Kantor 1980). The approach provides a direct mechanism for citizen participation. Everyone can look at the target from their residence or place of work. Under proper conditions, its accuracy is beyond question. However, the method operates under the same set of contextual constraints identified below for primary data.

Iconic Two-Dimensional

Since the Rennaissance, designers have used drawings, including plan, section, and perspectives, to develop project concepts. These tools are iconic (they look like the real objects), and two dimensional (they are on flat sheets). Photography and video are modern updates of this format.

The method of analyzing viewsheds from maps was developed by the French military to solve the defilade problem: "... to arrange, plan and profile of a fort so that their lines should be protected from ... fire" (Oxford Universal Dictionary). The basic method is shown in Figure 16.3. Sightlines are established on the topographic map, and a cross-section is constructed for each. Straight lines may then be drafted on the section to simulate sightlines from an observer position (or a proposed project) to the environment, indicating hidden and visible points. The locus of these points on the base map represents hidden and visible areas.

This approach can be adapted to incorporate all components of the environmental model. Often the analyst uses vertical exaggeration of the cross-section to enhance the interpretation process. This has no effect on the legitimacy of the method due to the fundamental assumption of straight sight lines. Nontechnical reviewers of this analysis may, however, be somewhat confused or misinformed by greatly distorted landscapes and very tall proposed facilities.

Three-Dimensional Iconic

The use of scale models in design development to visualize general relationships has been common throughout history. In order to adapt models for prediction of physical phenomena, mathematical principles of similitude must be established. For example, an environmental wind tunnel must replicate the complex nonlinear relationship between air velocity, turbulence, object shape, and surface roughness. If we assume that sightlines are straight, then visual similitude may be obtained by simply maintaining scale consistency within each x, y, and z dimension of the model. (Note that vertical distortion will not affect viewshed mapping.)

Scale models may readily include all the visibility components except atmosphere. Two problems inherent in the use of scale models are the simulation of the phenomena (in this case, sightlines), and the extraction of data from the simulation.

A simple, yet powerful solution to this problem is the use of a point light source, as shown in Figure 4.14. A photograph of the illuminated surfaces provides a direct record. Enhancements to this approach include masking a portion of the light to simulate a cone of vision, and exposing a time series of points to simulate moving visibility. This type of simulation produces only viewshed outputs.

If both viewsheds and perspective scenes are required, then photography or video recording, through a modelscope is necessary. In order to simulate linear experiences, either the model or the modelscope (mounted on a gantry) must move. A simple gantry arrangement is shown in Figure 4.15.

Analog

In analog simulations, the form of energy transmission used is different than the form which occurs in nature. A simple example is the use of an electrical circuit to analyze the flow of water in pipes where the current represents flow rate, and voltage is analogous to water pressure. To date, there has been little development of analog visibility methods. One unique study involved intervisibility of a landscape where terrain was gentle and hedgerows dominated visibility limits. The method used optical transforms to classify field shapes and resultant visible areas (McCullagh 1981).

Numeric-Digital

Landscape interposition can be directly translated into a simple trigonometric relationship as shown in Figure 4.2. If the vertical angle between observer and target is greater than the angle between observer and intermediate objects then the target is visible; if not, it's hidden. The extension of this algorithm to an area can generate a viewshed map.

Although these computations can be done by hand, they are much more cost-effective when done on a computer. As discussed above under data sampling, major analytical issues involve data texture and algorithm logic.

The texture issue concerns the size and shape of the data unit. Common cell formats are square. Other shapes include rectangles and triangles. Even though the line of sight algorithm is simple and computers are powerful, there are cost and capacity limits in computerized visibility studies. Since only the orthagonal locations and prime diagonals involve inputted data, before the decision rule may be applied to other locations, intermediate elevations must be interpreted (see Figure 4.16).

This interpretation raises the more fundamental question as to whether all cells need to be individually classified. One approach to reducing interpretation costs is to sample with decreasing

FIGURE 4.14. Point light source scale model.

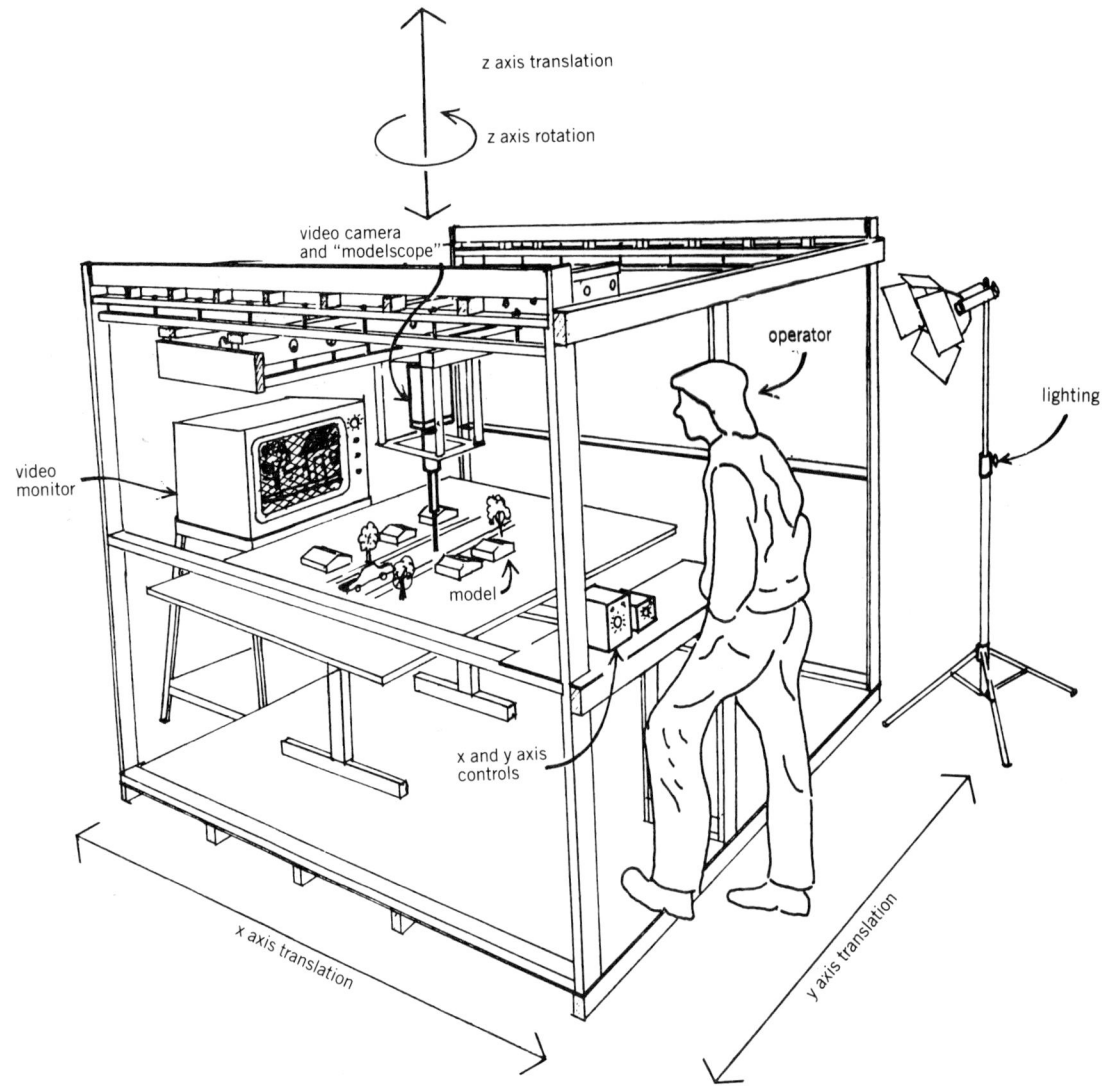

Schematic View of the SUNY ESF Environmental Simulator

Illustrating the 4 degrees of freedom of movement of the modelscope in the model (x, y, & z translation and 2 rotation), as well as the principal components of the simulator.

FIGURE 4.15. Modelscope and gantry. *Credit:* G. Willmott.

density as distance from the observer (or project) increases (Steinitz and Paulson 1976, 184). The rationale behind this simplification is that as distance increases, the apparent visible size of the cell decreases.

All of the visibility components can be incorporated in a digital simulation. It should be noted that the cell size may not be fine enough to make specific local viewer environment determinations.

The approach can produce visibility maps and perspectives as shown in Figure 4.2. In addition, the method lends itself to complex analyses, such as weighting distances, terrain slope and aspect, and multiple times seen (Travis et al. 1975). When combined with a suitable land cover data base, it is possible to make statistical statements about the probable composition (and thus visual quality) of views from each cell (Steinitz and Paulson 1976).

Hybrid methods involve combinations. There are often orchestrated sequentially to optimize resource use. For example, a study design may utilize a computerized approach to establish general visibility zones, with selected field checks for error detection and fine tuning.

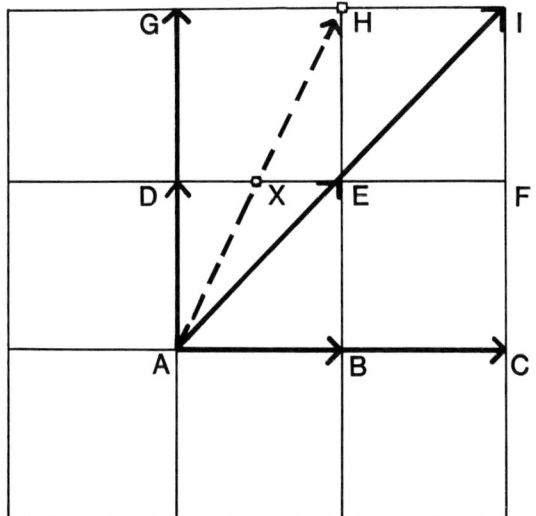

FIGURE 4.16. Grid cell visibility interpolation. *Source:* Felleman, 1979, 53.

ENVIRONMENTAL DATA

As seen from the discussion of physics, the general principles of landscape visibility are well understood. What makes the analytical problem difficult is the complex diversity of the environment itself. The challenge to the analyst is to efficiently simplify the environmental description while maintaining the integrity of the physical principles. This is done by constructing a data model of the environment.

Once the simulation method(s) has been selected, the analyst must construct a data model of the environment which addresses each operational component of the physics model (Figure 4.3) and is consistent in format with the simulation requirements. Two major factors to be considered are data type and sampling strategy. Careful consideration to both factors provides a sound basis for subsequent sensitivity analysis and potential litigation.

Data Types

It is useful to classify data on the basis of the degree it has been processed. In visibility studies, five levels are discernible. Primary data is information collected onsite. Examples include photos, sketches, video tapes, leaf samples, and so forth.

Although highly desirable, there are some major limitations inherent in primary data. Site access may be expensive and possibly infeasible. Field work is by necessity influenced by situational climatic conditions.

Secondary data involves information that is already existing which was generated for an application similar to the study under consideration. Examples include the terrain shown on 1:24000 U.S.G.S. Survey maps. This data is often convenient and inexpensive. One potential limitation may be its vintage. Frequently, for example, recent air photos may be needed to check and update the surface cover information depicted on government maps.

Existing information that was developed for a use dissimilar in character to the investigation is classed as tertiary. This is often the most difficult type to successfully integrate into a study.

An example would be the forest cover depicted in the above mentioned 1:24000 maps. Is this data suitable to analyze the local viewer environment of roadside vegetation? If one checks the federal mapping criteria for vegetation, it can be found that the interpretive purpose is to hide military groups from areal detection (pre-infrared). Thus only stands above a certain size and mature crown density are recorded. In some locales, this may constitute all the existing vegetation, and the map is secondary data. However, in regions with single rows of roadside growth, the maps represent tertiary data.

When primary, secondary, or tertiary data is translated into digital format, it becomes quarternary (note we are now beginning to directly develop digital field data with equipment such as remote sensors, and laser survey equipment). Of particular importance in quality control are the spatial formatting and classification rules used in translating the data.

A simple example can be seen in the digitizing of terrain from a contour map. Spatial formatting includes shape and texture. Many programs utilize square grid cells, some rectangular, and some triangular facets. Texture is concerned with spacing. As texture increases, more and more detail is retained, but storage and analysis costs increase geometrically. Decision rules are needed to consistently code data. For example, for a square cell, what elevation is recorded: centroid, average, or maximum?

Pentenary data is processed quarternary data. Continuing the terrain example, a computer algorithm can be developed to estimate the slope

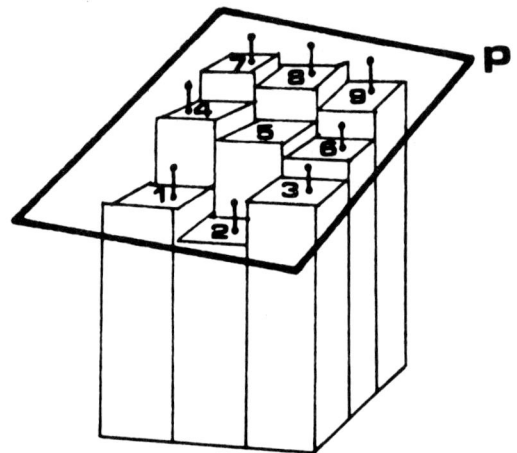

FIGURE 4.17. Slope analysis of grid cells. *Source:* Travis, M. et al., 1975 VIEWIT: Computation of Seen Areas, Slope and Aspect for Land Use Planning, US For Serv. Gen. Tech. Rpt. PSW-11, Pacific Southwest Forest and Range Exp. Stn., Berkeley, California, 12.

and aspect of each cell. A variety of alternatives exist. The slope could be assigned as the average of the slopes from the centroid to the centroids of the four orthogonal neighbor cells (see Figure 4.17). It could be the maximum of the four values investigated. The four diagonal cells could also be factored in. Once computed, the actual value could be stored, or a classification such as southwest could be retained. The major concern is whether the software documentation clearly articulates all algorithm and classification procedures.

Sampling

The second consideration in developing the data model is sampling. Environmental data is four dimensional—three dimensions in space and one in time. Since much information is in map form it is useful to distinguish between areas and elevations. (For example, using air photos, one method may be used to delineate vegetative cover and another vegetative height.)

Spatial sampling approaches can be grouped: areal, regular, random, stratified random, and selected. Areal methods record the entire surface. An air photo provides building cover, a topographic map continuous relief, a car-mounted video records roadside vegetation.

Regular samples include periodic spacing. The grid in Figure 4.16 is a common example. Power plant studies have utilized concentric grids (see Figure 4.18). Moving visibility is often analyzed by summing the views from evenly spaced points along the path.

Random samples are based on statistical principles and are efficient ways to determine variables such as surface cover height or average viewer environment. Stratified random samples are effective where spatial characteristics are clustered, such as establishing vegetative heights in an area that has distinct stands of different species.

Selected samples are utilized when the analyst needs to incorporate certain information, often to meet authoritative requirements. This is often the case in choosing viewer positions, such as the inclusion of views of a project from a national historic site.

The reader is encouraged to explore sample

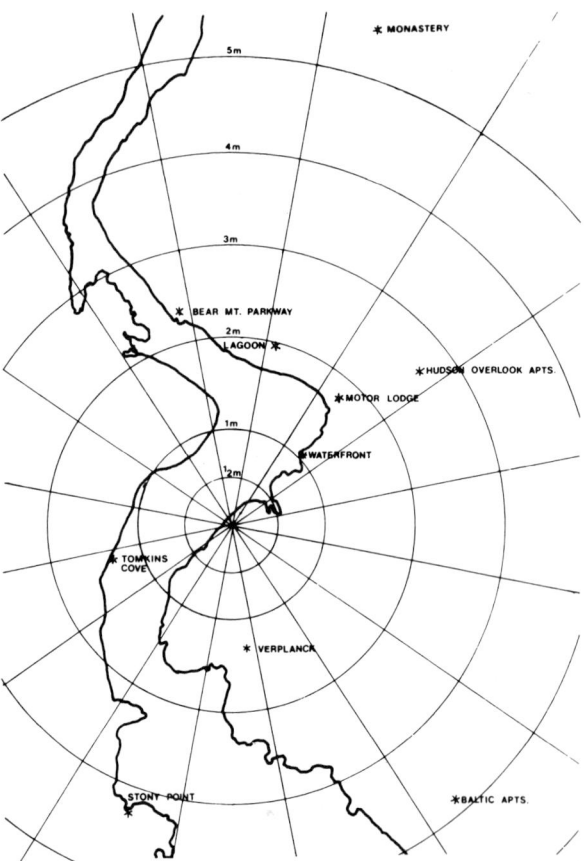

FIGURE 4.18. Concentric grid sampling. *Source:* Jones and Jones, 1975, 11.

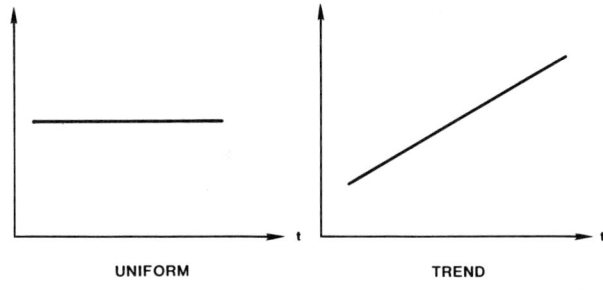
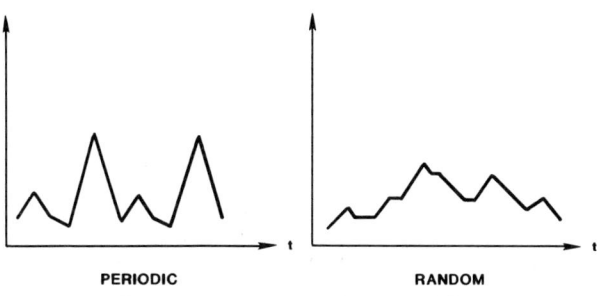

FIGURE 4.19. Types of temporal data.

design issues further in the many texts available on the subject.

Four basic types of temporal phenomena are uniform, trend, periodic, and random. These are shown schematically in Figure 4.19. Landform is often assumed to be uniform. Vegetative growth and suburban development often exhibit a trend line. Solar position, foliation, and snow cover are periodic. Some temporal phenomena tend to appear randomly.

Simply classifying temporal type is not sufficient to establish a sample. What is also needed is the decision-making prediction criteria. Two extremes could be a "worst case" scenario: short term, sunny day, sidelit, defoliate; versus an "average" scenario: 15-year future, slight overcast, partial foliation, adjacent infill.

It is useful in constructing the data model to record data type, areal and temporal sampling, and decision concept for each element of the physics model. This can be summarized in a matrix.

Sensitivity

All data collection and information processing involves error. The challenge to analysts is to establish acceptable limits to error, estimate the relative contribution of various factors to the expected error (sensitivity), and orchestrate resources to efficiently control error within the preestablished limits.

Generalizing, there are three common types of error: blunders, systematic errors, and random errors. Blunders are mistakes such as the misplacement of a decimal point in data entry. Large blunders may be found by repetitious checking; small blunders are difficult to eliminate.

Systematic errors occur when there is a bias in the human and/or mechanical-electrical processing system. An example would be a light meter that reads high. This could be corrected by calibration. Another common systematic error, the tendency of field observers to mistake an intermediate peak for a mountaintop, is described by Litton (1973). Random errors are always present due to the inherent limits of equipment and empirical formulas. All base maps have accuracy ranges. Measurements made from the sources can be expected to vary from the "real world" in accordance with statistical principles.

To date, very little attention has been given to the issue of error in visibility analysis. One pilot study of commonly used simulation methods concluded that for a test site in rolling terrain with varying forest cover, the error in visible area mapped may be on the magnitude of 20 percent (Felleman 1982).

A variety of approaches are available to address this situation. For all simulation approaches, checks can be made by changing key variables within their expected ranges. For example, if vegetative height may vary between 40 and 60 feet, viewsheds could be constructed for both extremes as well as for the mean. The result would be a map which shows three classes of area—visible, hidden, and ambiguous. If the latter contains geographic factors critical to the study, such as residential exposure, then field checks may be justified to clarify the situation.

In a more comprehensive framework, contrary to popular opinion, errors do not cancel each other. Rather, they propagate cumulatively throughout an analysis. A computerized approach of dealing with multiple factors each of which contains error is to utilize Monte Carlo simulation techniques. An example of a project application is the route location summary shown in Figure 4.20. If the decision was to be made on the average values, one alternative would be selected.

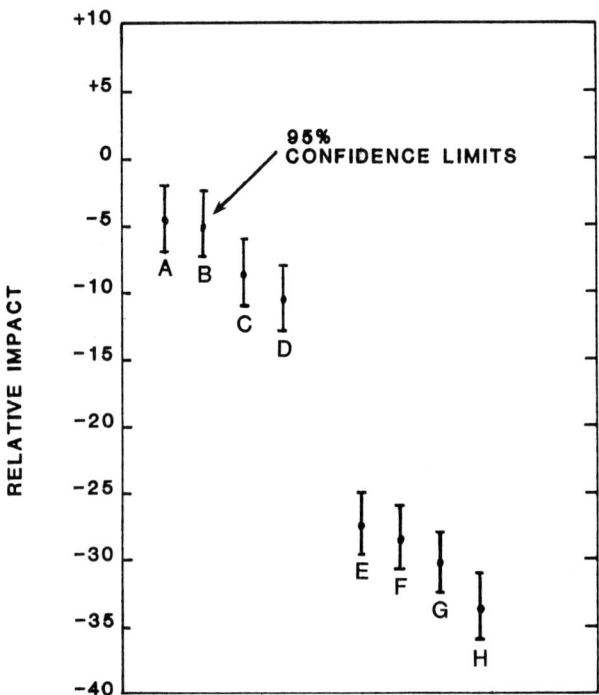

FIGURE 4.20. Route Impact sensivity. *Source:* Odum, E. et al., 1971, Optimum Pathway Matrix Analysis Approach to Environmental Decision-Making Process, Institute of Ecology, University of Georgia, Athens.

An examination of the associated error ranges reveals that the top two alternatives are essentially equivalent. Note the expected error ranges for each are different. This is due to the fact that the corridors cross different resource areas, with varying internal data quality.

SUMMARY

Visibility is a central component of all scenic analyses. Analytically, the determination of existing or future views is a subset of the more general field of predicting environmental performance. The first and most critical step is to establish an operational set of objectives for the study.

The physics of light in the environment are well known. Theoretically, it should be a straightforward process to establish visibility. Under closer scrutiny, the problem becomes quite complex due to the diversity of environmental conditions and the broad range of potential viewer positions. The analyst is thus presented with the need to construct a simplified model of the environment for subsequent evaluation.

A variety of sightline delineation methods are available. Each has different resource needs. Each will potentially yield different results.

As yet, there is no standardization of visibility mapping methods. Until such time, it is the responsibility of the analyst to assess the quality of his or her study in the context of subsequent use in scenic analysis and potential substantive litigation.

CHAPTER 5

ENVIRONMENTAL PERCEPTION

James F. Palmer

INTRODUCTION

Science has come a long way to provide rigorous neurophysiological explanations of visual perception. This is to say that the knowledge of perception related to the physics of vision, the physiology of the eye, and the dynamics of single visual neurons are now relatively well understood. While the sophistication of this microknowledge is rather great, we are unable to answer the question "How are the neural and the mental domains linked?" (Utall 1981, 28). The science of psychology as it relates to perceptual and cognitive processes is still in a very descriptive phase. In his review of more than a dozen macrotheories, Utall (1981, 68) identifies three dimensions to characterize the range of descriptions proposed to explain the perceptual and cognitive processes associated with vision.

1. Is perception mainly innate or is it mainly learned?
2. Is perception mainly a directed and automated outcome of the stimulus information acting on a passive perceptual system, or is it mainly mediated by deductive, epistemic, logical, symbolic, inferential, or rational processes in a highly active way?
3. Is perception mainly influenced by the overall configuration of stimuli, or are percepts mainly the results of processes more sensitive to the individual features or parts of stimuli?

Most of the possible combinations are represented in Utall's review and the reader with an interest in more detail is referred to his work.

A macrotheory of perception useful as a hueristic for those conducting landscape assessment is a somewhat more limited problem, however, and has some special requirements. Visual landscape assessment is an applied field with a primary task of describing the perceived or perceivable environmental condition. Most perceptual and cognitive psychological investigations concentrate on the workings of isolated organs or individuals in contrived laboratory settings. However, visual assessments must evaluate real, or at least potential, environments. The holistic study of the relationship between living organisms and their normal environment is generally termed the ecological or environmental approach. Proshansky (1976) has articulated the need for an environmentally based psychology. The past two decades have seen substantial interest and some activity but relatively little in the way of ecologically based psychological theory. Barker (1968) provides a notable exception in the area of social psychology and Gibson (1966) in perceptual psychology.

Gibson has consciously developed his ecological theory as an alternative to the abstract physical analogies that prevade most of psychology.

The world of physical reality does not consist of meaningful things. The world of ecological reality, as I have been trying to describe it, does. If what we perceived were the entities of physics and mathematics, meaning would have to be imposed on them. But if what we perceive are the entities of environmental science, their meanings can be discovered. (Gibson 1979, 33)

Gibson has evolved his theory of ecological perception over the past 20 years. Using Utall's scheme of classification, it would be considered in the middle of the innate-learned dimension, actively rather than passively directed but certainly not mediated or rational, and very holistic in its orientation. Gibson capsulizes his theory in this way:

To perceive is to be aware of the surfaces of the environment and of oneself in it. The interchange between hidden and unhidden surfaces is essential to this awareness. These are existing surfaces; they are specified at some points of observation. Perceiving gets wider and finer and longer and richer and fuller as the observer explores the environment. The full awareness of surfaces includes their layout, their substances, their events, their affordances. Note how this definition includes with perception a part of memory, expectation, knowledge, and meaning some part but not all of those mental processes in each case. (Gibson 1979, 255)

If Utall is correct in his survey of the field, then none of the available cognitive or perceptual theories have advanced beyond the hypothetical descriptive phase of science. However, among the available theories, Gibson's holds the most promise for environmental professionals seeking to understand the possible relationships between psychology and their own field because he attempts to describe the phenomenon of perception as we encounter it. If at some future date scientific evidence is forthcoming that indicates these ideas wrong in some absolute sense, they would still have value to us. This is much the same situation as a ship's navigator finds herself. The earth may no longer be considered the center around which the universe turns, but it still provides a very useful and workable hueristic for navigation.

The following chapter is derived from Gibson's latter work, particularly *The Ecological Approach to Visual Perception* (Gibson 1979). While it is a radical departure from current perceptual theories, Gibson makes a persuasive case incorporating experimental findings and theoretical points. The present author must accept any shortcomings of the synopsis presented in this chapter. The first section presents a description of the environmental structure as we experience it—a medium surrounding substances and surfaces. The second section describes the types of ecological meaning that the environment has for us—its layout, events, and affordances. It also describes how light makes information available to us in an ambient optic array and discusses some notions about how active perception takes place. The third section considers four theories concerning pictures and picture perception. The final section reviews the principles associated with creating perspective pictures, line drawings, and motion pictures.

ENVIRONMENTAL STRUCTURE

The environment refers to our surroundings or more properly that which surrounds any perceiving and behaving organisms in the environment. Similarly, the environment requires the presence of an animal.[1] This mutuality of animal and environment is not implied by the physical sciences which concentrates on the basic concepts of space, time, matter, and energy. The difference between these two approaches provides the key to answering the child's riddle: "Does a tree falling in an uninhabited forest make any sound?" The answer is: "Of course not, it only makes energy *waves* because someone must be there to hear it before it becomes sound." As this question highlights, the reality of physics does not necessarily provide a proper understanding of perception. The structure of physical reality ranges from atomic to cosmic. Within this range is the intermediate or terrestrial scale that we can perceive. Our environment consists of valleys nestled within mountains, trees growing within valleys, leaves growing on trees, and cells within leaves. The environment has this nested structure where things are components of other things. Gibson (1979, 16–32) proposes that this perceivable environment is most meaningfully described in terms of the medium, substances, and surfaces.

Medium

Air is the medium of the terrestrial environment. It is insubstantial and therefore affords animals locomotion. It is also important that a medium is usually transparent or transmits light, while substances are generally opaque and reflect light. Light is also absorbed by substances and needs to be continually replenished to maintain the environment's ambient level of illumination. The normal condition of illumination is termed ambient because, as illustrated in Figure 5.1, it reverberates through and fills the medium so that light is normally coming to any point from all directions. This light is not random, however, but is structured and contains information that affords seeing. Other important characteristics of the medium are that it transmits vibrations such as sound waves and allows rapid chemical diffusion. Therefore, the medium also affords hearing and smelling. The medium is relatively homogenous and constant in its makeup. This characteristic assures the availability of oxygen for breathing; it also assures there will not be any sharp transitions or surfaces to affect the travel of light or sound waves. Finally, gravity provides an intrinsic polarity so that there is an up and a down within the medium. Radiant light normally comes from the upper hemisphere or sky. The sun also rises and sets, providing another referent axis. These axes in the medium are related to the environment in an absolute sense. This is in contrast to the concept of physical space where the reference axes are arbitrarily oriented.

---

[1] Since plants are generally not considered perceiving organisms, for the purposes of this discussion, they will be considered as only part of the environment.

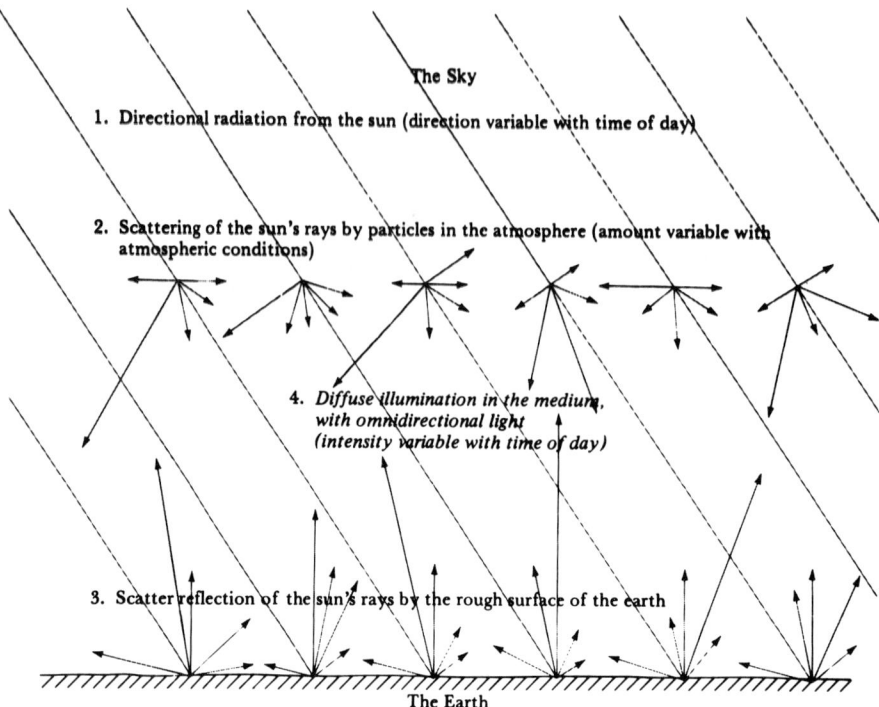

FIGURE 5.1. The creation of ambient light conditions. *Source:* Gibson, J.J., 1979, *The Ecological Approach to Visual Perception* Boston: Houghton Miffin, 49.

Substances

In contrast to the insubstantial medium are the substantial portions of the environment. Substances are characterized as more or less solid, rigid, resistant to deformation, impenetrable by other substances, and permanent in shape. Substances usually do not transmit light; they are opaque. Finally, most substances are normally heterogeneous mixtures of elements and compounds. While substances have a more or less specific composition, they are generally aggregates rather than pure compounds. This brief characterization refers to substances at the ecological state. There are, of course, other levels of analysis for substances, but they need not concern us now.

Surfaces

The medium is separated from environmental substances by surfaces. Most ecological action happens at the surface. Light is reflected or absorbed by the surface, not by the interior substance. We touch the surface, not the interior substance of objects. We do not see the medium or substances; what we see is information available at their interface, the surface. Gibson (1979, 23–31) has begun to formalize a set of principles or ecological laws of surfaces:

1. *All persisting substances have surfaces, and all surfaces have a layout.* Layout refers to the persisting arrangement of surfaces relative to one another and to the ground. The perception of layout takes the place of space and depth in the traditional terminology of abstract geometry.

2. *Any surface has resistance to deformation, depending on the viscosity of the substance.* Viscosity is the resistance of a substance, the penetrability of the surface. Some substances are very fluid and can be poured or slashed; others are simply plastic and can be easily molded or smeared, while others are quite rigid, such as steel. Combined with the first law, this explains why we can walk on the ground and cannot walk through walls or other objects. It also explains why a light animal is easily supported by a bog and a water spider by a still pond's surface, but why a heavy animal cannot be supported by either.

3. *Any surface has resistance to disintegration depending on the cohesion of the substance.* Some substances disintegrate easily, such as sugar cubes and sand castles, while others do not. In general, viscoelastic substances will stretch and remain continuous with the application of pressure while rigid substances may be disrupted and made discontinuous.

4. *Any surface has a characteristic texture, depending on the composition of the substance. It generally has both a layout texture and a pigment texture.* The environment is structured, as previously mentioned, with units nested within each other. Texture is the term used to describe structure at the scale of centimeters and millimeters when viewed at arm's length. Natural substances are seldom homogeneous but are composed of an aggregate or conglomerate with various chemical and physical properties. This gives rise to the fact that speckled surfaces have pigment texture and rough surfaces have layout texture. The relative size of these aggregated units determines whether the texture is fine or coarse.

5. *Any substance has a characteristic shape, or large-scale layout.* If texture refers to the microstructure of surfaces, then shape refers to the macrostructure at the scale of environmental enclosures and objects. Obviously, different shapes afford different possibilities for manipulation and behavior. The analysis of an object's facets or the ground's slope aspect describes whether a portion of the surface is or is not facing a point of observation or a source of illumination. Complex geometrical solids can be analyzed in terms of faces, edges, and vertices. These terms also have important implications for understanding perception.

6. *A surface may be strongly or weakly illuminated in light or shade.* The intensity of incident light falling on a surface may be high or low, intense or dim. In the natural environment, there is normally some illumination, even if it is night. Incident light is also ambient, that is, more or less omnidirectional. However, there is normally a prevailing illumination or a direction from which incident light is most intense. A surface facing the prevailing illumination will be more brightly lit, while one not facing it will be relatively shaded. Since the sun normally determines the prevailing direction of illumination, the pattern of bright and shaded illumination changes throughout the day as the sun traverses the sky.

7. *An illuminated surface may absorb either much or little of the illumination falling on it.* The chemical composition of a substance determines whether more or less of the illumination falling on the surface will be absorbed. Substances that absorb much light, such as coal, are black, while those that absorb little, such as chalk, are white. Light that is not absorbed is either transmitted or reflected. There are not perfectly transmitting substances, and relatively few that are as transparent as optical glass or pure, still water.

8. *A surface has a characteristic reflectance, depending on the substance.* Normally light that is not absorbed is reflected. Each homogenous compound has a characteristic proportion of incident light that is reflected. A conglomerated substance, such as granite, therefore appears speckled or mottled. This is pigment texture.

9. *A surface has a characteristic distribution of the reflectance ratios of the different wavelengths of the light, depending on the substance. This property is what I will call color, in the sense that different distributions constitute different colors.* Color, here, refers to hue or chroma rather than variations in white, gray and black. The color and texture of a surface provide the information that specifies the composition of a substance or what it is made of.

This section presents the basic concepts and vocabulary Gibson uses to describe the environment. The next section outlines what there is in the environment for us to perceive and why we perceive it.

ENVIRONMENTAL MEANING

The environment is most simply conceived as being composed of medium, substances, and surfaces. Yet, these terms do not really describe what we see or why we see it. Surfaces in the environment must be patterned in ways that have intrinsic meaning for animal behavior. In particular, environmental meaning can be understood from the layout of surfaces, from changes in this layout or events, and from what the environment offers or affords animals. Once these concepts are understood, the ambient optic array that carries visual information can be introduced. Finally, the question of how we perceive this information can be addressed.

Layout

The theory of layout is proposed as a way to describe environmental arrangement. It is not based on abstract geometry but on the world as we experience it. Therefore, we refer to surfaces which have color and texture rather than planes which have neither. In geometry, the initial placement of coordinate axis is arbitrary, but in the environment, the vertical axis is determined by gravity and one horizontal axis by the passage of the sun. In the vocabulary of layout, the surface of the earth is referred to as ground. It is generally horizontal and serves as a reference for all other surfaces. Objects are surfaces that are more or less surrounded by the medium. A detached object is completely surrounded by the medium and can be moved without breaking the continuity of its surface. An attached object is not completely surrounded by the medium and may even be a simple convexity or protuberance. It is continuous with the substance of another surface and generally not movable. A weed in a garden is an attached object, but once pulled its continuity with the ground is broken and it becomes a detached object.

When a surface more or less surrounds the medium, it is termed an enclosure. A concavity that partly encloses the medium is a partial enclosure, such as an overhang that provides shelter in the rain. In a hollow object, such as vase, part of the total surface faces outside like an object, while part faces inside like an enclosure.

A place is an extended surface in the environment. It is a location, but not in the sense of a point in geometry. Places do not move around; rather, locomotion consists of going from place to place. At one level, what can be seen from here or hereabouts is a place. Places can be nested, so a home place may consist of a sleeping place and an eating place. Places also have an order of adjacency that cannot be rearranged in the environment. Way-finding is, therefore, possible.

Events

In general, an event refers to any change in an object, place, or surface. It is tempting to consider events in terms of mechanics, time, and space. However, time constitutes an even, linear flow while ecological events are differentiated into parts and are perceived to flow in an uneven fashion. Some of the differences between geometry and ecological layout have already been suggested. Another difference concerns the treatment of time as a fourth dimension by modern physics. However, time is an order of events and spatial layout concerns the order of objects. These types of order are not even analogous since objects can be shuffled or reordered while events cannot.

Events can take several forms. One type of event concerns the reshaping or repositioning of surfaces. For instance, surfaces can be rotated or translated. They can be deformed, such as waves or the complex movements of animals. There can be collisions of objects and even disruptions such as cracking or disintegration. Some of these events are reversible, such as a pendulum swing, while others are not, such as a plate breaking.

Another class of events concerns change in color or texture. For instance, iron rusts, leaves turn color in the Fall, and fur becomes less thick in the summer. Many of these changes correspond to chemical reactions, such as a ripening apple turning red. A final type of event concerns a change in state of matter. For instance, water can turn from liquid to gas through evaporation or to a solid by freezing. These chemical changes and changes in state are not perceptually reversible. Ripening, rusting, and burning are progressive events without meaningful reciprocals; the process of water evaporating is ecologically not the reverse of steam condensing.

Affordances

In order to survive, animals must be able to interpret their environment. Affordances are what the environment offers an animal: what to approach and what to avoid. The medium, substances, and surfaces of the environment are the same for all animals. However, their meaning is different to different animals. Water affords support to a spider, but not to the elephant for whom it affords a cool bath. The concept of affordances draws our attention to Gibson's view of mutuality between animal and environment. He suggests that the ecologist's concept of niche is similar to a set of affordances—to how an animal lives. This is in contrast, though related, to where an animal lives—the collection of places that constitute its habitat.

Some examples might prove instructive. The medium, air, affords us respiration. When supported by our feet on the ground, it affords us unimpeded walking, while for the bird it affords flight. It also affords us visual, sound, and odor perceptions. Substances afford us different things. Water affords drinking, pouring, and bathing. Some solid substances afford manufacture, such as clay being molded into a pot. Some solids afford nutrition while others do not, depending on the type of animal. Such perceptions are made on the basis of ecological characteristics such as surface color and shape. Even so, animals can frequently misconstrue the food value of substances. Surfaces are particularly important to affordance perception. The ground, a rigid surface, affords support. Walking is guided away from surfaces that indicate barriers towards openings that indicate the medium. A surface with a sharp edge, a knife, affords cutting. An elongated flexible surface, such as string, affords tying. Finally, animals interact with each other; behavior affords behavior.

The theory of affordances is a radical departure from other theories that describe perception as value-free. Perception includes apprehension of the value-richness of ecological objects. This perception is not of subjective values such as feelings of pleasure or pain, but of positive and negative properties of the environment in reference to the perceiving animal.

Ambient Optic Array

It now becomes necessary to describe how this information is made available to the observer. Ecological optics are quite different from the optical realities described by physics, geometry and physiology. The orthodox description (see Chapter 3) of vision begins with a ray of radiant light that is focused by the eye to form a retinal image. These focused rays stimulate sensors on the retina and the image is transmitted along the optic nerve to be perceived or processed by the brain. The perception of motion is simply the perception of a series of images processed in sequence. It is a theory appropriate for an image-oriented culture. Vision becomes analogous to light being projected from the physical world, focused by the lens of the eye onto the screen of the retina and perceived by the brain. Various experiments demonstrate these processes. For instance, one can see an image focused onto the transparent retina of a dissected open eye. But Gibson cautions against drawing hasty conclusions. Who is there to "see" the image projected onto our retina? Is there a homunculus, a little man in our brain that perceives this image as we perceive the image through an open eye? Who sees for the homunculus, Descartes asked? And even more awkward, what system of optics do we use for insects that see through compound eyes without lenses?

Gibson's alternative is an ecological theory of optics and visual perception. Its central concept is the ambient optic array. Each of the words in this term has a particular meaning that contrasts with the orthodox theory. Light in the environment is unlike the simplified focused rays of radiant energy studied by physicists. The nature of light in the environment is ambient. Light may begin as radiant energy from the sun, but it is scattered by the atmosphere and reflected by surfaces to such an extent that it becomes omnidirectional or ambient. This reverberation of radiant light is so extensive that even shelters not open to the sun or sky can be illuminated.

This theory only concerns light as it converges at a point of observation, or a point where an observer could potentially be. In this sense, it is an optical theory, one that is only concerned with light as it reaches the eyes of an observer.

The flow of light in the environment normally has structure, as schematically represented in Figure 5.2. At the point of observation, it is an array composed of densely packed solid angles nested into a spherical angle. The envelope of each solid angle intercepts a face, facet, or aperture in the layout; it is that portion of the ambient light projected to the point of observation. The pattern of nested solid angles provides the structure that we perceive. Light without struc-

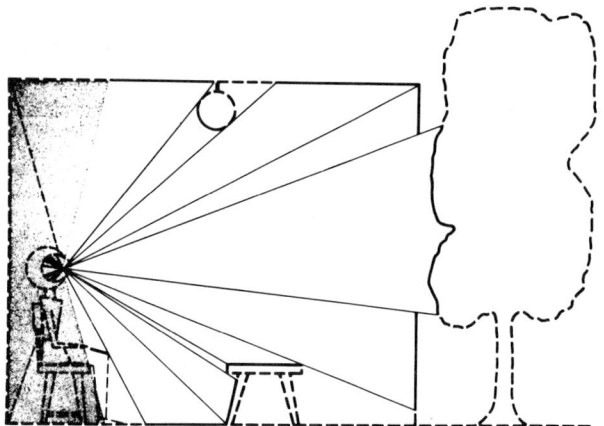

FIGURE 5.2. The ambient optic array in a room with the point of observation occupied by a person. *Source:* Gibson, J.J., 1979, *The Ecological Approach to Visual Perception*, Boston: Houghton Miffin, 79.

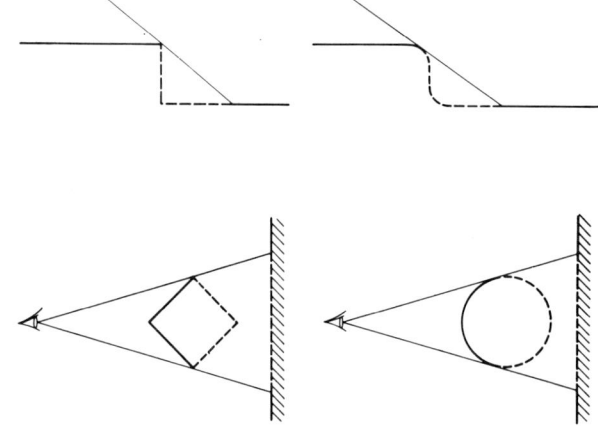

FIGURE 5.3. Occlusion by surfaces and objects with sharp and rounded edges. The hidden or occluded surfaces are indicated by dotted lines *Source:* Gibson, J.J., 1979, *The Ecological Approach to Visual Perception*, Boston: Houghton Miffin, 80.

ture, such as the perfectly diffuse light of a dense fog, cannot provide information about the environment.

Perception

Visual perception is not just an activity of the eyes. Rather, it results from using a visual system: the eyes-in-the-head-on-the-body-resting-on-the-ground. This visual system does not passively receive light stimuli. Instead, perception is an act of attention. People actively scan the visual field to obtain foveal detail as well as actively sampling the ambient array by moving their head and body.

In general, perception involves the concurrent awareness of persistence and change in the ambient array. Information concerning persistence comes from various invarients such as ratios, gradients, discontinuities, and other relationships in the ambient array that are due to persisting features of the environment.

Change in the ambient array is indicated by three forms of going out of and coming into sight. First, surfaces may cease to be illuminated, that is, the solid angles become dark. Surfaces in darkness have not disappeared or ceased to exist, but we are not able to see them. Second, surfaces go out of sight at great distances. This occurs because their projected solid angle is of insufficient size to be seen at the point of vision. Finally, surfaces can go out of sight, as shown by Figure 5.3, because of occlusion. This is specified by progressive decrements of structure along the leading edge of the contour of an ambient array. Coming into sight is similarly specified by accretion. In all three cases, the change in structure of the ambient array may be reversed. That is, surfaces may go into and come out of darkness. They may pass out of sight in the distance and come into sight from the distance; and occlusion may involve both decretion and accretion.

Perception is not simply the geometric analysis of change and invariants in the ambient array. Perception is an achievement of the individual, a keeping in touch with the world. Information about the observer's environment is specified by the ambient array. This information is not communicated to the observer. The world does not speak to us or convey information in the way of words or pictures. It is simply there, specifying the qualities of the environment. Moreover, the active picking up of information happens in an unbroken stream. Animals perceive places, objects, and substances together with events which are changes in these things. Information in ambient light is also inexhaustible. There is no threshold of information; the observer can notice new facts without reaching a limit. This is the most decisive difference between mediated perception such as in an image and environmental information from ambient light. The observer cannot gain more information from a picture by changing his or her position relative to the illustrated objects.

Finally, knowing is simply an extension of perceiving. They both are processes of extracting and abstracting environmental information from the ambient array; different only in degree rather than kind. Therefore, the basic affordances are usually perceived directly from the environment once we learn to attend to the information available in the ambient array.

THEORIES OF PICTURE PERCEPTION

The previous two sections attempt to describe visual perception as an ecological phenomenon. It is important that those who would assess and evaluate landscape visual quality appreciate the ecological nature of perception. This is because actual or potential environments are often visually simulated in order to conduct these assessments (see Chapter 11). It is improbable that a reader of this book would believe an object and an image of that object to be identical. Pictures are not duplications, but merely visual representations. However, it is our responsibility to provide simulations that provide sufficient information to make reasonable judgments.

There seem to be four useful types of explanations concerning how images can represent objects (Gibson 1971; Kennedy 1974). These four theories respectively consider pictures as (1) being mere conventions, (2) being similar to what they depict, (3) providing the same elements of light as the actual scene, and (4) providing the same optic information as the actual scene. There are clear lessons to be learned from each of these explanations.

Conventions

The first theory proposes that pictures are merely conventions—composed of symbols arranged according to rules similar to the grammar and syntax of a language. It is advocated primarily by artists, art critics, and art historians. Arnheim clearly represents this view in stating:

> As a rule in a given cultural context, the familiar style of pictoral representation is not perceived at all—the image looks simply like a faithful reproduction of the object itself. [To attuned observers] the Picasso, the Braques, or the Klees look exactly like the things they represent. Anyone who is concerned with modern art will find it increasingly difficult to remain aware of the deviations from realistic rendition that strike the newcomer so forcefully. . . . As far as the artists themselves are concerned, there seems to be little doubt that they see their works as nothing but the exact equivalent of the object. . . . Pictoral representations that come from the observer's own cultural environment appear to him as "styleness," that is, as done in the only natural and correct way. (Arnheim 1954, 117–119)

On its surface, most of us would reject this position as contradicting everyday experience. Most pictures do transmit some information, even to the very young who could not possibly have yet been trained to read them (Hochberg and Brooks 1962). Gibson (1971) dismisses the adherents to the convention theory as artists who reject projective perspective because "it seems to prescribe and constrain what they should do."

However, the literature in cross-cultural perception does lend some credance to the acceptance of picture perception as an convention. For instance, Serpell and Deregowski (1980) review a study where adults shown pictures of local animals for the first time "sniffed at them, licked them and explored them manually as well as visually, showing no signs of recognition of the items represented in them." When we look at a photograph, by convention, we ignore many of its most striking aspects: the glossiness of the surface, the white band around the picture, and the sharp rectangular shape of the paper. Training in photographic conventions has provided us the insight that important visual information is available if we attend to the fuzzy contours and blotches of contrasting tones. Further investigation of the use and acceptance of pictoral conventions could provide useful information for landscape simulation and assessment.

Similarity

The second theory defines picture as a "likeness" to that which they depict. The general notion is that pictures have common qualities or represent the essential character of an object. This position is represented by Langer (1951, 68) when she states that "the only characteristic that a picture must have in order to be a picture ... is an arrangement of elements analogous to the arrangement of salient visual elements in the object." This conception begins to address representational issues such as caricatures which can obviously be powerful portrayals even though they are not projective, perspective representations. However, it suffers from a lack of specificity that leads to circularity.

Elements of Light

The third theory of pictoral representation is based on principles of projective geometry. This approach was well capsulated by Taylor, the eighteenth-century mathematician, who asserted that in a perfect painting "the light ought to come from the Picture to the spectator's Eye in the very same manner as it would do from the Objects themselves" (Gibson 1971). Instant credibility is given this approach because light can be focused by the eye's lens to form a projected image on the retina.

True pictures, in the sense of this theory, have been created only under very special controlled circumstances (Gibson 1960; Hochberg 1962). However, the normal conditions for viewing a picture do not even approximate the assumptions of this theory (Gibson 1971). For instance, a particular station point is specified by the projective perspective. When viewed from any other point, the picture should become distorted. Another limitation is that light intensities from the viewed picture cannot match the range of the real scene. In addition, the faithfulness of color cannot be matched even by the best photograph while a line drawing does not even portray color or brightness. Finally, the problem of caricature arises once again. The whole point of caricature is to distort the image to *better* portray the object's significant aspects.

As argued earlier in this chapter, the credibility of perspective images seems to be based on the confusion caused by the analogy between projecting light onto a screen and into the "mind's eye." There are, for instance, repeated examples in the cross-cultural literature of cultural groups with a pictoral tradition that have difficulty interpreting perspective clues such as depth (Miller 1973; Pick and Pick 1978; Serpell and Deregowski 1980). However, the power of projective perspective cannot be denied and experience has shown that its principles are quickly learned (Miller 1973).

Optic Information

The final theory of pictures is derived from Gibson's concept of ecological perception.

> *In short the optic array from a picture and the optic array from a world can provide the same information without providing the same stimulation. (Gibson 1971)*

It is important not to be limited by thinking of a picture as simply a cross-section of a frozen optic array, though it may be that.

> *A picture is not an imitation of past seeing. It is not a substitute for going back and looking again. What it records, registers, or consolidates is information, not sense data. (Gibson 1979, 280)*

Information is available from the invariants of the ambient optic array; perception and knowing are the processes of extracting and abstracting this information. These invariants are preserved under transformation, which includes pictoral recording as well as changes during the flow of the optic array.

It should now be obvious that the reason we are not misled by caricatures is because they convey the essential information. Kennedy (1974, 144–145) reviews several studies where caricatures or cartoon drawings provided viewers a better understanding than photographs or high-fidelity line drawings. In his review of the cross-cultural literature, Miller (1973, 139) also found that "too much non-essential detail detracts from comprehension." However, it is also possible to oversimplify: "the recognition of single objects is dependent upon there being enough cues which characterize that object, and which are relevant within the environment of the viewer." These same principles led Cuff (1979) to construct a "conglomerate drawing" representing distinctive elements of a site in a hypothetical perspective rendering to better communicate the sense of place.

PRINCIPLES OF PICTORAL DEPICTION

The use of visual simulations to depict existing or potential environmental conditions is a major concern in landscape assessment. This section reviews the pictoral or graphic principles that make it possible to perceive three-dimensional relationships from a two-dimensional depiction. The methods for creating different types of simulations and issues associated with their use are described by Sheppard in Chapter 11. Vining and Stevens, in Chapter 10, present the procedures for people to evaluate landscape quality using these simulations.

In actuality, a picture is simply pigment on a sheet of paper or film. How is it that we are able to make the sensory shift from awareness of markings on a paper to an awareness of a depicted environment? The principles or clues of perspective are used to depict in two dimensions the three-dimensional space, or in Gibson's terminology, surface layout. These clues are derived in part from projective geometry and therefore tend to be thought of as natural rules or laws. They have been used in place of or to simulate real environments in most of the perceptual psychology research. There is some evidence from cross-cultural studies that the ability to interpret a perspective picture is an acquired skill. However, it is reasonable to expect that anyone from a middle-class Western cultural background will appropriately interpret perspective images using various media and degrees of abstraction. Their use among other populations should be with caution, however. Gibson (1950) has described in detail the stationary monocular clues of perspective representation as they would apply to photographs or other "realistic" depictions. Kennedy (1974) has shown that many of these clues can be abstracted and represented by line drawings. Finally, the perspective clues related to motion or parallax (Gibson 1950) and the perception of motion pictures (Hochberg and Brooks 1978) are considered.

Stationary Monocular Perspective

The following depth or layout clues are present even when all the objects are stationary and viewed with only one eye—the type of situation represented in a photograph or perspective painting. Figure 5.4 schematically represents each of these perspective clues.

1. *Texture perspective.* As the texture of a depicted surface gradually becomes finer and denser, it appears to recede from the observer. This is true for both pigment and layout textures.
2. *Size perspective.* As objects are depicted in relatively decreasing size, they appear to re-

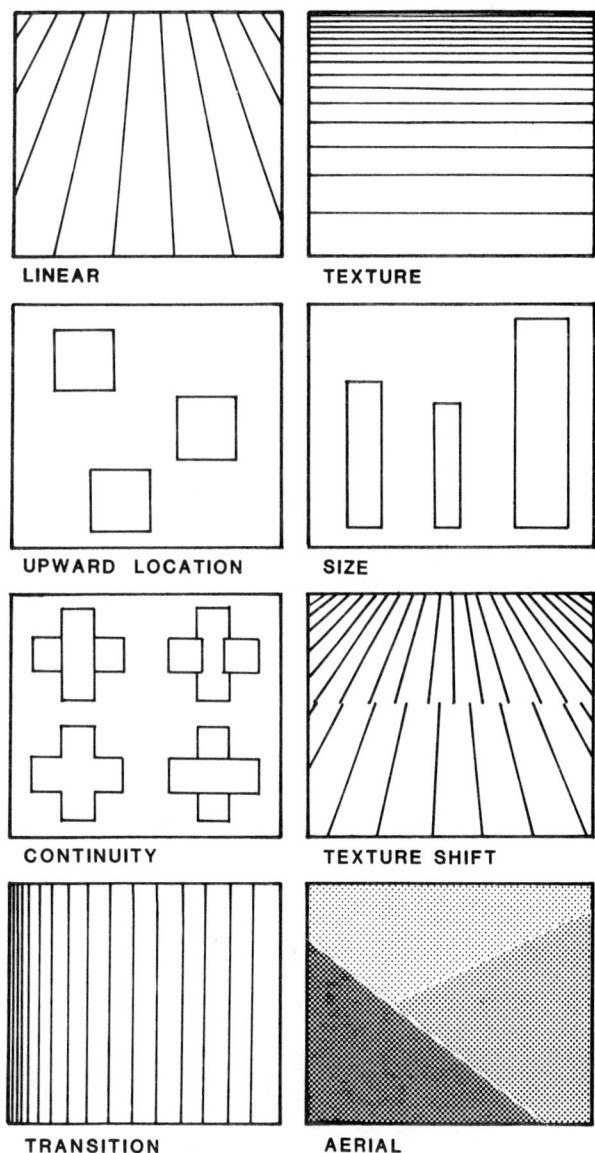

FIGURE 5.4. The stationary monocular clues that specify perspective. *Source:* Gibson, J.J., 1979, *The Ecological Approach to Visual Perception*, Boston: Houghton Miffin, 81.

cede from the observer. This condition presupposes the perception of the objects as contours or figures on a background.

3. *Linear perspective.* The spacing of equidistant edges or objects is depicted as decreasing and converging toward a point on the horizon as they recede from the observer. This phenomenon is commonly illustrated by a view looking down a highway or railroad tracks. It was one of the most favored and highly developed techniques of Renaissance painters and has since become equated by the public with the meaning of perspective. It is possible that persons in Western cultures have become overly reliant on this clue and are more sensitive to it than individuals from other cultures.

4. *Aerial perspective.* As the distance of objects from the observer increases, they are depicted as hazy with less detail and loss of sharp outline. In addition, color desaturation and bluishness is associated with increasing distance. In Chapter 4, Felleman discusses the atmospheric causes of aerial perspective. It has not been as precisely described as the other clues because it is affected by variations in illumination and atmospheric quality. While it may be difficult to measure for these reasons, it will nevertheless be an important consideration when preparing project simulations that relate to air quality (for example, EPA 1979).

5. *Relative upward location in the visual field.* The horizontal ground plane is depicted as rising from the picture's lower margin as distance from the observer increases. It is as if the surface climbs from one's feet to eye level. The implication for objects resting on the ground is that their bases will raise in the picture or approach the horizon line as their distance from the observer increases.

6. *Shift of texture density.* An occluding edge is indicated by a sudden rather than gradual shift in pigment or layout texture. The overall effect is like looking at a valley beyond the edge of a cliff on which the observer is standing.

7. *Completeness or continuity of outline.* When depicted objects overlap, the tendency is to perceive the one with a regular outline and simpler form as being nearer the observer. This clue of overlaying is associated with the Gestalt laws of continuity and simplicity. The perception of a figure and ground relationship is a special case of this principle.

8. *Transitions between light and shade.* Sharp contrasts in light and shade or abrupt shifts in brightness indicate an edge. Gradual shifts in brightness are the principle indication of roundness or surface modeling. These transitions are determined by the degree of bright direct compared to indirect illumination. The relatively shaded area is termed an attached shadow to distinguish it from a cast shadow which is projected by an object that intercepts light. Cast shadows do not indicate overall layout, but at their contour, they are important indications of surface relief.

Line Drawings

When thinking of "realistic" pictures, photographs or detailed paintings usually come to mind. Yet our everyday experience indicates that a few simple lines can frequently convey a significant amount of environmental information. How is it that mere lines can be so versatile? The answer lies in Gibson's suggestion that information lies in the invariants and change apparently in the optic array. In a sense, the lines represent the envelope or outline of the intercepted solid angles in the arrested or frozen optic array represented by the picture. In particular, a line drawing can specify the following invariants of surface layout (Gibson 1979; Kennedy 1974).

1. *A corner.* The concave intersection of two planes forms a corner and may be represented by one line. The intersection of three perpendicular planes, such as the floor and two walls of a room, is represented by three lines meeting at the apex of the joint intersection.

2. *An edge.* The convex intersection of two planes forms an edge. The information whether a line represents an edge and a corner is provided by the context of the drawing. An ambiguous context is the basis for one type of optical illusion.

3. *An occluding edge.* A line may also represent the occluding edge where an object

visually obscures another object. Properly speaking, if the line of occlusion represents a sharp transition, such as the peak of a roof, then it is an edge. However, if the line represents an occlusion defined by a surface with gradual transition, such as the brow of a hill, it is termed a bound.

4. *A fiber.* The substance of a thin fiber, such as a wire, is represented by a single line. However, as extended substances become thicker, it is expected that their outline will be represented.

5. *A fissure.* A thin crack in a surface, such as a closed mouth, is also represented by a line. However, as cracks become wider, such as an open mouth, it is represented by its inlines.

6. *Skyline.* The bound between earth and sky is also represented by a line. In a sense, this is occlusion of the medium, without the presence of an obscured background object.

The following invariants cannot be fully represented by a line. However, a line can specify abrupt discontinuity if it exists.

7. *Change in reflectance.* Abrupt changes in color are indicated by a line, though information about the particular colors cannot be indicated.

8. *Shading on a curved surface.* A line can be used to outline highlights on a curved surface.

9. *Cast shadows.* The penumbra of a cast shadow can be outlined.

10. *Changes in texture.* The abrupt change in texture, such as the juncture between mown and unmown grass, is indicated by a line.

Figure 5.5 demonstrates the pictoral richness that simple lines can represent; the use of lines to represent these invariants follows certain rules or laws. For instance, the lines must connect as they divide the picture into superordinate and subordinate areas. While all the monocular stationary perspective clues cannot be fully and unambiguously specified by lines, our knowledge about the environment and/or skill in reading line drawings makes this a powerful form of depiction.

FIGURE 5.5. Simple line drawings are part of our everyday experience. Advertisements and childrens coloring books provide instructive examples. Can you identify lines used to indicate corners, edges, occulding edges, fibers, fissures, skyline and changes in color, texture or shading?

Motion Perspective and Motion Pictures

Three additional clues of perspective are made possible by motion parallax. This is depicted information made available by a sequence of pictures, or pictures seen from slightly different points.

1. *Binocular perspective.* It is possible to provide some information about surface layout by preparing two monocular depictions, one specified for each eye. This technique is used in photogrammetry to interpret depth using stereo pairs of aerial photographs. Stereoscopic depiction was once popular in American parlors as a way to represent stereoscopic landscape scenes, and more recently, it has been the basis of so-called "3-D movies." However, it is not particularly useful unless the depictions are viewed at a specified distance.

2. *Motion perspective.* As one moves forward, stationary objects appear to move toward you. As the distance between objects and viewer decreases, this motion appears to become faster. Likewise, if two objects are moving at equal speeds, the one closer to the observer will move more rapidly across the visual field. These phenomena are respectively recorded in moving pictures by dolly shots where the camera is moved toward an object and by tracking shots where the camera is moved laterally across a scene.
3. *Shift in the rate of motion.* Additional perspective clues are provided when the observer moves his or her head or body. At an occluding edge, the texture of a more distant object is displaced more rapidly than it is for a nearer object. This information is recorded by a motion picture through a panning action of the camera. This is distinct from a zoom shot which only magnifies but does not have displacement along occluding edges.

The use of motion pictures, either film or video, has yet to be extensively explored for either landscape documentation or simulation. Hochberg and Brooks (1978, 260) list at least five things that moving pictures can portray, but still pictures cannot.

1. They can provide movement-dependent information about tri-dimensional spatial arrangement (motion depth cues) that are unavailable in still pictures and that contradict by their absence whatever depth is otherwise protrayed in stills.
2. Scenes that are very much larger than the size of the motion picture screen (or television tube) can be represented by successive views, calling upon a storage capacity for visual information that we must use in normal perceptual integration, as well.
3. The motion picture characteristically permits—in fact, depends on—change per se, making possible a level of interest-maintenance that cannot be sustained in an equivalent still picture.
4. Motion pictures permit scenes and events to be represented piecemeal, by juxtaposing views of objects that were not in the same place when they were photographed.
5. Redundant sections of actions, periods of time, or extents of space can be elided, and series of events can thereby be reduced to their minimal communicative features.

From a perceptual aspect, moving pictures provide a special experience because the camera is moving in relation to the scene, whereas the viewer is stationary with respect to the projection screen. The viewer's initial glances are directed toward parts of the field that are likely to be informative or prominent. However, interest rapidly declines as information is apprehended and the viewer becomes aware of not being able to redirect his or her view. One way to maintain visual momentum is through discontinuous cuts between places that are separated in space, time, or both. The cutting rate presumably affects interest by introducing an element of surprise or information arousal. In addition, visual momentum can be maintained through substantive content. Shots that are more meaningful, more unexpected, or more complex require longer presentation times and therefore can sustain a lower cutting rate. Hochberg and Brooks (1978, 297) report that "film editors say, in fact, that good, rapidly comprehended cuts are those that provide the viewer with the answer to the visual question he would normally be free to answer for himself." This is the question we will have to learn to answer in order to create effective motion picture simulations.

SUMMARY

This chapter discusses an ecological approach to understanding visual perception and cognition. It is presented in a general and descriptive way because a reasonably comprehensive prescriptive theory for this material has yet to be developed. Much of the detailed cognitive research that exists has not been brought out of the laboratory and evaluated in an everyday setting. However, our application requires a framework to help us understand how people as perceivers fit into the everyday environment. The following table lists the major perception topics discussed and some of their major implications of landscape analyses and assessment.

TABLE 5.1. Perception and Analysis Topics

Perception Topic	Analysis Topic
Ecological approach	Study definition and context
Surfaces	Visual characteristics
Layout	Visibility; spatial notation
Events	Route analysis and notation
Affordances	Environmental meaning
Ambient optic array and perception	Simulatable condition
Pictures as convention	Sampling of respondents, media limitations
Pictures as light	Construction of simulation
Pictures as information	Sampling environments and character simulating
Monocular perspective	Photographic and pictoral simulation
Line drawings	Line-drawn simulations
Motion perspective	Video and film simulations

PART 3

LANDSCAPE DESCRIPTION AND ANALYSIS

This section contains three chapters (6, 7, and 8) addressing visual landscape inventory and analysis—each for a different landscape context. Chenoweth and Gobster address wildland landscapes; Schauman addresses the rural countryside, and Smardon et al. address urban landscape inventory and analysis.

Chenoweth and Gobster start their chapter by defining wildlands and wilderness landscape and by giving the reader some background on legislation, ownership, distribution, and management of wildlands in the United States. The next section of Chapter 6 reviews the purposes, methods of choice, and criteria for wildland description and analysis. The latter includes discussions on professionally based versus publicly based landscape analysis methods and quantitative versus nonquantitative approaches. Chapter 6 ends with discussion of sets of landscape analysis criteria for choosing and guidance for selection of a procedure.

Sally Schauman's Chapter 7, on countryside landscape analysis, begins by setting an assessment context, for example, why the landscape is heavily laden with cultural associations, and a short exploration of attitudes toward rural countryside held by different groups of users. Schauman then describes some of the unique physical attributes of countryside landscapes, then summarizes concepts for evaluation of countryside landscape quality. An overall process for countryside landscape assessment concludes Chapter 7.

The final chapter by Smardon, Costello, and Eggink addresses visual inventory and analysis of urban landscapes. Chapter 8 starts with a brief history of urban physical planning, then addresses five types of decisions or applications for which visual analysis could be used. A brief history of recent professional approaches to urban image analysis is followed by a professional step-by-step approach to visual inventory and analysis using case study material. The latter includes a discussion of positive and negative attributes of qualities of light, including glare analysis. The professional approach is then contrasted to a public assessment/social science approach. Potential combinations of professional and public participation approaches are discussed. Procedural guidance for urban visual studies and a brief discussion of new technologies and techniques closes Chapter 8.

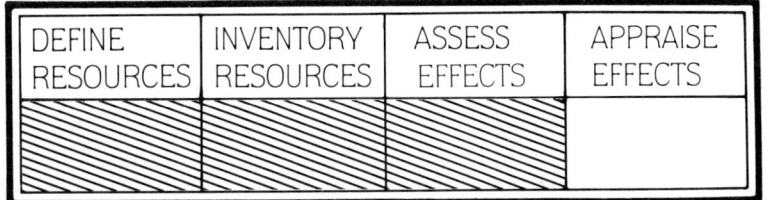

CHAPTER 6

WILDLAND DESCRIPTION AND ANALYSIS

Richard E. Chenoweth and Paul H. Gobster

INTRODUCTION

During the past two decades, the public and its governmental institutions have become increasingly concerned with the allocation and use of wildland resources. Wild landscapes are highly valued both for utilitarian and nonutilitarian purposes such as the enjoyment of natural beauty. Some are even valued for their ability to be changed into other landscapes altogether, such as the filling of wetlands to become rural agricultural landscapes or suburban landscapes.

Legislatively declared wilderness areas are afforded a strong measure of protection from resource extraction and development activities (U.S. Laws, Statutes, etc. 1964). But few wildlands are designated wilderness areas. Wildlands can be either publicly or privately owned and are often prime candidates for mineral extraction, energy-fuel extraction, wood fiber production, the harnessing of water resources, sand and gravel extraction, and other nonagricultural production activities that are required to feed our hunger for a materially comfortable quality of life. Construed as organic entities, industrial, urban, suburban, and even rural landscapes must feed upon the resources of wild landscapes to maintain themselves and grow just as surely as human organisms must feed upon the resources of agricultural landscapes to maintain themselves and grow.

In return, the wildland edge is penetrated by visitors from other landscapes who seek to enjoy the beauty, the wildlife, the recreational opportunities, and spiritual quality of life associated with wild landscapes. In addition to more common means, off-road vehicles, airboats, and recent advances in lightweight gear have permitted entrance to wild landscapes by unprecedented numbers of people. In the midst of this active exchange of people and resources for an enhanced spiritual and material quality of life, the resident wildlife seek a diminishing base of the necessities of life within their wildland habitat.

In this chapter, the means are provided for arriving at the most basic kind of understanding of the visual properties of particular wildlands, that is, description. Wildlands are defined and relevant legislation, ownership, and distribution patterns and management authorities are briefly discussed. Since no one method is likely to be applicable to all descriptive situations, a set of considerations involved in wildland description is provided along with appropriate examples drawn from the literature. These considerations begin with being clear about the purpose for conducting the description, alternative options for choosing a particular type of method, and criteria to be employed in ascertaining the quality with which a particular procedure is administered. Special attention is given to alternative concepts which may be used to portray the visual properties of wildlands.

WILDLANDS DEFINED

No single definition is likely to be sufficiently precise to allow totally reliable distinctions between wild landscapes and other landscapes. After all, the entire landscape is graduated in multifaceted ways and is indifferent to the labels placed on it by humans. Nevertheless, definitions are useful in conveying the sense of a place and are necessary for land use classification systems. One way of defining wildlands is to say that they occupy a space on a continuum of landscapes between wilderness and urban landscapes, a conceptual space closer to the former than the latter. Early wilderness advocates, such as Leopold (1921) and Marshall (1933), defined wilderness as landscapes substantially devoid of human alteration, where the natural environment remains essentially intact. More recently, Section 2 of the U.S. Wilderness Act of 1964 [16 U.S.C.§ 1133 (c)] formally defined wilderness areas for the purpose of land use classification and protection under provisions of the Act:

> *A wilderness, in contrast with areas where man and his own works dominate the landscape, is hereby recognized as an area where the earth and its community of life are untrammeled by man, where man himself is a visitor who does not remain. An area of wilderness is further defined to mean in this Act an undeveloped area of Federal land retaining its primeval character and influence, without permanent improvements or human habitation, which is protected and managed so as to preserve its natural conditions, and which (1) generally appears to have been affected primarily by the forces of nature with the imprint of man's work substantially unnoticeable; (2) has outstanding opportunities for solitude or*

a primitive and unconfined type of recreation; (3) has at least five thousand acres or is of sufficient size as to make practicable its preservation and use in an unimpaired condition; and (4) may also contain ecological, geological, or other features of scientific, education, scenic, or historical value.

This definition specifies physical conditions related to minimum size, naturalness, and absence of improvements or human habitation. However, it also includes criteria which relate to human perception (that is, noticeability) and experiential qualities (that is, solitude and unconfined recreation).

The legal definition of wilderness is too restrictive to encompass the breadth of landscapes intended in this chapter. Nevertheless, it appears that wildlands can best be defined not only as physical or geographic entities, but also as areas that are likely to provide opportunities for experiences that are tied to the natural qualities of the land. Therefore a useful working definition of wildlands should reference not only characteristics of the land, but also the human perceptual and value aspects presumed to be produced by these characteristics:

Wildlands are those landscapes in which there are few if any permanent human inhabitants and where the land remains, is managed, or has been restored such that natural features and processes substantially dominate over man-made development or extractive or consumptive activities. Wildlands are valued or potentially valued for their opportunities for outdoor recreational pursuits including the enjoyment of natural beauty, observation of wildlife, and other pursuits dependent on the special characteristics of the natural features and processes.

In contrast to the definition of wilderness, this definition allows that the presence of humans may be more in evidence and that the wildland may be a result of management and restoration practices. Other similar definitions of wildlands have been offered by Brockman and Merriam (1979), the University of California Wildland Research Center (1959), Ford-Robertson (1971), Schwarz (1976), and Wagar (1964).

WILDLANDS IN THE UNITED STATES

Legislation

The protection of wildlands in the United States has been legislated at federal and state levels of government. Early in U.S. history, large land withdrawals were made by executive order to preserve national treasures such as Yellowstone and Yosemite; later additions to the system were made under the National Park Act of 1916. However, these early parks were created with a "resort" concept in mind, and it wasn't until the 1920s that National Park management shifted to a policy of maintaining wildland characteristics (Nash 1978, 32). Other important early legislation withdrawing federal lands for wildland conservation includes the Organic Act of 1897, which established the authority for the Forest Service to acquire and manage lands for forest and range conservation purposes, and the Migratory Bird Treaty Act of 1918 and Migratory Bird Conservation Act of 1929, which established wildlife refuges across the United States (Cox and Wilkinson 1980).

Additional wildland preservation systems were established in the 1960s with passage of the Wilderness Act of 1964 and the Wild and Scenic Rivers Act of 1968. These Acts added important pieces to the wildland system for primarily recreational and aesthetic use, but like National Parks and Refuges, they were aimed at specific land areas and therefore gave little attention to management of wildland values across the rest of federal land holdings.

Comprehensive federal landscape management came with the passage of the Multiple Use-Sustained Yield Act of 1960. Despite the ambiguity and lack of implementation authority in the Act, agencies began to consider the importance of multiple use in landscape decision making. Recognition of nonutilitarian landscape values in federal agency planning received a boost with the passage of the National Environmental Policy Act (NEPA) in 1969. This law required all federal agencies to consider the impact of land development proposals which would have a significant effect on the human environment. The Act was important because for the first time in U.S. history aesthetic and cultural values were given explicit recognition, along with economic values, on all federal lands. By implication, this includes all federal wildlands and is not limited just to designated parks and wilderness areas. Subsequent legislation for the Forest Service (National Forest Management Act of 1974) and the Bureau of Land Management (Federal Land Policy and Management Act of 1976) gave these agencies the authority to classify and manage lands for a spectrum of uses and gave wildland aesthetic and recreational values equal status with economic values.

At the same time the federal interest in wildlands grew, the individual states became interested in wildland planning and management for their lands. State parks and forest systems were established through federal transfer of lands to the states by laws such as the Swampland Act of 1850, and through condemnation and fee simple acquisition of private lands. Wilderness and wild river legislation was passed during the 1960s and 1970s in some states, and many states passed their own versions of NEPA during this period of environmental awareness.

States, especially those without significant public land holdings, have often adopted innovative techniques for protecting wildland aesthetics and recreational access to private lands. In Wisconsin, for example, progressive state and county zoning regulation for rural areas has gone far to preserve wildland amenities in lakeshore, river, and forest environments. Scenic easements have been established in areas such as the Great River Road along the Mississippi River in order to control rural development. This is accomplished by paying landowners a portion of the value of their land for them to maintain it in a scenic condition as specified in contract agreements. And in Northern Wisconsin commercial foresters are given tax incentives to maintain land in forest land use and to allow public access to these lands. Many other states and local levels of government have similar laws and incentive programs.

Ownership

Approximately 68 percent or 1.56 billion acres of the U.S. land base today remains in wildlands. Many landscape types are represented—forest, coastal, river, mountain, and desert (see Figures 6.1, 6.2, 6.3, 6.4), but in general about half is considered forest and the other half rangelands.

The federal government owns 755.4 million acres or about 48.5 percent of the nation's wild-

FIGURE 6.1. Forest wildland scene. *Source:* Litton, R.B., Jr., 1968, Forest Landscape Description and Inventors-a basis for land planning and design, USDA For. Serv. Res. Paper PSW-49, Pacific Southwest Forest and Range Exp. Stn., Berkeley, California, 31.

FIGURE 6.2. River wilderness scene. *Photo credit:* G. Coniff.

FIGURE 6.3. Desert wildland scene. *Photo credit:* R. Smardon.

FIGURE 6.4. Coastal wildland scene. *Photo credit:* R. Smardon.

lands. These lands are distributed among many federal agencies, but the Bureau of Land Management and the Forest Service are the major landholders (Table 6.1). Although established for a variety of purposes, each agency is concerned with wildland management to some degree.

About 77 million acres or five percent of the wildland resource base is supplied by state and local governments. These lands exist as state and county park and forest lands, school forests, and other holdings.

Private landowners account for the remainder of wildland holdings. About 47.5 percent or 740 million acres of wildlands are owned by 34 million different owners, most (90 percent) of whom are individuals or married couples (Cordell and Hendee 1982).

Distribution

While the total U.S. wildland resource base looks impressive at first glance, this supply must be re-considered in terms of "effective acreage." In this sense, the supply is quite sparse because most wildlands are located far from the population centers. Sixteen percent is in Alaska and 72 percent is in the West. Thus 88 percent of wildlands are readily accessible to less than 20 percent of the nation's population (ORRRC 1962). Table 6.2 shows this disparity in terms of per capita distribution of wildlands. Additionally, federal effective acreage is somewhat less than what is stated, due to restricted access on some lands owned by the Department of Defense (30 million acres), the Fish and Wildlife Service, and Bureau of Indian Affairs.

While the concentration of federal lands in the West and Alaska is responsible for the bulk of disparity, it is clear that state, local, and privately owned wildlands become ever more valuable assets as one moves eastward. These lands are likely to be more evenly distributed relative to population and thus provide a potentially greater level of access than federal lands (Diamond et al. 1983).

Management

While there is disparity in access to wildlands between the western versus midwestern and eastern states, so too is there a disparity in management practices among federal, state, and local land management agencies. As will be seen in subsequent chapters, agencies of the federal government, particularly the Forest Service and Bureau of Land Management, have developed visual management techniques and methods to deal with project development on the federal estate. Considerable progress has been made by these agencies in dealing with aesthetic issues which here-

TABLE 6.1. Federal Land Holdings by Agency (1980)

Agency	Millions of Acres	Percent of Total Federal Holdings
Bureau of Land Management	320.0	42
Forest Service	191.0	25
Fish and Wildlife Service	87.0	12
National Park Service	76.7	0
Department of Defense	30.3	4
Native American Lands	15.1	2
Army Corps of Engineer	8.2	1
Bureau of Reclamation	6.6	1
Tennessee Valley Authority	0.1	--
Other Federal Agencies	20.0	3
	755.0	100

Source: General Service Administration, Inventory Report on Federal Real Property (Washington, DC: U.S. Government, Printing Office, 1980).

TABLE 6.2. Wildland Acreage per Capita, by Region and Ownership, 1980

Region	Population (1981) (millions)	Federal	State & Local	Public (Fed. & State)	Private
North	111.2/48.4%	.12	.20	.33	1.15
South	68.3/29.7%	.27	.29	.57	4.16
Rocky Mtn & Gt. Plains	17.3/7.5%	15.39	1.06	16.46	15.29
Pacific Coast	33.0/14.4%	17.72	.96	18.69	1.92
TOTAL	229.8/100%	3.10	.40	3.50	3.22

tofore have been ignored or slighted due to lack of experience in this area. At the same time, state and local governments and private landowners have neither developed nor received much assistance in dealing with aesthetic management problems of their wildlands. Undoubtedly, state and local public constituencies value wildlands, and the high degree of aesthetic value private landowners themselves place on their wildlands has been shown by Brush (1984). Therefore landscape architects and others with knowledge of visual management approaches have an opportunity to play a significant role in determining the future of nonfederal wild landscapes.

PURPOSES, METHODS OF CHOICE, AND CRITERIA FOR WILDLAND DESCRIPTION

Purposes

Conducting a description of any landscape is not a trivial undertaking. This is especially so for wildlands where difficulties associated with accessibility and relatively large areas of land may compound the problem of description. It is important, therefore, to be clear about the purpose behind a description or inventory prior to deciding upon the general type of method to be used, the specific procedures, and the criteria for quality against which the success or failure of the method might be ascertained.

Nine purposes for conducting a description of wildlands have been identified and are briefly discussed below. They are not mutually exclusive. Furthermore, any given description is likely to have more than one reason which would justify the time, labor, and expense necessary for its completion. Nevertheless, the somewhat artificial classification can be useful, assisting those who describe wildlands in being clear about the purpose behind whatever method is chosen.

Conveying a Whole Image

The most basic purpose of a description of the visual characteristics of wildlands is to convey an image of the appearance of the land to those who have not seen it. This is not as inconsequential an endeavor as it may at first seem. Nor is it simple if one is aware of the numerous choices that must be made by those who describe. While field personnel in land management agencies are often intimately acquainted with the specific landscapes for which they are responsible, often policy and decision-making personnel have not directly experienced the particular piece of real estate whose fate is to be decided. Broad descriptions conveying an image may be especially appropriate in forums where fundamental decisions about land use classifications are to be made, such as the conversion of wild landscapes to recreational tourist attractions.

Comparing and Contrasting Different Wildlands

This purpose is not one that is prevalent. Nevertheless, as the number of wildlands diminish in response to the material needs of urban, industrial, and suburban landscapes, descriptions that compare wildlands will be necessary to assist decision makers in selecting some wildlands for special protection, those which might absorb the most change with the least visual impact, or those whose conversion to other types of landscapes are required to meet the needs of an expanding society.

Comparing and Contrasting Wildlands with Other Landscape Types

While at first such a purpose may seem to require the comparison of apples and oranges, such comparisons may be useful in land allocation decisions. In fact, such comparisons are implicit in the body of research that contains perhaps the most replicated result to be found anywhere in the literature. People find natural appearing landscapes more aesthetically pleasing than those containing man-made structures.

Discriminating Between Areas Within a Single Wildland

This is a common type of purpose for description. Trail and road locations, recreation site development, utility corridor selection, and resource extraction activities will all require the ability to make relatively fine discriminations between the visual attributes of alternative locations within a wild landscape.

Anticipate Visual Impact of Proposed Development

This situation will often confront those responsible for landscape planning, management, and design. In cases such as this, special skills may be required to effectively describe the appearance of a currently nonexistent visual situation. The ability to portray the expected visual impacts and possible mitigative alternatives is often paramount in the landscape description appropriate to this purpose.

Appraise the Economic Value of the Visual Aspects of Wildlands

While not a common purpose, it may become so. Land condemned for public purposes and the evolution of the value of scenic easements are two examples that could require a separate analysis of the dollar value of the landscape considered as a visual resource.

In one case, wildlands in the North Central Cascades in Washington were condemned for inclusion into the Alpine Lakes Wilderness Area. Based largely on land appraisal techniques that favor the value of timber, the U.S. Forest Service initially offered the wildland owners $13 million. James Graaskamp, a professor at the University of Wisconsin-Madison, utilized a market-comparables approach to estimating the value of the real estate that was based on wilderness values, including scenic beauty (Landmark Research, Inc. 1980). The scenic beauty description and analysis was undertaken by Chenoweth and Niemann (1981) and the results used to establish the dollar value of the scenic resource for each 10-acre parcel of land. The case was settled out of court for $27 million, a portion of that directly attributable to the visual quality of the wildlands. This suggests that landscape architects and others who acquire expertise in describing the visual quality of wildland and other landscapes may find that there are opportunities for a new role to be played in the real estate appraisal area.

Assign a Scenic Value for Possible Trade-offs with Other Landscape Resources

The need to assign scenic value for consideration along with other resources most often occurs within governmental agencies. Often planning, management, and even design decisions are made with the input of foresters, wildlife managers, ecologists, air- and water-quality specialists, and so forth, each with their own measurement procedures and favorite resource to advocate during the proceedings. Lacking defensible procedures for establishing scenic value and articulate spokespersons for the visual resource, it is likely to be given short shrift in decisions regarding wildlands. This situation is particularly acute in state departments with responsibilities for natural resources. While there may be bureaus galore reflecting many academic disciplines, there are not bureaus of beauty, and landscape architects are often called in to mitigate visual impacts only after the important resource trade-offs have already been established.

Use in Legal Adversarial Settings

As legislation at all levels of governments adopts language that refers to aesthetic value, scenic beauty, visual resource, visual quality, natural beauty, and so forth, legal challenges either for failure to implement or for implementations that affect economic interests in wildlands can be expected to occur. An examination of Table 2.1 (Chapter 2) shows major court cases and hearings involving aesthetic issues. The bulk of these cases arose in disputes over allocation and use in wild landscapes. Undoubtedly future opportunities to use wildland descriptions in legal and quasilegal settings will occur.

Use in Professional/Client Relationships

Since 20 percent of wildlands are in private ownership distributed among 34 million different owners, there are probably numerous untapped opportunities for applying landscape management skills for the maintenance, enhancement, or restoration of visual quality in wildlands. Whether as technical assistance through government and university extension activities or as private consulting arrangements, the ability to portray visual possibilities for wildland owners is an unexplored area for those wih expertise in visual resource management.

Choice of Methods

Once clear about the purpose or purposes for conducting a description, one is in a better position to select a method or develop a new one that directly fits the original purpose.

Even when clear about the purpose of conducting a description of a particular wild landscape, one faces a bewildering array of procedures from which to choose. The breadth of available methods that have been used in landscape quality assessments is apparent in reviews by Arthur, Daniel and Boster (1977), Bagley, et al. (1973), Brush (1976), Dearden (1980), Fabos (1971), Palmer (1980), and Wohlwill (1976).

There is no one "best" choice, and the purpose of this chapter certainly is not to detail *the* method for conducting a wildland visual analysis. Rather, a more rational and useful procedure would be to present a framework for the consideration of some major aspects of wildland descriptive and evaluative methods and allow the potential investigator a choice of those that best fulfill the original purpose for conducting a description.

Figure 6.5 presents such a framework. The framework is given in the form of a "branching-tree" diagram. As additional considerations are added at levels 1, 2, and 3, the appropriate choice of methods becomes more circumscribed. Table 6.3 can be used in conjunction with Figure 6.5 to find specific examples of the use of different types of wildland descriptors within each major branch of the tree, given that one has initially selected a systematic approach rather than an historic or popular approach to wildland description.

Historical and Popular Perspectives

Before discussion of systematic methods of wildland visual analysis begins, let it first be men-

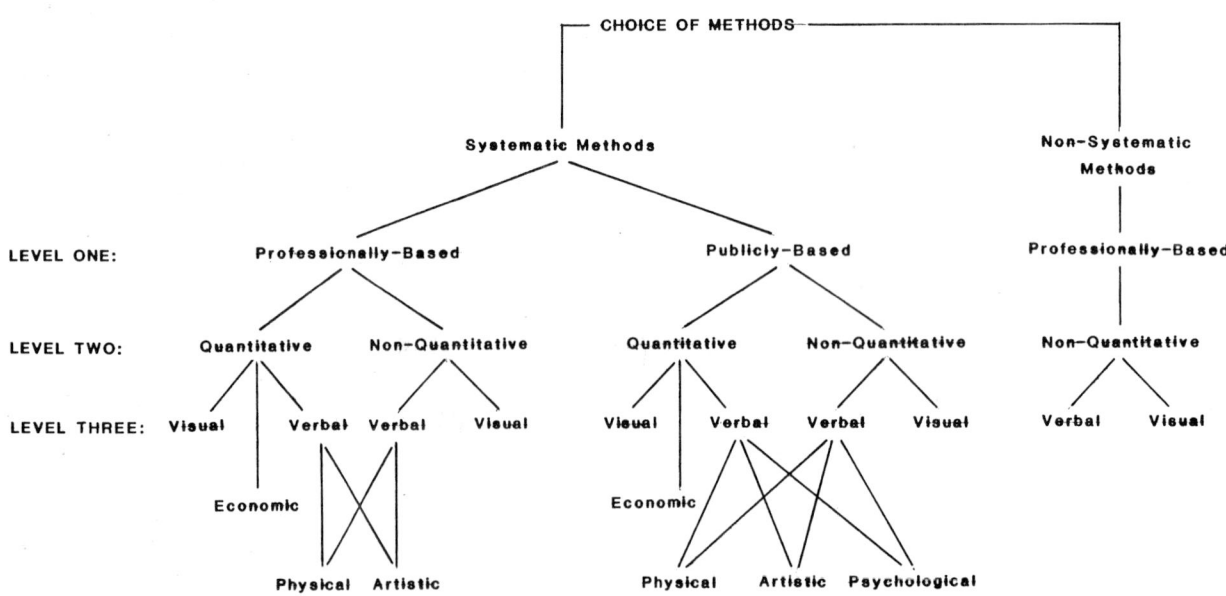

FIGURE 6.5. Choice of methods for wildland description and evaluation.

TABLE 6.3. Examples of Systematic Methods of Wildland Description and Evaluation

EXAMPLES:	Professionally-Based		Publicly-Based	
	A. Quantitative	B. Non-Quantitative	C. Quantitative	D. Non-Quantitative

A. Quantitative

1. Visual
   - Fines, 1968
2. Economic
   a. Travel Cost Method
      - Clawson, 1959
      - Johnson & Haspel, 1983
   b. Cost-Benefit Analysis
      - Coomber & Biswas, 1973
      - Krutilla & Fisher, 1975
   c. Real Estate Appraisal
      - Conner, Gibbs, & Reynolds, 1973
      - Landmark Research, 1981
      - Reynolds, 1978
3. Verbal
   a. Physical
      - Anderson, et al., 1979
      - Leopold, 1969
      - Linton, 1968
      - Zube, 1970
   b. Artistic
      - Hart & Graham, 1967
      - Mann, 1975
      - Jones & Jones, 1975
      - Scheele & Johnson, 1979
      - USDI BLM, 1980

B. Non-Quantitative

1. Visual
   - Litton, 1968 ('scenic notation')
   - Litton & Tetlow, 1978 (maps & aerial photos)
   - U.S. Forest Service, 1974 (maps & photos used in conjunction with description)
2. Verbal
   a. Physical
      - Litton & Tetlow, 1978
      - Lewis, 1963
      - Zube & Dega, 1964
   b. Artistic
      - Litton, 1968
      - Litton, et al., 1971
      - Tetlow & Sheppard, 1979
      - U.S. Forest Service, 1974

C. Quantitative

1. Visual
   a. Visitor Employed Photography
      - Chenoweth, 1984
   b. Multidimensional Scaling
      - Chenoweth, 1983
      - Pearce & Waters, 1983
      - Ward, 1977
2. Economic
   a. Willingness to Pay
      - Cicchetti & Smith, 1973
   b. Contingent Valuation
      - Boyle & Bishop, 1984
      - Brookshire, et al., 1976
3. Verbal
   a. Physical
      - Anderson, Zube, & MacConnell, 1976
      - Arthur, 1977
      - Brush, 1981
      - Buhyoff, et al., 1979
      - Pitt, 1976
   b. Artistic
      - Arthur, 1977
      - Craik, 1972
   c. Psychological
      - Echelberger, 1979
      - Herzog, 1984
      - Evans & Wood, 1980
      - Russell, Ward, & Pratt, 1980
      - Wohlwill & Harris, 1980
   d. Multidimensional Scaling
      - Ullrich & Ullrich, 1976

D. Non-Quantitative

1. Visual
   a. Cluster Analytic Techniques
      - Palmer, 1979
   b. Visitor Employed Photography
      - Cherem, 1972, 1977
   c. Graphic Landscape Typology
      - Craik, 1972
2. Verbal
   a. Questionnaires & Surveys
      - Arthur, Daniel, & Boster 1977
      - Chenoweth & Niemann, 1983
   b. Physical
      - Craik, 1972 [Landscape Adjective Checklist (LACL)]
      - Palmer & Zube, 1976 (cluster analysis)
      - Zube, Pitt, & Anderson (Landscape Feature Checklist)
   c. Artistic
      - Craik, 1972 (LACL)
   d. Psychological
      - Craik, 1972

tioned that artists and authors have been describing wild landscapes in their own terms for many years.

Eloquent verbal descriptions, such as those provided by early lovers of wildlands, can evoke powerful images. Henry David Thoreau's description of Walden Pond (1960, 128), Aldo Leopold's description of a Wisconsin marsh (1949, 95), and Clarence Dutton's description of the Kanob Desert (1882, 122–125) are just a few examples of the power of the written word to evoke images that can be consistent with the actual appearance of the wild landscape. The same can be said of

FIGURE 6.6. Thomas Cole (1801–1848), *Schroon Mountain, the Adirondacks 1833. Source:* Prown. J.D., 1980, *American Painting from its Beginning to the Armory Show,* Geneva: Albert Skira S.A., 67. Reprinted with permission.

FIGURE 6.7. Albert Bierstadt (1830–1902), *Lake Tahoe, 1868. Source:* Prown, J.D., 1980, *American Painting from its Beginning to the Armory Show,* Geneva: Albert Skira S.A., 69. Reprinted with permission.

FIGURE 6.8. Frederick E. Church (1826–1902), *Twilight in the Wilderness, 1860. Source:* Prown, J.D., 1980, *American Painting from its Beginning to the Armory Show,* Geneva: Albert Skira, S.A., 70. Reprinted with permission.

current writers such as Edward Abbey (1971) and John McPhee (1977, whose novels have become the modern classics of today's wilderness enthusiasts.

Artistic renderings, such as the ink drawings of the Grand Canyon by William Holmes and paintings by Thomas Cole, Alfred Bierstadt, and Thomas Moran, may also serve to convey relatively realistic, albeit dramatic, images of wildlands to those who will not directly experience them (see Figs. 6.6, 6.7 & 6.8).

Contemporary photographic equipment and techniques, low-cost video apparatus, stereo aerial photography, and other advances in the visual arts and sciences now make extremely faithful visual representations of even large expanses of wildland areas possible.

Professionally Based versus Publicly Based Methods

Perhaps the most fundamental division of wildland visual analysis methods is between the professionally based and publicly based methods. These categories are largely self-explanatory. Professionally based methods rely principally upon "experts" in the selection and evaluation of method components and in the assignment of descriptive labels to the wildland. Public methods rely on public groups, frequently user and interest groups, either to make some judgment of landscape quality or to define content categories for the analysis, or both.

The professional approach is characteristic of "early" or traditional approaches to wildland description and evaluation. Such approaches are associated with the fine arts tradition and include disciplines such as landscape architecture, art criticism, and philosophical aesthetics (Figure 6.9). According to an analysis of the landscape perception literature by Zube, Sell, and Taylor (1982), the professional approach or "expert" paradigm dominated other types of studies throughout the 1960s and into the 1970s, while in the mid-1970s publicly based methods started becoming equally prevalent.

Professional approaches have some clear advantages over publicly based methods. There is no need to assemble public groups for experimental preference testing, for most of the analysis can be done in-house. Expert approaches are flexible in that they can be applied to a wide range of landscape types at a variety of scales (Daniel and Boster 1976). Depending upon the specific parameters chosen for analysis, analysis and evaluation can be done using data collected in the field, or in some cases secondary data sources (for example, maps and air photos) can be used. Due to its versatility and its strong traditional grounding in the design arts, expert approaches will continue to be a major method of landscape description and evaluation.

Expert approaches are not without their disadvantages, however. Numerous authors (for example, Arthur, Daniel, and Boster 1977; Cerney 1974; Gilg 1975; Jaques 1980; Ribe 1982) have criticized this type of method. For instance, the methods have been called elitist (Jaques 1980; Arthur, Daniel, and Boster 1977) in that they assume that the expert is a better judge for what is good for the public than is the public itself (for example, Carlson 1977). A somewhat different objection to the use of expert approaches is that expert evaluations of landscapes may differ from those of the public. It would follow that expert approaches are inappropriate in situations where consideration of visual quality is mandated in the public interest. Empirical studies of expert versus lay judgments of landscape quality suggest that this objection may be a valid one (for example, Buhyoff et al. 1978; R. Kaplan 1973). Expert approaches have also been criticized on the scientific grounds that the arbitrary selection, weighting, and combining of landscape components to form an overall index of landscape value (for example, Hamill 1976) is not valid. Finally, empirical tests assessing the reliability of certain

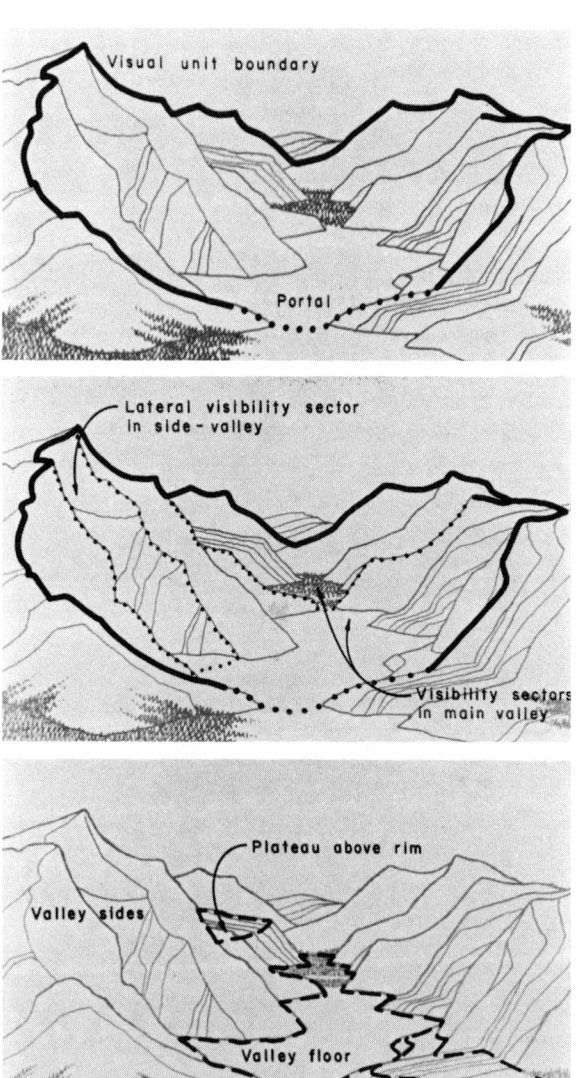

FIGURE 6.9. Example of a professional approach to landscape inventory. *Source:* Tetlow, R.J. and Sheppard, S.R.J., 1977, Visual Resources of the Northeast Coal Study Area 1976–1977, Resource Analysis Branch, Ministry of Environment, Province of British Columbia, Canada, 10.

professionally based approaches have indicated that experts often do not agree in their assignment of ratings (Feimer et al. 1979).

Public approaches to wildland description and evaluation take various forms as do the expert approaches, but all concern themselves with tapping some aspect of public perception of the visual aspects of wildlands. Daniel and Boster (1976) make a distinction between public assessments involving surveys and questionnaires and those that use graphic means of representation to elicit judgments and perceptions of the landscape. More will be said about verbal and visual types of representation and response formats later, but it should be said now that most public approaches use some means of visual stimuli presented to observers.

Public approaches have come out of a different tradition than expert approaches and have their grounding in the empirical social sciences. Because of this tradition, there has been a greater concern for scientific rigor. Studies have been conducted to test the reliability and validity of various aspects of these methods (see, for example, Daniel and Boster 1976; Buhyoff, Lueschner, and Arndt 1980). These types of concerns are important in assessing the meaningfulness and utility of study results. In addition to responding to scientific criteria, the results of public approaches may serve to satisfy requirements for citizen input into public land use issues (Figure 6.10).

The user of public approaches is confronted with a host of methodological choices: sampling of respondent groups, sampling of the environment under study, choice of response formats, and so on. While beyond the scope of this chapter, detailed discussions can be found in Chapter 10

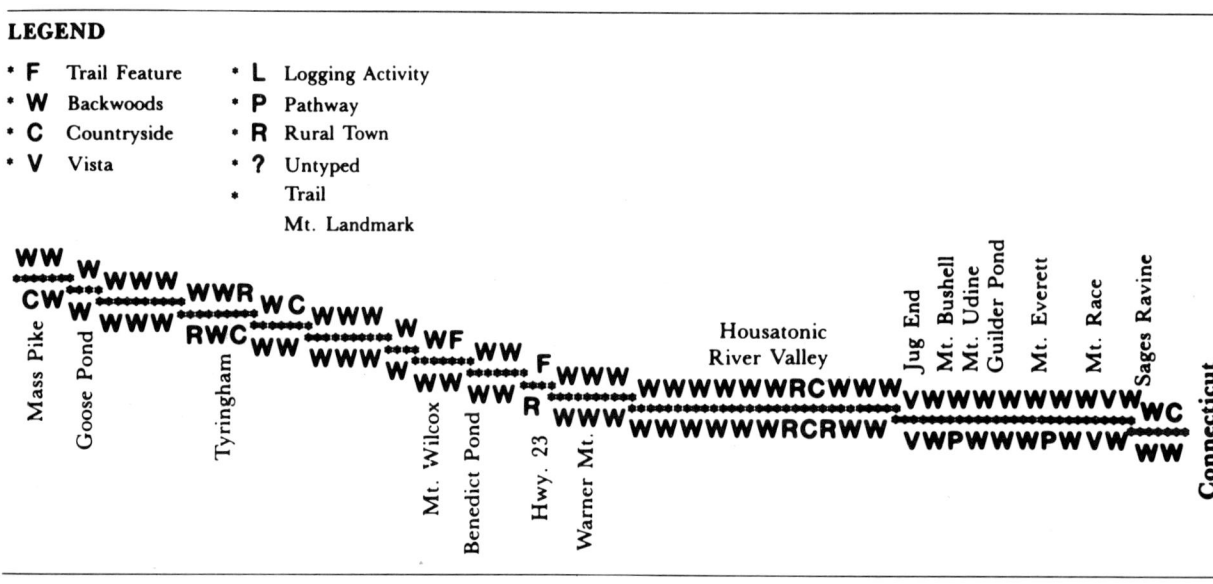

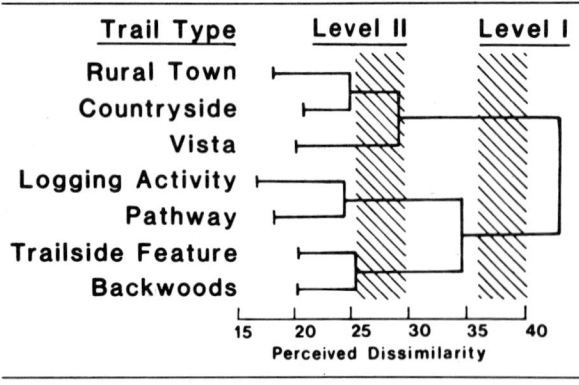

FIGURE 6.10. Perceptual inventory of the Appalachian Trail. *Source:* Palmer, J.F., 1983a, A visual character approach to the classification of backcountry trail environments, *Landscape Journal* (University of Wisconsin Press), 2, (1), 11.

of this volume, as well as articles by Daniel and Boster (1976) and Wohlwill (1976). These discussions should be considered as required reading for those planning to conduct a wildland description or evaluation using a publicly based approach.

Public approaches clearly sidestep some of the criticisms inherent in professionally based approaches, but they, too, have been criticized on some accounts. Powell (1981) has criticized public approaches for treating "the public" in a generic manner, discounting the possibility of judgmental variability. While this is indeed an important concern, empirically based research designs have been used to test for and study individual (Craik 1975), group (Daniel and Boster 1976), and cross-cultural (Zube and Mills 1976) perceptions of landscape quality. Kreimer (1977) and Carlson (1977) have also criticized public methods on various substantive and procedural grounds. Rebuttals to these perceived inadequacies have been presented by Buhyoff and Wellman (1979) and Ribe (1982).

Quantitative versus Nonquantitative Approaches

The next division of categorizing methods of choice in wildland description of the visual landscape concerns quantitative and nonquantitative methods of analysis. This choice again is a fundamental one that should be given consideration at the outset of the proposal stage. Is the need to simply describe the appearance of the landscape as a whole, realistically and accurately? If so, a nonquantitative approach would suffice. Most methods in use today, however, are selected with the purpose of evaluating some aspect of landscape, frequently landscape quality or scenic beauty. In this case, it is necessary to supplement description and classification with some form of quantitative measure of landscape components and/or judgmental responses to the landscape.

Quantitative and nonquantitative approaches have been utilized within both public and expert modes of landscape analysis. Landscape architects and others in the design arts have traditionally described landscapes in nonquantitative terms. "Vividness," "unity," and "variety" in line, color, form, and texture, for example, are properties of landscapes thought to be related to scenic beauty (Litton 1982; U.S. Forest Service 1974). Such descriptors have the advantage of applying to landscapes that differ widely in their physical characteristics. But they also carry ambiguous meanings that make it difficult for nondesigners to understand or to know what physical features in the landscape can be manipulated to achieve aesthetic goals (Arthur, Daniel, and Boster 1977). Other nonquantitative techniques merely explain what is present in the landscape in physical terms, amounting to an inventory of features (for example, Lewis 1963) or classification of landscape types (for example, Zube and Dega 1964; Litton and Tetlow 1978). Such analyses are useful for further planning because they initiate a base vocabulary or inventory from which evaluation may take place at a further stage, if desired.

Nonquantitative public approaches are useful for obtaining user-defined landscape components. Surveys and questionnaires with appropriately defined questions can be used to elicit properties of the wildland environment relevant to user perceptions. For example, in a study of river environments (Chenoweth and Niemann 1983), canoeists and other river floaters were asked in a questionnaire format to list elements of the landscape that they felt contributed to scenic beauty. Results of this task gave investigators a useful taxonomy of user-defined landscape components. In a different study, Palmer (1979) used photographs of landscape scenes along a wildland trail to develop a taxonomy of user-defined landscape components. Trail hikers were asked to separate scenes of the trail into piles based upon their similarity. As with the questionnaire study, Palmer's results provide a useful tool for understanding user perceptions and for managing recreational wildland environments (see Figure 6.10).

Expert approaches have evolved such that they are increasingly quantitative in nature; numbers are usually assigned to landscape elements relative to their presence or absence, or their degree of presence. These numbers are then combined in some fashion to produce an overall evaluation of landscape quality. There are numerous examples including studies by Fines (1968), Leopold (1968), Linton (1968), and the U.S. Bureau of Land Management (1980).

Quantitative methods comprise the bulk of public approaches used in wildland description and assessment. Usually viewing the landscape through photographic stimuli, public groups judge some aspect of the quality of the scene. This judgment might be a single response measure, such as scenic beauty (for example, Daniel and Boster 1976), but in some cases judgments are made on a number of scales describing various physical dimensions or affective qualities of the scene (for example, Craik 1972; Zube, 1973; Wohlwill, and Harris 1980). In other cases, scenes are judged for their overall quality by public groups, and properties of individual scenes are independently scaled. Using public preference judgments as the dependent variable, statistical correlational techniques are then applied to test the importance of various landscape attributes in predicting landscape preference. Examples of these types of studies applied to wildland environments include those by Anderson, Zube, and

MacConnell (1976), Arthur (1977), Schroeder and Daniel (1981), and Shafer, Hamilton, and Schmidt (1969).

One particular type of quantitative approach not already discussed deserves mention. These are the economic approaches to landscape valuation. Again approaches vary considerably. They may be expert-based, such as the "travel-cost" method developed by Clawson and colleagues (1959). In this approach it is assumed that the attractiveness of an area can be valued on the basis of how many people visit the area and how much it costs them to get there. Other expert economic types of analysis include cost-benefit analysis (Krutilla and Fisher 1975; Coomber and Biswas 1973) and real estate appraisal techniques (Landmark Research, Inc. 1981; Conner, Gibbs and Reynolds 1973). Publicly based economic approaches are receiving increased attention by researchers who wish to find out how the public values nonmarket resources, such as aesthetics. These approaches have been labelled "willingness to pay" or contingent valuation methods. Respondents are asked how much they would be willing to pay for a good, such as visiting a wildland environment, contingent on conditions specified (for example, degradations of scenic quality, crowding). Examples of contingent evaluation methods pertaining to wildland aesthetics include papers by Brookshire et al. (1976) and Boyle and Bishop (1984). More general reviews of the contingent technique are available in Brookshire and Crocker (1981) and Schulze et al. (1980).

Verbal versus Visual Approaches

Another facet which can be used in the selection of a particular method involves the choice between verbal and visual means of description and representation. In professionally based methods, visual approaches have been used to help convey landscape qualities and treatments that are often hard to express in words. A visual notation system developed by Lynch in *The Image of the City* (1960) presents one example of this type of system. Litton (1968) presents a similar type of "scenic notation" for wildland environments (see Figure 6.11). These systems can aid designers in detailing spatial qualities and other properties of the landscape, but by themselves offer little communicability between designers and nondesigners or the general public.

An improvement over abstract visual approaches is the use of photographs and sketches to describe and represent landscapes. Most notable examples of this type are handbooks on Visual Resource Management published by the Forest Service (1974) and Bureau of Land Management (1980). These agencies use both verbal description and visual representation to convey information about their landscape evaluation processes, to make them understandable both to design and nondesign professionals, as well as to the interested public.

Visual methods have been already mentioned as the dominant means used in publicly based approaches for representing and describing the wildland environment. The popularity of this approach lies mainly in the fact that visual images are easily understood and responded to by the public. In terms of representing the landscape, photographs and sketches can give accurate, common images to respondents. Visual means of representation are also amenable to a wide variety of verbal response and descriptive formats, which will be discussed shortly.

Sampling the environment photographically is an inexpensive means of landscape representation, especially if the alternatives are actual field visits. Furthermore, the validity of photographic representation of the landscape has been established in numerous studies (see, for example, Shafer and Richards 1974; Daniel and Boster 1976; Shuttleworth 1980; Nassauer 1983). See Example 1.

Although visual representation of landscape images is a popular method for public approaches of wildland visual analysis, visual description is rarely used. One technique for visual description used by Palmer (1979) has already been mentioned. Another technique developed by Cherem (1972) and refined by Chenoweth and his associates (Chenoweth 1984) is *visitor employed photography*. In this technique, respondents are given cameras and response forms as they enter the landscape study area. They are asked to photograph things around them they feel add to or detract from the scenic beauty of the area. When a photograph is taken, respondents write the name of the feature in the space provided, rate the degree to which the feature adds to or detracts from

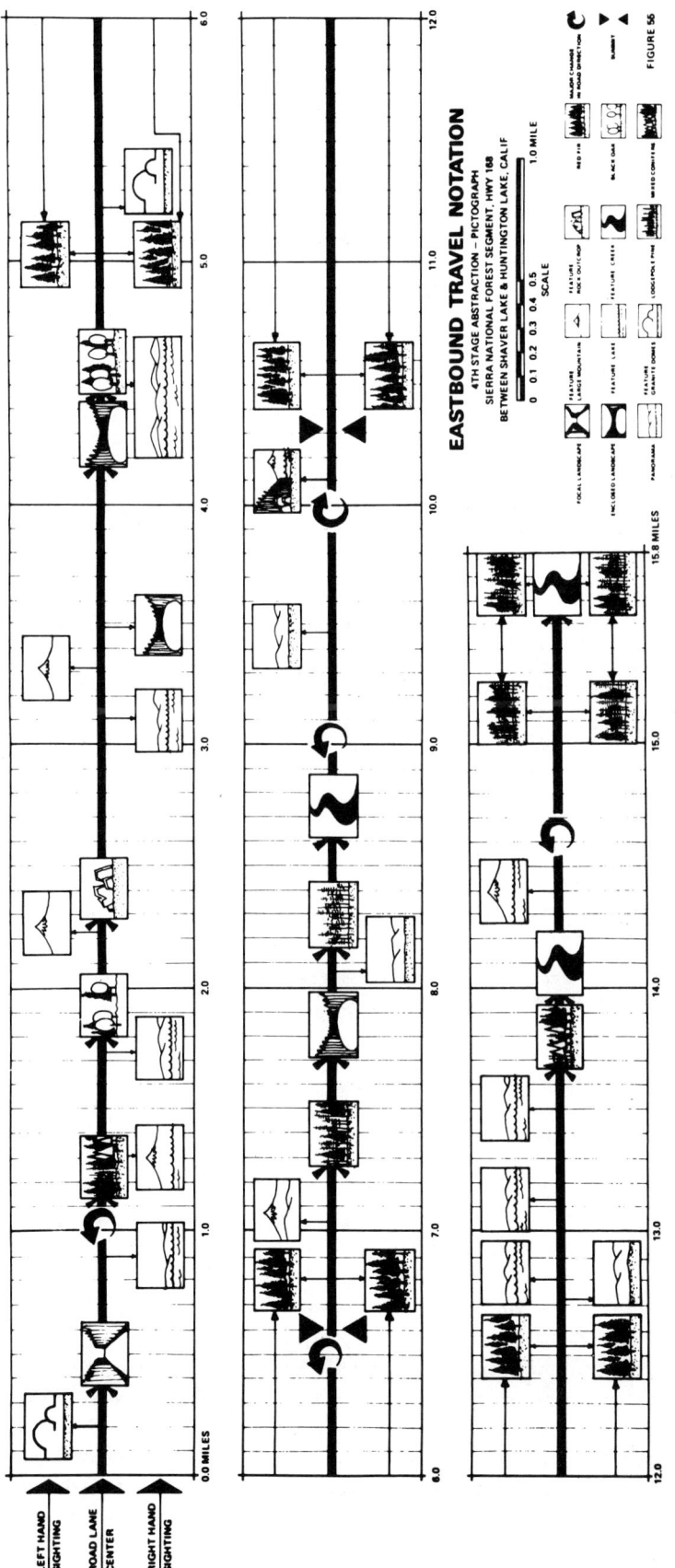

FIGURE 6.11. Litton's notation system. *Source*: Litton, R.B., Jr., 1968, Forest Landscape Description and Inventories—a basis for land planning and design, USDA For. Serv. Res. Paper PSW-49, Pacific Southwest Forest and Range Exp. Stn, Berkeley, California, 56.

EXAMPLE 1

LOWER WISCONSIN

VISITOR EMPLOYED PHOTOGRAPHY

Department of Landscape Architecture
School of Agricultural and Life Sciences
University of Wisconsin-Madison

| month | day | year | put in | take out | film # |

INSTRUCTIONS: During your trip on the river today, please take photographs of features in the riverway or rivervalley which <u>detract from</u> or <u>add to your experience of scenic beauty</u> while on the river. The features which detract from or add to your experience of scenic beauty of the river may be very near you or as far away as you can see, they may be people or activites, natural features or man-made features, wildlife, whole views or specific objects. In addition, we would like you to answer several questions about each photograph that you take.

STEP 1 Once you have taken a photograph of some feature in the riverway or rivervalley which detracts from or adds to yur experience of scenic beauty while on the river, name the features on the line next to the number of the photograph which appears in the camera window.

STEP 2 Without consulting other members of your group, circle the number which indicates how much you think the feature detracts from or adds to your experience of scenic beauty.

STEP 3 Without consulting other members of your group, please circle the number which indicates how beautiful the whole scene in the viewfinder is to you.

STEP 4 Record <u>your location</u> and the <u>number of the photograph</u> using the accompanying maps.

STEP 5 Draw an arrow from your location to the feature which was photographed using the accompanying maps.

YOU HAVE 20 PHOTOGRAPHS. PLEASE TRY TO USE THEM ALL!

CAMERA RETURN

Please return all materials to Blackhawk Ridge

THANK YOU FOR YOUR CONCERN AND COOPERATION!

---

the scenic beauty, and finally rate the beauty of scene as a whole. Results from such a study can be valuable in a number of ways. The photographs are taken in the study area by respondents themselves and not imposed upon them by the investigator. In this way the respondent samples and self-selects landscape features rather than responding to the investigator's selection, which might include features the respondent would not have even noticed in the study area. Public consensus can be readily determined by ratings of common scenes taken by respondents. Also, descriptive features of scenes are user-defined and often include things ignored by conventional sampling procedures such as details, sequences, and ephemeral effects. Finally, written descriptions and the photographs themselves provide a user-defined record of pertinent features, again direct evidence of public perceptions put in publicly defined terms, not those imposed by the researcher or predicted statistically through regression analysis.

EXAMPLE 1

LOWER WISCONSIN RIVER - VISITOR EMPLOYED PHOTOGRAPHY

STEP 1		STEP 2		STEP 3		STEP 4
number in camera window	Feature in Photograph	Feature detracts from experience of scenic beauty detracts	Feature adds to experience of scenic beauty adds to	Extremely low scenic beauty	Extremely high scenic beauty	Record photo location on map
1		-3 -2 -1	+1 +2 +3	1 2 3 4 5 6 7 8 9 10		
2		-3 -2 -1	+1 +2 +3	1 2 3 4 5 6 7 8 9 10		STEP 5
3		-3 -2 -1	+1 +2 +3	1 2 3 4 5 6 7 8 9 10		
4		-3 -2 -1	+1 +2 +3	1 2 3 4 5 6 7 8 9 10		Draw an arrow from photo location
5		-3 -2 -1	+1 +2 +3	1 2 3 4 5 6 7 8 9 10		
6		-3 -2 -1	+1 +2 +3	1 2 3 4 5 6 7 8 9 10		
7		-3 -2 -1	+1 +2 +3	1 2 3 4 5 6 7 8 9 10		
8		-3 -2 -1	+1 +2 +3	1 2 3 4 5 6 7 8 9 10		
9		-3 -2 -1	+1 +2 +3	1 2 3 4 5 6 7 8 9 10		
10		-3 -2 -1	+1 +2 +3	1 2 3 4 5 6 7 8 9 10		
11		-3 -2 -1	+1 +2 +3	1 2 3 4 5 6 7 8 9 10		
12		-3 -2 -1	+1 +2 +3	1 2 3 4 5 6 7 8 9 10		
13		-3 -2 -1	+1 +2 +3	1 2 3 4 5 6 7 8 9 10		
14		-3 -2 -1	+1 +2 +3	1 2 3 4 5 6 7 8 9 10		
15		-3 -2 -1	+1 +2 +3	1 2 3 4 5 6 7 8 9 10		
16		-3 -2 -1	+1 +2 +3	1 2 3 4 5 6 7 8 9 10		
17		-3 -2 -1	+1 +2 +3	1 2 3 4 5 6 7 8 9 10		
18		-3 -2 -1	+1 +2 +3	1 2 3 4 5 6 7 8 9 10		
19		-3 -2 -1	+1 +2 +3	1 2 3 4 5 6 7 8 9 10		
20		-3 -2 -1	+1 +2 +3	1 2 3 4 5 6 7 8 9 10		

Describing and representing the environment verbally can also be done in many ways. Terms for the description and analysis of wild landscapes have evolved from a number of disciplines, including landscape architecture, geography, geomorphology, psychology, art history, and philosophical aesthetics. The disciplines involved often constitute a bias where methods and terminology are transferred to the relatively young field of landscape assessment. While cross-disciplinary input has been of great value to the field, it has also caused communication problems due to the diverse nature of environmental description.

Landscape architects and design professionals tend to describe the wildland environment in terms of *artistic* nature. Terms such as those in Table 6.4 connote abstract properties of the landscape in that they are based upon a synthesis of readily observable landscape elements rather than

TABLE 6.4. Examples of Artistic Landscape Descriptors

River[a]	Forests[b]	Regional Landscape Study[c]
vividness	focal view	line
intactness	prominence	form
unity	observer position	color
expansiveness	lighting effects	texture
enclosure	contrast	spacial character
sequence	detail	visual dominance

[a] from Jones and Jones, 1975.
[b] from Arthur, 1977.
[c] from Yeomans, 1982.

Sources: Jones and Jones, 1975; Arthur, 1977; Yeomans, 1982.

TABLE 6.5. Examples of Pyschological Landscape Descriptor

Rivers[a]	Forests[b]	Regional Landscape Study[c]
ordinary-unusual	honest-dishonest	active
pleasant-unpleasant	pleasant-unpleasant	adventurous
interesting-boring	valuable-worthless	alive
harmonious-inharmonious	relaxed-tense	arid
ugly-beautiful	large-small	autumnal

[a]from Wohlwill, 1977
[b]from Moeller, MacLachlin, and Morrison, 1974
[c]from Craik, 1972

Sources: Wohwill, 1977, Moeller, MacLachlin, and Morrison, 1974; Craik, 1972.

a straight physical description of tangible landscape elements.

Environmental psychologists and related professions also tend to describe wild landscapes in terms of abstractions. In this case, however, terms relate to affective and evaluative responses elicited from those who view the landscape. These are called *psychological* descriptions in that the terms connote the psychological effect the landscape has on the observer. In other words, scenes shown to observers might elicit such feelings as harmony, coherence, unity, complexity, or mystery. Other examples of psychological descriptions are shown in Table 6.5

Finally, there are the *physical* descriptions of landscape employed most frequently by geographers, foresters, and other physical science disciplines to describe wild landscape. These describe landscapes in terms of the physical elements present: rocks, trees, water, and so forth. Further examples are shown in Table 6.6.

Physical, artistic, and psychological descriptive types can be used both in professionally based assessments as well as in public evaluation methods. Combinations of the three types are often used within a single study. There are literally thousands of environmental descriptors and combinations proposed and used in past studies of the

TABLE 6.6. Examples of Physical Landscape Descriptions

Rivers[a]	Forests[b]	Regional Landscape Study[c]
River Width (ft)	Amount of Downed Wood	Length of View
River Depth (ft)	Density of Trees	Percentage Tree Cover
Velocity	Size of Trees	Absolute Relavite Relief
Bank Height (ft)	Amount of Ground Cover	Water Edge Density
Biological Diversity	Variety of Tree Sizes	Mean Elevation
Amount of Trash & Litter	Percent Crown Cover	Area of View

[a]from Leopold and Marchand, 1968.
[b]from Arthur, 1977.
[c]from Anders, Zube, and MacConnell, 1976.

Sources: Leopold and Marchand, 1968; Arthur, 1977; Andrews, Zube, MacConnell, 1976.

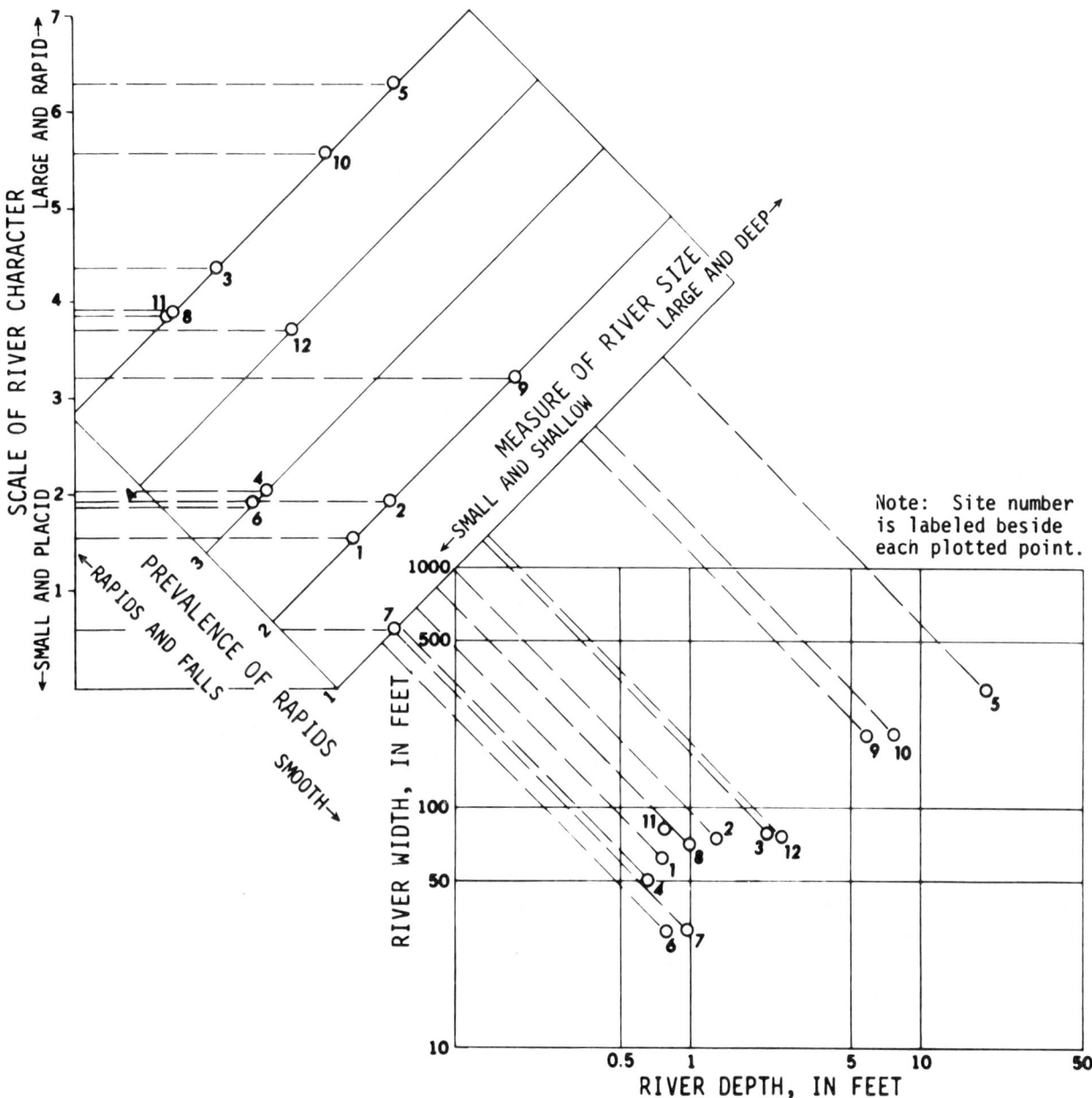

FIGURE 6.12. Leopold's uniqueness assessment system. *Source:* Leopold, L.B., 1969, Quantitative Comparison of Some Aesthetic Factors Among Rivers, US Geological Survey Circular 620, Office of Scientific Publications, 904 National Center, Reston, Virginia.

landscape. While there is some preliminary consensus on which variables might satisfy the effectiveness criteria mentioned previously, the overall picture is one of lack of agreement on their use both within and between descriptor types and landscape types. For example, some techniques, like the descriptive inventory proposed by Leopold (1968), use many (31) physical descriptors that are weighted and summed to produce an overall Index of Uniqueness Value for River Environments (see Figure 6.12) Other techniques, like the Forest Service's (1974) inventory, utilize relatively few parameters that can be classified artistic. These are subjectively cumulated to give an overall judgment. Still others, like Daniel and Boster's (1976) Scenic Beauty Estimation Method, use only one overall judgment of "scenic beauty."

Sets of Available Criteria

Having clearly identified the purpose of description and the major methodological choices, there remains the problem of quality control over the specific procedures to be adopted. The criteria to be chosen and the rigor with which they should be met will vary according to the extent to which the procedures are likely to be challenged by competing interests, as well as practical considerations, such as the time and resources available to execute the description. For example, if one simply wishes to convey an image of the existing wildlands to people in a nonpolitical climate, one may need to consider nothing further than commonly accepted rules for good photography. Alternatively, if one's purpose is to appraise the economic value of wildland aesthetics for a pending land transaction or to anticipate the visual impacts of proposed development in controversial cases that may lead to legal action, firm criteria rigorously adhered to will be necessary.

The sets of available criteria for selection of a methodology described below come from a variety of sources and disciplines. While each set includes some criteria worth consideration for any methodology, certain points seem more appropriate to particular methodologies. These criteria can be divided roughly into two types. First are "design" criteria, considerations applicable to project simulation, design and planning situations, and the like. Criteria of this type pertain primarily to visual or graphic forms of description and representation, but are also of a concern in verbal descriptions as well.

Emphasis in this set of criteria is on the following factors suggested by Appleyard (1977):

Accuracy and Realism. Method should accurately and realistically portray existing or proposed environmental conditions;

Comprehensibility and Evaluatability. Method should be understandable to a diverse set of public and interest groups;

Engagement. Methods and procedures should hold interest or attention, and encourage involvement;

Cost Effectiveness. Both initial costs and production costs should be efficient in terms of size and scope of the project;

Flexibility. Method can be flexibly applied to different groups, landscape types, and situations.

A second set of criteria pertains to "scientific" considerations in landscape description. These criteria are relevant to the methodological effectiveness of an approach, although they parallel some of the concerns mentioned in design criteria. Bagley et al. (1973), Craik and Feimer (1979), Daniel and Vining (1983), and others have discussed the following scientific considerations as they apply to landscape description:

Reliability. Method can yield consistent results when applied in similar situations or by different persons.

Validity. A method measures what is intended; should include relevant aesthetic aspects inherent in problem.

Sensitivity. A method has the ability to discriminate between objectives of concern to the investigator.

Generalizability. The method can be applied to different landscape types and situations without substantial modification. Generalizability also includes the flexibility of the approache's application to diverse user and interest groups.

Utility. Method should yield useful information for planning and management. Interpretation should be straightforward and unambiguous. Usefulness is also gauged in terms of fulfilling legal or planning requirements such as public input.

Appropriateness and Comprehensiveness. Techniques and results should be capable of being comprehended by a variety of interest groups, including those in traditional design disciplines, physical and social sciences, and the untrained public.

Selecting a Procedure

Being clear about one's purpose for describing a wild landscape does not lead ineluctably to the choice of one particular type of method. Nor is the choice of method the sole determinant of a particular set of criteria for ascertaining the quality of procedures used within that method type. After all, practical constraints associated with time, labor, and costs will color many of the decisions that must be made in planning for the conduct of a wildland description.

Well-considered judgments by those planning a wildland description in site-specific situations cannot be replaced by a set of robotically applied decision rules. Nevertheless, it is possible to suggest some general guidelines that assist in the choice of method and criteria once the purpose of the description has been clearly identified.

If the purpose is simply to convey a whole image to others, then nonsystematic methods may suffice. The systematic methods may not only be unwarranted in terms of time and expense, but may even detract from achieving the purpose. Accuracy, realism, engagingness and other design criteria are most appropriate for the nonsystematic methods.

When attempting to describe the visual impacts of proposed development in wildlands, professionally based, nonquantitative visual methods will often be the most appropriate and again the design criteria will be relevant. The same choice is commonly made for use in professional-client relationships. Wildland alterations associated with mineral extraction, energy-fuel extraction, wood fiber production, harnessing of water resources, and so forth can all be simulated. These visual descriptions of currently nonexisting environments can later be used in conjunction with evaluative methods to determine the acceptability of the alternatives as described. For example, simulations can serve as visual stimuli in publicly based quantitative methods, the results of which might be used in legal or quasilegal adversarial settings. For the latter purpose, rigorous adherence to scientific criteria is advisable.

When the purpose is to compare and contrast different wildlands, to discriminate between areas within a single wildland, or to assign a scenic value for possible trade-offs with other landscape resources, a quantitative verbal approach using physical descriptors may be the best choice. In these situations, scientific criteria, especially sensitivity, generalizability, and utility, should be carefully considered during the planning of a wildland description.

It is true that the total number of possible final procedures that could be used to describe wild landscapes is quite large. However, the decision about a particular procedure will be greatly facilitated if it is the product of a clear purpose, conscious selection of a type of method from a set of known alternatives, and the diligent application of appropriate criteria.

CONCLUSION

Wild landscapes will continue to be required to provide for a materially comfortable quality of life in urban, industrial, and suburban landscapes. Simultaneously, demands for a spiritually satisfying quality of life associated with journeys to wildlands are not likely to diminish. The obvious dilemma cannot be resolved without a better understanding of wildlands. Careful descriptions presented in a variety of forums will be needed to serve as a basis for understanding the visual properties of wildlands and their relationship to other resources and human values.

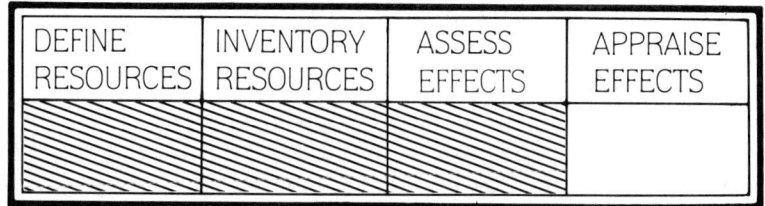

CHAPTER 7

COUNTRYSIDE LANDSCAPE VISUAL ASSESSMENT

Sally Schauman

Countryside is a recognizable unit containing a predominance of agricultural patterns and activities and defined by both cultural interpretations and the physical setting.

SCHAUMAN AND PFENDER 1982

Countryside is a comfortable concept. It is the landscape we believe we know and love. Public interest in this landscape is widespread and growing. The federal government admonishes us to save prime farmland, advertisers use quaint scenes of farm life to sell their products, and interest groups form national coalitions to conserve countryside life and land. Our reactions to countryside go beyond buying coffee mugs with cows painted on them. Thousands of people have moved to rural areas in the past decade (Economic Research Service 1981). This dramatic population shift has resulted in growth and change in areas which had changed only slightly in the past. New factories, shopping centers, bypass roads, five-acre estates, farmettes, recreational vehicle campgrounds, and water resource projects transform landscapes where previously only the crop may have changed through the years. These landscapes are often the sites for surface mining, transmission lines, slurry conveyors, oil-gas pipelines, and water supply conduits. Clearly, the countryside is a landscape of present change—a landscape that is going to look different in the future.

Visual changes are often the least understood and yet the most controversial aspect of land use change. The process of assessing visual changes in countryside landscapes can be understood by considering the five following facets:

1. Assessment context
2. Client/user
3. Landscape
4. Evaluation
5. Overall process

ASSESSMENT CONTEXT

Understanding the context is the first step in developing a visual assessment. Context means the ultimate use of the assessment. Contexts vary (see Figure 7.1) from those in which a calculated answer is most important to those in which the dialogue is most important. Some visual assessments serve best as catalysts for community action. This is particularly true in small countryside communities where few, if any, professional planners are on staff. The main purpose of these assessments is not the professional's evaluation, but the local

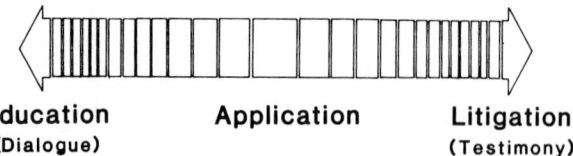

FIGURE 7.1. Assessment context.

residents' increased awareness of their visual environment and its probable future appearance. The professional's role is to facilitate this enhanced awareness. To do this, the professional may use any one of the many visual assessment techniques from preference testing (Kaplan 1979) to rating forms listing visual factors such as color and form (BLM 1980a; Smardon et al. 1983). For example, the U.S. Soil Conservation Service (SCS) helped the town of Acton, Massachusetts, conduct visual quality assessment. A citizen's committee photographed local scenes and buildings and administered a Q-sort (forced rating) preference test (Pitt and Zube 1979) to neighbors. Although the test did not meet the standards of research protocol, it was highly effective. Developers were interested in what landscapes people preferred, and the town government moved to acquire visual easements on pastoral landscapes located at the entrance to town. Practitioners who use visual assessment in the dialogue-important context understand the role of the social interaction plays in countryside areas.

Even when people live great distances apart, they may consider themselves neighbors within a community. People in small towns *expect* to be involved. In the experience of this author, the dialogue of visual assessment provides more opportunity than any other planning technique for dealing with visual change in countryside areas. At its best, the visual assessment process can help the visually illiterate to read their landscape. As Penning-Rowsell states, "We need to identify what people believe are the facets of landscape value, rather than what the researcher, the historian, the landscape architect and planner think they believe." (Penning-Rowsell, 1981). Dialogue important visual assessment should be tried first unless the context is clearly an impact assessment of a highly controversial project where the battle lines have already been etched.

On the other end of the continuum are visual assessments done in the context of litigation. In these instances, the process and its methods of quantification must stand up to intense scrutiny. The professional conducting the visual assessment can depend upon testifying as to the validity of the methods. In these cases, the visual assessment resembles research and the measurement methods must be reliable, valid and generalizable. These assessments must validate answers to narrowly defined questions. Practitioners must scrupulously document everything from the process design to field notes. For example, if photos are used, the practitioner must be prepared to testify that he or she took Photo A and can verify the photographic specifications as to lens, location, time of day, and so forth. Obviously, the cost of documentation can be great and often may be overlooked by the inexperienced. Sometimes practitioners believe they are operating in the middle range of the assessment context (Figure 7.1) only to find themselves backtracking to verify data that was gathered haphazardly earlier in the process.

CLIENT/USER

After establishing the assessment context, the practitioner then must ascertain the users' attitudes and values for that special landscape. Even when the client/user group seems to be well understood, care should be taken to unveil the symbolic meanings associated with countryside landscapes, for more often it is symbolic meaning, not preference, which motivates our value judgements and reactions. More than any other landscape, the countryside conjures nostalgic rather than real interpretations. Often this symbolism goes beyond and does *not include the actual physical realities of the landscape.* Understanding landscape symbolism is crucial to our understanding of peoples' reactions to landscapes. To date, research on landscape meaning is nascent, but nevertheless has shown interesting results.

In one study, the author asked more than 70 students in four universities to describe and draw a typical countryside landscape. Similarities of the descriptions were striking—most featured simple barns, pastures, woodlots, and fields. The students gave very little recognition to the distinctive appearance of their regional landscapes. Students in Mississippi, Indiana, Washington, and California described the countryside as if it were all the same. Since these were design students trained to observe the landscape, the study seemed to indicate that a nostalgic image of the countryside may be more influential than the actual landscapes. The countryside nostalgia may have early beginnings. In another study conducted at the University of Washington, researchers evaluated the pictorial descriptions of countryside landscapes in 200 children's books. The pictures of farm scenes in these books were nostalgic stereotypes of farms prevalent more than 50 years ago. Even when other pictorial descriptions in a story were modern (characters were ethnically and racially mixed, gender stereotyping was eliminated, and modern events such as space exploration were included), the farm scenes were very similar—nostalgic and old-fashioned. They depicted farming as a gentle occupation in which every family had a few cows and other animals, fruit trees, vegetable gardens, and a small acreage on which all crops were grown. In this author's judgement, nostalgic stereotypes rather than real images form a strong basis for the existing attitudes and values held toward countryside and potential visual changes.

It is useful to understand these stereotypes for they are voiced by users. The research and discussion by cultural geographers, sociologists, and historians has made it easier to sort out these stereotypical versions. One stereotype sees the landscape as sanctified because farming is a noble endeavor basic to all economic pursuits—perhaps even to democracy. This view is rooted in agrarianism, a concept popularized by Thomas Jefferson (Flinn and Johnson 1974). Since the farm family is a respected American ideal, to tamper with the sanctity of agricultural landscapes is to tamper with a fundamental freedom. It has been interesting for this author to note how strongly the agrarian attitude is held by those who neither farm nor live in countryside areas. These agrarian values often are transferred to corporate agricultural landscapes which are managed at a distance and which contain no farm family. Because agrarianism implies self-sufficiency, however, one should not assume farmers are interested only in utilitarian values for the landscape and not interested in beauty. Some farmers take great pride in the appearance of their work—examples are the careful choices of colors for new metal buildings to match existing ones, meticulous fence painting, and opposition to no-till farming because it looks "messy."

The back-to-basics/flee-from-the-city user exemplifies another stereotypical attitude. This attitude places higher value on anything nonurban than on anything resembling the urban scene. Some researchers describe this as ruralism (Buttell and Flinn 1977; Falk and Pinkey 1978) and use it to explain the nonfarming rural resident's decision to live in the countryside. In this author's judgement, this attitude is the hardest to deal with because it is ambivalent and inconsistent. People holding this attitude have fled from the city to something else not defined clearly yet desired passionately. Sometimes ruralism values are in direct conflict with agrarianism and often lead to a no-growth stance for a community.

A third attitude and potent value system is related to the first two but is more straightforward. It is the attitude of pastoralism or as Marx (1968) explains, our search for happiness, order, and the meaning of life in the countryside. Pastoralism requires no utilitarian function of the landscape. The resulting perception is a romantic notion of peace, tranquility, and scenic beauty which has lured people to countryside retreats for centuries (Marx 1968; Vance 1972). People who hold these values and move to the countryside have a certain visual expectation. They can tolerate visual change as long as it is not perceived as a threat to beauty and tranquility. Unlike ruralism, but similar to agrarianism, pastoralism is an attitude often held from afar. These are people who value the appearance of a serene countryside even though they do not live in it or use it.

To lump all countryside attitudes within one of these three categories is simplistic. The point of the distinction is to remind ourselves that present demographic trends result in a heterogeneous set of often conflicting attitudes among countryside residents. Often these attitudes are not conscious and do not surface until changes are contemplated. Most importantly, all of the attitudes involve symbolic rather than utilitarian values. As the geographers Sauer (1925) and Hart (1975) have long contended, the landscape is both a physical and a cultural concept. Perhaps more than any other landscape, the tended fields of the countryside symbolize our most revered meld of man, nature, and time. Those who attempt to assess visual change must understand this and integrate the physical and cultural components of countryside.

LANDSCAPE

In any visual assessment, one must choose a landscape unit and consistently describe its visual resource. Choosing an appropriate landscape unit would be easier if perceptual research had given us a clearer notion of the optimum size for human comprehension—a perceptual unit in the landscape. Unfortunately, research has not done this. Therefore, choosing a unit size becomes a function of the landscape's homoheterogeneity and the objectives of the assessment. Generally, the more homogeneous-appearing the landscape, the larger the units. In impact assessments, the unit size should relate to the scale of the proposed changes. In other assessments, size may vary. For example, if the purpose of the assessment is to designate countywide scenic easement areas, the units should relate to local viewsheds and to political boundaries. In other words, determining the size of landscape units is a judgment based on visibility and diversity of the landscape and the purpose of the assessment. With regard to the visual resource, research indicates several considerations.

First, deceptive descriptions such as *natural* and *human-made* should be avoided. The countryside is the inbetween landscape and consists of natural (riparian vegetation), man-made (fiberglass silos), human modifications of nature (croplands), and nature's modifications of human-made (oil fields and decaying barns). *Natural* and *human-made* are terms which have ambiguous interpretations in the countryside. Are the dark/light ribbons of dry land wheat farming natural because they follow the contour, or human-modified because they are evenly spaced? (See Figure 7.2.)

The visual resource is the consistently definable appearance of the landscape and may be described by the measurable visual elements; topography, water, vegetation, sky, human/animals and structures and the pattern of interacting among these elements. (adapted from U.S.D.A.S.C.S. 1978)

Considering the elements individually, some conclusions are reasonable. Topography is not as important visually in the countryside as in other landscapes because rugged topography usually is

FIGURE 7.2. Ground level view of dry-land wheat cropland. *Photo credit:* Soil Conservation Service, USDA.

not farmed in this country. Flatter crop and pasture lands account for more than 25 percent of all nonurban U.S. lands. This percentage rises significantly when parklands, wilderness and federal forests are excluded from the nonurban base. Since countryside areas often are rolling or flat, the horizon line tends to be a uniform visual edge. Any change which breaks up the uniformity becomes conspicuous. The horizontal nature of croplands makes them visually sensitive to the presence of vertical elements such as shelter-belt trees, windmills and transmission towers. When slight topographic relief exists, it often is visually exaggerated by contouring farm practices such as terracing and strip cropping (see Figure 7.2). Since there are fewer elevated viewpoints in the countryside than in more rugged landscapes, the plan views of ground surface patterns are seen less extensively. Thus disruptive patterns to the surface can be screened more easily.

Vegetation, in many ways, is the essential element of countryside landscapes—crops, lands, pastures, rangeland, and woodlots. As crops flower, fruit, and ripen, they provide a continuing visual focus. Some crops such as mature corn or evergreen citrus trees act as visual screens since at ground level little can be seen through them. In very flat agricultural landscape, irrigated row crops set up strong visual linear matrices. Any nonlinear form located amid these straight lines will stand out.

Most researchers agree that water is one of the most preferred visual elements in the landscape (Zube et al. 1974; Litton et al. 1974). Although most research has focused on nonagricultural landscapes, there is no evidence to indicate that irrigation, farm ponds, and other agriculturally related water would be viewed less favorably. It may be that irrigation water sparkling in the sunlight of an arid landscape provides a unique visual resource.

At first glance, the sky seems to be too ephemeral to be considered as a measurable visual unit. Yet visibility can be modified by pollution and is measurable. In some Western states, residents have long acknowledged the importance of a clear, expansive sky. For example, Montana auto plates proclaim the state to be "big sky country."

In this author's judgement, human activity or animals and structures provide reactions that are strong and negative, but beyond that are not easily predictable. The image of a green pasture with contented cows is a vivid, perhaps quintessential, stereotype of farm activity. Does the same pasture with cows munching under concrete transmission lines receive the same praise? The farmer turning dark, moist earth in the spring to begin again the cycle of life evokes a feeling of goodness. Yet, the same farmer spreading manure may not win such a positive public reaction. We know people like to look at wooden barns and quaint farmsteads. Do the structures of modern farm technology evoke similar pleasant reactions? What is the function of Figure 7.3, and how do you think people react to it? It is not a grain elevator. To date, no research has been done to effectively sort out these ambiguities. The unpredictability of the public's reaction is another reason why the cultural component in the countryside should be given equal consideration with the physical landscape in all visual assessments.

Another consideration in landscape description is the pattern of interaction among the landscape elements. Recent research indicates that land use/cover or the pattern of interaction is an important factor in our perception of agricultural landscape. This finding varies from conventional professional wisdom, which to date has declared topography a single element and to be the most important basis in classifying land for visual analysis. However, previous classifications and most research has been focused on wildlands and forested landscapes. In one of the few research studies to focus on cropland, Nassauer decided that "land use is the most important indicator of meaning" and "meaning seems to be the most fundamental determinant of visual quality" (Nassauer 1979). In other studies done recently for the Soil Conservation Service, researchers concluded that "land form was not sensitive enough to be used as the basis for a classification system of predominantly agricultural landscapes, but that it should be included as a modifier" and "as part of . . . evaluation" (Schauman and Pfender 1982). These researchers proposed a hierarchical taxonomic (place-independent) classification system based on land use/cover adjusted by local place dependent modifiers. The proposed classification, Table 7.1, incorporates SCS definitions, classifications proposed by the U.S. Geological Survey for remote sensing data (Anderson et al. 1976), and common visual sense.

In the proposed system, modifiers are local landscape elements which do change our perceptions. They need not necessarily be contiguous to but are seen in combination with the classified land use/cover. At a regional scale, modifiers are mountains/hills, all forms of water

FIGURE 7.3. Catfish food storage facility. *Photo credit:* S. Schauman.

TABLE 7.1. Countryside Classification System

LEVEL I	LEVEL II	LEVEL III
CULTIVATED LANDS	Row crops Solid-seeded crops Crops requiring cultivation	Type of crop Farming method Cultivation factors
ORCHARDS	Deciduous Evergreen Palms	Patterned and spacing Species Local/special cultivation factors
GRAZABLE LANDS	Range lands Pasture Grazable woodlands	Herbaceous Shrub and brush Mixed Native Improved Species composition-variety Proportion of species-density Height variation
FOREST LANDS	Deciduous Evergreen Mixed	Crown cover Species-variety Status e.g., old field, etc.
BUILT-UP LANDS	Farmsteads, non-dairy Farmstead, dairy Confined animal production Towns and villages Scattered development	Thoroughbred horses Cattle ranches Mixed crop farms Single-crop farms Open-pastured animals Confined animals, no pastures Roofed structures, chickens Non-roofed structures, corrals, etc. Special facilities, aquaculture, etc. 20,000 to 5,000 15,000 to 20,000 5,000 to 15,000 Less than 5,000 Crossroads ag. service center Residential, resort and recreation Industrial and commercial-isolated and remote from urban areas
BARREN LAND	Natural Human impacted	Salt flats Beaches, dunes Bare rock
COMBINATION LANDSCAPES		

Source: S. Schauman and M. Pfender, 1982.

including irrigation, nonagricultural structures, and sky. For example, perception of land use seen in the Pacific Northwest changes if one of the Cascade peaks is visible (see Figure 7.4). Similarly, our perception of land use in Long Island will be modified when highrise skylines form a backdrop. At a local level, mountains/hills, water, and structures remain important, but other modifiers such as human activity, animals, and noncrop vegetation become more significant. For example, hedgerows and solitary trees modify our perception of nearby fields and pastures (see Figure 7.5).

EVALUATION

Evaluation involves decisions as to who will evaluate and what criteria will be used. Most visual assessment professionals agree that a solitary practitioner can no longer make professional visual judgments in isolation and expect that these

FIGURE 7.4. Mountains and hills as modifiers. *Photo credit:* Soil Conservation Service, USDA.

FIGURE 7.5. Vegetation (hedgerows and single trees) as modifiers. *Photo credit:* Soil Conservation Service, USDA.

will be implemented or withstand legal scrutiny. One method of dealing with evaluation has been to use trained observers to rate landscapes. This method has had mixed success (Smardon et al. 1983; Vermont Transportation Board 1979). In the judgment of this author, visual assessment in the countryside is so intertwined with poorly understood cultural interpretations that neither professional nor lay-trained observers should be used as surrogates for the public in rating the landscape. The user—the public—should be the key player from the beginning. If the assessment context (see Figure 7.1) is community planning, then the widest participation of residents in the dialogue is preferable. If the context is litigation, then data from a cross-section of users in proportion to their use is important.

In evaluation, one can choose among the plethora of criteria emerging from research during the past 20 years (see Table 7.2). Some of the criteria measure the landscape's ability to absorb change, others evaluate inherent visual qualities of the landscape which contribute to a higher quality visual resource, and a few criteria reckon with peoples' preferences for certain landscape scenes. Visual resource quality criteria have emerged from a variety of research sources. Some of these include environmental psychologists studying peoples' preferences for landscape and landscape architects analyzing various landscapes and the impact of change on these landscapes. Some of the criteria, their derivation and their applicability to countryside landscapes are:

1. Fragility or visual absorption capabilities (VAC). This is a measurement of the landscape's range of abilities to absorb change. The criteria is a function of landform, vegetation, and visibility through the landscape. First proposed in 1969 (Jacobs and Way 1969a), it has been researched and applied extensively (Litton 1974; Yeomans 1979; Anderson et al. 1979). Although much of the discussion has focused on the VAC of forested landscapes, translation to countryside landscapes is possible. For projects where multiple sites are available, fragility/VAC can help determine the best site to either enhance visibility or to hide a project.

2. Character or congruence or contrast. Given various labels, this criteria is a judgment based on traditional visual design factors of form, line, color, texture, and scale. This fundamental notion is as old as landscape architecture (Hubbard and Kimball 1917; Simonds 1961; Laurie 1975), most recently reappearing as a contrast rating scheme

TABLE 7.2. Comparison of Landscape Indicators

Litton & Tetlow (1978)	Nassauer (1979a)	Zube et al. (1974)	Kaplan (1979a)	Brown, Itami and King (1979)
(DESCRIPTIVE) ONLY, NO EVALUATION	QUALITY INDICATORS	PHYSICAL DIMENSIONS CORRELATING WITH POSITIVE SCENIC VALUE	PERCEPTUAL CONTENT/ CONTEXT	DIMENSIONS OF SCENIC RESOURCE VALUE
boundaries & edges	spatial definition		spatial configuration: --coherence --complexity --legibility --mystery	landform: --edge contrast } predicted --spatial diversity } information
landform & topography	relief	landform		--slope } --relative relief } legibility
plant cover	ground plane patterns	natural features of vegetative cover		land cover:
water	water	water	particular content "things"	--high contrast } predicted --internal variety } information
focal attractions	siting vertical features	farm buildings		--naturalism } --land use compatibility } legibility
	land use	--agricultural elements --pastures --tilled and abandoned fields		

Source: S. Schauman and M. Pfender, 1982.

for evaluating the visual impact of projects proposed on federally managed lands (BLM 1980a). While easily used by landscape architects, the criterion is fraught with application problems in the countryside. First, it is much harder to describe form/line/color/texture/scale changes in a melded landscape than to describe these changes in one which is either predominantly natural or human-made. Secondly, there is only scant evidence that lay people see, much less can consistently rate, these visual factors (Smardon et al. 1983; Feimer et al. 1981). In this author's judgement, character/congruence/contrast can be used very effectively in community planning to help residents see the visual character of the countryside. A community planning example is the application by Vermont to designate scenic roads rated by local citizens (Vermont Transportation Board 1979). It should be used carefully as a precise measurement for rating visual impact in predominantly agricultural landscapes.

3. Fitness. This criterion measures the range of landscape conditions resulting from human stewardship—tidy, conserved, reclaimed, littered, battered, derelict. It is more a measurement of the care of the people who inhabit the landscape than of the landscape itself. As such, it is difficult to use this criterion in community planning because it can be insulting to some participants. On the other hand, it is an index which might be useful to demonstrate how a project might improve fitness or at least not diminish the local standard. It is a commonsense notion, correlated with preference (Ellsworth 1982) and is particularly relevant in the countryside. For these reasons, it was proposed recently to SCS (Schauman and Pfender 1982).

4. Structure or spatial definition. This is a measure of the "range of landscape conditions from those which offer limited but undefined views to those which offer no vista or where all views are blocked" (Schauman and Pfender 1982). Geographers' theories (Appleton 1975), environmental psychologists' research (Kaplan and Kaplan 1982) and classic landscape architectural wisdom (Simonds 1961) all conclude that humans are more comfortable in and therefore need or prefer landscapes which fall in the middle range of this criterion. In the flatter countryside, land cover contributes to spatial definition. At one end of the range are the flat, wide-open views characteristic of alfalfa fields; at the other end are the citrus groves which block all visual access. Structure or spatial definition may be the most important visual criterion contributing to quality in the countryside.

5. Information. This is a "range of landscape conditions from those which provide maximum information, in which all of the parts may be visible at first glance, to those which contain no interest or little information or contain disordered information" (Schauman and Pfender 1982). This criterion relates to structures or spatial definition, but is not the same. Psychologists tell us that the quantity of information is important to our comprehension of and comfort in the landscape (Kaplan and Kaplan 1982). Simply put, we try to make sense out of our visual world and, at times, it can be too bland or too chaotic. Information can emanate from natural or human-made elements. This criterion relates to "variety" as proposed as a visual quality criterion by the U.S. Forest Service (1974). This author prefers the term *information* over *variety* because the latter can be confused with other variety indices in the environment, for example, ecological factors. Landscape architects have researched and long maintained that visual interest relates to visual quality (McCarthy 1979; Greenbie 1976). This criterion focuses on the nature of that interest.

6. Preference. This ranges from "like very much" to "dislike very much." It is a judgment on the whole scene derived from both conscious and unconscious notions. Since it seems similar to a vote, it can be used effectively in community planning to reduce resistance to visual assessment. It is useful as a planning tool (Kaplan and Kaplan 1982), as a part of a research protocol, and to calibrate the evaluation criteria listed above within a local context. Preference tests range from Q-sorts of photos and simple black/white rating sheets to sophisticated videotapes for rating simulated models of proposed changes.

7. Uniqueness. This is a rating of the special or one-of-a-kind quality of certain landscapes or artifacts. This criterion is most obvious and usually emerges early. In the countryside, it relates to the urban landmark described by Lynch (1960).

8. Vividness/intactness/unity. These are three criteria used together to evaluate visual quality. Applied extensively by one landscape architectural firm (Blair et al. 1979; Gray et al. 1979), they

were derived from the evaluation factors—unity, variety, and vividness proposed by Litton et al. (1974) for waterscapes. Essentially, the three criteria combine many of the evaluation factors noted above. The terms are familiar to visual designers but not necessarily to lay people. There is no research indicating that humans organize perceptions into these three factors. Caution should be taken when using these terms to simplify visual assessments. In one application, eight separate ratings were used to gather data for just one of the factors (Burnham et al. 1974).

OVERALL PROCESS

The context, user/client, landscape, and evaluation are all facets which must be finally integrated into an assessment process (see Figure 7.6 and Table 7.3). In search of an established visual process for the countryside, researchers recently surveyed the visual assessment literature of the past 16 years and concluded:

1. Visual assessments done in other countries are difficult to translate to the American countryside because our agricultural practices differ significantly.
2. Most of the studies have not been researched but have been visual impact assessments. These have tended to describe the countryside with less detail than the visual character of the proposed changes.
3. More research has been done for forests, wildlands, and coastal landscapes than for the countryside (Schauman and Pfender 1982).

In other words, no handy visual assessment process for the countryside exists such as the one developed and researched by the U.S. Forest Service for forest and wildlands (U.S. Forest Service 1974). For example, SCS, which provides technical information on the countryside, maintains that no one visual assessment process will work in all SCS contexts because of the paucity of research on the wide diversity of project scales, users, and landscape types. We should not be disconcerted by the fact that there is no established visual assessment process for the countryside. This is desirable because the practitioner should develop a process appropriate to the specific assessment objectives rather than try to modify a

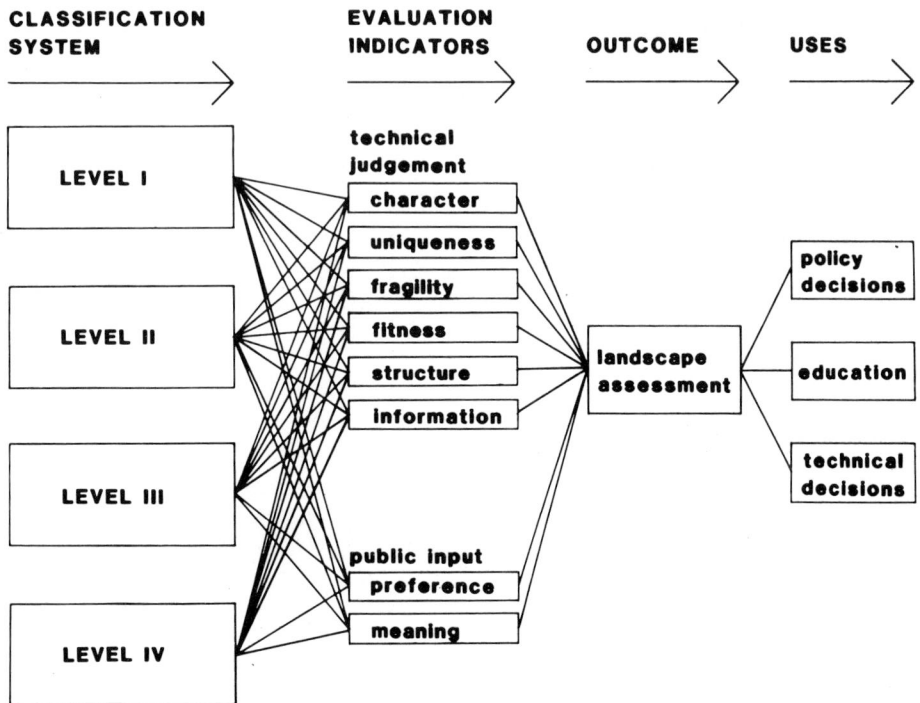

FIGURE 7.6. Countrywide assessment system. *Source:* S. Schauman and M. Pfender, 1982.

TABLE 7.3. Proposed Hierarchy of Classification

TAXONOMIC UNITS		GEOGRAPHICAL BASE-FRAME OF REFERENCE
Level I	National	SCS Land Resource Region
Level II	Regional	SCS Major Land Resource Area
Level III	Local	Watershed or other natural resource unit
Level IV	Site	Project site

Source: S. Schauman and M. Pfender, 1982.

process developed to meet other objectives. There are guidelines for developing an assessment process when the objective is to assess the visual impacts of a federal project as required by the National Environmental Policy Act. For example, a comprehensive set of guidelines has been written for evaluating impacts on water resource projects (U.S. Water Resources Council 1983).

While the visual assessment process needs to be developed specific to the project in question, some common notions do prevail. The following guidelines should be kept in mind:

1. Ask the right questions. In one visual assessment, the public stated that it objected to the color and shape of a project while it really objected to the project's view-blocking (Schauman 1982).

2. Conduct a preliminary analysis to determine the visibility (Felleman 1979, 1982), viewer, and the visual resource. Generally, the client/user has only a partial notion as to visibility and the range of viewers involved. One process for doing this is a procedure used by SCS (U.S.D.A.S.C.S. 1978). Also see Chapter 9.

3. Set clear limits for the assessment. Is the problem only visual or are other aesthetic considerations such as noise or odor involved?

4. Learn about existing and future farm practices. Many agricultural activities will change in the future. For example, dairy farming practices of confining cows in loafing sheds rather than putting them out to pasture affects visual quality. This is a trend which is increasing and somewhat predictable.

5. Keep the assessment process as free from the practitioner's own stereotypes and biases as possible.

6. Keep abreast of recent research. This is not an impossible task and is well worth the effort. Research conclusions often emerge and challenge our notions of evaluating visual quality. For example, a recent dissertation by Sheppard gives us much needed new information concerning the technology and application of visual simulation techniques (Sheppard 1982). Also see Chapter 11.

7. Do your own homework. Don't assume that factors and techniques cited in reports have been based on research. Nothing can harm the credibility of visual assessment more than conclusions derived from shallow investigation. Remember that repetitive use by a wide variety of practitioners does not always indicate an accurate, researched fact.

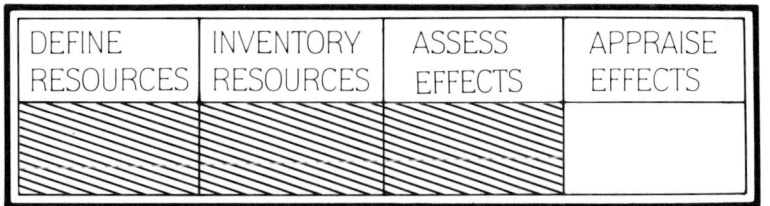

CHAPTER 8

URBAN VISUAL DESCRIPTION AND ANALYSIS

Richard C. Smardon with Tony Costello
and Harry Eggink

INTRODUCTION

Of all the environments that we perceive, record, and analyze, the only one that we classify as "urban in nature" is the most complex. The multiple interactions and interfaces of the built components—whether that be the overall plan, infrastructure, buildings, or streetscapes— with the natural ones—geographic location, topography, water bodies, or flora—generate this complexity and provide the environmental planner and designer with a rich, diverse, and multilayered context in which to practice.

There are many examples of strong form-giving urban planning practices in European cities, culminating with the Hausmann effort in Paris under Napoleon III. By contrast, roughshod early settlements in the United States developed with minimum planning and control. Early exceptions included planned industrial towns like Lowell, Massachusetts.

No cohesive planning movement related to cities' physical form took place until the Chicago World's Fair in 1893 exposed the public to an orderly, articulated plan with generous open spaces, regular cornice lines, trees, canals, and other bodies of water, The so-called "City Beautiful" movement resulted in Burnham's plan for Chicago and influenced physical planning for Washington, D.C. and Philadelphia in fragmentary ways. During the next 25 years, much of city planning was focused on control of physical development through zoning and planning streets, transportation, and recreation—so called "comprehensive planning" which really was not comprehensive in that socioeconomic concerns were not addressed. However, the major positive contribution of the early nineteenth century to urbanism was the great central park—the large, romantic naturalistic oasis—characterized by the designs of Frederick Law Olmsted. Examples include Central Park in Manhattan, Prospect Park in Brooklyn and others in St. Louis, San Francisco, Boston, Hartford, and Trenton.

Basic or organic city planning in the 1930s was a counterreaction to prior planning efforts and focused on slum-like housing conditions and the need to remedy basic living conditions in cities. The intent of the U.S. Housing Act of 1937 was to spread the need or requirement for community planning. A series of federal legislative enactments followed which focused on specific socioeconomic defects of previous legislation, until 1969 when physical environmental concerns came back into concern.

The 1930s was also typified by the socially oriented planning group that stood "above the melee." The professional planner and city planning commission assumed the sacred tenet of professional neutrality, and activity was focused on the evolution of the single, "right" plan. From the initial scope and purpose of orderly and spatial development, utilities, and transit system along with some architectural awareness or emphasis, there came the input of social, economic, and even psychological thinking. The planner became more the orchestrator—no longer the architect or engineer—but more of a manager. Public hearings soon became more than a formality, and formidable opposition to proposed plans and projects became a reality in the 1960s. This was especially true for "urban renewal" projects in many U.S. cities as well as major transportation planning efforts in New York, Philadelphia, San Francisco, and Boston.

Twentieth-century planning can be characterized as major movements toward city and town extensions, suburbs without distinction, urban renewal which was often ill-fated, tenuous model cities or demonstration cities, selected new towns and communities, and some metropolitan and regional planning. Probably the new communities of Reston, Columbia, and Radisson are the most physical or tangible form-giving results.

The complexity of urban environments has posed problems for designers, social scientists, and urban dwellers. How complex should urban environments be? Some designers propose simplifying urban environments (Ashihara 1983) to make them more aesthetically pleasing and understandable. Social scientists have stated that a certain amount of ambiguity and complexity in urban environments is desirable (Rapoport and Hawks 1970; Rapoport and Kanter 1967). Still other social scientists inform us that urban visual material has excessive complexity compared to natural environments (Kaplan, Kaplan, and Wendtt 1972; Wohlwill 1968). Are we to trust the designer or the social scientist when are are inventorying, analyzing, and assessing visual qualities of urban environments? This chapter will assist us in dealing with this question as well as in arriving at a generic framework for doing urban visual analysis.

We will first review the types of decisions or actions which visual analysis can affect. Given the tasks at hand, we will historically review how urban designers and architects approached these problems. Then we will explore in detail the expert designer approach for a more detailed analysis of scale, design elements, light effects, and static versus dynamic viewing of the environment. This will be contrasted with a social science framework which can be used to choose environments to be sampled, environmental displays, stimulus material, and choosing respondents. Finally, we will discuss how we can combine approaches in a generic overview, and describe new emerging methods and technologies.

DECISIONS/ACTIONS

Let us start from the largest scale and work down to smaller-scale urban activities. On the largest scale, the activity addressing urban environments would be deciding which regions are suitable for urbanization or increased density of development. In other words, can visual analysis assist us in determining which geographic areas are suitable for urbanization? In the United States, this would apply to new town development or to areas which are threatened with urbanization from belt-line highways (Jacobs and Way 1969a, 1969b; Yuill and Joyner 1979). In other areas of the world, visual analysis has been used as part of an assessment for suitability for urban development [for example, Australia (Wright 1974) and Yugoslavia (Pogacnik 1979a, 1979b)]. Lynch has also given us some general approaches in his book *Managing the Sense of a Region* (1976).

The second application would be the siting and design of major new transitways in urban areas or analyzing existing ones (for example, the view from the road or "city as a trip"). Much of the urban visual analysis work has been done from this perspective and it's true that we perceive much of urban environments from major highways and transitways (see Appleyard et al. 1964; Carr and Schissler 1969; Craik 1975; Smardon and Goukas 1984; Winkel 1969).

The third application is deciding what to keep at the district or neighborhood level because of its inherent or associated visual quality via neighborhood or historic district preservation, or what to develop because of its loss of visual quality through downtown or waterfront revitalization (Frey 1981; Palmer 1983; Robinson 1980; Huspeth 1982; Lambe and Phillips 1981; Peterson 1967; Willmott et al. 1983; Zoelling 1981). An important aspect of any analysis technique at this scale is to facilitate a sound reflection of citizen values and attitudes within the process.

The fourth application is control of undersirable land uses which create visual environmental problems. Commercial strips are the typical example of a mixture of land uses which create traffic safety problems as well as visual disorder. A common misconception is that the two problems are separate. They are not—they are interdependent; visual disorder due to too many signs and other artifacts creates cognitive confusion and way-finding problems which may cause traffic accidents. Only a few studies have attempted to address this problem (Carr and Schissler 1969; Ewald and Mandelker 1969; Smardon and Goukas 1984). A more positive aspect to this problem would be saving or preserving high-quality streetscapes, where the first object would be to document environmental quality (Craik and Appleyard 1980; Ulrich 1974), and the second step would be to involve appropriate parties in the process of redesign or rehabilitation of the streetscape (Ramati 1981; Willmott et al 1983).

The fifth application would be the siting and design of specific urban structures. The object would be to minimize incompatable building scale or materials, unless intended contrast is the design objective, and to avoid unintended physical effects such as view blockage, shadow and glare effects, as well as surface wind acceleration (Appleyard and Fishman 1977). Some cities, such as Seattle, Washington (Erickson 1980) and San Francisco, California (Bosselman 1982), have made great strides in review processes to attempt to avoid such impacts.

The introduction to this chapter included an extremely short history of public physical planning relating to the physical form of cities. What about control of private development? Since Euclidan zoning in the 1930s, there have been extremely sporadic and spotty applications of general zoning and architectural controls to private development in cities. Courts have rarely upheld aesthetic controls on architectural development, and most of the cases are concerned with outdoor advertising. There are two interesting developments from legal and administrative aspects of aesthetic development control. One is a recent Supreme Court case which addresses the right to control private development when historic and aesthetic issues are at stake, and the second is the use of urban design review processes to review private projects. One of the most sensitive areas is the use of police power to restrict uses of an historic property or building without providing compensation. The Supreme Court recently decided that New York City did not violate the Penn Central Transportation Company's Fifth Amendment property rights when it designated Grand Central Terminal as an historic landmark, thus blocking the company's proposal for an office tower above the facility.

The company is not entitled to compensation as a result of the city's denial of permits for the office project, the court said in a decision which is expected to spark similar preservation efforts in other cities. The court gave historic preservation constitutional status similar to that enjoyed by zoning and other conventional land use controls. Over the last 50 years, the court noted, over 500 cities and states have adopted landmark protection laws "to encourage or require the preservation of buildings and areas with historic or aesthetic importance."

In Justice William Brennan's opinion, the court rejected Penn Central arguments that the landmark designation constituted a "taking" of property for which "just compensation" is required under the Fifth Amendment. The restrictions imposed on the terminal site, Brennan said, "are substantially related to the promotion of the general welfare" and "permit reasonable beneficial use of the landmark site," namely, the terminal itself. The facility was described in the opinion as "one of New York City's most famous buildings."

Some interesting possibilities are suggested by the decision. While it emphasizes "historic" preservation, Justic William Brennan's opinion also stresses the need to protect areas of *aesthetic importance*. That phrase could be sufficiently vague to protect communities seeking to block development proposals on specific sites which may have no real "historic" significance. The court's ruling seems to expand a city's authority to single out certain sites for protection.

Urban design review is a process whereby a public entity can review private development within a city's jurisdiction, and subject matter can include aesthetic aspects of design. In his recent book, *Urban Design Review: A Guide for Planners*, Hamid Shirvani characterizes the nature of urban design review as performance-based or prescriptive or whether standards are accompanied by comprehensive prototypes or specific design components (Shirvani 1981, 26).

On a more specific level, Shirvani addresses specific elements addressing issues of concern or scope of issues. He gives the example of design review process for the City of Palm Springs as an outstanding example of an aesthetic guideline that includes aesthetic issues. The standards state that building design, material, and colors are to be "sympathetic with desert surroundings" and that there should be a "harmony of materials, colors and composition of those structures which are visible simultaneously" (Shirvani 1981, 28). He also gives an example from the process for Santa Barbara which states that "skyline trees be incorporated into the landscape plan when practical" and that "building components such as windows, doors, and arches should have appropriate proportions to the structure" (Shirvani 1981, 29). The former standard from Palm Springs is a performance standard whereas the latter example from Santa Barbara is both prescriptive and performance-based. A standard which would be descriptive would merely state that aesthetic issues be addressed.

Let us now explore approaches to urban visual analysis that attempt to address some of the five applications or problems listed above. For a broader review of architecture and perception of urban environments, the reader is referred to Prak (1977) and Ashihara (1983). For an overview of urban environmental aesthesis from a multidisciplinary perspective, the reader is referred to recent reviews by Porteous (1982) and Lynch (1981).

DEVELOPMENT OF EXPERT APPROACH

Kevin Lynch's *Image of the City* (1960) stands as the seminal work and influence on how we as environmental designer—architects, landscape architects, urban designers, planners—have, subsequently, viewed and analyzed the urbanscape. Lynch's work introduced concern for the importance of finding out how humans experience and relate to their environments. It also lead to a comprehensive approach to analyzing how people see, perceive, use, and remember their surroundings. It alerted the design and planning professions to the importance of taking the lay person's perceptions of the physical environment into consideration. Lynch developed one of the first notational and mapping systems that allowed for the recording of individual "images" and, subsequently, composites that showed commonly held perceptions. The terms *path, edge, node, district* and *landmark*, taken from *Image of the City* (see Figure 8.1), became commonplace in the environmental planning and design community.

Lynch's greatest contribution, however, lies in his introduction of the notion of *imageability* which was originally derived from Boulding. As early as 1915, Paul Stern addressed this issue of environmental sensory response when he dealt with *apparency*. As an initial probe of the inner

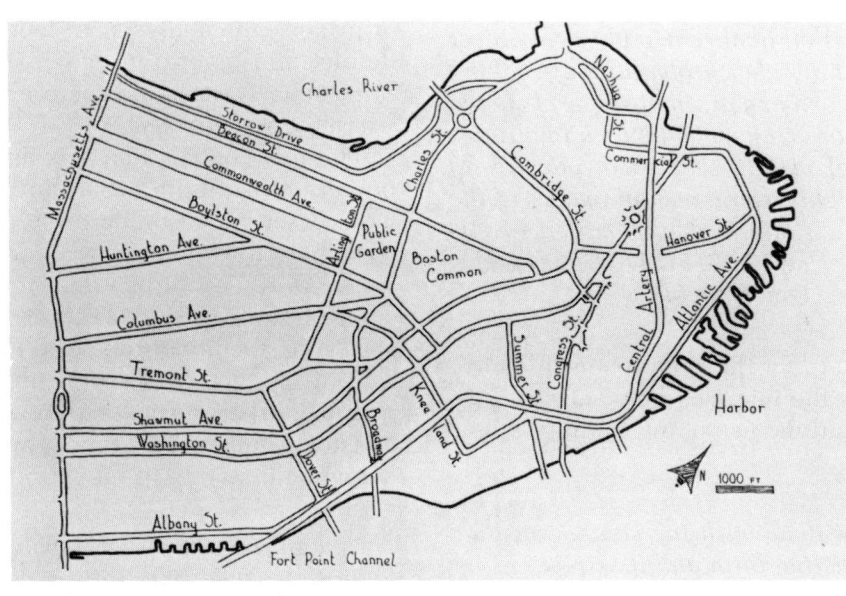

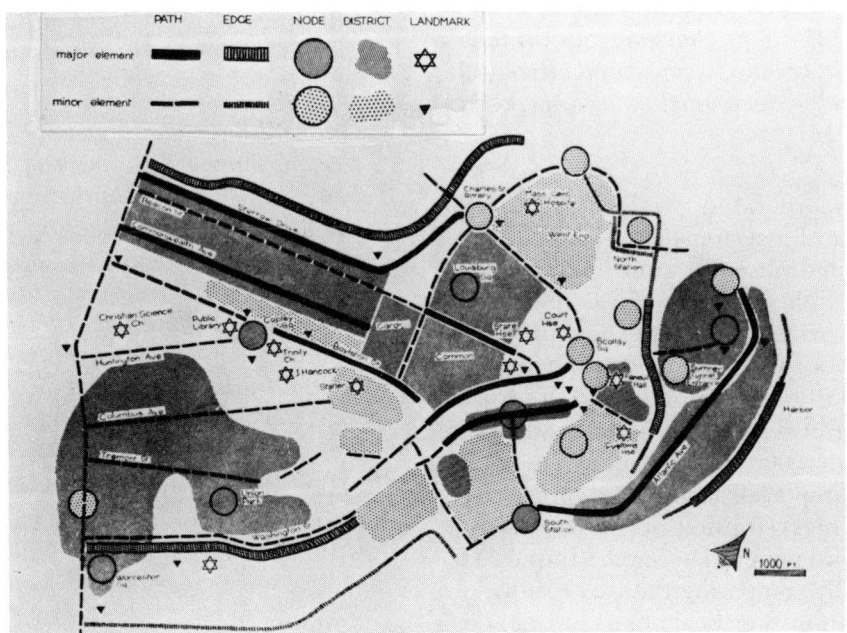

FIGURE 8.1. Examples of visual nodes, edges, paths, landmarks and districts. *Source:* Lynch, K., 1960, *The Image of the City*, Cambridge, MA: MIT Press, 18–19.

meaning of art objects, he felt that the clarity and harmony of a form elicit a response during the observer's search for an appearance that is comprehensible.

Lynch's definition of *imageability* is worth noting, for it not only describes the qualities that make an impression on any observer, but, in fact, it provides a very applicable conceptual framework for the structuring of an inventory and analysis of the urbanscape. It reads:

> *Imageability: that quality in a physical object which gives it a higher probability of evoking a strong image in any given observer. It is the shape, color, or arrangement which facilitates the making of vividly identified, powerfully structured, highly useful mental images of the environment. It might also be called LEGIBILITY, or perhaps VISIBILITY in a heightened sense . . . (Lynch 1960, 9).*

In Lynch's concern for the comprehensible city, he clearly states the interface between the analytical process and the use of the findings when he states:

> *The work was done with the conviction that analysis of existing form and its effect on the citizen is one of the foundation stones of city design, and in the hope that some useful techniques for field reconnaissance and citizen interview might be developed as a by-product. (Lynch 1960, 14)*

His research incorporated two basic analytical techniques: that of a systematic field reconnaissance by a trained observer, and lengthy interviews with a sample of city residents in order to ascertain their images. This latter technique included requests for descriptions, locations, sketches, and performances of "problem" trips.

In Lynch's brief section on the method as the basis for design (1960, 156), he recommends an improved two-step approach based on the two concurrent sources—trained observers (two or three) and general population (large sample). He points out that by comparing the two results, an initial identification of critical points, sequences, or patterns can be made. A second, more detailed, and intensive investigation by both trained observer and a small public sample would deal with identity and structure under many field conditions of light, distance, activity, and movement. All the material would be synthesized in a series of maps and reports that would give the basic public image, the visual problems and strengths, the critical elements, and their interrelationships and possibilities for change.

Gordon Cullen's book, *Townscape*, published in 1961 (also *Concise Townscape* 1971) was quickly recognized by architects and planners as a major contribution to the concept and method of urbanscape analysis. In fact, it affected academics and practitioners who were seeking to bring cohesiveness and comprehension to the urban environment.

The first contribution was that specific visual perceptions of both urban building and spaces were based on aesthetic principles. The second contribution was an exploration of what makes a town "work"—in urban design terms. The third contribution was the quality of Cullen's graphic analysis of the urbanscape (see Figure 8.2). Taken collectively then, *Townscape* truly introduced the notion of urban design (a term he did not use and one not common at the time) as process and product when he wrote in his introduciton:

> *Now turn to the visual impact which a city has on those who live in it or visit it. . . . [b]ring buildings together and collectively they can give visual pleasure which none can give separately.*
>
> *One building standing alone in the countryside is experienced as a work of architecture, but bring half a dozen buildings together and an art other than architecture is made possible. Several things begin to happen in the group which would be impossible in the isolated building. We may walk through and past buildings, and as a corner is turned an unsuspected building is suddenly revealed. (Cullen 1961, 7)*

He also spoke to the idea of the analysis of the buildings, their elements or characteristics, and how those relate to context when he wrote:

> *Suppose that we are just looking at the temple by itself, it would stand in front of us and all its qualities, size, color and intricacies would be evident. But put the temple back amongst*

DEVELOPMENT OF EXPERT APPROACH 121

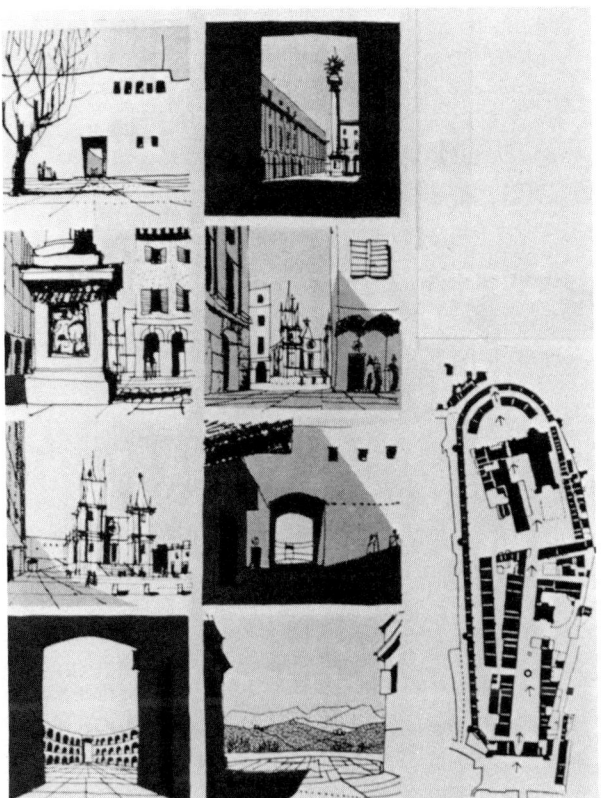

FIGURE 8.2. Spatial sequence. *Source:* Cullen, G., 1971, *The Concise Townscape*, New York: Van Nostrand Rhinehold, 17.

the small houses and immediately its size is made more real and more obvious by comparison between the two scales. Instead of being a big temple, it TOWERS. The difference in meaning between bigness and towering is the measure of relationship. In fact, there is an ART OF RELATIONSHIP just as there is an art of architecture. Its purpose is to take all the elements that go to create the environment, buildings, trees, nature, water, traffic, advertisements and so on, and to weave them together in such a way that drama is released. For a city is a dramatic event in the environment. (Cullen 1961, 7, 8)

Additionally, he addressed the process of looking, analyzing, and extracting information pertinent to the design process. In what he calls *optics/serial vision*, he discusses the concept sequence—existing view and emerging view (see Figure 8.2). Through what Cullen calls *place* he explores "...

the continuous habit of the body to relate itself to the environment, this sense of position cannot be ignored; it becomes a factor in the design of the environment...." The third category is *content*, which addresses the exactness of the fabric of towns; color, texture, scale, style, character, personality, and uniqueness.

The work of Appleyard, made familiar in his book *The View From the Road* (with Lynch and Myer 1964), established the foundation for the critical concept of dynamic perceptions. Since the users of the urban environment are, most often, in motion, either on foot or in an automobile, coming or going, the understanding of the complexity involved in changing vistas, unfolding views, ever-changing "images," becomes critical to the urban design process.

Since publication of *The View from the Road* in 1964, the inclusion of an analysis of an urbanscape as perceived when *moving through it* has become more commonplace. A quote from the preface underscores the importance.

Design involves a balanced judgment about many factors, of which visual requirements are only one set. We are convinced, however, that these requirements are among the most important that the road must satisfy.... [i]t is also a good example of a design issue typical of the city: the problem of designing visual sequences for the observer in motion. (Appleyard et al. 1964, 2)

It is important to note that movement implies a sequence of events, views, perceptions, and interpretations. Therefore, the recording of the existing situation/context/environment and proposals for their alteration requires specialized graphic and notational systems. These were first investigated and presented in *The View From the Road* (see Figure 8.3), also developed by Philip Thiel (1961) in his sequence-experience notation system, and futher investigated and developed by reknowned landscape architect Lawrence Halprin in *RSVP Cycle*, published in 1969. In developing the notion of *scores*, Thiel displayed a series of graphic techniques to record, analyze, and set forth events involving a sequence of human actions and interactions. A short passage from the conclusion of *The View From the Road* underscores the importance of the application of findings when it states:

122 URBAN VISUAL DESCRIPTION AND ANALYSIS

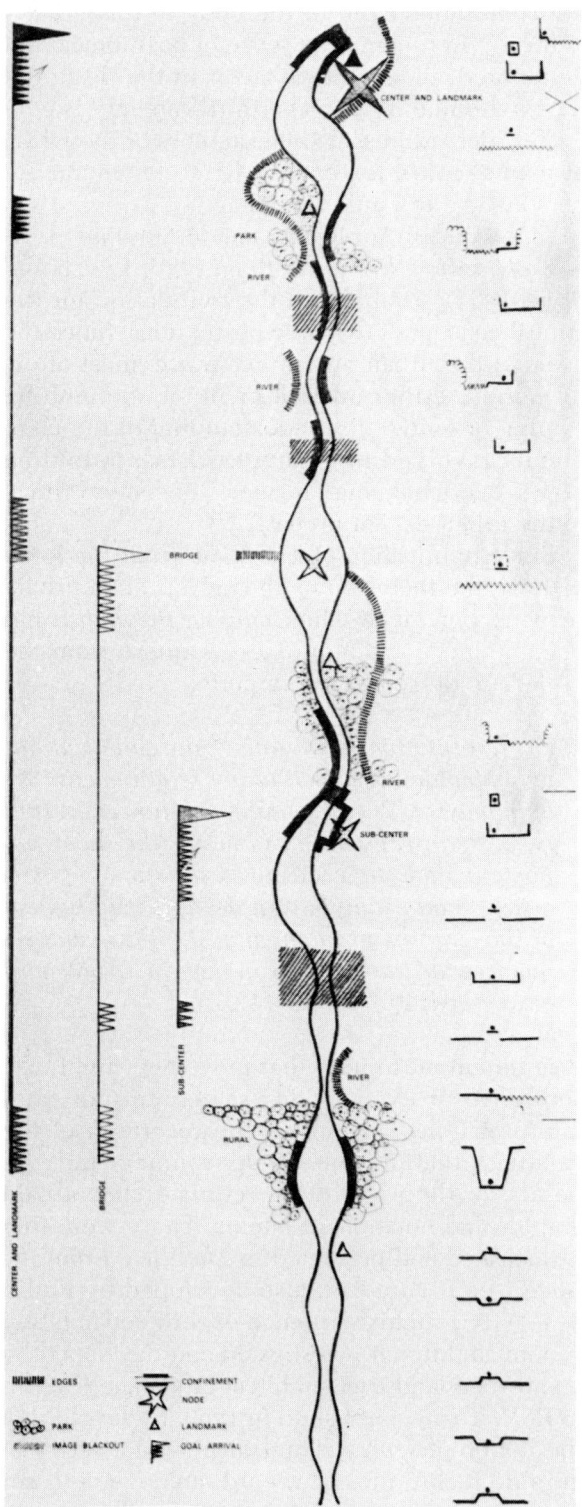

FIGURE 8.3. Sequential notation. *Source:* Appleyard, D. et al., 1964, *The View from the Road*, Cambridge, MA: MIT Press, 38.

The crucial test will come in applying these ideas to actual design problems, and in evaluating the results obtained. Here the techniques of design and of analysis can be refined, and our grip on principles strengthened.... An experimental road would be the proof of the pudding. (Appleyard et al. 1964, 63)

PROFESSIONAL OR EXPERT RECORDING AND ANALYSIS TECHNIQUES

In regard to this matter of "graphic skills," it is usually the expert's belief that the process of recording and analyzing is integrally tied to examination of relationships through graphic exploration. The expert approach is based on the premise that in the process of graphically recording and analyzing the urbanscape, one continually discovers relationships, commonalities, juxtapositions, and sequences that are not evident upon first, or even subsequent, visual examination (see Figure 8.4).

In similar fashion to the methodology by which an architect analyzes a single building or a landscape architect a specific landscape, the urban designer must develop a basic vocabulary process which is then used to structure the analysis. This primary "process" can then be modified, refined, and detailed so as to allow for application to any given project.

Process

The first step for expert visual inventory and analysis is to prepare an overall process. Within Figure 8.5, we can trace some of the major steps in urban visual analysis. Critical steps include determining what observation points we will use to inventory the urban visual environment, how to describe the visual landscape, how to represent the urban visual environment with specific scenes, and how to evaluate visual quality.

Establishing Visual Control Points

One of the early, but important, decisions is how to visually record the characteristics of the urban visual environment. A standard technique from a professional perspective would be to take 35 mm photographs or slides from intersections or areas where people would congregate (see Figures 8.6a

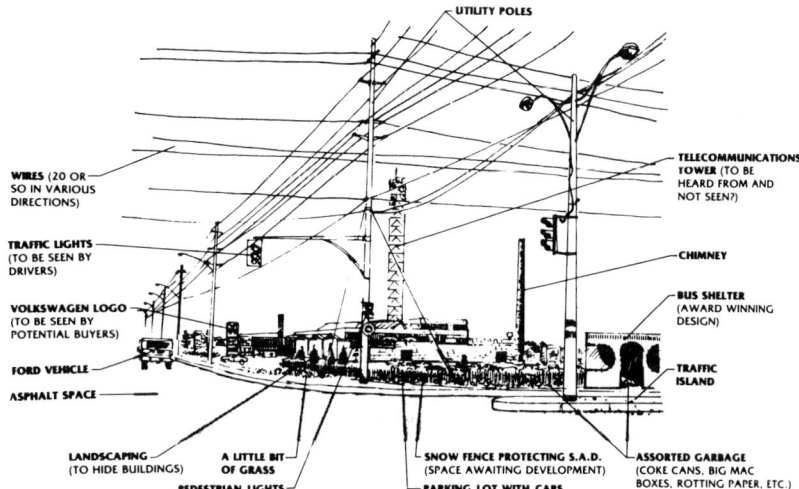

FIGURE 8.4. Example of expert graphic analysis. *Source:* Sadler, B. and A. Carlson, eds., 1982, Environmental Aesthetics: Essays In Interpretation, Department of Geography, University of Victoria, Victoria, Canada, 55.

and b) and then to record on a map of some type the position and direction that these photographs were taken. These individual positions where single or multiple photographs were taken would be called visual control points (after Litton 1973) and become the anchoring points for our visual data base.

A different approach would be to take totally random photographs of the urban environment (Milgram 1972), or to give subjects cameras and have them take pictures of what they think best represents the urban environment (user-employed photography; Chenoweth 1984). Still another method would document the experiences of the view in motion by using video or movie cameras to take tape or film while moving down a street. The latter technique has been used by the author (Smardon and Goukas 1984) and others (Appleyard et al. 1964; Craik 1975; Carr and Schissler 1969) as well. Chapter 5 on environmental perception tells us why these decisions are important.

Visual Elements

Beside recording images visually, one needs a procedure or method to characterize visual elements in the environment. The analyst needs to note a number of characteristics on a data sheet while looking at the specific view. The following typology of visual elements was derived from a number of sources (Velasques 1979; Erickson, 1980). Such notations can include:

1. The type of view: vista, wide angle, or panorama.
2. Viewer distance: close, intermediate, far.
3. Viewer elevation: inferior, normal, superior (see Figure 8.7a).

Specific physical attributes of views which may be recorded include:

1. Paths: grid, irregular, or radial.
2. Degree of enclosure: ratio, distant view, open-ended versus close-ended (see Figure 8.7b).
3. Street trees: height, distribution, canopy, and scale (see Figure 8.7c).
4. Architectural pattern/distribution/land use.
5. Activity pattern (see Figure 8.7d).

With physical elements recorded, one can then attempt to distribute them on a map in a geographic sense or begin to characterize sequences of views.

Analysis

Notation systems can be developed (see Figure 8.8) to begin to document sequential visual experiences. Such an approach was also utilized by

124 URBAN VISUAL DESCRIPTION AND ANALYSIS

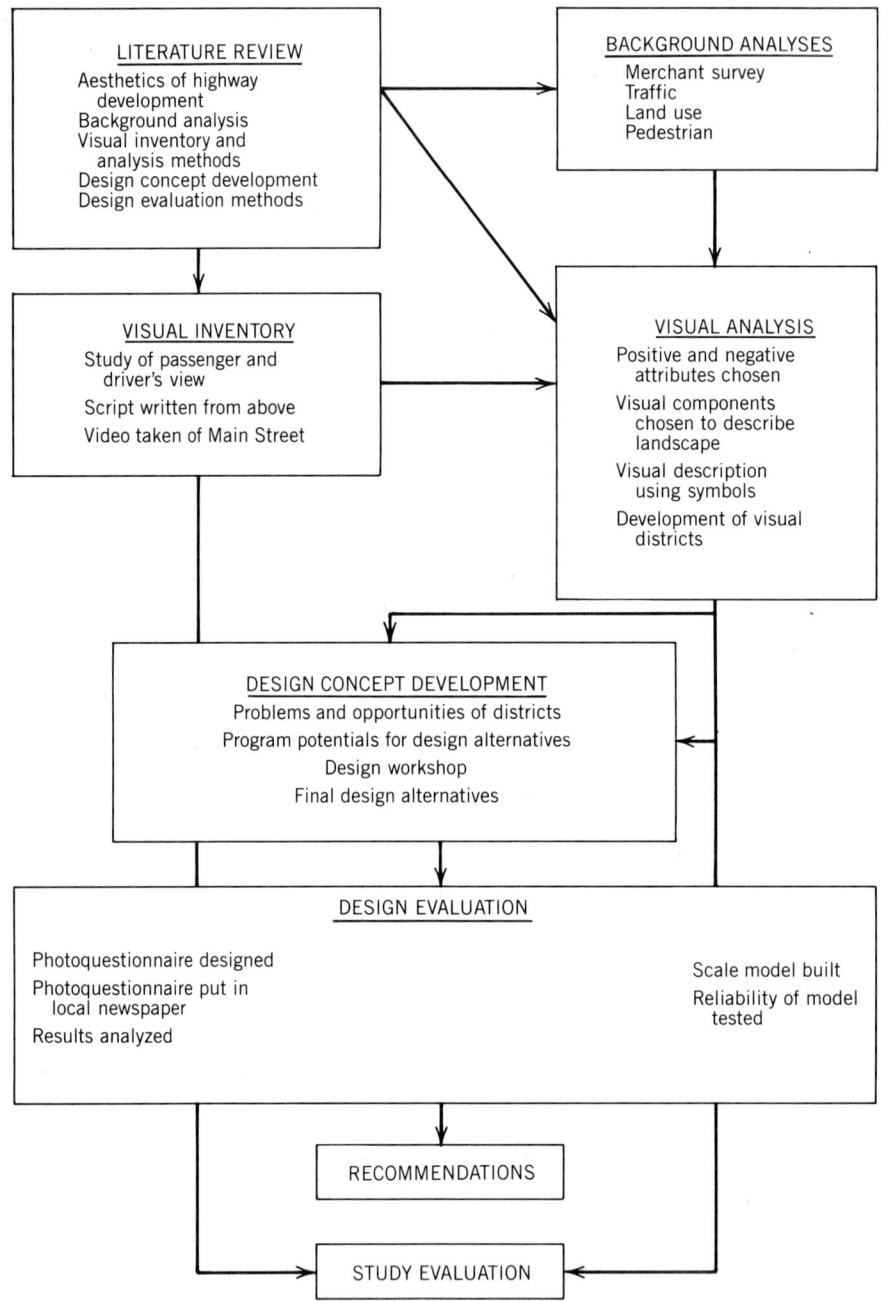

FIGURE 8.5. Sample visual inventory process.

Appleyard in *The View From the Road* (Appleyard et al. 1964) and Philip Thiel (1961) and in a recent North Syracuse Commercial Strip project (Smardon and Goukas 1984). Notation systems can also be used to classify urban landscapes into visual districts as orginally conceived by Lynch (1960). This is illustrated in Figure 8.9 for the North Syracuse commercial strip. The visual units were derived from layers of notations which, in turn, were derived from video footage replayed many times.

Visibility

Once an analyst has developed a visual data base and notational system, there should also be thought given to visibility assessment of the urban landscape (see Chapter 4). This is a fairly complex

FIGURE 8.6a. Photo inventory sequence.

undertaking for urban landscapes since elevated highways and walks as well as buildings give the observer many different vantage points, and hence changes the viewable area drastically. Even at the street level, large buildings block or obscure sections of a stationary view (see Figure 8.10); but if the observer walks to a street corner, the viewshed changes drastically.

Some thought needs to be given to visibility criteria for foreground, middleground, and background zones of any given viewshed (see Figures 8.10 and 8.11). Then activities and use of the urban environment should be studied to develop a rationale for determining which visual control points viewsheds should be constructed from. Then any number of viewsheds should be developed based on methods discussed in Chapter 4.

Light

In the perception of any urbanscape, light plays an important role for it is a well-known fact that the quality of an urban space, in fact the entire "image" of a particular city, is determined in part by the quality of light. London, in the shrouded translucency caused by the fog, or the Greek hilltowns of the Aegean bathed in the Mediterranean sunlight are prime examples, as the ambiance and mood of both are greatly created by the light that pervades the urbanscape.

In addition to the idea of a lighting quality analysis which, by its very nature, is subjective, the more pragmatic study of shades and shadows is an important component of an analytical process. With the ever-increasing concern for energy

126 URBAN VISUAL DESCRIPTION AND ANALYSIS

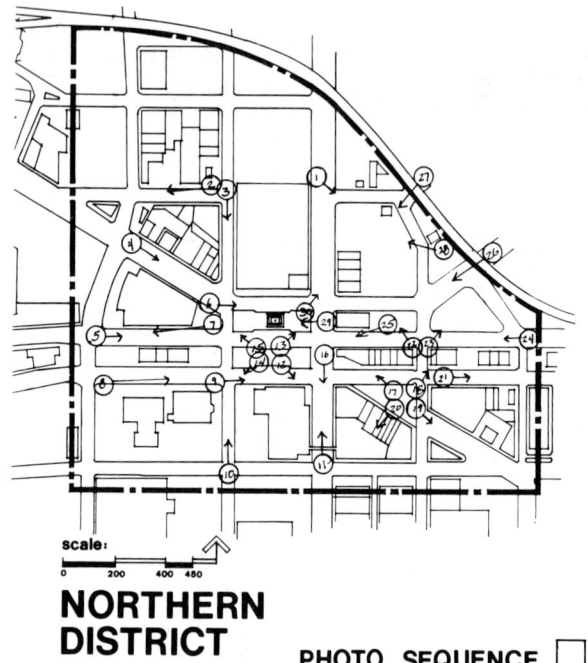

FIGURE 8.6b. Photo inventory sequence.

considerations, a detailed study of an urban site or existing building in terms of "sun access" is of great importance. Critical factors dealing with the sun's relationship on the "celestial sphere" to an urban site, street, and so forth constitute a comprehensive, analytical technique (see Chapter 3 for more detail).

The impact of natural light considerations must be paralleled by an investigation of artificial light so that a total understanding of an urbanscape at night is ascertained (see Hack et al. 1974). Terms like *the Great White Way* (New York City's Broadway Theatre District), and *pearl necklace of car lights* are terms which refer to a quality of a specific urban context created at night. Appleyard, Lynch, and Myer (*The View From the Road*, 1964) reinforce this notion:

> At night a new order reigns in the city. The chaotic skylines, jagged shapes, erratic signs, forms, and shapes disappear into the darkness, to be replaced by the luminous dots, stripes, and diffused light. The path system becomes clearer.... The more prominent intersections or nodal points can gain extra emphasis...; certain areas ... become nocturnal landmarks. (Appleyard et al. 1964, 57).

The above are positive aspects of lighting. There are negative aspects as well.

Seattle, Washington (see Erickson, 1980) adopted an ordinance in 1978 to help correct the adverse effects of lighting and glare by limiting:

The reflective qualities of surface materials that can be used in development;

The area and intensity of illumination;

The location or angle of illumination; and

The hours of illumination.

Glare is generally described as being either *primary* or *secondary*. Primary glare pertains to glare caused by a direct light source, whereas secondary glare is from reflected light, also often referred to as reflective glare. Reflective glare is generally of two types: "spot" glare in which parallel light rays from the source are reflected parallel from the reflective surface; and "scattered" glare when

MATRIX - ILLUSTRATED DEFINITIONS

In order to inventory views from public sites in Syracuse a matrix was developed that classified and quantified site and location, view description, view angle and direction, view type, viewing distance, view elevation, and urban physical view descriptors.

In order to ensure consistency in categorizing views, a series of illustrated definitions was prepared for use by those working in the field.

[One of the reasons a qualitative approach was not taken was the difficulty in deciding what was or was not a good view. (For example, an unattractive daytime view can be quite attractive at night.)]

VIEW DESCRIPTION — short phrase depicting location.

VIEW ANGLE : DIRECTION — assumed breakdown of cone of vision, in degrees, of specific view.

KEY	VIEW TYPOLOGY
	VISTA — an intermediate to far view which is restricted on either side by natural or man-made elements. Street corridor views are of this type. Viewing angle may range from 10 to 60 degrees.
	WIDE ANGLE — a view encompassing a considerable viewing angle. The actual viewing angle may range from 60 to 180 degrees.
	PANORAMA — a view which provides the observer with a great sweep of the natural setting and/or city scape. Viewing angle may range from 180 to 360 degrees.
	VIEWER DISTANCE
	CLOSE — viewer only sees part of building facade.
	INTERMEDIATE — viewer has entire building in sight.
	FAR — building and its immediate environs are seen.
	VIEW ELEVATION
	INFERIOR — below object viewed.
	NORMAL — eye level or ground level typical of viewer.
	SUPERIOR — above specific view giving overall perspective.

FIGURE 8.7a. Key view typology.

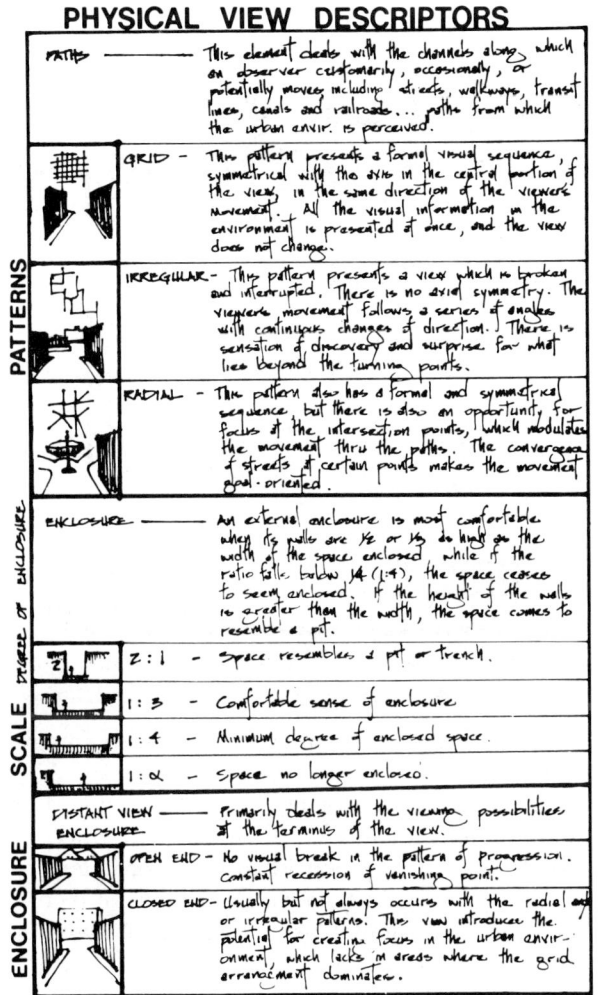

FIGURE 8.7b. Typical view descriptors—patterns, scale, enclosure.

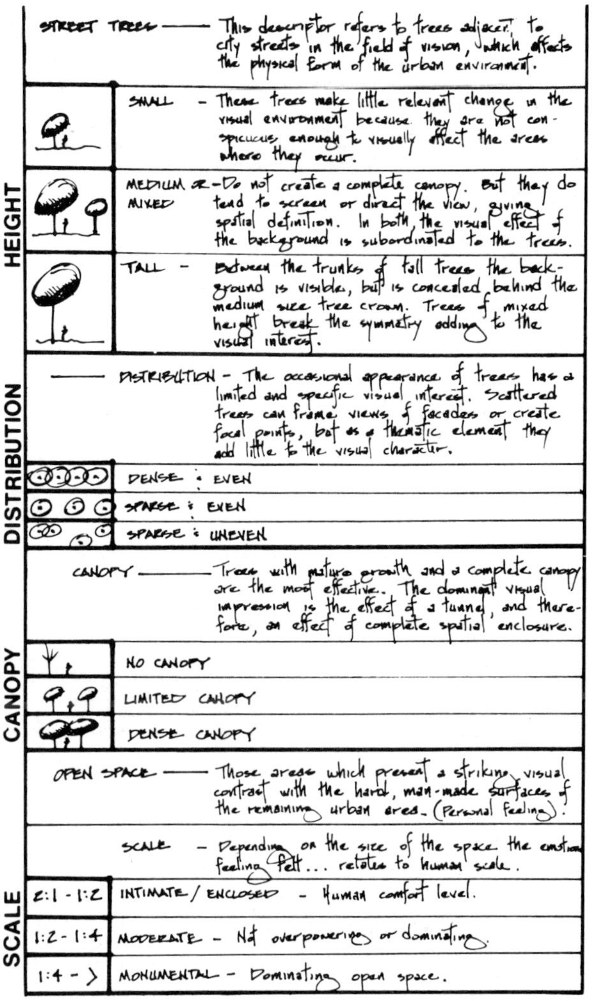

FIGURE 8.7c. Typical view descriptors—vegetation height, distribution, canopy, and scale.

parallel light rays from a source such as the sun are reflected from a surface in a nonparallel fashion. With spot glare, one usually sees an image of the source on the reflecting surface, whereas with diffused flare the whole surface appears illuminated and one does not see the image of the source.

The adverse effects of glare on vision are often analyzed in terms of visual disability and visual discomfort. The former occurs when one's eyes cannot adjust simultaneously to a bright light source against a dark background, which might happen one one looks at bright headlights of an oncoming car at night. Spot glare directly viewed also weakens vision if the source is intense enough. Visual discomfort results when a relatively intense source of light suddenly appears before one's eyes have the opportunity to adapt to it. Squinting and visual avoidance of the source are signs of visual discomfort from glare.

Spot glare from reflected sunlight is actually quite common in our environment but rarely creates a visual nuisance since the angles of reflectance are usually sufficiently large so that the angle of incidence with the horizon is greater than 30 degrees and does not intrude on vision unless one looks up. Reflected glare from the sun is not noticeable during the early or late hours of the day when the altitude of the sun is still relatively low or during the winter months when the sun is continuously at an angle of less than 30 degrees. At other times, reflected spot glare may occur

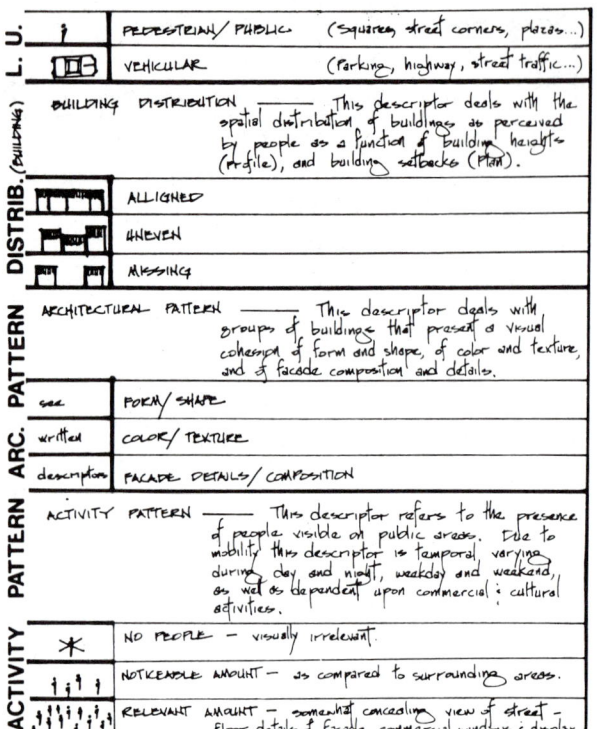

FIGURE 8.7d. Typical view descriptors—land use, building distribution, architectural pattern, activity pattern.

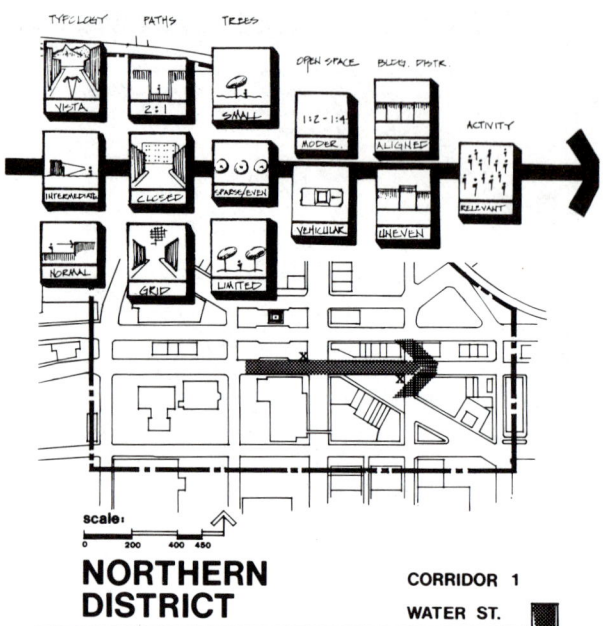

FIGURE 8.8. View corridor with notations.

when one looks up at an object and the glare from it is within one's field of vision or when one feels the heat of reflected sunlight. Parking lots full of cars with reflective bumpers and windshields often cause solar spot glare, especially when viewed from nearby buildings above it.

The major determinants of direct glare are the intensity of the source and the brightness of the surroundings. Two factors significantly affecting reflective glare are the brightness of the light source and the reflectivity of the surface which reflects the light. Solar reflective glare is often most noticeable off highly reflective surfaces such as metal, glass, or water. Car bumpers and windshields, large glassed surfaces, and large bodies of water often function as reflectors of direct sunlight.

Just as the brightness of the light source has a major bearing on reflective glare, so also does the reflective power of the surface the source strikes. Smooth, nonporous metal surfaces were found to have the highest degree of reflectivity (50 to 95 percent), followed by lighter colors. Flat white has the highest degree of reflectivity (85 to 89 percent) followed by yellow (70 percent) and then diminishing as the spectrum of shades grows darker.

Also, the degree or coefficient of reflectivity alone cannot always be depended on since the visual impact varies considerably according to the surface type. Smooth specular surfaces reflect the sun's rays in a parallel fashion (spot glare) whereas a porous surface such as concrete painted white scatters the sun's rays in a number of directions, thereby diffusing it (scattered glare).

Besides metal surfaces, the other major type of specular surface is glass. All smooth glass gives off some spot glare, although the intensity varies considerably with the type of glass and the angle of incidence of the light source's rays. For example, *nonreflective* glass (a misnomer) reflects at an average of about eight percent whereas reflective glass reflects at an average, depending on type, of between 14 and 44 percent. As the angle of incidence of the source light increases above 70 degrees, however, nonreflective glass takes on approximately the same degree of reflectivity as reflected coated glass.

The applications of light and glare evaluation are obvious as we progress toward visual impact assessment in urban environments with Chapter 13. As part of a visual inventory, however, we could start to note existing "problem" areas in the urban environment. This is exactly what was done

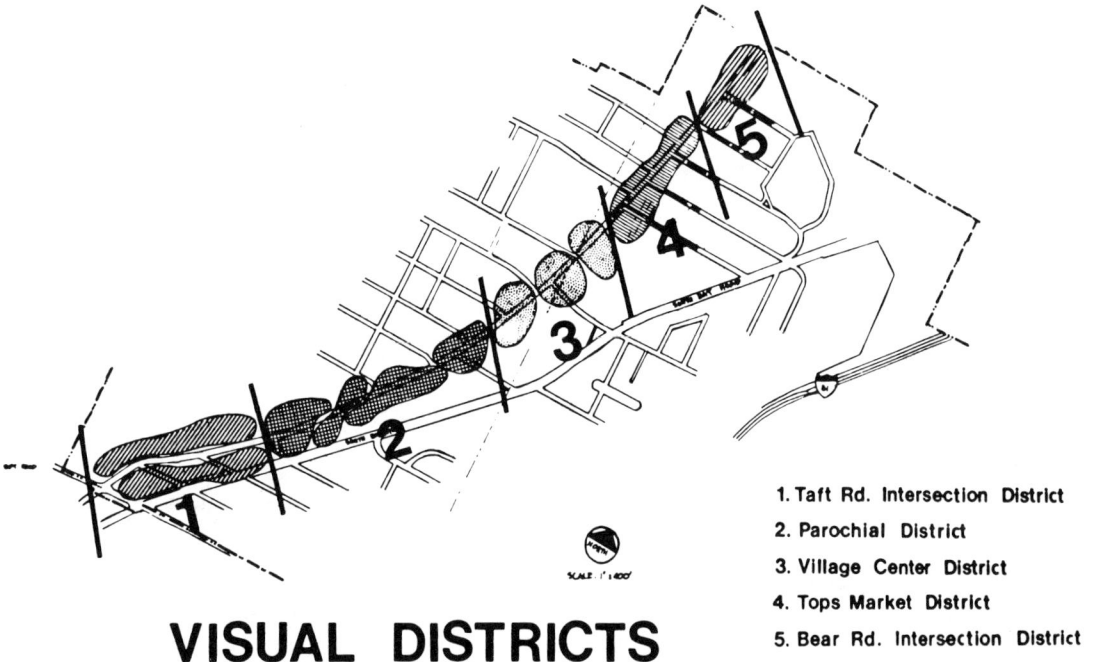

FIGURE 8.9. Village of North Syracuse visual districts.

1. Taft Rd. Intersection District
2. Parochial District
3. Village Center District
4. Tops Market District
5. Bear Rd. Intersection District

for our visual inventory of the Northern District. A simple procedure (see Figures 8.12 and 8.13) of using a light meter at different locations, atmospheric conditions, and times yielded some problem areas, especially near some building facades and parking lots.

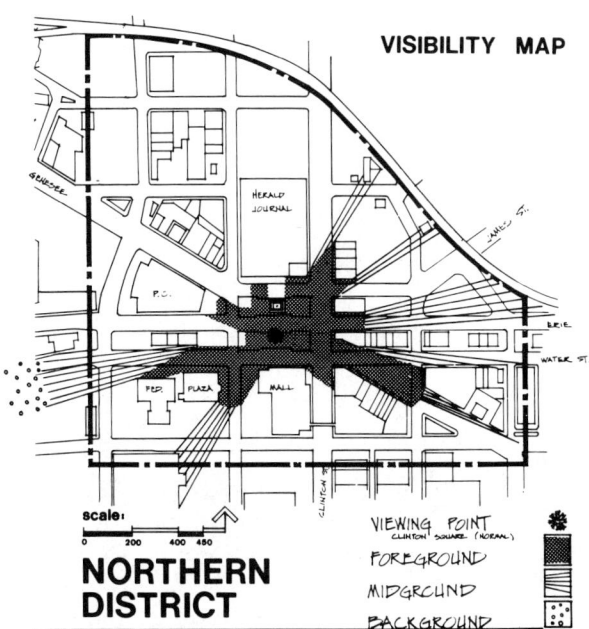

FIGURE 8.10. Visibility map from one point.

Other analyses of shadow effects at different times of the day and season could be undertaken (Bosselman, 1982) as well as night illumination studies (Hack et al. 1973).

Summary of Expert Approach

After all inventories and analyses are completed, many professionals attempt to develop one composite map of an area. This composite map is often intended to represent all the incremental factors studied thus far in a holistic summary of an impression. This still does not address evaluation of visual quality in the urban environment. Evaluative assessments are best done with some sampling of respondents who experience the actual area in question, for example, people who live, work or visit the urban landscape.

A SOCIAL SCIENCE APPROACH TO URBAN VISUAL ASSESSMENTS

In the late 1960s and 1970s, there was increasing social science work performed by environmental psychologists, sociologists, planners and designers to improve our understanding of man-environment relationships in urban settings. Much of

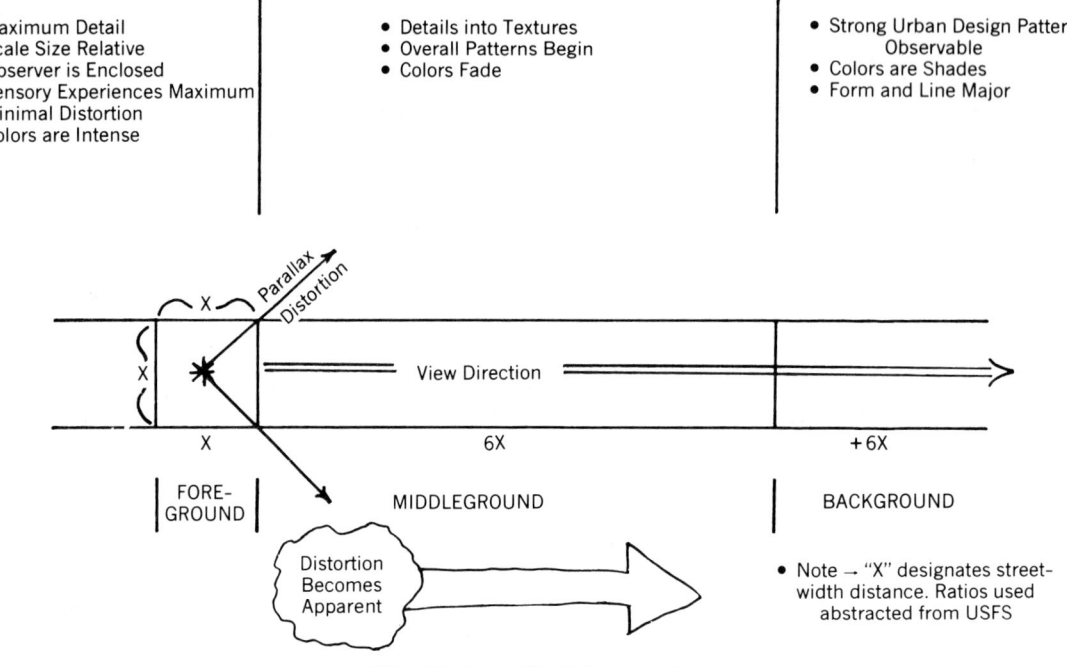

FIGURE 8.11. Visibility criteria.

this work centered around issues of whether increasing amounts of stimulus complexity or ambiguity was good for urban living or not (Wohlwill 1968; Rapoport and Hawks 1970; Kaplan et al. 1982; Rapoport and Kanter 1967), whether familiarity increased people's preference for certain urban environments (Herzog et al. 1976), the role of personality in assessment of urban environments (Craik 1975; Winkel et al. 1969), the role of perceptual selection and memory (Carr and Schissler 1969) and the role of symbols and meaning (Appleyard 1969; Harrison and Howard 1972).

Of course, planners and designers would find more immediate utility in studies that attempted to correlate specific physical attributes of the physical environment with respondent preference (Carp et al. 1976; Peterson 1967) and less immediate utility in more sophisticated psychological statistical treatment of data (Garling 1976). It is interesting to note after a period of relative inactivity in urban perception studies that recent studies are being reported which assess specific types of urban environmental situations such as highrise buildings and their residents (Zoelling 1981; Ulrich 1984) or specific attributes such as the role of vegetation in urban environments (Palmer 1984; Thayer and Atwood 1978).

For the average environmental analyst or designer, this may not help much with the specific decision of which type of study to do, if one is to ask respondents about quality of the urban environment. To the author's mind, one of the most useful papers in this regard is Craik's paper, "The Comprehension of the Everyday Physical Environment" (1968). Within this paper, he addresses methodological situations in general but presents four elements that must be considered in research on the comprehension of the physical environment (see Figure 8.14). These elements are: (1) media of presentation, (2) observers, (3) environmental displays, and (4) response formats.

Media of Presentation

The first choice to be made is what medium or mediums of display are to be used. Typical choices might include: (1) direct exploration of the site, (2) viewing a model, (3) viewing photographic slide series, or (4) viewing a complete set of architectural elevations, and plans. Obviously, the first option would be most desirable but too expensive, and the last option would not be optimum because most people have a difficult time reading architectural elevations, plans, and perspectives. A choice between (2) and (3) would

GLARE PHOTOS & METER READINGS

A study of the degree of glare produced by buildings and vehicles has been conducted in the Syracuse Central Business District, Northern District. The results will hopefully aid in assessing those areas producing hazard, distraction, or stress. The procedure required a site visit on two different occasions, differing distinctly in lighting and weather.

DATE NO. 1 : April 8, 1982   NO. 2 : April 12, 1982

CLIMATIC
CONDITIONS: windy, gusty   : windy
TEMPERATURE: 35°F   : 43°F
TIME: 12:15 – 1:45 PM   : 3:30 P.M
WEATHER: 100% sunshine   : overcast
         20% snow covering

View Description	View Direction	View Distance	"F" stop	Shutter Speed	"F" stop	Shutter Speed
1. SOUTH FACING FACADES HANOVER SQUARE	NORTH	CLOSE	5.6	500	2.8	500
2. HERALD JOURNAL BLG	N. WEST	Interm.	5.6	"	2.8	"
3. FRONT OF HANOVER SQUARE	South		5.6	"	2.8–1.7	"
4. HERALD JOURNAL WEST-SIDE	North	close	8.0	"	2.8–4.0	"
5. SURFACE PARKING ISLAND BY ERIE	S West	Interm.	4.0	"	2.8	"
6. SOUTH CLINTON BY CLINTON SQUARE	South		8.0	"	2.8	"
7. HERALD - JOURNAL CT. TO CLINTON SQ.	South	Interm.	4.0	"	2.8–1.7	"
8. ERIE, SOUTH SIDE OF POST OFFICE	East		4.0	"	2.8	"
9. ROYS FACADE	East	close	4.0–5.6	"	2.8	"
10. WAREHOUSE FACE	North		4.0	"	2.8–4.0	"

FIGURE 8.12. Glare photos and meter readings.

depend upon which option would allow the most realistic depiction of the environment to the observer given the relative cost. (Also see Chapter 11.) Work by Seaton and Collins (1972) supports the use of color slide simulations to represent buildings. Furthermore, if one is addressing a moving sequential experience, video photography of the actual site may be a new optimum. Feimer (1984) has recently compared different types of media and their effects on observers, especially for viewer sequences along highways. Also, note in Table 8.1 that the visual stimulus materials often include multiple types and more use of dynamic media, for example, video and modelscope photography in later studies.

FIGURE 8.13. Glare analysis.

Observers

One must first decide whether one is concerned with individual or group differences in comprehension of the environment. In most cases, we are concerned with comparing one group's reactions to another, such as in the Clayton Study (Willmott et al. 1983), where we compare three different populations' reactions (year-round resident, summer resident, and day visitor) to waterfront revitalization differences. Sometimes we want to compare designer/planner preferences or evaluations with the public reactions. In most cases, we want to ensure that we have representation of most groups who use the urban environ-

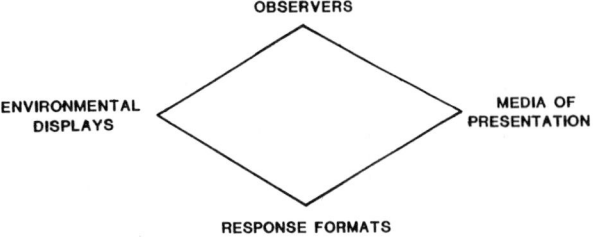

FIGURE 8.14. Craik's model. *Source:* Craik, K.H., 1968, The comprehension of the everyday physical environment, *Journal of the American Institute of Planners*, 34:29–37, Figure 2, 34.

TABLE 8.1. Progression of Community Image Perception Studies

Citation	Location & Time	Study Environment	Participants	Visual Stimulus	Survey Instrument	Special Technology
Lambe & Phillips (1981)	Lancaster, New Hampshire 1980	small town main street	2 graduate students	photographic slides	maps & slides	none
			local residents	none	questionnaire	none
Lambe & Smardon (1982)	Fredonia, New York 1981	small town commercial strip	25 local landowners	none	questionnaire door-to-door	none
			35 local business & community leaders	plans & color simulations	verbal responses at workshops	color photocopy simulations
Zoelling (1981)	Syracuse, New York 1981	high-rise structures near CBD	78 high-rise & low-rise residents	respondents' own views	direct interview w/ questionnaire & cognitive mapping	area maps & color markers for marking pedestrian routes
Willmott (1982) Willmott et al. (1983)	Clayton, New York 1982	small town waterfront	local residents & businesses	B & W photos	direct interview/ open ended questionnaire	none
			designers	videotape	design workshop	video inventory from streets, water and rooftops
			year-round residents, seasonal residents, day visitors	photo simulations, plans & descriptions	mail back ballot & questionnaire	black & white photomontage simulations developed in photo darkroom
Smardon (1983)	Syracuse, New York 1982	downtown CBD	25 students in 4 teams	field video, still photos, video of CBD scale models	team developed visual impact rating forms	video camera & recording equipment & editing lab, equipment for scale model production, modelscope & gantry
Smardon & Goukas, (1984)	Village of North Syracuse, New York 1983	small village w/ large regional commercial strip	6 local residents	actual views	tape recorder	scriptwriting ability to record video sequence
			30 students	videotape	open ended survey form	videotaping equipment to record passenger & driver's experiences
			12 member village board	videotape	verbal responses in workshop	scale models of strip video footage & equipment to record dynamic simulations through the modelscope/stop action recorder to do analysis on tv monitor
			92 local newspaper subscribers	B & W photo simulations w/ descriptions	tear-off mail back ballot/ questionnaire	B & W photomontage 35 mm camera & equipped darkroom

ments that are being assessed (see Table 8.1 under column *Participants*).

Response Formats

We need to record observers' reactions somehow and there are many different formats to do this. This aspect of survey design is covered in detail in Chapter 10. We have found in several community service projects that open-ended responses are very useful in the beginning of a study to uncover the range of qualitative attributes of urban environments (Smardon 1984). Cognitive mapping exercises are very interesting to the scientists, but often very intimidating to the subject (Zoelling 1981). Finally, high-quality black and white photoquestionnaires with rating scales and/or attached questionnaires have prove very useful in eliciting responses to existing qualities or proposed changes in urban environments (Frey 1981; Robinson 1980; Grant 1982; Hudspeth 1982; Willmott et al. 1983). (See Figure 8.15.)

Purpose of Environmental Display

The basic structure which ties everything together is the purpose for the study. It is (1) *descriptive assessment* whose purpose is to uncover qualitative attributes or dimensions of urban environments, or (2) an *evaluative assessment* which compares, rates, or ranks one environmental setting with another or (3) *a preconstruction predictive assessment* used to assess possible changes in the environment before it happens.

COMBINING EXPERT AND SOCIAL SCIENCE APPROACHES

At this point, let us attempt to bring the expert approach together with the public sampling approach. As a basic framework, we can array the four paradigms of landscape assessment (from Zube et al. 1982)—expert, psychophysical, cognitive, and experiential—against four application scales or environmental contexts—urbanizing region, transportation corridor/roadside view, neighborhood/district, and streetscape/place. As one can see from Table 8.2, many of the previously mentioned studies can be placed with this array.

As one can see from Table 8.2, most urban visual studies have been at the regional or citywide scale and are psychophysical or cognitive in nature. In other words, they were attempting to find correlations between preference or scenic evaluation and specific attributes in the environment, or were concerned with perceived meanings in the urban environment, respectively.

Transportation corridor or roadside view studies are scattered throughout the paradigms' spread but concentrated primarily in psychophysical and experiential work. An experiential approach to the view from the road is a logical approach since one wants to gauge a subject's reaction while traveling through a stimulus sequence.

Many district or neighborhood studies are psychophysical in nature, attempting to correlate physical attributes or urban districts and neighborhoods with preference or scenic evaluation. There are some notable professional approaches as well as cognitive approaches seeking meaning and cognitive structure of urban districts.

Finally, there are very few studies addressing visual quality perception at the streetscape or place scale with the notable exception of Cullen's (1971) work from an expert or professional perspective.

There are interesting trends in subgroups of studies. These include assessment of views from highrise buildings (Zoelling 1981) and hospitals (Ulrich 1984).

PROCEDURAL GUIDANCE FOR URBAN VISUAL STUDIES

1. As a general rule of thumb, more public involvement is needed to solicit qualities of the environment as the scale of application decreases, unless one is dealing with strictly physical phenomena—shadow, solar glare, wind—where professionals should be able to describe and assess existing conditions.
2. Symbolically rich historical and multicultural urban environments will necessitate some type of cognitive approach to address the various meanings contained within the environment.
3. Environments rich in multisensory attributes, for example, the observer's experiences, visual motion, olfactory sensations, water sounds, or tactile sensations of a number of unusual surfaces, will need an experiential approach.

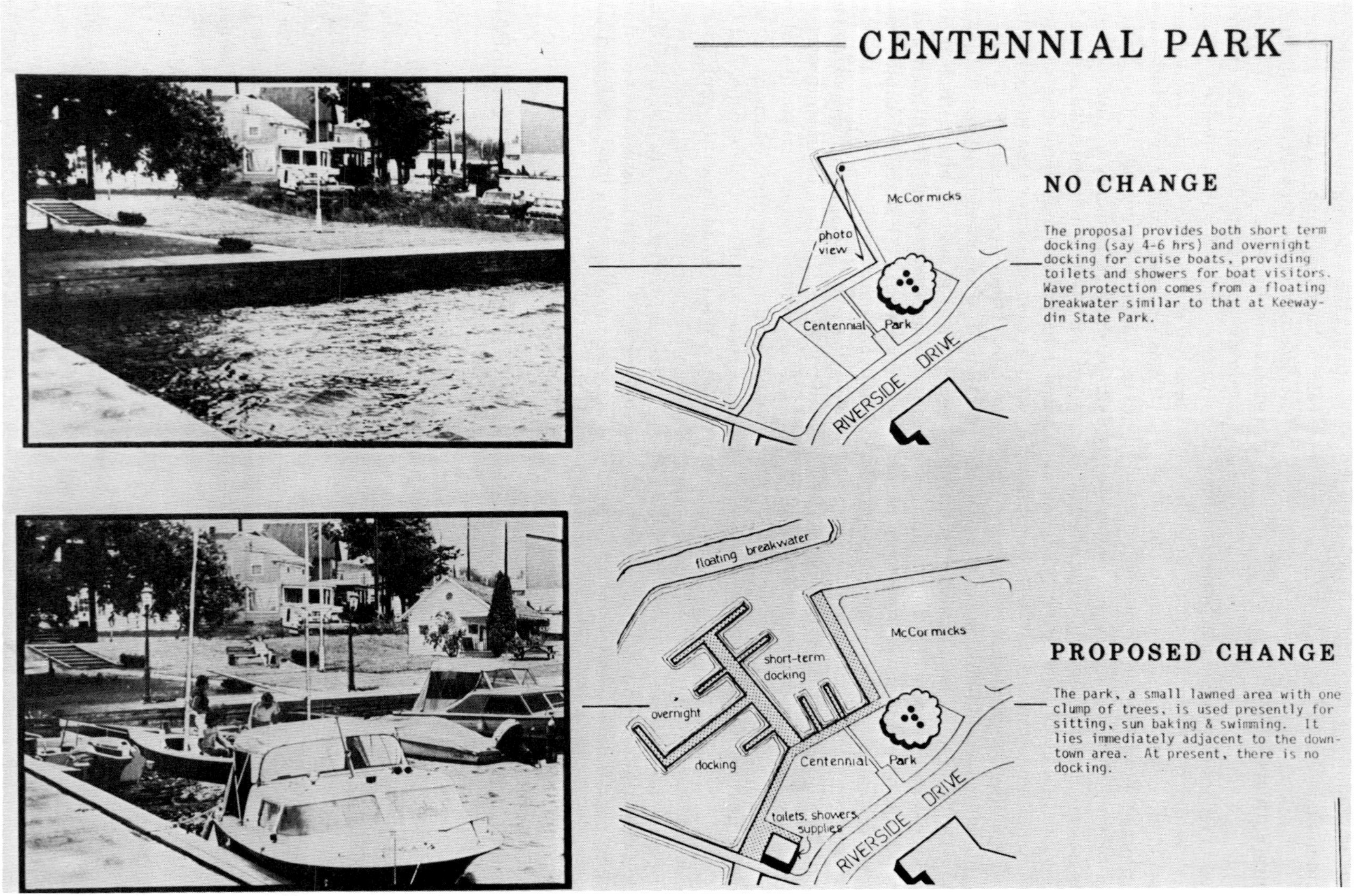

FIGURE 8.15. Example of photoquestionnaire.

TABLE 8.2. Landscape Assessment Paradigms and Urban Environmental Contexts

LANDSCAPE ASSESSMENT PARADIGM	WHOLE CITY OR TOWN URBANIZING REGION	TRANSPORTATION CORRIDOR/ROADSIDE VIEW	DISTRICT/ NEIGHBORHOOD	STREETSCAPE/ PLACE
EXPERT	City of Seattle (1971) Yuill & Joyner (1979) Kansas City (1967)	Appleyard et al. (1964) Jacobs & Way (1969a, 1969b)	Lambe & Phillips (1981) Lynch (1960) Smardon (1983)	Ramati (1981) Cullen (1971) Willmott et al. (1983)
PSYCHO-PHYSICAL	Anderson & Schroeder (1983) Garling (1976) Brush & Palmer (1979) Thayer & Atwood (1978) Palmer (1983) Carp et al. (1976) Crystal & Brush (1978) Wright (1974)	Ulrich (1974) Craig (1975) Smardon & Goukas (1984)	Peterson (1967) Palmer (1984) Frey (1981) Robinson (1980) Zoelling (1981) Hudspeth (1982)	Willmott et al. (1983) Craik & Appleyard (1980)
COGNITIVE	Herzog, Kaplan & Kaplan (1976) Appleyard (1970) Appleyard (1969) Harrison & Howard (1972) Kansas City (1967)	Winkel, Malek & Thiel (1969)	Downs (1970) Zoelling (1981) Lynch (1960)	Groat (1982)
EXPERIENTIAL		Carr & Schissler (1969) Smardon & Goukas (1984) Craik (1975) Feimer (1984)	Hack et al. (1974)	Hack et al. (1974)

4. A mixed approach of professional assessment combined with either psychophysical, cognitive, or experiential studies (as originally proposed by Lynch in 1960) would probably be most practical and thorough for most urban visual studies, especially descriptive and evaluative assessments.

5. Approaches for visual urban predictive appraisals are treated in Chapter 13.

NEW TECHNIQUES

Because of the complexity of urban environments and the richnesses of multisensory experience, new techniques and technology will be needed to more fully "capture" aspects of urban environments. For basic field inventory and recording of experiences, video offers many advantages for urban visual inventories (Kopka 1979; Mertes and Smardon 1984). We have used video in a number of urban community service projects already (Smardon 1984 and see Table 8.1). Other techniques include building scale models and exploring them through use of modelscopes (Felleman 1983; Bosselman 1983) which has increasing utility for visual impact assessment (Smardon 1983). This will be covered in Chapter 13 for urban environments.

Finally, visual inventories should broaden to include all aspects of the aesthetic experience including sound (Southworth 1969), shadow effects, excessive daytime glare (Erickson, 1980) or nighttime light intrusion (Hack et al. 1974), pedestrian wind effects (Cohen et al. 1977) and air quality (Stewart et al. 1983). These are covered to some extent in Chapter 13, but basic inventory techniques need to be developed that ensure adequate preparation of urban aesthetic data bases.

PART 4

LANDSCAPE ASSESSMENT AND EVALUATION

Whereas the previous chapters gives us means to describe, inventory, and to some degree analyze attributes of wildland, rural, and urban landscapes, the five chapters within this section are written specifically to address questions of evaluation. This includes landscape evaluation of two types: (1) existing landscape quality, and (2) proposed landscape changes and their visual impact.

Chapter 9 by Smardon is, as its title says, a review of agency methodology for visual project analysis. Much of the early innovation in methodology for incorporation of landscape values in project planning and analysis was done by federal agencies such as the U.S. Forest Service, the U.S. Department of Interior's Bureau of Land Management, and the U.S. Department of Agriculture's Soil Conservation Service. A brief history of these agencies' internal procedures development is followed by a step-by-step comparison of the actual methods used for areawide visual landscape assessment and evaluation. This is followed by a discussion of methods of "scoping" or identifying at an early stage the visual effects of proposed projects. The approaches of New York State's Environmental Quality Review Act, the Federal Highway Administration, and the Housing and Urban Development Administration to "scoping" are presented. Finally, detailed visual impact assessment procedures that are used by the U.S. Forest Service, Bureau of Land Management, and Federal Highway Administration are presented and are followed by a summary comparison of all agencies and procedures described within Chapter 9.

Chapter 10 by Vining and Stevens lays the foundation for understanding basic principles for psychological assessment of landscape quality. After presenting a rationale for why assessments that involve public groups need to be used, Vining and Stevens present different assessment methods such as surveys and questionnaires, perceptual preference, and behavioral measures, which all can be used to collect information about landscape quality. These tools can be used for different assessment designs which include case studies, experimental designs, correlational methods and quasiexperimental designs. Finally, Vining and Stevens offer criteria for evaluating the appropriateness of assessment methods including reliability, validity, and sampling. Examples of actual methods, in four steps, are included as inserts.

Sheppard, in Chapter 11, offers another critical foundation chapter on visual simulation methodology. Before we can ask questions about a project's visual impacts, we must know how to design approaches to eliciting responses from affected parties (Chapter 10) and be able simulate what the project will look like from all appropriate vantage points (Chapter 11). Sheppard has four purposes which organize his chapter. They are: (1) to identify the primary research findings and information sources which are applicable to visual simulation, (2) to establish principles of visual simulation for use at the project scale, (3) to review problems and advantages associated with simulation methods, and (4) to illustrate key procedures by means of simulation examples included as inserts.

With the three background Chapters 9, 10, and 11 in hand, one can proceed to Chapters 12 and 13, which address visual impact assessment (VIA) for natural/rural and urban environments, respectively.

Yeomans traces the demand for rural and wildland areas as well as the types of activities most likely to affect such environments, in Chapter 12. He then quickly summarizes visual impact assessment (VIA) methods used by agencies in the United States and Canada and then reviews VIA methodology research. Yeomans provides a summary of VIA criteria and six major steps within the VIA process: (1) conducting the landscape description or inventory, (2) assessing user (or viewer) characteristics, (3) making preliminary line-of-site determinations, (4) establishing key viewpoints, (5) assessing impact activity/land use characteristics, and (6) preparing a visual impact

PART 4: LANDSCAPE ASSESSMENT AND EVALUATION

assessment and mitigation summary. Additional guidance is given on project aesthetics including internal, relational, and environmental aesthetics and design guidelines.

Similarly, in Chapter 13 Blair outlines a VIA process for urban environments which contains: (1) a definition of the visual characteristics of the project, (2) a definition of the visual environment of the project, (3) a determination of visual impacts of project alternatives, (4) evaluation of visual impacts, and (5) identification of ways to mitigate significant visual impacts. Key contributions to methodology include means to involve publics in VIA and to address shadow and glare impacts in urban environments.

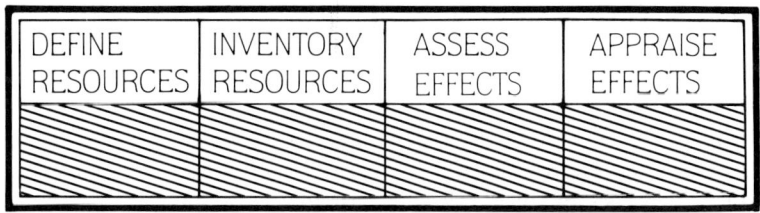

CHAPTER 9

REVIEW OF AGENCY METHODOLOGY FOR VISUAL PROJECT ANALYSIS

Richard C. Smardon

Portions of this chapter were previously published by R.C. Smardon. An organizational analysis of Federal agency visual management systems. (Ann Arbor, Michigan: University Microfilms International); and U.S. Dept. of Transportation, 1981, Visual impact assessment for highway projects (Washington, DC: U.S.D.O.T. and U.S. Govt. Print. Office); and State of New York, Department of Environmental Conservation, 1980, SEQRA Handbook (Albany: D.E.C.). All are reproduced with permission of the publishers.

INTRODUCTION

Before the reader becomes involved in the following chapters addressing landscape evaluation, let us review, in brief, the history of visual resource management (VRM) system development, and then review existing procedures utilized by the federal agencies for visual analysis and evaluation.

Recent History of VRM System Development

Simultaneous to the public emphasis on natural beauty and elimination of ugliness, a new spatial dimension of landscape policy emerged. This dimension was the scenic corridor concept which recognized that the aesthetic experience of moving through the landscape was a sequential spatial experience involving time and motion.

The concept of linear sequential experience of spaces, as pointed out by Litton, was probably first articulated for public use by Frank Waugh in 1918 in his pamphlet on landscape engineering in the National Forests (Waugh 1918). This approach later evolved in the scenic corridor concept used for roads and wild and scenic rivers. The Highway Beautification Act sought to provide the states with legal tools to preserve and enhance these linear scenic corridors.

The social need for outdoor recreation concept received public policy recognition when Congress authorized establishment of an Outdoor Recreational Resources Review Commission in 1958 (ORRRC 1962). One of ORRRC's principal recommendations was the establishment of a uniform system for classifying outdoor recreation resources. This system comprised six categories and was adapted by the Forest Service, the Bureau of Land Management, and the National Park Service. Five of the six classes of land under the system pertain to areas where the retention of natural beauty is a major objective: high density recreation areas (Class I), general outdoor recreation areas (Class II), unique natural areas (Class IV), primitive areas (Class V), and historic and cultural sites (Class VI) (ORRRC 1962, 109). This classification was not always used consistently by federal agencies but did signify the beginning of the idea that landscapes could be classified for varying qualities and intensity of usage.

Landscape inventories conducted in the early 1960s for statewide recreation planning programs as a outgrowth of the Outdoor Recreation Resources Review Commission Report (ORRRC 1962) still tended to focus on the identification of specific sites. However, Lewis's (1968) efforts in the State of Wisconsin marked a sharp departure from this site-oriented approach by encompassing continuous linear sections of the landscape which he called environmental corridors. This coincided with the move to assess the regional landscape, as proposed by Twiss and Burton, or what was later called the landscape "continuum" by Zube (1973, 126).

A number of water resources planning studies included specific efforts to assess the visual quality of the regional landscape continuum in 1969–70. Several similar studies were conducted in Great Britain, Germany, and the United States related to general regional planning programs from 1969 to 1971.

The proposed standards for water resource planning by the special task force of the Water Resources Council (1970) give further credence to the importance of the landscape continuum as well as to discrete sites when incorporating scenic values into resource planning programs. The report of the Public Land Law Review Commission (1970) and the hearings on the proposed National Land Use Act (Senate Committee) suggested the need for broad-scale regional land inventories including scenic values.

Landscape values can be applied to single sites, corridors, and landscape continuums (See Figure 9.1). We can expand the geographic context of value attribution one more step to include the whole atmospheric envelope as opposed to just the land surface. The atmospheric envelope was explained well by Udall (1979) in his retrospective discussion of the realization by the Johnson administration that certain land and water areas that they succeeded in preserving were susceptible to the insidious threats of air, water, and noise pollution from offsite sources. The Clean Air Act Amendments of 1977 is one such Act which attempts to meet the threat of air quality degradation to landscape already preserved as National Parks, Wilderness Areas, and so forth.

The landscape image as aesthetic is the primary theoretical basis that visual resource management systems have been postulated upon. There is also a strong naturalistic bias in the way in which these systems are used. There are also ongoing arguments about whether quantification of the visual

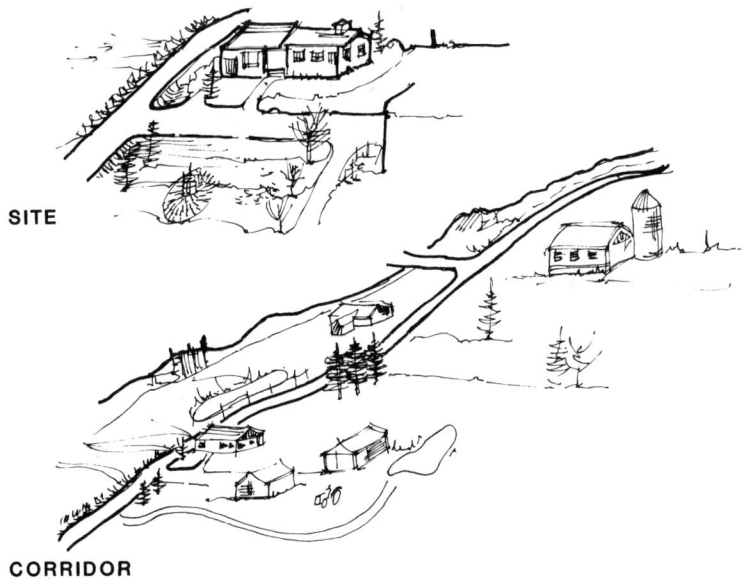

FIGURE 9.1. Geographic constructs of landscape analysis.

attributes of landscape is desirable or possible (Carlson 1977). This debate is strongest in academic circles, but resource management agencies are under pressure to incorporate visual resource values into land management and environmental review procedures.

VRM is generally used in analyses and decisions about utilization of the publicly owned land areas, decisions concerned with permitting activities to take place on the public landscape, and decisions about whether publicly financed activities should take place on private lands. VRM procedures generally facilitate the integration of scenic or visual values into the decision-making process, to be considered along with many other resource values. Visual or scenic resource values are rarely the major determining values in environmental decision making but are becoming increasingly significant in some cases (Smardon 1984). As one can surmise, most of the activity regarding visual resource management is concerned with federal agency activities and management of the federal lands. This emphasis is directly attributable to legal activity dealing with the adequacy of environmental resource decision making.

The need for development of VRM systems can be traced to certain publics' concern with aesthetic and environmental issues related to specific land management activities, for example, wilderness designation, strip mining, timber harvesting practices, highway funding and construction, park maintenance, and so forth. This concern is exemplified by several major federal court cases in the last decade (Smardon 1982, 1984). It is also exemplified by several pieces of major environmental legislation which call for explicit consideration of aesthetic or visual resources as part of the environmental decision-making process (See Chapters 1 and 2).

As can be seen from the historiographs (Tables 9.1, 9.2 and 9.3), development of visual resource management systems have occurred only recently for three federal agencies in the United States. In fact, most developmental work was done in the 1970s and 1980s. Generally, these systems were developed quite rapidly with little time for in-house research to meet multiple resource management decision needs. However, incorporation of aesthetics into agency decision-making processes was often enthusiastically supported by key agency administrators, as one can see from Tables 9.1, 9.2, and 9.3.

Visual resource management systems were developed by federal agencies to deal with three classes of problems: (1) visual inventory and analysis systems for large landscape areas needing landscape planning; (2) systems for scoping of

TABLE 9.1. VRM Development within the Forest Service

Period	Year	Specific Event
Recreational Design Era	1965	
	1968	Burt Litton's Research at PSW is finally published.
Strong Impetus Buildup for VRM	1968–69	F.S. Chief Ed Cliff visits England—discovers Sylvia Crowe's work with Forestry Commission. Work ongoing in England.
	1968	Director of Recreation Dick Costley caused meeting to be held in St. Louis, developed outlines for total VRM system.
Development Stage for Region 6 VRM	1970	Bacon assimilates ideas from F.S. Regions 5, 8 and 6. Bacon moves to Region 6 in Portland. Received directive from Jack Usher to develop 'more objective way'.
	1971	Number of timber management plans for Region 6 were unapproved:—strong impetus for VRM. *Forest Land Management* Published in Region 1.
Implementation of VRM. Development & Publishing Chapters.	1972	Washington Office decides to go with Region 6 system—it was developed and some inventory was done in Region 5 and 6. Model study application done on the Gifford Pinchot National Forest.
	1972	Regional Forester Rex Ressler liked the system—wanted it implemented. Burt Litton reviews proposed VRM system/methodological problems. Major split between Bacon, Region 6 and Orr, Region 8. Orr's ideas went to BLM via Leopold.
Implementation of system in other regions	1975–76	Majority of inventory done for Region 6 and Region 5—other regions slower to implement.

Key People:
                              Administration
    Ed Cliff, Chief of F.S. (1968–69)
    Dick Costley, Dir. of F.S. Recreation (1968–69)
    Jack Usher, Asst. Dir. of Timber Management, Region 6 (1970)
    Rex Ressler, Regional Forester, Region 6 (1972)
    Craig Rupp, Regional Forester, Region 2 (1976)
                          Methodology Development
    Ed Stone, Warren Bacon, Howard Orr, Wayne Iverson, Gerald Coutant
                                Research
    Burt Litton, Gary Elsner, PSW

Source: Smardon, 1982.

TABLE 9.2. VRM Development within the BLM

Period	Year	Specific Event
Partial implementation of scenic quality component of RIS	1965 1966	Recreation Information System (RIS) included scenic quality component. (Lynn Fergus and Del Price).
Integration in Bureau Planning system & development of support for comprehensive VRM system.	1971	Review of existing visual analysis. Prepared position papers for Congress. Started integrating visual analysis into planning system (Fergus).
	1972	Established National Advisory Task Force on visual resources (1 meeting each year). Few landscape architects hired.
	1974	Leopold was hired in Washington. With input from Orr, Regions 8 & 5 awareness program developed. VRM program put into BLM Manual.
	1975	Support from top BLM decision-makers. Development of training program.
	Nov. 1975	System signed officially by Director. Full training program initiated. Hiring of State Office L.A.'s.
Training, implementation & improvement	1977	Task Force met in Santa Fe. Research resulted in contrast rating commission.
	1978	Passage of BLM's Organic Act with specific visual resources language (possible result of earlier position papers).
	1978	Second Task Force on revamping of VRM system/first computer graphics workshop. More investigation into Planning System.
	1979	Elimination of Denver Service Center staff. Ross takes over for Leopold in Washington. Second computer graphics workshop.
	1980	New BLM publications came out of GPO.

Key People: Assistant Director for Resources and BLM Director George Turcott
Methodology: Lynn Fergus, Del Price, Bob Leopold, Bob Ross in that order for developing methodology.

Source: Smardon, 1982.

potential visual impact or determining thresholds, and (3) systems for detailed evaluation of visual impact.

REVIEW OF VRM METHODS FOR LANDSCAPE PLANNING

The following section describes the use of VRM systems within federal agencies.

VRM systems are utilized within the Forest Service, and the Bureau of Land Management (BLM) as part of broad regional planning and assessment. In the Forest Service, these exercises are known as regional guides and are prepared as part of the Resource Planning Assessment Act of 1974. Regional assessments for BLM are either for special uses, for example, energy development for the state of North Dakota (U.S.D.I. BLM et al. 1978), or special areas such as the Desert Conservation Area Plan which covers the southwestern one-third of California.

Visual resource management is used forest-wide for preparation of 10-year timber management plans for the U.S. Forest Service. These plans are multiple resource plans which array the major resource groups against different goals of timber output from the forest. Timber management plans are supposed to (but do not always) interface with land use forest planning for specific geographic subareas of national forests. The VRM practitioners prepare their own visual inventory

TABLE 9.3. LMS Development within the Soil Conservation Service

Period	Year	Specific Event
Development phase of landscape architecture system.	1970	Passage of NEPA—need felt for landscape architect within SCS.
	1972	Sally Schauman hired as first LA in Washington.
	1978	Publishing of in-house technical document TR-65.
Implementation of material in TR-65. Development of more complex range of investigation techniques.	1980	

Key People: Administrators
  Director of SCS (1970)
  Engineering Division in general

Methodology: Sally Schauman

evaluations, sensitivity analyses, and visual management objectives for these specific land areas. Decisions concerning development and maintenance of the visual management objectives are worked out by an interdisciplinary land use planning team which the VRM practitioner is a member of. The ultimate decision regarding visual management objectives, however, rests with the Forest Ranger or a Forest Supervisor depending on the scale of land area involved. Forest Service VRM practitioners also do visual corridor analyses for roads and visual absorption capability analyses for visual impacts from a range of activities.

BLM, like the Forest Service, is heavily involved with permit processing activity to determine whether private parties should be allowed to do many different kinds of activities on federal lands. These activities include timber harvesting, vegetation conversion, recreational activities, recreational development, water resource development, energy development and mining activity, and agricultural and range-related activities. For each permit action, both Forest Service and BLM need to check the existing visual quality or management objective of the site in question and do a visual impact analysis via an environmental assessment or full environmental impact assessment if the project may cause significant environmental impact or is controversial. Even after visual impact assessment is done, there may be a need to have visual mitigation work done to remedy the severity of visual impact. This is the range of situations in which the Forest Service and BLM would use VRM.

The Soil Conservation Service (SCS) would use its LMS system on a similar geographical range of project scales—from very large to very small—but the activity types would be much more restrictive. The landscape resource management systems would be used for water resource planning projects under the Small Watershed Development Projects Act of 1966 or local agricultural or soil conservation projects sponsored by a local conservation district. The LMS system would be used to identify visual resources of a land area which may be affected by planning alternatives or those areas that need to be considered in an environmental assessment or environmental impact statement. These identified high-priority areas would then be analyzed by a landscape architect.

The following paragraphs will examine the

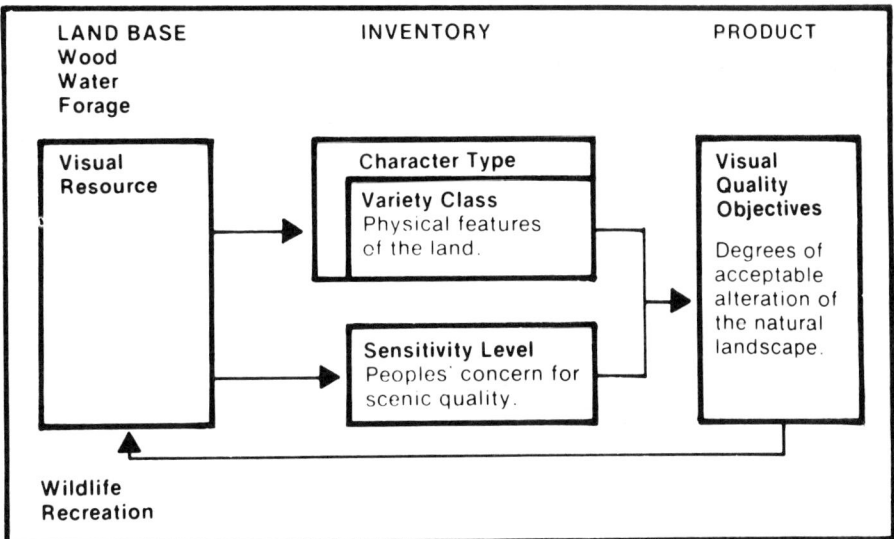

FIGURE 9.2. Overview chart of Forest Service Visual Management System. *Source:* USDA, Forest Service, 1974, vol. 2, chapt. 1, USDA Handbook No. 462, U.S. Government Printing Office, Washington, DC, 9.

specific methodologies, procedural steps and key terminology for each of these three VRM systems.

Two of the three systems to be treated are called visual resource management systems (U.S.D.A. For. Serv. 1974; U.S.D.I. B.L.M. 1980) (see Figures 9.2 and 9.3), and third is called a landscape management system by the Soil Conservation Service (1978). All three systems contain common elements, including: (1) subsystems for physically based landscape visual quality inventory and evaluation; (2) subsystems for assessing peoples' use, visibility of landscape, or attitude toward the landscape; and (3) geographic mapping of these factors to yield classified areas for certain management objectives, visual quality maintenance levels; or priorities for a professional landscape architect's attention.

Two of the agencies concerned, the U.S. Forest Service and the Bureau of Land Management, have actual federal lands within their jurisdiction with which they are charged with management responsibilities. The Soil Conservation Service does not own land and only advises groups and individuals about maintaining landscape quality as part of soil conservation or small watershed development services. This latter fact accounts for some of the differences between the systems. They are, however, on the whole, quite similar. The following paragraphs will identify further similarities and differences which can be attributed to these systems.

Both the Forest Service and Bureau of Land Management's VRM's physical landscape inventory and evaluation subsystems utilize the basic variables of form, line, color, and texture as modifying descriptors of landscape quality as it is found in physical attributes of the landscape such as landforms, rock form, vegetation, and so forth (see Figures 9.4 and 9.5).

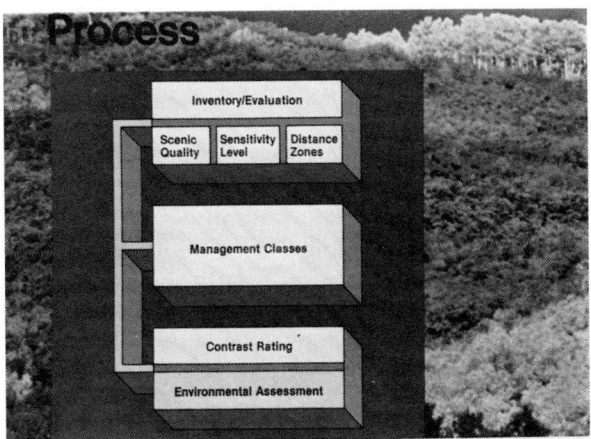

FIGURE 9.3. BLM Visual Resource Management System. *Source:* USDI, BLM, 1980a, Visual Resource Management, U.S. Government Printing Office, Washington, DC, 16.

	CLASS A DISTINCTIVE	CLASS B COMMON	CLASS C MINIMAL
Landform	Over 60 percent slopes which are dissected, uneven, sharp exposed ridges or large dominant features.	30-60 percent slopes which are moderately dissected or rolling.	0-30 percent slopes which have little variety. No dissection and no dominant features.
Rock Form	Features stand out on landform. Unusual or outstanding, avalanche chutes, talus slopes, outcrops, etc., in size, shape, and location.	Features obvious but do not stand out. Common but not outstanding avalanche chutes, talus slopes, boulders and rock outcrops.	Small to nonexistent features. No avalanche chutes, talus slopes, boulders and rock outcrops.
Vegetation	High degree of patterns in vegetation. Large old-growth timber. Unusual or outstanding diversity in plant species.	Continuous vegetative cover with interspersed patterns. Mature but not outstanding old-growth. Common diversity in plant species.	Continuous vegetative cover with little or no pattern. No understory, overstory or ground cover.
Water Forms, Lakes	50 acres or larger. Those smaller than 50 acres with one or more of the following: (1) Unusual or outstanding shoreline configuration, (2) reflects major features, (3) islands, (4) Class A shoreline vegetation or rock forms.	5 to 50 acres. Some shoreline irregularity. Minor reflections only. Class B shoreline vegetation.	Less than 5 acres. No irregularity or reflection.
Water Forms, Streams	Drainage with numerous or unusual changing flow characteristics, falls, rapids, pools and meanders or large volume.	Drainage, with common meandering and flow characteristics.	Intermittent streams or small perennial streams with little or no fluctuation in flow or falls, rapids, or meandering.

FIGURE 9.4. Forest Service's variety classes. *Source:* USDA, Forest Service, 1974, vol. 2, chapt. 1, USDA Handbook No. 462, U.S. Government Printing Office, Washington, DC, 13.

As can be seen in Figures 9.4 and 9.5, the physical attributes are arrayed for both VRM Systems. Note that BLM's A, B, C Scenery Classifications correspond to the Forest Service's Class A-Distinctive, Class B-Common, and Class C-Minimal. Note that some of the physically based attributes are the same for both systems, for example, landform, vegetation, water (forms), and that some are quite different (Forest Service's rock form) or are not included in the other system, for example, BLM's color, adjacent scenery, scarcity, and cultural modifications.

Note within SCS's visual quality table in Figure 9.6 that everything is described in terms of distinctive, average, or minimal visual resource quality, and the physical attributes are similar to those used by BLM and the Forest Service. It should be noted that the Forest Service's and BLM's physical landscape attributes as presented in Figures 9.7 and 9.8 are specific in application to certain general geographic locales. The Forest Service's descriptors are specific to the heavily vegetated mountain landscapes in the Pacific Northwest and Rocky Mountains, while BLM's descriptors are specific to the sparsely vegetated and semiarid Southwest, basin and range grasslands, and the Great Plains. SCS, on the other hand, has utilized a range of color photographs (U.S.D.A. S.C.S. 1978) taken from many different geographical localities to illustrate ranges of dis-

Scenic Quality Inventory/Evaluation
Rating Criteria and Score

	Landform	Vegetation	Water	Color	Adjacent Scenery	Scarcity	Cultural Modifications
	High vertical relief such as prominent cliffs, spires or massive rock outcrops; or severe surface variation or highly eroded formations including major badlands or dune systems; or detail features dominant and exceptionally striking and intriguing such as glaciers. 5	A variety of vegetative types in interesting forms, textures, and patterns 5	Clear and clean appearing, still, or cascading white water, any of which are a dominant factor in the landscape. 5	Rich color combinations, variety or vivid color; or pleasing contrasts in the soil, rock, vegetation, water or snow fields. 5	Adjacent scenery greatly enhances visual quality. 5	One of a kind; or unusually memorable, or very rare within region. Consistent chance for exceptional wildlife or wildflower viewing. 6	Free from esthetically undesirable or discordant sights and influences, or modifications add favorably to visual variety. 2
	Steep canyons, mesas, buttes, cinder cones and drumlins; or interesting erosional patterns or variety in size and shape of landforms; or detail features present and interesting though not dominant or exceptional. 3	Some variety of vegetation, but only one or two types. 3	Flowing or still, but not dominant in the landscape. 3	Some intensity or variety in colors and contrast of the soil, rock and vegetation, but not a dominant scenic element. 3	Adjacent scenery moderately enhances overall visual quality. 3	Distinctive, though somewhat similar to others within the region. 2	Scenic quality is somewhat depreciated by inharmonious intrusions, but not so extensively that they are entirely negated; or modifications add little or no visual variety to the area. 0
	Low, rolling hills, foothills or flat valley bottoms. Interesting, detailed landscape features few or lacking. 1	Little or no variety or contrast in vegetation. 1	Absent, or not noticeable. 0	Subtle color variations, contrast or interest; generally muted tones. 1	Adjacent scenery has little or no influence on overall visual quality. 0	Interesting within its setting, but fairly common within the region. 1	Modifications are so extensive that scenic qualities are mostly nullified or substantially reduced. -4

FIGURE 9.5. BLM's, scenery classifications. *Source:* USDI, BLM, 1980a, Visual Resource Management, U.S. Government Printing Office, Washington, DC, 19.

tinctive, average, and minimal visual resource quality.

Both the BLM's and the Forest Service's VRM's have similar subsystems that are used to assess sensitivity level. Sensitivity level, as used by these agencies, is an indicator of the sensitivity of the landscape to the viewer as expressed by its visibility (can it be seen by many people?), its importance or intensity of use, or interpretations of how people actually feel about the landscape in question. Both the Forest Service and BLM utilize use volume criteria (see Figures 9.7, 9.8, and 9.9). Many different measures of frequency

Visual Resource Quality

visual resource element	Distinctive VRQ³	Average VRQ²	Minimal VRQ¹
Landform	·Visually dominant geomorphology. ·Topography patterns that provide visual diversity to an otherwise homogeneous landscape.	·Visible but not dominant geomorphology.	·Unapparent geomorphology. ·Homogeneous topography patterns providing no visual diversity
Vegetation	·Vegetative patterns that provide visual diversity to an otherwise homogeneous landscape. ·Unique plant specimens or communities.	·Vegetative patterns providing limited diversity to an otherwise homogeneous landscape.	·Homogeneous topography patterns providing no visual diversity
Water	·Shores of estuaries, oceans and great lakes. ·Waterbodies and streams with high clarity and diverse bottom material and/or side slopes.	·Waterbodies and streams with clarity.	·Waterbodies and streams with visible pollution and unapparent visual interest
Structures (man-made development)	·Unique visual identity (i.e. barns,fence). ·Development where high concern for the landscape appearance is obvious.	·Typical structural element/pattern. ·Development where no concern for appearance is obvious.	·Visual structure identity "blighted." ·Development where no concern for appearance is obvious.
Combinations	·Unique combinations of any visual elements. ·Proposed or designated scenic areas and locally recognized scenic or special areas.	·Typical combinations of any visual elements.	·Combinations which are visually incongruous visual intrusions. ·Designated visual eyesores

FIGURE 9.6. SCS's visual resource quality rating criteria. *Source:* USDA, SCS, 1978, p. 4.

Sensitivity Level Matrix

Sensitivity	High				Medium		Low	
User Attitude	H	H	M	H	L	M	M	L	L
Use Volume	H	M	H	L	H	M	L	M	L

FIGURE 9.7. BLM's sensitivity level matrix. *Source:* USDI, BLM, 1980a, Visual Resource Management, U.S. Government Printing Office, Washington, DC, 21.

	primary importance	secondary importance
Travel Route	National importance High use volume Long use duration Forest land access roads	Local importance Low use volume Short use duration Project roads
Use Areas	National importance High use volume Long use duration Large size	Local importance Low use volume Short use duration Small size
Water Bodies	National importance High fishing use High boating use High swimming use	Local importance Low fishing use Low boating use Low swimming use

FIGURE 9.8. Forest Service's travel route, use area and water body importance criteria. *Source:* USDA, Forest Service, vol. 2, Chapt. 1, USDA Handbook No. 462, U.S. Government Printing Office, Washington, DC, 18.

of travel are used to assign a high, medium, or low rating in both cases. The Forest Service sensitivity subsystem adds consideration of intensity of usage of recreation areas and water bodies to this criteria (see Figures 9.11 and 9.12).

BLM, unlike the Forest Service, considers the specific user attitude towards the landscape area by familiarizing public groups with the area and asking them to respond to activities that will modify that landscape (see Figure 9.7). The concern they express about proposed changes in scenic quality is rated high, medium, or low. Final sensitivity levels are set using matrices, as can be seen in Figures 9.7 and 9.9 for both the Forest Service and BLM.

BLM and the Forest Service also delineate distance zones on maps. These zones show how far landscapes are from convenient viewpoints or frequently traveled viewing corridors. The Forest Service uses the distance zones of foreground, middle ground, and background; and BLM utilizes foreground/middle ground, background, and seldom seen.

SCS, unlike BLM and the Forest Service, separates landscape use from visibility of the landscape. Figure 9.10 depicts the type of factors considered by SCS in landscape use in terms of rating direct, indirect, or combinations of use. Figure 9.11 illustrates the types of concepts used in assigning high, average, or low visibility to a landscape area by utilizing the factors of number, frequency and duration of view, view expectations, location, and viewer's position.

All three subsystems are then combined by the agencies to yield mapped data and three-way matrices. These tools are utilized by the Forest Service to delineate geographic areas with certain visual management objectives (see Figure 9.12). Likewise, BLM delineates certain areas for visual management classes (see Figure 9.14). SCS utilizes this information to delineate areas for priority of landscape architecture treatment (see Figure 9.13). The latter delineation is used to flag areas where a certain level of expertise is needed for

Summary Table for all Sensitivity Levels:			
	Sensitivity Level		
Use	1	2	3
Primary Travel Routes, Use Areas, and Water Bodies	At least ¼ of users have MAJOR concern for scenic qualities	Less than ¼ of users have MAJOR concern for scenic qualities	
Secondary Travel Routes, Use Areas, and Water Bodies	At least ¾ of users have MAJOR concern for scenic qualities	At least ¼ and not more than ¾ of users have MAJOR concern for scenic qualities	Less than ¼ of users have MAJOR concern for scenic qualities

FIGURE 9.9. Forest Service's summary table for sensitivity levels. *Source:* USDA, Forest Service, vol. 2, Chapt. 1, USDA Handbook No. 462, U.S. Government Printing Office, Washington, DC, 21.

Landscape Use			
rating type of use	Most Important LU³	Important LU²	Minimal Importance LU¹
Direct	· One of a kind · Intensive use (volume, frequency)	· Ordinary availability · Normal use	· One of many available · Occasional use (infrequent)
Indirect	· Highly valuable environmental controls (size, shape, location, seasonal factors)	· Valuable environmental controls	· Limited environmental controls
Combinations	· High cultural, scientific, or educational value · One of a kind	· Ordinary cultural, scientific or educational value · Ordinary	· Limited cultural, scientific or educational value · One of many

FIGURE 9.10. SCS's landscape use criteria. *Source:* USDA, SCS, 1978, 10

Visibility			
rating viewer factor	High Visibility V³	Average Visibility V²	Low Visibility V¹
Number, Frequency and Duration	· Large number of viewers · Very frequently (daily) · Long viewing time, i.e. canoeing, pedestrian	· Frequent (occasionally) · Intermediate viewing time (normal traffic)	· Few viewers · Infrequent viewing (rarely) · Very short viewing time
Expectations	· Homeowner or tourist	· General public	· Transient, nontourist
Location and Viewers Position	· Elevated in landscape >20 feet · View from home, school, hospital, recreation area, major highways, and scenic areas	· Elevated < 20 feet · View from general community areas and roads	· Ground level · View from cropland, industrial areas, minor roads or from within dense forests

FIGURE 9.11. SCS's visibility criteria. *Source:* USDA, SCS, 1978, 12

	Sensitivity Level						
	fg1	mg1	bg1	fg2	mg2	bg2	3
Variety Class — class A	R	R	R	PR	PR	PR	PR
class B	R	PR	PR	PR	M	M	M / MM
class C	PR	PR	M	M	M	MM	MM

FIGURE 9.12. Forest Service matrix yielding management classes. *Source:* USDA Forest Service, vol. 2, chapt. 1, USDA Handbook No. 462, U.S. Government Printing Office, Washington, DC, 43.

Landscape Architecture Priority Matrix

	V^3			V^2			V^1		
VRQ^3	H^9	H^8	M^7	H^8	M^7	M^6	M^7	M^6	M^5
VRQ^2	H^8	M^7	M^6	M^7	M^6	M^5	M^6	M^5	L^4
VRQ^1	M^7	M^6	M^5	M^6	M^5	L^4	M^5	L^4	L^3
	LU^3	LU^2	LU^1	LU^3	LU^2	LU^1	LU^3	LU^2	LU^1

FIGURE 9.13. SCS's landscape architecture priority matrix. *Source:* USDA, SCS, 1978, 14

Visual Sensitivity	H			M			L	
Special Areas	1	1	1	1	1	1	1	
Scenic Quality A	2	2	2	2	2	2	2	
B	2	3	3	3	4	4	4	
C	3	4	4	4	4	4	4	
Distance Zones	FG MG	BG	SS	FG MG	BG	SS	SS	

Note: Class 5 areas are those that have been identified in the VRM planning system which require rehabilitation or enhancement and therefore are not included in this chart.

FIGURE 9.14. BLM's visual management class matrix. *Source:* USDI, BLM, 1980a, Visual Resource Management, U.S. Government Printing Office, Washington, DC, 24.

SCOPING THE VISUAL IMPACT ASSESSMENT 151

further evaluation. The Forest Service and BLM want to assign a certain level of visual quality at which a section of landscape is to be managed or maintained. Both BLM's management classes and the Forest Service's visual management objectives determine the different degrees of modification or change allowed for a specific landscape area.

SCOPING THE VISUAL IMPACT ASSESSMENT

This approach was intended to help agency personnel identify the visual effects, if any, that are likely to be significant on a particular project. This identification was intended to help determine the scope of visual impact assessments under NEPA as well as state mini-NEPAs and to suggest appropriate mitigation measures for study.

CEQ Regulations and Scoping

In November 1978, regulations were issued for the implementation of NEPA. These are designed to increase the usefulness of environmental analysis in project decision making, as well as to reduce the paperwork and delays sometimes associated with the preparation and review of environmental impact statements (EISs).

The regulations employ several means to achieve these purposes. One set of measures limits preparation of a full EIS to projects which are likely to have significant environmental effects. If the significance of a project's environmental effects is in doubt, agencies can perform a brief environmental assessment to determine whether a finding of no significant impact (FONSI) can be issued or if a full EIS is needed. The regulations also allow agencies to establish categorical exclusions for actions which do not require environmental review except under extraordinary circumstances.

Another set of measures governs EIS preparation. Every EIS is to be "concise, clear, and to the point." To this end, "there shall be an early and open process for determining the scope of issues to be addressed and for identifying the significant issues related to a proposed action. This process shall be termed scoping" (CEQ, 1979, 763). A similar consideration applies to mini-NEPAs as well.

Scoping Visual Impacts

There are many different types of visual issues. For a few major projects, one may have to address all of them and the next section will present three approaches to do this. The three approaches include: (1) a visual checklist which is used for SEQRA, New York State's Environmental Quality Review Act; (2) a questionnaire for federal highway projects; and (3) a series of visual thresholds used for screening federally funded housing projects.

New York's State Environmental Quality Review Act: Visual Scoping Process

The SEQR process calls for an environmental impact statement when an action may have a significant effect on the environment. The visual aspects of the environment, both man-made and natural, are an important environmental resource value. A commonly held viewpoint is that making a determination of significance based on aesthetic values is hopelessly subjective ("beauty is in the eye of the beholder"). This discourages one from addressing the visual resource when considering potential environmental effects.

This guideline offers a model process to preserve and enhance the visual resources of a community. It is a flexible process recognizing the inherent diversity in community values across the state. The following simplified process provides the practical tools for a lay person to evaluate potential visual impacts and make a defensible determination of significance under SEQR. The process includes three basic stages:

> *Stage 1:* Conduct an inventory of visual resources to establish or clarify community values, policies, and priorities related to existing visual resources *before* projects of controversy arise.
>
> *Stage 2:* Establish practical visual criteria to guide decisions related to the undertaking, funding, or approval of future projects.
>
> *Stage 3:* Use the visual-environmental assessment form addendum to supplement SEQR's full Environmental Assessment Form (EAF) and focus on a project's potential visual impacts. Such impacts may require preparation of a draft EIS. The form is an orderly method that can be used to support a determination of nonsignificance.

Stage 1: Suggested Visual Inventory Process

A. **Identify Community Visual Resource Values**
   1. Describe and define the general character of the existing area.
   2. Document visual resource and/or visually sensitive land including:
      a. State parks or state forest preserves, municipal parks;
      b. wild, scenic, or recreational water bodies designated by a state governmental agency;
      c. publicly or privately operated recreation areas;
      d. publicly or privately operated areas (including areas used for recreation) primarily devoted to conservation or the preservation of natural environmental features;
      e. hiking or ski-touring trails designated as such by a state or municipal government agency;
      f. architectural structures and sites of traditional importance;
      g. historic or archaeological sites designated as such by the National Register or State Register of Historic Places;
      h. parkways, highways, or scenic overlooks and vistas designated as such by a federal, state, or municipal government agency;
      i. important urban landscapes including visual corridors, monuments, sculpture, landscape plantings, and urban "green space";
      j. important architectural elements and structures representing community style and neighborhood character.

B. **Public Participation**
   1. Notify the public of the proposed inventory process and its purpose.
   2. Conduct a survey of local resident/viewer perceptions:
      a. identify positive visual attractions;
      b. identify visual detractions or "mis-

fits" (car dumps, gravel pits, waste disposal areas, and so forth).

Results of the survey should indicate a preliminary consensus of the public's perceptions and values regarding its visual resources.

3. Conduct public meeting(s) to inform residents of the public's perceptions and values regarding its visual resources.
4. Adopt the municipal visual resource inventory.
5. Formalize community visual standards through creation of sign ordinances, architectural boards' of review adopted standards, or other appropriate techniques.

C. **Establish "Critical Areas of Environmental Concern" in Accordance with SEQR**

Special visual resources that are considered highly valued by the community and are sensitive to change may be established as Critical Areas of Environmental Concern under SEQR (see 617.4(j)). Thereafter, any action that takes place within, partially within, or adjacent to the critical areas would be treated as a Type I action and receive a fully coordinated environmental review process.

Stage 2: Practical Visual Criteria

Agency decision makers can protect the visual character and quality of a project and its environmental setting by early consideration of the general siting and design criteria listed below. Municipalities and agencies may wish to use these suggested criteria as a base, adding their own criteria to reflect community values.

1. Locate new facilities where they are intrinsically suitable to their visual environment.
2. Insure that agency decisions prevent the exposure or creation of visual misfits (such as car dumps or waste disposal areas adjacent to scenic vistas) unless visual mitigation measures are adequate.
3. Whenever possible protect the visual privacy of residential sites.
4. Actively preserve future access to public viewing points.
5. Emphasize shared infrastructure space for public utilities.
6. In areas of high scenic quality, avoid commercial advertising, overhead utility service, and other man-made distractions.
7. Avoid development on steep slopes.
8. Take special care to enhance the visual quality of the physical entranceway to a community. The entranceway, usually a public roadway, sets the tone for the perceived visual expectation of the community.
9. Protect the integrity of visually important building facades by utilizing transfer of development rights techniques.
10. Promptly remove, refurbish, or replace abandoned facilities.
11. Be aware that visual spaces can be as important as physical objects. In this sense, air pollution can affect the visual quality of important spaces by obscuring or diminishing views.
12. Insure that transmission line corridors are not silhouetted against the skyline and traverse slopes on a diagonal rather than perpendicular basis.
13. As appropriate, either remove existing vegetation along travel corridors in order to create or enhance views or vistas, or retain existing vegetation along travel corridors to enhance the natural character.
14. Consider all possible mitigation measures. Use vegetation, landforms, or structural techniques to screen visually intrusive characteristics of a proposed development.
15. Enhance views to bodies of water.
16. Avoid adverse visual effects caused by the introduction of materials, colors, and/or forms incompatible with the surrounding landscape.

Stage 3: Visual EAF Addendum

The following Visual EAF Addendum is to be completed by the lead agency to provide information for determining whether a proposed action may have significant impacts on the visual resources.

The EAF addendum focuses on four categories for measuring the visual significance of a project:

1. description of the existing visual/scenic environment;
2. identification of the degree to which the proposed action will be visible;
3. determination of who will see the project and in what context, for example, worker, tourist, local resident;
4. identification of the degree of visual compatibility or incompatibility of the project with the existing environment or the "projected" environment.

While this conceptual approach for determining visual significance relies heavily on objective measurements, there will always remain some degree of subjective discretion on the part of the agency decision maker.

VISUAL EAF ADDENDUM

This form is to be used in conjunction with the SEQR Full EAF. Once the potential visual impacts have been identified by the following questions, proceed to Step 2 of the EAF.

Step 1

1. Is the project within or adjacent to a Critical Area of Environmental Cancer established under the State Environment Quality Review Act (see 617.4(j))?
   Yes ☐   No ☐

Description of Existing Visual Environment

2. Area surrounding project site can be identified by one or more of the following terms:

	Within	
	*1/4 mile	*1 mile
Essentially undeveloped	☐	☐
Forested	☐	☐
Agricultural	☐	☐
Suburban residential	☐	☐
Industrial	☐	☐
Commercial	☐	☐
Urban	☐	☐
River, Lake, Pond	☐	☐
Cliffs, Overlooks	☐	☐
Designated Open Space	☐	☐
Flat	☐	☐
Hilly	☐	☐
Mountains	☐	☐
Other _____	☐	☐

3. Are there visually similar projects within:
   * One Mile   Yes ☐   No ☐
   * Two Miles   Yes ☐   No ☐
   * Three Miles   Yes ☐   No ☐
   Adjacent   Yes ☐   No ☐

*Distances from project site are provided for assistance. Substitute other distances as appropriate.

Degree of Project Visibility

4. Will the project be visible from outside the limits of the project site?
   Yes ☐   No ☐

5. The project may be visible from:
   Site or Structure on the National Register or State Register of Historic Places ☐
   Palisades ☐
   State or County Park ☐
   Parkway ☐
   Interstate Route ☐
   State Highway ☐
   County Road ☐
   Local Road ☐
   Bridge ☐
   Railroad ☐
   Existing Residences ☐
   Existing Public Facility ☐
   Adjacent Property Owners(s) ☐
   Designated Scenic Vistas ☐
   Other _____ ☐

6. Will the project eliminate, block, partially screen, or detract from views or vistas known to be important to the area?
   Yes ☐   No ☐

7. Is the visibility of the project seasonal? (For example, screened by summer foliage, etc. but visible Fall/Winter/Spring)
   Yes ☐   No ☐
   If yes, which season(s) is project visible:
   Summer ☐
   Winter ☐
   Spring ☐
   Fall ☐

8. How many linear feet of frontage along a public thoroughfare does the project occupy?
   _____ Feet

9. Will project open new access to or create new scenic views or vistas?
   Yes ☐   No ☐

10. Does proposed project or action plan to:
    a. maintain existing natural screening
       Yes ☐   No ☐
    b. introduce new screening to minimize project visibility
       Yes ☐   No ☐

If yes, is screening:
1.) vegetative ☐
2.) structural ☐

Viewing Context
11. Viewers will **likely** be in which of the following situations when the project is visible to them?

Activity	Daily	Weekly	Frequency Holidays Weekends	Seasonally
Travel to and from work	☐	☐	☐	☐
Involved in recreational activities	☐	☐	☐	☐
Routine travel by residents	☐	☐	☐	☐
At a residence	☐	☐	☐	☐
At worksite	☐	☐	☐	☐
Other _____	☐	☐	☐	☐

Visual Compatibility
12. Are the visual characteristics of the project obviously different from those of the surrounding area?
    Yes ☐   No ☐
    If yes the visual difference is because of:
    Type of project ☐
    Design style ☐
    Size (including length, width, height, number of structures, etc. ☐
    Coloration ☐
    Condition of surroundings ☐
    Construction material ☐
    Other _____ ☐

13. Is there local opposition to the project entirely, or in part, because of visual aspects?
    Yes ☐   No ☐

14. Is there public support for the project because of its visual qualities?
    Yes ☐   No ☐

Step 2

By answering the questions in the Visual EAF Addendum, you have identified the visual relationship between the proposed action and its surrounding environment. With this information, return to the Full EAF, Part 2, Question 10, that addresses Visual Resources. Here you will identify the degree (size amount) of each significant visual impact. For example, the proposed action may only be visible after the leaves have fallen. This gives an indication of the time of exposure associated with a particular visual impact.

Once an impact's **magnitude** has been identified as potentially large, proceed to Part 3 on the SEQR Full EAF to determine the importance of the identified visual impacts. The community's established Visual Resource Inventory can be used as a practical measure of the importance of the potential impact. If the project will significantly affect a recognized visually sensitive area, facility, or site of visual importance, there should be sufficient information on the Visual Resource Inventory to warrant the preparation of a Draft Environmental Impact Statement.

If your agency or municipality has not developed a Visual Resource Inventory, there is a potential problem of having to conduct the inventory during a time of public controversy. This would make it even more difficult to establish a true consensus on community values. Conducting a visual resource inventory at an early stage would avoid this potential problem.

The Full EAF, Part 3, provides a series of questions to help determine the importance of each visual impact. These include:
1. What is the probability of the (visual) effect occuring?
2. What will the duration of the (visual) impact be?
3. Is the nature of the (visual) impact irreversible and will the (visual) character of the community be permanently altered?
4. Can the (visual) impact be controlled?
5. Is there a regional or statewide consequence to this (visual) impact?
6. Will the potential (visual) impact be detrimental to local goals and values?

The answers to these questions will indicate whether or not the potential impact is important. If one or more impact is found to be potentially large and important, sufficient reason exists to require the preparation of a Draft Environmental Impact Statement.

Federal Highway Administration Scoping Questionnaire

The major questions for the highway questionnaire are grouped under five main headings discussed in the following paragraphs.

Project Characteristics

The first set of questions calls attention to project characteristics that may have a significant effect on project appearance. Alternatives may involve changes in these characteristics. For instance, a viaduct structure may be an alternative to a massive fill section across a low-lying area.

Visual Environment or Project

The next set of questions helps to identify and differentiate the visual environment of the project within the meaning of the terms of *affected environment* and *human environment* defined in NEPA regulations. The questions are intended to clarify the need for detailed analysis such as viewshed mapping.

Significant Visual Resource Issues

We can often identify the nature and likelihood of significant visual resource effects before we perform a detailed visual impact assessment.

Sometimes visual resource effects are significant in themselves; for example, high visual quality is generally worth conserving wherever it exists. In most cases, however, the significance of these resource effects must be interpreted in combination with viewer response (the next set of questions).

For instance, the visual quality of an urban residential district may not be very high, but local residents may still value its visual character. On the other hand, highway projects are often related to urban improvement and redevelopment proposals. In these cases, community groups may be very concerned about improving the visual quality of urban travel routes by facility design and even the appropriate incorporation of art.

Significant Viewer Response Issues

Often, we can also identify the general nature of viewer response to a project before we undertake a detailed visual assessment although the values and goals of local viewer groups may not become fully apparent until later in the process. For example, we can safely predict that residential and recreational viewer groups will be concerned about the appearance of their visual environment. We also know that various federal laws and regulations impose what we may call the test of visual compatibility on projects located close to visual resources that are recognized for their cultural signficance. Where this recognition is based on "scenic values," effects on visual quality will be equally important.

Visual Impacts and Impact Management

The last group of questions is intended to summarize the major visual effects—adverse or beneficial—that are likely to be associated with project alternatives. It is also intended to help identify potential visual mitigation measures for study in the assessment process. Mitigation can include avoiding, minimizing, and reducing impacts, as well as rectifying them or compensating for them. A mitigation measure should be related to a specific impact, or it may not only be ineffective but also compound the problem. For example, a color chosen to enhance the appearance of a bridge may prove incompatible with the surroundings of the bridge.

Sample Scoping Questionnaire

To help, there is included a scoping questionnaire—an example for an urban freeway on new location for comparison.

Project Introduction

The project is a freeway spur that would provide access to the downtown core of a medium-sized western coastal city, as well as a bypass route for traffic bound to the north and east of the core. It includes a 1.3-mile link between a major interstate freeway to the south and a limited access parkway to the north, with two interchanges in the core itself. The north-south leg would be located along a waterway that is the eastern boundary of the urban core. The project also includes a 2.3-mile east-west connection across the waterway, leading to industrial port lands. Project alternatives include alignment options to reduce adverse effects on a redevelopment area along the waterway and on an historic rail station.

EXAMPLE 1: Highway Scoping Questionnaire

1. *Project Characteristics*
A. What are the major project design standards (capacity, access, speed, geometry)? Alternatives?

- Two travel lanes in each direction, with up to 50,000 total ADT
- Fully controlled access
- 50 miles per hour design speed on mainline, 35 on ramps
- Minimum radius curves can be used

B. What is the typical highway cross-section (roadway, roadside slopes and drainage, right-of-way)? What major structures and appurtenances will be required? Alternatives?

- Mainline (2-lane) roadways = 42 feet
- Ramp (1-lane) roadways = 28 feet
- Right-of-way = 120 to 400 feet
- Waterway and river crossings: 340 feet (45 feet clear) and 400 feet (52 feet clear)
- All of N-S roadways, much of E-W roadways elevated on structure over railroad tracks (23 feet clear)
- Balance of roadway elevated on fill, 1½:1 side slopes
- Lighting and sign bridges required

C. Are any highway-related facilities (such as rest areas or maintenance yards) part of the project? What construction areas (borrow pits, spoil areas) will be needed? Alternatives.

- Possible point-use beneath structures
- Potential uses include parking, outdoor storage, industrial use, and parks

D. What secondary effects (such as development at interchanges or conversion of land from rural to urban uses) may result from the project?

- Increased potential for redevelopment of downtown and adjacent waterway
- Possible urban deterioration immediately next to right-of-way

2. *Visual Environment of Project*

A. What landscape components (landform, water, vegetation, and manmade development) are characteristic of the regional landscape and the immediate project area?

- Landform: glacial terraces and small bluffs, estuarine deposits and landfill on valley floor
- Water, stream (partially culverted), river, waterway, sound
- Vegetation: weedy species on disturbed uplands, including blackberry and Scotch broom; lowland vegetation includes stands of red alder and black cottonwood;
- Manmade development: highrise office core, brick warehouse and railroad district, port industry, recreational marinas, hillside residential neighborhoods

B. Where is the project likely to be seen from?

- Existing city streets, existing freeway and parkway, and new highway itself
- Downtown core, historic warehouse and rail station district
- Waterway, new parks, new marinas
- Residential areas
- Industrial areas

C. What visually distinct landscape units or urban districts can be identified within the immediate project area?

- Downtown core, warehouse and rail station district, waterway district, port industry area

D. Which major viewer groups are likely to see the project?

- Commuters, office workers and shoppers, recreational boaters, neighborhood residents, industrial workers

3. *Significant Visual Resource Issues*

A. What landscape components are now present within the visual environment of the project and how would project alternatives change these?

- Landform: heavily modified hillside terraces and estuarine lowlands; little additional modification
- Water: stream valley at south end of corridor may be further disturbed; waterway and river would be crossed by bridges
- Vegetation: stands of trees in stream valley and on lowland floor may be reduced in size
- Manmade development: highway would require clearing some industrial buildings; brick warehouses would not be removed

B. What is the present visual character of the project environment (e.g., form, line, color, texture and dominance, scale, diversity, continuity) and how compatible would project alternatives be with this character?

Prominent aspects of existing character include:
- Form: hillside terraces and bluffs; buildings generally rectilinear, except rail station dome
- Line: horizontal bluff edges, rail lines, waterway shore, roofs of warehouses
- Diversity: very great, because of close juxtaposition of districts, and profusion of industrial structures and equipment
- Continuity: relatively low, due to demolition and high proportion of vacant land

Project alternatives may or may not visually interrupt rail station dome, bluff and shore edges; may further increase diversity and decrease continuity

C. What levels of visual quality now exist (evaluated by criteria such as vividness, intactness, and unity or by other indicators) and how much would project alternatives affect these?

Existing visual quality is low in foreground, moderated by good background views of sound and mountains
- Vividness: moderate due to rail station dome, waterway, towers in downtown core
- Intactness: low, due to demolition, vacant land, and lack of maintenance
- Unity: low, due to high diversity of development and lack of continuity

Project could adversely affect waterway and rail station; it could also improve intactness and unity, and thus improve overall visual quality significantly.

4. *Significant Viewer Response Issues*

A. What is the viewer exposure to project alternatives for different groups (numbers, distance, duration and speed of view, etc.) and how much would these alternatives block important existing views?

View from road: improved visibility of downtown for entering drivers (up to 50,000 daily); view duration approximately 30 seconds

View of road:
- Neighborhood residents—several thousand, middle-ground to background, permanent view
- Recreational boaters—several hundred (may increase significantly in future), foreground, intermittent view

- Office workers and shoppers—several tens of thousands, foreground, intermittent view
- Industrial workers—several thousand, middleground to background, intermittent view

Project may block views between rail station and waterway, downtown and waterway

B. How are viewer activity and awareness likely to affect the attention that different groups pay to the project and its visual environment?

View from the road: drivers will have clearer orientation, limited ability to focus on foreground
View of the road:
- Residents may have high concern about effect of road on views
- Recreational boaters and users of waterway, redevelopment area may also have high concern
- Office workers and shoppers probably will have moderate to low concern
- Industrial workers may be expected to have low concern

C. Are there any visual resources in the project environment that are particularly important to local viewers? Are there any districts, sites, or features that are regionally or nationally recognized for their cultural significance?

- Rail station is on National Register and is important to community
- Warehouse district around it is also important to community and may be eligible for Register
- Waterway views are valued, where available
- Tree stands in lowlands and in stream valley at south end of north-south leg are important to environmental groups

D. Is the project thought to threaten or support expectations for the future appearance of any areas it traverses? How might viewer response be affected by superior project design or the incorporation of art?

Community is divided:
- Businessmen and most city officials anticipate project improving visibility of downtown and contributing to revitalization; project design could enhance downtown
- Widespread community concern over possible adverse visual effects on historic rail station and warehouse district; compatible design could reduce concerns
- Additional concern over possible adverse visual effects on redevelopment of waterway for commercial and recreation use

5. *Visual Impacts and Impact Management*

A. In summary, what significant visual impacts, if any, appear likely? Include both adverse and beneficial impacts.

Beneficial effects (potential):
- Improved visibility of downtown core
- Improved visual quality of city entry

Adverse effects (potential):
- Lower visibility of rail station and waterway
- Visual incompatibility between elevated road, rail station area, and waterway redevelopment
- Decreased visual quality of expected views of rail station area and waterway redevelopment (present views are low in visual quality)

B. What alternatives might avoid, minimize, or reduce any adverse visual impacts and by how much?

- Minimum profile elevated road could considerably decrease obstruction of views from rail station and waterway areas
- Lower profile could enhance compatibility of elevated road by making it appear continuous with bluff edge of first terrace

C. What actions might rectify or compensate for adverse visual impacts and by how much?

- Structural concepts, landscape and development, and joint-use alternatives may enhance visual compatibility of elevated road somewhat and greatly improve general visual quality over present condition.

HUD Threshold Approach

The variety of factors that influence the individual's perception of the surrounding visual scene may be said to define visual quality. Good quality should provide the individual with a sense of place and should contribute to the individual's ability to orient himself or herself in space. Because of the highly perceptual and subjective nature of this component, it is perhaps one of the most difficult aspects of the environment to analyze and measure.

In terms of visual quality, the perceptions of the project residents, as well as those of the existing area residents, must be considered. This requires a determination of how the project relates to the existing visual quality and an analysis of resident satisfaction with the visual quality of the surrounding area (see Tables 9.4 and 9.5).

Subcomponents

Visual content
Area and structure coherence
Apparent access

Visual Content

Description

Visual content refers to the structures and spaces of an area which provide input information for the

TABLE 9.4. Visual quality assessment summary table

1	2	3	4	5	6	7
Subcomponent	Goals/ Objectives	Impacts	Necessary Information	Methodology	Findings/ Measurements	Standard/ Guidelines
Visual Content	Sense of time and place; social and civic attachment.	Will the content of the visual scene perceived by the residents of the surrounding area be adversely affected by the project? Will the visual content of the surrounding area have an adverse effect on project residents?	Project plans; site observations; signing; building design characteristics; pictorial images, etc.	Photographic analysis of intrusion; semantic differential techniques; standard classification for landscape analysis; open ended questions.	Analyst defined scales of visual intrusion, design compatibility, urban character, etc.	
Area and Structural Coherence	Clarity of area structure; sense of harmony; integration of activities.	Will the coherence of the surrounding area be reduced by the project action?	Plan, building and landscape descriptions; visual observations.	Descriptive evaluation; sketch mapping	Activity-image map, judgment of coherence	
Apparent Access	Access to activities and areas	Will the project obscure or eliminate access information required for the use of activities and areas?	Visual observations; project plan.	Descriptive evaluation of observed diversity of activity; access to window displays, etc.; question users.	Judgment of access to activities and areas of interest and use.	

Notes: (L. Min)—Legal Minimum Allowable   (Reco)—Recommended, a Goal
(L. Max)—Legal Maximum Allowable   (Ave)—Average or "Rule-of-Thumb" Guide
Source: Planning Environment International, 1975.

individual to use in structuring his or her perceptions. This information contributes to the development of a sense of place and provides markers for use in orientation. In this way, visual content is closely related to area coherence and apparent access—the two other subcomponents of visual quality.

Impact

Will the content of the visual scene perceived by the residents of the surrounding area be adversely affected by the project?
Will the visual content of the surrounding area have an adverse effect on project residents?

Scale of Impact

A+   There will be an improvement or positive impact on the visual content of an area.
A   There will be no effective change in the perceived visual content of the project or from the project.
B   There will be changes in content but mitigative action can reduce or alleviate the problem.
C   Overall visual content will definitely be reduced by the project action.
C−   N.A. (Generally accepted standards have not been developed).

TABLE 9.5. Visual quality: types of environmental information necessary for assessment

Subcomponent	Initial Screening Test		Higher Level Tests	
	Informational Needs	Source	Informational Needs	Specialist
Visual Content	Description of views before and after project; description of potential views from outside project looking in; description of potential views from inside project looking out.	Site visit; 1"–100' scale maps of existing site area; photos of site with project drawn in.	Judgment of residents and users of area. Results of semantic differential techniques. Further description of content.	Small groups of residents. Environmental psychologist. Urban designer; architect; landscape architect.
Area and Structure Coherence	Extent to which project area has formal coherence as described by qualities of "articulation, direction, landmarks, clarity, harmony, and rhythm". Project plan.	Site visit; area residents. Developer.	Opinion of residents and design professional; opinion of design professional.	Small groups of residents, architect; urban designer; landscape architect.
Apparent Access	Major access and linkages of project to surrounding area. Any qualities which improve apparent access such as: —Visible points of entry and exit —Lack of visual or apparent physical barriers —Lack of conflicting activities —Inviting spaces.	Site visit; site plan; existing land use map. Site visit; site plan.	Opinion of design professional.	Architect; urban designer; landscape architect.

Source: Planning Environment International, 1975.

Initial Screening Test

(Note: The nature of the analysis allows the concerns of project on environment and environment on project to be addressed jointly.)

1. Review appropriately scaled maps (preferably 1" = 100' scale) of the existing area surrounding the site and site plans for the project. Walk around the site and surrounding area, preferably with project plans in hand.

2. Describe the following:
   Views before and after the project. Use photographs of the area or neutral drawings derived from them with the new project drawn in.

Views from outside the project looking in.
Views from inside the project looking out.

Descriptions of views from several points in and around the project should be made. Observation points should be indicated, visually or with photographs, on a map or plan with the direction of the view indicated by arrows. Observations may then be described verbally or through the use of simple diagrams (see Figures 9.15 and 9.16).

3. The evaluation of environmental impact relative to visual content will be made in terms of changes in the quality of these views. A positive (beneficial) impact occurs if the project screens objectionable objects from view, presents informative or appealing vistas, or helps to improve the definition of spaces or areas in the surrounding environment. A negative (adverse) impact occurs if existing pleasant vistas are blocked, unpleasant views are created, or if views become less defined. The lack of strict criteria or standards means that judgment will be required in assessing the results of the tests. If a rating of A$^+$ or A cannot be given based on the supporting descriptions, higher-level-tests should be done.
4. If there are adverse effects which can be ameliorated by changing the project design or plan, the project should be rated B.

VIEW OF TOWER BLOCKED, FACTORY BUILDING IN FOREGROUND

TOWER MORE FULLY REVEALED, ADDITIONAL SKYLINE, LANDSCAPING IN FOREGROUND

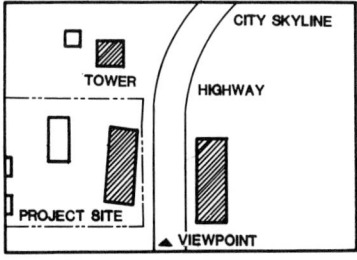

PLAN VIEW

FIGURE 9.15. Observing image content before and after project implemenatation. *Source:* Planning Environmental International, 1975.

Higher-Level Tests

The judgment of the residents or users of an area should be solicited. The pictorial data—photographs and drawings—developed during the initial screening tests can be used to help the residents or users gain a sense of the proposed change. A simple interview or semantic differential techniques could be helpful in describing the judgments and opinions of the residents or users. An environmental psychologist should be consulted for administration of the semantic differential technique. Using that technique, individuals are asked to rate a situation on a scale of distinct steps between terms describing extremes, such as very pleasant ... very unpleasant. Correlation analyses are then made to attempt to identify what it is about the situation which leads to the judgment.

Area and Structure Coherence

Description

Coherence refers to the degree to which the internal organizing framework of an area or structure can be perceived by the users so that they can move freely within it. Coherence also refers to the success with which buildings or spaces are integrated. As examples, buildings or open spaces which are out of scale and spaces which offer no guidance as to location or movement through them will generally be considered unsatisfactory by the people using them.

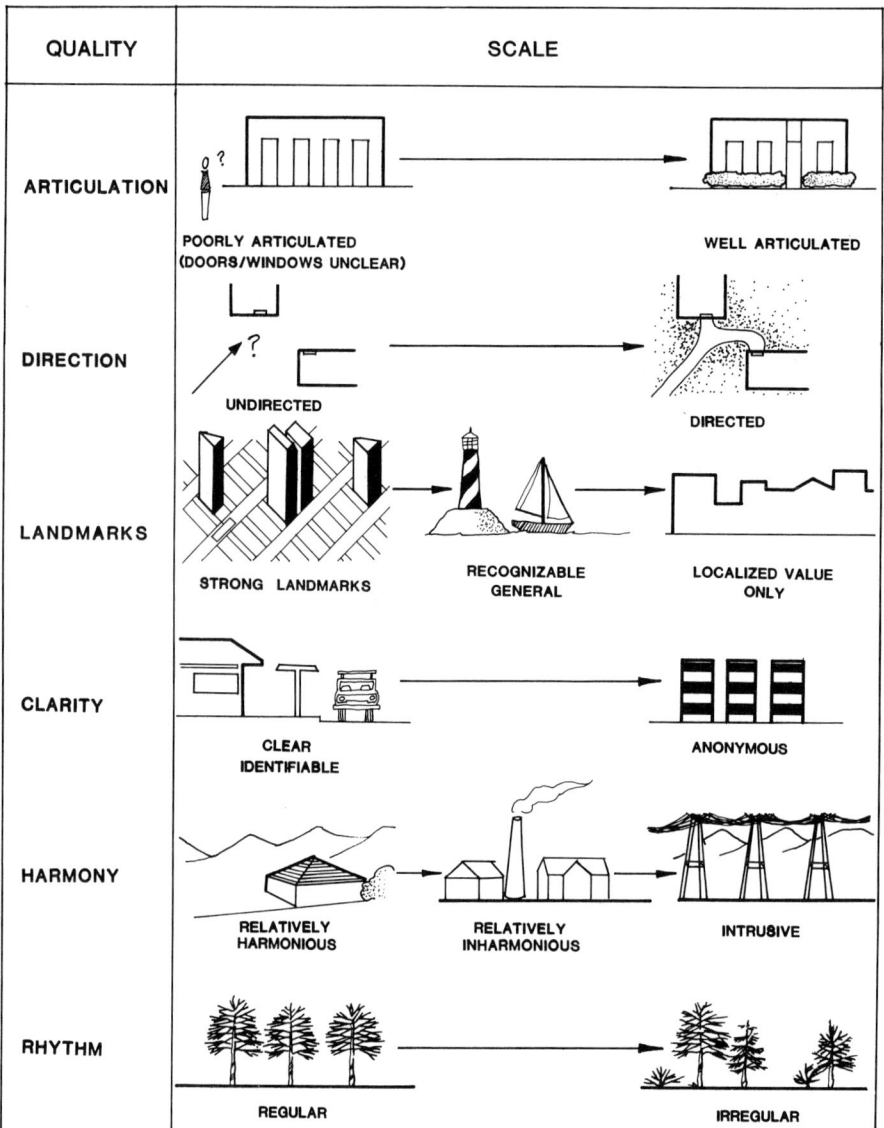

FIGURE 9.16. Qualities describing coherence. *Source:* Planning Environmental International, 1975.

Impact

Will the coherence of the surrounding area be reduced by the project action?

Scale of Impact

A+ The project itself is coherent and will improve the coherence of the surrounding area.

A There is no notable visual conflict between the project and its surroundings which might reduce coherence.

B There is likely to be some loss of coherence due to the project action; however, mitigative measures can be taken.

C There is likely to be a loss of coherence due to the project action. No mitigative measures are planned.

C− N.A. (Generally accepted standards have not been developed).

Initial Screening Test

1. Through site vistas and the examination of proposed project plans, describe the extent to which the surroundings of the project have coherence. Table 9.5 provides a framework for this description. Photographs, discussion with area residents, and construction of maps using methods described by Lynch (1960) may assist and support this description.
2. Note any aspects of the project plan which are likely to cause changes on the scales suggested in Table 9.5. Careful consideration should be given to projects which represent a definite change in land use type or intensity.
3. Judgment will be required to address the critical concern. If a rating of A+ or A cannot be given and supported by reasonable argument, higher-level tests should be done.

Higher-Level Tests

Higher-level tests will require securing the opinions of residents or users. The services of a professional such as an urban designer, architect, or landscape architect may also be of assistance.

Apparent Access

Description

The organization of spaces and buildings and the design of the building themselves influence the individual's perception of his or her access to the associated activities and spaces. An environment which is interesting and enjoyable is one which invites the individual to explore. Apparent access refers to the extent to which an area or structure provides information to the individual on approaching and moving through it so that the structure or area can be used or experienced.

Impact

Will the project obscure or eliminate access information required for the use of activities and areas?

Scale of Impact

A+	There are measures taken to improve the apparent access to a variety of activities.
A	There is no serious diminution of apparent access to a variety of activities.
B	There are conflicts of apparent access which may prevent a variety of activities, but modifications can be made which will enhance the accessibility.
C	There is a definite conflict between apparent access as compared to actual physical access.
C−	N.A. (Generally accepted standards have not been developed).

Initial Screening Test

1. Using a plan of the project and its surroundings, identify the major access and linkages which should exist. For example, pedestrians should be clearly invited to walk through commercial areas. Note should also be made of linkages and activities which are undesirable. For example, in a pedestrian mall it might not be desirable to include provision for direct access of automobiles.
2. Based upon site visits and examination of project plans, judge the apparent access which is actually afforded using the examples given in Table 9.6 for assessing the quality

TABLE 9.6. Evaluation of Apparent Access

Qualities Improving Apparent Access	Illustrations
Visible points of entrance/exit	Doors
	Openings between buildings
Lack of visual or apparent physical barriers	Roads that are not heavily travelled
	Low shrubbery or lawn areas
	No fence and walls
Lack of conflicting activity	Sidewalks with room for window shopping
	Buffered noisy activities
Inviting spaces	Well-lighted interior
	Attractive features such as open space, fountains, park benches

Source: Planning Environment International.

and clarity of the access information that is given.
3. A listing of opportunities for apparent access should be made and an overall assessment made. If the project does not qualify for an A^+ or A rating, higher-level tests should be done.

Higher-Level Tests

The judgment of a qualified design professional (urban designer, architect, or landscape architect) should be employed.

DETAILED VISUAL IMPACT ASSESSMENT

There is one additional component to visual resource management systems. This additional component is a means of assessing the severity of visual impact or the capability of specific landscape sites to absorb visual impact. BLM has used its contrast rating procedure for this purpose, and the Forest Service has developed a process entitled Visual Absorption Capability or VAC (Anderson et al. 1979), and the Federal Highway Administration has a visual impact guidance procedure. The philosophical precepts behind the development of these three subsystems are quite different. VAC is used to determine how much can be done to a landscape site before its visual absorption capability is exceeded. Contrast rating is used by BLM (1980), on the other hand, is used to determine whether a proposed change to the landscape would cause an acceptable or unacceptable level of contrast with that specific site according to professional judgment. The Federal Highway Administration system is different because it advocates public reactions to visual impact from simulations.

VAC combines physical factors of the existing landscape, highly changeable perceptual factors, existing visual quality factors (form, line, color, texture), and proposed activities factors (scale, configuration, duration, frequency, and so forth) to determine the VAC score for that particular landscape (see Figure 9.17). A low VAC score is very restrictive, and a high score means much more activity can be allowed. The VAC score range is then compared to the existing visual management objective(s) already determined for that area (see Figure 9.18).

The contrast rating procedure as used by BLM operates in the following manner:

1. The landscape character as expressed by land features or water bodies, vegetation, and structures is described in terms of form, line, color, and texture.
2. The proposed activity for that particular locale is described in terms of form, line, color, and texture introduced or modified.
3. A contrast rating is then made by multiplying preestablished numerical values of form, line, color, and texture *for* land/water bodies, vegetation, and structures *by* the estimated degree of contrast (strong-3, moderate-2, weak-1, none-0) to yield subtotals of contrast for land/water texture, vegetation, and structures (see Figure 9.19).
4. If the contrast ratings exceed "allowable" levels set according to the BLM Manual, then the project feature/element of greatest contrast is to be redesigned, the basic presumption being in most cases that too much contrast is "bad" or "not desirable."
5. The process is then repeated after the redesign.

This process is useful in that it provides a record of the landscape as is and the landscape with the proposed project. It can be used to document which physical portion of the project needs to be reworked or redesigned, for example, landfill cuts reduced, less vegetation disturbed, structures reduced in size, and so forth. If mitigation measures are not implemented, it can provide the legal documentation for taking action to ensure the mitigating actions are implemented. Thus from an administrative procedural point of view, the process provides many advantages.

For Highway Projects

The approach suggested by U.S.D.O.T. (1981) here is flexible but is also strongly related to the elements of visual experience. There are five general steps in this approach:

Define the visual environment of the project.
Analyze existing visual resources and viewer response.

Factors		Variables	Rating	Viewpoints		
				V1	V2	V3
Observer Position	Superior	+300' – +500'	1			
	Normal	+100' – +300'	2	2	2	
		±100'	3			
		−100' – −300'	4			
	Inferior	−300' – −500'	5			
Observer Distance	Foreground	0 – ¼ mi.	1			
		¼ – ½ mi.	2			
	Middle-ground	½ – 1 mi.	3	3	3	
		1 – 2 mi.	4			4
	Background	2+				
View Duration	Long	30+ sec.	1		1	
		10 – 30 sec.	1		1	
	Short	5 – 10 sec.	3			3
		3 – 5 sec.	4	4		
	Glimpse	0 – 3 sec.	5			
Landscape Description		Feature	1			
		Focal	2			2
		Enclosed	3	3	3	
		Panoramic	4			
		Other	5			
Slope	Very Steep	45+%	1			
	Steep	00 – 45%	2			
	Moderate	20 – 30%	3			
	Gentle	10 – 20%	4			
	Very Gentle	0 – 10%	5	5	5	5
Lowest rating is the Key Viewpoint				17	14	18

Summary

Visual Absorption Capability

5–13 Low
14–16 Intermediate
17–23 High

FIGURE 9.17. Rating system devised for development of visual absorption capability.

REVIEW OF AGENCY METHODOLOGY FOR VISUAL PROJECT ANALYSIS

LANDSCAPE MANAGEMENT GUIDE MATRIX					
I-Most Restrictive ↓ V-Least Restrictive		VISUAL QUALITY OBJECTIVE			
		Retention	Partial Retention	Modification	Maximum Modification
Visual Absorption Capability	Low	I	II	III	V
	Intermediate	I	III	IV	V
	High	II	III	IV	V

FIGURE 9.18. Matrix for identification of appropriate landscape management guides.

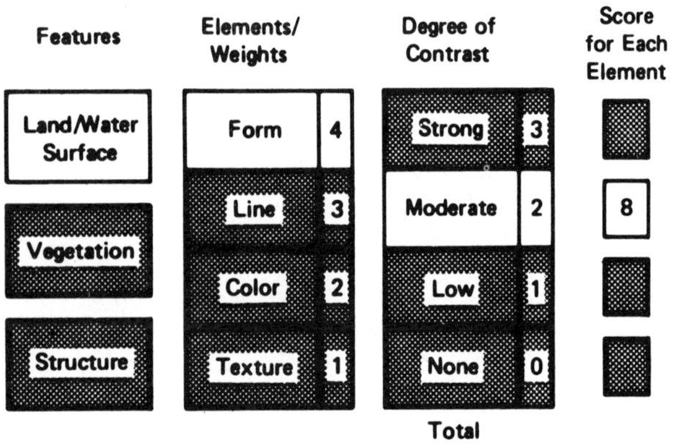

FIGURE 9.19. BLM's contrast rating system. *Source:* USDI, BLM, 1980a, Visual Resource Management, U.S. Government Printing Office, Washington, DC, 30.

Depict the visual appearance of project alternatives.

Assess the visual impacts of project alternatives.

Determine ways to mitigate adverse visual impacts.

In practice, the content of these steps will depend on the visual issues specific to a project. Special considerations are the linear dynamic experience of the driver and/or passenger, which complicates the VIA analysis. More detailed treatment of VIA procedures is presented in Chapters 12 and 13.

SUMMARY

In summary, visual resource management systems were designed by these agencies to:

FS, BLM, SCS	1. Inventory and simultaneously evaluate visual landscape quality based on primarily physical landscape factors with aesthetic modifiers (form, line, color, texture).
FS, BLM, SCS, FHWA	2. Inventory amount of use of the landscape, travel through the landscape, or attitudes towards the landscape, indicating degree of sensitivity.
FS, BLM, SCS, FHWA	3. Map degree of visibility or distance zones from which the landscape can be seen.
FS, BLM	4. Combine this information to establish appropriate levels of management of visual quality. Under these management levels, certain intensities and types of activities are allowed or not allowed.
SCS	In SCS's case, priorities for appropriate level of professional involvement are established.
FHWA, HUD	5. Assess whether significant visual impact may occur.
FS, BLM, FHWA	6. Assess visual impact absorption limits or thresholds to severity of visual impact allowed for specific landscape sites and provide guidance for ameliorative redesign or change in location of the impacting activity.
FS, BLM, SCS, FHWA, HUD	7. Integrate all of the above into appropriate levels and times of environmental decision making.

CHAPTER 10

THE ASSESSMENT OF LANDSCAPE QUALITY: MAJOR METHODOLOGICAL CONSIDERATIONS

Joanne Vining and Joseph J. Stevens

The authors gratefully acknowledge the contribution made by Dr. Terry Daniel to the development of the conceptual basis of this chapter.

INTRODUCTION

Numerous methodological approaches have been applied to the assessment of the landscape, but they differ in scope, purpose, logic, and utility. The purpose of this chapter is to provide an overview of those methods. Several general categories of assessment methods will be distinguished, defined, and evaluated. The primary emphasis in this chapter is on the assessment of *perceived* landscape quality via observer-based measures.

Landscapes are managed for two basic purposes: to obtain certain tangible commodities or products from the land, such as water, timber, or forage, and for production of intangible commodities. These "intangibles" may be divided into two classes—symbolic and aesthetic. The landscape, or some particular landscape feature, can serve as a symbol or representation of some entity that has value. For example, a mountainous landscape might represent a challenge for one person or a mystical experience for another. Other symbolic goals for landscape management are the so-called "existence values." That is, even though a wilderness area, wildlife preserve, or urban forest might rarely be contacted directly, the knowledge that it exists is an important symbolic value for many.

The aesthetic value of a landscape is embodied in its visual merit. Of course, there is considerable overlap between symbolic and aesthetic values. Symbolic values may interact with the perception of the visual quality of a scene (Anderson 1981), or, conversely, aesthetic quality may enhance the symbolic image. However, symbolic values are not dependent on the features of a specific landscape: symbolism transcends the immediate experience of the landscape. On the other hand, aesthetic values are linked to the experience of a particular landscape at a specific time and therefore involve a more direct interaction between a person and particular landscape features.

Traditionally, two approaches have been taken in assessing landscape aesthetics. Arthur, Daniel, and Boster (1977) termed these two approaches the descriptive inventory and public preference models. The descriptive model, also called the formal aesthetic model by Daniel and Vining (1983), assumes that aesthetics are inherent in the landscape so that a description of landscape characteristics can presumably provide an evaluation of its aesthetic quality. Descriptive approaches typically rely on the standards of trained experts (Smardon Chapter 9 this volume) and do not assess the perceptions of the public (Palmer, this volume; Daniel and Vining 1983; Arthur et al. 1977; Zube, Sell, and Taylor 1982).

Arthur et al. (1977) questioned the validity of the assumptions of descriptive models and suggested that an assessment approach based on the preferences of the general public is more practical and appropriate. Daniel and Vining (1983) echoed this concern and further stated that the concept *landscape quality* requires human perceptual and judgmental processes, preferably those of the general public. The conceptual basis for the public preference approach to landscape quality assessment is diagrammed in Figure 10.1. This model views design or the assessment processes as a function of the characteristics of the environment, the actions of designers and managers, plus the needs, demands, and perceptions of the observing public or user. This is in contrast to the descriptive approach in which only the environmental characteristics and activities of designers or managers are explicitly considered.

The user-based or public preference approach explicitly incorporates the viewpoint of the public. More importantly, it provides a double feedback loop represented by the clockwise and counterclockwise circles of arrows in Figure 10.1. In the inner counterclockwise loop, management actions produce changes in the environment which elicit perceptions and judgments of the landscape from the observing public. These perceptions and judgments then constitute feedback to the manager regarding the landscape, thus affecting future designs and plans. The outer clockwise loop represents a similar feedback system operating in a different direction. Here, the actions of the public produce certain environmental effects which then influence the manager's perception of environmental capacities and constraints. The manager then completes the feedback loop to the public through education and communication regarding the environmental consequences of users' behavior, thereby affecting their behavior. This model, which explicity and overtly incorporates the actions, perceptions, and judgments of the public in the design or assessment process, forms the conceptual basis for the landscape quality assessment methods presented in this chapter.

INTRODUCTION

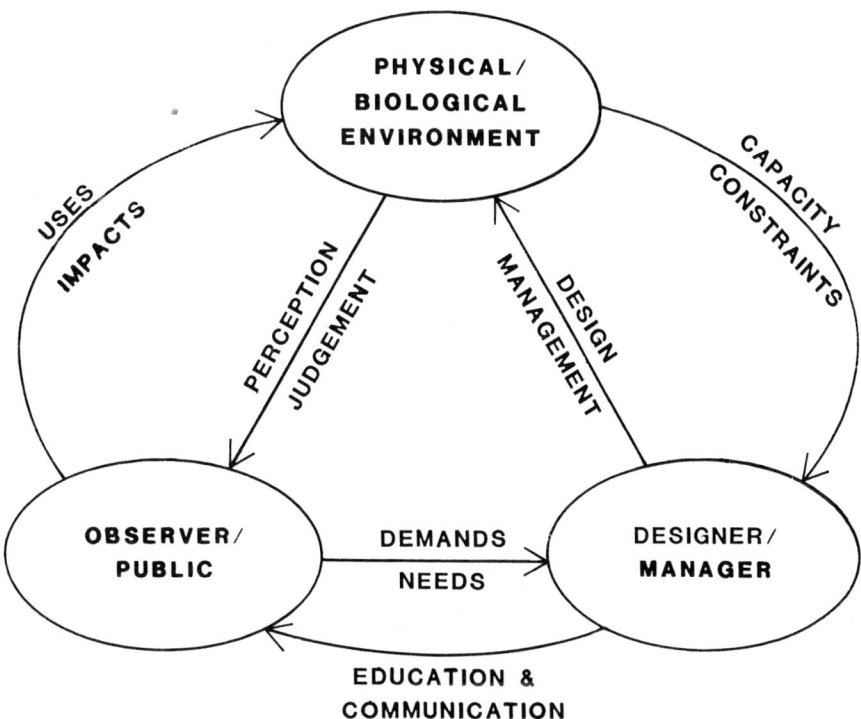

FIGURE 10.1. Public preference model of landscape quality assessment.

There are several reasons why a conceptual link is needed between the user or observer of the landscape, designers and managers, and the landscape itself. First, understanding the interaction between people and environments is important, regardless of whether immediate applications or requirements exist. As with other areas of basic science, the study of this interaction may yield useful information or lead to unexpected gains in more utilitarian applications.

A second reason is legal. The National Environmental Policy Act of 1969 and other legislation addressing specific actions or agencies require the evaluation of the aesthetic effects of most land management decisions (see Smardon et al. Chapter 2 this volume). Evaluation of scenic consequences is often done by landscape professionals, but the addition of user-based landscape quality assessment may be advisable. Legal challenges of management decisions are commonplace. Systematic assessment of the public's perception of scenic effects of landscape management and design enables more informed planning decisions, provides important communication and educational messages for the public, and may help to circumvent costly legal battles.

Although fulfilling legal requirements and decreasing the number of angry, court-bound citizens are worthy reasons for the assessment of perceived landscape quality, a more compelling ethical reason also exists. Public lands are held in trust for all citizens and should be managed with their best interests in mind. User-based assessment of perceived landscape quality is therefore one way of obtaining public opinions that may be used in the formation of policy or in environmental planning decisions. Participation of the public has been mandated legally; for the responsible planner it is also an ethical mandate.

A fourth reason for obtaining systematic assessments of public landscape preference is to improve the design or planning process. Like the postoccupancy evaluation in architecture, a postmanagement evaluation of landscape quality can provide useful feedback to planners. This information may then be used to avoid past errors, imitate past successes, and plan new projects more intelligently, responsibly, and responsively. The public preference model of landscape quality assessment provides a conceptual basis from which assessment methods may be generated, utilized, and evaluated.

It is important for landscape designers and planners to understand these methods in order to (1) conduct their own assessment for planning and evaluation purposes, and (2) properly interpret the results of assessments conducted by others. The remainder of this chapter will review major procedural and methodological issues that should be considered when attempting to assess perceived landscape quality or to evaluate the assessment efforts of others.

ASSESSMENT METHODS

Assessment of landscape quality is a three-step process. The first phase entails the design and planning of the assessment. The second phase consists of the actual measurement procedures: characteristics of interest, whether they be attitudes, judgments, or perceptions, are systematically assessed. The third stage of landscape quality assessment involves drawing inferences about measurement data collected in the second phase. For example, one might measure attitudes or perceptions of a specific group in a particular environment and then attempt to make inferences to other groups or environments. In this section three measurement methods will be described: the survey or questionnaire, perceptual preference assessment, and behavioral measures. The following section will describe four assessment designs which allow varying degrees of inferential power.

To unify this discussion, the problem of determining a site for a nuclear power plant will be used as an illustrative example. Assessment of public preference for such a plant would obviously enhance the planning process and might also defuse opposition to the project. When appropriate, Petrich's (1979) study of nuclear power plant sites will be used as a case study. Otherwise, a similar hypothetical nuclear plant project will serve as an example.

Surveys and Questionnaires

Surveys and questionnaires have been a very popular means of assessing the opinions, attitudes, and perceptions of the general public and can be very useful for probing complex management options or issues. Generally, a series of questions is submitted in written or oral form to a sample of people representative of those likely to experience the impact of the proposed management action. Surveys and questionnaires are deceptively easy to compose and distribute, and are often used when other methods might be more appropriate. The correct use of surveys and questionnaires, however, demands consideration of many issues, only a few of which are described here. Dillman (1978) provides a thorough discussion of the issues involved in the use of surveys or questionnaires.

Sampling is a critical issue for users of surveys and questionnaires. It must be determined in advance which people will be the appropriate respondents. For our nuclear plant example one might survey all those who might benefit from lower rates or better service, or residents of a geographic area surrounding the proposed development. Once the appropriate population is identified, a sampling procedure may be used to select the respondents. A basic rule is that results may be generalized only to those individuals who in principle had an equal chance of being included in the survey sample.

A related issue critical to survey administration is the proportion of responses received from sampled individuals. Phone surveys generally result in high response rates, but may discriminate against people who do not own phones. Surveys distributed through the mail or onsite may, for various reasons unknown to the surveyor, not be returned. For example, a questionnaire might be lost and therefore not returned by an interested individual, or not returned because an individual is disinterested. Those surveys that are returned may then constitute a biased sample and the surveyor will have no idea of the reason for or direction of the bias.

Interviews are perhaps the most effective means of administering surveys primarily because personal contact usually results in a higher response rate. Furthermore, the interviewer may probe for explanations of ambiguous or intriguing responses. However, because of this personal contact, and the unique interactions between particular respondents and surveys, the results of interviews may vary and often differ substantially from those obtained from identical written surveys.

Survey questions may be phrased in many different ways, any of which may introduce bias. For example, the management option preferred by the surveyor may be presented in a favorable light, or the wording of the questions may constrain or preclude some responses. Relatively subtle differences in labeling of stimulus scenes (Anderson 1981) and in emphasis of problem issues (Vining 1983) have been shown to influence responses to judgmental or problem-solving tasks similar to those in the public participation process. For instance, asking for a response to *neighborhood noise* could produce a different answer than a question about *neighborhood sound quality*.

EXAMPLE 1: Methods and Procedures of Response Measurement

This section will briefly describe several of the most common procedures for quantifying the response of the observer. Each of the methods is characterized by certain advantages and disadvantages. The actual performance of each method, however, is largely dependent on the specific procedures used to implement the method in the particular assessment application. The utility and interpretability of the method is also dependent on the manner in which the resulting observer responses are analyzed (Example 4 presents one such analysis method). A more complete discussion and comparison of different response methods can be found in Baird and Noma (1978), Engen (1971), Hake and Rodwan (1966), and Torgerson (1958).

The central purpose of the different response methods is to provide an observable indicator or response from which a scale of measurement may be derived. It is possible to use "direct" response scales similar to the measurements that might be performed in physics. For example, the observer might judge the length of an object by reporting its length proportional to a second object used as a standard. The observer's judgment of length would represent a "direct" psychological scale of length. Often, however, direct scales of measurement are neither feasible nor attainable. This often occurs when the property to be measured has no immediately definable physical scale. For example, a concept such as beauty does not automatically suggest a physical measure of beauty. Many response methods are an attempt to provide an indirect scale of measurement that allows the quantitative representation of the observer's response where no other scale is available.

The Method of Paired Comparisons. This response method consists of the systematic pairing of objects or stimuli. As each pair is presented, the observer makes a judgment indicating which member of the pair has a greater value of some attribute. For example, scenic beauty of several landscapes might be assessed by presenting pairs of landscape scenes to the observer. On each presentation, the observer would indicate which scene is perceived to have greater scenic beauty.

The method of paired comparisons is a relatively simple task for the observer. Only two environmental stimuli or objects must be judged on a given occasion and the simultaneity of judgment often allows the observer to make fine discriminations among objects. Usually, all possible pairs of the objects ($N[N-1]/2$ pairs) are presented to the observer in a random order. The number of pairs increases rapidly as more objects are used in the task and, therefore, the method is cumbersome when many objects are judged. Analysis of observers' responses typically involves the calculation of the proportion of times each object was judged as "greater" than every other object. These proportions are then transformed to standardized values that represent the scaled judgments of the objects (Torgerson 1958).

Categorical Rating Scales. The most common response procedure is the rating method. This method requires the observer to choose which of a number of categories best reflects his or her perception of objects or stimuli presented one at a time. The observer's rating of the object may be expressed by numerical or nominal categories. In practice many rating scales combine a numerical scale with nominal adjectives that describe some or all of the numerical categories. For example, a landscape view might be presented to the observer whose task would be to rate the scenic beauty of the landscape on one of the following scales.

Low Beauty   High Beauty
1   2   3   4   5   6   7   8   9   10

Very Low Scenic Beauty	Low Scenic Beauty	Neutral	High Scenic Beauty	Very High Scenic Beauty
1	2	3	4	5

Rating methods are also commonly used for the assessment of attitudes, beliefs, or statements. For example, a survey might incorporate the rating method by asking the respondent to rate his or her agreement with a particular statement:

Preservation of the natural landscape is very important to me.

Agree Strongly	Agree	Disagree	Disagree Strongly
1	2	3	4

The number of rating categories should probably be limited to 10 or fewer. There is some disagreement as to whether a neutral middle point should be included in the scale. It has been argued that the omission of a neutral center category forces the observer to make a more definite choice, resulting in a more reliable measurement. Others have argued that omission of the neutral point results in the use of two interior categories of the scale as a neutral point, thereby reducing the true number of categories (Tzeng 1983). Whether a neutral category is used depends on the nature of the observers, the task, and the stimuli to be rated. If, for example, very fine distinctions must be made, a neutral category might be overused, resulting in decreased reliability. The type of labels associated with the rating categories can also influence the observer's response (Lam and Klockars 1982). Caution should therefore be exercised in the construction and design of rating scales. It is also important to use a method of analysis that incorporates some standard of comparison or scaling of the obtained ratings. Without such a procedure, it is difficult to interpret how high a rating is "high" (Daniel and Boster 1976; Torgerson 1958). Overall, however, the method of rating is relatively easy to administer and is quite tractable for inclusion in a wide range of assessment procedures and designs.

Sorting Methods. A number of procedures have been used in which the observer arranges several objects or stimuli into piles or categories. These procedures are quite similar to the method of rating in that the observer assigns each object to a particular category. The sorting procedures differ from rating methods in that the procedure usually entails the direct physical manipulation of placing objects into the piles. The piles or categories may be labeled as in the rating methods. For example, several landscape scenes might be sorted by the observer into five piles, ranging from pile 1, low aesthetic value, to pile 5, high aesthetic value. Or one might ask the observer to sort scenes based on his or her own idea of intrinsic differences between them. The sorting procedures usually require that all objects are available throughout the sorting process. In some sense, the observer's task involves the simultaneous comparison of all objects. As a result, sorting procedures often become quite difficult for the observer as the number of objects sorted becomes large.

A useful variation of the sorting procedure that facilitates the analysis of observer's responses has been used by Pitt and Zube (1979). This procedure requires that a certain number of objects are sorted into each pile or category. This standardizes the sorting process so that every observer creates categories of equal size, thereby facilitating the analysis of responses.

The Method of Magnitude Estimation. This method represents the most direct approach to the scaling of the observer's perceptions. The observer examines an object or stimulus and assigns a number to his or her perception of the object on a stated attribute. For example, the observer might be instructed to assess the scenic beauty of a series of landscape scenes and to provide a numeric estimation of the scenic quality of each scene. No constraints are placed on the range of the numbers the observer may assign. This procedure is sometimes altered by first presenting the observer with a standard object that is assigned a predetermined value or anchor. For example, a standard landscape might be presented to the observer with the instruction that the scene represented a "100." The observer would then be instructed to judge the magnitude of all other objects given that the standard was a "100." Use of such an anchor, however, usually influences the rest of the magnitudes obtained from the observer.

With the method of magnitude estimation, a wide range of objects are presented to the observer, one at a time, in random order. The method is also used most commonly when the observer's judgments can be compared with a corresponding physical continuum, such as particulate air pollution. Since different observers are certain to assign different values and ranges of values to the objects, analysis of observers' responses should include some form of standardization of the estimates.

The response given by a survey participant depends on the way in which the question is worded. There are two basic formats for survey questions: open-ended and closed-ended. An open-ended question elicits a more variable response from the participant. For example, a participant at a public forum might be asked what he thinks of a proposed nuclear power plant development near his home, and why he feels as he does. A closed-ended question narrows the response ahead of time. A participant might be asked to rank several alternatives in order of attractiveness or suitability, or to specify which of several alternatives she favors. Open-ended questions provide rich information at the cost of coding, analyzing, and interpreting those data. Because responses are more variable, they may be difficult to interpret. Closed-ended questions provide more precise and analyzable information, but at the expense of constraining the respondents' answers. For example, if a respondent is asked only to choose one of three sites for a nuclear power plant, the surveyor will not know why or with what level of conviction the response was made. Open-ended questions are optimal in pilot studies where issues must be identified. After this point, closed-ended questions should primarily be used, but questions must be written carefully and tested to ensure they measure the intended information.

A final issue with survey and questionnaire use is the distinction between attitudes and behavior. Briefly, the nature of this distinction is that people occasionally will behave contrary to, or at least not strictly in accordance with, their expressed attitudes and beliefs. For example, a respondent may indicate that conservation is preferable to any new power plant, but fail to use conservation or alternative energy systems at home. The nature of this distinction is complex, and research on the issue is equivocal at this point (Bell, Fisher, and Loomis 1978). The best approach is to employ more than one method for collecting data, and to interpret data cautiously. That is, an attitudinal survey is not necessarily a direct indication of the behavior of respondents.

EXAMPLE 2: Psychophysics and the Representation of the Observer's Response

Several of the methods of landscape assessment can be traced to the methods of *psychophysics*. Psychophysics is the study of the relationship between the occurrence of environmental events (the *physical* world) and the resultant perceptual response (the psychological world) of the observer. To the extent that we rely on the perceptions of the observer in landscape assessment, the methods of psychophysics are particularly relevant.

In analyzing and interpreting the observer's perceptual response, it is often assumed that the response is more than a simple reaction to environmental events. For example, suppose an observer has been presented with a photograph of a landscape view and asked to rate the "scenic value" of the landscape using a five-point scale ranging from 1 (very low scenic value) to 5 (very high scenic value). Most would agree that the representation below, Figure 10.2, is an oversimplified diagram of the observer's perceptual/judgmental process. In essence, the observer's rating (r = 4) arises directly from the sensory process of observing the scene. This representation is quite mechanical and does not consider the observer's cognitive or mental processes that mediate the response to a stimulus. Although these intervening processes are not directly observable, a more satisfying account of landscape perception would include at least several such processes. The purpose of theoretical psychophysics is to study, albeit indirectly, these hypothesized processes and their relation to the observer's response.

Therefore, there is a useful link between the assessment of perceived landscape quality and psychophysics. In order for the landscape professional to benefit from psychophysical methods, this link must be explicit and avoid the oversimplification of Figure 10.2. The observer's response is a function of several complex and interactive processes. The interpretation of that response should acknowledge the operation of cognitive processes such as judg-

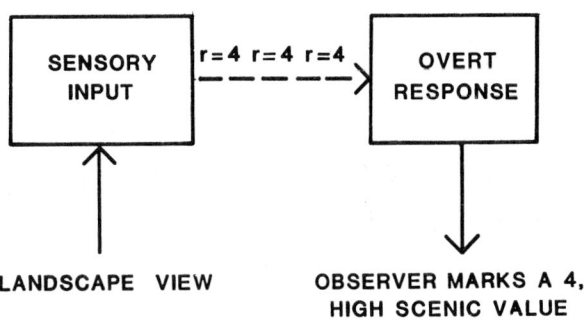

FIGURE 10.2. Model I.

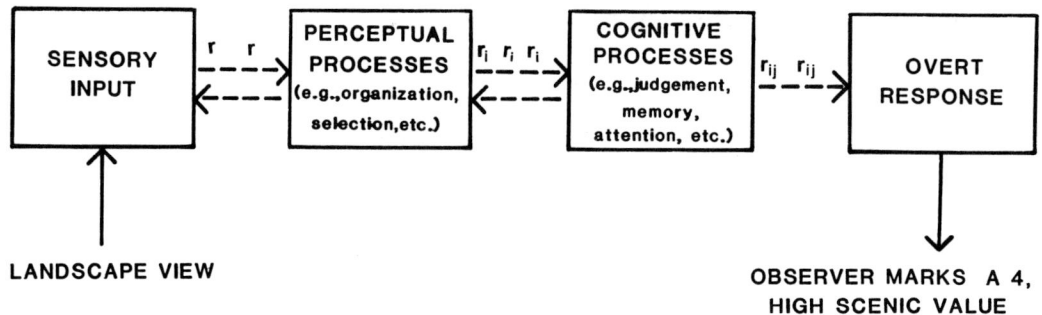

FIGURE 10.3. Model II.

ment or decision making, as well as the observer's particular experiences and frame of reference. Therefore, the Figure 10.2 representation of perception must be modified to include, at the least, several intervening processes as diagrammed below. The diagram in Figure 10.3 emphasizes two intervening processes: cognition (for example, judgment, memory) and perception. These processes are mutually interactive and may influence or alter the interpretation of the observer's response (as indicated by the ith and jth influences on the rating r) from that obtained in a simple, isomorphic sensory system (for example, Figure 10.2).

A complete discussion of theoretical psychophysics is far beyond the scope of this chapter (see Baird and Noma 1979; Torgerson 1958). However, it is important to understand the difficulties of simplistic or direct interpretations of assessment information. In Model 1 (Fig. 10.2) the observer has rated the scenic value of a landscape by marking a "4" on the rating scale. Many would interpret this response as a direct indication that the observer's *perceived value* of the landscape was quite high (a "4" out of 5). However, if the observer never used scale values below 4, the rating might actually be low. In this case, memory or experience with particular landscapes might intervene in the perceptual/judgmental process. A direct interpretation of the rating of "4," common in many assessment studies, is tantamount to accepting the representation of perception given by Figure 10.2. If we accept the richer conceptualization of perception afforded by Figure 10.3 (or any other complex model), the processes that contribute to the observer's response may be considered. Through such an analysis, the interpretation of the observer's perception becomes more meaningful and possibly more accurate. One example of this type of analysis is the Theory of Signal Detection (TSD) which has documented the interaction between perceptual and judgmental processes (see Green and Swets 1966; Swets 1973).

Assessment and the interpretation of assessment can be enhanced through the use of methods that are designed to accommodate the complexities of the perceptual response. In Model 1, (Fig. 10.2) if we accept the more complex view, the rating of "4" may be directly due to the landscape presented *or* due to intervening processes. To best understand the observer's response both alternatives should be considered.

Perceptual Preference Assessment

The goal of perceptual preference assessment is to measure environmental quality judgments more directly. Typically, participants are shown a landscape, either in person or simulated with a photograph or videotape, and asked to indicate the extent of their preference for that landscape. The landscape quality assessment may thus be more directly related to the actual features of the landscape than when only verbal surveys are used. For example, Petrich (1979) asked his subjects to provide landscape quality judgments for slides of proposed power plant sites with and without superimposed power and cement plants and air pollution. Subjects' ratings could therefore be meaningfully compared across three types of land use (cement plant, power plant, undeveloped) all with or without air pollution that might result from development (see Figure 10.4). Rather than relying on verbal descriptions or memory for a site, the perceptual preference method measures

1 2 3 4 5   AS IS

1 2 3 4 5   WITH CEMENT PLANT

1 2 3 4 5   WITH COOLING TOWER

FIGURE 10.4. Sample visual stimulus and rating scales. *Source:* Petrich, 1979

the perceptual response to the environment and relates it to a specific environmental feature.

One critical issue in perceptual preference assessment is the manner in which the landscape is presented. Ideally, perceptions are assessed while the observer is in the environment in question. However this is not always practical, and, in the case of proposed future development, not always possible. Thus the environment is often represented with photographs, drawings, or models. Of these, the color slide is most commonly used. Several studies have examined the validity of the color slide representation of landscapes (Daniel and Boster 1976; Seaton and Collins 1972), and it appears that color slides provide good surrogates for landscapes, especially if the landscapes are relatively homogeneous. For example, Petrich (1979) successfully assessed two reasonably similar landscapes in the same geographic region with forty photographs. Responses to radically different sites can prove difficult to interpret, particularly if those sites are not well represented photographically. Daniel and Ittelson (1981) point out that responses to very diverse environments reflect stereotypical reactions to the symbolic environment rather than a perceptual response based on specific landscape characteristics. If perceptual responses are desired, environmental representations should be restricted to a reasonable range of environments and those environments should be sampled well. The validity of pictoral representation generally increases with the number of photographs or drawings used to represent an environment.

EXAMPLE 3: The Measurement of the Observer's Response

Example 2 discussed some aspects of theoretical psychophysics and the implications of simple versus more complex representations of the observer's response. If a complex representation of perception is accepted, analytic procedures and methods that are sensitive to these complexities should be employed. Methodological psychophysics is devoted to the development and refinement of such procedures, usually called scaling methods. Methodological psychophysics focuses on three distinct tasks: scaling of observers, scaling of objects or stimuli, and the scaling of both observers and stimuli. In the first case, interest lies in differences among people. The second case is concerned with the measurement of the physical world through the judgments of observers. This case is most relevant to landscape assessment where the interest is most often in the measurement of perceptions of landscape qualities. Thus, methods that separate assessment differences into observer differences and landscape quality differences are needed. Once this separation has been performed, observer differences may be held constant to obtain a "pure" measure of differences in landscape qualities.

This process of separation commences with the statistical standardization of each observer's internal measurement system. When the attitudes, beliefs judgments, perceptions, or aesthetic preferences of the observer are assessed, an implicit assumption is that some continuum exists within the observers. Thus the human observer is viewed as a measuring instrument with some internal "yardstick" of measurement. Unfortunately, we do not have direct access to the observer's "yardstick" and, therefore, must attempt to infer or scale each observer's measurement. This is especially important in that other cognitive processes (for example, attention to the perceptual task or judgmental criteria) may influence the observer's use of his or her "yardstick." A simple scheme of the observer as a measurement instrument might be illustrated as shown in Figure 10.5.

This scheme conforms to the example used earlier in which an observer has rated the scenic value of a landscape view. In this example, Observer A had responded to the slide presentation by marking a rating of "4." Observer B has rated the same landscape view as "2." A direct interpretation of this example would be that Observer A perceived the slide as possessing greater scenic value than Observer B (actually, a 4 on Observer A's scale is quite similar to a 2 on Observer B's scale). But, as discussed earlier, neither rating can be interpreted as a direct representation of the perception of the observers (as in Figure 10.2) because the ratings are influenced by cognitive processes which are likely to differ from one observer to the next. The task of both observers, however, is to translate their own "yardsticks" into ratings on the one to five scale. Although both observers use the same rating scale, each may use it in a different way. Thus the rating obtained from the observer is a representation of both perception of the landscape *and* the observer's translation of his or her own internal "yardstick" to the response method.

The purpose of stimulus-centered (that is, landscape-centered) scaling methods is to equate or standardize the "yardsticks" of several observers. Following this process of standardization, remaining response differences among landscapes are interpreted as differences in the *perception* of landscape qualities. Example 4 will present an example of this approach to the analysis of the observer's response, the Scenic Beauty Estimation Method (Daniel and Boster 1976).

A second major issue in perception preference assessment is the measurement of the response of the participant. Many different methods have been used. Daniel and Boster (1976) used a categorical rating scale for their Scenic Beauty Estimation Method. Participants were asked to rate landscapes represented by color slides on a scale from 1 to 10, where 1 indicated low scenic quality and 10 high scenic quality. Others have used rank order (Buhyoff, Wellman, Harvey, and Fraser 1978), paired comparison (Buhyoff and Wellman 1979), magnitude estimation (Buhyoff, Wellman, and Daniel 1982), and Q-sort procedures (Pitt and Zube 1979). Each of these methods has characteristic advantages and disadvantages (Daniel and Boster 1976; Torgerson 1958; also see Example 1). Consideration of such issues should guide method selection since empirical comparison of several of these techniques has shown them to be comparable (Buhyoff et al. 1982).

Treatment of preference data can be complex and often involves fairly sophisticated statistical treatment (see Example 4). However, perceptual preference data are relatively easy to collect, and, if properly gathered, can provide a link between the perceiver and the environment that is often more direct and interpretable than that obtained by either survey or behavioral observation methods.

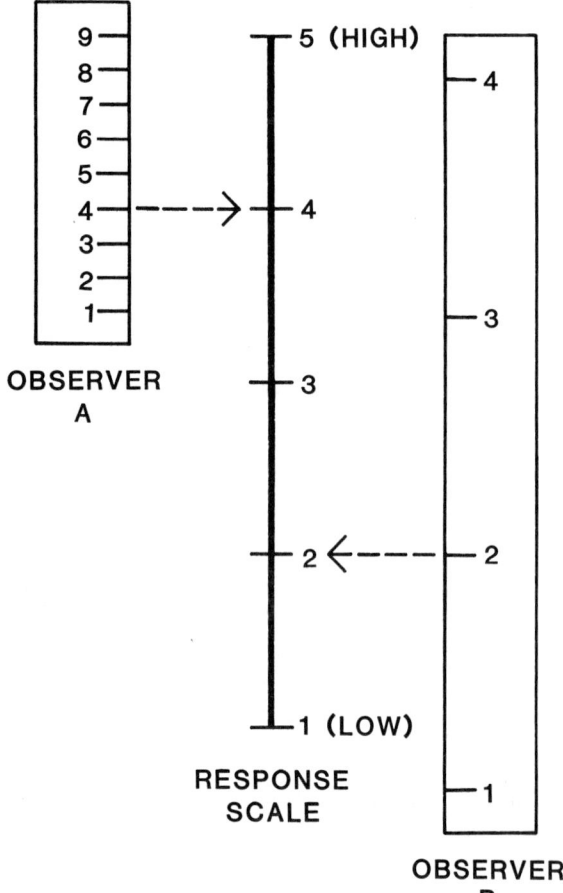

FIGURE 10.5. Perceptual yardsticks.

EXAMPLE 4: Analyzing the Observer's Response; An Example of Scaling Using the SBE Model

The observer's response is not necessarily a simple or direct function of visible landscape properties. Rather, the response of the observer is determined by at least several cognitive factors that are involved in the perceptual process, and direct interpretation of the observer's response can be quite misleading. This problem can be minimized through the use of several methods for the scaling and analysis of observer responses (see Baird and Noma 1978; Bock and Jones 1968; Torgerson 1958). One method that has been developed specifically for the analysis of perceptual preference of landscapes is the Scenic Beauty Estimation (SBE) model (Daniel and Boster 1976).

The SBE model assumes that categorical ratings assigned to a landscape scene by the observer are determined by two factors: the "true" perceived scenic beauty of the landscape and the judgmental

TABLE 10.1. SBE Method Frequencies (f), Cumulative Frequencies (cf), Cumulative Probabilities (cp), z Scores (z), and the Mean z Score ($\bar{z}$) for Each of Three Observers Rating Three Landscapes

		LANDSCAPE I				LANDSCAPE II				LANDSCAPE III			
	Rating	f	cf	cp	z	f	cf	cp	z	f	cf	cp	z
OBSERVER A	1	6	20	1.00	--	6	20	1.00	--	6	20	1.00	--
	2	8	14	.70	.52	8	14	.70	.52	8	14	.70	.52
	3	3	6	.30	-.52	3	6	.30	-.52	3	6	.30	-.52
	4	2	3	.15	-1.04	2	3	.15	-1.04	2	3	.15	-1.04
	5	1	1	.05	-1.64	1	1	.05	-1.64	1	1	.05	-1.64
				Σz = -2.68				Σz = -2.68				Σz = -2.68	
				$\bar{z}$ = -.67				$\bar{z}$ = -.67				$\bar{z}$ = -.67	
				SBE = [-.67-(-.67)] x100=0				SBE = [-.67-(-.67)] x100=0				SBE = [-.67-(-.67)] x100=0	
OBSERVER B	1	12	20	1.00	--	10	20	1.00	--	9	20	1.00	--
	2	6	8	.40	-.25	8	10	.50	0.00	10	11	.55	.13
	3	1	2	.10	-1.28	1	2	.10	-1.28	1	1	.05	-1.64
	4	1	1	.05	-1.64	1	1	.05	-1.64	0	0	0.00	-1.96
	5	0	0	0.00	-1.96	0	0	0.00	-1.96	0	0	0.00	-1.96
				Σz = -5.13				Σz = -4.88				Σz = -5.43	
				$\bar{z}$ = -1.28				$\bar{z}$ = -1.22				$\bar{z}$ = -1.36	
				SBE = [-1.28-(-1.28)] x100=0				SBE = [-1.22-(-1.28)] x100=6				SBE = [-1.36-(-1.28)] x100=-8	
OBSERVER C	1	0	20	1.00	--	0	20	1.00	--	0	20	1.00	--
	2	1	20	1.00	1.96	1	20	1.00	1.96	0	20	1.00	1.96
	3	1	19	.95	1.64	1	19	.95	1.64	0	20	1.00	1.96
	4	12	18	.90	1.28	8	18	.90	1.28	9	20	1.00	1.96
	5	6	6	.30	-.52	10	10	.50	0.00	11	11	.55	.13
				Σz = 4.36				Σz = 4.88				Σz = 6.01	
				$\bar{z}$ = 1.09				$\bar{z}$ = 1.22				$\bar{z}$ = 1.50	
				SBE = [1.09-(1.09)] x100=0				SBE = [1.22-(1.09)] x100=13				SBE = [1.50-(1.09)] x100=41	

NOTE: There will always be a cp=1.00 at the lowest rating category (1), so no information is added by a z-score entry identical for all observers. The $\bar{z}$ is therefore based on one less than the total number of rating categories (i.e., 5-1=4). In all other cases where cp=1.00 or 0.00 (z=$\pm\infty$), the convention is followed that cp=1-1/(2N) or cp=1/(2N), respectively (see Bock and Jones, 1968). In the example above, N=20, therefore cp=1-1/40 or 1/40, yielding z scores of 1.96 and -1.96, respectively.

criteria applied by the observer. Further, it assumes that the scenic beauty of the landscape is not a single value, but is best represented by a distribution of values such as that which might result from the rating of several scenes from a particular landscape. Simple inspection of a distribution of ratings will not reveal which of the two factors ("true" versus judgment) are responsible for differences in observer ratings. Comparison of the distribution of ratings for several different landscapes, however, allows the distinction of actual differences in perceived scenic beauty from differences in the judgmental criteria of the observer. True perceptual differences will be manifested by consistent differences in the ratings assigned to the several landscapes by the same observer. Differences in ratings that are due to the observer's judgmental criteria will result in distributions of ratings that are overlapping or equal for the landscapes. The purpose of the SBE model is to eliminate the ambiguity introduced by differences in the observer's judgmental criteria. The resulting Scenic Beauty Estimates (SBEs) provide a quantitative index of the perceived scenic beauty of the landscapes.

Table 10.1 illustrates the use of the SBE method in the analysis of the hypothetical perceptual preference ratings of three observers for three different landscapes. Each observer has rated a number of scenes of each landscape on a five-point categorical rating scale. The frequency (f), cumulative frequency (cf), and cumulative probability (cp) values are shown for each observer and landscape. The z values are the standard normal deviates associated with each of the cumulative probability values. Mean z values are also shown.

The SBE analysis compares the observer's ratings distribution for one landscape with the distributions for several other landscapes. The resulting SBEs represent a more interpretable index of the perceived scenic beauty of the landscapes than the original ratings themselves. It can be seen in Figure 10.6, in fact, that direct interpretation of the "unscaled" ratings (in this case, mean average ratings for each landscape) might result in substantially different conclusions regarding perceived scenic beauty than interpretation of the SBEs.

Behavioral Measures

A problem with both survey and perceptual preference assessments is that the link between preference, or attitudes and opinions, and actual behavior in the landscape may not be explicitly evaluated. Observing or measuring behavior in the target setting, although not feasible in many cases, is a useful means for obtaining this information. Behavioral measures are a broad class of methods for directly observing and measuring human activities which have many advantages, the most obvious of which is their face validity. Recording people's behavior provides a direct indicator of human activities in a particular environment.

A missing element in behavioral approaches, however, is the reason for the behavior. For example, in investigating the suitability of various sites for nuclear power plants one might assume, as did Petrich (1979), that the more scenic a site is, the less appropriate it might be for industrial development. One might then assess the attractiveness of several sites indirectly by measuring and comparing the number of visitors to each site. However, several factors, such as the proximity of a site or its accessibility, might mitigate the decision to visit a particular site. These intervening causes are always a threat to the conclusions that can be reached because measures of behavior, whether a rating on a 10-point scale, or the number of visits to a site each year, are always indirect indices of perceived landscape quality. One way to compensate for this disadvantage would be to combine behavioral observation with preference or survey data.

Another disadvantage of behavioral observation methods is that the behavior of nonusers or nonparticipants is not recorded. Although this may seem a trivial point, consideration of an example will clarify its importance. If visitation rates are used to assess visitors' perception of scenic quality, no information will be gained about those who opted not to visit a particular site. The reasons for not visiting an area are as important as reasons

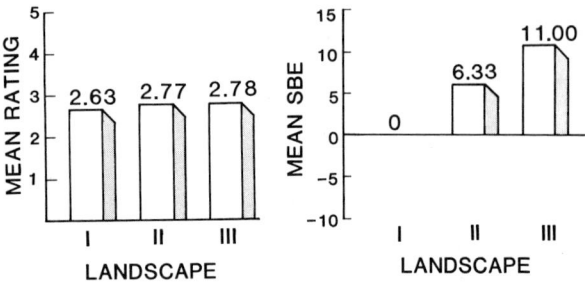

FIGURE 10.6. Mean scores of scenic beauty estimation.

for visiting and could be critical in planning or managing those areas. Finally, behavior may not be observed at projects which have not yet been constructed.

ASSESSMENT DESIGNS

The assessment methods discussed above represent alternative approaches to the collection of information about landscape quality. These methods differ both procedurally and in their assessment focus (that is, what is measured). We can also contrast different approaches to landscape assessment on the basis of the design of the assessment process. The assessment design is the plan that specifies what is to be done and how it will be accomplished. Some assessment designs are characterized by formal and explicit "blueprints" that embody generally accepted requirements for assessment. Others are less formal. With varying degrees of success, any may serve as the basis from which to organize and draw inferences from data collected via the three assessment methods presented in the previous section.

We will discuss four general types of assessment designs: the case study, the experiment, the correlational design, and the quasi-experiment. These four categories of assessment design reflect substantive differences in the philosophy, logic, methodology, and purpose of assessment. However, clear distinctions among the categories may not always be present or readily apparent in practice. The categories of designs will be contrasted primarily on the basis of three criteria. First, the goal of a particular design may be either the description, prediction, or explanation of the assessment outcome. Second, the categories of assessment designs will be examined in terms of the degree of control that is exerted over the assessment process. Third, the utility and difficulty of interpretation of the assessment outcome will be considered for each type of design.

The choice of an appropriate assessment design is complicated by numerous competing considerations. A complete discussion of the advantages and disadvantages of particular designs is far beyond the scope of this chapter. The reader is therefore referred to excellent source books on assessment and design by Babbie (1979), Cook and Campbell (1979), and Kerlinger (1973). It should also be emphasized that no design fulfills the needs of all assessments. The ultimate evaluation of the effectiveness of an assessment design is its concordance with the constraints, needs, and purposes of assessment within the unique context in which the particular assessment occurs.

Case Study

A case study involves the assessment of a single environment or environmental problem, and often emphasizes the uniqueness of a site rather than features it may have in common with other sites. The goal of this type of assessment is description, and the optimal case study will combine public preference data with assessments of various physical, cultural, or cognitive characteristics of the landscape. For example, Petrich (1979) examined not only preference data, but also historical and cultural values of the landscape, and scenic features such as visibility and land-use diversity. Petrich examined two sites, however, and therefore his study is most correctly viewed as two related case studies.

Of the four designs presented in this chapter, the case study is most frequently used for assessments of perceived landscape quality, and examples abound. Daniel, Anderson, Schroeder, and Wheeler (1977) created computer-generated maps of relative perceived scenic quality in an Arizona forest. Schroeder and Daniel (1980) investigated the perceived scenic quality of several road corridors, and Zube et al. (1974) examined the aesthetic quality of the Connecticut River Valley.

Compared with other assessment designs, however, the case study method suffers from several characteristic disadvantages. Because case study data essentially describe a single geographic area, comparisons with and generalizations to other environments are highly restricted. Petrich's (1979) pair of case studies of nuclear plant sites are comparable but generalizations to other sites, or even to other environmental development problems, would be limited.

The case study also suffers from a lack of control over the assessment process and can essentially be characterized as an anecdotal method wherein only a single site or environment is assessed. Further, the choice of the site and the variables to be measured is not accomplished systematically. Neither the variables of interest nor extraneous variables are subject to control by the investigator. Thus inferences from or interpretations of case study assessments are threatened by uncontrolled and competing explanations (extraneous variables). The report of the case study may also be somewhat anecdotal and it is often not possible to determine from case study results exactly how information was collected.

Thus inference from case study designs is limited by the inability to control variables or sample sites and/or observers. For example, one section of Petrich's (1979) evaluation of nuclear plant sites provided only two site options, both of which received high scenic quality ratings and very low ratings of suitability as sites for any power plant development. Petrich concluded that neither site should be used. It is uncertain, however, whether Petrich's conclusion was warranted. Since there was no standard of comparison to help interpret survey results, high or low ratings might have been due to attitudes toward power plants, wording of questions, or other unknown factors. It is also uncertain how these results can be generalized to other settings.

It is also difficult to evaluate the effectiveness (for example, reliability, validity, and so forth) of the assessment, since the case study typically makes only singular measures of a particular site. For example, a scenic beauty map of a forest (for example, Daniel et al. 1977) will indicate which parts of an area are attractive (description), but not why (explanation) or whether they will remain so in the future (prediction).

The case study method does have some advantages, however. It is often less expensive of time and resources than other methods. Case studies are appropriate when a single site or problem is of consequence; they are also very useful for exploratory or pilot studies. Finally, the usefulness of the case study method can be vastly improved through the standardization of measures, sampling, and definition of variables so that comparisons can be made across separate sites and studies.

Experimental Designs

The general logic of the classical approach to experimentation is well known. Preferences for a site, for example, might be compared before and after some management action or treatment had taken place. In this example, physical change in the environment is controlled by the experimenter. This treatment is therefore called an *independent variable*. Some measure of the observer's perceptions or judgments is used as an indicator of the effects of that treatment and is called the *dependent variable*. The dependent variable is not manipulated by the experimenter; it is only measured. It might also be useful to consider or identify other variables that might influence the experiment, such as environmental attitudes, differences in the observers' cultural or geographic backgrounds, and so forth. Such variables are termed *extraneous variables*.

Experimental designs have three identifying characteristics. First, the emphasis is on explanation rather than description. The purpose of an experiment is to provide evidence that changes in the dependent variables can be explained as a function of the changes induced in the independent variable by the experimenter. This kind of explanatory evidence supports inferences about the cause of events.

A second identifying characteristic of the experiment is the ability to exert control over the assessment process. Experimental control is manifested in three ways. First, the dependent variables to be measured are explicitly chosen and defined by the experimenter. The level or occurence of the independent variable is controlled by the experimenter, and extraneous variables are often controlled to ensure that their effects are not confounded with those of the independent variable.

Experimental control is also manifested in the assignment of sampling units to groups or conditions. For example, in the traditional experiment consisting of an experimental group and a control group, the assignment of experimental subjects to each group is completely controlled by the experimenter. Two types of control of assignment are most common: matching and random assignment. Matching of experimental groups involves balancing the composition of the groups such that, prior to the experiment, the groups are equal or comparable. Though this procedure seems logically satisfactory, in practice it is somewhat costly. Furthermore, it is seldom certain that all relevant characteristics of the group members have been identified and matched. A more acceptable procedure is random assignment, which results in groups whose composition is solely due to chance. This procedure supports much of the rationale of experimentation and greatly enhances the interpretation of experimental results.

The third type of control manifested in the experiment involves the ability to control the experimental setting or the surrounding conditions of the experiment. At one extreme, this type of control is exemplified by the laboratory experiment, where all conditions surrounding the experiment are held constant. Controlled conditions minimize the risk that an unknown extraneous variable may influence experimental results.

A third identifying characteristic of the experiment is complete specification of methods and procedures before observation has begun. Specification entails the definition of the experimental variables, statement of hypotheses predicting the outcomes of the experiment, and precise description of the exact methods and procedures to be used in the experiment. This process, known as operationalization, must fulfill the requirement that any independent experimenter could duplicate the experiment in all relevant details.

In our example of the assessment of sites for a nuclear power plant, Petrich (1979) manipulated the type of site development and its effects by superimposing cement plants, nuclear plants, and air pollution on photographs of the two geographic areas under consideration (see Figure 10.7). Observers examined scenes of the same geographic areas with and without development and air pollution. Because of this control over the independent variable (kind of development superimposed), Petrich was able to interpret observers' perceptions of the two sites by comparing reactions to the various developments. More importantly, he could conclude that superimposed air pollution or development provided causal evidence of a decline in scenic preference because those were the only variables manipulated; extraneous variation was eliminated through experimental control.

Thus the experiment is characterized by formal requirements for operationalization, a great degree of control over the assessment process, and a focus on explanation and causal inference. The outcome of the well-designed experiment is particularly amenable to interpretation because competing interpretations are eliminated by experimental control. A potential difficulty of the experiment is its "artificial" nature. It may be questionable whether the results of a particular experiment can be generalized to other samples of people, environments, or variables. Also, formal experiments are often costly or impossible to conduct in the natural setting or field environment, and the requirements for experimental control are often

FIGURE 10.7. View of proposed power plant from historic site Olana. *Source:* Petrich, 1979.

quite intrusive in the field setting. Therefore, although the experiment may yield the most precise and interpretable assessment information, it may be very difficult to generalize from the artificiality of the experiment to the setting of interest.

Correlational Methods

The goals of correlation methods are description, explanation, and prediction. In contrast to experimental designs, correlational methods institute statistical, rather than experimental, control over the variables of interest. Typically a set of candidate variables are identified *a priori* and measured as they vary naturally. These independent variables are then systematically associated with a dependent, or criterion variable, typically preference, via simple or multiple regression procedures. The result of this process is an equation predicting preference from levels of a number of environmental characteristics. Additionally, regression procedures provide a measure of the strength of the relationship between preference and the independent variables. Tabachnick and Fidell (1983) provide a readable and useful description of regression techniques and available computerized statistical packages for their calculation. A more rigorous treatment of multivariate techniques may be found in Pedhazur (1982).

The human or psychological half of the equation is usually measured with perceptual preference techniques. Generally, a numeric value is assigned to a landscape via a rating scale, rank order, paired comparison, magnitude estimation, or Q-sort assessment method (see Example 1). Behavioral or survey measures could also serve as dependent variables as long as they constituted a response to a specific environment or scene in an environment and may be quantified in some way.

The environmental half of the equation is composed of any number of characteristics which range from objective to subjective, depending on the goals of the assessment. Objective measures are generally made either onsite or from photographs. For example, Latimer, Hogo, and Daniel (1981) and Malm, Kelley, Molenar, and Daniel (1981) associated high levels of particulate air pollution with low preference for western canyons. Arthur (1977) and Daniel and Schroeder (1979) measured physical characteristics of forests onsite and found that large trees, large amounts of ground cover and shrubs, and small amounts of downed wood and small trees were associated with high perceived scenic quality. Buhyoff and Wellman (1980) measured characteristics of scenic vistas from photographs and developed the following prediction model:

Landscape preference =

  10.83 (area in sharp mountains)
 −0.59 (area in sharp mountains)^2
  1.57 (area in distant forest)
 −8.60 (middle ground area of insect-damaged trees)
 −64.59 (proportion of forested area)
  0.97 (area in flat topography)

The numbers preceding each variable in parentheses are beta coefficients for the regression equation and represent the relative contribution of each variable in predicting the criterion variable, landscape preference. Thus, although sharp mountains and distant forests are both positively associated with landscape preference, sharp mountains are roughly eleven times more important as predictors. In this model, sharp mountains were associated with landscape preference in a curvilinear function. That is, sharp mountains are preferred only up to a certain point: if too much of the photograph is taken up with sharp mountain peaks (the squared second term of the equation), their contribution is negative.

Subjective measures of environmental characteristics are generally obtained from judges' ratings of photographs. For example, Vining, Schroeder, and Daniel (1984) used ratings of subjective characteristics of homes and homesites (for example, design congruity, fittingness, obtrusiveness) to develop models of preference for forested residential sites. R. Kaplan (1975), S. Kaplan (1975), and Ulrich (1977) found that mystery, a subjective or psychological property of the environment, predicted preference well. Other examples of subjective environmental characteristics are offered by Daniel and Vining (1983) and Zube, Sell, and Taylor (1982).

Subjective measures of landscape characteristics suffer two important disadvantages. First, since they are evaluated by independent judges, the agreement among those judges, or reliability, is a critical element of their usefulness. If judges do not agree in their assessments, the variables assessed are of questionable validity (Cook and Campbell 1979). Second, in project-level assessment, the applications of the analysis are more important than its theoretical value. The relationship between subjective properties of the environment such as mystery or fittingness and actual physical or biological features of the environment has not yet been determined. Thus specifying that an increase in mystery will increase preference provides little guidance to an environmental manager. Furthermore, it may be much more difficult to measure changes in these subjective determinants of environmental preference than to measure the preferences directly.

Correlational approaches have important advantages over the case study method and may, in some cases, be more useful or more practical than experimental or quasi-experimental designs. Although some correlational assessments may seem like case studies because they may be done in single environments, an important distinction must be made. In the correlational approach, preference in one environment is systematically and mathematically associated with the characteristics of the environment. For example, a correlational approach to Petrich's (1979) nuclear plant site might have associated measures of vegetative characteristics, air pollution, or visual obstruction (objective), or of cultural and historical values (subjective) with perceived suitability of various sites. Assuming that drab vegetation, short site lines, air pollution, and low cultural values would be associated with the suitability of a site for nuclear plant development (or with low scenic preference), one might attempt to generalize these findings to other similar sites. Specifically, one would use the multiple-R^2 statistic, which indicates the amount of variance in preference ratings accounted for by the predictor variables, to determine the extent of the same relationship for other sites. Obviously, even a correlational approach would benefit by comparison across several sites, and this approach may be combined with experimental or quasi-experimental methods to generate even more predictive power.

The greatest difference between correlational and experimental methods is in the degree to which causal relationships (that is, prediction *and* explanation) may be specified. The explicit manipulation of predictor variables is absent in correlational approaches. In the above example, there is no way to know whether it is vegetation, or some correlate of vegetation, such as topography, that *causes* low scenic preference. Thus to a certain extent correlational designs are restricted to less powerful inference and interpretation than experimental designs. They are often much more practical, however, and are based on a different, but not necessarily inferior, tradition and logic (Brogden 1972; Cronbach 1957).

Quasi-Experimental Designs

The quasi-experiment, characterized by incomplete control of the assessment process, is often a good compromise between the case study and the experiment. As with the experiment, the foci are explanation and prediction. Quasi-experimental designs often attempt to apply experimental methods within the existing constraints of a natural setting, where random assignment to groups may not be possible. This inability to control the composition of experimental groups poses a serious difficulty in the interpretation of the experiment because results may be attributable either to the effects of the independent variable or to differences in the composition of the groups. A number of tactics of design and statistical control are available to minimize this difficulty and the reader is referred to Cook and Campbell (1979) for further details.

In addition to a lack of control over group assignment, the quasi-experiment seldom attains the precision of control over the experimental setting that is achieved in the experiment. As a result, interpretation of assessment outcomes is usually less precise. This problem, however, may be tempered by the utility of assessment information from the field setting and by the ability to circumvent problems of experimental control through statistical procedures of control. Furthermore, the choice of true versus quasi-experiment may not be at issue. It is often the case that the quasi-experiment is the only viable design available. As Weisberg (1979) has pointed out, the use of quasi-experimental methods may be a necessity, especially given flaws that may intrude on assessments initially planned as true experiments.

The quasi-experiment may be illustrated by considering a situation that might have arisen in Petrich's study of the nuclear power plant sites had he chosen to study visitors to the two proposed sites. This procedure would constitute a nonrandom sampling technique, but might be used because it better represents the most concerned groups, that is, actual visitors to the site. Although this group might be more likely to suffer the impact of a nuclear plant development, and thus might be the most appropriate group to sample, it might also be true that visitors to each site differ in some systematic manner. For example, visitors to a site farther from the city might be more affluent or more prone to antidevelopment attitudes than visitors to the second, closer site. Control of these extraneous variables is possible (as through covariance analysis), if they are recognized and measured. Thus a major issue in the use of quasi-experimental designs is the identification and measurement of extraneous, or uncontrolled, sources of variation so that statistical control is possible.

CRITERIA FOR EVALUATING ASSESSMENT METHODS

Extensive criteria are available for evaluating the effectiveness of assessment. Three primary criteria will be discussed here: reliability, validity, and sampling. The use of these criteria aid in the determination of the adequacy of assessment.

Reliability

Reliability is often termed the consistency or stability of measurement. When a particular event is measured, we want to be sure that the measuring instrument is consistent. If we obtain a different measurement each time we measure the same event, our instrument is not reliable. The measurement instrument must be sensitive enough to reflect changes in the event of interest, but insensitive to changes in irrelevant events.

Depending on the design of the particular assessment, we may wish to assess different aspects of reliability. For example, if the assessment depends on the judgments of two or more observers, we would want to establish the consistency among judges. This type of reliability is usually termed *inter-observer reliability* or *between-observer agreement*. Agreement can be calculated by determining the number of times the observers agreed divided by the total number of observer judgments. A second method of estimating inter-observer reliability is useful when observers are using a rating technique. In this case, the correlations of one observer's judgments or ratings to the second observer's ratings is calculated.

A second aspect of reliability involves the consistency of measurement over time. Usually, we want to ensure that the assessment was not influenced by the particular time of measurement. A second assessment, perhaps at a slightly different time of day or year, can be compared or correlated with the first assessment. A high consistency or correlation between measurements at the two different times demonstrates the temporal consistency of measurement. This type of reliability is traditionally termed *test-retest reliability*.

Thus the calculation of reliability allows us to check our measurements to ensure that unwanted or extraneous events have not influenced the obtained measurement. The demonstration of reliability enhances our confidence that the measurements obtained reflect actual changes in the event of interest.

Validity

This criterion denotes the degree to which the assessment method measures what was intended. Validity is the accuracy of measurement and can be evaluated in several ways. First, we would want general agreement that the method is appropriate. This type of evidence is called *face validity*: on the face of things the method appears accurate. Face validity may be determined by judges, but most often is determined by the general acceptance of the assessment method.

A second type of validity is termed *content validity* or the degree to which the substance, topic, or items of the assessment instrument reflect the purpose of measurement. For example, in the use of a survey, each survey item should reflect the purpose of the survey. As with face validity, content validity can be established by judges. Further evidence of content validity can be established through statistical procedures such as factor analysis.

A third demonstration of validity is obtained through the comparison of the assessment method with previously established methods or results. This form of cross-validation or conjoint validity is usually obtained by correlation. Agreement between the assessment method and another accepted independent measure of the event of interest demonstrates that the assessment method also measures the event of interest.

Two important aspects of validity are the sensitivity and utility of the assessment method. Essentially, these aspects modify our previous definition of validity: the degree to which what is intended is measured for what purpose. The utility of an assessment method refers to the requirement that measurement produces useful information that can be applied. The sensitivity of the assessment method is the ability of measurement to detect important changes in the event measured. For example, a measurement system which designated landscapes as either pretty or ugly would be neither as sensitive nor as useful as one that provided finer distinctions or gradations between "prettiest and ugliest."

An interplay exists between these different facets of validity and between validity and reliability. It is often the case that different assessment methods display different degrees of the types of validity. Examination of the costs and benefits of each potential assessment method is necessary for an informed choice of methods. For example, the method with highest overall validity may be rejected in favor of a method with lower overall validity but particularly high utility. Similarly, sacrifices in reliability may be necessary in order to use a method with high validity. It must be stressed that reliability is prerequisite to effective measurement; however, methods must ultimately be evaluated within the context of the entire milieu of measurement and its intended purpose.

Sampling

The third criterion for evaluation of assessment regards the way in which units (for example, people, landscapes, and so forth) are chosen for measurement. Because it is seldom feasible to measure every unit, some procedure must be used to choose measurement units. If human perception is the subject of assessment, then people as well as landscapes are likely to be chosen.

Two major kinds of procedures are available for the sampling of units: intuitive procedures and probability procedures. Intuitive procedures do not incorporate explicit rules for the selection of measurement units. Units are chosen on the basis of perceived appropriateness, informal logic or reasoning, or, quite commonly, on the basis of convenience. Such procedures are prone to error and can greatly inhibit the interpretability of assessment and the ability to generalize from results.

Probability procedures specify the likelihood or chance of any unit being chosen. The first step in these procedures is determining the domain or population of all units that might be chosen. Units are then selected from the domain by one of two major methods—random or stratified sampling. Random sampling operates on the principle that every unit has an equal chance of being chosen. For example, all units in the domain may be assigned an arbitrary number. Using a table of random numbers, a previously specified number of units are chosen from the domain. This procedure guards against unwanted influences on unit choice (for example, experimenter bias). Units are chosen by random chance and the choice of each unit is equally probable.

Stratified sampling adjusts the units chosen to match the domain on some characteristic of interest. For example, if the assessment measures attitudes about the environment, and if political party affiliation is known to be related to attitude, then the sample could be stratified on party affiliation. If there are 30 percent Republicans and 70 percent Democrats in the domain of interest, the units can be chosen so that the resulting sample contains a comparable percentage of Democrats and Republicans. Within this constraint, however, units are chosen randomly. The resulting sample would be more representative of the domain with respect to party affiliation. Whenever knowledge of a relationship of such a characteristic with the measure of interest is available, stratification provides an improvement over simple random sampling.

Often, assessment methods are only concerned with the sampling of observers or judges. It may also be necessary, however, to consider the sampling of other units such as environments, times of measurement, orientations of landscape views, and so forth. The use of precise sampling methods is directly related to the ability to interpret results and generalize results to other hypothetical assessment situations. Precise sampling requires the specification of the unit domain and the objective choice of units through explicit rules. It is often most cost efficient to restrict the size of the domain and accept the resulting limits on generalization. Use of these procedures usually allows

TABLE 10.2. Assessment Methods and Designs

	Case Study	Experiment	Correlational Design	Quasi-Experiment
Surveys & Questionnaires	*	*	*	*
Perceptual Preference	*	*	*	*
Behavioral Measures	*	*	*	*

the interpretation of results free from errors of selection and allows generalization of results to the entire domain.

SUMMARY AND CONCLUSIONS

This chapter has provided a brief overview of methods for landscape quality assessment. Many different approaches are used to gather landscape assessment information and it is beyond the scope of this chapter to discuss all these approaches in detail. Rather, we have considered three assessment methods and designs based on several distinctions. In practice, these distinctions may not be clear or obvious, and a given project may incorporate features of any of several different types of designs. For example, an experimental design would be poorly suited to a project with the goal of obtaining initial descriptive information characterizing perceptions of a particular landscape. Conversely, a project whose goal was to establish the causal relationship between the degree of air pollution and perceived air quality is not amenable to the case study approach. In either case, the ultimate utility of assessment information is closely related to the appropriateness and adequacy of the application of methods to the goals of the particular project.

As can be seen in Table 10.2, each assessment method can be incorporated into any of the assessment designs. In fact, considerable inferential power and validity may be gained if more than one assessment method is used in a particular design. The quality of an assessment is less a function of which cell of Table 10.2 is used than of the care with which the assessment is executed. From consideration of cost-effectiveness, the case study and experimental methods are least desirable. Though the case study may be inexpensive in several ways, the outcomes of assessment are difficult to interpret and generalize; thus little time is spent, but little is gained. On the other hand, the experiment is often quite difficult to implement in the field setting and may be intrusive. As a result, in most landscape quality assessment projects the most practical choice of assessment design is likely to be the quasi-experiment or the correlational study. These approaches can be matched to any of the three assessment methods to fulfill the particular requirements of the project.

Regardless of the assessment method or design used, the consumer of assessment information must be critical of the quality of that information. To this end, several evaluative criteria were described. Foremost among these criteria is the establishment of the reliability of measurement. If measurement is capricious, no confidence can be placed in an assessment. Given reliability, it must also be determined whether the particular assessment displays adequate validity for the purpose of the project. It is also crucial to determine the adequacy of sampling. How project results are generalized to other observers and settings depends on the sampling methods used. Few assessment projects entirely satisfy all evaluative criteria. Rather, it is usually the case that precise methodology is tempered by needs for project relevance, utility, and cost-effectiveness.

Finally, we have presented a conceptual basis for landscape quality assessment emphasizing the need for a user-based or observer-sensitive approach. In addition to obvious physical and biological characteristics, the landscape manifests the impacts of past human use and the goals and hopes of plans for the future. Explicit consideration of the perceptions, judgments, needs, and demands of the observing public can contribute to wiser resource use and more effective and intelligent planning of future landscapes.

DEFINE RESOURCES	INVENTORY RESOURCES	ASSESS EFFECTS	APPRAISE EFFECTS
		/////	

CHAPTER 11

SIMULATING CHANGES IN THE LANDSCAPE

Stephen R.J. Sheppard

INTRODUCTION

This chapter is concerned with the role of visual simulations in project visual analysis. Visual simulations are pictures, images, or models of an environment, object, or design, whether real or imagined. They are coming to be recognized as a key tool in project visual analysis, because they make it much simpler for people to visualize the change in the landscape which would result from a proposed project.

The purpose of this discussion is to provide an introduction to and some insights into the current and potential use of visual simulations in visual analysis. Specifically, this entails:

1. Identifying the primary research findings and information sources which are applicable to practice.
2. Establishing principles of visual simulation for use in project visual analysis.
3. In the context of these principles, reviewing the problems and advantages associated with simulation methods in routine use.
4. Illustrating key procedures by means of simulation examples.

THE ROLE OF SIMULATIONS IN VISUAL IMPACT ANALYSIS

Visual simulations take many forms: so-called "artist's impressions," photographs, maps, television, theatre sets, and holograms, to list a few. Anything which visually represents or creates a picture of something else is a visual simulation.

For the purpose of this chapter, simulations will be given a more limited definition: a simulation creates a two- or three-dimensional image of a *future* or *proposed* environment or condition (often the proposed project itself). Simulations used in visual analysis of projects commonly include plans, diagrams, elevations, perspective sketches and renderings, modified photographs, scale models, and computer graphics. This chapter will focus still more narrowly upon those simulations which depict a view in perspective (Figure 11.1). Excluded from the discussion will be the more widely used plan views, elevations, axonometrics, and so forth, which show only limited, dimensionally correct aspects of a project or site.

FIGURE 11.1. Rendering of proposed geothermal powerplant, by S. Sheppard, courtesy of Bureau of Land Management (BLM).

Simulations are used in a variety of ways which bear upon project analysis:

1. As a design tool in the development of a project.
2. As an analytical tool for those reviewing the project, for example, the project client, government agencies with regulatory powers, and third-party environmental consultants.
3. As an information device in presentations about the project to the public and interested parties.
4. As a stimulus for eliciting certain responses toward the project from public, key informant, or other groups.
5. As documentary evidence in environmental reports and legal testimony.

The recent rise in demand for visual simulations in project analysis may be attributed in part to the overall growth in demand for visual assessment in environmental review, and in part to a dissatisfaction with or lack of confidence in existing methods of visual assessment. The findings of a complicated or questionable methodology for visual analysis may be vividly confirmed by simulations, almost at a glance. They permit laypeople and experts alike to put the project into an actual context, focus on specific hard issues, and form opinions independently of any methodology. People tend to feel comfortable in interpreting conventional pictures of various types. In some cases, it may even be thought that simulations make professional visual impact assessments and aesthetic quality judgments unnecessary.

However, all simulations may not be equally useful or acceptable to the users. Furthermore, there is a danger that so influential and powerful a tool may carry hidden biases. The call for more use of simulations in project analysis should not obscure the fact that there may be right simulations for the job and wrong ones, and, indeed, all shades in between. What information and what guidelines can we draw upon in considering valid methods of simulation?

SIMULATION RESEARCH AND INFORMATION SOURCES

The body of knowledge currently available on visual simulations stems from three main sources: research (theory and experimental findings); manuals or descriptions of various simulation techniques; and environmental reports and studies making use of simulations for actual projects. This discussion attempts only to identify selected key sources of information of most use to the practitioner.

Research

A considerable body of research in various disciplines has employed simulations in order to test people's preference for and reactions to landscapes. However, much of this work has used simulations of existing environments, for example, photographs of real scenes. The research which is most germane to the use of simulations in visual impact assessment is that which includes simulations of future conditions, and in some way compares these with other simulated or real views of the project.

Another consideration in reviewing research which uses simulations is that a significant proportion of studies have sought to establish broad preferences for or reactions to different kinds of environment or scenery, rather than different types of landscape change or specific projects.

Care must be taken in applying these findings to the role of simulations in predicting the consequences of visual change.

The study which provides the most comprehensive analysis of the principles and purposes of simulation is Appleyard's (1977) review of professional media. Appleyard describes the differences between experiential simulations, which attempt to duplicate one or more aspects of a place or project as it would be experienced in reality, and conceptual simulations, which are simplifications or abstractions showing the underlying structure or relationships of a place or project. He provides a "communications model" which identifies the components and participants normally involved in project review. Since these participants hold different opinions of simulation effectiveness and validity according to their attitudes towards the project, Appleyard suggests objective criteria for evaluating simulations (discussed in The Principles of Simulation).

A number of researchers have conducted experiments to test the effectiveness or validity of simulations. Craik (1971) developed a "process model for the assessment of environmental displays," where the critical test of validity is the similarity or equivalence between responses to simulations and responses to reality. Experimentation by Wood (1972), Cunningham et al. (1973), Zube (1973), Acking and Kuller (1973), Sims (1974), Schomaker (1979), Craik et al. (1980), and Sheppard (1982a, 1983), among others, has provided no clear consensus on levels of response equivalence of simulations to reality, or the determining factors.

Studies by Wood (1972), Acking and Kuller (1973), and Sheppard (1982a) comprise the principal attempts to test the success of simulations used in actual project review in predicting responses prior to construction against responses to the real project as built. All these studies found some substantial response differences between simulations and the corresponding built projects.

The traditional research approach has been to test for differences in the relative equivalence or bias of different *simulation media*, for example, renderings versus models. However, many variables (for example, level of detail, color characteristics, quality of reproduction, environmental conditions depicted, conditions in which the simulation is seen) can influence a simulation within any given medium, so that interpretation and generalizing from the results are very difficult.

One theory which appears to be commonly held (McKechnie 1976; Appleyard 1977; Schomaker 1978; Sheppard 1982b), at least for aesthetic evaluations, is that the more accurate a simulation is in depciting the appearance of a project, the closer respnses will be to those obtained in reality. This theory has not been adequately tested. Sims (1974) and Schomaker (1978) both found that increasing the accuracy of renderings improved aesthetic response equivalence, but Sheppard (1982a) was unable to establish any strong overall relationship between accuracy and response equivalence. Highly accurate simulations rarely led to response bias, but inaccurate or abstract simulations did achieve good response equivalence in several cases. It appears that other factors, such as certain intrinsic project characteristics, or the evaluator's familiarity with particular project types, may contribute to correct predictions of visual impacts without accurate simulations. It is, however, not as yet clear in which conditions this may apply.

Very few studies have attempted to document and analyze how simulations are used in practice, and how they have influenced or been influenced by the project review process. There is considerable need, therefore, for more systematic and comprehensive research on typical levels of simulation validity and effectiveness in practice.

Technical Guides

A wide variety of simulation techniques is available, and most of these have some sort of manual or descriptive guide. Many books have been produced on perspective drawing techniques. Martin (1976), for example, describes in detail the technical procedures of perspective construction. Caution should be exercised, however, in the use of books on rendering techniques. For the purposes of objective visual assessment, the approach of preparing attractive "sales" drawings, as endorsed by many professional illustrators, must be avoided. Recommended texts which place emphasis on avoiding deliberate distortions include works by Oles (1979) and Lockard (1977).

A variety of computer programs are applicable to simulation for project review. They include the Perspective Plot Program (Nickerson 1980) (see Figure 11.2), SCOPE (Twito 1978), MOSAIC (Stevenson et al. 1979), and PREVIEW (Wagar and Myklestad 1976). All of these provide line or symbolic drawings of terrain and structures or vegetation. More sophisticated programs and hardware employing color computer graphics in perspective views are being developed (for example, Treiman et al. 1979; Paullson 1979).

A number of methods of photomanipulation exist. Techniques of photomontage, that is, superimposing parts of one photograph or a rendering onto another photograph, are described by Gerdes and Bosselmann (1980) and Blair et al. (1982). Procedures for direct photosimulation by retouching or painting onto a print are described by Baird et al. (1979), Sunwoo et al. (1977), and Blair et al. (1982). An optical method of achieving a similar result by multiple projection of transparencies is explained by the U.S. Forest Service (1977).

Scale models have long been used in project presentations (Janke 1978). Appleyard and Craik (1978) describe the sophisticated Environmental Simulation Laboratory at the University of California, Berkeley, (Figure 11.3), which can provide eye-level moving views through scale models of considerable size. Photography of such models can be used in a variety of media, such as video, 16 mm movie film, and stills for photomontage. Less complicated but still effective simulators are in more common usage (for example, Smardon 1982).

A useful report which compares most of these methods is the Bureau of Land Management (1980) manual on Visual Simulation Techniques. It shares with most of the individual technique manuals one main drawback, however: it does not provide much guidance on the general principles and potential problems in preparing valid and effective simulations for objective visual assessments.

Simulation Examples in Practice

A review of simulations used in practice raises many issues and provides useful opportunities for criticism and learning. The author (Sheppard 1982a, 1983) found that visual simulations typically used in environmental impact documents and public meetings frequently bear little or no relation to the visual assessment process, if any. Furthermore, they are seldom accompanied by information on the assumptions made in depicting

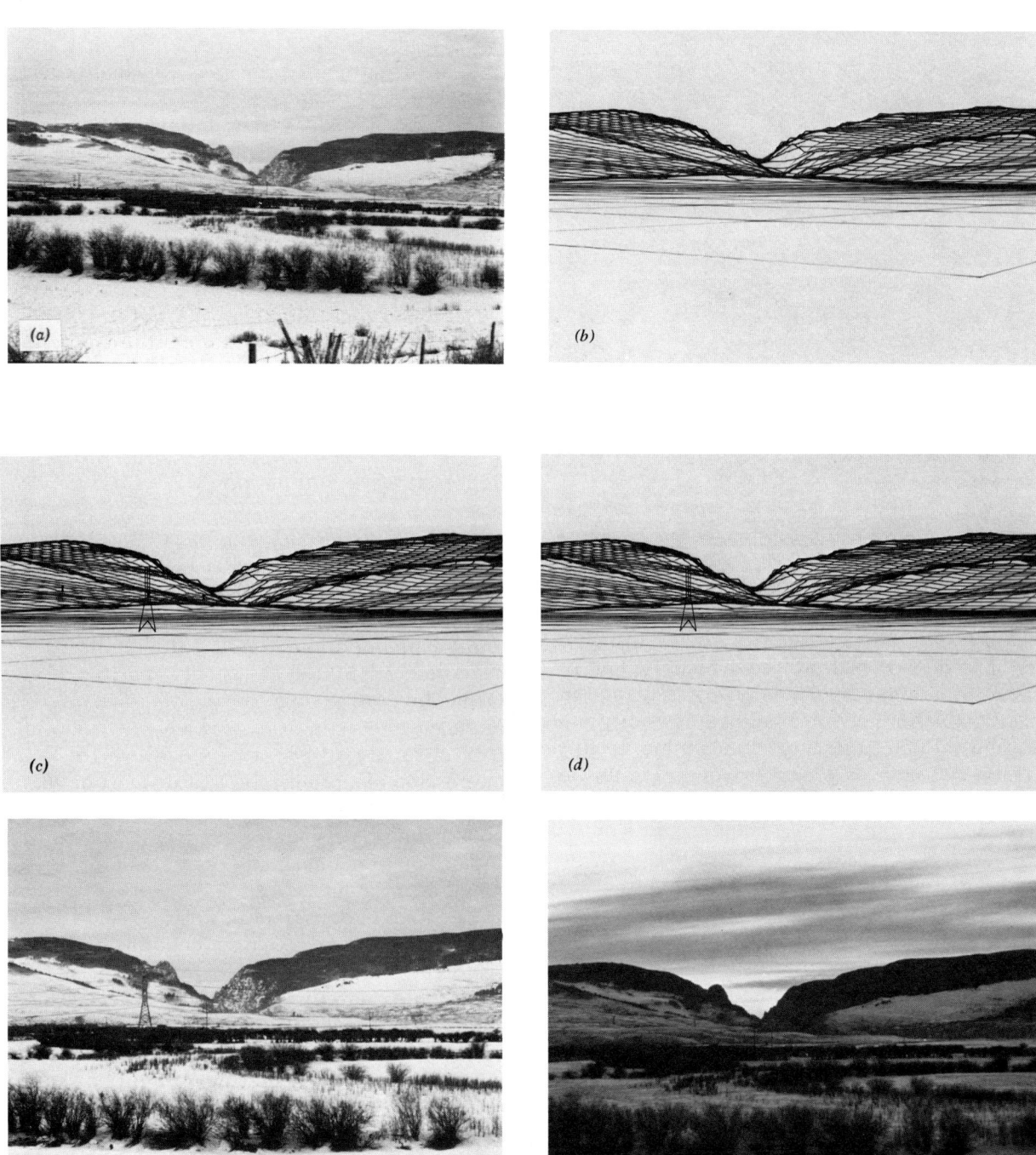

FIGURE 11.2. Use of computer-drawn perspectives in photosimulation. Courtesy of Tri-State Generation & Transmission Association Inc. *a,e,f* by WIRTH Environmental Services (Dames and Moore), *b,c,d* by D. Nickerson (Visual Simulations). The following sequence of figures illustrate an application of the Perspective Plot program to photosimulation of a proposed transmission line near Kremmling, Colorado. *(a)* Color photograph of the existing view towards Gore Canyon from a residential area. *(b)* A digital terrain model was generated by digitizing contours from a topographic map, and this view produced by matching the viewpoint, angle of view, and scale of the photograph in the computer perspective. *(c,d)* Transmission tower designs were also digitized, the locations of two alternative routes entered into the computer, and a view of each generated from the same viewpoint. *(e)* The closer transmission line alternative in the computer perspective was transferred to the photograph on a light table, and subsequently painted in. *(f)* Because local residents had expressed concern over the effect of a transmission line on westward views of Gore Canyon at sunset, the more distant alternative was also simulated towards dusk.

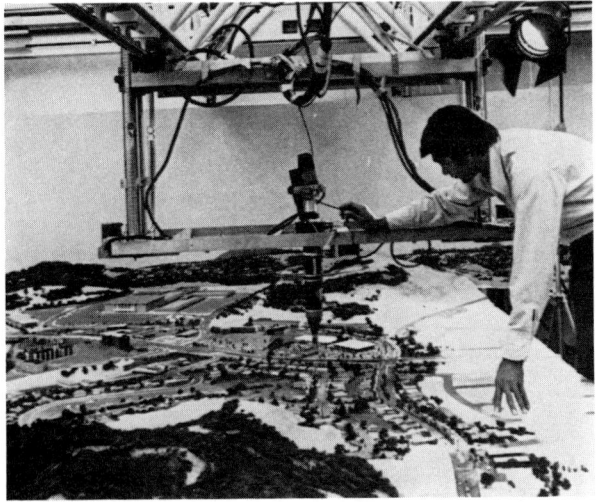

FIGURE 11.3. Modelscope simulator being used on a model at the Environmental Simulation Laboratory, University of California, Berkeley.

the project, the methods employed, or the likely accuracy. There is, however, an increasing number of studies on real projects which include series of simulations as documentary evidence integral to the findings, and simulation quality and/or sophistication appears to be increasing steadily. Notable examples of projects or studies with simulations include, for transmission lines, the Garrison-Spokane 500kV line (Scherer and Embree 1983), and Fort Peck-Havre Final Environmental Impact Statement (EIS) (U.S. Department of Energy/Wirth Associates 1983), both in Montana; for power plants, the Rawhide Energy Project in Colorado (EDAW 1978); for port facilities, the Seattle port terminal facilities (Jones and Jones 1980); for mining, the Alton Coal Mine Unsuitability Petition hearings in Utah (Sheppard and Tetherow 1983); for wind turbines, the San Gorgonio Wind Resource Study in California (Wagstaff and Brady 1982); for timber management, the Ant Hill proposed Timber sale in Montana (Tlusty 1979); for ski-hill development, the Sunshine Ski Area Expansion in British Columbia (Angelo 1979); for highways, the Blue Ridge Parkway in Virginia (Sunwoo et al. 1977); and for office buildings, the Trans Pacific Centre Phase II EIR in Oakland, California (City of Oakland 1982).

THE PRINCIPLES OF SIMULATION

Based upon a review of the research and practical simulation experience outlined above, it is possible to suggest basic principles which are central to creating valid and effective simulations for project visual analysis. The following principles are set forth in the realization that the time and money available for simulation will always be very limited and that the amount of visual information on the project which simulations can communicate will be miniscule in relation to the overall viewing opportunities which the real project would permit. Therefore, it is essential that simulation effort focus upon the key issues and important conditions of the project and avoid procedures which add to uncertainty over the true consequences of a project.

Representative Simulation

Simulations should depict project views and conditions which would prevail in reality. They should show typical views which would be experienced by significant numbers of people at regular or important times. Viewpoints which have been identified as visually sensitive at the visual inventory stage of analysis are obvious candidates. Selecting views which will "show off" particular design features or give the best impression of a project, be it at its most dramatic or least intrusive, is *not* valid. Aerial views of a project are very useful for general understanding and orientation, but should not be relied upon for visual assessments.

The time of day (see Figure 11.2e and f), time of year, lighting and weather conditions, and the age of the project should be considered also. The aim should be to illustrate typical worst-case situations, and at different stages in the life of the project if conditions would change. Ideally, a range of views and conditions should be shown. Litton (1973) provides useful guidelines for establishing representative viewpoints or landscape control points.

Accurate Simulation

In the absence of a precisely understood relationship between simulation accuracy and responses, it is safest to aim for visual accuracy rather than inaccuracy wherever experiential simulations are being used for purposes of visual evaluation. It should be incumbent upon the creator of a simulation to justify any and all known inaccuracies. There is, for example, some evidence (Sheppard 1982a) that moderate levels of abstraction, particularly in renderings, can lead to valid landscape evaluations. Even here, however, visual attributes which strongly influence assessments of visual impact, such as scale relative to the setting, profile in relation to skyline, and color contrast, should be shown with reasonable accuracy.

A further reason for requiring simulation accuracy is that all uses to which a simulation may be put cannot be predicted. Theoretically, it could be proven that an inaccurate or abstract simulation may be valid for a certain kind of project evaluation, for example, view blockage or scale relationship; however, should another issue arise, such as color harmony or privacy afforded by vegetative screening, the limitations on the simulation may make it totally inadequate in helping to answer the questions posed. Accuracy, therefore, may permit greater flexibility in applications of the simulation.

Credible Simulation

If a simulation is to communicate information effectively, it must be believable or convincing to its users. Whether the information it presents is correct is of little consequence if people reject it as false. Credibility of a simulation may be assured in two ways: by creating a "realistic" or lifelike appearance, and by providing documentary evidence demonstrating how accuracy was achieved.

In general, people seem to prefer "realistic" simulations (Sims 1974; Kaplan 1977; Schomaker 1979; Sheppard 1982a), in the belief that they are more accurate and/or less misleading (Figure 11.4). Appleyard (1977) calls this "apparent realism." However, it has been proved conclusively (Wood 1972; Sheppard 1982a) that high credibility of simulations alone is no guide to either accuracy or response equivalence.

Comprehensible Simulation

Related to credibility of simulations is the ease with which they may be understood by users and applied to project evaluation. If a simulation is confusing or incomplete, people may feel unable to make a judgment based upon it. This is particularly likely with lay audiences or users unfamiliar with a particular simulation medium. It is therefore essential that the medium and presen-

FIGURE 11.4. Comparison of an existing view (a) and a simulated powerplant (b) illustrates the high "apparent realism" which photosimulation can achieve. Courtesy of MAP Associates, (a) by D. Wormhoudt, MAP Associates, (b) by S. Sheppard.

tation technique be selected with the range of users in mind. Simulations used as an analytical tool by visual assessment experts should be screened for their suitability for a wider audience before they are incorporated into reports or public presentations.

Bias-free Simulations

Response equivalence or freedom from bias is the overriding principle of simulation validity (Appleyard 1977). The aim of simulation should always be to avoid misleading the user and to elicit project evaluations which are as unbiased as possible. There are enough sources of personal bias and subjective opinion in every user, without compounding the problem with simulation bias.

There is, unfortunately, evidence that a simulation which is valid for one kind of response may bias responses of another kind (for example, Wood 1972; Acking and Kuller 1973). In particular, simulations which are optimal for unbiased cognitive responses, that is, evaluations based on a person's knowledge or beliefs about characteristics of the project, may be misleading in affective responses, that is, sentiments or personal feelings associated with the project. Most visual evaluations of proposed projects include both cognitive and affective elements. Some simulations may elicit unbiased judgments of a project's visual impact while leading to biased evaluations of the overall visual quality of the scene (Sheppard 1982a).

Response bias can be either positive (in favor of the project) or negative (unfavorable to the project). It does, however, seem that simulations rarely lead to significantly favorable bias on one kind of aesthetic response and significantly unfavorable bias on another (Sheppard 1982a).

The five principles outlined above are not equally simple to follow in practice. A thorough visual analysis provides the information on which the representativeness of a simulation may be judged. The credibility and comprehension of a simulation may be estimated with a knowledge of how similar presentations have been received in the past; moreover, any serious shortcomings will normally be revealed at the time of use.

Accuracy, however, is impossible to predict precisely, because so many unknown factors may intervene to alter the situation before the project is completed. Furthermore, the visual reality of the built project is infinitely changeable due to normal environmental phenomena such as lighting. Therefore, the accuracy of a simulation at the time it is created or used may be judged only against the project information available and in terms of a broad comparison between salient visual characteristics of the project and its surroundings. These kinds of judgments are best made by a comprehensive professional evaluation of the full project specifications, the site, and its visual setting.

Response equivalence or bias is still harder to predict, and, ultimately, can be assessed only after project construction. Clues to what does and does not constitute a misleading simulation can be gleaned from some of the other criteria mentioned above. A simulation which is unrepresentative, poorly understood, or demonstrably inaccurate runs the risk of misleading users. Until such time as the factors, alone or in combination, which cause response bias have been clearly demonstrated, the only defensible course is to adhere as closely as possible to procedures and principles which may reduce the probability of bias. As more postconstruction evaluation of simulations in research and practice is documented, it may become possible to predict response equivalence based on past experience.

A SELECTIVE CRITIQUE OF SIMULATION METHODS

The following analysis outlines the pros and cons of some typical simulation methods, focusing principally upon their validity. This can be influenced by the type of simulation medium as well as by a number of general factors which apply to several, if not all, media.

Selected Simulation Media

Scale models, if they include the project and setting and can be viewed through a movable modelscope (Figure 11.3), provide a large number of potential views and the impression of motion, unlike static images from fixed viewpoints. With sufficient skill, care, and expense, highly accurate models can be built. The belief that films of such models are in fact films of real places can be absolute (Craik et al. 1980; Anderson 1970). Craik et al. (1980) and Acking and Kuller (1973) report high response equivalence with detailed colored models. However, more abstract models can have poor credibility and lead to response bias (Cunningham et al. 1973; Sims 1974; Sheppard 1982a).

Renderings (sketches, drawings, and paintings) suffer the restrictions of all fixed views, but offer the greatest flexibility in depicting different conditions of weather, lighting, project age, and so forth. As an overall medium, rendering is familiar and attractive to most people, but the credibility of an individual rendering varies widely according to its level of abstraction; line renderings appear to instill less confidence in users than tonal or full-color renderings (Sheppard 1982a). Accuracy, too, can vary enormously; renderings, because of their strong association with the creative or expressive arts, are perhaps most susceptible to influence by the creator's approach (see below). Renderings have been associated with generally high levels of response equivalence by some researchers (Sims 1974; Schomaker 1979; Sheppard

1982a). However, there is strong evidence that bias in favor of a project occurs more with renderings than any other medium (Wood 1972; Sheppard 1982a).

Methods of photomanipulation, primarily by photomontage, have proven to be an increasingly useful medium. Selection of a base photograph usually commits the creator of the simulation to showing the project in relation to its setting. It also encourages him or her to use a real and accessible viewpoint, and restricts the urge to exercise the imagination. To be fully convincing, visual conditions and graphic techniques used in depicting the project must be compatible with the surrounding photograph. The demands and constraints this imposes on creators have led many to resort to highly abstract "massing studies," capable of depicting accurately only the scale and profile of the project (Figure 11.5). Although this may be useful in indicating view blockage, it risks severe credibility and bias problems. Although comprehensive research results on the validity of this medium are lacking, the author has documented, both in practice and experimental conditions, considerable lack of confidence in more abstract black-and-white photomontages (Sheppard 1982). There is also indication that such simulations may unfavorably bias visual impact assessments due to exaggeration of visual contrasts. Full-color and more precise photosimulations, as produced by retouching (Figure 11.6) or montage with photographic material (Figure 11.7), are likely to have higher credibility. A simple method which may avoid some of the drawbacks of abstract black-and-white photomontage is to project a slide onto photosensitive paper, and then alter the resultant image by sketching in and hand-coloring on the paper with markers, using the original slide as a reference for color and detail.

Computer graphics have become an almost routine method of producing simulations in some quarters. They offer advantages in speed and cost if many simulations are to be produced for a single area, in the ability to select any viewpoint desired, and in attaining a level of "objectivity" free of the creator's influence. In fact, however, most of the currently available programs have severe limitations in credibility and accuracy. The abstraction and/or omission of terrain, vegetation, and structural detail in most simple programs with line-drawing output makes the medium more suitable as an analysis tool or preliminary step in simulation preparation, than as a final presentation device (Figure 11.2). Use for this purpose can confuse a lay audience still unfamiliar with the medium and lead to allegations of graphic overemphasis and consequent exaggerated assessments of visual impact severity (Sheppard 1982a; Wagstaff and Brady 1982). Less obviously, accuracy of computer graphics can be significantly constrained by their resolution, terrain information used, and the software options for data interpretation and terrain smoothing.

More sophisticated computer programs and equipment for producing tonal, full-color, or high resolution images (Figure 11.8) have yet to be extensively used in project review. Accuracy of the more common methods can be substantially enhanced by a combination of computer graphics with other media (Figure 11.9). However, the response equivalence obtained with various computer graphic simulations has not been comprehensively demonstrated.

General Simulation Techniques

Among the many factors influencing simulation validity independent of the media chosen are the data-gathering process, the skill and intent of the creator, the reproduction of the simulation, and the presentation to users.

Many simulations in practice display inaccuracies due to a lack of, or errors in, data on the project and setting. Due to the early stage in proj-

FIGURE 11.5. Abstract line drawings or "massing studies" may receive considerable public criticism where aesthetic character is a major issue. By Peter Szasz & Associates, courtesy of Whistler-Patri.

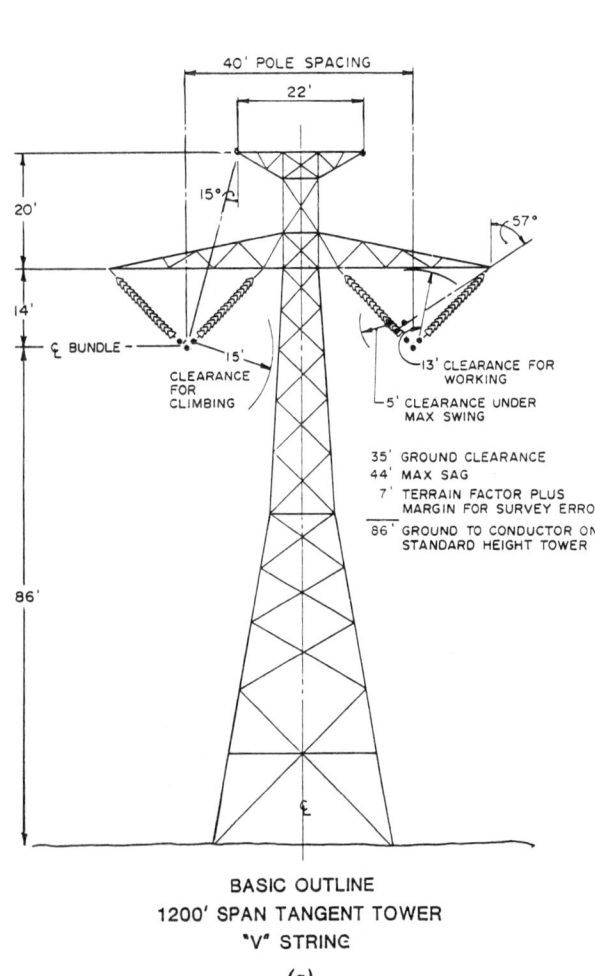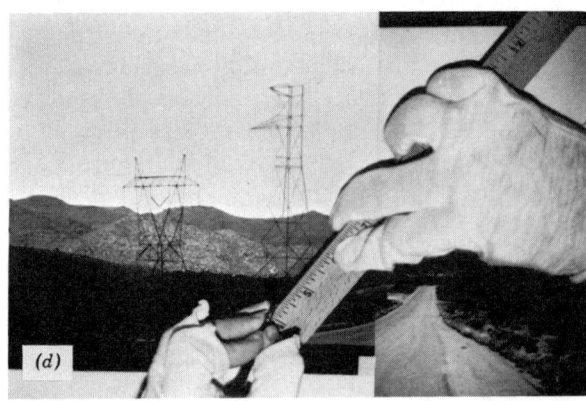

FIGURE 11.6. The photosimulation process. By WIRTH Environmental Services (Dames and Moore), courtesy of Salt River Project. Preparing simulations on photographs by manual perspective techniques requires the use of three sets of materials: data on the proposed development, plans or maps, and photographs of the chosen views. The following figures illustrate how these are used to prepare a photosimulation. (a) Design specifications, usually in the form of elevations, plans and sections, are necessary for determining correct scale, position and shape of the proposed development, in this case a lattice-tower transmission line. (b) Topographic maps or plans, and aerial photographs are necessary to establish angle-of-view between existing objects and the distance from the viewpoint. These measurements are proportional to the horizontal distance between objects measured on the photograph and to their size in the photograph, respectively. (c) Proposed structures can be located by the horizontal angles from known objects. Their size can be calculated from the size of objects of known height in the photography (image), and the distance to the structure, using the following equation:

$$\text{image size of proposed structure} = \frac{\text{image size of known object}}{\text{actual size of known object}} \times \text{actual size of proposed structure} \times \frac{\text{distance to known object}}{\text{distance to proposed structure}}$$

(d) With the aid of color samples, and photographs of similar developments, and taking into account the effect of lighting and distance, color can be selected and applied by painting with opaque gouache or transparent dyes.

FIGURE 11.7. Slide-projected montage. By Larry Green, The Design Studio, Courtesy of BLM. Using two slide projectors, two images can be combined to show a project, originally photographed in one location, set into a photograph of another location. (a) Photograph of an existing power plant. (b) The background around the power plant is masked out in black. (c) Photograph of the site on which the power plant is to be simulated, with similar lighting conditions and color balance to those in the power plant photograph. (d) The silhouette of the power plant from the other photograph, registered precisely, is masked out. (e) Both images are photographed to create 35 mm slides. (f) With correct registration, the two projected images blend.

198 SIMULATING CHANGES IN THE LANDSCAPE

FIGURE 11.8. A technique for simulating air pollution effects. By Energy Systems & Economic Analysis Group, Los Alamos Scientific Laboratory, courtesy of U.S. Forest Service. A sophisticated method for illustrating the effects of dispersed haze or smoke plumes from air pollution sources such as coal-fired power plants has been developed using computer image-processing (Treimen et al. 1979). The following views simulate air quality impacts on a view from Capitol Reef National Park. (a) The film densities of this original color slide of the unaltered landscape were digitized, and the brightness of red, blue, and green wavelength light analyzed. (b) By calculating the effect of light scattering and absorption by a particular plume on film density, a revised image is created and displayed on a TV screen. This view shows a plume downwind from a large power plant, with stable morning air in February with a wind of 2 meters/second. (c) This view shows the same conditions but with a higher wind speed (5 meters/second), leading to a more dispersed plume.

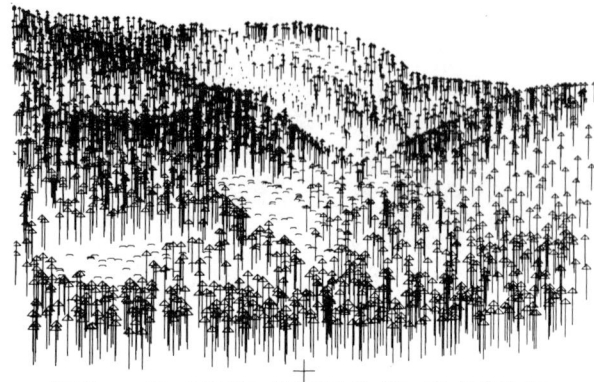

FIGURE 11.9. Computer simulation of timber harvesting (a), enhanced by rendering with color markers (b). Courtesy of BLM, (a) by A. Wagar, U.S. Forest Service and (b) by S. Sheppard.

ect design when many environmental assessments are made, the project descriptions available often fail to give crucial information on appearance, such as new and aged surface colors, architectural detail, height of vegetation plantings, amount and nature of ancillary facilities such as utilities, vehicles, temporary structures and so forth. Typically, also, the creator does not gather sufficient site information on soil and vegetation colors, seasonal variations, or other planned developments unrelated to the project but affecting its visual impact on the setting. The result is too often a "clean," uncluttered, or abstract simulation, presented without a statement of its limitations. This can cause users to fear that the project's visual impact is being underestimated or overestimated (Sheppard 1982a). Depending on the project and the evaluator's attitude toward it, users may also be led into making false or stereotypical judgments (Sims 1974).

The influence of the creator of the simulation on its validity is potentially absolute. Lack of skill, particularly in attempting to use more precise media, can quickly result in criticism by users, possibly with negative consequences for the entire project review process. Exhibition of too much artistic prowess or expression may provoke suspicion, particularly among environmental professionals who are familiar with the deliberate attempts of many project proponents to persuade the audience in favor of the project (Appleyard 1977). Indeed, in one study the author found that renderings prepared by project designers and professional illustrators accounted for virtually all instances of favorable bias, while renderings by third-party environmental consultants were associated with unfavorable bias or none at all (Sheppard 1982a). Nonetheless, much of this effect may not be due to deliberate distortion, so much as to traditional methods of training illustrators without emphasis on restraint and accuracy.

Once an original simulation is completed, the process is not over. Accurate reproduction of the original is crucial for effective presentations, in meetings or reports. Black-and-white processes are normally much cheaper for faithful reproduction of detail in originals, but important information on color contrast may be lost. There is also some evidence that, in certain circumstances, black-and-white simulations may reduce apparent visual quality of a scene in comparison with full-color simulations (Sheppard 1982a). Many reports fail to reproduce graphics clearly, and quality of base photographs is often given insufficient attention, which can negate attempts earlier in the process to produce accurate simulations.

Tied to reproduction quality is the presentation stage. Whether in report format or in meetings or demonstrations, it is important to present the simulations at a sufficient size and with sufficient clarity for the audience or users. Many simulations are presented at too small a size to recreate the true scale/distance relationship which would occur in reality (Appleyard 1977; Sheppard 1982a). Ideally, the angle of view from viewpoint to object in reality would be matched by that from the viewer to the simulation image. Presentation of simulations should include a means of comparison with the existing view, an explanation of the methods used to ensure accuracy and representativeness, and mention of crucial assumptions or unavoidable omissions which could affect visual impact.

CONCLUSION

This chapter has attempted to outline some principles for preparation and use of valid simulations for project analysis. By becoming aware of common pitfalls and inadequacies in routine simulation use, it is possible to derive improved procedures. Much needs to be done to develop, articulate, and demonstrate the techniques by which validity and effectiveness can be assured. Comprehensive research on the determinants of bias-free simulation is necessary, but much can also be learned by postconstruction monitoring of everyday projects by practitioners, for purposes of comparison with preconstruction simulations. Review agencies could encourage an improvement in simulation use by establishing policies or simulation requirements where appropriate, as part of environmental impact assessment, permitting, or management procedures.

Overall, it must be accepted that visual simulation should be an integral part of visual analysis, and not an adjunct, luxury, or cosmetic. Simulation, to be valid, must conform to the same requirements of objectivity, defensibility, and ease of understanding as do visual resource assessments of high professional quality. Indeed, a good simulation both draws information from visual assessment techniques and provides information for the visual impact evaluation.

CHAPTER 12

VISUAL IMPACT ASSESSMENT: CHANGES IN NATURAL AND RURAL ENVIRONMENT

William C. Yeomans

INTRODUCTION

The Demand for Rural and Wildland Areas: Trends in Public Use

Rural and natural environments in the United States and Canada are much in demand within today's changing land use patterns. They have become increasingly valuable in view of their advantages: high visual values, clean air, inexpensive land acquisition costs, and contiguity to attractive scenic and recreational surroundings.

These factors are exacerbated by the fact that distances between urban areas and their outlying rural and hinterland zones have shrunk in terms of real time. Thus once-remote areas have come to be within easy driving distance of most large urban centers. In addition, technology continues to bring sophisticated networks of available power, light, water, and transportation facilities to satellite communities and recreation centers in both rural and natural environments throughout the scenic mountain, valley, and coastal complexes of western United States and Canada (for example, Sunshine Valley, Aspen, Colorado).

Such trends promise to continue. Well-designed and professionally acceptable visual impact assessment (VIA) methodologies will be required to manage such lands *in consort with*, rather than *in opposition to*, introduced management activities.

Such management activities are numerous and complex. For a more comprehensive and detailed listing, see Dick and Smardon (1981). Their appearance in rural and wildland environments can be summarized as follows:

1. Commercial and cultural developments, for example, schools, colleges, cultural centers, shopping centers, and so forth. These primarily affect the rural environment.
2. Utility developments, for example, right-of-way access routes and utility towers; thermal plants, both coal and atomic; dams, spillways and pumping stations.
3. Energy exploration and extraction activities and developments, for example, attendant pipelines; coastal and mainland oil and gas storage plants and offshore platforms.
4. Transportation linkages, for example, scenic corridors, freeway intrusions within scenic rural and natural environments.
5. Agricultural developments, for example, megaprojects such as massive irrigation systems, monocultures (resulting in less diversified landscapes), canals and pumping stations, grain storage elevators, and so forth.
6. Forest products utilization, for example, pulp and plywood mills, sawmills, logging entries, and access haul roads.
7. Flood control developments, for example, river and stream channelization, dyking and diversion systems, artificial drainage schemes.
8. Miscellaneous industrial development beyond the urban core such as manufacturing and assembly plants seeking relaxed zoning restrictions and lower taxation rates in "countryside" settings.
9. Large and intensively developed outdoor recreation complexes where, all too often, the very qualities sought by the development and its users are destroyed by their intrusion of structures, parking lots, and "super highway" accessibility.

In reference to the above categories, a distinction should be drawn between *point*, or *view*-specific VIA applications and *area* or *lineal* studies (Yeomans, 1983).

Point or view-specific applications include mineral extraction, industrial or hydroelectric site installations and development, new townsite developments (viewpoints to and from) and site-specific logging operations, for example, harvesting activities.

Area or lineal studies include, but are not limited to the following: broad-level regional and strategic planning, systematic land inventories; transmission lines, pipelines, and highways and scenic corridors.

In developing any VIA methodology for dealing with the above land use activities, several factors should be considered. First, we should examine the meaning of "naturalness," and secondly, it is important to consider the unique qualities of both rural and wildland environments that pose special land use or specific siting problems.

The Meaning of Naturalness

Naturalness has no set of visual criteria in specific terms of form, line color, or texture; they change from place to place. The term may refer to the appearance of ecological/biological succession or the "natural" sight of rolling hills in a rural setting under agricultural use (Nassauer, 1979). In fact, the rural landscape lends itself well to design, for example, in the layout of fields, buildings, fences, and roadways whereas wildlands do not—or at least not so readily. Yet both hold high visual values. And in both cases visual management can enhance the capability of the landscape to retain its essential quality of naturalness.

Unique Qualities of Rural and Wildland Environments

Retention of "naturalness" in both rural and wildland environments nevertheless gives rise to some special problems in the siting of development projects or land use activities. Chief among these are the following:

1. Interruption of ecological/biophysical processes. For example, strip mining may easily destroy stream quality (color and purity), thus rendering it visually unattractive as well as ecologically unsound. In this regard, true wildlands can be considered as authentic "archetypes" (Nassauer 1979) from which we can learn much in ecological terms.

2. Disturbance of scenic environments, particularly in the American and Canadian west, where topography and vegetation give a high profile to the visual resource, can have a detrimental effect on tourism, which is becoming increasingly important as a source of state and provincial revenues.

3. There is a greater need in rural and wildland environments to work more subtly with existing form, line, color, and texture and blend development with these elements. In contrast, in urban environments structure (bridges, buildings, and so forth) can be manipulated more easily (Nassauer 1979).

4. User preferences for retention of natural qualities found in wildland settings are generally more evident and pronounced than in urban environments, where project and land use alterations are generally accepted as "true urban phenomena."

5. People tend to seek change in their visual environmental "events." Thus contrasts from urban congestion and structured architectural surroundings are sought in the rural and wildland environment. Siting of large industrial complexes such as atomic plants, pulp and paper plants, fuel storage tanks, and so forth in remote rural or wildland settings lessens these contrast values and tends to remind the observer of that which he or she has "left behind."

6. Rural settings often symbolize past historical events and present attitudes toward a particular expression or sequence of impressions in the landscape (symbolism and imageability). These become difficult factors to incorporate or accommodate in any VIA assessment. Examples would include the historical spirit exemplified by well-preserved split rail fences and old log houses in the Caribou country of central British Columbia or the historical imagery of old mining towns in and around Placerville, California.

7. Loss of farmland to urban and industrial development has become a matter of great concern to all serious regional planners throughout the American and Canadian West, particularly farmland contiguous to large urban centers (for example, the Santa Clara Valley in California). Rural aesthetics cannot readily be maintained within VIA assessments unless the rural environment receives some measure of zoning or similar protective measure.

VIA SYSTEMS APPLICATION AND RESEARCH ACTIVITY

VIA problems posed for rural and wildland environments outlined in the previous section have become a matter of concern to land management agencies, practitioners, and the research community in the United States, Canada and Europe. In light of their continuing efforts toward an effective VIA procedure, a brief review highlighting their contributions is appropriate, more so since the concluding section of this chapter draws upon their findings in outlining a recommended VIA procedure for rural and wildland environments.

The U.S. Forest Service

The U.S. Forest Service has developed a system of establishing visual quality objectives (VQO) for its designated forests and rangelands under federal jurisdiction (see Figure 9.18). This system is based on an assessment of variety classes and sensitivity levels. VQOs (preservation, retention, partial retention, modification, and maximum modification) are assigned to management units within each national forest following an inventory of the characteristic landscape in terms of form, line, color, and texture. Logging entries must be made in accordance with VQO restrictions or limitations. Visual absorption capability (VAC), or the ability of the land/water base to accommodate a specific management activity, then governs the nature of the logging entry, ski development, or homesite layout. In some cases, rehabilitation and enhancement may also be assigned as VQOs, where, in the first instance, an area previously affected by logging or mining is to be rehabilitated or enhanced by the introduction or removal of vegetation, redesigned (for logging entries), or scarified for replanting.

For a more detailed review of the USFS system, see Chapter 9, Bacon (1979), and the USDA Forest Service (1972, 1974, and 1979).

The U.S. Bureau of Land Management

The BLM system stresses contrast as its primary defining factor in visual assessment, for example, the degree to which a proposed or existing development contrasts with form, line, color, and texture in the natural or characteristic, environment (see Figure 9.9) (BLM, 1980a). Sensitivity levels, scenic quality, user attitudes, and volumes of use also contribute to a definition of Management Classes (One to Five) (see Figure 12.1) within which proposed activities may or may not meet contrast rating levels assigned to each of the five management classes, much as the USFS translates its visual quality objectives into map form for management purposes.

For a more detailed outline of the BLM system, see Chapter 9 as well as Smardon, Sheppard, and Newman (1984) and the BLM (1980a and 1980b).

British Columbia

In British Columbia, three government agencies are tangentially involved with VIA development: the Ministries of Forestry, Environment, and Energy, Mines, and Petroleum Resources. The Forest Landscape Handbook (B.C. Ministry of Forests, 1982) outlines visual prescriptions for logging entries and follows a methodology patterned largely after that of the U.S. Forest Service.

Visual Sensitivity	High			Moderate			Low
Special Class Zones (SZ)	I(SZ)	I(SZ)	I(SZ)	I	I	I	I
Scenic Quality A	II	II	II	II	II	II	II
B	II	III	III	III	IV	IV	IV
C	III	IV	IV	IV	IV	IV	IV
Distance Zones	FG MG	BG	SS	FG MG	BG	SS	all

DISTANCE ZONES.......................... FG - foreground
　　　　　　　　　　　　　　　　　　　MG - middleground
　　　　　　　　　　　　　　　　　　　BG - background
　　　　　　　　　　　　　　　　　　　SS - seldom seen

VISUAL RESOURCE
MANAGEMENT CLASSES..................... I, I(SZ), II, III, IV

Notes:

1. - If the area being evaluated is adjacent to any Management Class III or higher, select Class III; if lower, select Class IV

2. - Class I(SZ) applies only to classified or designated areas, e.g., parks, ecological reserves, natural areas, etc., as established through provincial or state legislation or policy

3. - Management Class V does not appear in the matrix. This Class applies only to areas identified in the scenic quality inventory where the quality class has been reduced because of unacceptable cultural modifications or areas that have the potential for enhancement or rehabilitation. Indicate the latter as V(E) or V(R) where appropriate.

4. - Each Management Class describes a different degree of modification allowed in the basic elements of the landscape. The primary character of the landscape should be retained regardless of the degree of modification allowed.

(modified from BLM VRM Manual, 1980)

FIGURE 12.1. Matrix for determining VR management classes. Modified from USDI, BLM, 1980a, Visual Resource Management, U.S. Government Printing Office, Washington, DC.

The B.C. Ministry of Environment recognizes the visual resource through an approval process jointly administered with the Ministry of Energy, Mines, and Petroleum Resources at the time a proponent makes application for a land use or a development activity on Crown (provincially owned) lands—other than those managed by the Ministry of Forests. For a fuller explanation of the B.C. system, see Yeomans (1983).

Private Practitioners

The private sector is presently drawn upon in both the western states and Canada by both the proponents for developments in rural and wildland settings and by federal, provincial, state or county agencies seeking VIA assistance beyond their own scope, capabilities, or mandate. Thus the role of the private practitioner has been and continues to be a significant one in the development of VIA methodologies for rural and wildland environments. In some cases, their work has been highly innovative (Jones and Jones' Nooksack Study 1975), or extensive in scale (EDAW

Inc. 1981). In other cases, they have introduced new methods of conducting visual analysis (Mann 1979) and initiated systems of evaluation unique to specific areas, for example, highways (Blair, Isaacson, and Jones 1979); Royston, Hanamoto, and Mayes—Smith River Study (Kunit and Calhoun 1974); recreation areas (Nieman and Futrell 1979) and Nassauer (1979) for rural environments.

Further elaboration of private practitioner contributions to VIA methodology is beyond the scope of this chapter, and the reader is referred to the publication *Our National Landscape* (Elsner and Smardon 1979) and to Smardon, Hunter, Resue, Zoelling, and Standiford (1982) for a more comprehensive review of professional expertise related to VIA application.

Research in VIA Methodology

It is difficult to regard VIA research activity as separate from agency and private practitioner applications, since within both the U.S. Forest Service and Bureau of Land Management professionals have carried out considerable research in preparation of their agency manuals and field guides. Likewise, some excellent research in the field of applied visual assessment has been done by private firms while carrying out their project assignments.

Nevertheless, the research community has made a number of specific contributions related to VIA methodology and terminology. These areas include unknown or untested aspects of VIA such as user attitudes, the true meaning of scenic beauty, psychological aspects involved in observer reactions to project or land use impactions, or simply reactions to the landscape itself. These and similar areas of research have been carried out at universities, Forest Range Experiment Stations and by private contractors throughout the United States in the course of VIA development. For example, Litton pioneered in developing concepts related to visual perception (1972, 1973, 1974, 1979) and, with Tetlow, has outlined a system for conducting large scale descriptive landscape inventories (Litton and Tetlow 1978). Smardon (1979) is known for his research into the legal aspects of VIA application and technical VIA publication interests (Smardon and Elsner 1979). Sheppard and Newman have conducted research leading toward a more precise visual contrast rating system (1982), while Feimer, Craik, Smardon, and Sheppard (1979) have critically appraised the reliability of current VIA methodologies.

Craik (1968) has made appreciable contributions to the psychological aspects of user demands for rural and wildland aesthetic experiences. Daniel, in concert with other researchers, developed the Scenic Beauty Estimation Model (Daniel and Boster 1976; Daniel and Schroeder 1979). Zube produced the only existing text on VIA application in 1975 and has made a number of research contributions toward the development of VIA methodologies (Pitt and Zube 1979; Zube 1974; Zube, Brush, and Fabos 1975). Elsner (1979) has been largely concerned with developing a technology for computer assistance in VIA applications; and in British Columbia, Yeomans (1979) generated biophysical studies related to Visual Absorption Capability (VAC) with parallel research in his field being done by Anderson, Mosier, and Chandler in the United States (1979).

A number of other researchers have made significant contributions to the enrichment of VIA procedures. See the publication *Our National Landscape* (1979) for specific areas of application. See also Smardon, Hunter, Resue, Zoelling, and Standiford (1982) for an annotated bibliography and expertise index related to the above publication.

VIA APPLICATIONS: A RECOMMENDED FRAMEWORK

The balance of this chapter will be concerned with a synthesis of agency, private practitioner, and research activity related to VIA systems and will propose a recommended framework for evaluating land use and specific project impacts, with particular emphasis on rural and wildland environments.

VIA Criteria: A Summary

Five major criteria governing the VIA assessment process have been posited by Starkey and Robinson (1969):

1. The land: its extent and quality.
2. The historical events that have been significant in influencing later land use.
3. The accumulation of structures on the land, including fields, buildings, routes, cities, and monuments.

4. The inhabitants: their numbers, character, culture, and rates of increase.
5. The income inhabitants earn and the economic structure within which they earn it.

Mann (1979) states that the probable impact of a facility (affecting the viewer) may be estimated through (1) delineation of viewing zones, (2) identification of size of presumably sensitive viewing populations, (3) description of visual characteristics of the facility, and (4) evaluation of facility visual impact on foreground and background landscapes. Smardon and Hunter, in their outline of procedures and methods for wetland and coastal area VIA (1983), outline six major steps involved in the VIA process:

1. Conducting the landscape description, or inventory.
2. Assessing user (or viewer) characteristics.
3. Making preliminary line-of-sight determinations.
4. Establishing key viewpoints.
5. Assessing impacting activity/land use characteristics.
6. Preparing a visual impact assessment and mitigation summary.

As can be seen by the above, there is considerable overlap in the steps outlined. It would appear there is a consensus on a general approach to VIA. What is needed is a more precise system of measurement utilizing principles and concepts that have been field tested and relate directly to project impaction.

A Model Format for VIA Procedures

With some modification and amplification, the author has adopted Smardon and Hunter's framework as a general model for application. Specifics in each step or phase have been drawn from a review of agency, practitioner, and research activities as noted in the previous section. Graphic examples and illustrations are included where appropriate. The model is intended as schematic only and should serve as a *procedural* guideline for visual impact assessment of rural and wildlands, bearing in mind that each project and each environment within which it is to be placed will have its own design requirements (see Figure 12.2 and the Appendix).

Phase One: Landscape Description

Fundamental to an accurate and reliable visual impact assessment is the landscape description or inventory stage which is basically a first step in any visual assessment.

Reference was made earlier to systematic visual assessment (assuming eventual visual impact) and one based upon a specific project or land use impact. The former is generally conducted by land management agencies, the latter where a proposed management activity will affect a specific land or water area—which may or may not be under a land management agency. Landscape inventory should proceed on a similar level *in both cases*, although the systematic inventory holds the advantages of time (to conduct the inventory) and scale (where entire regions are or may be related to visual management). In either event, the areas of investigation should be identical. These are: (1) general description, (2) boundaries and edges, (3) landform, (4) vegetation, (5) water bodies and river drainage systems, (6) focal attractions, (7) wildlife and obervable natural events, and (8) existing land use including cultural and historical modifications (Yeomans 1983; Grdén 1979). These factors should be examined with the implication that they are or will be seen by observers from selected visual viewpoints in terms of form, line, color, and texture related to scale and spatial dominance (Sheppard and Newman 1979).

The descriptive inventory is a rational documentation of observed landscapes and should be kept as objective as possible (Litton 1979). It becomes the matrix from which VIA procedures develop and through which eventual management activity or land use determinations are to be made. Thus it is essential that a careful record be kept of all field activities, areas covered by the inventory, photographs taken (and logged as to location, exposure, film's speed, atmospheric conditions: Smardon and Hunter, 1983; also see Figure 12.3). Air photo and topographic map coverage should likewise be carefully annotated as to scale, or approximation, date of notations, source data, and reliability. All these data should be kept for purposes of documentaton, presentation, and legal substantiation, where necessary, as will be noted in phase six.

Determination of regional and subregional inventory boundaries is an early essential in the landscape inventory. For this purpose, Fenneman (1931) is generally used in the western United

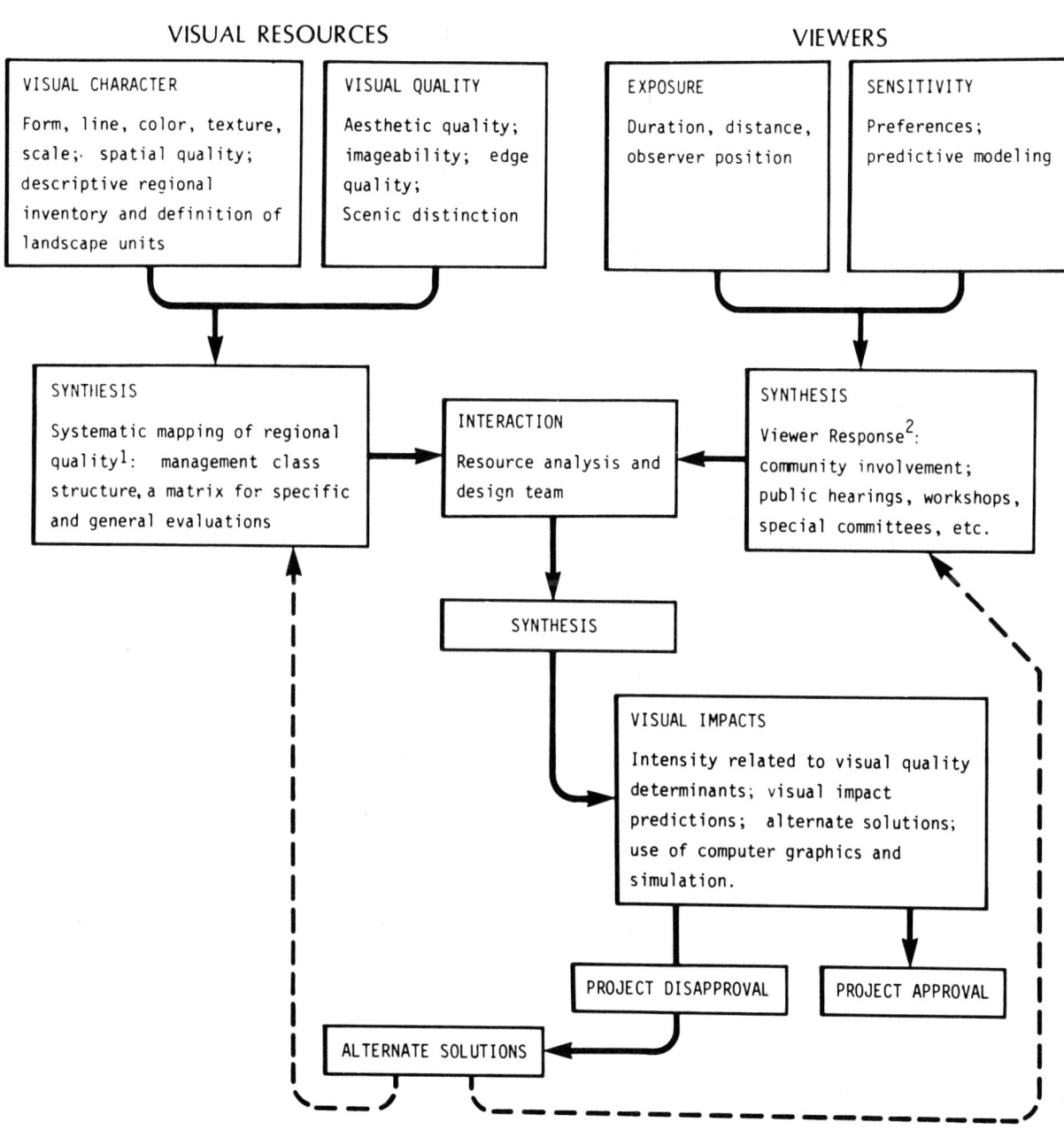

[1]Areal, lineal visual resource quality mapping precedes specific impact analysis.

[2]Relates to visual character and quality at site specific, view specific and route specific project.

FIGURE 12.2. A model for processing resource assessment and impact studies. *Source:* Yeomans, W.C., 1983, Visual Resource Assessment-A User Guide, B.C. Ministry of Environment, Victoria, British Columbia.

```
FILM REFERENCE NO: KM      ROLL NO: 1
FRAME NO(S): POLARIZER   UNDER      NORMAL
PANORAMA (180°)   LEFT    MIDDLE     RIGHT
       NORMAL     28       29         30
  2/3  UNDER      31       32         33
       POLARIZER  25       26         27
       OTHER      ___      ___        ___
```

FIGURE 12.3. Sample photo-log sheet. *Source:* Smardon, R.C. and Hunter, M., 1983, Procedures and Methods of Wetland and Coastal Area Visual Impact Assessment (VIA), in Smardon, R.C., ed., *The Future of Wetlands: Assessing Visual-Cultural Values*, Totowa, NJ:, Allanheld, Osmun, 197.

States and Holland (1964) in British Columbia. The *region* is determined primarily on the basis of similar landforms, river drainage systems, orogenic history, and climatic and vegetative characteristics. However, its definition depends as well upon the scale either of the systematic inventory or degree of influence of a specific management activity (see Figure 12.4).

While wildland descriptive inventories should emphasize landform, vegetation, water, and human use and development, the rural landscape under study must be closely examined for additional factors such as imageability and symbolism, that is, its thematic "story" in terms of history, agricultural patterns, and boundaries and edges.

Inventories may differ in their emphasis upon landscape description and character. Thus Litton, Tetlow, Sorenson, and Beatty (1974) should be consulted for guidance where interior water and wetlands prevail. Smardon and Hunter (1983), Mann (1979), Mills (1979), and EDAW (1982) give valuable direction on coastal inventories. Litton and Tetlow (1978) have drawn up a simple but effective framework for developing a large-scale inventory for the northern Great Plains in the United States. In Canada, Yeomans (1983) evolved a provincial inventory framework based on biotic regions (useful where biophysical factors

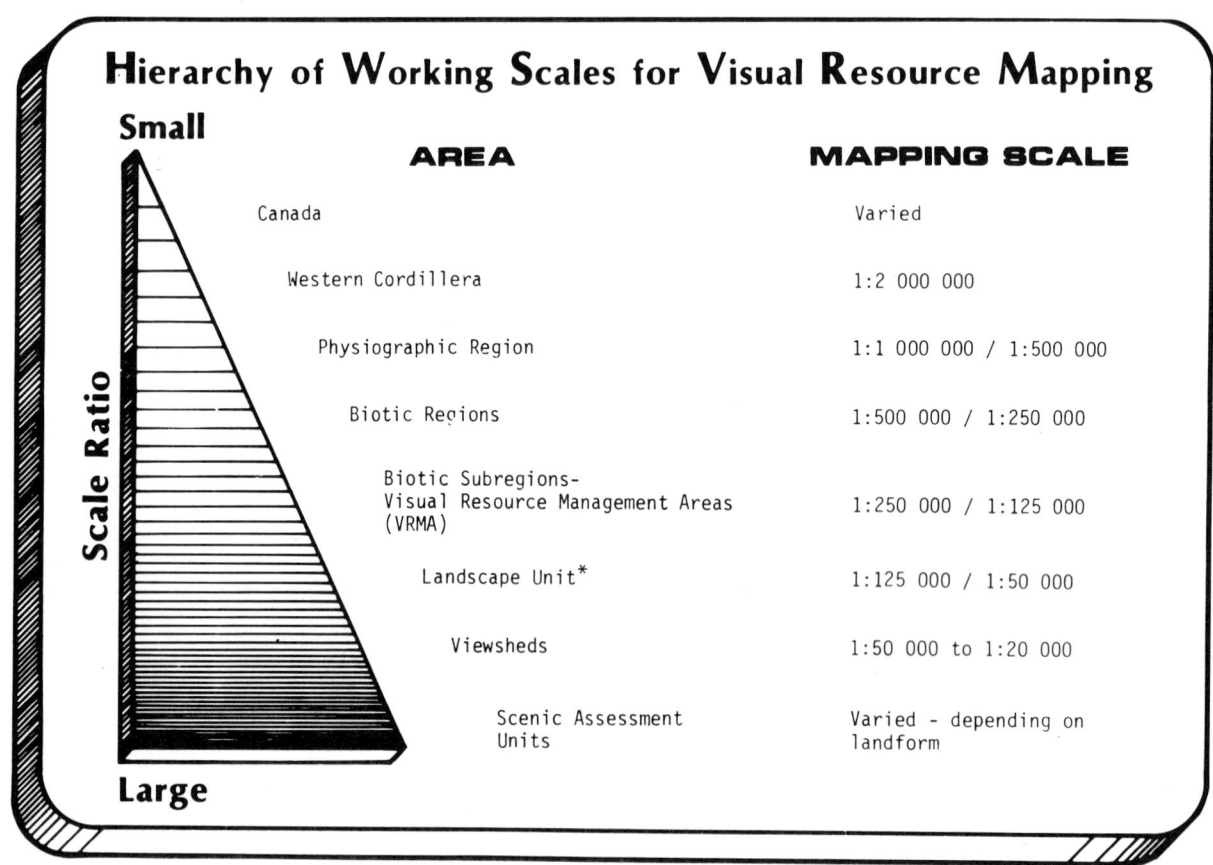

FIGURE 12.4. Hierarchy of working scales for visual resource mapping. *Note: Scales will vary as one approaches the area under study, depending upon intended level of inventory intensity. *Source:* Yeomans, W.C., 1983, Visual Resource Assessment—A User's Guide, B.C. Ministry of Environment, Victoria, British Columbia.

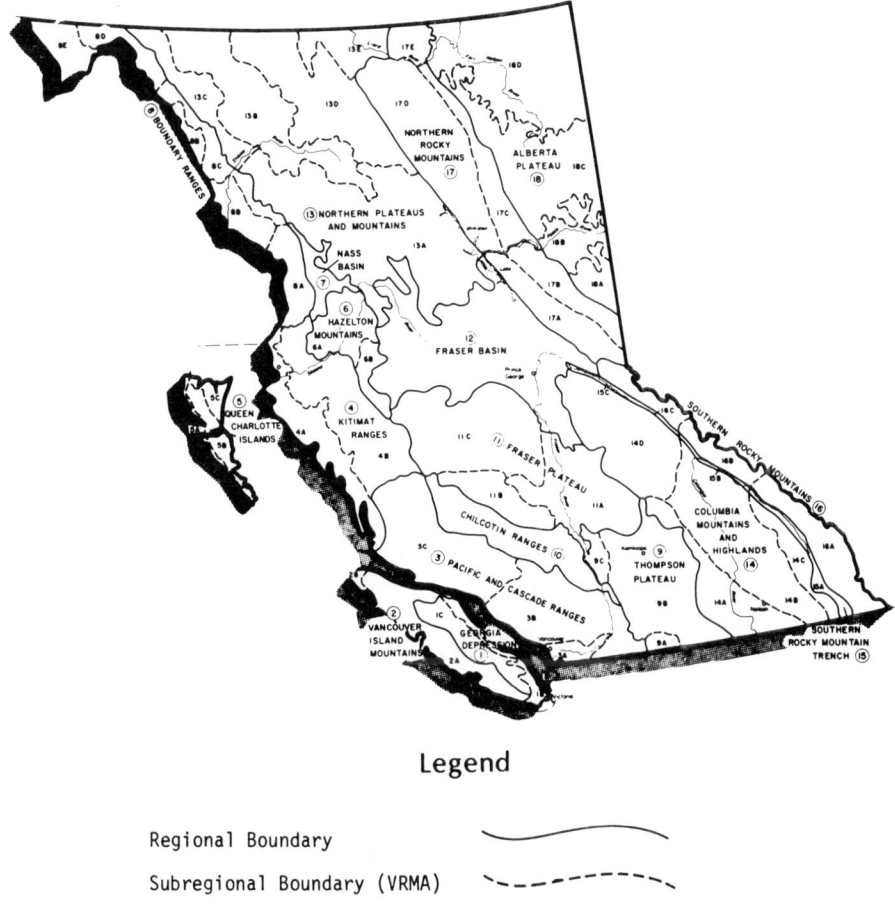

FIGURE 12.5. Biotic regions of British Columbia. *Source:* B.C. Ministry of Environment, Victoria, British Columbia, 1982.

must receive emphasis) (see Figure 12.5). And three reliable sources for describing the rural landscapes are found in Jones and Jones' Nooksack Study (1975), McHarg's *Design with Nature* (1969), and in British Columbia, the Spallumcheen study (Yeomans 1975).

Phase Two: Observer Characteristics

Determination of viewer characteristics can be made conjointly with landscape description and documentation or shortly thereafter. Assessing observer reaction to landscape effect is, of course, the basic intent of the entire VIA process. It is, therefore, of singular importance to obtain observer characteristics as they prevail in the area or region under analysis. Such questions as the following must be addressed:

1. Who are the people? (that is, demographic characteristics)
2. Where do they come from and where are they going?
3. What volume of use is the area experiencing, and during which time of the year does it take place?
4. What is the projected use of the subject area?
5. How do observers react to structures imposed on the landscape as opposed to landform, water body, and vegetational changes?

The above information may be obtained from census data, highway "origin and destination" studies, tourist travel statistics, land management, agency seasonal surveys (Smardon et al. 1980), personal interviews, carefully designed questionnaires, and on-the-ground observation. When involved in a team approach to visual assessment (which allows the benefit of additional judgement factors), the visual analyst may consult with a sociologist or statistician for specialized assistance. He or she may be required to conduct a recreational/activity survey if the above information is not readily available (Smardon and Hunter 1983).

Assessment of viewer attitudes is essential in any determination of the degree to which alteration may be desirable or acceptable (see Figure 12.6). Obtaining this information is not always easy or even reliable since studies in the measurement of user reaction to changes in the landscape are few in number. This factor is complicated by the reality that public attitudes and accessibility to project areas change over time (Grdén 1979).

There are other difficulties involved in sampling public opinion and basing the VIA summary form upon their conclusions. All too often, the public gives one set of reactions to a proposed development when queried in the field and quite another at a subsequent public hearing. The public is not always aware of its prejudices, socially conditioned attitudes, and general lack of awareness of the visual environment and may be unable to articulate its feelings at the time of questioning. In a parallel vein, professionals, or "experts," must be cautious of their own subjectivity, their own preferences and prejudices and—if they represent a land management agency—that agency's particular bias.

The best approach to assessment of viewer attitudes appears to be somewhere in the middle: a combination of public sampling with professional assessments based on training and experience in visual analytics (see Table 12.1). This will call for the development of sound sampling techniques and a well-designed VIA procedure readily understood at the public hearing roundtable. For guidance in this area, see Kaplan (1975), Craik (1968), Daniel and Boster (1976), Daniel and Schroeder (1979) and Chapter 10 in this volume. In British Columbia, see Fraser (1982) for public involvement guidelines and sampling techniques in forest environments where impacts have taken place. Continued research into the dynamics of public reaction to intrusions in the rural and wildland environments is of continuing importance to the VIA process but of one thing the analyst may be certain: he or she must assess viewer preferences for a particular environment *before* impaction takes place, since those who may not prefer such environments in the first place are hardly expected to be negatively affected by any environmental changes therein (Smardon and Hunter 1983).

Phase Three: Line-of-Sight Determinations

After the landscape description has been documented and observer characteristics assessed, the area or region under study can be divided into seen, partially seen, and unseen areas from existing roadways, trails, waterways, or other means of public access to and through the area. This phase leads to eventual selection of key viewpoint areas and must be carried out with a number of factors in mind. Chief among these are observer position (above, below, or level with the man-

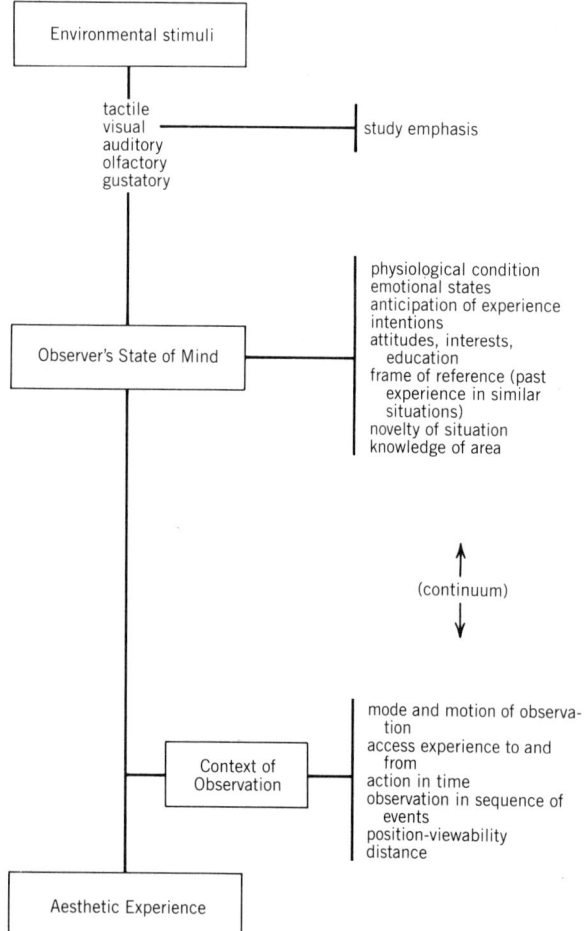

FIGURE 12.6. A model of aesthetic response. *Source:* Litton, Tetlow, Sorensen, and Beatty, 1974.

VIA APPLICATIONS: A RECOMMENDED FRAMEWORK   211

TABLE 12.1. Community Interaction Techniques

Information Gathering	Information Distribution	Interaction	Special Purpose
Existing sources: compiled statistics; descriptive information	Posters, billboards, and signs	Small group meetings	Referenda
	Mail notices, brochures, newsletters, fliers	Working meetings	Technical assistance
Working with local officials		Workshops	Mediation and arbitration
Monitoring new developments	Newspapers: Legal notices Advertisements News articles Feature columns and articles News releases Letters to the editor	Hearings and other large public meetings	Ombudsman
Analyzing plans, programs, and reports		Field offices	
		Public information centers	
Monitoring mass media: newspapers, radio and television other media		Advisory committees, steering commitees, other groups	
	Radio and television: Announcements News coverage Talk shows and community-oriented programs Documentaries		
Field work			
Surveys	Community organizations		
	Displays, maps, models		

FROM National Cooperative Highway Research Program Report #156 Transportation Research Board National Research Council, Washington, D.C., 1975.

agement activity); viewing distance zones, for example, foreground, middleground, and background; lighting conditions (front lighting, back lighting, and side lighting—the last being the best angle from which to judge visual perception in the study area (Smardon, Sheppard, and Newman 1984). Obstruction of view and compatibility within foreground areas are two other factors to be assessed (Mann 1979). Also see Chapters 4 and 16 for further methodological considerations.

At this point, the proposed location of the management activity or land use should be known since this activity becomes the focal point for line-of-sight determinations. To some degree, topographic maps and air photos, coupled with photographs taken during the initial ground reconnaisance phase, will be helpful in determining seen, partially seen, and unseen areas. If digital terrain data is available, computer assistance can prove of great value, particularly when dealing with large geographic areas. VIEWIT (Travis, Elsner et al. 1975); PERSPECTIVE PLOT (Twito 1978; Nickerson 1980) and PREVIEW (Mykelstad and Wager 1976) are the three computer-based graphic systems most commonly used today by visual analysts.

In more concise problem areas, or those reduced in scale, such as a single structure in the landscape, or where digital terrain data is unavailable, line-of-sight readings can be gained by establishing *landscape control points* (Litton 1973). Also see Figure 4.2. This involves establishment of cross-sectional diagrams from a point, or points of observation, thus determining seen and unseen areas. The process—a combined field and office operation—is valid and useful, but somewhat time-consuming, and does not allow for vegetative interspersions; these must be interpolated from forest cover maps (PREVIEW gives this information with prior digitizing).

Preliminary sketches and simulations should now be made of the management activity as it would look from each of the line-of-sight observation points. These will give the analyst some idea of levels of impaction involved from various locations in the study area and lead to final selection of *key viewpoints*, that is, those from which the activity appears most critical.

Phase Four: Key Viewpoint Analysis, Sensitivity Levels, and Scenic Assessment

Once the landscape description, observer characteristics, and preliminary line-of-sight determinations have been made (Phase One to Three), *key viewpoints* can then be determined and simulated.

Key viewpoints are determined on the basis of the number of times the activity will be seen, the duration of the view(s), the number of observers viewing the activity, and the distance over which the activity or land use is seen—for example, the closer the activity, the more severe the probable impact (see Figure 9.17). If field photographs have been carefully logged, these can be invaluable in depicting key viewpoint visibility characteristics.

Each key viewpoint should then be simulated. Sophisticated simulation technqiues have been developed at the agency, practitioner, and research levels. They range from superimposition of artist renderings on field photos (BLM 1980b) to computer graphic representations, balloon elevational studies (Yeomans 1982), perspective line drawings (Mann 1979), and touched-up color slides. Simulation details are beyond the scope of this chapter. For a concise and graphic summary of techniques involved, the reader should refer to the Bureau of Land Management publication "Visual Simulation Techniques" (1980). See also Baird, Sheppard, and Smardon (1979) and Feimer, Craik, Smardon, and Sheppard (1979) and Chapter 11 in this volume.

Although visual sensitivity levels and scenic assessments can be made at Step Three (line-of-sight determinations), it is the author's opinion that these factors are better understood *after* key viewpoints have been established since they reveal sensitivity to impaction *directly related to the point where scenic attributes are most affected.* Conversely, systematic agency evaluations literally "blanket" each administrative district or region with scenic and sensitivity levels in mapped form (BLM 1980a; U.S. Forest Service 1974). This is done prior to any development proposals, thus gaining an overall management class structure within which to evaluate any future project proposals. Disadvantages in this system lie in the isolation within which agency professionals tend to function, the tendency of the agency to protect its management mandate (by implication), and by virtue of changes normally taking place over time in both observer attitudes and the land base itself.

Sensitivity levels are obtained by running user attitudes (characteristics) and user volume (travel patterns) through a matrix where "highs" in each are matched to reveal various degrees of sensitivity (BLM 1980a). Thus an area seen by a large number of observers that is also in high user demand (evolving from an assessment of user attitudes—see Phase Two) has a high visual sensitivity level (see Chapter 9 for more detail).

The success of this assessment depends upon the accuracy with which travel patterns have been determined and the manner in which observer characteristics (attitudes) were recorded. Both factors may change between the time of the original field measurements and the time of visual impaction.

In the BLM system, *scenic assessment* is made on the basis of seven criteria: landform, vegetation, water, color, adjacent scenery, scarcity, and cultural modifications. These are then rated high, moderate, or low in value related to potential impaction.

The U.S. Forest Service makes its determinations on the basis of variety classes (A to C) and sensitivity levels (1 to 4) (see Figure 9.12). Jones and Jones (1977) use intactness, vividness, and variety to describe scenic quality. Both agency systems (BLM and USFS) tend to favor areas with strong topographic relief and abundant water, characteristic of the mountainous areas in the western states and British Columbia, whereas Jones and Jones were able to correct this deficiency in their criteria, which are generally applicable, but particularly so to rural and urban environments.

In any event, scenic beauty is not restricted to any firm parameters, a fact the analyst should keep in mind at all times. Protection of common landscapes may be just as important as with high scenic quality landscapes (Litton 1978) and, as Grdén points out (1979), "high scenic quality can exist in unfashionable or inaccessible deserts and plains as well as in popular and accessible areas of craggy peaks and crystal lakes." Even natural areas are not necessarily scenic, historically significant, or valuable for recreation but the need to preserve such areas lies in their distinctiveness from the overall landscape (Vermont Natural Resources Council 1978).

Although the rural environment is, in many

cases, unspectacular, it is nonetheless sensitive to visual encroachment; furthermore, it is seen by a greater number of people over a longer period of time than is the case with wildland environments. In addition, too little consideration is given in most current VIA assessments to either rural or wildland observation of wildlife or other special "watching and classifying" activities (for example, bird watching), which are growing in number and importance with the viewing public (Palmer 1979; Yeomans 1983).

Much remains to be done in refining techniques for measurement of scenic qualities in the landscape. Each visual analyst carries the responsibility of carefully annotating his or her own particular approach for documental defense in public hearings, for its research value, and for legal reasons as well. For specific examples of scenic assessment methodologies being followed today, see Tetlow and Sheppard (1977) (coal extraction in NE British Columbia); Blau, Bowie, and Hunsaker (1979) (natural area scenic inventory in Idaho); and EDAW, Inc. (1981) for coastal sensitivity levels and scenic attributes in California.

Phase Five: Assess Impacting Activity/Land Use Characteristics

Impact Assessment

The VIA procedure as outlined now requires the analyst to gain a full understanding of the impacting activity in order to prepare an assessment and mitigation summary form and subsequent report. Whatever simulation has been made up to this point should have maximized the realistic portrayal of impacting activity (Smardon and Hunter 1983), since component parts of the proposed land use may have differing effects on vegetation, landform, water bodies, and existing structures in the landscape. A large hydroelectric project, for example, most certainly affects the area's hydrology and the visual impact brought on by excessive drawdown. In addition, access to the dam may alter existing circulation patterns. The mass of the structure may dominate adjacent landforms or become the area's single dominant feature (spatial dominance). Aesthetics of its structure, in terms of form, line, color, and texture, may not be in harmony with the surrounding characteristic landscape. The above factors presume a stage of completion, while impaction of the landscape may become even more severe during stages required for its completion.

The above example can be replicated for many development projects proposed within the United States and British Columbia rural and wildland natural environments. It strongly suggests that the visual analyst familiarize himself or herself with direct and tangential effects the project may have from *all* key viewpoints as well as transit passage en route to the activity itself.

Two specific aids in gaining a better understanding of the relationships outlined above lie in an examination of project aesthetics and conducting a visual absorption capability (VAC) analysis.

Project Aesthetics

The proposed project or landscape should be questioned by the analyst in three principal design areas: internal aesthetics, relational aesthetics, and environmental aesthetics (Blair 1980; Yeomans 1983).

Internal Aesthetics

Three questions must be answered in regard to the internal aesthetics of a project:
1. Does the project design visually express its *internal* functions, that is, is it clear to the observer what the function symbolizes in the landscape?
2. Are details of the project visually consistent with one another?
3. Are there other aspects of internal aesthetics that vary with the nature of the project? For example, a scattered, undefined cluster of buildings generally creates a sense of disorder and confusion in the observer.

Relational Aesthetics

This term refers to the visual relationships *between a project and specific elements of its surroundings*. For example, although some degree of contrast is needed for highway informational signing, the contrast may be too extreme in terms of color or line. Signs may also block out important scenic views. Relational aesthetics are largely controlled by community approval of the proposed project, provided the information is adequate for review in the planning stage.

Environmental Aesthetics

A proposal to alter the landscape may also affect the surrounding regional environment, often outside the study area itself. This involves extended environmental aesthetics, a third area within the project analysis. Consequent effects may be to enhance the quality of the total environment, decrease its quality or, in some instances, have no effect whatsoever.

Visual Absorption Capability (VAC)

In addition to investigating the subtleties of project aesthetics, the visual analyst should understand *processes and subactivities* involved in the proposed activity/land use as they relate to earth processes. This becomes particularly important in the case of various forms of energy production, mineral extraction, road construction, and utility corridor manipulations. It does not necessarily involve a technical knowledge of engineering or architecture, but rather a basic understanding of structure placement and function related to the land's capability to accommodate that activity or land use. This is known in the VIA process as visual absorption capability, or VAC.

VAC is defined as the capacity of the landscape to screen or accommodate proposed development and still maintain its inherent character (Anderson et al. 1979; Yeomans 1979, 1983). Three major groupings of VAC factors are involved in the analysis: (1) biophysical factors (site conditions), (2) perceptual factors (observer-related); and (3) proposed activity factors (management or development activity) (Anderson et al. 1979).

Since we have already dealt in the preceding sections with the need for identifying *perceptual factors* (distance, visual magnitude, observer position, number of times the activity is seen, number of viewers, duration of view, and other variables) and *proposed activity factors* (scale, nature of development, and project aesthetics), something needs to be said relative to the *biophysical components* of VAC. These can be overlooked in the VIA process or given too little consideration. They include slope, soil stability, vegetation regeneration potential, vegetation diversity, and soil and rock color contrast—all of which may be affected by the proposed activity or land use.

Of the above biophysical factors, slope is the most critical since the steeper the slope, the more vulnerable it is to visual impact. Slope, therefore, becomes the multiplier for the formula:

$$VAC = S \times (E + R + D + C + V) \text{ (Yeomans 1983) where:}$$

S = Slope (the steeper the slope, the lower the VAC)

E = Soil stability and erosion potential (positive factors raise VAC; negative factors lower VAC)

R = Vegetation regeneration potential (high potential raises VAC)

D = Vegetation diversity (the greater the diversity, the greater the potential for high VAC)

C = Soil and rock color contrast (too great a contrast lowers VAC by virtue of exposure to view)

V = Soil/vegetation contrast (the higher the contrast, the higher the VAC)

Table 12.2 illustrates how the above formula can be applied in a quantitative rating system, for example, the higher the numerical score, the higher the VAC.

Biophysical base data can usually be obtained from soils, terrain, vegetation (forest cover), and geological maps in both the western United States (USGS 15-minute series) and British Columbia (NTS 1:50000 series). The latter may be obtained from the B.C. Ministry of Environment (1981). The analyst can then readily overlay the completed simulation(s) (Phase Four) over such base maps to determine VAC. Further overlays of visual sensitivity and scenic assessment findings on to the base map can reveal beyond the biophysical base (Blau et al. 1979).

Visual absorption capability varies with the visual characteristics of landscape alternatives, such as trail or road construction, clearcutting, or strip mining. Generally, as the *size* and/or duration of the activity increases, the project area's VAC decreases. Proposed activity factors interact with biophysical and perceptual factors to determine probable impact.

The following five-step procedure should serve as a guide to the analyst:

Step One: Define landscape units and/or viewsheds by air, ground, and air photo examination.

TABLE 12.2. VAC Values

Factor	Characteristics	VAC Values Verbal	VAC Values Numerical
Slope **S**	Steep (55%+ slope)	low	1(multiplier)
	Moderately steep (25%–55% slope)	mod.	2(multiplier)
	Relatively flat (0–25% slope)	high	3(multiplier)
Vegetation Diversity **D**	Barren, grass/brush	low	1
	Conifer, hardwood, cultivated altered	mod.	2
	Diversified (mixed open and woodland)	high	3
Soil Stability and erosion potential **E**	High constraint value derived from high erosion hazard and/or high instability hazard and/or poor regeneration potential	low	1
	Moderate constraint value derived from erosion hazard and/or instability hazard and/or regeneration potential	mod.	2
	Low constraint value derived from low erosion hazard and/or low instability hazard and/or good regeneration potential	high	3
Soil/ Vegetation contrast **V**	High visual contrast between exposed soil and adjacent vegetation	low	1
	Moderate visual contrast between exposed soil and adjacent vegetation (and all barren, cultivated, and diversified vegetation types)	mod.	2
	Low visual contrast between exposed soil and adjacent vegetation	high	3
Vegetation regeneration potential **R**	Low potential	low	1
	Moderate regeneration or Potential for regeneration	mod.	2
	High regeneration	high	3
Soil & rock color contrast **C**	High contrast	low	1
	Moderate contrast	mod.	2
	Low contrast	high	3

Adapted and modified from Blair, et al., 1979 and Yeomans, 1979

Step Two: Determine where VAC assessment is needed relative to probable project impacts.

Step Three: Review basic assumptions and visual quality objectives.

Step Four: Map slope, vegetation, soil, and rock color factors (Munsell Chart), and landscape diversity.

Step Five: Assign biophysical sensitivity ratings (high to low) with the formula VAC = S × (E + R + D + C + V) and rate accordingly.

Phase Six: The Visual Impact Assessment and Mitigation Summary

In the final Stage of the recommended VIA framework outlined in this chapter, the visual analyst completes his or her summary of what effects the proposed activity/land use will have on visual quality within the study area (see Figure 12.7). The summary should include:

1. A one-page rating sheet as shown in Figure 12.8 should adequately cover most projects and summarizes the evaluator's notations related to impacts experienced from kew viewpoints. At this point, the analyst is reminded that it is much easier for people to judge the visual impact of structures than landform, water bodies, or vegetation (Smardon and Hunter 1983). In filling out the rating sheet, it is also important to remember that variables that most consistently behave similarly to change in scenic beauty are scale contrast and

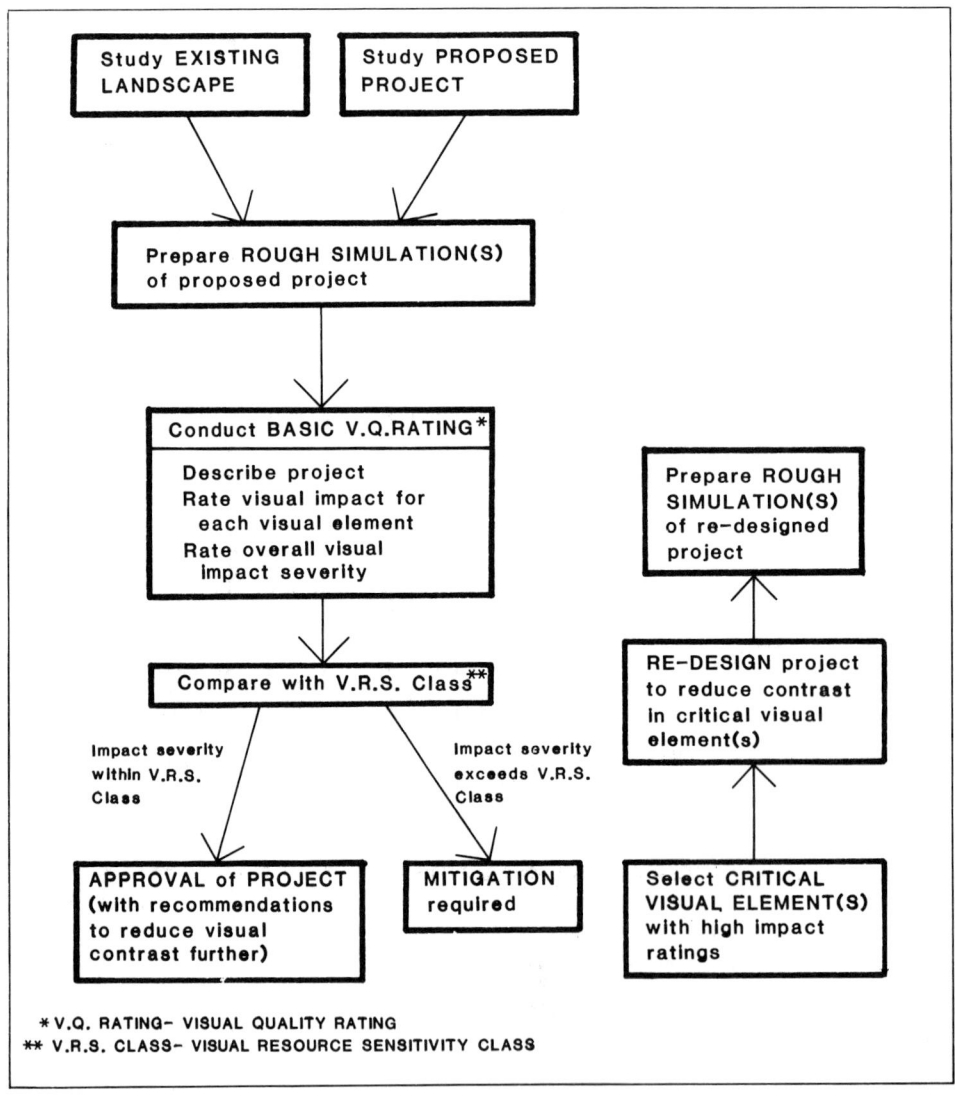

FIGURE 12.7. Mitigation procedure for typical projects. *Source:* Smardon, Sheppard, and Newman, 1984.

	Project Name			Date	
	Location	Map: _____		Scale: _____	
	Regional District: _____				
	Strategic Planning Area: _____				
	Section: _____	Range: _____		Township: _____	
	Longitude: _____	Latitude: _____			

Sketch Map	VRMA: _____
	Landscape Unit: _____
	Evaluated By: _____
	Checked By: _____
	Visual Resource Management Class: _____
	Key Observation Point _____

Characteristic Landscape

	Element	Descriptions[1]	Comments
LAND/WATER	Form	Landform (3-D) water, soil pattern	
	Line	Regularity/continuity	
	Color	Soil, rock, ice, snow, hue, value, chroma	
	Texture	Clarity, grain	
	Scale	Landform/waterform mass and area	
VEGETATION	Form	Regularity, simplicity, orientation	
	Line	Direction, regularity edge character	
	Color	Hue, value, chroma	
	Texture	Clarity, grain	
	Scale	Size, area surrounding objects	
STRUCTURES	Form	Regularity, simplicity orientation	
	Line	Direction, regularity continuity, simplicity	
	Color	Reflectivity, hue value, chroma	
	Texture	Clarity, grain	
	Scale	Size, height, width, surrounding areas	
LANDSCAPE	General Description	Define characteristic landscape, regional setting etc.	
	Scale	Expansive, bounded, area enclosure; visual unit	
	Spatial Composition	Focal, feature, enclosed, panoromic, canopied; weak to strong	

FIGURE 12.8. Visual contrast rating sheet. Adapted from Smardon, Sheppard, and Newman, 1984. Courtesy of Yeomans, W.C., 1983, Visual Resource Assessment—A User's Guide, B.C. Ministry of Environment, Victoria, British Columbia.

spatial dominance (for all situations) and texture, form, line, and color contrast for structures only. Landscape compatibility and the two variables—scale contrast and spatial dominance—should thus be given equal weightings in order to realistically relate elements (form, line, color, and texture) with significant variables (Smardon and Hunter 1983). See Figure 12.9.

2. Written documentation is a narrative summary of the procedures followed, original terms of reference, and items not covered by the project rating sheet. Written descriptions of landscape characteristics, compatibilities, and variables can be confusing if consistent terminology is not used. A glossary of terms is virtually a requirement if lay audiences are to understand written descriptions, and should conform with that found at the conclusion of this text.

3. Photographic documentation has been stressed throughout all phases of the VIA assessment model but becomes most essential at the time the final VIA summary is made. Photos should not only include landscape description backup material but should be logged for key viewpoints, project aesthetics and VAC details, for example, soils, vegetation, slope, aspect, and so forth. Photos should also be used to develop marker scenes to back up or support maps, diagrams, charts, or other documents where they can convey three-dimensional meaning to proposed concepts.

Summary Statement

The quality and utility of a measurement method is largely a function of four properties: reliability, validity, sensitivity, and generalizability (Smardon and Hunter 1983). *Reliability* is the degree to which different users come up with the same results or replicability. *Validity* represents the degree to which a measurement accurately reflects variation among landscape and land use conditions. *Sensitivity* refers to the degree to which a measure represents the construct of variability of interest, or the degree to which a method is able to capture meaningful variations in the aesthetic qualities of the landscape and depict impact of land use activities upon it. *Generalizability* refers to the universality of the system's potential application to different landscapes and user conditions.

In achieving the quality of visual impact assessment, the visual analyst should obtain multiple evaluations by different analysts working separately and cross-check these (Feimer et al. 1979). Where it is possible or feasible to achieve this, evaluations contained in the VIA and mitigation summary will be better able to hold up in both the professional community and in court—where it may well be contested by the proponent.

What is needed is a VIA system that incorporates previous methodology development (as briefly outlined in this chapter) but is also generally applicable to the land/water base and to coastal environments *regardless of agency management biases or specific locale* (Yeomans 1983; Smardon, Sheppard, and Newman 1984). In this regard, Grdén (1979) points out that there is an obvious need for a national visual management system and coordinated VIA approach. The author supports this statement. It seems that visual resources could be systematically inventoried and classified much as is presently done for soils, terrain, geology, forest management, and other earth sciences in the United States and Canada (B.C. Ministry of Environment 1977, 1981).

Lastly, the visual analyst is advised to maintain a close working relationship with current literature in the field of visual impact assessment, which is yet in its formative stage; to review agency and practitioner projects and procedures, and to utilize available research in field-testing his or her concepts and methodologies. In the final analysis, the decision to allow, mitigate, or disallow a project or land use activity in rural and wildland environments is a political and/or economic one. If the decision maker is given thorough and highly professional data that is nevertheless clear, concise, and well documented at the most objective level possible, that decision will most likely favor the maintenance of landscape quality. And quality should certainly be the essence and goal of any serious analyst, whether he or she be a professional, working with a land management agency, a private practitioner, or one in quest of VIA improvement by means of applied research.

APPENDIX: DESIGN GUIDELINES

Design guidelines are integral to the VIA process where the latter identifies unacceptable contrast ratings or improper siting of proposed develop-

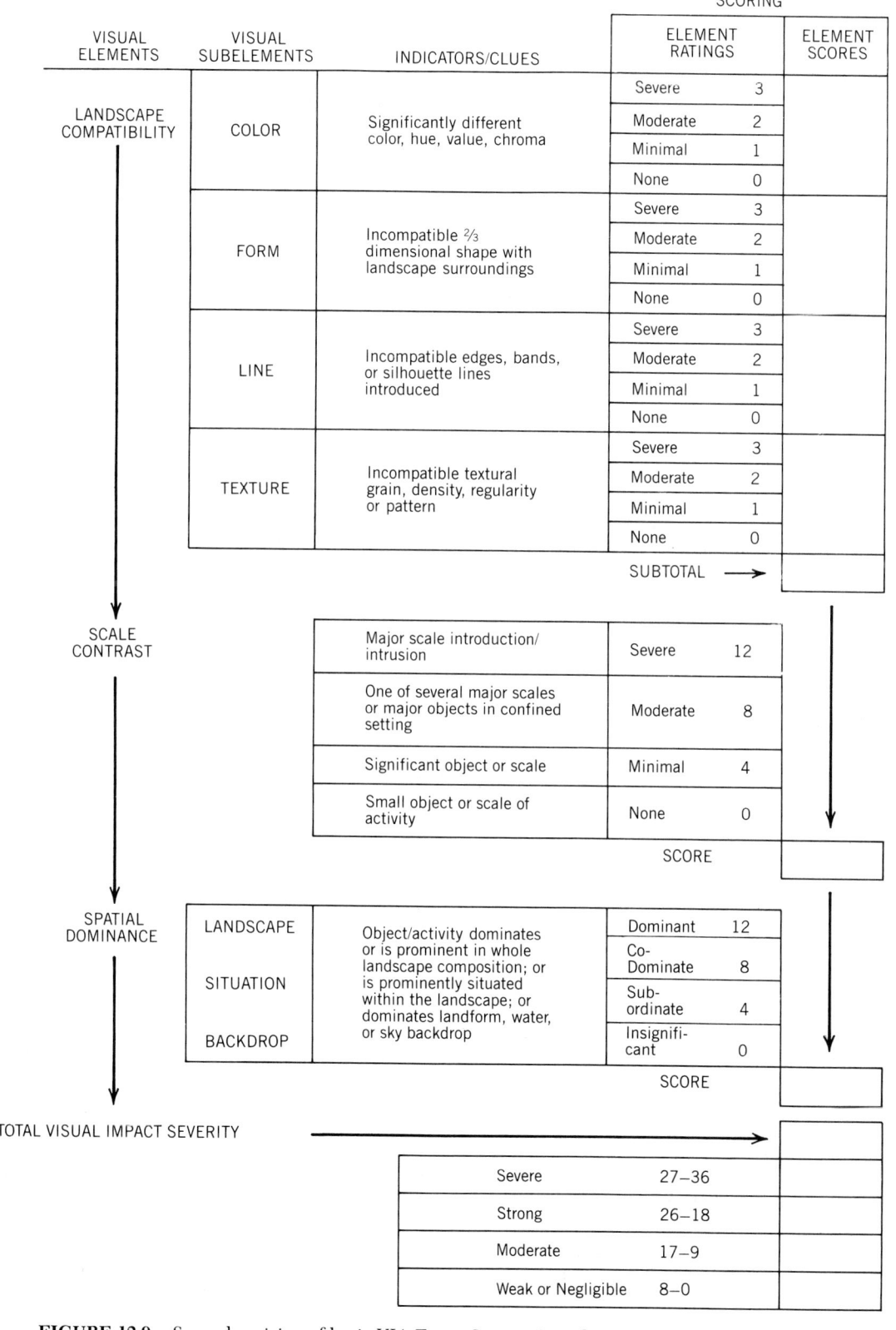

FIGURE 12.9. Second revision of basic VIA Form. *Source:* Smardon, R.C. and Hunter, M., 1983, Procedures and Methods for Wetland and Coastal Area Visual Impact Assessment (VIA). In R.C. Smardon, ed., *The Future of Wetlands: Assessing Visual-Cultural Values.* Totowa, NJ: Allenheld, Osmun, 202.

ment activities. Thus specific design measures may be required to mitigate, enhance, or rehabilitate the activity to conformance with the characteristic landscape.

The following design guidelines have been adapted, modified, and, in some cases, amplified from the following sources: U.S. Bureau of Land Management (1980a); U.S. Forest Service (1974); Litton et al. (1974); McHarg (1969); Blair (1981); and Yeomans (1983). They are not intended as all inclusive but rather as key standards and principles that can—and should—be amplified over time as architects, landscape architects, engineers and nonprofessionals apply their specific skills to project developments where visual impacts are involved.

General Guidelines

1. As a first principle, design *with* nature, not in opposition to it. The designer of landscapes should not forget sky and animals, sound, smell, taste and feeling (Litton, 1979). All affect the visual environment by association. For example, a dramatic scenic viewing experience is enhanced by clean, clear air; by the sound of wind or waves, or perhaps the chance observation of wildlife. Even the "taste" of salt spray can enrich a coastal marine encounter and render it memorable and lasting.

2. In theory, the design policies which promote either conspicuous or inconspicuous manmade changes can be equally satisfactory: both can have high quality through design control. For example, a well-designed sewage treatment plant, though conspicuous, can blend well with its surroundings if planned to reflect the characteristic form, line, color, texture, and scale of its surroundings.

3. Distribute management activities over space and time to reduce immediate negative visual impacts. Dam construction is a good example, where staging of construction may extend over years. Each stage should have minimum visual impact but long-term effects are of primary design concern.

4. Curves are less prominent to the eye than straight lines, therefore less obtrusive and easier to work with. There are few straight lines in nature. For example, undulating or sinuous river and valley systems are easier to design with than straight canals, dykes, or man-made channels. Conformity with natural gradients gives fewer visual design problems than straight and level lines.

5. Roads, paths, trails, and tramways are all directive. Design with constraint and in a manner that does not intrude on the natural landscape. Parking lots and entrance roads to a management activity should hold interest in themselves, that is, be designed for movement without confusion. Road systems are the keys to regional "images."

Color

In rural and wildland settings, color is usually the most dominant factor of impaction when in contrast with the landscape. Color accents function and can usually be seen from great distances. For living elements, color indicates season, age, organic health, soil condition, and other biophysical factors. Thus color is a significant factor in the determination of visual absorption capability (VAC).

Texture

Texture is readily apparent in foreground distances, less so in middleground, and seldom seen in the background. Therefore, vegetation, land surfaces and water textural patterns, although often subtle, should be recognized and reflected in the design of any imposed development seen at the foreground level. In this way, surrounding texture may be either complemented or contrasted.

Roadside Details

1. Signs are a significant force in the visual environment. There are two primary types of signing: promotional and official. Promotional signs (advertising places and events of a commercial nature) should be located within public information centers and/or screened from the main road. Special zoning may be required. Official signs (highway information, park and public area directional information) should be discreet and yet clearly legible. Generally, light-colored letters on a dark background blend most readily with the natural landscape (University of Michigan 1967).

2. Man-made elements can present satisfying visual images when forms are properly limited to

the scale of their surroundings and also reflect their functional requirements where these become visible through external design.

3. The more simple and straightforward the design, configuration, or development, the more easily its symbolism will be visually understood.

4. Roadside detail, color and texture of road surface, shape of objects at shoulders, retaining walls, bridges, overpasses—all set visual tone and are important in contributing to legibility/imageability of the landscape.

Water

Water makes the landscape more "visible" by extending vistas or by becoming a foil for surrounding landforms. Reflections and wave action create motion and variety in the landscape. Allow full play to these highly visible factors—particularly along edges in the landscape. Water edges in the landscape are generally "fragile" environments capable of withstanding little alteration. Therefore, water must be regarded as a sensitive and visually vulnerable design element. It is usually the most characteristic and imageable element in the landscape.

Diversity in the Landscape

1. Vegetation diversity, either natural or man-induced, creates both visual variety and biological diversity.

2. Principles of diversity: In the foreground, texture and color adds the most diversity; in the middleground, line is the most outstanding element; in the background, form is usually the most important element creating diversity. Segregation (combinations) and gradation (building toward a climax, or a sequence of events) are examples of repetition which can be used in creating diversity through design.

Edges

1. Major landscape elements can best be analyzed through consideration of edge. Each edge conveys a distinct feeling, depending on scale, mass, quality of elements, and manner in which elements come together.

2. Edges become extremely important as organizational features. Some examples where edges are visually important include stream banks, coastal shorelines, and forest edges. It is important to design in accordance with these natural configurations.

3. Edges can maximize the potential of features with high legibility/imageability and minimize those that do not.

Form

Irregular arrangement of forms, natural or man-made, may offer great variety but are generally less vivid (memorable) than regular, imposing arrangements. Also, the more regular the landform, the greater the contrast of an introduced project. A large dam, for example, is impossible to screen or disguise and can become a memorable visual experience. Irregular forms should be designed to blend rather than contrast with their surroundings.

Line

1. Boundaries (lines), whether natural or man-made, particularly straight sectional boundaries superimposed on irregular landscapes, are critical design features. Any proposed development should be located to either harmonize or blend with the direction of line or to contrast strongly with it.

2. Screening or softening in terms of color and texture can be effective. As an example, a strongly linear highway can dominate the natural landscape. Its design calls for sensitive vertical and horizontal curve alignment, median strip treatment, and sculpturing of cut banks to blend with adjacent side slopes.

3. Liner tree plantations can enhance and offer contrast to flat landscapes. For example, an introduced line of poplars or similar, highly vertical plantations serve to break the surrounding flatness, slow the eye and create visual interest.

Contrast

1. Depending upon site specifics, contrast in landscape pattern elements (form, line, color, texture, and scale) can either be emphasized or subdued, depending upon naturally existing dominance factors.

2. Man-made elements, such as monuments, piers, floats, and so forth, are more immediately

apparent to the eye than their surroundings since they are focal and draw the eye from their surroundings. Restraint in their placement should be practiced.

3. Extreme contrasts in form, line, color, and texture in the introduction of development activities to the landscape should be avoided.

4. Man-made elements not intended to be boundaries (power poles and lines, canals, highway alignments) are highly visible and deflect attention and interest by presenting extreme contrast in the landscape. They should either be relocated, screened, or accepted as necessary negative deviations.

5. Structural materials should not be directly imitative of nature (for example, using concrete to suggest rock masses), but should stand on their own as introduced elements designed to blend with nature.

6. Striking and eye-catching elements give the greatest contrast in the landscape (for example, waterfalls, high cliffs). Where dominant, they should be allowed prominence and not "countered" or opposed by structure.

Mitigation

This option can usually be carried out by means of project design. A harsh exterior can be softened by wood or masonry reflecting the color, hue, and intensity of the surrounding landscape. Storage tanks can be painted, utility towers modified, vertical buildings reduced in scale. Architectural, engineering, and landscape architectural treatments may often be the only requirements needed to bring the proposed development to a point of acceptance within the specified minimal management class requirement. Cost factors may preclude such treatment, in which case compensation will be required.

Enhancement

Another option is *enhancement* of visual attributes of a project or project area by design or improvement of existing site conditions. For example, additional visual interest can be created by introducing vegetation to soften harsh edges, removing it at critical viewpoints and, in some cases, by screening. Highway access routes can be visually enhanced with native plantations along median strips, by blending cutbanks with adjacent landforms, and through design of alignments to create variety and interest.

Rehabilitation

Rehabilitation differs from enhancement since it is directed toward site recovery rather than being additive. Nevertheless, design guidelines are needed. For example, where surface mining disturbs the visual quality of an area, rehabilitation to a point approximating original site or area conditions should be required. Another example would be scarifying and reseeding or replanting old logging, mining, or transmission line access routes when they have ceased to be functional. Filling and revegetating depleted gravel borrow pits and other byproducts of development are additional examples of such efforts.

CHAPTER 13

VISUAL IMPACT ASSESSMENT IN URBAN ENVIRONMENTS

William G.E. Blair

INTRODUCTION

Visual impact assessment can be an important component of environmental review for urban projects. The visual appearance of a project or structure can have significant effects on immediate project users, as well as on members of surrounding communities.

On the one hand, visual appearance can contribute greatly to user satisfaction, with such tangible results as low vacancy rates, high business volumes, maintenance of capital values, and evidence of physical care.

On the other hand, good visual relationships between a project and its setting can also help to secure project acceptance from the wider public. The visual character of our buildings, streets, and open spaces has cultural meaning and can support or erode our psychological well-being (Appleyard 1976). Community appearance, like the appearance of an individual project, also translates into economics. Where there are positive visual values in an existing community or open space, the visual appearance of a project should support or complement these values, which can include sunlight and distant views as well as harmonious building design. There is much room for improvement, however, in the appearance of many urban environments; in these settings, a new project may well present an opportunity to create beneficial visual impacts (Lynch 1976).

Because visual experience is a compound of physical stimulus and psychological response, some aspects of visual impacts are undeniably subjective. However, there is evidence that broad consensus exists for many visual issues. In recent years, extensive research has been conducted on visual perceptions and values. Much of this research has focused on rural areas and wildlands, where federal land-managing agencies have been charged with stewardship of visual resources, but researchers are also paying increased attention to urban environments (Elsner and Smardon 1979; Stone 1978).

Efforts at urban visual impact assessment, however, sometimes run counter to an older tradition of architecture and urban design. In that tradition, design is considered the province of an artistic elite. Members of the elite draw on personal aesthetic systems for design principles and may interpret public opposition to their designs as symptomatic of society's long-standing failure to understand advanced art. Practitioners who would assess the visual impacts of the designers' projects may be seen as on the side of the Philistines (Blair 1980).

During the environmental review process, the potential for conflict between the design tradition and the emerging field of visual assessment may be reduced if practitioners of the latter put their emphasis on examining (1) the effects of *alternatives* and (2) *offsite* visual impacts, leaving clients and market forces to deal with the visual effects of design on project users.

VISUAL IMPACT ASSESSMENT PROCESS

Visual impacts are somewhat different from many other environmental factors because their assessment requires information on *perceptions* as well as on *resources*. To understand and assess the visual effects of a project, we must understand not only the project and its context, but also the probable responses of the people who will see it (Zube et al, 1975; also see Chapters 3, 4, and 5).

It is important to obtain information on perceptions of a given project directly from the public, whenever possible. In this chapter, we will discuss ways to obtain such information during the assessment process, which can be organized into the following steps:

Define the visual characteristics of the project.
Define the visual environment of the project.
Determine the visual impacts of project alternatives.
Evaluate those visual impacts.
Identify ways to mitigate significant adverse impacts.

The balance of this chapter is structured around these steps. Before going into the process, however, let us discuss some major issues for urban visual impact assessment and some of its legal underpinnings.

MAJOR ISSUES IN URBAN VISUAL IMPACT ASSESSMENT

Determining the context, or *visually affected environment*, of the project is a critical step that guides subsequent visual analysis. What views and whose views will the project affect? These questions can be answered readily by using visibility analysis and mapping techniques (Chapter 4), in combination with land use and population information.

Because it is difficult to describe visual appearance in words, visual assessments of the existing environment and the consequences of project alternatives should be based on *illustrations of actual views* (Chapter 11). Because resources and time are always limited, it is also necessary to limit the number of views analyzed: it is essential that these be *representative views,* neither understating nor overstating the visual effects of the project. Viewpoint selection may be even more important to credible visual analysis than artistic sophistication. The visual consequences of a project can be illustrated by several simple but effective techniques which do not require artistic training.

The *visual resources* of a project site or an urban district are the stimuli upon which visual experience is based. Determination of project effects on these resources can involve several levels of analysis: a project may modify basic viewing conditions (shadow, glare, view obstruction); it may displace specific resources and replace them with others (trees, buildings, pavement); it may modify the visual character of existing resources (form, color, scale); and it may increase or decrease the overall visual quality of community views. Indicators of impact have been developed for each level, but consensus is best established for the more basic visual resource effects.

The recognition of *viewer constituencies* is also important in evaluating the visual impacts of a project, since these impacts are determined by perceptions as well as resources. Viewer sensitivity changes with activity, because vision is an active sense. That is, to a large extent we see what we are looking for. A direct examination of the perceptions of the people affected by a project is desirable but often difficult; land use is an example of a useful indirect indicator of likely viewer response.

Criteria for evaluating the visual relationships between a project and its setting often become more clear as the visual character of the setting becomes stronger. Many communities (Savannah, Georgia, and Lowell, Massachusetts, are two examples) have developed visual criteria for special review districts by abstracting the existing "visual vocabularies" of these districts. Once criteria for evaluating the visual impacts of a project are well determined, the effectiveness of alternative actions and mitigation strategies can also be readily evaluated.

LEGISLATIVE, JUDICIAL, AND ADMINISTRATIVE UNDERPINNINGS

Chapter 2 discussed the legal basis for incorporating aesthetic considerations in land use decisions, including the National Environmental Policy Act (NEPA) and the state environmental policy acts (SEPAs). That chapter also touched on the zoning and design review ordinances that have long been the vehicles for incorporating visual considerations into local government decision making.

Chapter 2 also covered federal administrative regulations for the implementation of NEPA. There are other federal regulations that deal with visual impacts in the urban environment. Perhaps the most relevant to urban programs and projects are the regulations that implement the Historic Preservation Act of 1966. Section 106 of the Act requires the consideration of project effects on any district, site, building, or object that is included in the National Register, or that is eligible for future inclusion. The implementing regulations define "criteria of adverse effect" to include visual elements "that are out of character with the property or alter its setting."

Various state environment policy act (SEPA) regulations and guidelines also require assessment of visual effects. To comply with these requirements, some local governments have adopted policies or regulations setting out the basis on which visual effects will be evaluated. For example, the City of Seattle has adopted specific policies on the disclosure and mitigation of view obstruction, shadow, and light and glare effects. Local design review procedures, such as those of Claremont, California, may also provide guidance for identifying and weighing visual impacts.

In the courts, the case law of urban aesthetics is predominantly concerned with zoning, billboards, junkyards, and urban renewal. In 1954, in the landmark case of *Berman v. Parker,* the U.S. Supreme Court upheld the use of eminent domain for aesthetic purposes, affirming that "it is within the power of the legislature to determine that the community should be beautiful as well as healthy." More recently, the courts have begun to receive cases stemming from the environmental legislation of the 1970s. In 1978, the U.S. Supreme Court affirmed a New York City rejection of a 53-story addition to Grand Central Station because of the adverse visual impacts on that historic landmark. In the same year, the Washington State Supreme Court affirmed a decision by the Building Superintendent of the City of Seattle denying a building permit because of visual impacts disclosed in an environmental impact statement (EIS). These and other decisions have confirmed that urban aesthetics is a legitimate concern of government and that visual considerations—if clearly stated and analyzed—can be incorporated into government decisions without violating fundamental personal and property rights (Brace 1980).

DEFINING THE VISUAL CHARACTERISTICS OF THE PROJECT

Although project design is usually schematic at the EIS stage, it is possible to determine basic visual impacts if the project submittal clearly identifies the primary visual characteristics of the project. In short, what will the project look like? Local codes often spell out submittal requirements, but it may be useful to briefly discuss these primary visual characteristics under three headings:

Structures.
Site improvements.
Uses.

Structures

Enough information should be provided to determine the location, dimensions, form, and exterior materials of principal and accessory structures.

With regard to location, it is particularly important to know the relation of proposed structures to existing site features. This information is not always provided as a matter of course and may have to be specifically requested or determined.

Project drawings usually give the basic dimensions of structures, but often omit the details of certain features that may have visual importance. These include roof configurations, stair towers,

FIGURE 13.1. Elevation of addition to existing apartment complex, indicating form, texture, and scale of proposed structure. *Source:* Preuss-Kovell International, Architects and Planners, Seattle, Washington.

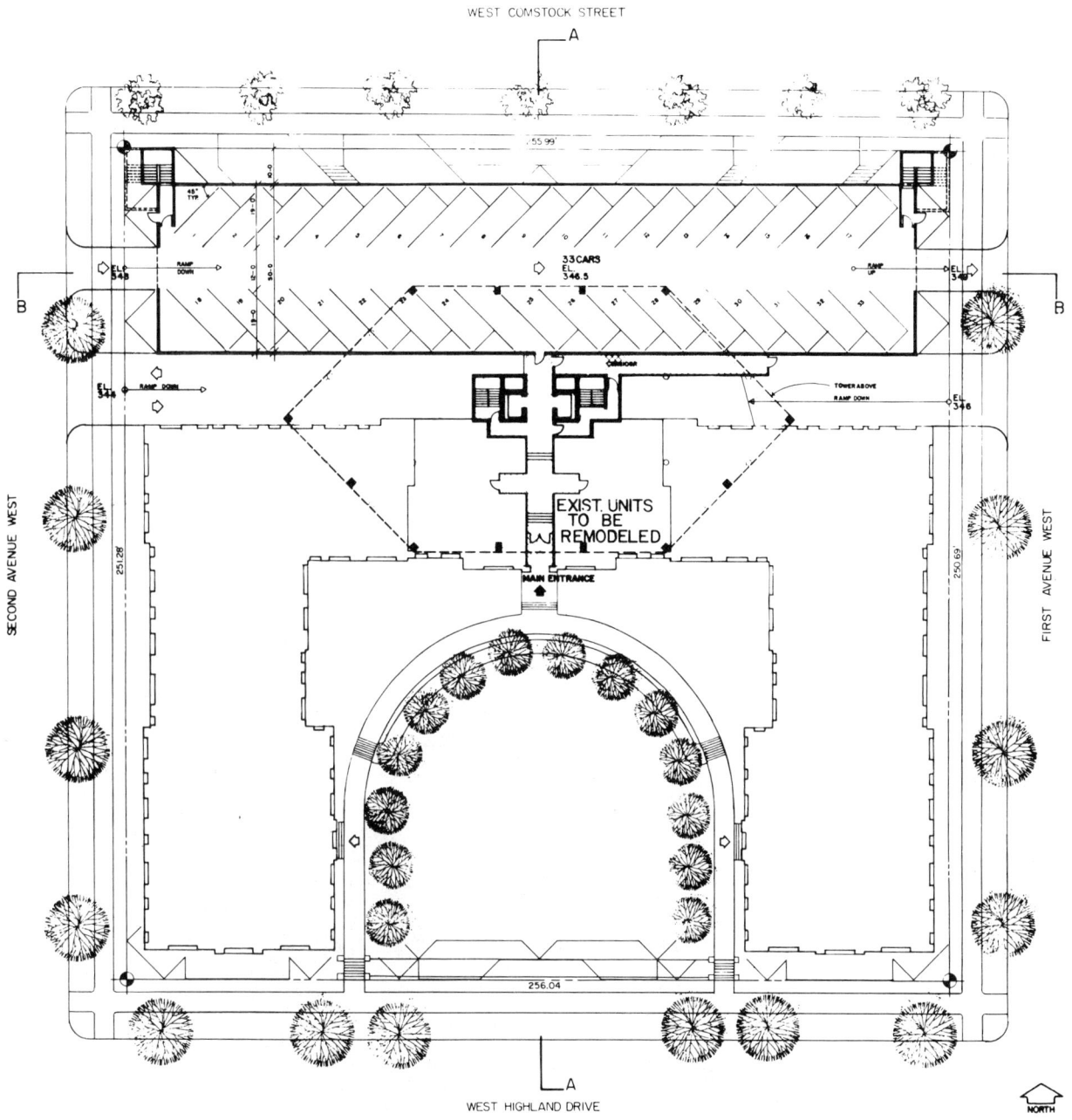

FIGURE 13.2. Plan of project shown in Figure 13.1, indicating relation to existing structure and streetscape. *Source:* Preuss-Kovell International, Architects and Planners, Seattle, Washington.

and mechanical penthouses, as well as accessory structures such as fences and service or utility enclosures.

The elevation drawings of structures should include all doors, windows, projections, and balconies to indicate the form and relative scale of structures. These drawings should also indicate the reflectivity, color, and texture of exterior surfaces (see Figure 13.1).

Site Improvements

Information on the project site should include existing visual resources as well as proposed conditions, to allow determination of the onsite effects of visual change and the integration of proposed improvements with existing resources. Written or drawn information should be supplemented by photographs of any notable existing features. The location of these photographs should be indicated on a site plan.

Landform information should include any special features such as rock outcroppings, as well as proposed grading and slope retention structures. Information on water features should include existing and proposed drainageways and surface water features, such as swales, wetlands, streams, and stormwater retention facilities. Vegetation data should include any mature trees or attractive native vegetation, as well as proposed planting.

Site information should also include existing structures, such as principal buildings, outbuildings, fences, walls, walkways, bridges, and other structures (see Figure 13.2). Special notice should be made of any man-made features that are historic, architecturally distinctive, attractive, or that reinforce regional visual character. Circulation and utilities should also be disclosed, including existing and proposed paths, roadways, parking areas, lighting, overhead utilities, transformers, pumping stations, and other utilities.

Uses

Uses intended for the project structures and site may require ancillary facilities and may have oth-

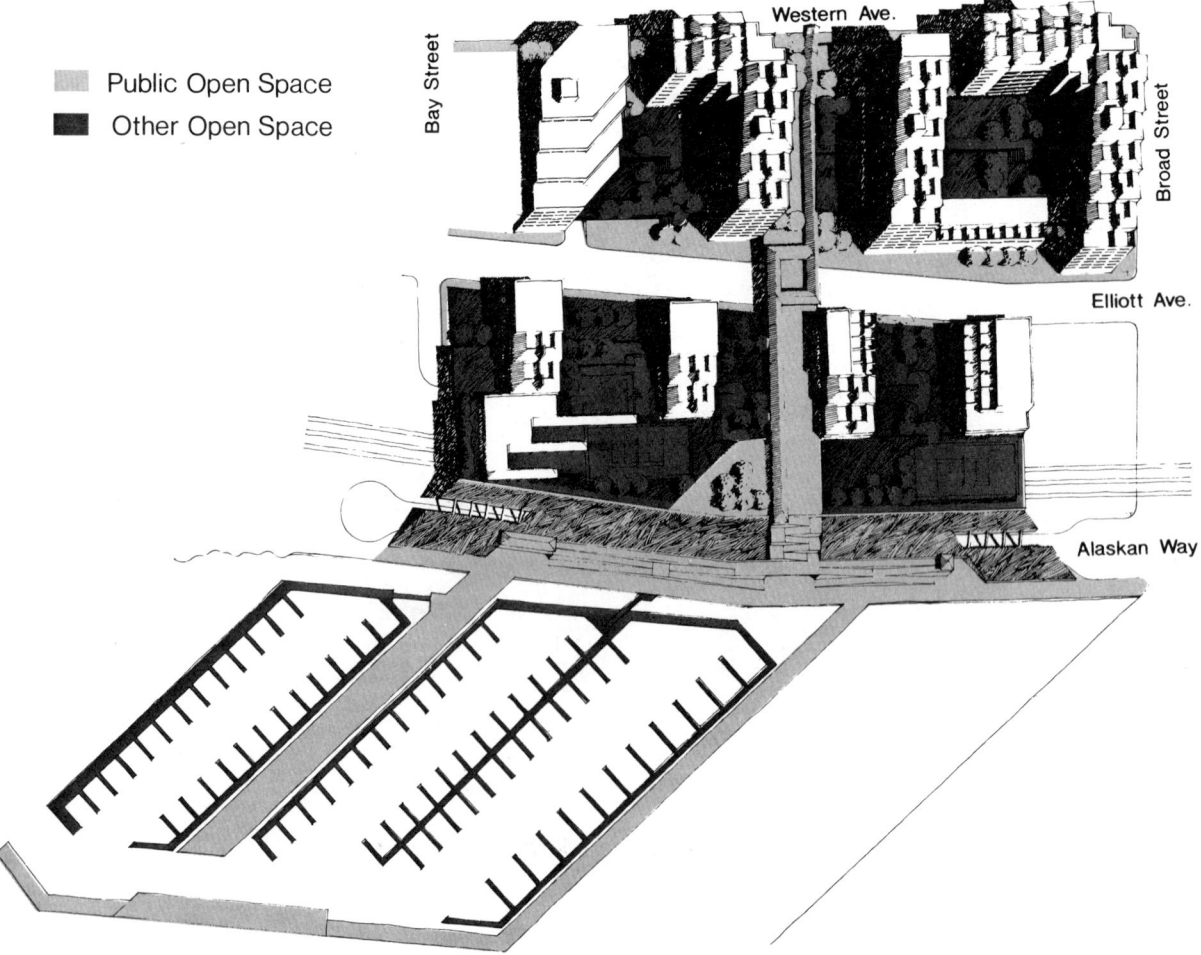

FIGURE 13.3. Project open space that is available for public use. *Source:* TRA, Architects and Planners, Seattle, Washington.

er visual implications. Certain uses may attract viewers onto the site; other uses may usually be considered unsightly by project neighbors.

Project information should therefore identify any public uses, including play areas, playfields, display gardens, sunning areas, public art, viewpoints, paths, and trails (see Figure 13.3). Private or semiprivate uses should also be identified. These may include garden plots, patios, play areas, laundry, outdoor storage, and vehicle maintenance areas. Service uses may pose visual issues on some projects. Such uses include repair, maintenance, storage, delivery, and refuse collection and disposal.

Physical facilities may be associated with any of the preceding types of uses. These facilities could include site furnishings, outdoor art, play equipment, lighting, screening, fencing, or other enclosures.

In summary, project information must be carefully reviewed to make sure that all the principal visual characteristics of the project are defined and disclosed. In the author's experience, important items of information are usually missing. In fact, it has sometimes seemed that visual impact assessment is one of the best vehicles in the environmental review process for tying down the often-elusive "project description."

DEFINING THE AFFECTED VISUAL ENVIRONMENT

The visual relationships between a project and its setting are the key to the visual impacts of the project on that setting. This is the subject on which many community concerns focus. Information on these visual relationships is central to visual impact assessment and is increasingly required by local governments for environmental clearances and approvals under planned unit development ordinances, coastal zone management programs, and similar planning mechanisms.

The critical questions include: "What is the viewshed of the project?" "Whose views will be affected?" "What are the existing characteristics of these views?" and "Which views of the project will be most important in establishing its impact?" The answers are commonly found in three sources:

Project information.
Existing documentation.
Field observations.

Project Information

Information in project applications and environmental documents should establish the visual context of the project and identify the major offsite viewing groups and their probable responses. While prediction of those responses may be possible, even better information is obtained if the project sponsor accommodates public involvement in the preparation of the EIS and if visual issues are explored in the involvement program. Citizens steeped in community history and values may be able to identify visually important features and views as well as, or better than, outside experts. Given this perspective, the information required from the sponsor should include the following types of data:

1. The visibility of the project: the areas from which the project will be seen (its viewshed) and any topography or tree cover that restricts visibility (Felleman 1982).
2. Project viewers (offsite): types, location, numbers, duration, and viewer activity (land use is an indication).
3. Visual characteristics of the immediate project setting, including any major views, important features, or eyesores.
4. Key views of the site and its setting from locations in the surrounding environment that are representative of the public and private viewpoints from which major viewing groups will actually see the project: these views should be illustrated by a limited number of photographs keyed to a plan and related to the analysis of project viewers (Blair, Walters, and Mah 1982).
5. Simulations of the visual appearance of the project in key views: these simulations should accurately illustrate both the project and its setting (Sheppard 1982b).

EXAMPLE: Key View Selection, Expert Analysis

Key views were selected for assessing the visual impacts of a controversial highrise project by (1) mapping the urban districts adjoining the project site (see Figure 13.4), (2) mapping the project viewshed (see Figure 13.5), (3) overlaying the first two maps to define visual assessment units, (see Figure 13.6), (4) selecting key views from a number of candidate views representing the assessment units (see Figure

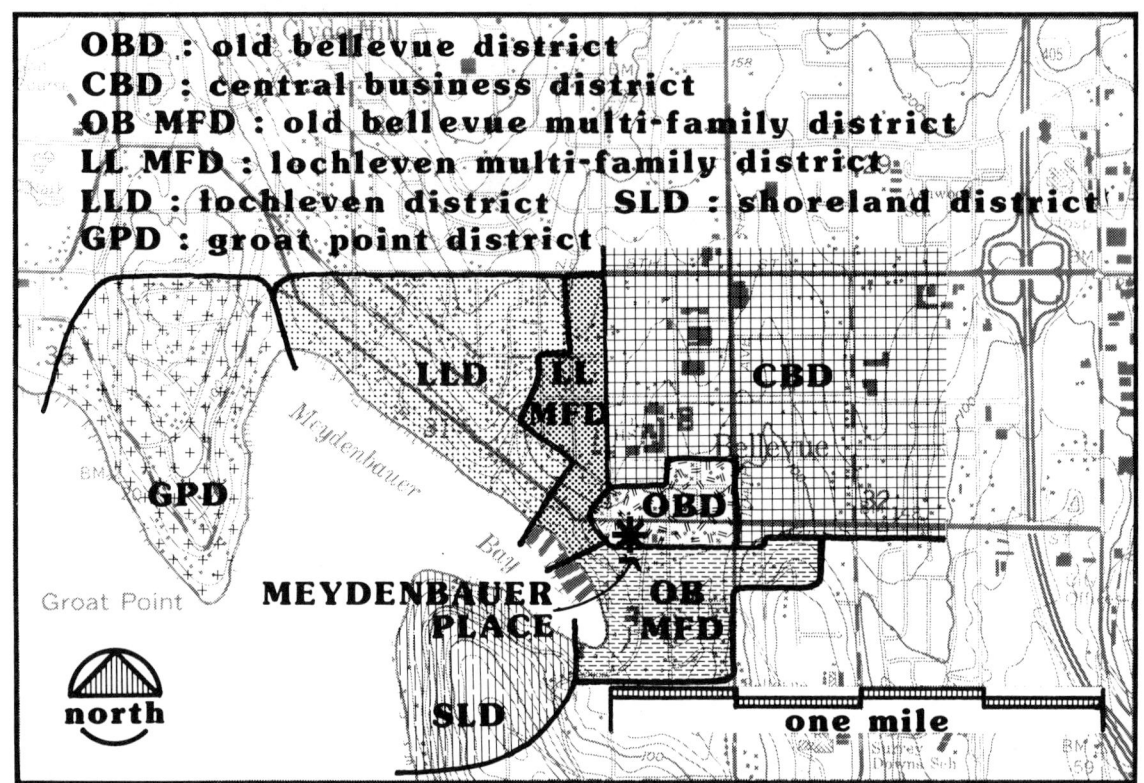

FIGURE 13.4. Urban districts adjoining project site. *Source:* Jones and Jones, Seattle, Washington.

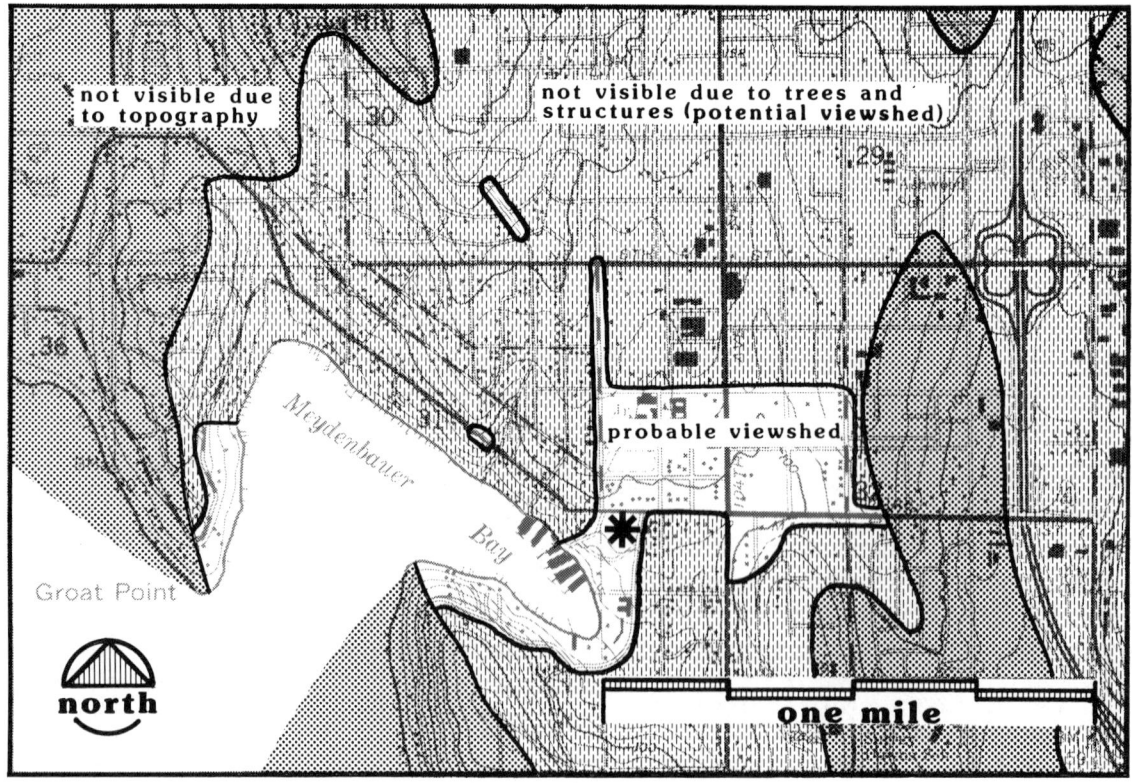

FIGURE 13.5. Project viewshed. *Source:* Jones and Jones, Seattle, Washington.

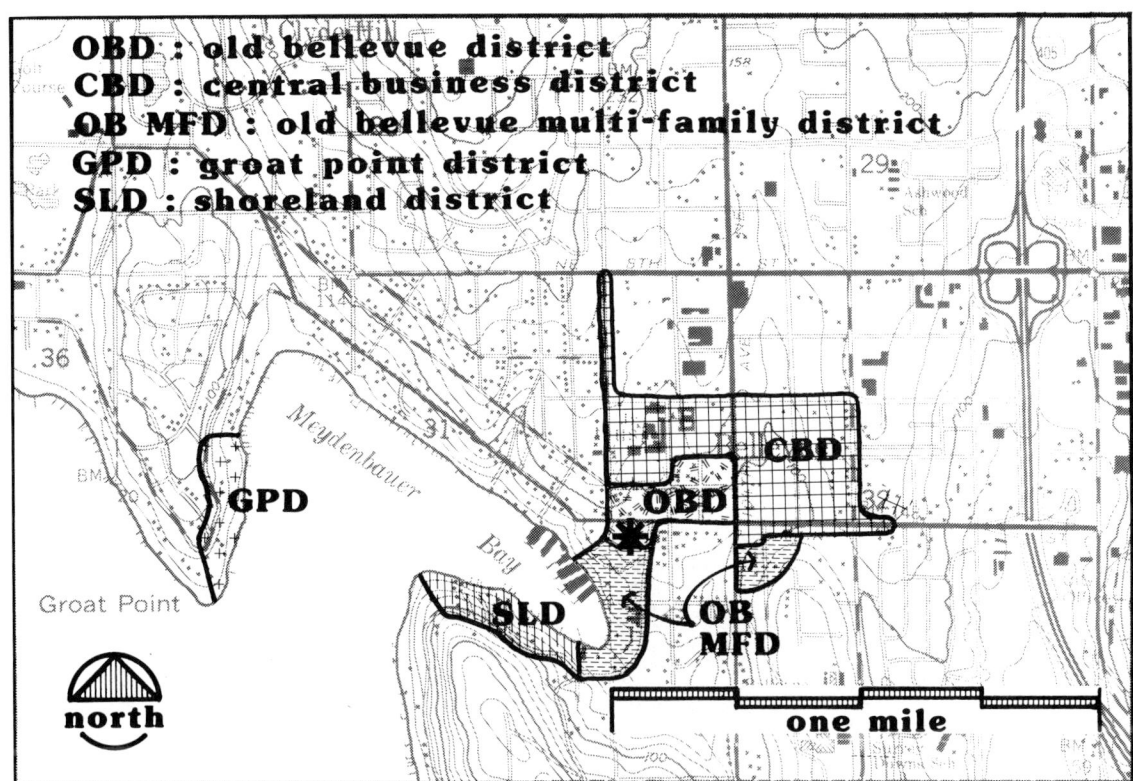

FIGURE 13.6. Project visual assessment units. *Source:* Jones and Jones, Seattle, Washington.

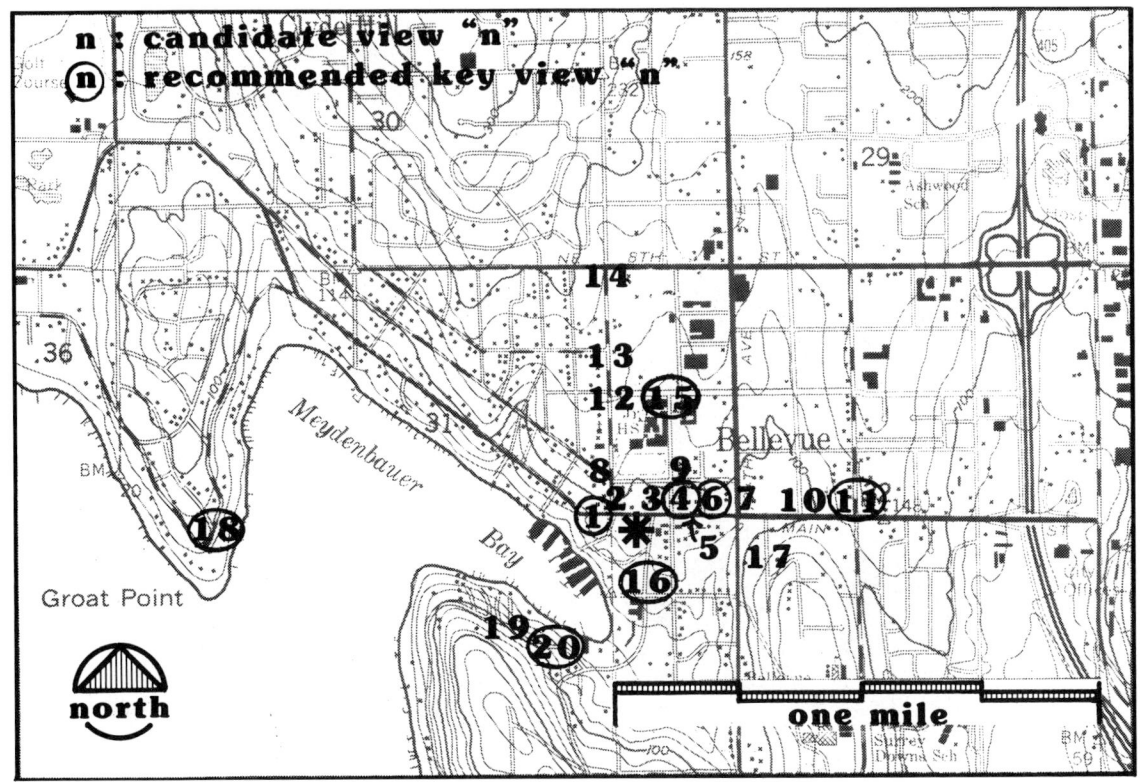

FIGURE 13.7. Location of candidate views and key views. *Source:* Jones and Jones, Seattle, Washington.

232 VISUAL IMPACT ASSESSMENT IN URBAN ENVIRONMENTS

13.7). The critieria for selection of the key views were:

- Inclusion of at least one view for each of the assessment units.
- Inclusion of foreground features characteristic of each assessment unit or important in that unit.
- Inclusion of background features characteristic of views toward the project from each unit.
- Complete disclosure of the appearance of the external features of the project.

EXAMPLE: Key View Selection, Public Involvement

When a project is extremely controversial, project opponents frequently challenge the key views selected by experts, charging that the selection favors the project or fails to disclose adverse visual impacts. This possibility was a concern for a visual assessment of a proposed marine terminal in Seattle.

A related concern was that the city had formally designated a large number of viewpoints for visual

Kinnear Park

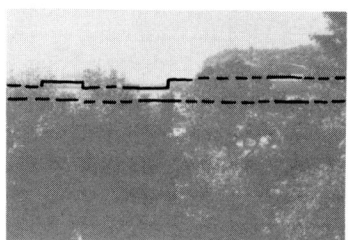

Marshall Park - B. Bowen VP

Soundview Terrace Park

Queen Anne Blvd., 8th & Lee

Queen Anne Blvd., 8th & Galer

Smith Cove Park

Near Magnolia E. S. Playground

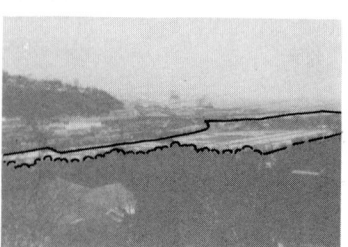

Near Bayview Playground

FIGURE 13.8. Designated views and scenic routes. *Source:* Jones and Jones, Seattle, Washington.

TABLE 13.1 Public Responses to Candidate Views

TABLE 1: Candidate views ranked in descending order of importance, based upon mean responses to daytime views.

RANK	CANDIDATE VIEW	MEAN IMPORTANCE		COMMENTS
		Day	Night	
1	Magnolia Bridge, westend	4.3	4.2	Key view (day)
2	Magnolia Way, to downtown	4.3	4.3	Similar to Magnolia Bridge
3	8th & Lee	4.3	4.4	Key view (day)
4	Kinnear Park	4.2	4.0	Similar to 8th & Lee
5	Magnolia Way, to Queen Anne	4.1	3.9	Key view (day and night)
6	21st & Halladay	4.1	4.0	Similar to 24th & Halladay (which is technically better for simulation
7	Smith Cove Park	3.9	3.4	Similar to Magnolia Bridge
8	24th & Halladay	3.9	3.8	Key view (day and night)
9	9th & Highland	3.8	3.9	Key view (night)
10	Soundview Terrace	3.7	3.8*	Similar to 12th & Raye (which is better for simulation)
11	27th & Smith	3.6	3.6	Too little of site in view
12	Betty Bowen Viewpoint	3.5	3.6	Similar to 8th & Lee
13	Magnolia Bridge, center	3.4	3.3	Similar to Magnolia Way, to Queen Anne
14	12th & Raye	3.3	3.2	Key view (day)
15	Magnolia	3.3	-	Too little site in view
16	Space Needle	3.2	-	Too far away
17	Myrtle Edwards Park	2.9	3.0	Too far away
18	26th & Fulton	2.7	3.1	Too little site in view
19	8th & Galer	2.6	2.9	Too little site in view
20	26th & Newton	2.3	2.4	Too little site in view
21	5th & Mercer	2.3	-	Too far away
22	Hamilton Viewpoint	2.2	2.5	Too far away
23	Ferry	2.2	2.4	Too far away
24	Waterfront Park	1.9	2.1	Too far away

Source: Jones and Jones, Seattle, Washington.

assessment purposes. Inclusion of all these in the assessment would have been cumbersome and also redundant, since many would be only slightly affected by the project.

The complete set of candidate views (including both day and night views) was shown to the public during the scoping meetings for the EIS (see Figure 13.8). Participants in the meetings were asked to score the *visual importance* of each view, defined as "the degree of consideration that should be given to possible changes in this view when examining alternatives for the (project) site." The mean scores were calculated for each view and the views were ranked in order of relative importance.

The final key views were selected from among the top-ranked candidate views, taking care to include views that showed all portions of the site and that represented major view types and major viewer groups. The accompanying table (see Table 13.1) lists the views in descending order of importance (daytime scores). It also indicates which views were selected as key views and why some views with high scores were not selected (Blair, Robertson, and Dingfield 1982).

234 VISUAL IMPACT ASSESSMENT IN URBAN ENVIRONMENTS

FIGURE 13.9. Weather balloons used to demonstrate height and bulk of proposed building. *Source:* David Nemens, Design and Development Department, City of Bellevue, Washington.

Chapter 11 discusses simulation techniques in considerable detail. Here, we note that simulations may be dynamic (film, video) or static. The greatest equivalence of response is achieved with dynamic simulations prepared with the aid of large three-dimensional models such as those constructed by the Berkeley Environmental Simulation Laboratory (see Figure 13.12). Static simulations may be quite adequate when the project to be assessed is a point feature (such as a building) and the sensitive viewpoints are themselves static—such as residences.

FIGURE 13.10. Line drawing overlay used to illustrate extent of view obstruction *Source:* Urban Regional Research, Planning Consultants, Seattle, Washington.

A number of graphic techniques may be employed, usually working from a photographic base. An artist's color "rendering" will provide the most realistic looking simulation, but can be costly (see Figure 13.11). A simple but effective technique is to superimpose the outline of project structures on a photograph of a key view (see Figure 13.10); this is particularly useful if the issue is view obstruction rather than the visual character or quality of the project itself. For some projects "story poles" have been erected on site to indicate the position and height of structures and to simplify the establishment of accurate perspectives. Weather balloons can serve the same purpose (see Figure 13.9).

Existing Documentation

The nature of regional visual resources and the value attached to views of these resources can be important background information for assessing the visual effects of a project. Regional planning studies, architectural guidebooks, and historic surveys will often provide this perspective. At a more detailed level, urban inventories and community plans may identify specific areas or features valued locally for their visual appearance.

If available and if they relate to the project site and its setting, the following types of information are useful:

FIGURE 13.11. Retouched photograph used to illustrate visual character of proposed marine terminal. *Source:* Jones and Jones, Seattle, Washington.

Distinctive regional visual characteristics, including landform, water, vegetation, and structures.

Adjacent urban districts or neighborhoods, their visual characteristics, and boundaries.

Important visual resources in the immediate vicinity, such as parks, landmarks, historic structures, and public art.

Viewpoints, including major travel routes, scenic routes, recreation areas, and residential areas.

FIGURE 13.12. Model set up for dynamic simulation of highway project in Berkeley Environmental Simulation Laboratory. *Source:* Jones and Jones, Seattle, Washington.

Field Observations

Field observations are often needed to test the adequacy of project information on views, visual resources, and viewers. Reviewers of environmental documents can check the following points by walking the project neighborhood and taking a brief photographic record:

Existing visual resources on the site and in the project setting.

Viewers: their types, relative numbers, activities, responses.

Available views from the project, to the project, and other important local views.

Representative viewpoints and key views of the project site.

DETERMINING VISUAL IMPACTS

The initial determination of the types and probable degree of visual impacts can be made directly from the information provided by the project proposal, documentation review, and field observations.

This section identifies situations in which specific visual impacts are likely and also identifies the information that should be developed when supplementary analysis is needed. Detailed descriptions of the techniques for such analysis are referenced throughout this chapter as well as chapter 12.

Viewing Conditions

A project may affect the amount and character of ambient light by casting shadows, creating solar glare, or introducing intense artificial light into residential areas. In turn, these effects may cause visual discomfort or interfere with activities such as driving. If one or more of the following effects is likely, information about neighboring uses and viewers will be needed to help determine the impact magnitude.

Shadow

Shadows cast by project structures may interfere with views and outdoor activity on neighboring sites. Shadow impacts are generally confined to areas northeast, north, or northwest of project structures. The likelihood of offsite shadows increase with latitude, the height and bulk of structures, and the proximity of structures to the north property line. The location and length of shadows changes with the season and time of day. They are longest on the winter solstice, December 21; at 10 A.M. on that day, the shadow of a structure will be two to four times as long as its height, depending on the latitude.

Because of limited shadow length, offsite shadow impacts are generally not significant for structures three stories (30 feet) or less in height. If offsite shadows appear probable for a taller structure and could fall on other structures or public use areas, the actual shadow pattern should be determined for the "heating season." This is the period including the autumn equinox, the winter solstice, and the spring equinox. The shadows on these three dates can be projected on a plan of the site and adjacent areas, using the sun's azimuth and altitude at 10 A.M., noon, and 2 P.M., the four-hour period of maximum daily solar radiation. This will establish the extent, location, and duration of offsite shadow impacts (see Figure 13.13).

Techniques for shadow projections are discussed in architectural drafting texts and handbooks such as *Graphic Standards*. An alternative approach is to simulate shadow patterns with building models (see Figure 13.14); *The Archi-*

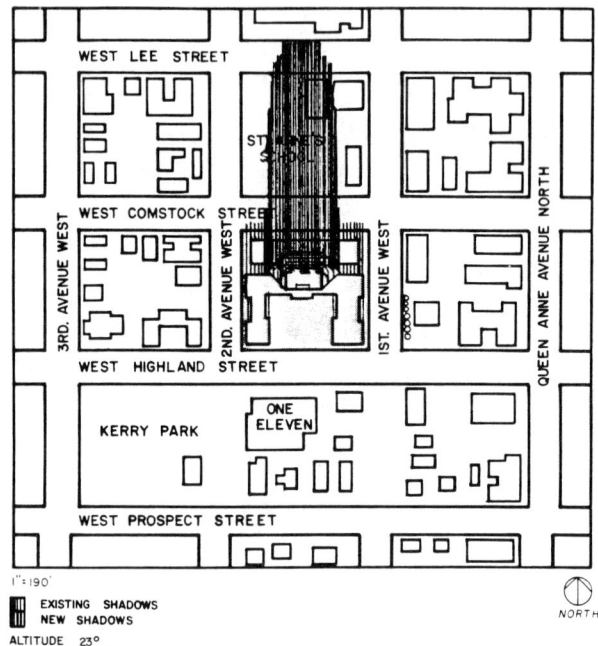

FIGURE 13.13. Shadow diagram, disclosing shading of school playground by proposed highrise. *Source:* Urban Regional Research, Planning Consultants, Seattle, Washington.

tect's Journal, a British magazine, has published a serial handbook that includes information sheets on such techniques (The Architect's Journal, 1968).

Solar Glare

Sunlight reflected from structures faced with highly polished or mirror-like materials may interfere with activities dependent on vision and make vision itself uncomfortable.

Glare from reflected sunlight is most likely whenever the altitude of the sun is below 30°. This generally includes the morning and evening hours, but the potential for solar glare may extend throughout the winter day in higher latitudes. The location of solar glare impacts depends on the orientation of reflective surfaces as well as on sun position, and these impacts can occur in any compass direction.

If the exterior materials of proposed structures make offsite solar glare appear probable and other structures, public use areas, major streets, or highways are located within 400 feet, actual glare patterns can be determined by geometric analysis. These patterns can be mapped on a plan of the site and its environs for the hours during the equinoxes and solstices when the sun's altitude

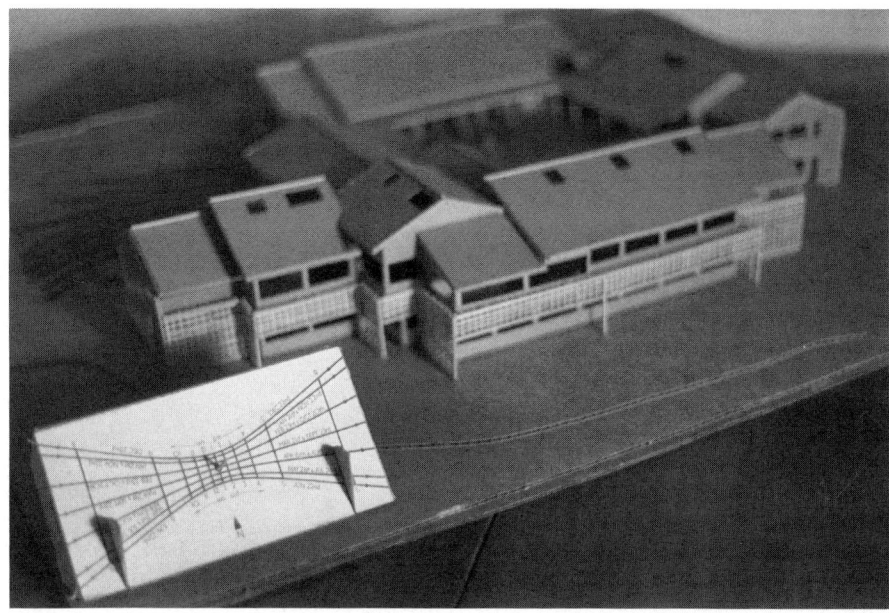

FIGURE 13.14. Building model and heliodon for direct simulation of shadow patterns.
Source: Iain Robertson, Jones and Jones, Seattle, Washington.

is below 30°. The extent, location, and duration of offsite impacts during the rest of the year can then be interpreted from the glare patterns on these days.

An article in *Environmental Comment* (Erickson 1980) demonstrates the potential severity of

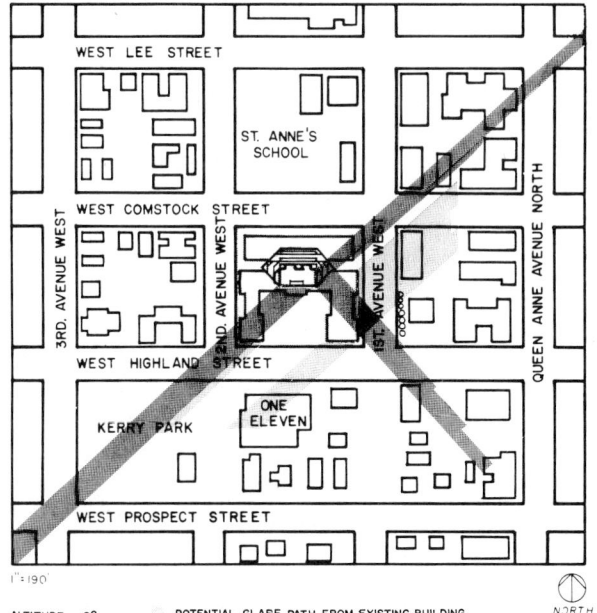

FIGURE 13.15. Plan of area subject to glare from sunlight reflected off glass surfaces in proposed highrise project. *Source:* Urban Regional Research, Planning Consultants, Seattle, Washington.

glare problems due to reflective building materials (see Figure 13.15).

Artificial Light

Bright lighting installations can intrude on nighttime views, cause visual discomfort, and even interfere with sleep patterns if the light sources themselves are visible.

Extensive nighttime lighting is often associated with proposals for industrial facilities, highways, large parking lots, playing fields, and institutions that operate late at night, such as hospitals and fire stations. Factors that contribute to the likelihood of offsite impacts from artificial lighting include the number of sources, source intensity (over 250 watts), mounting height (over 30 feet), and hours of operation (after midnight).

If offsite lighting effects appear probable and residential areas, major streets, or highways are located within 400 feet, a detailed lighting analysis may be necessary. The most important product of this analysis would be a plan or map of the area in which the sources that emit light would be directly visible. This area is determined by the "cutoff angle" of the fixtures that house the sources, the angles at which the fixtures are aimed, and any shielding that is added to the fixtures.

If artificial lighting appears to be a major proj-

FIGURE 13.16. Simulated lighting for proposed marine terminal. *Source:* Jones and Jones, Seattle, Washington.

ect issue, it may be necessary to develop a full mathematical projection of light intensity levels. This type of analysis is usually performed by an illumination engineer. It is also possible to simulate artificial lighting by means of retouched nighttime photographs (see Figure 13.16), using photos of comparable existing light systems as models (Blair, Robertson, and Dingfield 1982).

Site and Environs

This class of visual impacts results from the interaction between (1) the existing visual characteristics of the site and its environs, and (2) the visual characteristics of project alternatives. It includes effects on existing visual resources, view obstruction, visual contrast, and visual quality.

Existing Visual Resources

Complete or partial displacement of existing site features may have adverse visual effects if these features are valued for their visual appearance.

Existing visual resources may include site landform, water, vegetation, and structures. If an existing feature is recognized for some nonvisual characteristic such as rarity, scientific value, or historic meaning, the value of its visual appearance is usually enhanced. This recognition may occur at national, state, or local levels and is often documented by official means such as inclusion in a register. Official recognition may be accompanied by policies or regulations that protect the existing visual appearance of the feature and its setting (Federal Highway Adm. 1981).

The probable visual importance of existing site resources should be confirmed during field observations. If any existing resources are likely to be valued for their visual appearance, these resources should be located on a site plan. The plan should also indicate whether and to what degree these resources would be displaced by the project or integrated with it.

View Obstruction

Proposed structures or vegetation may cause view obstruction if existing middle-distance or long-distance views are available from the site or its environs and the project is located within the sightlines of these views. Obstruction of views of landmarks or other notable visual features may also constitute a visual impact, whatever the viewing distance (Parke 1966).

Unless a specific feature is involved, view obstruction generally does not become an issue until existing views extend to the middleground (1/4 to 3 miles) or background (greater than 3 miles). The lateral extent of distant views is also important. Views that fill or exceed the entire human field of vision, approximately 150°, are generally termed "panoramic" and are most highly valued. The content of distant views can further increase their importance: water, natural features, manmade landmarks, and urban skylines composed of highrise structures are particularly valued.

The existence of important views and the location of viewponts can best and most reliably be determined from field observations. If there is a likelihood that project structures or vegetation could seriously obstruct important existing views from public parks, residences, or other view-related use areas, a more detailed analysis can be performed. It could determine the location of obstructed views, the proportion of the middleground or background that would be obstructed, and the identity of any specific features that would be blocked out. The number of viewers affected can also be estimated and the nature of the obstruction can be illustrated by superimposing an outline of the project on photographs taken from key viewpoints (see Figure 13.10).

Visual Contrast

Strong contrast between the visual character of a project and that of its setting is an important indicator of potential visual impact (Appleyard and Fishman 1977). Contrast does not always have adverse visual effects, however; the evaluation of contrast is discussed later in this chapter.

Important aspects of visual character include form (the height, bulk, and shape of structures), line (setbacks, roof lines, floor and window levels), color and texture (structure materials, site improvements), scale or apparent size (plant materials and details of structures), proportion (the relationships between horizontal and vertical dimensions), and rhythm (the spacing of repeated elements).

The visual character of the project can be identified in project analysis; analysis of environmental context will reveal the visual character of its setting. If contrast is likely to be strong, a more detailed analysis can be based on accurate simulations of the project and its environs from representative viewpoints, preferably prepared from photographs, to illustrate the degree of contrast that is probable under actual viewing conditions. See Figure 13.17 for an example of a project that is widely felt to be in excessive contrast with its

FIGURE 13.17. Many questions about this proposed highrise focus on its relationship to the visual character and scale of the existing streetscape, which is considered to have historic value. *Source:* Bassetti/Norton/Metler, Seattle, Washington.

surroundings. A recent book, *Architecture In Context* (Brolin 1980), is largely concerned with the issue of contrast between historic structures and new buildings.

To supplement expert analysis, public involvement techniques may be used to help rate contrast. A principal difficulty with the use of direct public involvement in urban visual assessment is that feelings frequently run high. Therefore agencies and clients often fear that public response sessions will be "packed" by project opponents. This problem can be overcome by carefully designed sampling strategies, but such strategies are usually rather costly.

Visual Quality

A public project will usually be seen as one element in a larger visual setting. Therefore it should enhance or improve the visual quality of its environs, rather than diminish that quality.

Project effects on visual quality are particularly likely to be an issue in settings that are already recognized for their visual quality (designated scenic areas and viewpoints, natural areas, parks, design review districts, and historic areas). However, many other settings have visual qualities—picturesque architecture, mature trees, distant views—that are attractive and that encourage development. The visual quality of this development can be a very significant factor in whether such areas will continue to garner new investment. Underutilized urban shorelines, warehouse districts, and traditional small-town main streets are examples of settings where visually sensitive projects can make a critical difference in the economic future of an area.

Visual quality is difficult to evaluate from plans and elevations because it is based on three-dimensional visual relationships between a project and its environs. Nevertheless, when project plans are combined with field observations, reviewers can make an initial determination of likely visual quality effects. Research has confirmed that the general public regards certain project features as attractive in themselves (street trees, materials such as brick or stone), but regards other features as unattractive (parking, utilities, and refuse storage). The relative visibility of these features from the project surroundings is therefore a basic indicator of likely visual quality. Another is evidence of integration of the design arts in the proposed structures and exterior spaces: architectural detailing, site planting, play areas, viewpoints, sculpture, earthworks, site interpretation, and so on.

If visual quality appears likely to be an important issue, a complete analysis will require accurate illustrations of the project and its environs from representative viewpoints, as discussed earlier. Expert appraisals of these views can be acceptable surrogates for public opinion if the appraisals are based on well-defined criteria derived from research into viewer response. For example (Blair 1980), experts can use dimensions such as the following to assess visual quality and prescribe mitigation measures:

> The vividness or memorability of views that include the project.
>
> The presence of a visually recognizable order, man-made or natural, in these views and their freedom from elements encroaching on that order.
>
> The visual unity or compositional harmony of all the elements in these views.

In urban settings with many viewers, however, members of the public will freely volunteer opinions on visual quality. Further, John Costonis notes that the appropriate legal test may be the reaction of "the man in the street," rather than the opinion of the specially educated connoisseur. In this situation, expert opinion may be discounted and it may be more important to select representative views and prepare accurate and credible simulations that can "speak for themselves" (Costonis 1982).

On the other hand, it is also important to note that many communities have formally delegated aesthetic decision-making powers to experts. Thus the visual quality of the University of Washington is in the hands of the Campus Design Commission, and the visual quality of certain classes of private development in the City of Bellevue is subject to administrative design review by staff of the Planning Department.

EXAMPLE: Determination of Visual Impacts, Public Involvement

Plans for construction of a state highway across a lake in Shreveport, Louisiana, had been held up by court battles for many years. The issues were gradually narrowed to the relative visual impact of alternative routes on the lake and adjoining recreation lands.

Opposing expert witnesses had reached a standoff in courtroom testimony on these impacts. It appeared that the only way to reach a definite determination of the relative visual impacts would be to elicit public response to the alternatives. The highway agency was reluctant to do this because the community was so polarized over the project. Finally, however, the agency decided to try a public involvement program because of the enormous cost of further delay.

To ensure that participants in the response program were representative of the community as a whole, a rigorous sampling program was set up. Major viewer groups were distinguished on the basis of geographic location, because viewer exposure factors such as distance from the highway alternatives and angle of view were thought likely to affect viewer response. Another consideration that entered into the delineation of viewer groups was the minimum population size necessary to achieve statistical reliability.

Within the general project viewshed, seven groups of residential viewers were distinguished on the basis of their potential exposure to the alternatives (see Figure 13.18). The recruitment goal for participation in the response sessions was a randomly drawn sample of 20 persons from each of the seven residential groups. Each of the dwelling units within the seven areas was assigned a sequential

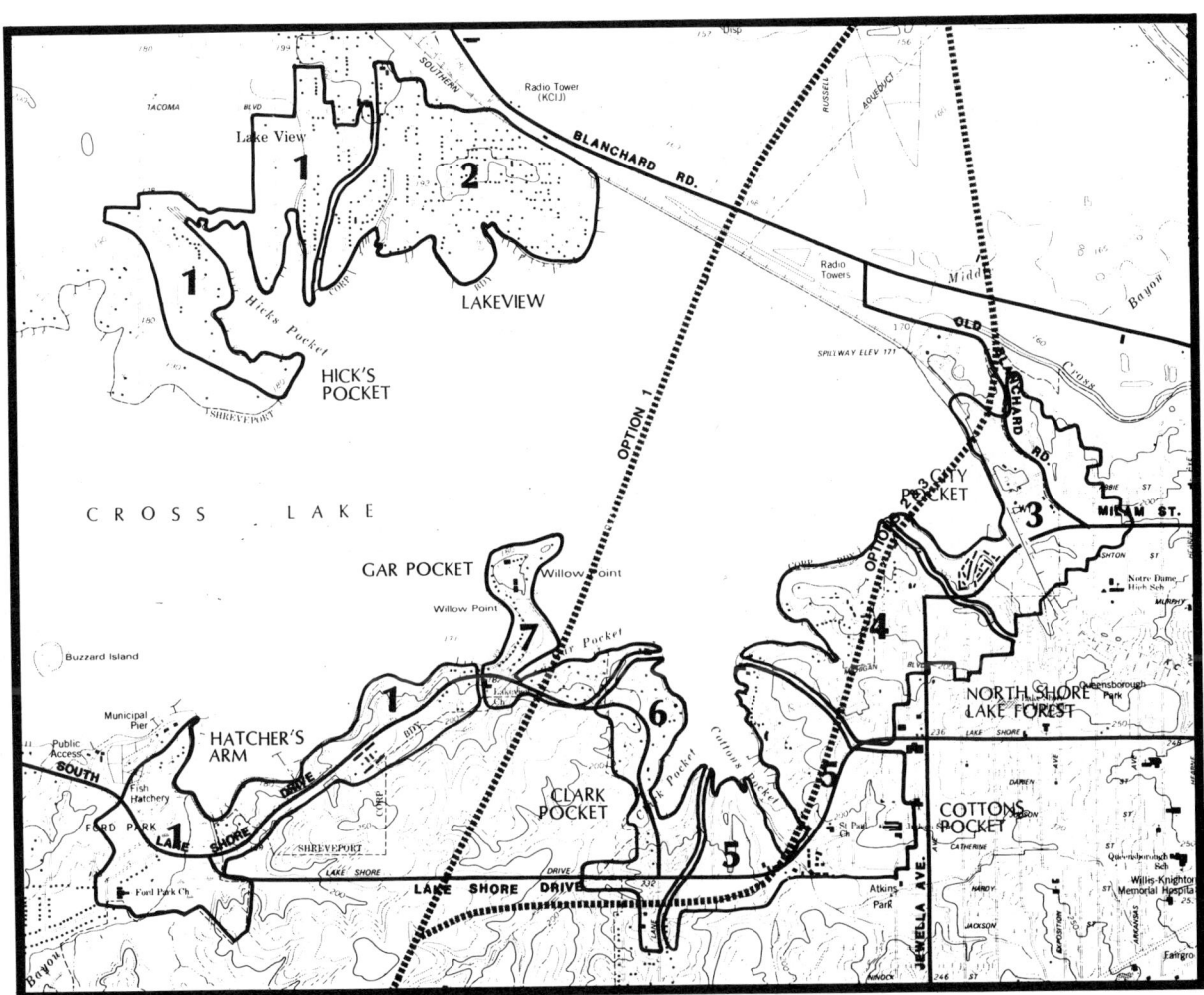

FIGURE 13.18. Location of residential viewer populations and highway options. *Source:* Jones and Jones, Seattle, Washington.

number. A random number program was then used to identify persons within each area; these people were contacted and their participation solicited until the quota for each area was met.

Responses were elicited in a series of small-group sessions (see Figure 13.19); in each, the participants viewed a series of film clips that simulated views of the highway and trips along it. The simulated views were divided into randomly ordered groups in which the participants were unlikely to be able to recognize "their" views, and into clearly organized presentations of the alternatives (Atkins and Blair 1983).

The results of the public response sessions appeared to show that the visual resource effects of the alternatives were roughly equivalent, but that one set of alternatives would expose roughly 10 times as many viewers to these resource effects as would the other alternative. Not surprisingly, the participants favored the low-exposure route by an overwhelming margin. This had never come out clearly before because the number of vocal spokespersons for each alternative was approximately equal.

EVALUATION OF VISUAL IMPACTS

Criteria

The evaluation of visual impacts cannot be reduced to a simple formula. Consideration must be given to all the types of visual effects discussed in the previous section, but there is no universal way of weighing these considerations against each other. In one case, a significant change and contrast in visual character may be acceptable if a

242 VISUAL IMPACT ASSESSMENT IN URBAN ENVIRONMENTS

FIGURE 13.19. Small group response session. *Source:* Jones and Jones, Seattle, Washington.

project helps to improve the overall visual quality of its surroundings. In another case, a project may be visually unacceptable because of the level of effect on a single consideration, such as view obstruction.

The project setting or existing features on the project site may trigger specific evaluation criteria in federal, state, or local laws and regulations. If so, these criteria must be addressed explicitly in the project EIS. Examples of such instances include the following:

1. Shadow. State environmental policy act regulations or local ordinances may control the extent of shadows that project structures cast on public areas offsite; other state or local legislation may control shadows indirectly, by protecting the solar access of existing structures adjoining the project site.

2. Solar glare. State and local environmental regulations may address offsite glare and heat gain from reflective project surfaces; such agencies as the Federal Highway Administration may be concerned with the safety effects of solar glare on drivers traveling high-speed freeways.

3. Artificial light. High-intensity lighting may be regulated in circumstances similar to those created by solar glare.

4. Existing visual resources. If site features are designated in federal, state, or local registers (or are eligible for designation), the project EIS must assess the visual effect of removing or modifying these features; other provisions, such as local tree protection ordinances, may also direct the assessment of effects on specific visual resources.

5. View obstruction. Views from public viewpoints or views of certain landmarks may be protected by means such as zoning codes, coastal management programs, or even scenic easements, as well as by environmental impact disclosure requirements.

6. Visual contrast. Legislation and regulatory programs commonly seek to minimize the introduction of visual contrast in areas valued for their existing visual character, such as historic districts, design review districts, and scenic rivers. In some cases, the evaluation of contrast may be intended to avoid the difficulties of evaluating visual quality directly.

7. Visual quality. The National Environmental Policy Act takes a direct approach to maintaining and enhancing all aspects of environmental quality, including visual quality. Several federal agencies with responsibilities in urban areas require the explicit evaluation and management of project effects on visual quality. Among these are the Federal Highway Administration, the Department of Housing and Urban Development, and the Soil Conservation Service. Further, many local communities have design

commissions or design review boards that try to maintain or enhance the quality of portions of the urban environment.

Significance

Factual information on the *degree* of effect is essential as a basis for evaluation of the *significance* of effect. In addition to the information on specific visual stimulus issues discussed earlier, evaluations of significance should also consider viewer response issues such as the types and numbers of viewers who will see the project onsite and offsite, and their perceptions and concerns. Thus the visual effects of projects must be evaluated in relation to both the visual setting of the project and the people who will see it. Whenever possible, evaluation should also be based on accurate (although not necessarily detailed) visual representations of the project in its setting.

The decision of "how much is too much" often must be based on local values and precedents. Once again, direct readings of viewer response provide extremely useful information for project evaluation and can help to corroborate expert judgments, particularly in adversary situations. Visual effects may be classified into five levels of significance:

Beneficial.
Acceptable.
Acceptable with mitigation.
Unacceptable.
Indeterminate.

1. The visual impacts of the project may be evaluated as *beneficial* if the appearance of the project evidences careful design and support of project functions, and if it complements the visual character of its setting or improves its visual quality.

2. The visual impacts of the project may be considered *acceptable* of there is reason to believe there will be no significant adverse visual effects onsite or offsite.

3. Visual impacts may be evaluated as *acceptable with mitigation* if there will be one or more significant adverse effects, but these can be eliminated, reduced, or offset to a major extent by specific mitigation measures.

4. Major adverse visual effects, onsite or offsite, that cannot be appreciably mitigated may compel an evaluation of the project's visual impacts as *unacceptable*.

5. If it appears that significant adverse visual effects are likely, but the extent to which they may occur and/or to which they may be mitigated cannot be determined, the visual impacts of the project may be rated as *indeterminate*. In this case, the specific visual effects at issue can be identified for more detailed study.

MITIGATION MEASURES

Mitigation measures for adverse visual impacts can transcend "cosmetics" if they address specific effects rather than dress up general project appearance. Each proposed mitigation measure should be clearly and logically related to the particular visual problem it is intended to correct. The degree to which the measure will correct the problem can also be identified. EIS reviewers, including members of the concerned public, may justifiably be suspicious of vaguely stated visual mitigation strategies.

Specific Measures

The following measures are examples of the types of actions that may help to mitigate adverse visual effects, grouped by categories of visual considerations:

1. Shadow. Reduce extent and duration of shadow impacts by modifying siting or orientation of structures and reducing their height or bulk.

2. Solar glare. Reduce extent and intensity of glare by reducing extent of reflective materials, reducing their reflectivity, and adjusting their vertical and horizontal orientation.

3. Artificial lighting. Reduce extent, intensity, and duration of lighting impacts by reducing number of fixtures, reducing source intensity, lowering fixture mounting height, providing source shielding, modifying fixture aiming, or limiting hours of operation.

4. Existing visual resources. Reduce impact on existing features valued for their visual appearance by retaining all or part of these features onsite, integrating these features into project de-

sign, relocating or salvaging the features, or providing interpretive materials about the features.

5. View obstruction. Reduce interference with offsite views by modifying placement, height, and shape of structures, including rooftop mechanical equipment and enclosures.

6. Visual contrast. When excessive visual contrast is an issue, reduce it by modifying spatial disposition of structures (setbacks, rhythm, and site coverage); modifying height, bulk, shape, and proportion of structures; manipulating visual scale (projections, doors and windows, materials); incorporating materials, textures, colors, and architectural details from the environs.

7. Visual quality. To increase the visual quality of the project and its setting, modify placement, height, form, and proportion of structures in relation to adjoining development and existing views; unify project with setting by plant materials, site furnishings, lighting, and paving; provide public activity space and/or viewing onsite; integrate design arts into project planning.

PART 5

INTERNATIONAL PERSPECTIVES

Part five presents three contributions from international authors: a report from Yugoslavia focusing on visual quality as an issue in urban planning; the second a report from Sweden of recent results from one of the oldest and most active environmental visual simulation laboratories; and finally a description of a comprehensive system for evaluating landscape visual quality used in Spain. At one time, consideration was given to including these contributions in their respective thematic parts. However, they have been collected together as a part of their own to illustrate the variety of state-of-the-art performance from other parts of the world. The United States is a large country and very active in the area of environmental protection. It is therefore only too easy for Americans to become smug in our own efforts and fail to appreciate the significant advances being made elsewhere. For instance, we should make it a habit to review the foreign journals that address issues of concern to our field. Those with texts in English include: *Landscape Australia, Garten und Landschaft* (Germany), *Landscape Planning* (International), *Anthos (Switzerland), and Landscape Research* (United Kingdom).

This section begins with Pogačnik's description of a geographic data base that incorporates visual as well as other landscape planning dimensions. It is applied to Ljubljana, Yugoslavia, for the purpose of developing visually sensitive project siting criteria. His outlook for integrating aesthetic and visual concerns within the planning and design process is very much in harmony with the intent of NEPA.

Janssens and Küller, in Chapter 15, describe the genesis of the environmental visual simulator at Lund, Sweden. Their report pays particular attention to the comparative efficacy of various representational techniques. Their simulation lab continues to be involved in helping designers and the general public to visualize the environmental implications of proposed projects. It should serve as a standard for others to emulate.

Finally, Alonso, Aguilo, and Ramos, from Spain, present a visual impact assessment procedure that seeks to optimize three considerations: visibility, visual quality, and fragility. Their work is particularly characterized by the careful articulation of a great many measured landscape parameters. The use of this procedure is illustrated through the siting of an industrial facility.

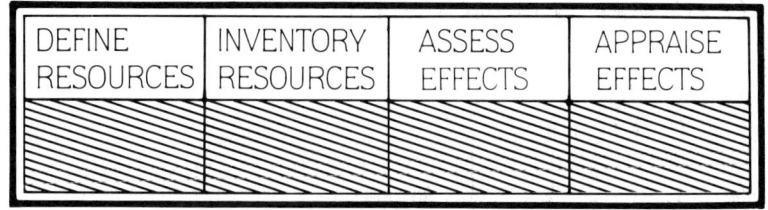

CHAPTER 14

VISUAL-AESTHETIC COMPONENTS IN THE CYBERNETICS OF URBAN PLANNING

Andrej B. Pogačnik

Portions of this chapter previously appeared in the following articles:
A. Pogačnik, Urban design: the case of Ljubljana, *Town & Country Planning*, Dec., 1977, 538–42; A systems approach to urban design, *Town Planning Review* 48: 187–92; A visual information system and its use in urban planning, *Urban Ecology* 4: 29–43; Environmental public preferences as obtained by method of photo-interpretation in the Ljubljana Region, *Urban Ecology* 4: 45–51.

INTRODUCTION

The research work summarized here has been conducted at the Cathedra for Urban Planning at the Faculty for Architecture, Engineering, and Geodesy of the University of Ljubljana, Slovenia, in Yugoslavia from 1972 to 1978. The theoretical and methodological foundations were tested successfully in the area of Kozarje near Ljubljana, and the research was extended to cover the whole metropolitan region of Ljubljana as part of the Year 2000 Master Plan worked out for the City Council of Ljubljana. One of the basic goals of this research was to find a scientific method of managing the visual environment which would enable society to control, simulate, and decide on changes in its aesthetic qualities. It is therefore necessary to encompass the visual message in some operational system, where it is quantifiable.

At this stage, it must be pointed out that the researcher's goal was not to develop mathematical aesthetics—beauty from a black box—but to rationalize visual-aesthetic relations in space, to determine objective conditions and *solution spaces* within which architectural creation could be realized. A flow diagram of the rational process used here is shown in Figure 14.1. A *classical* heuristic and intuitive approach in design problem solving can be qualitatively higher than the methodology shown here. However, rapid urbanization, personal mobility, behavioral changes, and the involvement of numerous designers all make control of the overall design of cities and regions increasingly difficult. The overall impact and interactive nature of visual phenomena seem to be impossible to govern without an objective, quantifiable model. The author has attempted to establish some objective limits to possible changes so that the basic visual-aesthetic qualities should not be lost but maintained.

HISTORICAL BACKGROUND, GOALS, AND ISSUES

Large-scale landscape design, as a part of urban and regional planning, began before the First World War with the introduction of garden architecture and theories of new cities. The period between the two wars saw the development of new theoretical work in the fields of visual aesthetics, perceptional psychology, and sociology. After the Second World War, ecology, system theory, integrated surveying, city and regional planning, and environmental sciences were included. With the work of Kevin Lynch (1960), the broader professional public became aware of and further developed the methodology of planning and visual environment. The approach outlined in this chapter is partly based on achievements of Appleyard et al. (1964), Steinitz (1970), Eckbo (1969), Andersson (1973), and others.

Changes and interactive visual relations in space, properly organized into an information system, should be included in a city or regional data bank and thus become integrated into the system of comprehensive planning. With such a system, the overall outlook, control, guidance, and planning of the visual environment is possible. The design team in the analysis and evaluation of the visual message can include public opinion, provide a simulation of possible changes, and so forth and thus, to a large extent, objectively optimize visual relations in space.

INFORMATION SOURCES

From the numerous feasible techniques for recording the visual message, black-and-white panoramic photography in a horizontal plane was chosen to represent views. It is thus possible to simulate the visual experience of pedestrians, vehicle users, and so forth. Ideally, we should be able to take photographs from any point in space and at any elevation angle. Costs, time, and operational constraints, however, limit the possibilities to selected photographic viewpoints that generalize visual characteristics for the given planning scale. Visual inventory should be compatible with the spatial information system. In Yugoslavia, an orthogonal geodetical[1] network has been accepted as a basis for data collection for different city and regional planning projects. Therefore its grid points are taken as the reference for visual inventory. At the urban planning scale, use is made of a 500 x 500 m grid; for a regional planning scale, a 1000 x 1000 m grid is used; 2000 x 2000 m is used for a macroregional scale, and so forth. Subdivision of the visual information network to architectural scale is also possible.

The visual information collected from one set of photographs should generalize the visual-aesthetic message within the grid cell from which

---

[1] Known as Gauß-Krüger network.

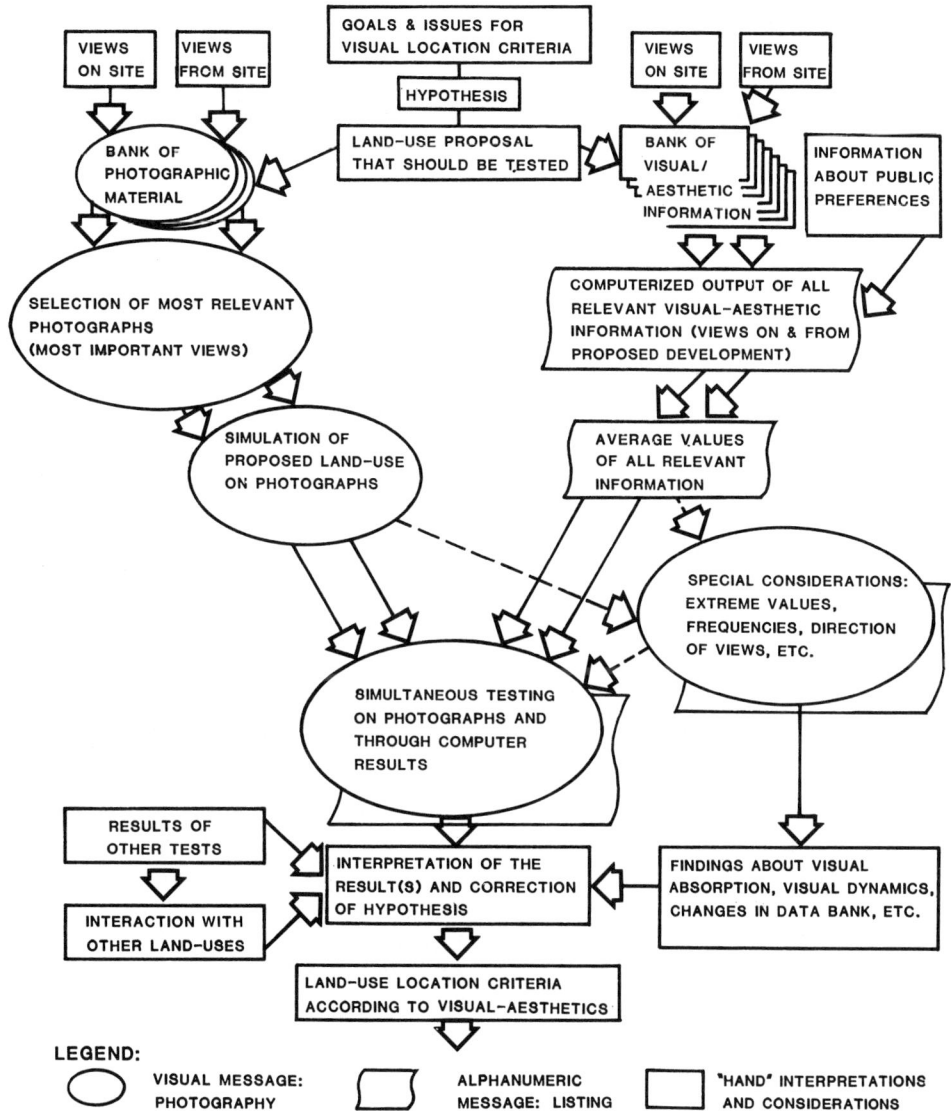

FIGURE 14.1. Generalized information flow in testing the locational preferences according to the visual-aesthetic optimization.

FIGURE 14.2. An example of the use of a visual data bank: portion of computer printout of decoded visual information scene from a selected viewing point towards a chosen area (square).

centroid the photographs were taken. It is thus necessary to extract from the photograph that information which is relevant to the planning scale, the defined goals, and the development tasks (Figure 14.2).

DESCRIPTION OF COLLECTED INFORMATION

What visual-aesthetic data should be collected? The basic pair of data is the coordinates of the photographic viewpoint and the centroid of the observed grid cell. We must know the location of the observation and what we observe. The computer data bank contains all possible pairs of coordinates of observation points and observed points. This *reserved space* in the data bank either contains information (when visual interaction exists) or not (when the observed point is hidden from the observer).

The first piece of visual information relevant to each view is called *visual topology:* it is factual, "quantifiable" information, stating whether the visual message means direct, real visibility of the space (in the grid square), or only scenery beyond the space (that is, the visible scene is behind the square, which is not itself visible). The first case is called *direct visibility*, the second *indirect visibility*. The third possibility, of course, is invisibility (that is, from the observation point neither the square nor anything beyond is seen).

The second piece of information concerning visual interaction gives the aesthetic, compositional distance of the observed scene—whether it lies in near, middle, or far distance. Such an evaluation of scenery is based on perceptive, semantic, compositional, and design components. This visual-aesthetic distance is generalized into three main categories—near, middle, and far distance or *screen*.

The third piece of information is essential as it describes the visual-aesthetic substance, that is, the meaning of the scene observed. With this information, the panoramic view is divided into meaningful visual entities or segments. This subdivision is also followed by detection and coding of *visual topology* and *distance*. This information contains basic aesthetic signals such as *points, nodes, edges, paths, surfaces,* and so forth, together with *semantic*, compositional, and planning interpretations. The coded information included: (1) *Ambient* (self-contained, readable, beautiful images); (2) *specific natural scenes* (mountains, vegetation groups, streams, and so forth, recognized as visual entities or parts of the overall view); (3) specific *man-made* scenes (settlements, streets, squares, architectural monuments, and so forth); (4) other specific meaningful scenes (historical sites, ethnographic, technological, and so forth). This information was interpreted into five planning categories.

The first category should be preserved accurately, while those in the second category could be subject to small changes in the overall scene of which they form part. The third category of coded topology includes natural or man-made environments without specific visual-aesthetic meaning (built-up areas, fields, forests, and so forth), and linear spaces (roads, valleys, coasts, and so forth). These scenes could all be subject to conditional changes. The fourth category includes the continuous, monotonous parts of the picture, that is, connection between its parts (suburban urbanization, poor vegetation, monocultures, flat land, continuous hills, and so forth). For this category, certain changes in the existing scene are requested. The fifth category includes the most unpleasant and unaesthetic visual entities (eroded, polluted land; poorly maintained, old, and abandoned structures, and so forth) that must be changed or hidden.

With the information described above, the basic visual inventory is covered together with the viewing position to be discussed later. For development and planning, this factual information is supplemented by evaluative information of natural–man-made relationships in the coded scene, or, in other words, information concerning the extent to which the area is built up visually. Finally, a category of summarized visual-aesthetic quality is added to the coded scene, based on previous information, together with the accepted value system goals and planning tasks. This is classified from highest to poorest quality.

For practical application and physical development purposes, the information system was broadened into the field of decision making. For any specific coded scene, a value was assigned, describing to what extent the existing situation could be changed (from absolute preservation to complete change) and in what way (by the introduction of man-made structures, plants and trees, demolition, and so forth). For this decision-making information, we must, of course, assume a certain planning requirement.

The last two pieces of required information try to measure viewing *heights*. They indicate from what height the coded scene is viewed, measured from the observation point, and also the height up to which one may change (that is, build, plant, destroy, preserve, and so forth) the existing visual environment, according to all the previously described planning issues. The heights have been generalized into groups for planning purposes—up to 2 m, up to 7 m, up to 18 m, up to 50 m, and over 50 m.

As can be seen, the basic visual information is quantitative. From this information is derived evaluative data and finally decision information. Thus it is possible to include in the process of visual identification, evaluation, decision making, teamwork, public opinion, and so forth. The visual information system can be broadened even further.

A certain area must be visually inventoried with panoramic photographs both inside the area and outside to the edges of visibility. Separate visual analysis of this type is reasonable in homogeneous, visually enclosed, and self-contained areas; otherwise, overall visual data banks are recommended.

SOME TECHNICAL ASPECTS OF THE VISUAL INFORMATION SYSTEM

This section describes some technical details of visual information systems which underlie the aforementioned theoretical work, as well as data processing.

Medium- or large-size computers are needed for the design, operation, and maintenance of such visual data banks which were researched in the late 1970s. The author used a CDC Cyber '72 computer and 1200 user active terminal on the batch basis. Fortran IV language was used for programming and is most suitable for spatial tasks.

The basis of the visual information system is two information types: one describing the "location" of the view, that is, the coordinates of the space observed (x,y), and the second describing the coordinates of the observing point (w,z). After fixing a particular view in the form of reserved space in computer memory, one can describe the particular visual message in a coded form. For instance, the coding $x_1\ y_2\ w_3\ z_4\ T\ L\ N\ 0\ 3\ 2\ 1\ 1$ means that the location x,y has been seen from the observing point w,z, as the direct view (T), to the near scenery (L), to the natural landscape (N), without man-made structures (0), with relatively good aesthetic characteristics (3), where few new buildings could be built (2); the height of visible structures is more than 7 meters (1), and new buildings should not exceed this height (1).

Our second important organizing point lies in the priorities of the information. Those data are first stored that are numeric and more constant; they then form the framework of the informative system. These are the coordinates of the observed space and viewing points, as already explained, the topography of the views, direct or indirect visibility of a certain space, and, finally, the visual height/elevation angle of the view expressed as a height of the visibility on the site:

| x | y | z | T | | | | | 1 | |

Next, partly factual and partly subjective information is stored. This information is obtained either through photo interpretation or through value interpretations via public questionnaires: and includes distance of the scenery observed, density of buildings, visual quality, and so on:

| x | y | w | z | T | N | 0 | | 1 | |

Finally, information that pertains to decision making is stored—information which is changeable and includes planning decisions, such as possibilities for building, future densities, possible heights of new structures, and so on—all relevant for the particular view, of course:

| x | y | w | z | T | N | 0 | 3 | 2 | 1 | 1 |

If necessary, more information could be added to the particular view.

Simple mathematical operations for visual analysis have been used. Primarily these have been average or mean values of the information within one space, assuming equal importance of all planning areas. Frequency of the views has shown us the visual sensitivity. Extreme values of certain information have indicated limiting factors that could not be included into the computing of mean values. Finally, ponderation factors, obtained through public opinion, affected results too. These items can be stated in mathematical form:

$$I_{x,y} = \frac{\sum_{i=1}^{i=n} I_{w_i v_i z_i}}{n} \cdot F_l$$

if $n > a$ then $I = I \cdot F_{la}$
$> n < b$ then $I = I$
$< n$ then $I = I \cdot F_{lb}$

if I includes any value U then $I = V_l$ where

I = value of the information
x,y = location of the information
w,z = source of the information
n = number of the information sources
F = ponderation factor
a,b = delimitations of visual frequency
U = extreme
V_l = assigned value of the information because of the extreme value

All basic information is scored in five levels such as highest, high, medium, low, lowest—quality, density, preference, and so forth. Such a polarization, which has been used by sociologists and gives relatively good and objective possibilities for further consideration, selection, or elimination of information. For instance, if the visual quality is being described from 1 to 5, from "ugliest" to the most "beautiful," we can, through public judgment, assign them new values—keeping the best view, eliminating the worst one, and taking into account medium values with different ponderations:

if $I = 5$ then $F = 1000$ $I_p = I \cdot F$ where
if $I = 4$ then $F = 2$
if $I = 3$ then $F = 1$ I_p = new value of information I after the ponderation
if $I = 2$ then $F = 0.5$
if $I = 1$ then $F = 0.001$

ROLE OF THE COMPUTER

Information thus gathered from panoramic photographs should first be related to the site through orientation and photo interpretation. This information is written into relevant grid cells and from there onto the code sheets (Figure 14.3). In the data bank, pairs of coordinates for each "view" are stored first, followed by other information describing details of the "view." Basic programs for handling the data bank include programs for storage and retrieval and simple listing of information in decoded form. Relatively large computer storage requirements are necessary.

More problem-oriented programs were developed giving certain analytical results. With the aid of the computer, it is possible to select certain relevant information ("views"), and summary information output (average values, and so forth) from these relatively simple programs can also be shown in graphic form using a digital plotter. Using differently shaded areas, the intensity of phenomena and suitability for various planning purposes can be illustrated (Figure 14.4). Drawn links between viewed and viewing points give graphs of directions of views (Figure 14.5). These graphs have been superimposed onto and reduced into grid cells to give the overall picture of visual relations.

More complicated programs have been developed for different tasks. Search routines can locate the relevant information in the data bank for any chosen spatial problem. This information is optimized with the use of median values, taking into account information frequency and extreme values. Different logical and do-statements were used. Completely automated interaction with a visual terminal has not been reached at this point. Interactive work is limited to automatic printout of values related to the panoramic photography, showing median information for each selected grid cell or "segment of view."

GENERAL USE OF VISUAL INFORMATION SYSTEM

There are many uses for such a visual information system. Sets of photographic material can be used for different simulations of possible or planned changes. From the generalized and coded information on all visual relations in space, it is possible to optimize future land use in visual terms; aesthetic images of the space can thus be incorporated into a system of comprehensive planning. Each "view" gives its own solution space with determined horizontal boundaries, heights, and degree and nature of possible changes in the vis-

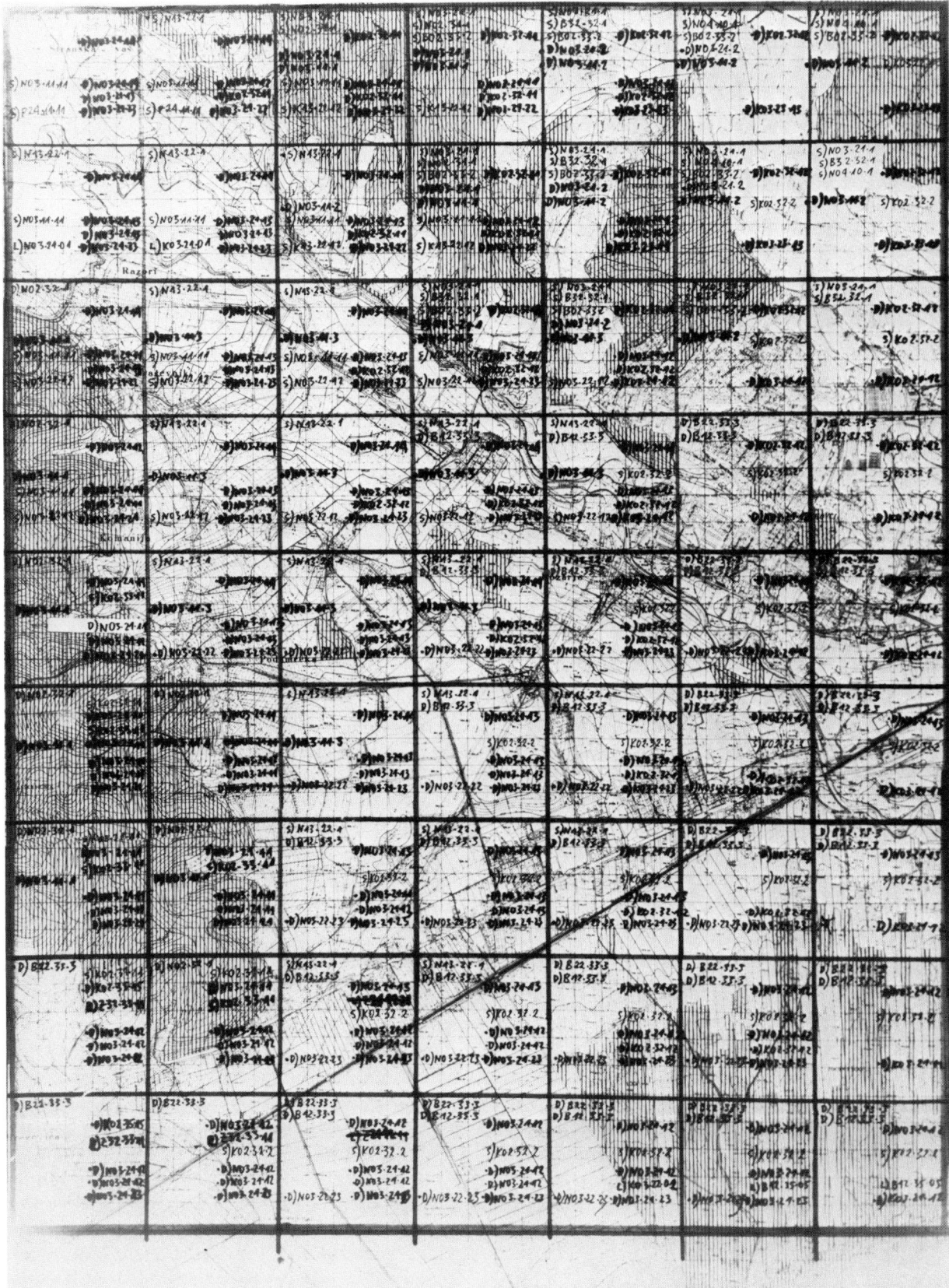

FIGURE 14.3. Example of information map: information from the photographs are transferred into relevant grid cells and from there via code sheets into the computer.

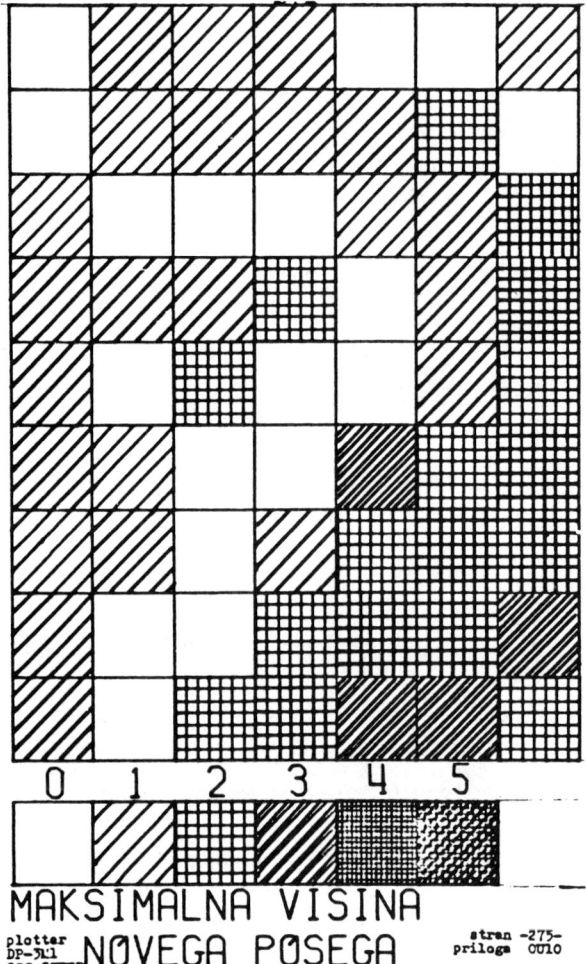

FIGURE 14.4. An example of geographical output showing aggregate values of information in site. The degree of possible change in the environment is shown here.

ual environment for each grid cell. With a method similar to that of linear programming, one can reach a final solution space that optimizes the conditions from all possible viewing points.

The results of the visual analysis can be obtained from the data bank in alphanumerics or in the form of decoded listings of information. Information from certain viewpoints, or the ones contained in certain grid cells, or combinations of both, can be called. Furthermore, it is possible to ask for only certain information or values, by introducing limits, constraints, and conditions, and thus come close to a particular planning task. Computer programs have been developed for the optimization of an average value of visual information in a grid cell, following qualitatively higher information and taking account of extreme values. These outputs are reported separately, enabling "hand" control and decision making. Graphical outputs can also be provided for synthetic maps of frequency distribution of information, simulations of visual quality, possibilities of change, possible heights of obstacles, and so forth. With the final synthesis of these thematic maps with "hand" optimization, we achieve the final result—a proposition for future land use in visual-aesthetic terms.

Especially interesting is the graphic presentation of the so-called "visual situation" on a map of the site that has been covered with the information grid. Projected into each grid cell is its visual relationship to the surrounding site, that is, to all viewing points, thus showing the visible scene for each grid cell. With these visual diagrams projected into each grid cell, it is possible from observing all of them to detect the main directions of view and all other visual phenomena such as *points, nodes, edges, paths, and surfaces*.

PRACTICAL TESTING OF VISUAL MODEL: FUTURE LAND USE OPTIMIZATION

All the theoretical approaches described above have been developed as part of a proposed methodology for visual optimization of the location of housing, industrial buildings, services, recreational areas, infrastructural corridors, protection and preservation areas, and so forth.

The hypothesis and theories have been tested on a site at Kozarje, near Ljubljana, Yugoslavia. As the scale of the problem was one of master planning, a grid 500 x 500 m was used. The test site was inventoried through 60 viewing points on 1000 x 1000 m grid. Photographs were taken inside the test site, at its limits, and outside to the limits of visibility. Panoramic photographs were laid out in a circular way, inventoried, evaluated, and coded (see Figure 14.6). Information maps were created following the orientation (that is, transfer of coded segments onto topographic maps and thus into grid cells), and through photo interpretation, that is, recognized geomorphology, vegetation, land use, and so forth.

The goal was to optimize future urban development of the site in visual terms, assuming equal importance throughout the test area and of all observation areas inside the test site and outside it. Thus the average values of data in each grid cell

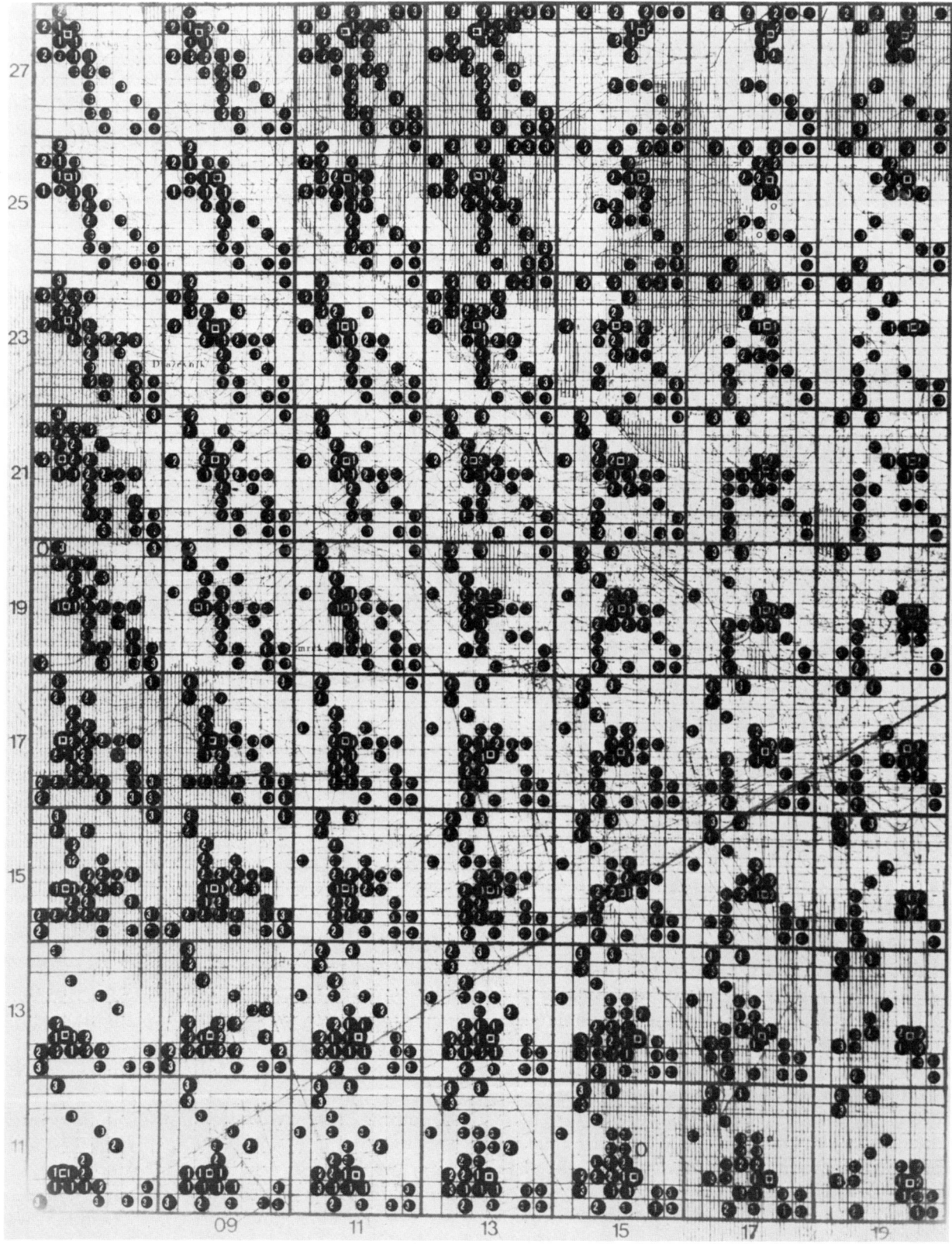

FIGURE 14.5. Computer-produced graph of visual relations in the site: map showing locations and sources of information within the site giving directions of views.

256 VISUAL-AESTHETIC COMPONENTS IN THE CYBERNETICS OF URBAN PLANNING

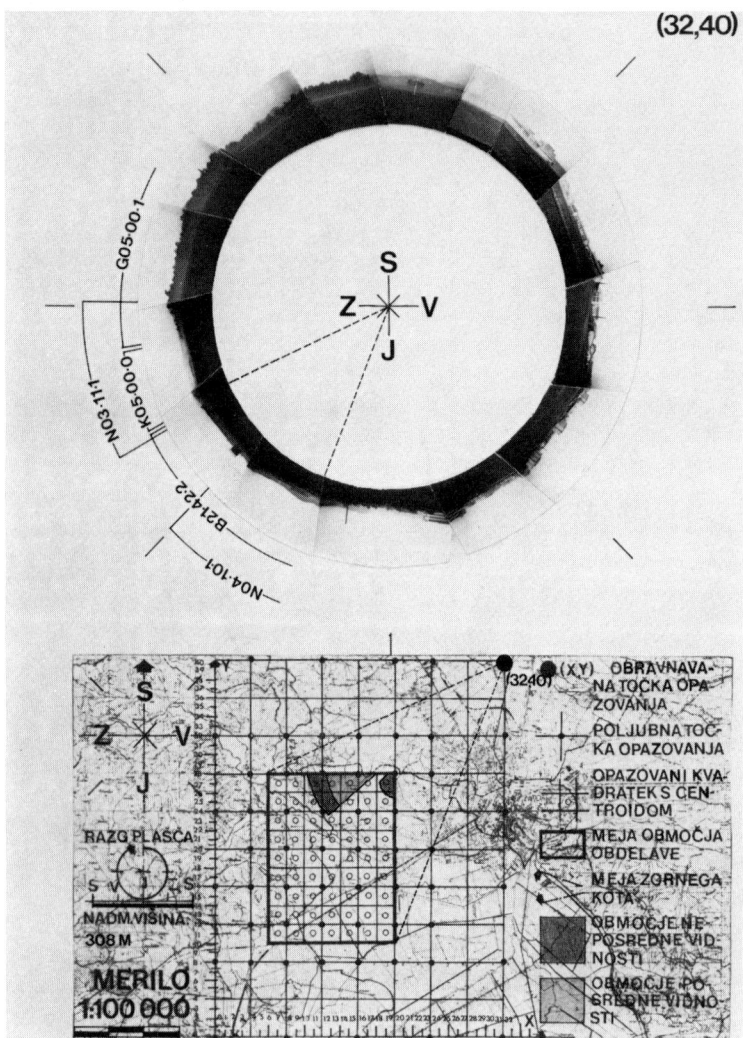

FIGURE 14.6. One of the 60 panoramic photographs used in this test. The map shows visible area—both direct and indirect—from this point.

were obtained. In the case of equal or dubious results, higher values were followed in order to preserve as many of the existing values as possible. Various decoded printouts of average values, frequency, extremes, and so forth were used. Graphical outputs of visual exposition (frequency), direction and topology of views (visual situations), possible degree, nature and height of changes in existing image, and so forth were required. After synthesizing these thematic maps and by manual interpretation, final results in the form of a land use map were produced. In this final step, of course, it was necessary to disaggregate the result from grid cells into real space again.

HIGHWAY TEST

The second important test on the same site was more application and problem-oriented by nature. The problem was to evaluate the future urban development on the site, following the proposed highway through this area. It was necessary then to optimize future developments from the visual-aesthetic point of view, with respect to the views from the highway (car driver's experience) and from the area to the highway (the experiences of residents, workers, and tourists). The solution was then obtained through optimization of average information, relevant to the grid cells in which the highway was located. The position of the

FIGURE 14.7. Photo simulation of highway: views from the road. At each segment, the computer prints out optimal values of visual-aesthetic characteristics to provide simultaneous man-machine dialogue and visual simulation.

highway was assumed to be fixed. The optimum solution was approached after many cycles, as the partial solutions were tested in photographic material and corrected data entered in the new run. Photographs, this time, were laid out in strips with the highway traced in (see Figure 14.7). Computer-produced average solutions were displayed at the corresponding segment of picture (grid cell observed), simultaneously from both aspects (looking from the highway and to the highway), separately for different visual distances (near, middle, far). Thus a dialogue between man, computer, and visual medium was possible; written results were traced onto the photograph, evaluated, and corrected. Final results were obtained in the form of sets of photographs redrawn, showing solution spaces for possible changes (urbanization, preservation, planting, demolition, and so forth) and in the form of a final land use map.

USE OF THE VISUAL MODEL IN THE MASTER PLAN OF LJUBLJANA

These first methodological approaches have been applied in the larger practical problem—in the future urban development of the city of Ljubljana as the part of the new Master Plan (Figure 14.8). All urban areas have been covered with 1km x 1km grid and inventoried with 60 observing points. A visual inventory and general public opinion results about the visual environment have been incorporated into the master planning process, for example, possible development and protection areas, possible changes in visual structure, building densities, heights, green screens, and so forth.

Within the third research stage summarized here, previous findings were made applicable to real planning situations. General goal formulation of this research could be defined as allocation criteria of different land uses, according to visual aesthetics. Before progressing, another problem had to be resolved that has not been addressed enough in previous studies; that is, visual inventory, evaluation, and decision making should be based, to a large extent, on public preferences, attitudes, and traditional values.

Therefore a broad public questionnaire was administered to ask people's opinions about typical *vistas*, scenes, and other environments; it was later incorporated within the research. These views—and the opinions about them—should represent all other similar visual environments. Results of the questionnaire were processed by computer and analyzed via correlations between social groups and their preferences, different types of scenes, people's attitudes, and so forth. Photographic material was then inventoried and evaluated according to public preferences, and such data was stored in the computer.

Based on social research and photo documentation, further research can become much more objective. As already defined, the basic goal was to define location criteria for new land uses, to research *visual absorption* of the landscape and the dynamics of visual changes, and so forth. All these problems were approached through numerous tests.

Each test, as mentioned above, consisted of an

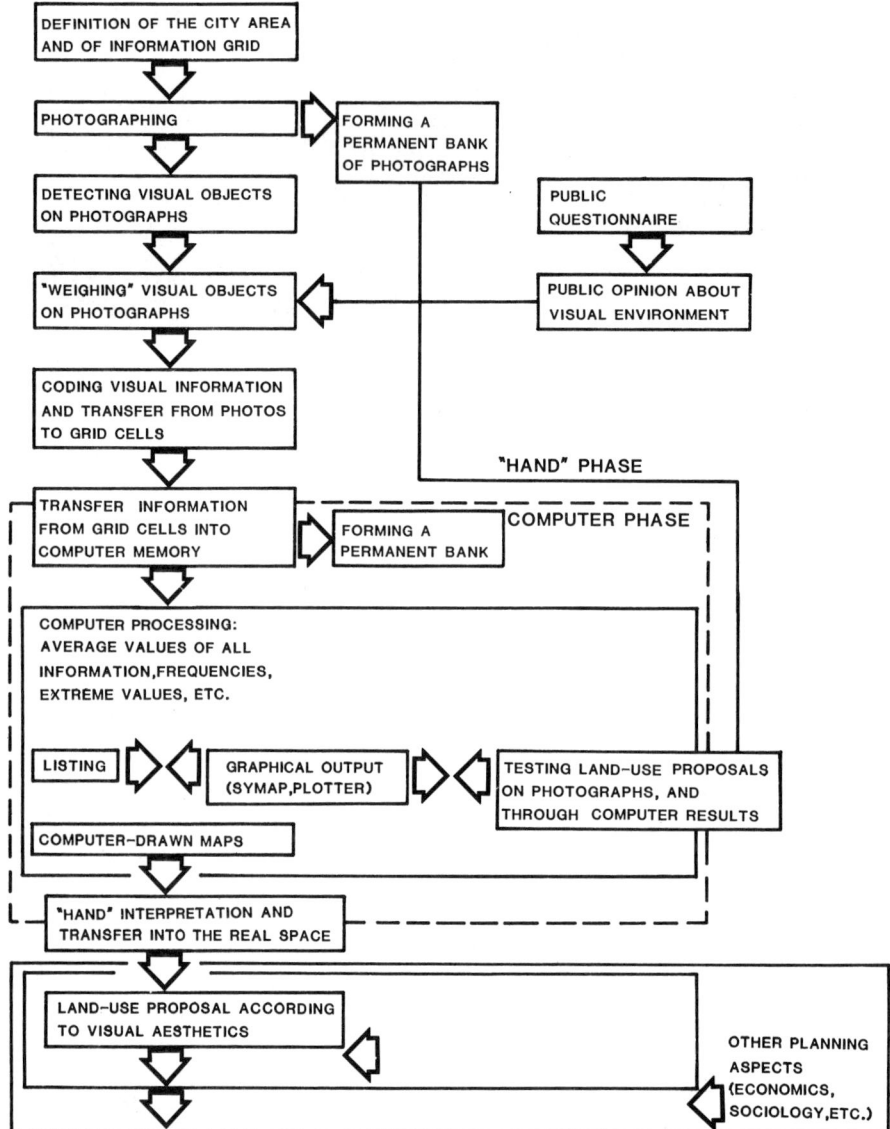

FIGURE 14.8. Generalized information flow in the system approach to the urban design/case study of the city of Ljubljana.

initial hypothesis about the visual location criteria. Such criteria was based on overall visual performance criteria such as: town centers should be visually well exposed, industry should be hidden in unattractive areas, and so forth. These hypotheses were tested in real planning situations. The results of the test should have some overall meaning; its inputs should be generalized as well. Thus industry, for instance, has always been assumed to be visually unattractive, city centers are interesting landmarks, housing is aesthetically neutral built-up scenery, and so on. On the other hand, the test sites should generalize the outlook and planning conditions of a typical Slovenian landscape. Therefore, an area of cca 500 hectares near the city of Ljubljana was chosen that was rich and diverse in its natural and built-up qualities.

First, the test site was fully visually inventoried and evaluated, according to the methodology explained before. Social values were computer processed and analyzed, and various visual characteristics of the site were determined through graphic routines.

In the first step of each particular test, the lo-

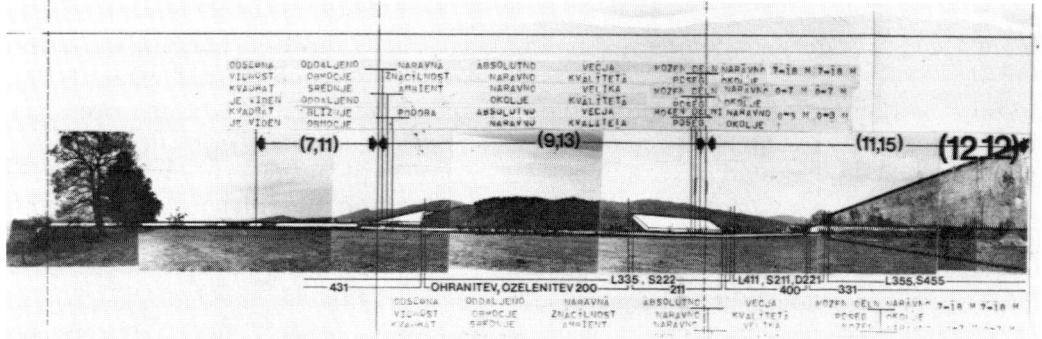

FIGURE 14.9. Close view of one segment of the photograph, corresponding to nearby grid-cell. In this cell there are possibilities for the extension of housing development.

cation of new land use, such as industry, housing, and so forth, was approximated into relevant grid cells. Summarized visual-aesthetic qualities of these grid cells were examined, yielding information about visual exposition, compositional qualities, scenic values, and so forth of that particular site. These synthesized data were presented in the form of various listings or computer graphs. This first part of the test already gave a certain feedback to the initial hypothesis. Much better results than those obtained through this automated technique have been obtained with visual simulations on the photographs. Proposed land use has been traced on the relevant part of panoramic photographs in the generalized form of a white strip (see Figure 14.9). Simultaneously, the computer-written information has been applied to the same segment of the photograph, giving aggregate information about that space. The result has been finally transformed in real space.

Different comparisons were made between the existing landscape and the one after new land development, or between successive developments. Comparisons were made with special attention to changes in visual message content and the data bank as a whole. After comparisons of visual simulation together with computer processing, the initial hypothesis was corrected, and new testings of different conditions were undertaken.

The author has described the general layout of the tests. The tests, however, have been interconnected, just as the visual relations in space are, in reality, influencing each other. All tests have been divided into three main "categories." First, different new and isolated land developments have been tested—housing, industry, urban centers, and so on. In the second group were the interactions between new land uses such as housing versus industry, recreation versus centers. Combinations also included three or more new developments up to the complete building development of the test site. The third "category" included tests that researched more delicate or "advanced" problems, like successive visual changes in the landscape—new developments occurring one after the other—visual absorption of natural landscape, congestion or "pollution" with various visual messages, and changes in "reading" the image.

LOCATION CRITERIA ACCORDING TO VISUAL AESTHETICS

First, the author examined housing development. The test indicated that housing—if assumed to look like monotonous structures without specific attractive characteristics—should be located in visually less exposed spaces, with relatively good views on green surroundings of city centers. New housing locations should tend to have a certain density and to connect scattered development, giving the observer clear interrelations and delimitations of natural landscape and built-up land. Low-density housing hidden in greenery should be favored where the green character of land should be retained for far views. Housing can be visually connected to recreational, tourism, or nature preservation areas. Proximity to traffic lines or industry should be avoided. Location close to energetic or long "strips" of continuous housing that cover between one-fourth and one-third or more of the 360° horizon should be interrupted with green sections. Orientation views on surrounding *landmarks* or distant mountains should be provided.

Second, industrial land use has been tested. Industry, including services and other commercial developments, should be located in visually hidden spaces with poor or no specific aesthetic qualities. Views from such sites are not of particular importance except in terms of psychological needs for the views of greenery from the working spaces. Views of industry are most often visually unfavorable and should be hidden with greenery, put in valleys, or should be part of neutral, intermediate scenes. Heights of development should be limited in order to promote distant vistas. Location could be close to traffic or communal infrastructure. Proximity to city centers, housing, or recreational areas should be avoided or hidden behind green screens. Location near the areas of protection of nature or monuments should be excluded.

City centers—commercial, tourist, sport center, and so forth—are regarded as attractive landmarks or visual *nodes*. Therefore they should be located in visually well-exposed spaces—cross-sections of paths or edges, as a summit of visual experience, or as a contrast to existing values. Views from the centers should be good as well, especially to the main traffic corridors, dependent housing, main city image, and so forth. Location should be near traffic corridors, housing, recreational, or other green areas, but far from industry, services, or communal infrastructure.

Recreational land use, as well as the areas of nature- or monument-protection, should be located in visually attractive, well-exposed, and distinct sites. Views on the green recreational land use are preferable from all other land uses; views from the location, however, should be insured to the surrounding landmarks, centers, and main city panoramas, while views on the housing or traffic corridors are just conditionally permitted. Views to industry, energy, or communal infrastructure should be excluded.

Traffic networks, such as roads, railways, paths, and so forth, have their visual locational criteria, too. It is important that the views from the networks are broad and good, giving the observer the sense of orientation, showing landmarks, far-distance scenes, and so on. Views to these networks are usually not favorable, and planners usually want to hide them from recreational, housing, or central land use. Limits of visually enclosed, unique spaces often match these contradictive criteria. Therefore locations along the visual paths, edges, and neutral spaces between visual entities is desirable. Cutting across valuable visual environments is critical.

Power plants, city supply systems, "heavy" industry, pipelines, disposals, and so forth are usually visually most unfavorable and require hiding. Therefore visually unexposed spaces without existing qualities are needed. Views from such sites are not important. Lower elevation, surrounding greenery, or other screens should hide them. Close location to industrial sites only is possible; all others require large buffering greenbelts.

Besides these basic tests, the author has started research in other fields of visual analysis, too. One field has been testing the visual absorption of the landscape for man-made structures. Absorption, of course, is dependent on topography, vegetation density, existing buildings, and so forth. However, a certain psychological limit has been found beyond which a landscape cannot be perceived any more as green, rural scenery, but as an urbanized built-up area if more built structures are located within it. In slightly hilly landscapes partly covered with forests, this limit is up to one-fourth of the 360° panoramic scene covered with built structures of "dense type" such as highrises, factories, streets, and so forth, up to one-third if covered with "lower density" structures such as row housing with small gardens, pedestrian paths, sport facilities, and up to one-half if covered with the structures of the "lowest density" such as individual housing in greenery.

In this research, the author has also started to use computer graphic simulation of the landscape, which could lead to a quicker, more automated, and cheaper visual simulation. At this point in the research, experiments have started with the program "Oblix," originally developed at the Center for Computer Graphics at Harvard University by Thomas Adrian (1972). It enabled axonometric or perspective pictures of a landscape to be generated, portrayed by a net layer over the topography and vertical cross-sections through the relief. The greatest advantage of this computer program is the one that enables drawings of the relief, stored in digital form.

One of the shortcomings of the research has certainly been that new buildings have always been generalized in the form of a white strip and their actual appearance has been neglected. Therefore the location criteria, cited above, should be regarded as only the most general planning principles. Specific realizations can overcome these considerations: a nuclear power-plant, for instance, could have an appearance of an attractive sculpture in green open space, while the most modern commercial center could look very unaesthetic and visually "polluted." Further research should be undertaken in the field of visual perception and cognitive experience of the visual world. Visual absorption should be connected with the meaning of visual messages, and "visual" should be broadened with other information channels that give the observer the most general and overwhelming *"gestalt"* of the aesthetic.

On the other hand, however, research of this sort could lead us more and more astray to specific and endless psychological questions that are too far removed from actual planning. Therefore we are forced to certain limitations, generalizations, and operational results that will actually help planners in land use decision making. Computer graphics that will replace our photographic documentation could be a great help, and many more endeavors will be applied to this research field in the future (see Chapters 4 and 16).

The importance of public opinion to "weigh" the visual information was mentioned in the introduction. From the year 1975 on, the author felt more and more that research must enter deeper into the sociological and psychological essence of the visual message. Therefore research was conducted in this field and was linked with the photographic and computer techniques previously described. In the following section some recent approaches and findings in this direction are explained.

ENVIRONMENTAL PREFERENCES AS PART OF THE VISUAL MODEL

Research in the field of environmental preferences has recently been done by several institutions in Yugoslavia. Studies include the Demonstration Study of Ljubljana Region, sociopsychological research on the new housing development in Belgrade, central parts of Sarajevo, and green spaces and public parks in Ljubljana. These studies, however, have largely been based on an abstract written questionnaires with a corresponding sociological interpretation.

Encouraged by similar research in foreign countries, especially that in the United States (Appleyard and Fishman 1977), Great Britain (Southworth 1971), and Sweden (see Chapter 15), and based on some of our previous studies, the author has recently conducted a large research project based on the method of the photo-interview. The goal was to discern public opinion regarding the protection of nature, urbanization, demolition, recreation, and so forth as obtained by and expressed directly on photographs. The final aim of such research (financed by the Research Community of Slovenia) has been the detection of sites most attractive for private housing, recreation, and other land uses so that they may be protected or used appropriately. Furthermore, the researchers intend to test what part environmental "beauty" plays in relationship to other factors such as land cost, existing roads and communal ducts, public services, land ownership or urban documentation.

First, a sociological study incorporated a typical written questionnaire without the visual presentation of the phenomena. The test site was Ljubljana, city of approximately 300,000 inhabitants, and capital of Slovenia, Yugoslavia. The pilot sample of 180 citizens was representative in sex, age, education, distance from the city center, and housing types. The subjects were asked different questions regarding the city and its surroundings. Subjects expressed their opinions regarding housing preferences, aesthetics of the city image, most important vistas, most favorable leisure grounds, worst city scenes, and so forth. The results did not differ very much from the ones expressed in previous similar studies. Citizens ask for quiet, peaceful neighborhoods with greenery and less industry and traffic noise. On the other hand, they would like efficient traffic flow, jobs close to the home, new shopping centers, and so on. One can see that the answers are, to a large extent, contradictory and abstract. Absence of the visual (graphical) presentation media seems to be a serious shortcoming since people can imagine any urban environment in response to the question or answer. This problem could be avoided using photographs, that is, the method of photo-interview.

A pilot sample of 60 citizens of Ljubljana was chosen stochastically and was representative in terms of sex, age, education, housing structure, distance from the city center, and so forth. Each was asked six questions looking at six groups of six panoramic photographs—altogether 36 city vistas. (Thus altogether 216 panoramic black-and-white photographs with the dimensions of 40 x 3 cm have been used). These panoramas displayed the typical "representative" scenes from Ljubljana and its near surroundings: the city, the suburbs, villages, green landscape, forests, and similar landscapes.

Each subject had to mark on each photograph at least one "place" that corresponded most to the question asked (marked with a circle), and at least one "place" that was the most unfavorable for the question (marked with a cross), or, in other words, the place that he or she "liked" and "disliked" the most. Where more sites than one were chosen, they all counted as one in the statistical overview. Subjects had to decide where they would build their own house, where they would protect nature, where to go for a walk, to play, to do sport activities, or where they would remove existing structures, and permit new urban development.

The sample was very small; a large convergence of the opinions, however, proved its representativeness. Some interesting results followed.

The most favorable sites chosen for land protection, recreation, and sports activities were open green spaces close to the city with various ambient qualities such as forest edges, hills, rivers or creeks, farmland, and so forth (93 percent). Practically the same percent (95 percent) would build their own private house in the same sites if they were in a position to do this. Although the open green space is very attractive for private housing, subjects (67 percent) would rather build their house in some connection with existing housing (close to or in between). Thirty-five percent would avoid building on empty, large, vacant, or remote spaces and out of the dense city fabric.

If subjects were in the position of "urban planners," they (88 percent) would permit housing only as infill of the existing urbanized areas or, partly, as the enlargement of them. In this role, subjects became real "ecologists" and wanted to protect green spaces to the highest degree (74 percent).

Subjects responded to the landscape details and indicated that the most favorable landscape features for sports, recreation, and leisure uses were forest edges (74 percent) and, to some extent, flat green fields (23 percent). In terms of housing preferences, respondents would largely prefer to live in groups of individual houses in green suburbs (50 percent); some would have chosen green open land relatively far from the city (21 percent), and some even inside the existing villages (17 percent). On the other hand, they disliked living inside the city (57 percent) or even in suburbia (26 percent); and 9 percent chose modern and sophisticated highrise apartments as the worst place to live!

In further research, the author tested the degree to which the ambient preferences were due to existing housing location. At this point, one should take into consideration the locations of unapproved housing in Ljubljana region only. Thus 53 percent of it is located in natural landscapes, and 18 percent at the forest edge (within 100 m). More dominant roles are played by other factors such as accessibility (87 percent is within 10 minutes isochrone to the public transport and 53 percent is within five minutes) to bus lines or local streets (73.5 percent is located at the local road). Fifteen percent is inside the gas network and 8 percent is located inside the water heating system. Only 18 percent are on the actual sites declared as the ones for housing developments; 33.5 percent is close to the existing local service center. More than half of the housing units are grouped in clusters, and very few are completely isolated.

These results prove that ambient preferences actually play a more minor role than expressed in photo-interviews. Location in greenery and grouping clusters seem here to be the only two significant factors largely expressed. Financial, practical, and other reasons seem to play much larger roles, and the ambient preferences remain, to a large extent, "castles in Spain."

The third research project attempted to test how the photo-interview can be used in practical decisions and planning proposals. The practical problem was chosen in the city of Piran on the Adriatic coast. This medieval, picturesque city, strictly historically preserved, has urgent traffic problems. A new ring road close to the city core was proposed. The road, as it would appear, was traced onto large photoposters from different viewpoints. A large sample of the citizens of Piran, tourists, experts, and Slovenes from other regions were asked for their opinions. People participated very actively; they would rather maintain a green belt around the city than have more efficient traffic. The method proved itself as a very powerful tool in planning decisions.

In the fourth research project, a final step was attempted regarding respondents' participation in the photo-interview. People actively participated in planning decisions: they traced onto the photos their proposals regarding new housing, roads, demolition, greenery, and so forth. Photographic copies were used as the material for the interview, or the transparent overlays were applied to the originals. Respondents were active in this interview, too (20–30 minutes for each person). However, large differences in the abilities of graphic expression seem to be a significant shortcoming of this method. The answers now were very direct and explicit, which was not the case with the questionnaires without the use of photographs. The mean and the most frequent answers were used to draw the plan of "people's wishes" and demands for the better urban environment in the center of Ljubljana. This "plan" differed substantially from the official urban planning regulations regarding traffic, green spaces and parks, historic preservation, sites for reconstruction, and urban renewal. In spite of the operational results that were obtained through this method, this method of the "active participation" in the photo-interview must be regarded as a marginal approach and technique. Difficulties in the graphic expression and large cost and time demands join to limit its use in urban and regional planning.

In the fifth research project, the method chosen seems to be the most powerful, fast, and inexpensive for a large experiment in different Slovenian regions. The technique of the "passive photo-interview" was used. Thus public preferences were examined regarding housing, recreation, leisure, and so on, evaluation of scenic beauty, and proposals for better urban and rural environments. This research was conducted in 10 different Slovenian regions. In each of them, a pilot sample of 30 people was chosen stochastically, which altogether yielded 300 subjects. The technique of using the transparent overlays applied over the photographic posters was very successful. Black-and-white photographs were used, covering 90°–160° angles with the dimensions approximately 5-by-30 centimeters. Photographs illustrated the most representative vistas in the relevant region, showing urban, rural, and vacant (natural) environments. A comparison between the results in each region was made, showing substantial regional differences. These differences, however, could be due to the unequal photographic material. In general, Slovenian subjects expressed, through this research, a profound love for nature, forests, mountains, and rural landscape. They refuse to live in the dense city fabric, especially in highrise apartments. They prefer living in individual homes in the greenery nearby the cities. They dislike industry and traffic corridors and would not like to see them in the vicinity. Differences between the preferences regarding housing location and leisure grounds can clearly be seen (they prefer the same types of landscape if asked on two different photographs).

The author feels that the method of photo-interview could play a great role in advocative and societal planning. Through this method, public opinion is expressed directly in a way that is usable for urban and regional planning. The author hopes that this methodology will become a permanent approach and an integral part of our planning as one of its self-management components.

CONCLUSION

Similar tests have been made for visual evaluation of other proposed land uses in the site (for example, housing and industrial zones). The research was concluded with a consideration of how to establish visual data banks on different scale levels (for example, local, architectural, urban, regional, statewide). Timing, financial, and personal needs have been estimated and identified for possible future users.

The approach described in this chapter is basically an exploration of visual interaction, a possible means of quantification, compatibility with other data banks, and a systems approach to the problems of visual aesthetics. This methodology should lead to a new stage in development of more cultural, more humanistic, and less economical, technocratic approaches to urban development. Visual-aesthetic analysis should be applied in any ecological method, and we have tried to make it more easily measurable, operable, and understandable.

Future directions of this methodology are in the automation of the whole system: direct digitizing of the photographic material (computer perspective of the grid with coded cells laid over the photograph) and automation of the visual message (computer perspective with land use characteristics, taken from the data bank and traced on it). Such future developments—which could never replace human judgment and the gestalt of the visual message—could lead to faster, cheaper, and easier-to-handle solutions. Of particular importance will be research into the following: visual dynamics, changes in visual environment, visual absorption of the landscape, and psychometry of different responses to visual messages.

The research is interdisciplinary by nature, which is both its strongest (because of new achievements) and weakest (because of the poor scientific basis for each field) feature. The methodology calls for continuous planning since the visual world is ever-changing; the visual data bank should be completed and reevaluated occasionally. We should be able to control these changes by introducing new qualities, but at the same time, retaining the specific, existing qualities.

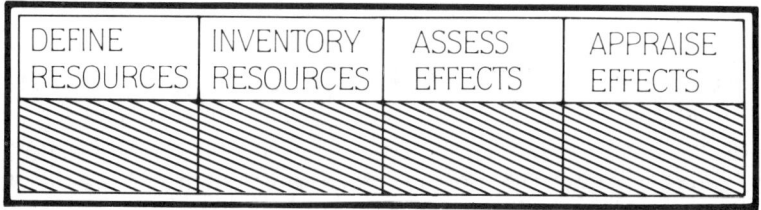

CHAPTER 15

UTILIZING AN ENVIRONMENTAL SIMULATION LABORATORY IN SWEDEN

Jan Janssens and
Rikard Küller

The construction of the simulator, as well as the writing of this chapter, was made possible through grants from the Swedish Council for Building Research.

THE DEVELOPMENT OF THE LUND SIMULATOR

Since the early seventies, researchers at the School of Architecture, the Lund Institute of Technology, have developed a procedure which can be used to simulate and evaluate planned physical environments. The emphasis with regard to representation has been on model filming, that is, filming from an eye level which is correct with regard to the scale of the three-dimensional, naturalistic model. Since movement through the model is also represented, the simulated reality is extended to include the time dimension as well, which makes the presentation more dynamic.

One of the first prototypes of this kind of simulating equipment was developed in the sixties at the Landbouwhogeschool in Wageningen, Holland (van Leeuwen and van Ingen 1968). This simulator consisted of a specially manufactured periscope connected to a television camera and fastened in an overhead crane system. It could be moved over a model environment by means of a servo-powered traveling system that made movement possible in the X, Y and Z axes. The movement of the periscope was guided by the filmer from a control desk situated beside the model environment. This early development, called *urbanoscope*, served as a model to a number of simulation plants, the largest and most advanced probably being the University of California at Berkeley simulator, developed by Appleyard et al. (1973).

After visiting these and other plants, the group in Lund, in order to investigate the advantages of the simulation method, carried out a study of different architectural presentation methods with simplified equipment (Figure 15.1). It was shown that all the conventional presentation methods, like plans, white models, and perspective drawings, gave inferior results concerning prediction of the real environment's actual qualities, in comparison to the model filming method, even if the equipment used at the time was rather primitive.

FIGURE 15.1. The first equipment used in Lund in order to compare various methods of presentation.

This conclusion resulted in an application to the Swedish Council for Building Research for the development of an advanced simulator. Based on practical considerations, the group decided on a 5.5 x 2.5 m overhead suspension system, permanently mounted in the ceiling of a laboratory room, bearing the television camera with the upside-down periscope, or *relatoscope*, as it is called. A direct steering system controls three servo motors which enable movement in the three axional directions. The model is placed on a table under the suspension system. The height of the relatoscope's lens over the model is adjustable and corresponds to the model's scale. A sensor at the bottom of the relatoscope automatically adjusts the eye level to the correct height for eventual level differences in the model (Figure 15.2).

In another room, the picture taken by the television camera is transmitted to a television screen in front of the filmer/subject, who has a steering wheel and a speed pedal at his or her disposal for direct movement of the relatoscope in any direction. In practice, running the equipment is comparable to driving a car and is very easy. The television circuit can be connected with several television monitors for research officers or observers, and all pictures may be recorded on videotape for later analyses or displayed over public communication systems.

If the equipment is to be used in order to obtain assessments of the simulated environment from test subjects, this can be done directly by means of a "semantic lever" connected to the research officer's screen where the evaluation is electronicaly displayed. The test subject's eye movements may be recorded simultaneously, for example, in connection with a particular sequence of the run through the model. These facilities make the Lund simulator an advanced piece of equipment with many possibilities. It serves to present models of interiors and exteriors in a realistic manner and can be used in both large- and small-model scales, that is, from individual rooms to parts of landscapes. It also enables the detailed

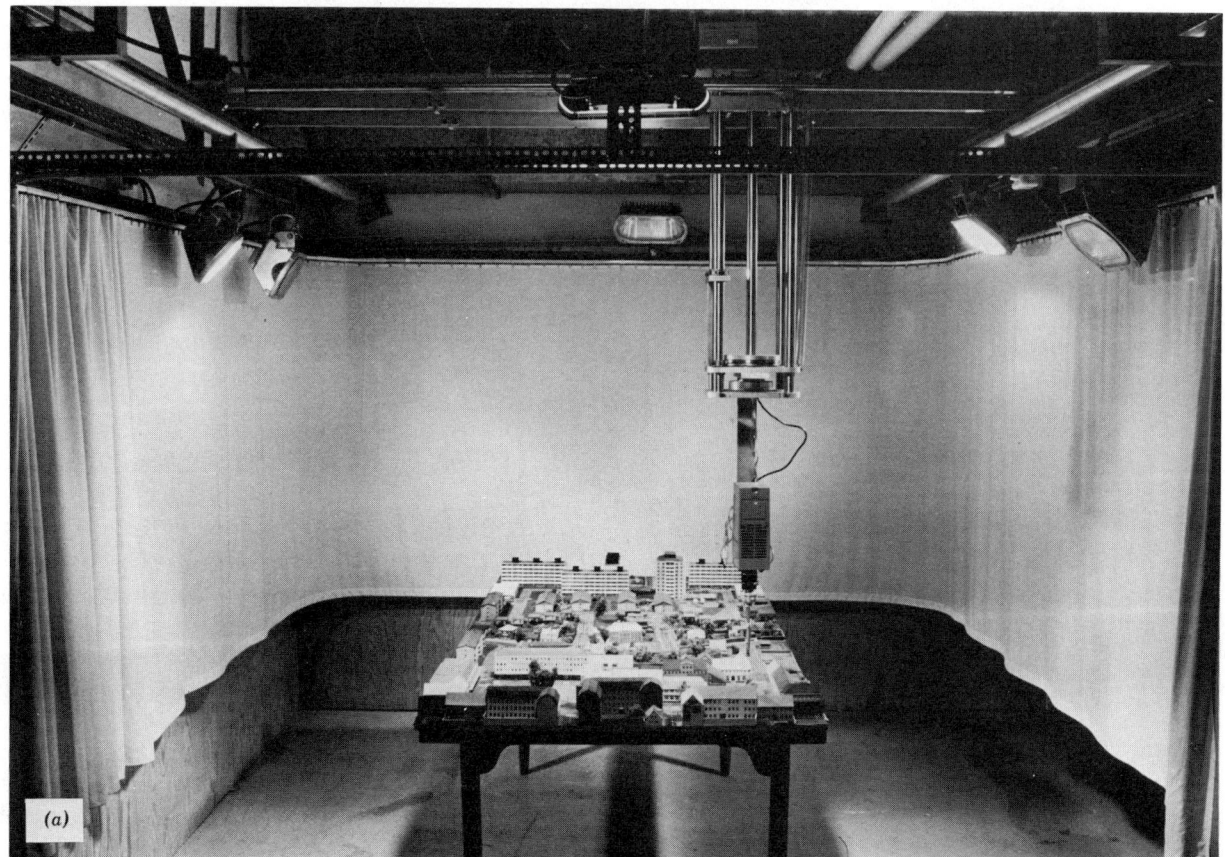

FIGURE 15.2.(a) The present simulator.

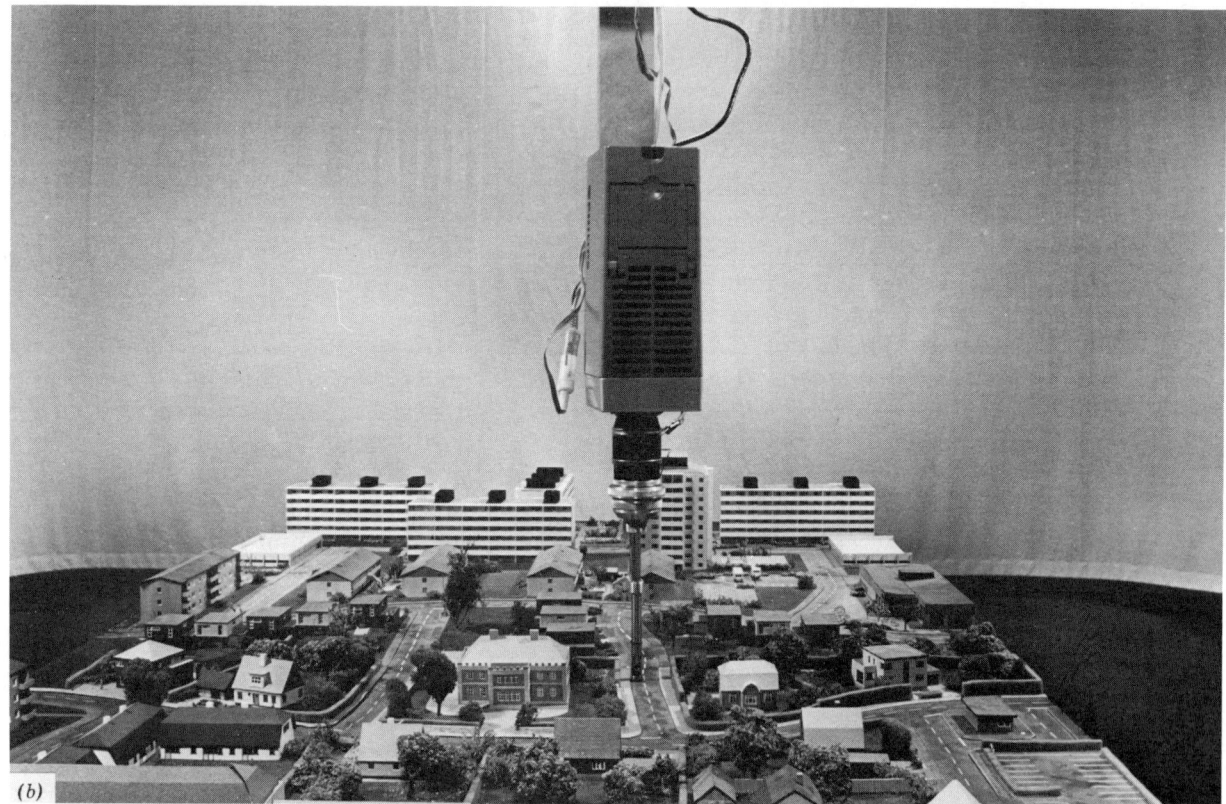

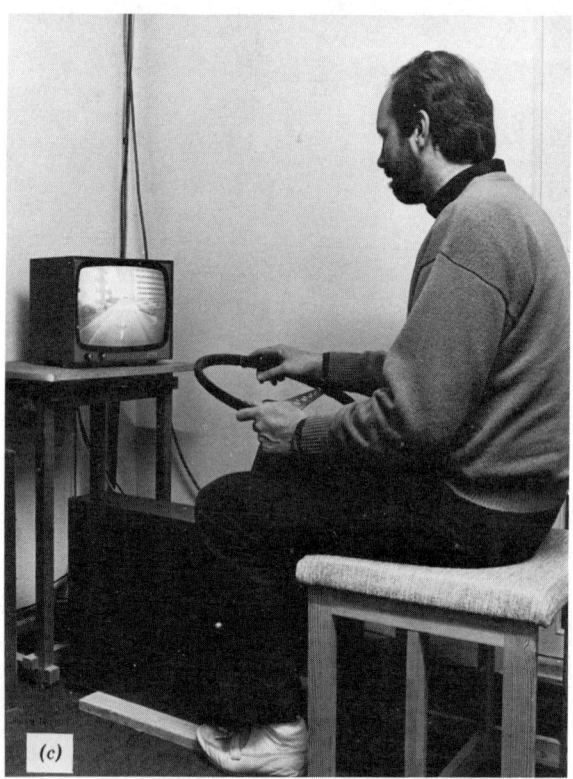

FIGURE 15.2(b,c). Closeups of simulator camera and control panel.

study of the subjective evaluation and objective eye movement behavior of the viewer. To date, the simulator is only equipped with a black-and-white video system, due to economic reasons. Pictures in color have to be taken on color film. Both 8 and 16 mm film equipment is available. The film camera is mounted on line with the video system, in front of the television camera (Figure 15.3).

THE NEED FOR SYSTEMATIC EVALUATION

The high-quality presentation, however, only constitutes one side of the coin, since there is also the need for qualified judgment. We know from several studies that the intuitive evaluation of the architect is highly subjective (Janssens 1984). For this reason alone, one could wish to establish a method for systematic evaluation based on intersubjective criteria. However, it was the need to assess the experiences of the common user that led the group in Lund to spend considerable effort on the development of various evaluation methods. One of these will be described in some detail.

In 1957, Osgood, Suci, and Tannenbaum had

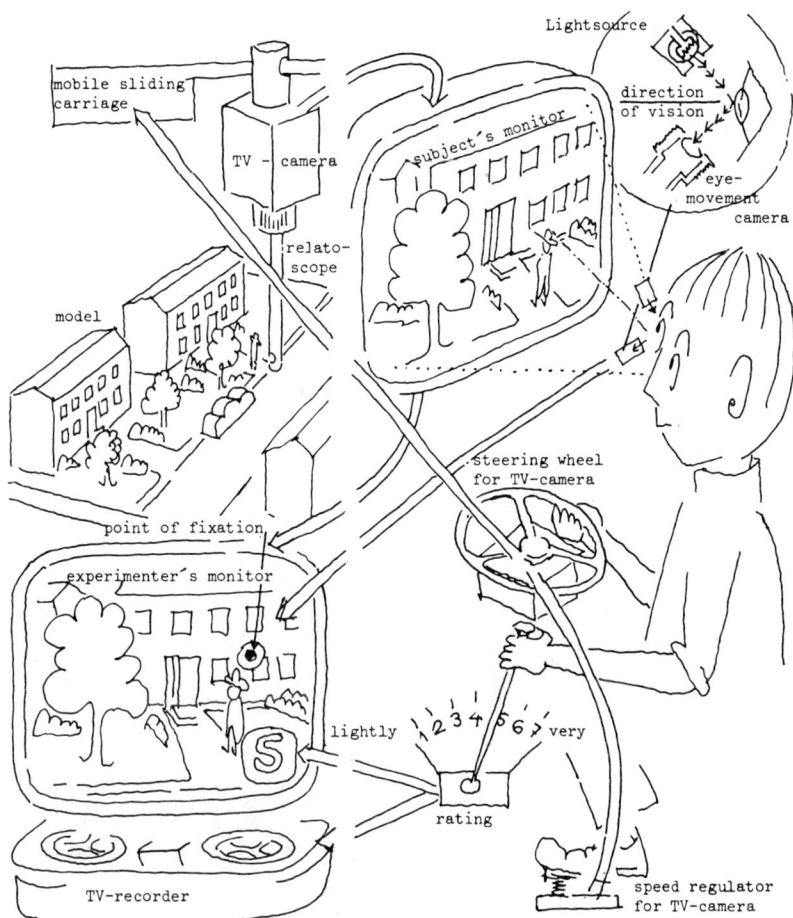

FIGURE 15.3. The principles of the Lund simulator. *Source:* W.F.E. Preiser, 1973.

shown that it was possible to obtain a relative simple semantic description model by using factor analysis (Osgood et al. 1957). By limiting the area of measurement to the perception of man-made environments, we hoped to obtain dimensions which could be easier to interpret and more meaningful when attempting to evaluate an environment, as well as measurable through a standardized approach. Like Osgood et al., we used seven-step semantic scales, but instead of letting these be defined by opposed pairs, only one descriptive word was, as a rule, used for each scale.

The type of scale used by Osgood et al.:
BAD 0 0 0 0 0 0 0 GOOD

The type of scale used in Lund:
              GOOD
slightly 0 0 0 0 0 0 0 very

Using a total of about 200 adjectives on a wide range of environments and subjects of different age, sex, and occupation, it could be shown by means of factor analysis that each of the adjectives related to one or more of the following eight dimensions: pleasantness, complexity, unity, enclosedness, potency, social status, affection, and originality. These eight perceptual qualities are now being used as a means of characterizing architecture and the built environment. The most reliable of the rating scales used have been compiled in a test where pleasantness is measured with eight different scales and the remaining dimensions with four scales each (Küller 1972, 1979).

Thanks to numerous validation studies including comparisons of perceptual and neuropsychological responses, the knowledge about the eight dimensions has increased considerably during the last few years, and the scales have become part of a theory of environmental psychology (Küller 1976, 1980).

In our opinion, semantic analysis has proven to be fruitful, not only in research, but also in application, for example, in simulation studies of various kinds. For example, how does a building that is to replace an older one correspond to it in various perceived qualities? The semantic method is also a good tool when it comes to comparing visually different alternatives for a projected environment. The study on presentation methods discussed later was carried out using this method.

In the Lund simulator, a rating lever, electronically connected with the other equipment, gives the subject the possibility to rate and evaluate the presented environments continuously in any of the eight semantic dimensions. Just like the scales, the lever has seven steps. It may be utilized while the subject is driving around in the model. A continuous evaluation of any sequence may thus be obtained and recorded, together with the picture from the drive, for later analysis.

COMPARING VARIOUS MODES OF REPRESENTATION

Planners and designers often feel the need to visualize their projects, not only to themselves and other professionals, but also to the general public. They commonly use representation methods, such as plans, perspective drawings, and three-dimensional white models. Depending on the type of method used, the experience of the environment will shift. The better it corresponds to the future experience of the real environment, the higher the value of the method as a predictive tool.

In order to investigate how different representations can predict the real environment, and how they eventually can be improved, an experimental study was carried out. In this study, two housing areas were depicted that existed in reality. Thus the judgment of reality could be used as a criterion. The following ways of presentation were compared:

1. *Surveys.* Illustrational plan in black and white, scale 1:400
   White schematic model, scale 1:400
   Colored naturalistic model, scale 1:400
2. *Pictures.* Perspective drawings in black and white
   Color slides from eye level in the naturalistic model
3. *Color movie.* Filmed from eye level in the naturalistic model

The two housing areas were about 10 years old and could be considered to have fairly clear physical boundaries. Area 1 consisted of one-family houses, situated in the town of Malmo. Although the different houses were alike and situated in a regular form, their inhabitants had given them rather individualistic looks by using different material in the fences, by planting different types of trees, bushes, and so forth. Area 2 consisted of three-story family houses situated in Lund. The families had no possibility to influence the exterior of the area. The buildings were grouped around a large open place with abundant vegetation. In this green area, there was a playground (Figure 15.4).

FIGURE 15.4. Relatoscope pictures from models of the two housing areas taken with the first rather primitive equipment.

The areas were judged in reality under two different conditions, nice and bad weather, each by a group consisting of 20 subjects. Comparable groups, each of 20 subjects, judged the two areas as presented by each of the methods mentioned above. The judgments were made with semantic rating scales, and measures were taken on the following five semantic dimensions: pleasantness, enclosedness, complexity, social status and unity.*

Comparisons between every method of presentation and judgments in reality were made by analysis of variance. When judged in reality, the two areas received a certain score in each of the five dimensions and could accordingly be related to each other. Suppose, for example, that the one-family area receives a higher score than the three-story area in reality in one of the dimensions. For a method of presentation to be good, it must show the same relationship. If not, the information from this method of presentation is useless. The analysis of variance permitted several comparisons of this kind of the different methods of presentation. This made it possible to rank the methods in the following way as shown in Table 15.1.

It can be seen that the illustrational plan, perspective drawing, and white model contained the most faulty information. This may have been expected but is still quite serious as those methods are the methods most often used in practice. The analysis also showed that pleasantness is the most difficult dimension to predict in a correct manner. This is equally serious, since pleasantness might be considered the most important dimension. It seems clear that the naturalistic model, especially when presented as filmed from eye level, is the best way of presenting a project. It contains the most valuable and least faulty information when one wants to predict the experience of an environment (Acking and Sorte 1972; Acking and Küller 1973).

THE SIMULATOR IN PRACTICE

The first requirement of any presentation is that it should be designed to suit the receivers. One of its prime purposes is to serve as a basis for discussion and decisions. Developments in this field have led to a breakdown of the project information so that today it is spread over a number of documents, each concerned with a particular sector of the work. Assembly drawings and quantity specifications are produced quite mechanically, with no overall conception of the planned project.

Because of this emphasis on specialization and the breakdown of information according to sector, there is an increasing need for a separate visual presentation of the project as a whole. In the course of planning and designing an environment, it is important to be able to get a visual perception of it at different stages before the project is finally implemented. Not only do the consumers need a way of visualizing the planned environment, but they would also appreciate the opportunity for gaining an insight into the process by which the environment is being shaped and for having their voices heard on points that concern them.

There is no method that produces our ideas about the environment with complete realism. It is, therefore, necessary to be clear in one's mind what the image is intended to convey, which methods are the most suitable, and for whom the presentation is intended. For adequate portrayal of a project by means of film or television, the model should incorporate sufficient detail. Three-dimensional models in cardboard or clay with smooth surfaces and facades are unsuitable for this purpose. On the other hand, the model need only be made in stage-set form, depicting just the parts of the planned environment required for the picture.

TABLE 15.1. Amount of Faulty Information for Different Representations in Five Semantic Dimensions

	Pleasantness	Enclosedness	Complexity	Social status	Unity	Total
Illustrational plan	3			1	2	6
Perspective drawing	1	2	1	1	1	6
White schematic model	2	1	1		1	5
Color slides from naturalistic model	1		2	1		4
Colored naturalistic model	2				1	3
Color movie from naturalistic model	1			1	1	3
Total	10	3	4	4	6	27

*At the time of the study, only these five semantic dimensions had been satisfactorily established.

A simple way of producing stage-set models of facades is to use copies of drawings. Scales of 1:50 and 1:100 are preferable here in order to facilitate the construction of the model. With too small a scale, it will be difficult to obtain enough detail. It should be pointed out that for the finished picture it is only the design and detail of the model, and not its scale, that are of significance. It should be noted, however, that in the preparation of these kinds of models, the amount of detail and stylization should be uniform over the whole model. To prepare realistic facades, it is important to use materials that ensure a correct rendering of textures and reflections. It is also essential to avoid stylized representation of vegetation, for example, by using paper and plastic balls; all shapes must be depicted and structured realistically.

The color intensity that it is intended to apply in reality should be used in the model since this method of presentation affords a direct natural reproduction of the colors employed. Even if the pictures are to be shown in black and white, a naturalistic use of color in the model is preferable since more grey tones give a more correct perception of the simulated environment.

With the relatoscope, it is possible to view models down to a scale of 1:400 at eye level (in relation to the model). An important advantage of the relatoscope is its small diameter (13mm). Its small base area and its tubular form afford easy access in the narrow passages and confined spaces in the model. With the relatoscope, a great depth of field is obtained in the picture. Because of the design of the lens system, however, the optical quality is lower than when, for instance, an inclined mirror is used. Moreover, the relatoscope has a very low light sensitivity, and very good lighting conditions are therefore necessary for filming (Acking et al. 1976).

The simulator has proven to be an excellent aid in environmental studies. It has become a fine pedagogic instrument in architectural education. Students of architecture may use the simulator for presenting their projects even at an early stage of their education. In that case, the technique does not require the exact model craftmanship that is otherwise used. Instead, models of various types may be put alongside in optional scenes and the alternative project solutions discussed before an audience (Figure 15.5).

The main purpose of the plant, however, was to assist designers, building committees, and the

FIGURE 15.5. The quality of the model and lighting has great impact on the truthfulness of the pictures. (Normally the picture will cover the screen of the monitor completely.)

general public in comprehending and foreseeing the impact on the real environment of plans for new constructions or rebuilding. Some of the projects carried out to date will be discussed below. These examples were selected, not because they were the most successful, but because in carrying them through we learned a great deal about environmental simulation.

One project dealt with the representation of a planned highway trace through a sensitive living area. The authorities had built a model with different solutions and traces. The model was constructed in wood and plastic and painted white. Level differences of the ground surface, as well as trees and houses, were represented in a rather stylized way. The scale of the model was 1:400. Here, also, the different solutions were filmed on black-and-white videotape. The results indicated the obvious difficulties in getting a naturalistic effect when filming a white snow landscape with circular trees and huge steps in the ground.

Another study tried to investigate the completion of a town square, where different design solutions would be tested. The model was built in a very naturalistic way in wood and cardboard and painted in naturalistic colors on a scale of 1:100. Different parts of the model could be exchanged for different solutions (Figure 15.6). Here, the model was filmed in color with a 16mm film camera mounted in front of the television camera. The results were very realistic, insofar that some local inhabitants thought the sequences with the existing buildings were taken in the real environment. Even so, small differences in lighting conditions caused minor color shifts in the different sequences.

After the Lund simulator had been presented in a number of architectural journals and bulletins, at conferences, and through the press, an investigation was carried out where all Swedish municipalities were asked for their opinion on the use of the simulator in their own environmental planning and design. Even though most of them answered in a positive way and expressed an interest in the equipment's possibilities as a supplement in decision making, not too many directly announced their willingness to cooperate in the near future. This rather disappointing result indicated several difficulties for the more general use of the simulator.

First, it was felt that the method would be more time demanding thus implying economic sacrifice in a time when local budgets were becoming even tighter. Furthermore, it was thought that certain

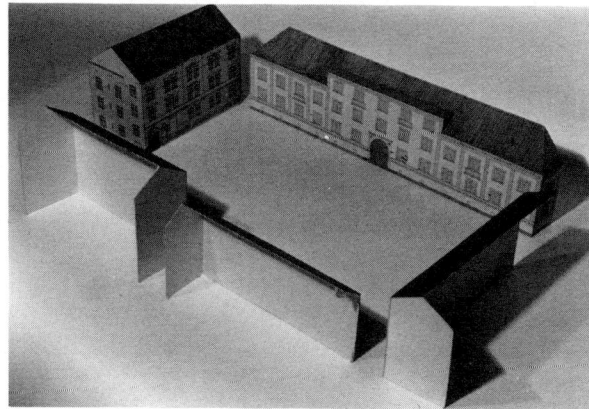

FIGURE 15.7. For filming purposes it may be sufficient to use building fronts made of drawing copies and cardboard.

parties might be able to manipulate the quality of the presentation in a way that best suited their private interests. Finally, the investigation indicated a fear of letting more people participate in the decision process. Since the simulator improves the comprehensiveness for the nonexpert, this would involve the right for common people to be consulted, a development that the authorities did not always seem happy about.

Nevertheless, a number of local housing committees got involved in the use of the simulator and cooperated with the research group, for example, in presenting planned environments to a larger public or for the benefit of their professional staff. For example, one municipality presented the results of an architectural competition in the form of alternative solutions for a planned downtown environment. They built a model where the different solutions could be inserted and then filmed on a scale of 1:100. The model was built in cardboard with drawing copies glued over it, colored in naturalistic colors (Figure 15.7). The different alternatives were filmed on black-and-white videotape and used both as a judging tool and as a presentation method for a larger public. Some other municipalities have cooperated in similar projects.

RECENT DEVELOPMENTS AND FUTURE PERSPECTIVES

It has been shown by ourselves and others that simulators are powerful research instruments. The special outfitting of the Lund simulator makes it

FIGURE 15.6. A flexible model with exchangeable parts may be used for studying alternative solutions.

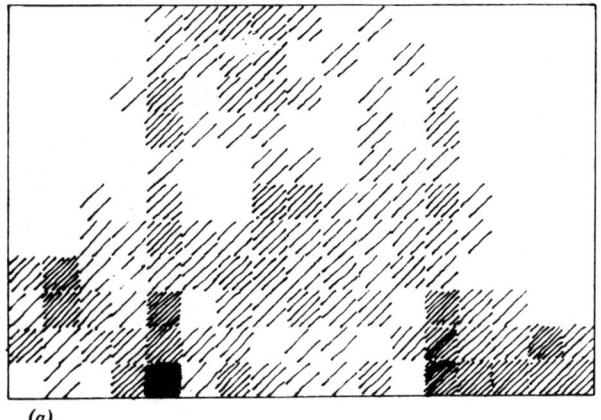

FIGURE 15.8. The Lund simulator may be used in order to study eye movements. The density plots in this figure represent fixations on the two buildings below.

potentially useful in basic studies on perception, attention, cognition, and so forth. Since the eye is always looking for points of interest in the environment, behavior dealing with searching for and dealing with environmental information may be studied.

In one basic study, subjects were shown a number of color slides representing different building exteriors, their task being to identify the functions of the structures presented. They were allowed to examine the slides for as long as they wanted. Looking time and eye movements were recorded as well as the time that each person required to identify the building. Afterward, the subjects had to recount the functions of the buildings presented and to explain their interpretations. They also judged the pictures according to a number of semantic variables describing different perceived qualities, for example, pleasantness.

Buildings that were harder to identify not only called for a longer verbal description time, but also for a longer looking and identification time and a more intensive eye movement behavior than did the other buildings. Windows and entries were shown to be the most frequently looked at parts in all the buildings (Figure 15.8). A simple straightforward connection between ease of identification and ratings of pleasantness had been hypothesized. However, no such relationship emerged in this study (Janssens 1984).

A study of the difference between architects and laypeople in eye movement behavior has recently been completed. Among the possible simulator applications of this research is a study of the design and placement of traffic signs, direction finding in urban environments, and the information content of building exteriors.

Another related basic research interest of the Lund group is to study environmental attention performance. To do this, a simulation technique was developed which uses two slide projectors. With the first projector, a color slide of a genuine built environment remains constant on a screen. Then, with the second projector, it is possible to project/dissolve grey rings into the background slide in a controlled way that corrects for contrast differences between each ring and its environment background by means of a computer. A subject's attentional performance is measured by two tasks: motoric reaction time to each grey ring and the ability to later recognize the environments he or she has been shown (Watzke and Kuller 1984).

Studies are currently underway in an attempt to find out what qualities in a given environment best explain a person's attentional performance. If this technique should prove to be useful, a next step would be to apply the same principles using the simulator equipment. With a second television camera, the grey rings could be made to appear on the monitor and subjects asked to respond to those cues as they move through various simulated environments. Such studies would have practical potential for questions about, for instance, traffic and transportation in built environments.

Until now, however, the climate for basic research involving the simulator has been rather cold. One reason for this is the suspicion shown by planners and authorities as indicated above.

Another reason has been the declining interest for perceptual studies during the seventies, since both the research councils and the researchers themselves became more inclined toward applied field studies (Küller 1986). However, at present there is once again a growing awareness of the need for basic research. It is felt that the Lund simulator will play its part in this development.

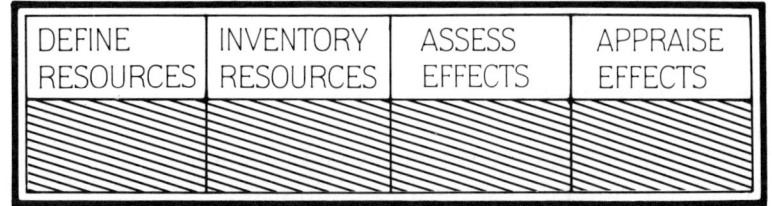

CHAPTER 16

VISUAL IMPACT ASSESSMENT METHODOLOGY FOR INDUSTRIAL DEVELOPMENT SITE REVIEW IN SPAIN

Santiago G. Alonso, Miguel Aguilo, and Angel Ramos

INTRODUCTION

This chapter addresses directions and techniques to follow in landscape studies undertaken as a requisite for official approval of industrial developments.[1]

The landscape is assessed for three qualities: Visibility, Visual Quality and Fragility. This is not a division corresponding to an analytic process that identifies different components which integrate into one reality, but three separate approaches or points of view. A complete analysis of the hypothetical visual impact produced by an industrial installation is achieved by: (1) a determination of what is actually seen; (2) consideration of its aesthetic value; and (3) a valuation of the capacity of response to impact, which, simultaneously, provide guidance to possible modifications or choices in case of conflict.

These approaches are first developed conceptually and then followed by an evaluation model for the possible visual impact. The techniques used in the application of these principles are described in the original report (Alonso et al. 1983). The landscape constraints are summarized in Table 16.1.

VISUAL FRAGILITY

The visual fragility concept addresses the whole of the characteristics of the landscape related to its capacity of response to the change of its specific properties. It is a concept associated with visual quality, although clearly independent. A territory of low visual fragility will preserve its landscape quality even if it suffers some modification that would have altered the quality of any other landscape with high fragility.

It constitutes an intrinsic territorial characteristic dependent on the conditions of the environment. The same industrial installation will offer the greatest visual impact where the fragility is high. The fragility being equal, the impact will be the highest where the activity of the largest amount of development is located. The fragility of the landscape or, more precisely, its visual vulnerability, carries a strength component or resistance capability independent of the landscape quality and the impacting activity.

The concept of visual fragility corresponds reciprocally to the capability of visual absorption, understood as "an ability of the territory to visually absorb the modifications or alterations without any loss of its landscape quality." The capability of visual absorption is a positive evaluation of the landscapes potential in regard to its use, opposite to the negative approach that corresponds with visual fragility.

Visual fragility is taken then as a quality or property of the land that helps in locating possible industrial installations or their elements, producing the lowest visual impact. It is not, therefore, a quality that is going to be affected by the future activities but is a guide for the location of those activities. Normally, the factors influencing visual fragility can be considered as belonging to three classes (Aguilo 1981):

Biophysical factors, mainly related to the slope, orientation, and land cover, determining the visual fragility in every point itself.

Perceptual factors, responsible for the readability or visual insight into the landscape and therefore defining the fragility conditions of the viewing point related to its environment.

Historic and cultural factors, explaining the character and shape of the landscape in terms of its historical process and determining the future compatibilities with the proposed activities.

These landscape qualities should be complemented by considering the real possibility that the activity could be seen by any observer. This theoretical or potential fragility becomes operational upon adding the concept of *potential accessibility* of the observation.

Potential accessibility depends, at the same time, on two factors: the distance from the "sources" of possible observers, or places where these can be gathered, and the visual accessibility of the territory from these sources, that is to say, the visibility from them. The most usual nuclei or sources of observers are the roads and the urban areas.

In the following paragraphs, the importance of the definition of every previously mentioned factor, its significance related to visual fragility, and the parameters or methods normally used to

---

[1] It is a part of a broader document, including ecological aspects, written by the same authors and supported by the Spanish Ministry of Industry (Alonso et al. 1983).

TABLE 16.1. Landscape Conditions

Affected Characteristics, Qualities or Processes	Parameters of measuring and contrast
Visual fragility of the spot Biophysical factors	— Vegetation density — Chromatic contrast ground-vegetation — Vegetation's height — Number of layers — Chromatic contrast within the vegetation — Vegetation seasonality — Slope — Orientation
Visual fragility of the spot's environment Perceptive factors	— Viewed areas — Percentage of hollow or shadow areas — Stretching of the shape — Observation position (in height)
Inherited fragility. Historical and cultural characteristics	— Global character of the landscape — Particular elements
Acquired fragility. Accessibility	— Proximity to villages, towns or roads — Visual exposure from villages and roads
Visibility. Viewshed	— Visual scope or reach — Distance areas — Angle of visual incidence — Visual intrusion — Properties of the viewshed, shape, eccentricity, compactness, surface, etc.
Visibility. Susceptibility	— Number of observers — Observer's attitude
Quality. Landscape components	— Water and land. Morphology, topography, slopes, water courses, lakes, etc. — Vegetation. Trees, bushes and vegetal cover — Human activity. Land uses, buildings
Quality. Visual elements	— Color contrast, shape, line, texture — Scale dominance — Intrusion by position
Quality. General character	— Lack of compatibility of the uses. Global character — Unique elements. Areas to protect

measure them are precisely described. The consideration of the visual (perceptual) factors is developed in the section devoted to visibility. The concepts applied to the industrial installation as a single viewpoint here are extended to a whole of the territory, describing its general conditions of visibility.

To clarify the role of every factor in the visual fragility analysis, an evaluation is included, with ordinal scales from 1 to 5 in which the increasing values correspond to situations of increasing visual fragility.

Visual Fragility: Biophysical Factors

Soil and Land Cover

The authors considered the possibilities of camouflage or enhancement that the combinations of soil and vegetation in the landscape offer as a support to future activity. The parameters or variables normally used include vegetative density, chromatic contrast of soil and vegetation, vegetative height, diversity of vegetative strata, chromatic contrast within the vegetation, and seasonal changes of vegetation, slope and orientation.

TABLE 16.2 Evaluation and Percentage of Land Cover

Evaluation	Percentage of Land Cover
1	$80 < x \leq 100$
2	$50 < x \leq 80$
3	$30 < x \leq 50$
4	$15 < x \leq 30$
5	$0 < x \leq 15$

Vegetative density

The more vegetative density, expressed by the percentage of soil covered by the horizontal projection of the woody species, the less the intrinsic visual fragility:

Chromatic contrast of soil and vegetation

The intrinsic visual fragility increases with the amount of color contrast between soil and vegetation. The highest color contrast furnishes the best camouflage or absorption.

Vegetative height

The power of vegetation to screen man-made structures increases with the vegetation's density and size. The largest vegetative sizes correspond to the least amount of visual fragility:

TABLE 16.3. Evaluation and Vegetative Height

Evaluation	Highest Size of the Upper Stratum of Plant Cover (in Meters)
1	$10 < x$
2	$3.0 < x \leq 10.0$
3	$1.0 < x \leq 3.0$
4	$0.5 < x \leq 1.0$
5	$0 < x \leq 0.5$

Diversity of vegetative strata

The land cover vegetative structure and organization determines its visual absorption capacity. As the complexity of this structure and the number and definition of vegetative strata increases, the visual fragility level decreases. It is necessary

TABLE 16.4. Evaluation and Land Cover Vegetative Cover Character

Evaluation	Characterization of Land Cover Vegetative Strata
1	Entirely organized vegetation: trees, shrubs, and herbaceous strata.
2	Vegetation generally lacking the shrub stratum, or if it exists, is very little defined.
3	Half-organized vegetation, normally with a thick tree stratum, a sparse shrub layer, and herbaceous stratum. Or, if the intermediate strata are well structured, they go with a poor tree layer.
4	Poorly organized monospecific vegetation: a well-defined tall-tree stratum, being accompanied only, as such a continuous stratum, by a low herbaceous layer.
5	Vegetation with no upper strata than small shrub layer; at most, some trees are scattered in open plantations or geometrically organized.

to point to the dominance of some of the strata upon the others related to the quantification of this fragility: the existence of a given number of the upper strata prevails upon that of the same number of the lower strata.

Chromatic contrast within the vegetation

The chromatic diversity within the land cover itself favors the "camouflage" of the human activity, especially if the large range of colors does not suit a clearly defined pattern and it is distributed in a chaotic way.

So the highest visual fragility situations are defined by the monochromatic spots (constants through the seasons—pinewoods—or changeable—dry farming land). Areas of intermediate visual fragility are composed of distinct homogenous color, while the least fragile or most absortive areas correspond to the heterogeneous colored vegetation masses.

Seasonal changes of vegetation

The loss of the opacity—the reduction of the screen effect which the deciduous leaves imply—is a factor that increases the visual fragility in areas that support deciduous vegetation even if it is a temporary effect in autumn and winter.

TABLE 16.5. Evaluation and Vegetation Seasonal Characteristics

Evaluation	Seasonal Characteristics of Land Cover
1	Evergreen vegetation dominant, especially in the upper strata.
3	Evergreen and deciduous species are well mixed up in the upper stratum.
5	Tree layer with majority of deciduous species.

All the above-considered factors do not have the same importance in the fragility evaluation. They are listed from the most important to the least in a hypothetical scale:

- Vegetation density.
- Chromatic contrast of soil and vegetation.
- Vegetation height.
- Strata diversity within the vegetation.
- Chromatic contrast within the vegetation.
- Seasonal change of vegetation.

Slope

The slope is the most important element in determining visual absorption capacity because it defines the visual angle of incidence of the observer. The increase of slope is intrinsically tied to the increase of visual fragility. If there are no physiographic factors to be considered, slope can be considered as a multiplier of the rest of the factors. A typical classification of slope and a possible evaluation could be:

TABLE 16.6. Slope Classification and Evaluation

Class and Value	Classification of the Slope	Range	Evaluation
1	Flat	$0\% \leq x \leq 5\%$	Low visual fragility
2	Gentle	$5\% < x \leq 15\%$	
3	Slight	$15\% < x \leq 30\%$	
4	Steep	$30\% < x \leq 45\%$	
5	Sheer	$45\% < x$	High visual fragility

Orientation

Orientation is directly related to the landform configuration. Its importance is not the same in a rugged landscape with well-defined exposures as in the gentle, ridged ones. It is related to visual fragility by a two-sided criterion:

- The highest illumination provides the highest visual fragility since it emphasizes possible contrasts. In this sense, the southern and western exposures are more fragile than northern and eastern exposures.
- Observation with backlighting. The areas to be normally observed opposite to the sunlight offer very little definition.

Taking into account both of these factors, the most fragile area would be the southern orientation, combining strong sunshine with the highest position of the sun when the observer is looking toward the landscape. The least fragile would be the north-northeastern exposure, receiving sunlight with a low angle of incidence.

Visual Fragility: Perceptual Factors

The visual relationship of each viewing point with its surroundings is complex and requires a sound definition. This can be approached through the study of the properties of viewshed or visual basin (see section on the viewshed).

Area Viewed

A stronger visual fragility is normally associated with larger areas viewed. Activities such as refuse disposal, for instance, will require sites of minimum visibility (small fragility).

Percentage of "Hollows" or Shadow Zones

Fragility decreases with percentage increase; the lack of shadow zones makes difficult the proper location of undesirable activities, that is, to hide them.

Shape of the Viewshed

Elongated shapes are more sensitive to visual impacts; visual intrusion tends to be emphasized within them, while in panoramic views only a sector is disturbed.

Position (in Altitude)

Position in altitude is a controversial matter. Some authors maintain that fragility is stronger when the point is seen from a higher position, but others maintain just the opposite. Both approaches may be reconciled insofar as a point is more fragile when it is clearly higher or lower than its viewshed. The "mean angle of incidence" is, then, the key parameter: With level visual rays, observation will be imperfect and fragility low; complete observation requires greater angles of incidence.

Historic and Cultural Factors

The accounting of historic and cultural characteristics, essential to the understanding of the landscape in its testimonial role and its formation process, is made in a double sense.

Global Character of the Landscape

Landscape character has its roots in the historical development of the landscape that has determined specific uses that give it its own sense. The history of the process of land taking, the beginnings of the different settlements, and the evolution of the man-environment relationship (especially farming systems and woodland uses) are essential to the understanding of the future problems of compatibility of land uses.

Special-Value Areas and Sites

Special-value areas and sites have a historical, cultural, traditional, and archaeological interest and function as focuses of experience, organizing the man-environment relationship and giving the special sense that transforms nature into landscape. These historical and cultural values, associated with specific sites or elements, are preserved by means of including them in protected areas. The criteria for selecting these sites, elements, or areas to protect are:

Uniqueness.

Buildings, monuments or places of unique or rare character.

Tradition.

Areas with strong significance at the local level, used as common references and being themselves regional symbols.

History.

Relevant monuments in the regional history.

Aesthetics.

Buildings, monuments, and areas recognized by their inhabitants and visitors to have aesthetic value.

Accessibility

In order to take into account possible observers, the concept of acessibility is introduced as an external modifier of the intrinsic fragility of the landscape. It is normally determined by two properties, proximity and visual exposure, related to the production nuclei of possible observers.

Proximity to Villages and Roads

The landscape's fragility increases in points close to places where a great number of observers can concentrate. It is necessary to take into account the number of visitors or observers related to the population in urban areas and the average intensity of the daily traffic on roads. In some cases, it is convenient to use a weighting system for different areas or districts of a nucleus, giving these areas a treatment according to their intensity of use.

Visual Exposure

As well as the number of potential observers, it is relevant to know the possibility of each point being seen. It is then a question of calculating and superimposing the viewsheds of nuclei and roads, protracting the zone exposed to the observers. For the roads, it is necessary to define a distance between viewpoints according to the road class and its traffic flow.

VISIBILITY

Apart from the inherent characteristics of the landscape and its sensory and cultural significance as defining elements of the visual quality of the landscape, it is absolutely necessary to determine the zone visually affected by the future man-made structure or industrial structure installation. Then the possible visual impact can be explicitly stated, with the severity of the impact defined in precise terms with regard to both its extent and the possible number of affected persons. The basic instrument for this analysis is the viewshed of the future installation. In the following paragraphs, this concept and the methods to determine it are explained. Nevertheless, it is advisable to apply the process with realism and rationality. The viewshed will be precisely defined but it must not be forgotten that it is only a simple means to predict, in relation to the visual effects, the area of influence of the installation.

In the same way, the parameters that control its extent, as well as the attributes used in the evaluation, ought to be applied on a trial-and-error basis. Their function is always to detect possible impacts. Their use in the opposite direction, that is, to prove the nonexistence of impacts, must be made with great care. For instance, if a maximum distance of visibility of 5 km is fixed to determine the visual impact, and there is a possible point of conflict at 5.5 km from the installation, the analysis is being improperly used. The values must be flexible enough to include possible abnormal or conflicting situations that must be always analyzed.

The methods, the values of the parameters, and the properties that are going to be explained must be taken into account in this sense, not being valid as a proof by themselves.

The Viewshed

The key element in a study of visibility conditions is the visual basin or viewshed. The viewshed, from a given point, is defined as the portion of the landscape seen from that point. By extension, this definition is applied to elements with appreciable physical dimensions, such as a dam or an industrial installation. The visual basin of these structures would be the sum of viewsheds of all their points.

The premises for these visibility analyses having been established, it could be interesting not only to include the building itself but auxiliary elements too, as access roads or the possible buildings that are surely going to appear near the main structure. Sometimes the effects of the installation ought to also be included in the analysis, as in the case of the steam clouds of the power station visible from several miles away.

EXAMPLE 1: Techniques for the Determination of the Visual Basin

DIRECT IN-SITU DETERMINATION (LITTON 1973)

The observer places himself or herself at the point from which the visual basin has to be determined, in order to transfer to a map the limits of his or her observations. The aim is to estimate the relative positions of the start and finish of shadowed areas with respect to accidents or characteristics of the terrain which are shown on the map, linking them to establish visible and shadowed areas, using a similar process to that used to fix the position of a real point on the map.

A scale around 1:25,000, where the localization of visual limits can be carried out with relative accuracy, is frequently used. Smaller scales yield better accuracy, but on the other hand will frequently require the use of many maps, which are difficult to handle, for in-field studies.

The process has to be carried out in the most advantageous conditions as far as illumination and visibility are concerned. Whenever possible, working in orientations with lateral illumination, as well as visiting the place at different times of the day would be preferred. Front or rear light tends to alter the shape of the terrain, thus introducing large errors in the determinations.

This is a fast technique (around one hour is a reasonable time for a normal determination) and enables a better knowledge of the terrain by the observer. Personal errors of the observer and characteristics of the area, however, yield variable reliability as a disadvantage. Errors tend to overestimate the visible area.

Summit lines are currently taken as vision limits, but they are not actually visible due to the convexity of the terrain; and limits are found far earlier.

MANUAL DETERMINATION BY PROFILES

This is the more common and simplest method to determine the visual basin. It can be used as a single procedure or in combination with the previous one, especially if available maps are thought to have inaccuracies. The procedure is as follows:

A visual direction, for example, north, is plotted on a map at the appropriate scale.

The transverse profile which corresponds to that visual direction is obtained by computing the intersections with the height curves (it is convenient to enlarge the vertical scale).

Visual rays are plotted in such a way that points, increasingly farther away from the obervation point, are linked with this by rays of increasing slope in order to maintain visibility. When a point such as F in Figure 16.1 is linked to the observer O, an initial ray OF is found which lies below another ray, thus indicating a point in an invisible area. In that way, points A,B,C,D,E indicate starting and finishing points for shadowed regions.

The points are plotted on the base map.

The visual ray is tilted a given angle, and all three previous points are repeated.

The previous step is repeated until the area of interest is scanned, and the corresponding points $A_1, A_2, \ldots B_1 B_2, \ldots$ are linked to find the shadowed areas.

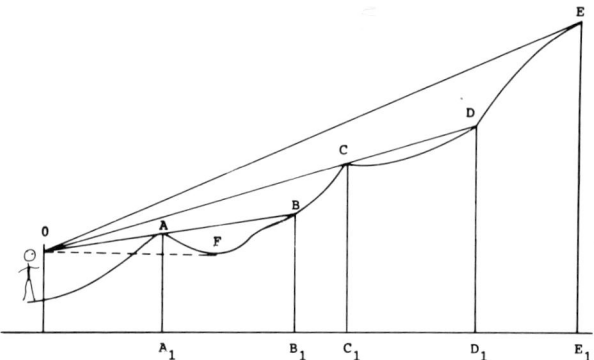

FIGURE 16.1. Vetical section of viewshed determination.

When accuracy is needed, 5° intervals are required; but, generally speaking, some 16 profiles are sufficient (22.5°).

Spacing of different profiles is frequently useful, according to topographic conditions in individual areas. Determinations without noticeable difficulties may allow fewer profiles without loss of accuracy, while potentially conflictive areas may require an increase in their number.

The most important difficulty lies in the limitation to include restrictions of visibility due to vegetal formations or buildings. Thus, it would be advisable for this, as well as for any other group method, to improve the determination by means of in-situ observation to account for likely deviations. A standard determination may take about 90 minutes without any special training.

HEBBLETHWAITE METHOD

A somewhat faster, manual procedure was developed by Hebblethwaite (Clark 1976) for the calculation of the visual impact for power plants. In order to use this method, a map with adequate scale, as well as two transparent plastic pieces, 10 to 15 cm wide and long enough to cover the maximum visible distance, are needed. For a typical 1:25,000 scale, 50 cm will generally be adequate. One of the pieces will have a straight line marked to indicate the visual line. The other piece will have parallel equidistant horizontal lines to represent different heights with the same distance as shown in the map. Parabolas or other curves may be preferred to account for curvature and refraction effects.

The procedure is as follows (Figure 16.2).

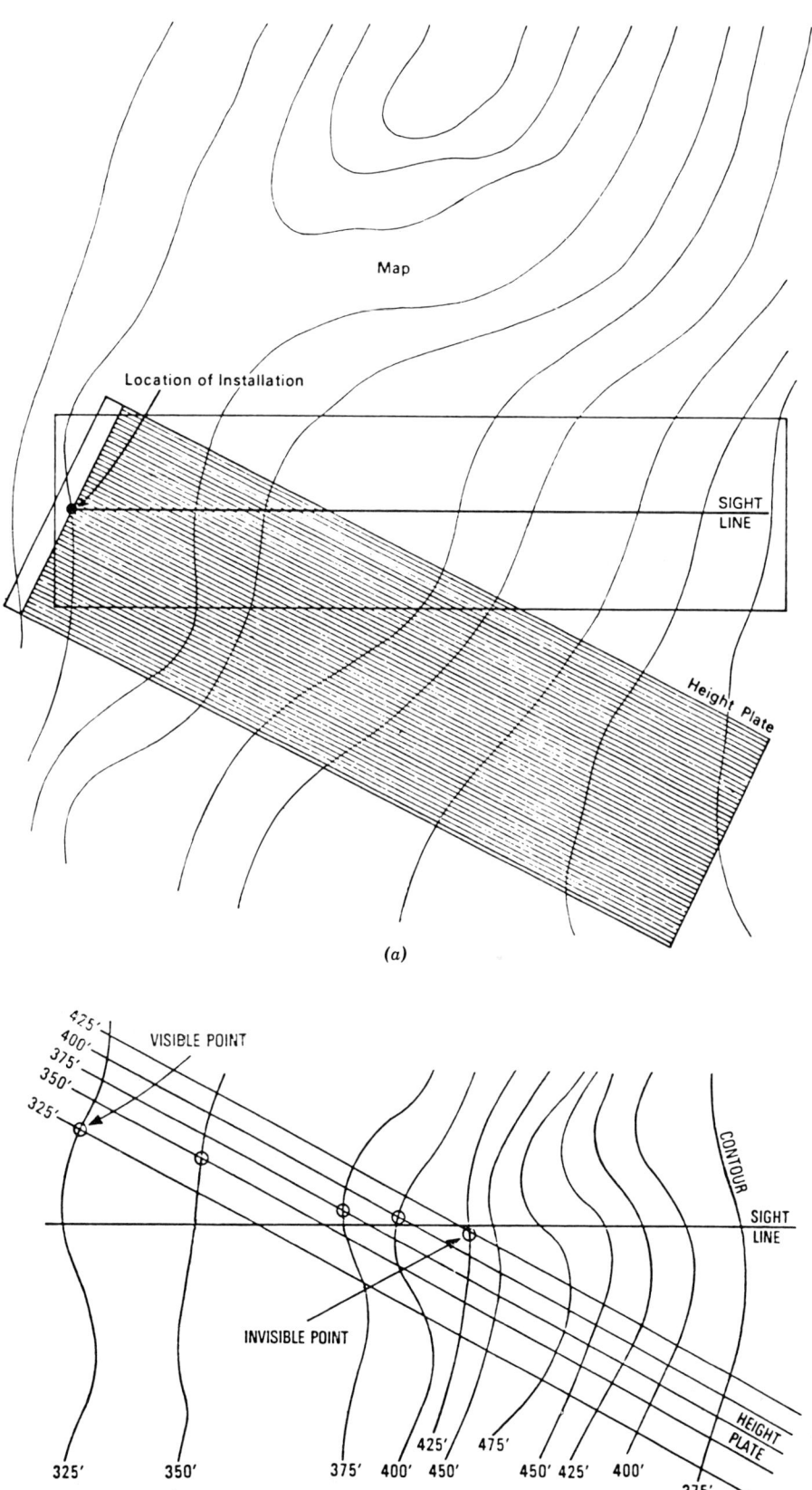

FIGURE 16.2. Viewshed determination. *Source:* Clark, 1976, Assessment of Major Industrial Applications. A Manual. Dept. of the Environment, London.

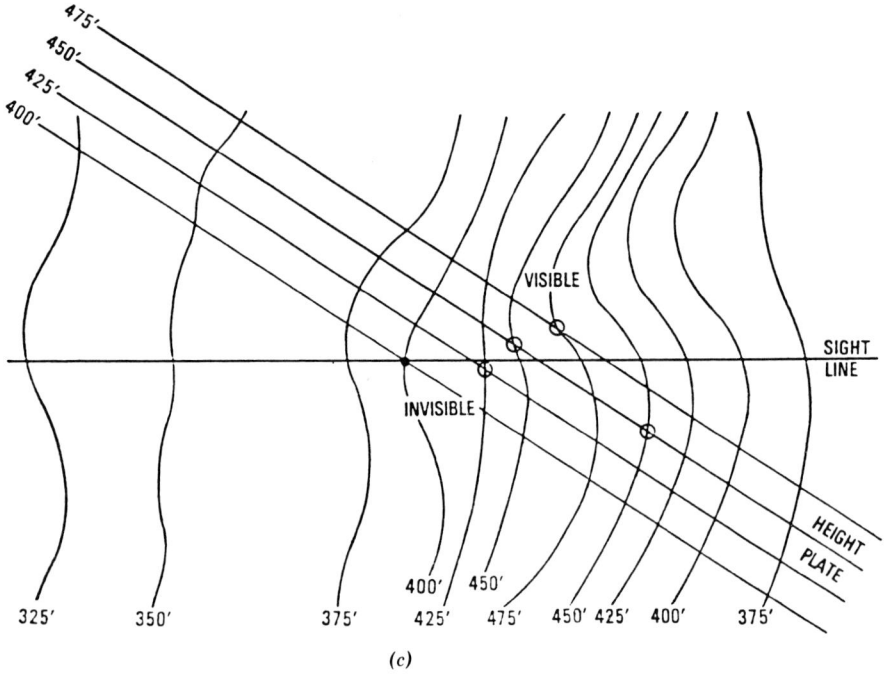

FIGURE 16.2. (continued)

The visual line plotter is based on the observation point according to a preset direction.

The height plotter is placed in such a way that the observation point coincides with the corresponding height line up to the height of that point (a in the figure).

The crossing point between the visual direction and the height curve is identified. The height plotter is guided in such a way that the height line which corresponds to that height curve coincides with the crossing point.

Following the visual direction, a point is reached where the next height curve is intersected. When this one and the height line cross above the visual direction, the point will be visible. Otherwise, the point will not be visible (b in the figure).

When an invisible point is reached, the latest visible point has to be taken again and the height plotter placed so that in that point visual line, height curve and height line cross (c in the figure).

The procedure is repeated with this location. All visible points are recorded until another invisible point is reached, and the height plotter is placed again there as described above.

The visual line is followed to the visibility limit.

The process is repeated at 5° or larger intervals.

When all visible points have been recorded for a given interval, they are linked in order to construct the visual basin or visual influence area.

AUTOMATIC METHODS

When the topography of the terrain is represented by a matrix of altitudes associated to a superimposed network, it is easy to identify visible and invisible areas by means of several simple routines. Several methods have become available since the VIEWIT program (Travis 1975) was set up, which are more or less efficient according to the aims of the project. Some of them do only identify the visible points in the network whilst several other methods may plot the visible areas and can compute several parameters which are associated with visual basins.

Well-known methods include VIEWIT, predetermination of cells in the visual ray, sectorial search, and cell-by-cell search.

Viewit

The procedure is similar to the manual procedure indicated in the section discussing manual determination by profiles. The program plots a visual direction, identifies cells which are intersected by that direction, and determines which of them are visible and which ones invisible. This implies a criterion for visibility to be defined. In fact, some of the visual rays might section a profile which allows visibility, and others may not be able to reach the network, leaving it in the shadow. It is thus reasonable to set up the condition that the visual ray segment, which is intercepted by the network, have a minimum length. When this is fulfilled, the network is considered to be visible from the observation point. A different condition could be that of the number of rays which are intercepted by the network. This has the drawback, however, that cells are discriminated according to distance, since the separation between rays increases with distance. It would be simpler to assume that a cell is visible whenever any of its points become so; this is not fully accurate but requires fewer additional operations.

The program will then store a 1 for visible cells and a 0 for invisible ones. If the number of times a point can be seen from a given set of points is larger, the program will place different origins and add another 1 to the corresponding memory. When all required origins have been scanned, the memory which corresponds to every cell will have stored the number of points from which the area is visible. The results are automatically plotted in numerical form or converted to a grey level scale.

Predetermination of Cells in the Visual Rays

This program, developed by Steinitz et al. (1974) for a visual quality model, acts in a different way. The area around the origin cell is divided into eight octants which are scanned by several beams in order to obtain a more efficient search algorithm. The user may select which octants and the number of rays he or she wants to use for the search; for example, he or she may select searching in the north-northeast octant with three visual rays and 26 cells range, which would mean reducing the search to some 70 cells instead of all 240 cells within 2.6 km in the octant (cell side, 100 m). With this, accuracy is lost in the interest of speed; but if the search is to be carried out from a set of origins, cells disregarded by an observation point will usually be taken into account by another one. Thus the loss of accuracy will be smaller. The program allows the land use for visible cells to be plotted and the search to be organized according to the land uses of the origin or other sought-after cells. This capability is very useful for identifying sensitivity levels for visible cells and allows the possible number of observers, as well as qualification of their attitude, according to the use to be computed (Figures 16.3, 16.4, and 16.5).

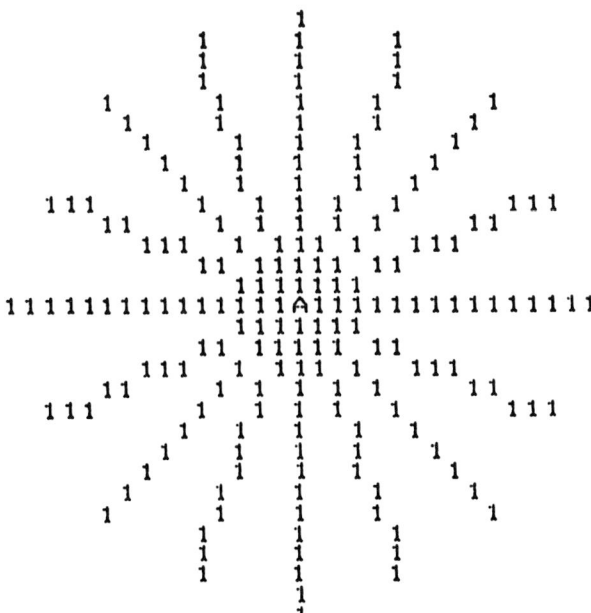

FIGURE 16.3. Predetermination of cells. Rays in octant, 3. Reach, 15 cells.

Sectorial Search (Aguilo 1981)

This is the automatic version for the manual method using profiles discussed previously. The search process is organized by means of rays which are made to scan the area under study from the origin or observation point. In every ray, which is considered to be representative of the corresponding circular sector, visible and invisible points are recorded. Also, the slope of the straight line linking every such point with the observation point is compared with slopes computed for previous points. If that

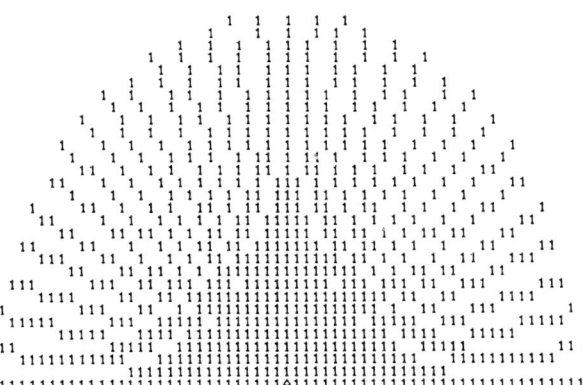

FIGURE 16.4. Predetermination of cells. Rays in octant, 9. Reach, 30 cells. Octants plotted, 1, 2, 7, and 8.

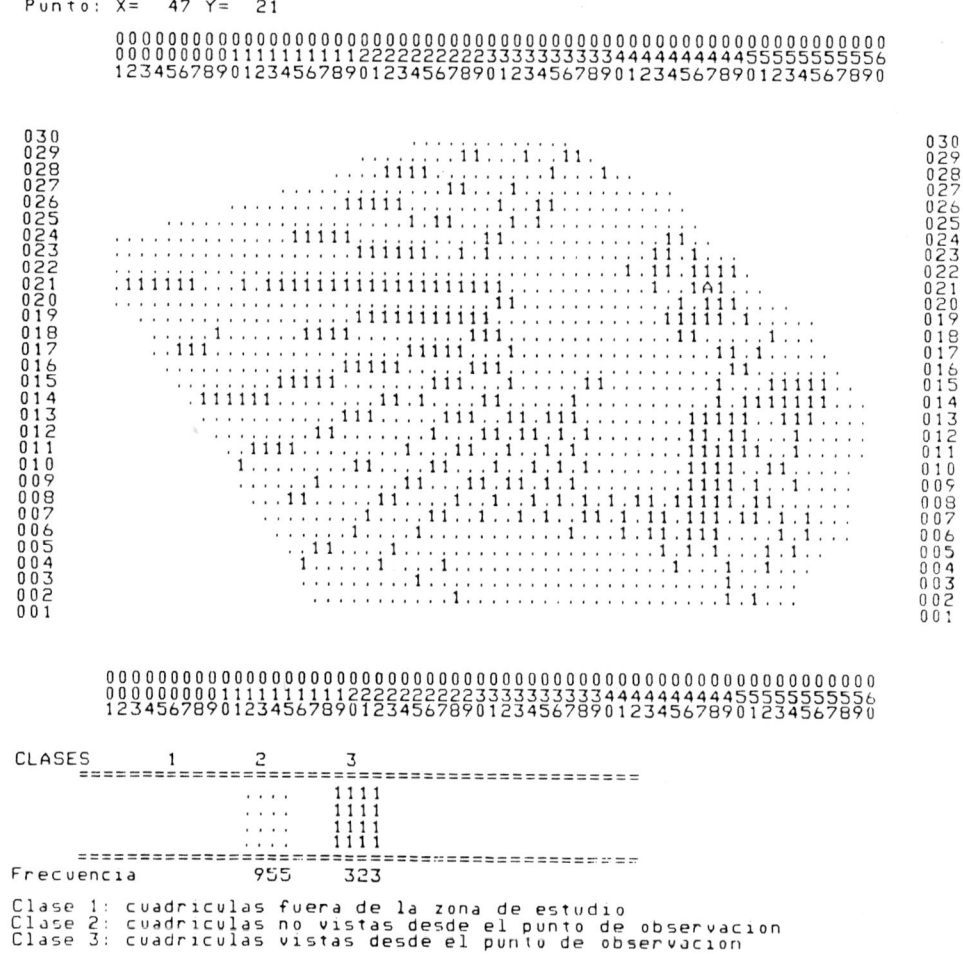

FIGURE 16.5. Predetermination of cells. Seen area.

slope is larger, the point—and thus its surrounding zone—will be visible; otherwise, it will have been covered by a previous point along the same ray.

Parameters which rule the process are the angle between two consecutive rays and the radius with which every ray is scanned up to the maximum visual range. Accuracy is regulated with these parameters; thus it is lower for more distant areas since the trapeze which is assigned to every point increases in area with distance from the observation point. This loss of accuracy, however, is similar to that which takes place from the physiological point of view and the process is accordingly well adapted to real conditions.

If a plotter is available with the computer, drawing of the basin can be carried out on a transparency which, placed on a conventional topographical map, will allow the identification of visible areas and their associate use. The program allows the shape and eccentricity parameters to be easily determined, as well as the calculus of maximum and minimum radii and diameters which are difficult to obtain with other means.

When the basin is plotted from a set of beams starting at the observation point but which are not drawn at the invisible areas, the strong relationship between the observation point and the visible areas is enhanced. Viewsheds are areas clearly focused, and it is advisable to employ a graphical representation which maintains such quality.

Cell-By-Cell Search

The search can be organized as a systematic scan of cells lying in the visual range circle. It is customary to scan only the central square submatrix around the observation point and size 2a x 2a where a is the range; every point is subject to a distance test $d \leq a$, and then to a visibility test.

```
Punto: X= 47 ,Y= 21
+++     000000000000000000000000000000000000000000000000000000000   +++
+++     000000000111111111122222222223333333333444444444455555555556  +++
+++     123456789012345678901234567890123456789012345678901234567890  +++

030                          ...1.11.......                            030
029                       ..11.111111.1111.11.                         029
028                     ...111111111...11.111.                         028
027                     ..11.1111111...1.1111....                      027
026                  ...1111111111111111...1..11..1...                 026
025                ......111111111111111...11.1...........1           025
024              ......1...1.111111111.11.1.11111..11.....111.         024
023          11.1........11111111111111.1.111111.11......11.11.        023
022          1.111.......11111111111111.1111111.1.....1111...111.      022
021          .111111....111111111111111111111111111.1....1..11A111.    021
020          .1111.111...11111111111111111111111...11.111.            020
019           1111111...111111111111111111111.....11.11111111....     019
018             11.1111....1111111111111111111.....111...111.1.1.111.  018
017             .111111.....1111111111111111111111111....11111.1111    017
016             .1111111...1111111111111111111111111......11.11...11.11 016
015             .11111111..1111111111111111111111111111.....111111.    015
014              .1111111..11111111111111111111111111......111111111.... 014
013              .1111111..1111111.1111111111111111.....111111...1.1.... 013
012               .1111111..11111111111111111111111111111......111..... 012
011                1111111..1111111111111111111111111111111111.....     011
010                 1111111..11111111111111111111111111111111.....      010
009                 1111111..1111111111111111111111111111111......      009
008                  ..1111.1.111111111111111111111111111111111111.....  008
007                   .111..1111111111111111111111111111111111111....   007
006                  .111.1111..1111.........11111111111111..11111....  006
005                   11111111...1................111.111111111.1      005
004                   1111.11.1.1111..............11.111.11..           004
003                    .11....1.1111.111...............111...            003
002                      11......11111...............1..1111...          002
001                                                                      001

+++     000000000000000000000000000000000000000000000000000000000   +++
+++     000000000111111111122222222223333333333444444444455555555556  +++
+++     123456789012345678901234567890123456789012345678901234567890  +++
CLASES       1        2        3
        ========================================
                           ....    1111
                           ....    1111
                           ....    1111
                           ....    1111
        ========================================
Frecuencia                  404     874

Clase 1: cuadriculas fuera de la zona de estudio
Clase 2: cuadriculas no vistas desde el punto de observacion
Clase 3: cuadricls vistas desde el punto de observacion
```

FIGURE 16.6. Seen area, according to cell by cell search.

This one is very simple. The observation point is linked with the center of the corresponding cell, and the straight line is followed comparing the altitudes on it with actual values for the terrain. If only a single point lies above the straight line, the center of the cell will not be visible. Only if the process is carried out without finding a point of more altitude will the cell be visible from the observation point. Drawing of the visual basin can be carried out then by means of a printer. The plot will be schematic, however, and will have the supplementary difficulty of inaccurate and generally different vertical and horizontal scales due to normalization conditions in the printers. Identification of visible areas will thus have to be carried out by manually translating them to a topographical map (Figure 16.6).

Taking into account the reciprocity of the visual fact, the viewshed includes all the possible observation sites from where the activity will be visible. Its fixing will mark the boundaries of the environment of the possible visual impacts of the installation with two main consequences:

1. To alter the view from all these observation sites by inserting a new artificial element, and
2. To modify the visual conditions of the landscape altering the visual flows produced by the almost simultaneous perception of viewsheds, crossing their different points, especially at a high speed.

This second effect requires the prior fixing of the visibility characteristics of the sites, especially given by the parameters stated in preceding sections.

Methods of drawing the viewshed can be found in Litton (1973), Hebblethwaite (1973), Clark

(1976), Travis (1975), Steinitz et al. (1974), Aguilo (1981), and Alonso (1983). They include simple manual methods to use in situ or at the office and more complex computer methods in case they would be needed.

To be considered next are the different qualities of the viewshed that can become altered by an industrial installation.

EXAMPLE 2: Selection of Observation Points

The visual impact of the new industrial plant reaches all the points in its visual basin, as has already been shown, and has a global character. As a complement of the evaluation of that global impact, which is analyzed when the effect on the character and the quality of the affected landscape is studied, it is very useful to select the points from which a more detailed analysis of the possible impact has to be continued.

The key observation points to carry out the analysis of the proposed activity are those which will more likely be used by possible observers. The aim is not to select a point from which the plant is best seen or its complete layout better understood. The purpose is to better establish a relationship between possible visual alterations and the people who have to suffer them, by an identification of its number and observation conditions, through the most representative points for every factor.

The procedure for the selection of these points requires a good knowledge of the project and the area where it is planned. Possible candidates should be selected according to three main criteria:

1. Number of observers. Population nuclei and roads are compulsory observation points and should always be considered. Parameters here will be number of inhabitants and average traffic density. Recreational areas are measured by the number of users or visitors.

2. Previsible attitudes and reactions. The use the observer makes of the visually affected area strongly influences the appreciation of the impact. Plants whose characters are strongly in disagreement with the use from which they are seen are valued very negatively. That is the case for recreational and cultural uses. Areas where such utilization is produced have to be very carefully considered since they are areas of potential conflict. Another important factor will be the special sensitivity of some social groups of potential observers, independently of the use they make of the area at the moment of the observation.

3. Observation conditions. They are related to the observer, the observed territory and atmospheric conditions and, together or separately, favor aesthetic behavior which is highly influential on the observation. These can be pointed out:

   a. Duration of the view on the spot. This applies especially to roads and railway lines. When the observer sees the plant for a limited amount of time, the corresponding impact will be much smaller because the time to detect contrast and misplacement is also limited.

   b. Single or repeated views. When the observation, for example, from the road, allows repeated views of the plant from different points, the appreciation of the impact will be more conscious and the plant-environment interaction will be more globally understood. On the other hand, the impact of a single view can be mitigated by the use of small modifications on the project, for example, screens.

   c. Seasonality. Both the appearance of the modifications that will be introduced by the future installation and the attitude of the observers can be modified by seasonal reasons. That is the case of snow, which can alter completely the relationship between the observer and the environment. A vegetal screen with non-perennial leaves will act in a completely different way according to the season by attraction, filtering, or repulsion of the view.

   d. Illumination. The season of the year as well as the time of the day may substantially alter visibility conditions and thus exert an influence on the selection of possible observation points. Views in the northern direction, for example, are characterized by a better illumination which enhances the contrast between the installation and its surroundings. In that direction, the observer will never be looking against the sun. An eastern view may yield a situation similar to sunset on a western view, but the average observer will scarcely see that view at sunrise time. On the contrary, the western view is more

likely to be appreciated and thus to have a larger implication with the surroundings.
  e. Spatial composition. Some landscapes direct or point the view in predetermined directions, and the visual flows in those directions are more likely to strengthen or weaken the attraction caused by the modification on the perceived landscape. A typical case could be the existence of a given point of special interest such as the top of a mountain. Possible observation points along the line linking such a singular point with the plant under evaluation are potentially conflictive. A similar case will take place when the installation obstructs the visual lines emerging from a valley, and the enhanced contrast will yield an increased effect.
  f. Parameters of the visual basins and situation within them. They collect the influence of topography of the surroundings of every possible viewpoint on the organization of the territory, as seen from every point, and from the plant with respect to the position of the basin. Shape, eccentricity, compactness, and relative height of the basin will have an important role as qualifiers of the possible viewsheds with strong importance in the process of appreciation of the match of the installation with its surroundings. Distance, angle of incidence, degree of intrusion with which the installation is seen have also their share.

These three groups of criteria will allow a careful selection of the viewpoints which are considered necessary for a detailed evaluation of the likely visual impact of the installation. The required number of points may vary according to the territory and the project under evaluation. If the project is small or the observation conditions are very uniform, a single point may suffice. More complicated projects may require two or more points to offer different aspects of the likely impact. In some cases, the impact produced by the project will only be ascertained by the use of a given sequence of points.

When the selection of points to be carried out is aimed at the evaluation of industrial actions of disperse localization, for example, power lines, lineal transport systems, pipelines for oil or gas, or large area developments, visual data will be obtained with the use of the parameters of the visual basins and selection of the more typical views among them.

This process requires the use of computerized methods due to the large number of basins and parameters to be determined and is very similar to the one used for the establishment of the visual control points (Aguilo 1981) which are used to evaluate the visual fragility of the landscape in a given territory. It is advisable (Smardon, Sheppard, and Newman 1984) to take into account the following:

1. Most critical points with respect to the number of observers or the crossing of areas of conflictive use, as stated above.
2. Most representative views at the main landscape types affected by the installation.
3. Any special characteristic of the project or the landscape which may prompt higher visual attraction such as river crossings, mountain tops, substations, and so forth.

In any case, for localized as well as for disperse localizations, the number of selected viewpoints should be small enough to allow the simulation processes to be carried out. If the characteristics of the project or the territory do not allow the selection of two or three viewpoints as a maximum, it is convenient to structure them in such a way that the accuracy of the simulations can be easily graded according to the importance of the viewpoints.

Visible Area

In an absolutely flat area, an object can be clearly seen until there is a distance from the observer in which the corrections by the earth's curvature and light refraction are equal to the object's height (size). The height reduction in meters, related to the distance in kilometers in refraction normal conditions, would be (Hebblethwaite 1973):

TABLE 16.7. Height Reduction

Distance in km	1	2	3	4	5	6	7	8	9	10
Height in m	0.07	0.27	0.61	1.08	1.69	2.43	3.31	4.32	5.47	6.75

(Example: Taking an object 8 m high, placed 10 km far away in a constant altitude area, only the 8 − 6.75 = 1.25 upper meters could be seen.)

If one were working in rough areas or at small scale, this reduction normally has no importance. In flat and large areas, it can be essential. Lighthouses are extreme examples of this problem. The processing of the visibility average conditions made to determine their range establishes the best approach to the problem (Soler Gaya 1972). In general and for reasons that we will explain, it is not necessary to take into account this effect, the range is fixed by trial and error, taking into account the effect of distance whose definition follows.

Loss of Sharpness at Distance

As objects are moving away from the observer, their details become unnoticeable. This fact has two immediate consequences:

> The quality of the visual perception decreases as the distance increases.
>
> It is possible to fix a distance, related to the conditions of the territory and the object to be seen, from where it is not interesting to pursue the visibility analyses.

The loss of sharpness in the distance can be represented by a function inversely proportional to the distance or its square (Aguilo 1981), though for practical purposes it could be enough to distinguish three zones of distance and apply decreasing weights to each one. Usually (Litton 1972; Burke 1968) three zones are considered:

1. *Foreground:* up to 200 or 500 meters. Observers have direct participation. They receive impressions from the near details. They realize color hue and chroma that will be lost far into the distance. They value all the architectural details of the man-made structure that take priority over any other considerations.
2. *Middle distance:* from the previous limit up to 3 or 5 k. It is the most critical zone to observe the activity environment system. This zone suffers all the adjustment or impact problems. Nearer, the detail has the priority, but further, the whole appears somewhat blurred. The attributes of the landscape group together and makes its character. "The hills become mountains, and the trees, forests" (Litton 1972). The industrial installation is not perceived as an isolated element and inserts itself into its environment.
3. *Background:* starting from 3 or 5 km. This threshold is the most variable. It is the outline that is emphasized. Color becomes indistinguishable. Masses and patches, against which the characteristics of the two other zones are detached, are perceived as a background.

The critical points to be considered for detailed analysis of the installation and its environment are found in the middle distance zone. Its boundaries, unavoidably vague, depend also on landforms and on the scale of the installation related to its environment. The concept of dominance plays an essential role.

Angle of Visual Incidence

If every point within an area is characterized by its normal vector, our impression of reflected light can be studied as a function of the angle formed by this vector and the view from the observation point. The smaller the angle, the nearer we are to the frontal observation of this area and the better we can value it. Big angles imply a level line of sight, of little significance.

In respect to the man-made structure itself, the angle of incidence has less significance in the quality of the observation since the facing is normally vertical. The only problems of level line of sight occur on the horizontal level and rarely in several faces at the same time. On the land, however, they reach great importance because this type of sight not only makes it impossible to perceive the landforms, but it also magnifies the structure by outlining its shape against the background.

Properties of Viewshed

Although it is common to use only the amount of area viewed as the sole parameter of visibility, the understanding of visual conditions of a piece of land can be improved by exploiting the possibilities offered by a more detailed study of the viewshed.

First, it is highly useful to investigate the land shape of the visual basin, that is, the geometrical shape of its delimitation in plan as a categorizing element of the land's visual conditions. Even though the visual basin cannot be directly related to the views, it contains a great deal of information. In the terminology of Gibson (1950), the visual basin would correspond to the visual world and views would form part of the visual field. The visual basin thus constitutes the objective land *seen* which, through a sensory organization process, we transform into a three-dimensional space *sensed*. Therefore, there is no direct, immediate relation, but the relation clearly exists. In fact, the shape, as one of the basin's spatial properties, explains how observation from a point is linked with the land's morphology, inasmuch as the view is supported or impeded by the content of the surroundings (Appleton 1975).

These concepts can be directly transferred to the study of the visual basin's shape drawn in plan. With the study of these shapes, numerous visual properties are inferred, not only of the observation point but of the land itself.

A circular shaped visual basin with its observation point near the center suggests a balanced position, either in an unstable way, as would happen if the observer were positioned at the top of a peak, or in a stable manner, if the observer is on the flat. In the latter case, it is possible to talk of an undifferentiated position, since the absence of obstacles to the views suggests that a displacement in either direction would not radically alter the land contemplated.

The elongated shape, with an observation point centered on the longest axis, is favored by the presence of side obstacles running parallel. These are the typical visual basins of valley bottoms. These basins will be characterized by the existence of long "diameters," that is, directions allowing large reaches in both senses.

When the morphology is not so clear and valleys cannot be clearly seen, the typical slope situations arise with very broad and highly off-centered visual basins. The typical shape is semicircular, with the observation point near the circle's center. Obstacles exist, the basin narrows and turns into a more or less closed view, depending on the reach. Something will always be seen toward the top of the slope, but it will be diminished.

Highly irregular basin edges are typical of highly blurred topography with a profusion of obstacles in all directions. The observation point usually has the close views restricted in some direction. This edge configuration is usually frequent in high-point visual basins on the slopes of land with rough topography, with basins in the shape of an irregular fan, cut off a great deal for a whole sector of the views.

Another main feature of visual basins as flat areas is the existence of "hollows" or shadow zones, which are not visible, inside the perimeter formed by the furthest viewed points. In general, the basins appear fragmented by innumerable intermediate obstacles which provide shadow zones but whose silhouette is drawn on a visible background, giving rise to a whole series of intermediate silhouettes. These silhouettes are taken by landscape drawers as points of support to build the land's morphology, and their perception constitutes the clearest sign of relief.

Visual basins full of "holes" are typical of very rough land. Moving from one observation point to another within them may mean a huge reduction in the areas viewed. Very nearby zones may be the zones with minimum or maximum visibility, thus in this kind of land the analyses of intervisibility are highly useful for locating actions.

Of the two ways mentioned earlier for calculating the visual basin, the one operating by visual rays is the most suitable, from a graphic point of view, for analyzing the shape of the edges and the presence of interior shadow zones. If a plotter is available, it is possible—with minimum modifications to the program—to draw the visual basins from a beam of rays originating at the observation point and break off in the shadow zones. With the grid division, the basins can also be drawn, but to a certain extent the strong link existing between each point and the observation point or pole is lost. Visual basins are clearly focalized areas, and it is advisable to use a representation that keeps and highlights this feature.

By representing this beam of rays on a survey graph with contour lines, recognition of obstacles or depressions giving rise to shadow zones is immediate, and rays "passing" between a group of obstacles reaching the furthest zones are easy to locate. Besides, this kind of representation needs no auxiliary symbolism to highlight the pole enhanced by the beam arising therefrom.

Very compact visual basins—whose visual rays

are not interrupted until they end—are typical of highly diaphanous land where everything is easily visible and the edges are clearly defined. They are zones with a high fragility. Everything done therein will have an immediate visual repercussion. There are no possibilities for hiding it since the shadow zones are scarce or do not exist.

The presence of hollows or shadow zones is, then, an important factor when the time comes to analyze the visual basin of a point. It constitutes an index of "roughness" of a landscape, as a feature defining its morphology, on a lesser scale than that anticipated by the overall shape of the visual basin.

The drawing of the visual basin on the topographical map not only enables the land viewed to be understood and to be related to the morphology, but it also anticipates the character of the land as it is observed from a certain point.

In Figure 16.7, representing a coastal area, four visual basins of a different character have been drawn. That of point (6,19) corresponds to a long view where the nearby land disappears under the feet. A sensation of being overhead, on a balcony, will be felt. The observer will be tempted to advance toward the edge in order to see the sea crashing onto the rocks.

Observation point (23,15) offers a very clear example of a panoramic view not very much broken in the whole circle. The foregoing phenomenon is repeated somewhat toward the left-hand side, but the same does not happen toward the right, where the sight is continuous from the feet to the limit of visual extension.

Point (8,7) has a typical hillside basin, very much closed. It is inside a crevice, and so its view toward both sides is small as it also is upwards, and it immediately stumbles into the once-again ascending contour lines which shut off the views thereof. Point (30,6), finally, has a somewhat irregular basin with certain nearby shadow zones, reaching cohesion when arriving at the sea.

Finally, although the amount of area viewed does not adequately reflect the whole of visual conditions, this simplified intervisibility measure is useful in regional planning studies and site analysis. It helps to find maximum visual repercussion sites, not only to see from (a fire tower's location, for example) but also to be seen (sites for a monument, a signal, or lighthouse).

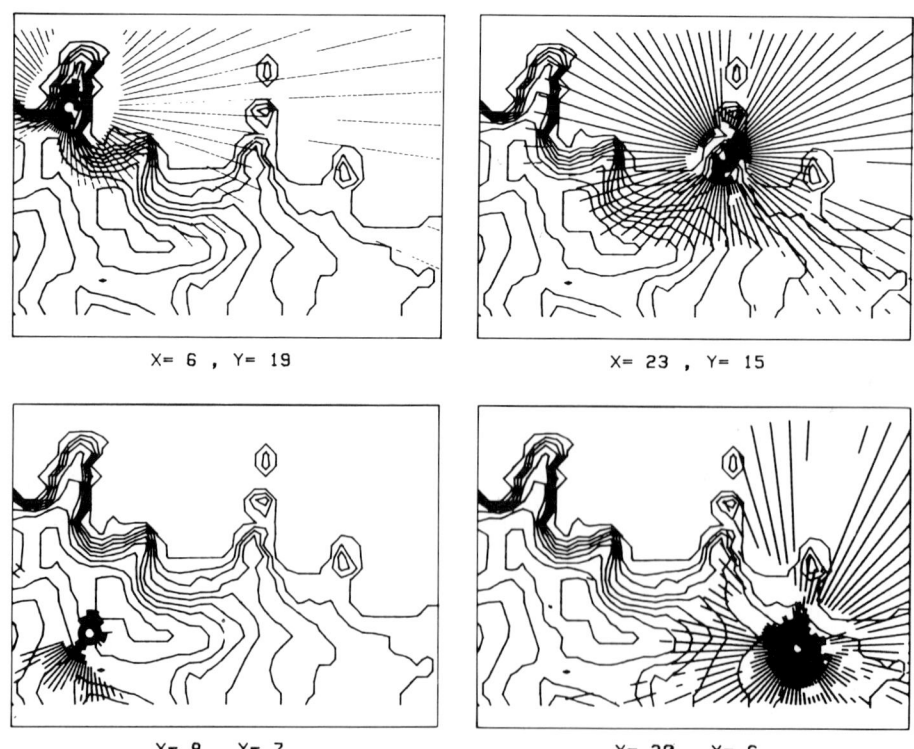

FIGURE 16.7. Viewsheds of four different points. NOTE: for figures 6 and 7. Class 1: cells outside the study area. Class 2: cells not seen from the observation point. Class 3: cells seen from the observation point.

Susceptibility

Apart from the viewed areas and their qualification, it is interesting to introduce the active subject of contemplation. It is clear that the visual impact will be more intense as long as the maximum number of observers will be capable of understanding it as it is. This interest or relation between the landscape and the observer is considered by means of two parameters: the number and the attitude of the possible observers.

1. Number of observers is usually proportional to the frequency of use of a particular area. The areas capable of producing observers are, generally, the inhabited areas, roads, and internal use places attracting a lot of people. The standard of observers can be quantified by managing the amount of population, the average intensity of daily traffic, and the population density per hectare.

2. The observer's attitude or reaction related to the degree of interest toward the landscape shown by the observer. The expected behavior of an average observer, in relation to site land use, is considered as a possible approach to the individual behavior. The people who drive along a rural or forest road during their free time or those who use a recreational area are expected to show a higher interest in the landscape than those who ordinarily travel or are forced to work in that place. It is a parameter difficult to evaluate and only its positive sense should be considered, as a further precaution standard in order to admit other possible spectators sincerely interested in the landscape because of its peculiar characteristics. It has special significance in tourist places and routes.

Supposing both parameters are measurable in three levels: high, medium, and low—or 3, 2 and 1—the following aggregation matrix can be established (USDI, B.L.M. 1980):

TABLE 16.8. Aggregation Matrix

Number of observers	3	3	2	1	3	2	1	2	1
Attitude	3	2	3	3	1	2	2	1	1
Susceptibility	High				Medium			Low	

An average number of observers (2) with an attitude of high interest in the landscape (3) give place to an area of high susceptibility.

Thus the possible visual impact can be magnified or decreased in relation to the area where it takes place. As will be explained later, this may compel more careful evaluation and modification of the design or the location of the industrial plant.

The notion of susceptibility is always relative and it should be considered in that sense. For example, a province or state with a high tourist potential will have more problems when placing an energy plant than those scarcely visited. Moreover, the different regions and areas of that same province or state will possibly have a variable flow of visitors. In each case, the concept is applicable in relative terms.

VISUAL QUALITY EVALUATION

The landscape's quality is an important element to be considered when placing an industrial plant. Quality evaluation is usually a comparative exercise, and it is not easy to determine the quality of a certain place independently. There are many methods for the evaluation of visual quality, but on the whole, they are all based on the classification of the land in comparative terms. The option for an industrial location will be determined by planning, and visual quality will be an element of the land's capacity models used. Nevertheless, the methods are useful as a strategy of approach of that complicated reality, the landscape, and also as indicators of the components, elements, and techniques to be used in each case. There is plenty of literature on compilation of methods (Dunn 1974; Aguilo et al. 1982; Blanco and Aguilo 1981) in which the principal series of methods are summarized in order to facilitate the appreciation of each one of them.

The landscape, in its double role as a sensitive mediator with the environment and as witness of man's historical activity, is capable of giving clear signs of acceptance or rejection toward our performances by adjusting the forms and contents of what is intended to the actual situation. The evaluation of this adjustment is not unanimous, but there are enough available methods so as to try.

Usually the evaluations of the landscape's quality are considered as subjective. It is clear that the subjective component plays an important role. The acquired education, the affective bonds, and the tastes represent a considerable part of the evaluating process, and it is unreasonable to ignore them. It is not so much a matter of leaving out the subjective component as a submission and rationalization of it, so that the evaluating process may be understood by the general public and not only by the operator. Still, there is no other way but to trust qualified professionals who are trained to face these problems as in many other fields of human activity.

Another of the great topics on the evaluation of the landscape's quality is the real value of the analysis systems which work through aggregation when the landscape is basically perceived as a whole. There is plenty of literature on this subject that implies the revision of the evaluating methods we have mentioned before. "The whole is not just a result of the addition of its parts." This is a powerful reason supporting the methods of direct and global evaluation, but we cannot deny the progress attained by the analytic methods in the gradual understanding of the landscape.

With the aim of helping to improve subjective and/or global evaluations, an orientative list of landscape components is given below. Its purpose is not to propitiate independent evaluations that can be later added up into one single value; on the contrary, it is meant to facilitate the approach to a complicated problem, making clear the several shades of that sole reality.

Landscape's Components

The landscape's components are the physical factors that form the landscape. They can be assembled in three groups:

Water and Land. Terrain's morphology, topography, slopes, rocky outcrops, ground surfaces, lakes, ice, snow, and so forth.

Vegetation. Trees, bushes, plant cover—all of them as individual tridimensional elements and also as homogeneous compounds or in contrast with the ground.

Human Performance. The various uses of the ground, structures, and buildings. Punctual character (buildings), linear (roads, railways, energy transport lines), or superficial (big installations, crops, and so forth), which gives out most of the testimonial function, which will determine the adjustment of the contents.

Sometimes, these components are intrinsically important, especially when certain conditions are present: scarcity, special characteristics of the component, aesthetic value, historical concern, and so forth. Usually, a component's importance for the evaluation depends more on its interactions with other elements originating compositions that provoke aesthetic emotions. The components as well as the compositions, or even the whole landscape, have their visual characteristics or basic elements organized in a certain way. On the other hand, the installation which we pretend to place there has its own visual characteristics, and the analysis of the presumable impact tries to determine the agreement or disagreement between both groups of visual basic elements.

Usually, a new industrial plant modifies several components of the actual landscape and supplies new ones, with particular visual characteristics. These components are also assembled in three groups, similar to those referred to above. For example (Smardon, Sheppard, and Newman 1984):

Water and Land

Altered or uncovered soils
Earth tracks and paths
Embankments
Rocky outcrops
Flooded areas
Refuse disposal areas

Vegetation

Sown fields or new plantations
Pruned or cut trees
Pruning remnants
Vegetation clearings

Structures

Buildings
Water pipes, wells, transmission towers
Concrete asphalt roads
Contention walls and complementary works
Basic material stores and uncovered manufactured products
Waste material

All of them play their part in the impact's evaluation. In many cases, the installation's secondary elements (belonging to any of these groups) produce a greater visual impact than the one produced by the principal building of the installation itself. And there is a further problem because these secondary elements are not carefully evaluated or designed, due to hasty and careless improvisations. It is necessary to insist on giving special attention to the work leading to the construction of the industrial installation—access, quarries, earth dumps, and so forth—which are generally ignored when evaluating, even if they are potentially capable of very serious alterations.

Basic Visual Elements

Any landscape or industrial structure may be described in visual terms by means of the basic elements: color, shape, line, texture, scale, and spatial character.

Color

Property of reflecting the light with a certain intensity and wavelength. It is defined by its tinge: red, blue, yellow; shade: light, dark; brightness: bright and dull. It is the most important visual property of a surface. The luminous and bright colors prevail over the dark and dull ones. They lose brightness with the distance acquiring a blue tinge.

Shape

Limited surfaces or volumes so as to acquire unity. It is explained in terms of geometry, complexity, and orientation. It depends on the observation's visual angle and is modified by the illumination.

Line

The border or limit perceived when there are different colors or textures. The special configuration or unidimensional arrangement of the objects. It is distinguished by its complexity, orientation, and strength—very intense, weak, and so forth. The strong and vertical lines tend to prevail over the weak and horizontal.

Texture

An aggregate of small combinations of shapes and colors forming a continuous superficial configuration. It is studied in terms of relative dimensions of the superficial variations and density or degree of surface scattering and regularity.

Scale

Relation of size between an object and its environment. Intimately related to the notions of dominancy and contrast. It is altered by the distance, the configuration of external space, and the relative position of the observer—considering his or her height.

Space

Determined by the tridimensional arrangement of solid bodies and empty spaces. Distinguished by the spatial composition which gives place to panoramic, closed, or focal landscapes, dominated by one particular component. Its perception is closely connected with the observer's position in relation to the landscape, vertically as well as horizontally.

Visual Impact Assessment

In addition to what we have already mentioned about the effects of the visibility conditions of the area, the industrial plant can produce a visual effect capable of altering the two ways by which the landscape displays itself: its role of sensorial measurement and its testimonial role.

The first is essentially displayed by a lack of adjustment, or by an excessive contrast between the visual elements of the components introduced by the installation. For example, consider the contrast of shapes and lines established between the building's geometry and the mild contours of the land, or the different scales or the chromatic contrast.

The contrast between the visual elements of the environment and the installation can be provoked by one or several of those elements. Its influence on the global impact can be classified in the following order: color, shape, scale, line, and texture. As a suggestion (Smardon, Sheppard, and Newman 1984), certain weights could be assigned: 3, 2, 2, 1, and 1, respectively. The impact can be graded into four classes which can act as multipliers of what has been mentioned before: null, low, medium, or high impact (0, 1, 2, 3).

As well as the visual contrast, the impact on the sensorial role becomes apparent by the visual dominancy of the introduced elements in relation to those already existent, especially in terms of scale and position in space. Frequently, it is the most important factor in the production of a possible visual impact. It is closely related to the visual characteristics of the land and the notion of visual intrusion already mentioned.

The dominance of scale is determined by the relative occupation of the viewshed in terms of area of the invaded visual plane. In order to appreciate this effect, the observation spot has to be situated at an appropriate distance so as to perceive the surrounding landscape (its morphology, organization, and imbrication in the region's geography) and simultaneously appreciate the installation. Spots must be chosen at medium distances, where these effects are observed in their real magnitude. The installation's components become directly connected with the components of the surrounding landscape. In some cases, the landscape can annul or diminish them, showing a dominant power. In other cases, the installation has such energy that it diminishes the resulting landscape, transforming itself into its most fundamental characteristic and blotting out the environment.

The visual intrusion depends on the situation of the industrial plant in relation to the dominant components of the landscape, or of the visibility conditions of its morphology. In areas with regular and defined parameters (viewsheds always stretched and in the same direction, for example), the visual flows are compelled to canalize the direction of the vistas and the observation positions. In this case, the presence of an industrial installation can provoke a fracture of the visual flow system, occupying prominent positions in most of the viewsheds of that area's spots. The problems of maximum intrusion, because of this reason, are normally found in narrow valleys when the installation is rather big and occupies a position near the center.

The spatial relation with certain principal components of the landscape is another source of potential problems. If a landscape is dominated by a mountain or a crest line, the partial or total hiding of the mountain or the interruption of the crest line will produce a strong visual impact. Even if the hidden components are artificial, the impact can be equally strong. The concealment of a village from an outstanding view spot is a clear example of it all. The effect, in this case, can be enhanced depending on the aesthetic quality of the components that have been hidden, interrupted, or altered. It also depends on the significance of the observation points.

Usually, and without considering the importance of the observation points that have been chosen, the most vulnerable landscapes in this sense are the focal landscapes (where all lines converge in one point), those dominated by a particular component (an interesting or isolated tree, a waterfall, and so forth) and the very closed-up landscapes. There are two other kinds of landscapes which suffer milder impacts: the panoramic landscapes with a predominant horizontal composition and without definite delimitation, or those landscapes dominated by a certain characteristic or component that is not very strong. The least vulnerable are the vague landscapes or those without any specific meaning.

In regard to position, the prominence of the installation is bigger when situated on top of a hill or half-way down a slope. When situated in a plateau (plain and high area with clearly defined borders) or in undulating open valleys or beside the foot of a hill, then the problem is usually less important. The background against which we observe the installation can increase or reduce the effect of dominance because of position. The outline of the structures or buildings against the sky or the water have more relevance than with a background of vegetation.

In relation to the landscape's testimonial role, the impact is basically due to a lack of compatibility between the historical land uses which have conformed it and the meaning of the installation in that place. An agricultural landscape, for example, typified by certain crops, acquires a peculiar morphology on which all further human activities have been registered.

Roads, paths, tracks, irrigation systems, agricultural buildings, houses—all interrelate and influence one another, giving place to a real cultural possession of the environment. With the passing of the years, the activity adjusts itself to the environment, generating new ways of behavior. For example, roads always use the "cuestas" to communicate the productive high lands with the bottom of the valleys, and the latter are spared because of their fertility, restricting the buildings to the border of the productive area. Fences' orientation is also determined by the morphological conditions. If in a landscape of this kind a road is built neglecting the context, or electric posts are set which have nothing to do with the place, or if the bottom of a valley is damaged by a building that does not profit from it, then the incongruity with the traditional use of the surrounding land becomes clear.

Finally, the respect for those singular elements which are for any reason positively valued by the local life, because of their uniqueness, history, or aesthetics (see prior section on fragility). Any building, monument, or component of the landscape possessing any singularity of this kind must be protected. Its use and enjoyment must be guaranteed, and the environment, as well, cannot suffer any change capable of altering the service it renders to the community.

OPERATIVE PROCESS

In order to determine the convenience of a certain location for an industrial plant, we have to evaluate its possible impact on the qualities and characteristics mentioned in the preceding pages. Depending on the magnitude and the conditions of the installation and on the characteristics of the chosen place, the evaluation will be more or less complete. We now describe the necessary stages to follow when it is a complicated case. Each stage may be submitted to detailed analysis, implying long time and procedures, or, it may be a simple estimation elaborated with good sense. In any case, and as we are trying to elude future problems, it is convenient to trust qualified professionals when considering the landscape's problems.

If we already have a duly documented plan of the chosen area, this will provide information about the visual quality of the different landscape units of the area. If there is no available plan, and if the area has landscape value, or is being used for activities which are potentially incompatible with those intended, it will then be necessary to do a previous study of fragility or visual vulnerability in order to support the first decisions about the selection of optional and alternative locations. From these previous studies, valuable suggestions for the external design of the installation will be obtained, also reducing future problems.

Unfortunately, it frequently happens that the consideration of conflicts begins when the principal characteristics of the installation and the location are totally decided. It is then necessary to evaluate the possible impact on the landscape and to propose the appropriate measures to mitigate impacts according to the following steps:

1. Information about the project, including built volumes, spatial organization, building materials, auxiliary elements, and so forth. Illustrated documents of the installation.
2. Description of the surrounding landscape. Identify its principal uses. Sketch of historical process. Identify all particularly interesting elements, and so forth.
3. Definition of the area visually affected by the installation. Viewshed. Calculation of the visual parameters (see Example 1).
4. Selection of observation points. Places which will probably concentrate observers. Probable visual elements to be affected. Routes, and so forth (see Example 2).
5. Definition of the new viewsheds of the chosen spots. Evaluation of the intrusion and dominance problems. Final selection of the observation points.
6. Fulfill a simulation from the chosen spots.
7. Definition of the probable impact, based on the simulation, studying (see Table 16.1):
   Contrast between the visual elements of the installation and the environment: lines, color, shape and texture.
   Scale dominance
   Disturbance of the visual parameters
8. Evaluation. With the following possible results:
   Acceptable impact. Installation is authorized.
   Nonacceptable impact, requiring a change of location. Go back in the process to Steps 3 or 2.
   Impact which can be corrected. Proposal of changes. Go back in the process to Steps 6 or 7. In some cases, it is necessary to reform from Step 3.

EXAMPLE 3: Figures 16.8, 16.9 and 16.10.

The following three computer programs to calculate visibility were written in BASIC computer language to be run on an HP-85 microcomputer. The approach taken by each is generally described in Example 1. The program in Figure 16.8 allows for the predetermination of cells in the visual ray to obtain greater calculating efficiency, as described by Steinitz, et al. (1974). The second program, Figure 16.9 uses a cell by cell search to identify seen areas. The program in Figure 16.10 uses the sectorial search method to calculate visibility described by Aguilo (1981).

PROGRAMA DE VISIBILIDAD.
METODO DE C. STEINITZ.

```
10 REM PROGRAMA DE VISIBILIDAD SEGUN STEINITZ.
20 CLEAR
30 OPTION BASE 1
40 DIM A$[100]
50 COM INTEGER Z(30,60)
60 COM L1,L2,L3,L4
70 V=1-L1
80 INTEGER A(67,9),C(30,60),R(17,17)
90 COM W4
100 DISP "PROGRAMA DE VISIBILIDAD.STEINITZ"
110 PRINT "Visibilidad. STEINITZ"
120 DISP "LONGITUD MAXIMA DEL RAYO: 67 cuadriculas"
130 ASSIGN# 1 TO "V1"
140 READ# 1 ; A(,)
150 ASSIGN# 1 TO *
160 FOR I=1 TO 30
170 FOR J=1 TO 60
180 C(I.J)=0
190 NEXT J
200 NEXT I
210 DISP "NUMERO DE RAYOS(3,5,9)"
220 INPUT A
230 DISP "LONGITUD DE LOS RAYOS"
240 INPUT B
250 DISP "COORDENADAS DEL PUNTO DE OBSERVACION (X/Y)"
260 INPUT F,G
270 W1,W2=0
280 FOR I=1 TO 17
290 FOR J=1 TO 17
300 R(I,J)=0
310 NEXT J
320 NEXT I
330 FOR C=1 TO 8
340 T=0
350 IF C=1 THEN M,N=1
360 IF C=4 THEN M=1 @ N=-1
370 IF C=5 THEN M=-1 @ N=-1
380 IF C=8 THEN M=-1 @ N=1
390 IF C=2 THEN M=1 @ N=1 @ T=1
400 IF C=3 THEN M=1 @ N=-1 @ T=1
410 IF C=6 THEN M=-1 @ N=-1 @ T=1
420 IF C=7 THEN M=-1 @ N=1 @ T=1
430 IF A=3 THEN V=4
440 IF A=5 THEN V=2
450 IF A=9 THEN V=1
460 L8=9
470 L7=1 @ L8=9
480 IF INT(C/2)=C/2 THEN L7=V+1 @ L8=9-V
490 FOR J=L7 TO L8 STEP V
500 S=-100
510 FOR I=1 TO B
520 X1=IP(A(I,J)/100)
530 Y1=FP(A(I,J)/100)*100
540 L=SQR(X1^2+Y1^2)
550 IF L>B THEN 770
560 IF T=0 THEN 600 ELSE 570
570 Y=G+X1*N
580 X=F+Y1*M
590 GOTO 620
600 Y=G+Y1*N
```

FIGURE 16.8.

```
610 X=F+X1*M
620 IF Y<L3 OR Y>L4 THEN 770
630 IF Y<L3 OR Y>L4 THEN 770
640 IF X<L1 OR X>L2 THEN 770
650 IF Z(Y,X)=-1 THEN 770
660 W=Z(Y,X)-Z(G,F)
670 Z=W/L
680 S=MAX(Z,S)
690 IF Z>=S THEN 700 ELSE 760
700 IF ABS(X-F)<=8 AND ABS(Y-G)<=8 THEN C(Y,X)=1 @ GOTO 730
710 W1=W1+1 @ C(Y,X)=1
720 GOTO 760
730 T1=X-F+9
740 T2=Y-G+9
750 R(T2,T1)=1
760 NEXT I
770 NEXT J
780 NEXT C
790 FOR I=1 TO 17
800 FOR J=1 TO 17
810 W2=W2+R(I,J)
820 NEXT J
830 NEXT I
840 PRINT "Punto: X= ";F;"Y= ";G
850 W3=IP((W1+W2)*100)/100
860 PRINT
880 GOSUB 1130
890 PRINT USING 900
900 IMAGE 3/
910 FOR I=L4 TO L3 STEP -1
920 A$[1]=VAL$(IP(I/100))
930 A$[2]=VAL$(IP(FP(I/100)*10))
940 A$[3]=VAL$(FP(I/10)*10)
950 FOR J=L1 TO L2
960 IF I=G AND J=F THEN A$[J+6+V]="A" @ GOTO 1000
970 IF Z(I,J)=-1 THEN A$[J+6+V]=" " @ GOTO 1000
980 IF C(I,J)=0 THEN A$[J+6+V]="." @ GOTO 1000
990 A$[J+6+V]=VAL$(C(I,J))
1000 NEXT J
1010 A$[L2+7+V,L2+9+V]="   "
1020 A$[L2+10+V]=A$[1]
1030 A$[L2+11+V]=A$[2]
1040 A$[L2+12+V]=A$[3,3]
1050 PRINT A$
1060 NEXT I
1070 PRINT USING 1080
1080 IMAGE 3/
1090 GOSUB 1130
1100 GOSUB 1270
1110 GOTO 160
1120 STOP
1130 FOR J=L1 TO L2
1140 A$[1,5]="     "
1150 A$[J+6+V]=VAL$(IP(J/100))
1160 NEXT J
1170 PRINT A$
1180 FOR J=L1 TO L2
1190 A$[J+6+V]=VAL$(IP(FP(J/100)*10))
1200 NEXT J
1210 PRINT A$
1220 FOR J=L1 TO L2
1230 A$[J+6+V]=VAL$(FP(J/10)*10)
1240 NEXT J
1250 PRINT A$
1260 RETURN
1270 PRINT USING 1280
1280 IMAGE 2/
1290 D$="  .1"
1300 PRINT "CLASES";
1310 FOR I=1 TO 3
1320 PRINT TAB(5+7*I),I;
1330 NEXT I
```

FIGURE 16.8. (continued)

```
1340 PRINT
1350 PRINT "      =========================================
====="
1360 FOR I=1 TO 100
1370 A$[I]=" "
1380 NEXT I
1390 FOR I=1 TO 4
1400 FOR J=1 TO 4
1410 A$[11+J,11+J]=D$[1,1]
1420 A$[18+J,18+J]=D$[2,2]
1430 A$[25+J,25+J]=D$[3,3]
1440 NEXT J
1450 PRINT A$
1460 NEXT I
1470 PRINT "      =========================================
====="
1480 PRINT "Frecuencia";TAB(19);W4-W3;TAB(26);W3
1490 PRINT USING 1500
1500 IMAGE /
1510 PRINT "Clase 1: cuadriculas fuera de la zona de est
udio"
1520 PRINT "Clase 2: cuadriculas no vistas desde el punt
o de observacion"
1530 PRINT "Clase 3: cuadriculas vistas desde el punto d
e observacion"
1540 RETURN
```

FIGURE 16.8. (continued)

Visibilidad por cuadriculas


```
10 REM   "CUADR1".VISIBILIDAD POR CUADRICULAS, CON CORREC
CION DE ALTITUDES.CINTA 2,14.XI.81.
20 CLEAR
30 OPTION BASE 1
40 COM INTEGER Z(30,60)
50 COM L1,L2,L3,L4
60 COM W4
70 V=1-L1
80 INTEGER A(30,60)
90 DIM A$[100]
100 DEF FNZ(Y)
110 IF X+1>L2 OR Y+1>L4 THEN FNZ=Z(Y,X) @ GOTO 180
120 IF Z(Y+1,X+1)=-1 THEN FNZ=Z(Y,X) @ GOTO 180
130 IF E>=R THEN 140 ELSE 160
140 IF Z(Y,X+1)=-1 THEN FNZ=Z(Y,X) @ GOTO 180
150 FNZ=Z(Y,X)*(1-E)+Z(Y,X+1)*(E-R)+Z(Y+1,X+1)*R @ GOTO
180
160 IF Z(Y+1,X)=-1 THEN FNZ=Z(Y,X) @ GOTO 180
170 FNZ=Z(Y,X)*(1-R)+Z(Y+1,X)*(R-E)+Z(Y+1,X+1)*E
180 FN END
190 DISP "ALC,SOBREL,PASO"
200 INPUT A,S,P
210 DISP "COORDENADAS DEL PUNTO DE OBSERVACION (X,Y)"
220 INPUT F,G
230 Y=G @ X=F
240 IF Z(G,F)=-1 THEN PRINT "PUNTO FUERA DE LA ZONA DE E
STUDIO" @ GOTO 210
250 E,R=.5
260 Z1=FNZ(Y)+S
270 D=0
280 FOR I=1 TO 30
290 FOR J=1 TO 60
300 A(I,J)=0
310 IF Z(I,J)=-1 THEN 490
```

FIGURE 16.9.

```
320 IF F=J AND G=I THEN 490
330 T=SQR((F-J)^2+(G-I)^2)
340 IF T>A THEN 490
350 M=(I-G)/T
360 N=(J-F)/T
370 O=Z(I,J)-Z1
380 FOR Q=1 TO T STEP P
390 Z=Q*O/T+Z1
400 X=Q*N+F @ E=X-INT(X) @ X=INT(X)
410 Y=Q*M+G @ R=Y-INT(Y) @ Y=INT(Y)
420 IF X<L1 OR X>L2 THEN 490
430 IF Y<L3 OR Y>L4 THEN 490
440 Z2=FNZ(Y)
450 IF Z2<=Z THEN 460 ELSE 490
460 NEXT Q
470 A(I,J)=1
480 D=D+A(I,J)
490 NEXT J
500 NEXT I
510 PRINT "Visibilidad cuadricula a cuadricula."
520 PRINT "ALCANCE:";A;" SOBREL:";S;" PASO:";P
530 PRINT "Punto: X=";F;",Y=";G
540 D=IP(D*100)/100
550 PRINT USING 560
560 IMAGE /
570 GOSUB 820
580 PRINT USING 590
590 IMAGE 3/
600 FOR I=L4 TO L3 STEP -1
610 A$[1]=VAL$(IP(I/100))
620 A$[2]=VAL$(IP(FP(I/100)*10))
630 A$[3]=VAL$(FP(I/10)*10)
640 FOR J=L1 TO L2
650 IF F=J AND G=I THEN A$[J+6+V]="A" @ GOTO 690
660 IF Z(I,J)=-1 THEN A$[J+6+V]=" " @ GOTO 690
670 IF A(I,J)=0 THEN A$[J+6+V]="." @ GOTO 690
680 A$[J+6+V]=VAL$(1)
690 NEXT J
700 A$[L2+7+V,L2+9+V]="   "
710 A$[L2+10+V]=A$[1]
720 A$[L2+11+V]=A$[2]
730 A$[L2+12+V]=A$[3,3]
740 PRINT A$
750 NEXT I
760 PRINT USING 770
770 IMAGE 3/
780 GOSUB 820
790 GOSUB 1000
800 GOTO 190
810 STOP
820 FOR J=L1 TO L2
830 A$[1,3]="+++"
840 A$[4,5]="  "
850 A$[J+6+V]=VAL$(IP(J/100))
860 NEXT J
870 A$[L2+10+V,L2+12+V]="+++"
880 PRINT A$
890 FOR J=L1 TO L2
900 A$[J+6+V]=VAL$(IP(FP(J/100)*10))
910 NEXT J
920 A$[L2+10+V,L2+12+V]="+++"
930 PRINT A$
940 FOR J=L1 TO L2
950 A$[J+6+V]=VAL$(FP(J/10)*10)
960 NEXT J
970 A$[L2+10+V,L2+12+V]="+++"
980 PRINT A$
990 RETURN
1000 PRINT USING 1010
1010 IMAGE /
1020 D$=" .1"
1030 PRINT "CLASES";
1040 FOR I=1 TO 3
```

FIGURE 16.9. (continued)

```
1050 PRINT TAB(5+7*I),I;
1060 NEXT I
1070 PRINT
1080 PRINT "     =========================================
===="
1090 FOR I=1 TO 100
1100 A$[I]=" "
1110 NEXT I
1120 FOR I=1 TO 4
1130 FOR J=1 TO 4
1140 A$[11+J,11+J]=D$[1,1]
1150 A$[18+J,18+J]=D$[2,2]
1160 A$[25+J,25+J]=D$[3,3]
1170 NEXT J
1180 PRINT A$
1190 NEXT I
1200 PRINT "     =========================================
===="
1210 PRINT "Frecuencia";TAB(19),W4-D;TAB(26),D
1220 PRINT USING 1230
1230 IMAGE /
1240 PRINT "Clase 1: cuadriculas fuera de la zona de est
udio"
1250 PRINT "Clase 2: cuadriculas no vistas desde el punt
o de observacion"
1260 PRINT "Clase 3: cuadricls vistas desde el punto de
observacion"
1270 RETURN
```

FIGURE 16.9. (continued)

Visibilidad por rayos.

```
10 REM PROGRAMA DE VISIBILIDAD POR RAYOS.
20 CLEAR
30 OPTION BASE 1
40 COM INTEGER Z(30,60)
50 COM L1,L2,L3,L4
60 COM W4
70 DEG
80 DISP "DIR,AMPL,ALC,PASO,ANG,SOBR"
90 INPUT A1,A2,A3,P,A4,A5
100 DISP "X,Y DEL PUNTO DE OBSERVACION"
110 INPUT F,G
120 H=Z(G,F)+A5
130 R,T=0
140 FOR W=A1-A2/2 TO A1+A2/2 STEP A4
150 B=COS(W) @ C=SIN(W) @ E=TAN(A4/2)
160 S=-100
170 FOR D=P TO A3 STEP P
180 X=D*B+F
190 Y=G-D*C
200 X=INT(X)
210 Y=INT(Y)
220 IF X<L1 OR X>L2 THEN 330
230 IF Y<L3 OR Y>L4 THEN 330
240 IF Z(Y,X)=-1 THEN 330
250 L=Z(Y,X)-H
260 M=L/D
270 R1=(2*D*P-P^2)*E
280 S=MAX(M,S)
290 IF M>=S THEN 300 ELSE 310
300 R=R+R1
310 T=T+R1
320 NEXT D
330 NEXT W
```

FIGURE 16.10.

```
340 PRINT "Punto: x=";F;",y=";G
350 PRINT USING 360 ; "Cuenca visual real:",R,"cuadricul
as"
360 IMAGE K,2X,DDDD.DD,X,K
370 PRINT USING 380 ; "Cuenca real esperada:",T,"cuadric
ulas"
380 IMAGE K,2X,DDDD.DD,X,K
390 PRINT USING 400 ; "Cuenca relativa:",R/T*100,"cuadri
culas"
400 IMAGE K,2X,DD.DD,X,K
410 GOTO 100
420 STOP
```

FIGURE 16.10. (continued)

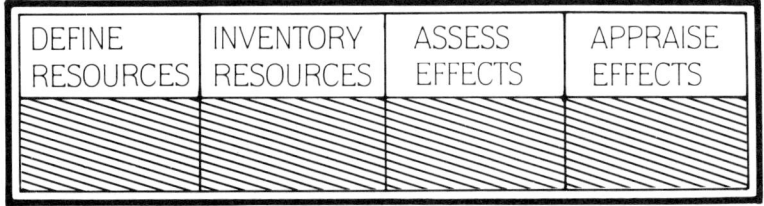

ILLUSTRATED GLOSSARY

Kate Grinde and Al Kopf

This book touches on many technical areas and we thought the reader would appreciate definitions of often used terms. We have compiled definitions for these terms as well as graphics which may aid understanding as well. The terms are not listed alphabetically, but are listed in families of similar terms. We have provided an alphabetized index at the beginning of the glossary so the reader can find definitions for a specific term.

ILLUSTRATED GLOSSARY

GLOSSARY INDEX

Terms	Page No.
absolute scale	329
absorption	318
accent	328
accessibility	323
accuracy	333
acuity	324
adverse visual impact	332
aerial perspective	318
aesthetic quality	310
aesthetic resource	310
aesthetic zoning	332
aesthetics	310
agrarianism	313
amenity	310
analog	321
angle of observation	318
angle of vision	318
aspect	318
association	323
asymmetry	328
atmospheric conditions	318
attribute	310
axis	328
background	320
back lighting	320, 318
balance	328
basic elements	314
binocular field	325
brightness	318
canopied	312
cardinal value	333
chroma	315
close-ended question	325
closure	327
codominant	329
cognitive	323
color	315
color contrast	318
compose	328
composite viewshed	322
composition	328
cones	325
congruence	329
continuity	328
contour	318
contrast	330
countryside	310
critical viewpoint	319
cross-section	319
dependent variable	325
designation	310
diffraction	318
digital/numeric	321
disability glare	330
discomfort glare	330
discontinuity	327
distance	319
distance zones	319
distinct	327
district	317
diversity	327
dominance	330
dominant	330, 327
dominant elements	330
edge	317
enclosed	312
environmental displays	326
environmental psychology	323
environmental quality	310
ephemeral	312
experimental psychology	323
feature	312
fitness	330
fixation	324
focal	312
focus	324
formal aesthetic attributes	328
foreground	319
foreshortening	324
form	314
fragility	330
front lighting	320
harmony	327
hue	315
hybrid	321
imageability	323
independent variable	325
inferior	321
intactness	327
internal scale	333
intervisibility	320
intrusion	330
key observer position	320
landscape	311
landscape attributes	327
landscape, beauty	311
landscape character	312
landscape compatibility	330
landscape composition types	312
landscape control points	330, 320
landscape, cultural	312
landscape features	316
landscape type	312
landscape unit	312
landscape values	313
land form	316
landmark	317
land use	317
land use intensity	317
legibility	323
lighting	320
lighting direction	320
line	315
mass	328
media of presentation	326
midground	319
mitigation	332
morphology	316

ILLUSTRATED GLOSSARY 309

motion perspective	324
monocular field	325
monotony	327
node	317
observer position	320
observer set	323
observers	326
ocular fixation	324
open-ended question	325
operationalism	325
optical field	324
order	329
ordinal value	333
orientation	324
panorama	312
pastoralism	313
path	317
pattern	329
perception	323
perspective	324
photomontage	333
picture plane	324
proportion	329
prototype	321
psychophysics	325
quality	313
random sampling	325
ratio scale	333
reflection	318
refraction	318
rehabilitation	332
relative scale	330
reliability	325
repetition	329
representativeness	333
response formats	326
retina	324
rhythm	329
rods	325
ruralism	313
sample	325
sampling	326
saturation	315
scale	330
scale contrast	331
scenery	313
scenic area	313
scenic corridor	313
scenic distinction	313
scenic quality	314
seasonal change	327
seen area	321
sequence	327
serial vision	325
shade	321
shadow	321
shape	329
side lighting	320
sightline	321
silhouette	329
similarity	327
simulation	333, 321
skyline	318
slope	318
space	329
spatial dominance	331
stratified sampling	326
structures	317
subordinate	331
superior	321
symmetry	329
texture	316
3-D iconic	321
tint	316
topographic viewshed	322
transition	329
transparency	325
2-D iconic	321
uniqueness	327
unity	327
user activity	323
value	316
validity	326
variety	327
vegetative patterns	316
view	321
viewer activity	323, 321
viewer awareness	323, 321
viewer exposure	321
viewer sensitivity	322
viewing angle	322
viewshed	322
visibility	322
visibility models	322
visual absorption	331
visual character	314
visual character type	314
visual compatibility	331
visual contrast	331
visual corridor	314
visual dominance	331
visual field	325
visual impact	331
visual landscape character	314
visual management classes	332
visual perception	324
visual quality	314
visual resource	314
visual sensitivity	332
visual vulnerability	332
vividness	328
water bodies	317
weighting	333

AESTHETICS:

1. Evaluations and considerations with the sensory quality of resources (sight, sound, smell, taste, and touch) and especially with respect to judgment about their pleasurable qualities (U.S. Bur. of Land Manage. 1977.)
2. Pertaining to the quality of human perceptual experience (including sight, sound, smell, touch, taste, and movement) evoked by phenomena or elements or configurations of elements in the environment. (Schwarz et al. 1976.)
3. Giving visual pleasure. (Hubbard and Kimball 1917.)
4. The theory of perception of susceptibility. (Santayana 1955.)
5. Generally, the study, science, philosophy, and beauty extending to all the arts, as well as to all factors of cultural endeavor. (Wolf 1951.)

Aesthetic(s):
(a) generally, the study, science, or philosophy dealing with beauty and with judgements concerning beauty.
(b) Giving visual pleasure.
(c) The theory of perception or of susceptibility.
(d) The quality of being aesthetic is not the opposite of the qualities of "practicality" or "reality" but rather another aspect or way of experiencing the same real world phenomena. Thus blue skies, uncontaminated water, and uncluttered urban landscapes all have aesthetic value because they imply health, pleasure, and security.
(e) In terms of visual assessment, aesthetics can be thought of in three primary aspects: (1) internal, (2) rational, and (3) extended environmental aesthetics. (Blair 1980.)

Aesthetic Quality: The aesthetic significance given to a landscape determined by cultural values and the landscape's intrinsic physical properties. (A.C.E. 1984.)

Aesthetic Resource: Those natural and cultural features of the environment which elicit one or more sensory reactions and evaluations by the observer, particularly in regard to their pleasurable effects. (A.C.E. 1984.)

AMENITY (Amenity value):

1. An object, feature, quality, or experience that gives pleasure or is pleasing to the mind or senses. (After Webster 1963.)
2. The pleasurable or aesthetic, as contrasted with the utilitarian, features of a plan, project, location, or resource. The term amenity is now used so broadly that it can refer to just about anything that makes life more agreeable—from a temperate climate to an intellectual climate. (Abrams 1971.)
3. (Amenity value). Typically used in land use planning to describe those resource properties for which market values (or proxy values) are not or cannot be established. (Schwarz et al. 1976.)
4. Quality of being pleasant or agreeable as in respect to situation, climate, disposition. (Webster 1960.)

ATTRIBUTE:

The ecological, cultural, and aesthetic properties of natural and cultural resources that sustain and enrich human life. (A.C.E. 1984.)

COUNTRYSIDE:

Widely used to designate a place apart from urban and wilderness areas, rather than a particular landscape. It connotes both physical and cultural components. Countryside is a recognizable landscape unit containing a predominance of agricultural patterns and activities and defined by both cultural interpretations and the physical setting. (Schauman et al. 1982.)

DESIGNATION:

Landscapes and special districts formally or informally recognized for their historic, educational, scientific, recreational, or aesthetic value. Designation may affect viewer expectations about these areas. (Jones and Jones 1977.)

ENVIRONMENTAL QUALITY:

1. Natural environmental quality. Heyman and Twiss in evaluating management practices on federal public lands speak of *environmental quality* as referring "primarily to the continuance, to the extent feasible, of the natural ecosystems existing on public lands especially as that ecosystem is important to human health and safety, the provision of direct sensory experiences, and

the continued viability of life forms and biotic communities that exist naturally on, and surrounding, the public lands." (Heyman and Twiss 1971.)

2. In general, definition 1 must be expanded to include all environments experienced by man and include aspects of environmental psychology. Even though qualities may exist without man, it is man who makes the judgments that define qualities. The qualities are both individual and consensual. The "group" may attach some value or measure of quality to some environment, and each individual may give a somewhat different value to the same environment. "Quality" is a "separate reality" for each individual, but may contain universals for a great many individuals. Thus the environment may be a wilderness or a city street, with each person having his or her own value judgment as to the quality of the environment, but together they may reach a consensus which forms an "environmental quality" basis for planning. (Schwarz et al. 1976.)

3. U.S. Water Resources Council (WRC) usage. Enhancing environmental quality by the management, conservation, preservation, creation, restoration or improvement of the quality of certain national and cultural resources and ecological systems is one of the two main objectives for programs involving water and related land resources administered by federal agencies whose activities involve planning and development of water resources, as contained in the Water Resources Council's Principles and Standards. An evaluation of environmental quality effects should include: (1) areas of natural beauty; (2) water, land, and air quality; (3) biological resources and selected ecosystems; (4) geological, archeological, and historical resources; and (5) irretrievable commitments of resources to future use. (After U.S. Dept. of Agric. 1974.)

4. One of the four "required accounts" for categorizing, displaying, or "accounting" the beneficial and adverse effects of each alternative plan formulation for water and related land resources planning specified in the Water Resources Council's Principles and Standards and the U.S. Department of Agriculture's "Procedures" for adhering to them. (After U.S. Dept. of Agric. 1974.)

5. The sum total of the forces and factors which influence people's satisfactions with their work, leisure, living conditions, and community. (Barron 1972.)

LANDSCAPE:

1. Landform and land cover forming a distance visual pattern. Land cover comprises water, vegetation, and man-made development, including cities. (Jones and Jones 1977.)

2. An expanse of natural scenery seen by the eye in one view (Webster 1960.)

3. The natural landscape is an indeterminate object; it contains enough diversity to allow the eye a great liberty in selecting, emphasizing, and grouping its elements; and it is furthermore rich in suggestion and in vague emotional stimulus. (Santayana 1955.)

4. The surface features of an area including not only landforms, but all other objects and aspects, both of natural and human origin. (Monkhouse 1970.)

5. Countryside, the environment in which natural features dominate even though often controlled and ordered by man. (Robinson et al. 1976.)

6. An areal entity which is a composite of all of the characteristics that distinguish a certain area on the earth's surface from other areas. (Holland 1971.)

7. An expanse of natural scenery seen by the eye in one view. (Webster 1963.)

8. An area made up of a distinct association of forms, both physical and cultural. (Stamp 1961.)

9. The sum total of the characteristics that distinguish a certain area on the earth's surface from other areas. These characteristics are a result not only of natural forces but of human occupancy and use of the land. (U.S. For. Serv. 1973).

LANDSCAPE, BEAUTY:

(a) When it reveals a moral or ethical truth (historical);

(b) when the energy-flow system is functioning with the unimpeded efficiency (19th–20th century);

(c) where natural environment is seen as a setting for an experience rather than experience itself, (modern). (Jackson 1984.)

LANDSCAPE CHARACTER:

1. The arrangement of a particular landscape as formed by the variety and intensity of the landscape features and the four basic elements of form, line, color, and texture. These factors give the area a distinctive quality which distinguishes it from its immediate surroundings. (U.S. Bur. of Land Manage. 1977.)

2. A mode of aesthetic organization which is a result of the operation of the forces of nature not guided by man. (Hubbard and Kimball 1917.)

LANDSCAPE COMPOSITION:

1. The arrangement of objects and voids in the landscape that can be categorized by their spatial arrangement. Some spatial compositions, especially those which are distinctly focal, enclosed, detail, or feature-oriented landscape, are more vulnerable to modifications than panoramic, canopied, or ephemeral landscapes.

2. Arrangement of the elements of a design into an ordered whole. (Hubbard and Kimball 1917.)

Landscape Composition Types:

(a) Canopy, Canopied: Covered or bridged by the uppermost spreading branchy layer of a forest. (U.S. For. Serv. 1973.) See Figure (*a*).

(b) Enclosed: Enveloped or surrounded; bounded or encompassed. (U.S. For. Serv. 1973.) See Figure (*b*).

(c) Ephemeral: Anything lasting but a brief time. (U.S. For. Serv. 1973.) See Figure (*c*).

(d) Feature: A distinct or outstanding part, quality, or characteristic of something. (Webster 1960.) See Figure (*d*).

(e) Focal: Of or placed at a focus; as a focal point. (Webster 1960.) See Figure (*e*).

(f) Panoramic: A continuous series of scenes or events, constantly changing scene. See Figure (*f*).

(a) **Canopied Landscape.** Source: Yeomans, W.C, 1983.

(b) **Enclosed Landscape.** Adapted from: U.S. Forest Service, 1973.

(c) **Ephemeral Landscape.** Adapted from: Yeomans, W.C., 1983.

(d) **Feature Landscape.** Source: Yeomans, W.C., 1983.

(e) **Focal Landscape.** Adapted from: Yeomans, W.C., 1983.

(f) **Panoramic Landscape.** Adapted from: Yeomans, W.C., 1983.

LANDSCAPE, CULTURAL:

The attachment of a particular culture or historical value to a familiar local landscape. (Robinson et al. 1976.)

LANDSCAPE TYPE:

An area of landform plus land cover forming a distinct, homogenous component of a landscape, differentiated from other areas by its degree of slope plus a single pattern of land cover. A landscape type is a unique segment of the environment. This segment or portion of the environment can be separated from other segments on the basis of the land cover and the landform. Any landscape type can be subdivided into unique landscape subtypes, through definition of the desired homogenity of the landscape type. For example, a forest is composed of different tree types, and each tree is itself made up of branches, a trunk, foliage, and so on. (Vaughn 1974.)

LANDSCAPE UNIT:

An area of volume of distinct landscape character which forms a unit spatially enclosed or partially enclosed at ground level; the extent of a landscape type which forms the dominant character of an area of landscape which is not spatially enclosed.

LANDSCALE VALUE (VALUE SYSTEM):
1. The particular (frequently subjective) point of view of an individual or the common point of view of a group on an issue, way of life, or concerning the worth of things or experiences. (Schwarz et al. 1976.)
2. An individual or collective conception of that which is desirable. This conception usually has both emotional and symbolic components. Values may range from those that are subjectively meaningful to a given individual to those that are shared cultural norms. They influence the selection of the means and ends of actions, and they serve as criteria by which objects or actions are evaluated. (O'Connell 1974.)

(Landscape Value):

(a) Agrarianism—A value system of rural origin typified by high values attached to independence, self-sufficiency, family farms, and the occupation of farming. (Schauman et al. 1982.)

(b) Ruralism—A value system of urban origin. A back-to-nature and antiurban philosophy. (Schauman et al. 1982.)

(c) Pastoralism—It is an attitude of urbanites to the countryside. It is a romantic vision of peacefulness and retreat amid scenic beauty, and it carries none of the functional or economic attitudes that the farmer, of necessity, must hold toward the land. (Schauman et al. 1982.)

QUALITY:
A degree of excellence; superior in kind; a distinguishing attribute.

SCENERY:
The general appearances of a place; the features of a landscape (Webster 1960.)

SCENIC AREA:
1. U.S. Forest Service usage. A place which has been designated by the Forest Service as containing outstanding or matchless beauty which requires special management to preserve these qualities. (U.S. For. Serv., FSM 2362.41, June 1975). Areas of this type and all other special interest areas are identified and formally classified primarily because of their recreational values. (Schwarz et al. 1976.)
2. An area preserved primarily because of its present beauty, such as cliffs, streams, vistas, vegetation, and wildlife. (U.S. Bur. Outdoor Recreation 1974.)
3. A place which has been designated by the Bureau as containing outstanding scenic quality and requires special management to preserve or enhance this quality. (U.S. Bur. of Land Manage. 1977.)
4. An area whose landscape character exhibits a high degree of variety, harmony, and contrast among the basic visual elements which results in a pleasant landscape to view.

SCENIC CORRIDOR:
The visible land area outside the highway right-of-way and generally described as "the view from the road." (Calif. Counc. on Intergov. Relat. 1973.)

SCENIC DISTINCTION:
An indicator of scenic quality derived from the combination of distinct elements seen in a landscape. High scenic distinction is attributed to vivid and attractive features in unified and memorable settings, or to extensive, cohesive, and visually rich landscapes. The following terms may be used to describe the range of scenic qualities exhibited by landscapes:

Scenic Qualities:

(a) Vivid: Of very high clarity and contrast; visually outstanding; making a very strong and memorable impression the senses.

(b) Conspicuous: Obviously contrasting and widely visible; a focus for attention; easily distinguished in a complex visual setting; memorable.

(c) Definite: Sufficiently contrasting to be identified in form and extent, but not particularly noticeable in its setting.

(d) Distinct: Obviously contrasting and widely visible; a focus for attention; easily distinguished in a complex visual setting; memorable; contrasting; distinguishable as to color and form; visually separable from its setting; clearly recognizable.

(e) Indefinite: Obscure, subdued, or of low contrast; concealed or partly identifiable in some settings. (Tetlow et al. 1977.)

SCENIC QUALITY:

The degree of harmony, contrast, and variety within a landscape; the overall impression retained after driving through, walking through, or flying over an area of land and/or water.

VISUAL CHARACTER:

The visual character of a landscape is formed by the order of the patterns composing it. The elements of these patterns are the form, line, color, and texture of the landscape's visual resources. Their interrelationships can be objectively described in terms of dominance, diversity, continuity, and so on. (Jones and Jones 1977.)

VISUAL CHARACTER TYPE (Character type, visual type):

U.S. Forest Service, Visual Management System usage. A large area of land that has common distinguishing visual characteristics of landform, rock formations, water forms, and vegetation patterns. (U.S. For. Serv. 1974.)

VISUAL LANDSCAPE CHARACTER (Characteristic landscape):

1. U.S. Forest Service, Visual Management System usage. The overall impression created by a landscape's unique combination of visual features (such as land, vegetation, water, structures) as seen in terms of form, line, color, and texture. (U.S. For. Serv. 1973.)

2. The naturally established landscape being viewed as visually represented by the basic vegetative patterns, landforms, rock formations, and water forms which are in view. (U.S. For. Serv. 1974.)

3. A visual landscape character unit usually makes up a small portion of a visual character subtype, depending upon how much of the subtype unit can be viewed at one time. (After U.S. For. Serv. 1974.)

VISUAL CORRIDOR:

A continuous succession of visually and spatially distinct experiences; series of consecutive or composite viewsheds. Each visually and spatially distinct experience. (Jones and Jones 1977.) See following figure.

Visual Corridor. Adapted from: Yeomans, W.C., 1983.

VISUAL QUALITY:

The visual significance given to a landscape determined by cultural values and the landscape's intrinsic physical properties. (A.C.E. 1984). While many factors contribute to a landscape's visual quality, they can ultimately be grouped under three headings: vividness, intactness, and unity. Analogous concepts: scenery quality rating (B.L.M.), variety class (U.S.F.S.). (Jones and Jones 1977.)

VISUAL RESOURCE(S):

Those natural and cultural features of the environment which can potentially be viewed. (A.C.E. "V.I.A. Manual" 1984.)

1. The composite of basin terrain, geologic features, water features, vegetative patterns, and land use effects that typify a land unit and influence the visual appeal the unit may have for visitors. (Sandpoint Zone Plann. Team 1974.)

2. The land, water, vegetative, animal, and other features that are visible on all lands. (U.S. Bur. of Land Manage. 1977).

3. The appearance of the features that make up the visible landscape. Includes the land, water, vegetative, animal, and other features that are visible on all national resource lands. (U.S. For. Serv. 1973).

BASIC ELEMENTS:

The four major elements (form, line, color, and texture) which determine how the character of a landscape is perceived. (U.S. Bur. of Land Manage. 1977.)

Form:

(a) The perceived aggregation of elements in which there is a consciousness of the distinc-

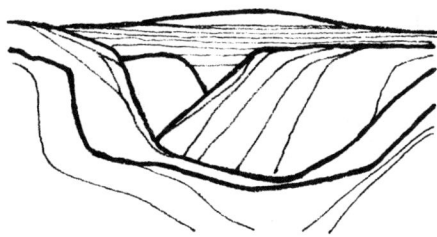

Form. Source: Yeomans, W.C., 1983.

tion and relation of a whole to its parts (Santayana 1955.)

(b) One of the four basic elements of visual pattern (usually the strongest); the mass or shape of an object. (Jones and Jones 1977.)

(c) The mass or shape of an object or objects that appear unified, such as in the shape of the land surface or pattern placed on the landscape. (U.S. Bur. of Land Manage. 1977.)

(d) In visual arts, shape, especially solid shape, as in statement that the form, color are elements in art. Also made of arranging or co-ordinating the factors in a work of art. As distinct from physical form of the object. (Runes and Sehrickel 1946.)

Line:

(a) A very thin, threadlike mark; a border or boundary; a division between conditions, and so forth; limit; demarcation. (Webster 1960.)

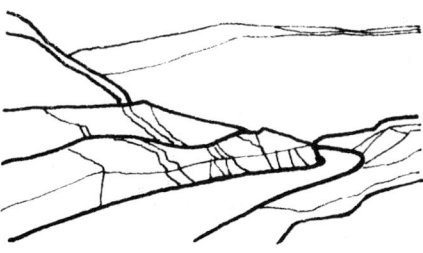

Line. Source: Yeomans, W.C., 1983.

(b) One of 7 elements of art: point, line, plane, texture, color, mass, space; the point is the easiest element to understand, but line is the easiest to follow; has direction as well as position. (Baldinger 1960.)

(c) Geometrically, a point that has been extended, or the intersection of two planes, for example, a silhouette, or a boundary between patterns in the landscape. The second strongest of the four basic visual pattern elements. (Jones and Jones 1977.)

(d) The path, real or imagined, that the eye follows when perceiving abrupt differences in form, color, or texture. Within landscapes, lines may be found as ridges, skylines, structures, changes in vegetative types, or individual trees and branches. (U.S. Bur. of Land Manage. 1977.)

Color:

(a) Is the general name for the nonspatial component of the sensation arising from the activity of the retina of the eye and its associated nerve systems. (Runes and Sehrickel 1946.)

Color. Source: Yeomans, W.C., 1983

(b) The property of reflecting light of a particular wavelength of otherwise identifiable objects. (U.S. Bur. Land Mgt. 1977.)

(c) A phenomena of light (as red, brown, pink, and so forth) or visual perception that enables one to differentiate otherwise identical objects. A hue, as contrasted with black, white, or grey. (U.S. For. Serv. 1973.)

(d) The third of the four basic elements of visual pattern; the hue (for example, red or blue) and value (for example, light or dark) of the light reflected or emitted by an object. (Jones and Jones 1977.)

Chroma: Purity of a color, or its freedom from white or grey. (Burnhart 1963.)

Hue: That attribute of certain colors which enables them to be classified as reddish, greenish, bluish, yellowish, or purplish. (Runes and Sehrickel 1946.)

Saturation: The measure of the actual color content in a given sensation. (Kepes 1944.)

Tint: Any color tone which has more or less brilliance than it would have in its spectral hue. (Runes and Sehrickel 1946.)

Value: Relative lightness or darkness of a color. (U.S. For. Serv. 1973.)

Texture:

(a) The arrangement of the particles or constituent parts of any material, as wood, metal, and so forth, structure, composition. (Webster 1960.)

Texture. Source: Yeomans, W.C., 1983.

(b) The structural quality of a work of art; a visual "feel" of material: rough, smooth, hard, soft, and so forth. (Baldinger 1960.)

(c) Aggregate of parts so small as to register as a continuous surface and not as discrete parts or objects in a composition; an aggregation of forms. (Hubbard and Kimball 1917.)

(d) The visual or tactile surface characteristics of something. (U.S. For. Serv. 1973.)

LANDSCAPE FEATURES:

The land and water form, vegetation, and structures which compose the characteristic landscape. (U.S. Bur. of Land Manage. 1977.)

Landscape Features. Adapted form: Yeomans, W.C., 1983.

Land Form:

(a) The form of the surface of the land. The three-dimensional shape of the surface of the ground. *Land form* may have a different meaning than *landform* when used in a geomorphological context. *Landform* is always used for surface features whose origin can be attributed to particular geological processes or particular structures. (After Savigear 1965.)

Landform. Adapted from: Yeomans, W.C., 1983.

(b) Term used to describe the many types of land surfaces which exist as a result of geological activity, such as a plateau, plain, basin, mountain, and so forth. (U.S. For. Serv. 1974.)

(c) A feature of the earth's surface with distinctive form characters which can be attributed to the dominance of particular processes or particular structures in the course of its development and to which the feature can be clearly related. (Savigear 1965.)

(d) *Land form* may have a different meaning than *landform* when used in geomorphological contexts. *Land form* is sometimes used when referring only to the three-dimensional shape of the ground surface—without any reference to the processes responsible for that shape. (Savigear 1965.)

(e) A term used to describe the many types of land surfaces which exist as the result of geologic activity and weathering, for example, pleateaus, mountains, plains, and valleys. (U.S. Bur. of Land Manage. 1977.)

Morphology: Within the subject matter of geomorphology, the meaning of *morphology* is restricted to studies of the surface form of the earth—without any reference to the processes responsible for those forms. *Morphology* is not synonymous with *geomorphology*. (After Savigear 1965.)

Vegetative Patterns: General plant community types in an area such as nature and exotic species, debris, and so forth.

Structures: Things which are built or constructed by man such as buildings, dams, hardtop roads, and so forth.

Water Bodies: The water of an ocean, river, stream, pond, and so forth.

LAND USE:

Various human activities which impact the landscape in a variety of ways. Examples of land use types are: industrial, commercial, residential, agricultural, recreational, and undeveloped. (A.C.E. 1984.)

LAND USE INTENSITY:

The degree to which a landscape is used by human activities. Examples of landscape intensity are: urban, suburban, rural, and wilderness. (A.C.E. 1984.)

NODE(S):

1. A point of concentration; a central point. (Webster 1960.)

2. Points, the strategic spots in a city into which an observer can enter, and which are the intensive foci to and from which he or she is traveling. They may be primarily junctions, places of a break in transportation, a crossing or convergence of paths, moments of shift from one structure to another. Or the nodes may be simply concentrations, which gain their importance from being the condensation of some use or physical character. (Lynch 1960.)

LANDMARK(S):

1. Another type of point reference into which one may not enter, rather the experience of which is external. (Lynch 1960.)

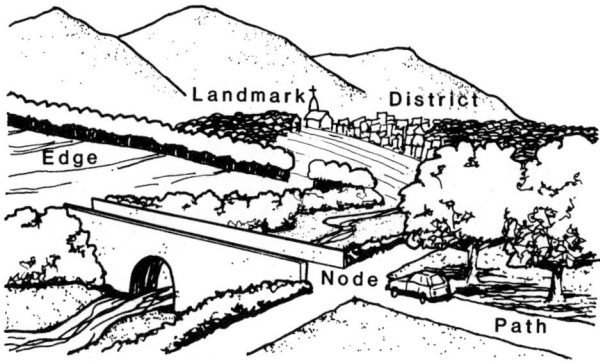

Urban Image Elements. Source: R. Lambe, 1983.

2. Another type of point reference, but in this case the observer does not enter within them; they are external. They are usually a rather simply defined physical object: building, sign, store, or mountain. Some landmarks are distant ones, typically seen from many angles and distances, over the tops of smaller elements, and used as radial references. They may be within the city or at such a distance that for all practical purposes they symbolize a constant direction. (Lynch 1976.)

PATH(S):

1. Path (route) along which the observer moves. Context: urban highway. (Lynch 1960.)

2. The channels along which the observer customarily, occasionally, or potentially moves. They may be streets, walkways, transit lines, canals, railroads. For many people, these are the predominant elements in their image. People observe the city while moving through it, and along these paths the other environmental elements are arranged and related. (Lynch 1976.)

DISTRICT:

1. Medium to large sections of the city having some recognizable character (elements forming city image: district, edge, landmark, node, path).

2. The medium to large sections of the city, conceived of as having two-dimensional extent, which the observer mentally enters "inside of," and which are recognizable as having some common, identifying character. Always identifiable from the inside, they are also used for exterior reference if visible from the outside. (Lynch 1960.)

EDGES:

The linear elements not used or considered as paths by the observer. They are the boundaries between two phases, linear breaks in continuity: shores, railroad cuts, edges of development, walls. They are lateral references rather less penetrable, which close one region off from another; or they may be seams, lines along which two regions are related and joined together. These edge elements, although probably not as dominant as paths, are for many people important organizing features. (Lynch 1960.) Linear elements noted or considered as edges by the observer; serve as boundaries. (Baldinger 1960.)

CONTOUR:
The outline of a figure, mass, land, and so forth. (Webster 1960.)

SKYLINE:
The line along which the sky seems to touch the earth; the visible horizon; the outline (as of a city) seen against the sky. (Webster 1960.)

SLOPE:
An area of landform surface differentiated from other areas by its degree of slope. It is a component of landforms but is not limited in place or extent, for example, cliff, gentle slope, flat plain. Analogous concept: landtype. (U.S. For. Serv. 1974.)

ASPECT:
The side or surface facing a given direction. (Am. Coll. Dict. 1963.)

AERIAL PERSPECTIVE:
Concerning the effects of distance from the viewer upon the color and distinctness of objects—especially as due to the transparency of the intervening air. Typically objects become bluer, greyer, edges less distinct, and there is less contrast of light and shade with increasing distance from the viewer. (After Runes and Sehrickel 1946.)

ANGLE OF OBSERVATION:
The vertical angle between a viewer's line of sight and the slope or object being viewed. (U.S. Bur. of Land Manage. 1977.)

ANGLE OF VISION:
About 20 degrees. The pictorial compositional relation within this angle can be perceived well without being distracted by the necessity of turning the eye or head. (Hubbard and Kimball 1917.)

ATMOSPHERIC CONDITIONS:
Fog, precipitation, pollution, and so forth which affect the visibility of an object or objects. These conditions can greatly impact the visual contrast of form, line, color, and texture.

Atmospheric Conditions:
(a) Absorbtion: The wavelengths of light are selectively absorbed or "taken up"; as a result,

Atmospheric Conditions. Adapted from: Yeomans, W.C., 1983.

different colors are seen. They can also have a uniform shift which results in a contrast change.

(b) Reflection: Light is often redirected or "cast back"; as a result, changes in color or intensity are seen.

(c) Refraction: the change of direction of a ray of light in passing obliquely from one medium into another in which its speed is different.

(d) Diffraction: A modification that light undergoes when it passes by an edge of an opaque body, or is sent through small apertures, resulting in the formation of a series of light and dark bands, prism colors, or spectra. (Burnhart 1963.)

BACKLIGHTING:
A situation where the light source is coming from behind the object being viewed; objects are generally in shadow with highlighted edge. See figure Lighting Direction on page 320.

BACKGROUND LIGHTING:
This is the distance in the landscape where elements lose detail distinctions. Emphasis is on the outline or edge of one land mass against another with a strong skyline element. See figure Lighting Direction on page 320.

BRIGHTNESS:
1. Brightness, that is, the sensation that one color appears lighter or darker than another, governs the value of the color. (Kepes 1944.)
2. The amount of reflected light of an object relative to its field (Arnheim 1954.)

COLOR CONTRAST:
Value and hue tend to be the more significant subelements of color in determining visual contrast between colors.

CRITICAL VIEWPOINT:

The point(s) commonly in use or potentially in use where the view of a management activity is the most disclosing. (U.S. Bur. of Land Manage. 1977.) See figure Viewpoints on page 320.

CROSS-SECTION (X section):

1. Graphic methods usage. A two-dimensional pictoral representation method which shows the characteristics and relationship between land (and/or water) characteristics that would be observed in a vertical slice through that portion of the earth. (After Durrenberger 1973.)

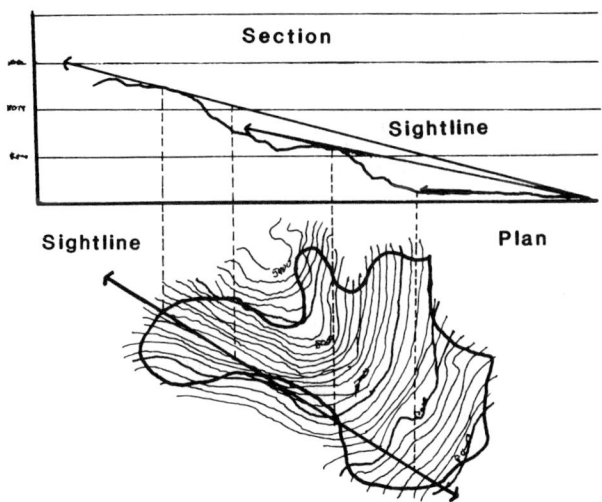

Cross-Section. Source: Ministry of Forests B.C., 1981.

2. In land use planning, cross-sections frequently only show land surface conditions (soil, soil moisture, vegetation type distributions, elevation, slope steepness, and so forth), though they may also be used to illustrate subsurface geological structures, groundwater relationships, and so forth. The vertical scale of projection is frequently exaggerated in relation to the horizontal to emphasize topographic relationships, for example, while the scale of horizontal projection may be 1 in. = 10 ft., the vertical projection scale may be 1 in. = 1 ft. Thus slopes will appear steeper and elevation changes more rapid than they truly are. This geographical method is frequently used to analyze or show the impacts that would result from potential land uses or use practices on an area, by superimposing over the natural profile the changes in land surface (and/or subsurface) conditions that would result. (Schwarz et al. 1976.)

DISTANCE:

The spatial separation between an observer and subject (that is, visual); categorized as foreground, middleground, and background. (A.C.E. 1984.)

DISTANCE ZONES:

1. The area that can be seen as foreground-middleground-background, or seldom seen (see previous definitions). (U.S. Bur. of Land Manage. 1977.)

2. Three conventional terms in painting—foreground, middleground, background—which can be helpful in describing distance relationships. (Jones and Jones 1977.)

Distance Zones:

(a) Foreground (0 to ¼–½ mile): That area which can be designated with clarity and simplicity not possible in middle and background because the observer is a direct participant. The observer can have the impressions of immediate details—bark, pattern, boulder forms, or degraded parts. This is a zone of important linkage because it sets a tone of quality or its absence. Intensity of color and its value will be at a maximum level, lacking the effect of color diminution due to atmospheric scattering of light rays. At greater distances, the intensification of aerial perspective becomes an important means of discrimination. (Jones and Jones 1977.)

Distance Zones. Adapted from: Yeomans, W.C., 1983.

(b) Middleground (¼–½ to 3–5 miles): A critical area for two reasons: This is where the parts of the landscape can be seen to join together, where hills become a range or trees make a forest. This is also where man-made changes may be revealed as sitting comfortably upon the landscape, or where conflicts of form, color, shape or scale show up. Colors will be unmistakable, but they will be more blue, softer than those of the foreground. Some of the sharpness of value contrasts will be reduced. (Jones and Jones 1977.)

(c) Background (3–5 to infinite miles): That area where distance effects are primarily explained by aerial perspective. Surfaces of landforms will lose detail distinctions, emphasis will be on outline or edge, with background becoming an effective foil against which foreground or background is more clearly seen—a figure-ground relationship. Silhouettes and ridges of one land mass against another are the conspicuous visual parts of the background with skyline the strongest line of all. (Litton 1972.)

INTERVISIBILITY:

The principle that from any point visible to an observer, the observer can also be seen. (Jones and Jones 1977.)

KEY OBSERVER POSITION (K.O.P.):

One or a series of observer positions on a travel route or at a use area or a potential use area. (U.S. Bur. of Land Manage. 1977.)

LIGHT:

Has been recognized as part of the electromagnetic field, the visible radiations being of such magnitude that they must be measured in fractions of microns (one thousandth of a millimeter), falling within the range of approximately 380 to 740 millimicrons. (Runes and Sehrickel 1946.) (a) The sensation aroused by stimulation of the visual receptors. (b) Something which makes vision possible. (U.S. For. Serv. 1973.)

LIGHTING DIRECTION:

Backlighting. A viewing situation in which sunlight is coming toward the observer from behind a feature or elements in a scene. (Jones and Jones 1977.)

Front Lighting: A situation where the light source is coming from behind the observer and falling directly upon the area being viewed. (Jones and Jones 1977.)

Sidelighting (Side Lighting):

(a) A viewing situation in which sunlight is coming from the side of the observer to a feature or elements in a scene. (Jones and Jones 1977.)

(b) A situation where the light source is coming from one side of a scene or object being viewed, usually the most critical for displaying contrast. (U.S. Bur. of Land Manage. 1977.)

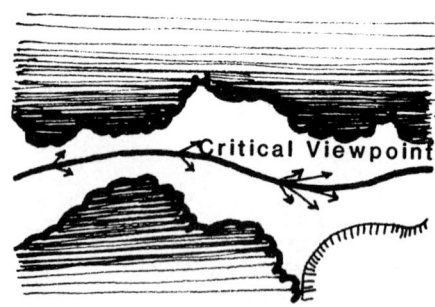

Viewpoints. Adapted from: Felleman, J.P., 1979.

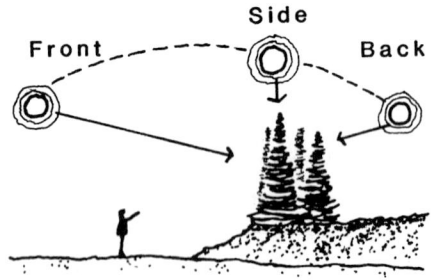

Lighting Direction. Source: Felleman, J.P., 1979.

LANDSCAPE CONTROL POINTS:

A network of permanently established observation sites which provide the means of studying the visual impact of alternatives to the landscape (Similar terms: observation points, observer viewpoints). (Litton, 1972.) See figure above.

OBSERVER POSITION:

1. The placement and relationship of a viewer to the landscape which is being perceived. (U.S. Bur. of Land Manage. 1977.)

2. A term employed to describe the observer's elevational relationship between himself or herself and the landscape he or she sees. It is used

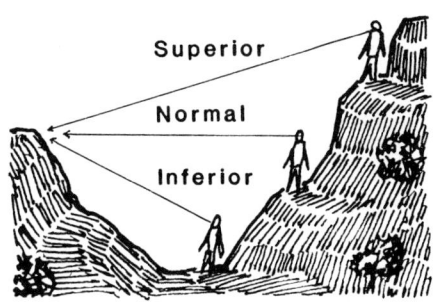

Observer Position. Adapted from: Yeomans, W.C., 1983.

to indicate whether the observer is essentially below, at the same level, or above the visual objective. Three specific terms are used: (a) observer inferior—viewer below object; (b) observer normal—viewer on level of object; (c) observer superior—viewer above object. (Jones and Jones 1977.)

SEEN AREA:
That portion of the landscape which can be viewed from one or more observer positions. The extent of area that can be viewed is normally limited by land form, vegetation, or distance. (U.S. Bur. of Land Manage. 1977.)

SHADE:
1. Darkness of certain areas on objects caused by those parts being faced away from the source of light. (Runes and Sehrickel 1946.)
2. Any hue moved in the direction of black. (Baldinger 1960.)

SHADOW:
Darkness due to light being cut off by some intercepting material. (Runes and Sehrickel 1946.)

SIGHTLINE:
The unobstructed line of sight between an observer and viewed object. (Jones and Jones 1977.)

SIMULATION:
1. The realistic visual portrayal which demonstrates the perceivable changes in the landscape features of a proposed management activity through the use of photography, artwork, computer graphics, and other such techniques. (U.S. Bur. of Land Manage. 1977.)
2. An abstraction or simplification of a real-world situation. In its broadest sense, any model is a simulation since it is designed to represent the most important features of some existential conditions. (U.S. Gen. Account. Off. 1969.)

Simulation Types:
(a) Real-world prototype: Simulation method which uses field testing to portray changes in the environment such as balloons representing a tower structure.
(b) 2-D iconic: Simulation method which uses graphics, such as perspective sketches to represent a change in the environment; a two-dimensional representation.
(c) 3-D iconic: Simulation method which uses a three-dimensional representation of the environment such as a model.
(d) Digital/math: Simulation method which uses formulas and/or computers to represent the environment.
(e) Analog: Simulation method which uses a phenomena which behaves in the same way as another yet are based on different energy systems in representing the environment.
(f) Hybrid: Simulation method which combines two or more of the aforementioned methods.

VIEW:
Something, especially a broad landscape or panorama, that is looked toward or kept in sight; the act of looking toward this object or scene. (U.S. Forest Service 1977.)

VIEWER ACTIVITY:
The extent of a viewer's ability to perceive the landscape and its detail may be heightened or decreased by the visual requirements of his or her current activity and past experience of the landscape. (Jones and Jones 1977.)

VIEWER AWARENESS:
A viewer's receptivity to the visual character of the landscape can be affected by elements and relationships in the landscape setting itself or by expectations about the setting. Visual experience contrary to expectation may be suppressed or heightened, depending on the degree of disagreement. (Jones and Jones 1977.)

VIEWER EXPOSURE:
The degree to which viewers are exposed to a view by their physical location, number of viewings and duration of view. (Jones and Jones 1977.)

VIEWER SENSITIVITY:

The viewer's variable receptivity to the elements within the environment that he is viewing, affected by viewer activity and awareness. A person cannot readily notice every object and all the attributes of the objects that compose the total visual environment. Analogous concept: sensitive level. (U.S. For. Serv. 1974; U.S. Bur. of Land Manage. 1977.)

VIEWING ANGLE:

The angle at which an object is seen. This angle may affect the perception of that object by: (1) perspective foreshortening when seen obliquely or at a low viewing angle, thereby reducing apparent sizes of surfaces or areas, (2) increasing the object's relative scale when seen perpendicularly.

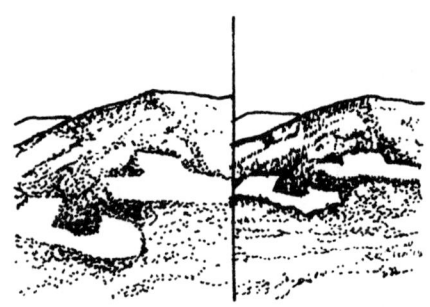

Viewing Angle. Source: Yeomans, W.C., 1983.

VIEWSHEDS:

1. All the surface areas visible from an observer's viewpoint.
2. Surface areas from which a critical object or viewpoint is seen. Analogous terms: seen area, visible area. (Jones and Jones 1977.)

Viewsheds, Existing and Topographic:

(a) Existing viewshed: The area normally visible from an observer's viewpoint, including the screening effects of intermediate vegetation and structures.

(b) Topographic viewshed: The area which would be visible from a viewpoint based on landform alone, without the screening effect of vegetation and structures.

Viewsheds Composite: Composite of overlapping areas visible from a continuous sequence of viewpoints along a road; or a network of viewpoints surrounding a road (or object).

VISIBILITY:

The geographic extent of a resource and legibility of its features which can be seen by an observer(s), determined by his or her location. (A.C.E. 1984.)

VISIBILITY MODEL: See figure below.

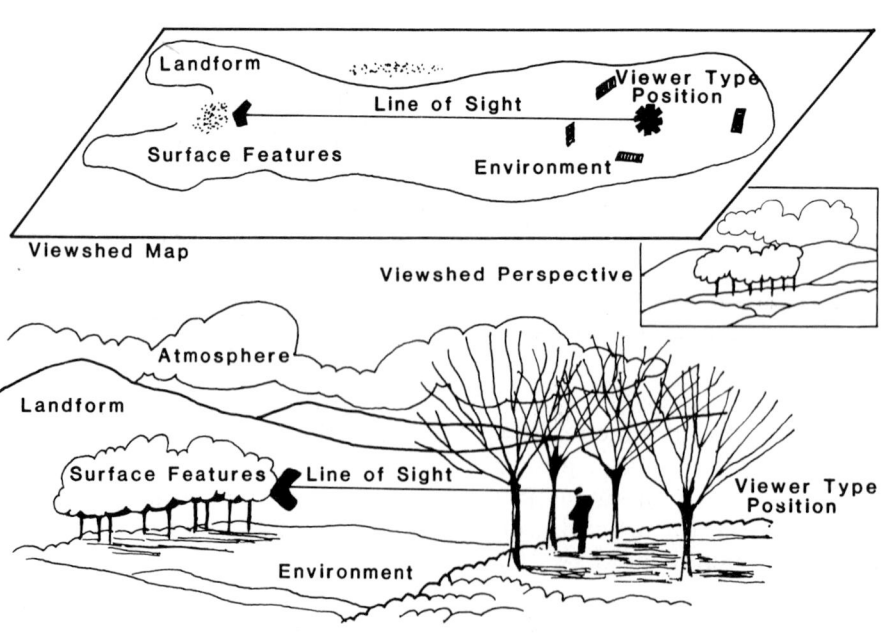

Visibility Model. Source: Felleman, J.P., 1979.

ACCESSIBILITY:

General proximity in terms of time of all points in the region to a given kind of activity or facility (elements of spatial pattern: grain, focal organization, accessibility). (Lynch 1961.) The degree to which a resource can be approached. (A.C.E. 1974.)

ENVIRONMENTAL PSYCHOLOGY:

That area of psychology which deals with environmentally induced behavior or mental states of individuals or groups, for example, whereas psychoanalysis probes for subconscious motivations derived from past experience, or behavioral psychology attempts to alter self-concepts through operant conditioning, environmental psychology seeks to determine how the everyday physical environment affects human behavior. Also, the study of human perception of elements in the environment or of different types of environmental settings. Perception in this context is understood to mean not only direct sensory knowledge but also cognitive discrimination expressed in terms of preferences rated on a scale of desirability versus undesirability. (Schwarz et al. 1976.)

EXPERIMENTAL PSYCHOLOGY:

1. The investigation of psychological phenomena by experimental methods.
2. The methods and the results obtained by experiment, systematically set forth (often arbitrarily limited to the psychology of the laboratory).

OBSERVER SET:

The tendency of the observer to perceive a landscape in a manner conditioned by his or her education, habits, psychological state, and previous experience. (Tetlow et al. 1977.)

USER ACTIVITY:

Human behavior which can be evaluated in terms of kind (the variety of activities), use (the number of participating people), and degree (the frequency of the activity).

VIEWER ACTIVITY:

The extent of a viewer's ability to perceive the landscape and its detail may be heightened or decreased by the visual requirements of his or her current activity and past experience of the landscape. (Jones and Jones 1977.)

VIEWER AWARENESS:

A viewer's receptivity to the visual character of the landscape can be affected by elements and relationships in the landscape setting itself or by expectations about the setting. Visual experience contrary to expectation may be suppressed or heightened, depending on the degree of disagreement. (Jones and Jones 1977.)

ASSOCIATION:

The mental connection or bond existing between any sensations, perceptions, ideas, or feelings that to an observer have a relational significance with one another. (U.S. For. Serv. 1973.)

COGNITIVE:

The mental operations involved in the receiving, storing, and processing of information; includes sensory perceptions, memory, thinking, and learning.* (*Differs from usual definition which does not include sensory perception.) (Arnheim 1969.)

IMAGEABILITY:

That quality in a physical object which gives it a high probability of evoking a strong image in any given observer. It is that shape, color, or arrangement which provides a strongly identified, powerfully structural, highly useful mental image of the environment. (Jones and Jones 1977.)

LEGIBILITY:

Ease with which (a city's) parts can be recognized and organized into a coherent pattern. Urban context. (Lynch 1960.)

PERCEPTION:

1. To become aware of, and grasp mentally through primarily sight, but also hearing, touch, taste, and smell. (U.S. Bur. of Land Manage. 1977.)
2. From sensations, we come to be able by experience and habit to perceive the existence of objects in the world, and to attribute to them the characteristics which our senses discover to us; and also, building from our memories of real objects, we may imagine objects which have their characteristics related differently from any which we have actually known. (Hubbard and Kimball 1917.)

VISUAL PERCEPTION:
The visual thinking, the active performance of focusing, scanning and exploration of visual information. (Arnheim 1969.)

ACUITY:
The sharpness or acuteness of vision. (Burnhart 1963.)

FIXATION:
The eye movements that help to select the targets of vision that direct the eyes in a way that the area of the visual field to be scrutinized comes within the narrow range of sharpest vision. Sharpness decreases at a deviation of 10 degrees from the axis of fixation, where it is at a maximum. Retinal sensitivity is so restricted that the eye can and must single out some particular spot, which becomes isolated, dominant, central. This means taking up one thing at a time, and distinguishing the primary objective from its surroundings. (Arnheim 1969.)

FIXATION, OCULAR:
A move from tension to tension reduction by shifting an eccentric stimulus to the center of the visual field. (Arnheim 1969.)

FOCUS:
The point where rays of light and so forth come together, or from which they spread or seem to spread; any center of activity, attention, and so forth. (Webster 1960.)

FORESHORTENING:
The apparent diminuation of intervening spaces because they are seen from an acute angle. (Runes and Sehrickel 1946.)

MOTION PERSPECTIVE:
As with an observer riding in an open car, the horizon and stars (upward) field of view are motionless, whereas the world and the ground below flow past in a continuous stream.

OPTICAL FIELD:
The combination of forces of visual attraction—a point, a line, an area—and the background. (Kepes 1944.)

ORIENTATION:
The necessary information and opportunities to see significant features indicating location, direction, and progress.

Orientation Needs:
(a) Sense of location: The driver's awareness of his or her location in the environment at any point during travel.
(b) Sense of direction: The driver's sense of travel direction, both compass direction (north-south) and geographic direction (for example, along the shore).
(c) Sense of progress: The driver's sense of making progress from his or her origin to his or her destination.

Orientation Satisfiers:
(a) Landmark feature: A prominent or conspicuous object in the landscape that serves as a guide.
(b) Landmark areas: An area having distinctive characteristics and definable boundaries that are useful to the traveler in determining where he or she is.
(c) Linear elements: Features in the landscape with directional characteristics because they lie on a perceived axis and/or connect other features. (Hornbeck et al. 1975.)

PERSPECTIVE:
That which suggest the effects of distance upon the appearance of objects. (Runes and Sehrickel 1946.)

PICTURE PLANE:
1. The theoretical transparent surface of the picture. Perspective reference. (Runes and Sehrickel 1946.)
2. The two-dimensional surface when a view is enclosed by four borders. The two-dimensional picture plane assumes the center of the spatial field and every optical event appears to advance or recede from it. A point, a line, or a shape on the picture surface is seen as possessing spatial qualities. (Kepes 1944.)

RETINA:
The innermost coat of the posterior part of the eyeball consisting of a layer of light-sensitive cells connecting with the optic nerve. (Burnhart 1963.)

Cone: One of the cone-shaped cells of the retina used in color vision.

Rods: Rod-shaped cells in the retina which are thought to be the specific structures for the reception of light for vision at the lower intensities. Rod vision is achromatic—in shades of grey.

SERIAL VISION:

While moving at uniform speed, the environment is often revealed to us in a series of jerks or revelations; such vision is dependent upon contrasts, physical or imagined; two elements: emerging view and existing view. (Cullen 1961.)

TRANSPARENCY:

Mutual overlapping of two objects in different planes so that the overlapped area is made paradoxically to belong to more than one object as if one object were a plane made of glass. (Arnheim 1954.)

VISUAL FIELD:

The boundaries of the visual field are 180° laterally and 150° up and down.

Binocular Field: The field of vision seen by two eyes at one time.

Monocular Field: The field of vision seen by one eye at one time.

CLOSE-ENDED QUESTION:

Any question which is structured in such a way that the person must respond in a prescribed form. (Rubin and Elder 1980.)

Does your office ever get
warm enough to make
you feel uncomfortable?

( ) often
( ) sometimes
( ) only occasionally
( ) never

Close-Ended Question. Source: Rubin, A.I. & Elder, J., 1980.

DEPENDENT VARIABLE:

The variable whose value changes as a result of the experimenter's changes in another variable, the independent variable. (Rubin and Elder "Building" 1980.)

INDEPENDENT VARIABLE:

1. A variable that can be observed and assessed as a determinant of behavior. (Rubin and Elder 1980.)
2. The variable that is altered independently of any other variable, usually by the experimenter. (Rubin and Elder 1980.)

OPEN-ENDED QUESTION:

Any question which allows the person answering flexibility of form and substance in his response. (Rubin and Elder "Building" 1980.)

What do you think of
your environment?

Open-Ended Question. Source: Rubin, A.I. & Elder, J., 1980.

OPERATIONALISM:

The doctrine that scientific concepts secure their meaning from the relative set of operations involved. (Burnhart 1963.)

PSYCHOPHYSICS:

The branch of psychology which investigates the relationships between physical stimulus magnitudes, or the differences between stimuli and the corresponding sensory experiences. (Rubin and Elder 1980.)

RELIABILITY:

The degree to which results are consistent upon repetition of an experiment or test.

SAMPLE:

A part of a larger set, usually selected deliberately, to investigate the properties of the parent population. (Rubin and Elder 1980.)

Random Sample: A sample selected by using a random selection procedure. Each individual or object in the population most have a known (for example, equal) chance of being included. Selection of one individual or object should not affect the selection of another.

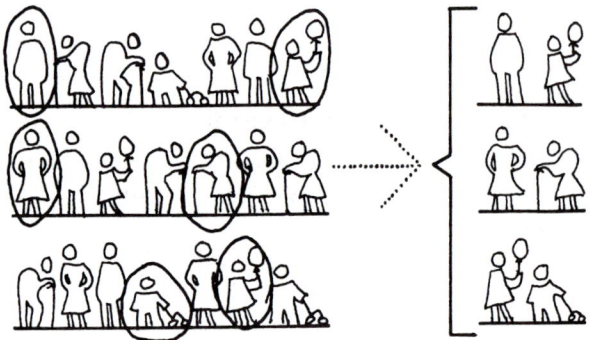

Random Sample. Source: Rubin, A.I. & Elder, J., 1980.

Stratified Sample: A sample selected from a population which has been divided into parts, a portion of the sample coming from each stratum.

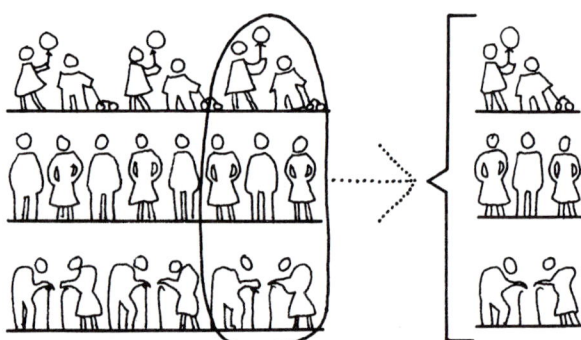

Stratified Sample. Source: Rubin, A.I. & Elder, J., 1980.

SAMPLING:
To select a number and type of individual or object members from a class. (Rubin and Elder 1980.)

VALIDITY:
The degree to which a research study or test can predict performance in a realistic situation—that is, where the problem investigated actually exists.

ENVIRONMENTAL DISPLAYS:
The researcher must define the environment to be assessed. This may be a clearly defined geographical area (for example, Manhattan Island, Yosemite National Park) or a general environmental type (for example, metropolitan environments, wildlands). In either case, it is unlikely that observers will be able to comprehend the whole environment from one viewpoint. The researcher must select those views that best represent the environment. Three strategies are commonly used: (1) random selection, (2) rational selection, and (3) public selection.

OBSERVERS:
It is normally not possible to ask every potential user's opinion. Total user populations are frequently very large and difficult to identify. Therefore researchers must find their observer group by sampling (1) randomly, (2) according to availability, or (3) by proposing a surrogate group.

PRESENTATION MEDIA:
The visual quality of landscape must be simulated if potential visual impacts are going to be assessed. Among the media available for simulation are: (1) sketches, (2) models, (3) computer graphics, (4) photographs, and (5) graphic montages. The use of simulations raises questions concerning the validity of such techniques.

RESPONSE FORMATS:
It is necessary for the researcher to establish a method to elicit observer descriptions and perceptions of the landscape. While there are well-established and widely recognized methods available, a host of conceptual and methodological issues are associated with their use. (Craik and Feimer 1979; Daniel 1976; Wohlwill 1976.) These issues include: (1) the reliability that the results can be replicated; (2) the validity that the method measures what it purports to measure; (3) the sensitivity of the method to distinguish actual differences; (4) the generality of the method's application across diverse environments and observers; and (5) the utility of the method for the landscape planners and managers needing to assess visual quality and impacts. These issues have not been comprehensively addressed for any visual assessment response format. However, the past decade has seen repeated use of several methods without any obvious difficulties that would eliminate them from further consideration. These methods for quantifying visual qualities include: (1) rating scales, (2) Q-sorts, (3) rank ordering, and (4) checklists. They also include more holistic cognitive methods for systematically describing visual qualities such as: (5) similarity sorts, (6) observer-employed photography, and (7)

cognitive maps. This list should not be considered exhaustive.

LANDSCAPE ATTRIBUTES:
Qualities, characteristics, or properties pertaining to the landscape.

Closure: Forces of organization driving toward spatial order, toward stability, tend to shape optical units into closed compact wholes. Confronted with a complex optical situation, the beholder searches for the form with the most stable unity, or with the least disturbed relationships to the environment. (Kepes 1944.)

Discontinuity: Lack of continuity or cohesion. (U.S. For. Serv. 1973.)

Distinct: A resource or activity which is considered unique and as an asset of an area. It is typically known as a visual/aesthetic draw and/or has many distinctive attributes. Diversity and compatibility are characteristic in such a resource. (A.C.E. 1980.) Clearly marking a landscape or landscape feature as different from others.

Diversity: The number of pattern elements as well as the variety among them and edge relationships between them. (Jones and Jones 1977.)

Dominant:
(a) Ruling: governing; predominant; exercising influence. (Webster 1960.)
(b) One of two contrasting elements must clearly dominate the other. One is the feature, the other the supporting backdrop. (Simonds 1961.)

Harmony: The representation of all opposed elements (in a work of art) in such a way as to become a pleasing unity; generally the task of art is to bring the distinct parts into a unified whole, or to demonstrate them as components of one unified law and thus excite aesthetic satisfaction—harmony is the main requirement of every art. (Runes and Sehrickel 1946.)

Intactness: The integrity of visual order in the natural and man-built landscape, and the extent to which the landscape is free from visual encroachment. (Jones and Jones 1977.)

Monotony: Complete repetition; tedious sameness. (U.S. For. Serv. 1973.)

Seasonal Change: Change brought about by seasonal variation (that is, vegetation color, density of foliage) which may affect aesthetic perception of an area. (A.C.E. 1984.)

Sequence:
(a) Units arranged that motion of attention from unit to unit is easiest in a certain direction. Progressive change of at least one characteristic in a series of objects. (Hubbard and Kimball 1917.)
(b) A succession of perceptions or experiences having continuity. (Simonds 1961.)

Similarity: A physiographic area of land which has common characteristics of ecoregions, land use, land use intensity and water resource. Similarity zones are assigned a specific management classification. (A.C.E. 1984.)

Uniqueness: A resource-oriented criterion: a visual resource, visual character, or visual quality which is rare or uncommonly found at a regional or national scale. (Jones and Jones 1977.)

Unity:
(a) Harmony of the total scene. (Simonds 1961.)
(b) The degree to which the visual resources of the landscape join together to form a coherent, harmonious visual pattern. Unity refers to the compositional harmony or intercompatibility between landscape elements. (Jones and Jones 1977.)

Variety: An intermixture of succession of different things, or qualities. (U.S. For. Serv. 1973.)

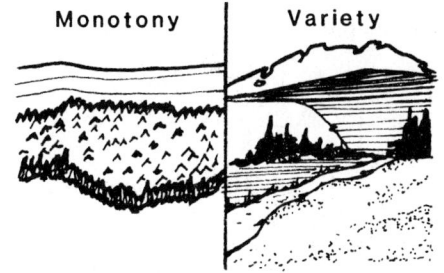

Monotony/Variety. Source: Grinde, K., 1984.

(a) Relief from monotony; not a principle of organization, but the pleasure of its perception is a principle of the organization of the human mind. (Hubbard and Kimball 1917.)

(b) The state or quality of being varied and having the absence of monotony or sameness. (U.S. Bur. of Land Manage. 1977.)

Vividness:

(a) The memorability of the visual impression received from contrasting landscape elements as they combine to form a striking and distinctive visual pattern. (Jones and Jones 1977.)

(b) The quality in a landscape which gives distinction and makes it visually striking. (Litton et al. 1971.)

FORMAL AESTHETIC ATTRIBUTES:

Accent:

(a) A detail or area emphasized.

(b) Emphasis laid on a part of a design or composition.

(c) A small detail or area emphasized.

(d) An object used for emphasis.

Asymmetry: (See Balance, asymmetrical).

Axis:

(a) A main line of direction, motion, growth, or extension.

(b) A straight line with respect to which a body, figure, or system of points is symmetrical.

Axis. Adapted from: Yeomans, W.C., 1983.

Balance:

(a) Stability produced by even distribution of masses.

(b) An aesthetically pleasing integration of elements; harmony.

Balance (symmetrical or formal): An imaginary line drawn vertically through the center of the arrangement will divide it into two equal parts, and each part will appear as the reverse of the other.

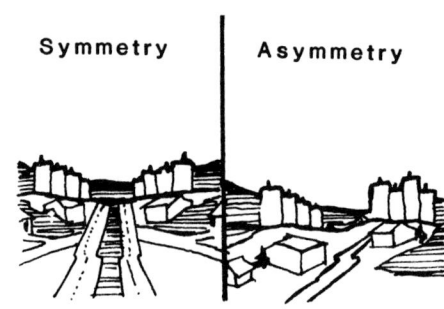

Symmetry/Asymmetry. Adapted from: Jones and Jones, 1977.

Balance (asymmetrical): Occult balance. Disposition of objects neither similar nor similarly placed but still so chosen and arranged that the sum of the attractions on one side of the vertical axis is equal to the sum of the attraction on the other side.

Compose: To form by uniting two or more things; to put together; to form, frame, or fashion; to create.

Composition: The putting together and organization of components in a work of art; the product of such organization.

Continuity: Uninterrupted connection, succession, or union.

Mass: A quantity of matter cohering together so as to make one body, usually of indefinite shape.

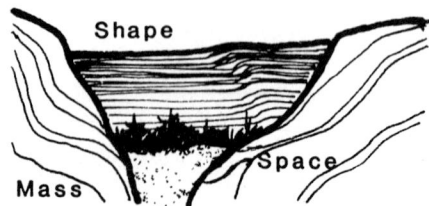

Shape, Mass, Space. Source: Kopf A. B., 1984.

(a) A quality of matter forming a body of indefinite shape and size, usually of relatively large size; a lump. (Webster 1960.)

(b) One of the elements of art: bulk or quantity of matter. (Baldinger 1960.)

Order:
(a) The manner in which one thing succeeds another; arrangement, sequence, or succession in space or time. (b) The totality of arrangements composing some sphere of action or being.

Pattern: An arrangement of parts, elements, or details that suggests a design or somewhat orderly distribution.

Proportion: The relation of one part to another or to the whole with respect to magnitude, quantity, or degree.

Repetition: Units all the same in interest and ability to attract attention, or at least the same throughout in some characteristic.

Rhythm: Harmonious or orderly movement, fluctuation, or variation with recurrences of action of situation at fairly regular intervals.

Shape:
(a) Spatial aspects of appearance. (Arnheim 1954.) See figure on bottom page 328.
(b) Perceived relation of an object's parts. (Hubbard and Kimball 1917.)
(c) The grasping of structural features found in, or imposed upon, the stimulus material. Perception of shape consists in fitting the stimulus material with templates of relatively simple shape, visual concepts, or categories. (Arnheim 1954.)

Silhouette: Any dark shape or outline seen against a light background.

Silhouette. Adapted from: Yeomans, W.C., 1983.

Space:
(a) Distance, interval, or area between or within things; extent, room. (Webster 1960.) See figure on bottom of page 328.
(b) That which in three dimensions corresponds to "background" in two dimensions. (Rasmussen 1959.)
(c) A limited extention in one, two or three dimensions; a volume.

Symmetry: Balanced proportions; the correspondence of parts in size, shape, and relative position, especially on opposite sides of a dividing line or about an axis.

Transition: A passing from one state, stage, place, or subject to another, especially without abruptness.

VISUAL IMPACT ATTRIBUTES:

Absolute Scale: Absolute size; relation of the size of any given object to a definitely designated standard (generally in relation to man). (Hubbard and Kimball 1917.) The absolute size of an object obtained by relating the size of the object to definitely designated (that is, measured) standard. (A.C.E. 1984.)

Absolute Scale. Adapted from: U.S.D.A. Forest Service, 1973.

Codominance: Two dominating features of relatively equal visual importance in one scene. (U.S. For. Serv. 1973.)

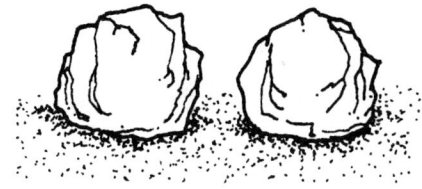

Codominance. Source: U.S.D.A. Forest Service, 1973.

Congruence: Agreeing or harmonious in character of the landscape.

Contrast:
(a) Diversity of adjacent parts, as in color, tone, or emotions.
(b) The closer the juxtaposition of two dissimilar perceptions, in time or space, the more powerful the appeal to the attention. (U.S. For. Serv. 1973.)

Disability Glare: Glare resulting in reduced visual performance and visibility. (Rubin and Elder 1980.)

Discomfort Glare: Glare which results in a feeling of annoyance. It does not necessarily interfere with visual performance or visibility. (Rubin and Elder 1980.)

Dominance: Dominance of components or specific features in a scene may be dominant because of prominent positioning, contrast, extent, or importance of pattern elements. (Jones and Jones 1977.)

Dominant:
(a) Ruling; governing, predominant; exercising influence. (Webster 1960.)

Dominance. Source: U.S.D.A. Forest Service, 1973.

(b) One of two contrasting elements must clearly dominate the other. One is the feature, the other the supporting backdrop. (Simonds 1961.)

Dominant Elements: The basic elements (form, line, color, texture) in a particular landscape which exert the greatest influence on the visual character of the landscape. (U.S. Bur. of Land Manage. 1977.)

Fitness: A judgment of how much the landscape exhibits the care of the people who tend it.

Fragility: A judgment of the landscape's ability to accept development without diminishing visual quality. (Schauman et al. 1982.)

Intrusion: A feature (land and water form, vegetation, or structure) which is generally considered out of context with the characteristic landscape. (U.S. Bur. of Land Manage. 1977.)

Landscape Compatibility: The degree to which landscape elements/characteristics are unified with their setting. (A.C.E. 1984.)

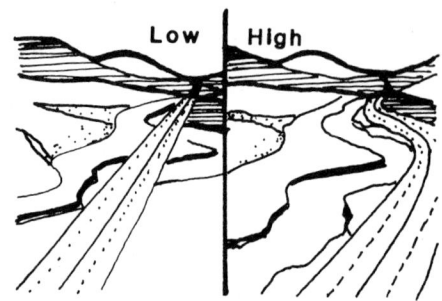

Landscape Compatibility. Source: Jones and Jones, 1977.

Landscape Control Points: A network of permanently established observation sites which provide the means of studying the visual impact of alterations to the landscape (similar terms: observation points, observer viewpoints). (Litton 1972.)

Relative Scale: The apparent size relationship between landscape components and their surroundings. (A.C.E. 1984.)

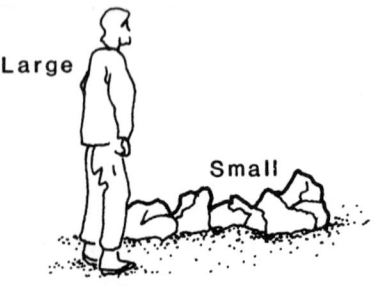

Relative Scale. Adapted from: U.S.D.A. Forest Service, 1973.

Scale:

(a) Visual scale is the apparent size relationships between landscape components or features and their surroundings. (Jones and Jones 1977.)

(b) A system of grouping or classifying in a series of steps or degrees according to a standard of relative size, amount, importance, perfection, and so forth; progressive graduated series. (Webster 1960.)

(c) The amount of open space around an object creates a factor called scale. Scale, too, is a matter of relationship. (Baldinger 1960.)

(d) Relative size of objects. (Hubbard and Kimball 1917.)

(e) Graphics usage. The proportional relationship (ratio) between the reduced size at which something is being represented on a map or other type of drawing and its true distance or size relationships. (Schwarz et al. 1976.)

(f) The proportionate size relationship between an object and the surroundings in which the object is placed. (U.S. Bur. of Land Manage. 1977.)

Scale Contrast: The difference in absolute or relative scale in relation to other distinct objects or areas in the landscape. (A.C.E. 1984.)

Spatial Dominance: The prevalent occupation of a space in a landscape by an object(s) or landscape element. (A.C.E. 1984.)

Subordinate: Inferior or placed below another in size, brightness, and so forth; secondary in visual impact. (U.S. For. Serv. 1973.)

Visual Absorption: The physical capacity of a landscape to screen proposed development and still maintain its inherent visual character. The degree of visual penetration and the complexity of the landscape affect this capacity. (A.C.E. 1984.) Two major factors affecting the absorption capacity of a landscape are: (1) the degree of visual penetration, and (2) the complexity of the landscape. The degree of visual penetration (that is, the distance into the landscape that you can see from a vantage point) is affected both by vegetation and topography. The higher the visual penetration, the lower the ability of the landscape to visually absorb development and still maintain its existing visual character. Also, the higher the visual complexity within a landscape, the greater the visual absorption. (Vaughn 1974.)

Visual Absorption. Adapted from: Yeomans, W.C., 1983.

Visual Compatibility: The degree to which development with specific visual characteristics is visually unified with its setting. (A.C.E. 1984.) Visual compatibility can be evaluated with reference to pattern elements and pattern character. Analogous concepts: contrast rating (B.L.M.), visual absorption criteria (U.S.F.S.), external harmony. (Tunnard and Pushkarev 1963.)

Visual Contrast: The difference in appearance between two (or more) elements and/or an element and its background. (A.C.E. 1984.)

Visual Dominance: That visual object(s) which exerts the greatest influence on the visual character of the landscape. (A.C.E. 1984.)

Visual Dominance. Adapted from: Jones and Jones, 1977.

Visual Impact: The significance and/or severity of visual resource quality change as a result of anticipated activities or land use that are to take place (or have taken place) on or adjacent to the landscape. (A.C.E. 1984.)

(a) A contrasting intrusion in the unified order of landscape, seen and appreciated as a misfit in appearance or function. A visual impact contributes to a reduction in scenic values. (Tetlow et al. 1977.)

(b) The degree of change in visual resources and viewer response to those resources caused by highway development and operations. (Jones and Jones 1977.)

Adverse Visual Impact: Any impact on the land or water form, vegetation, or any introduction of a structure which adversely changes or interrupts the visual character of the landscape and disrupts the harmony of the natural elements. (U.S. Bur. of Land Manage. 1977.)

Visual Sensitivity: The degree of observer interest in visual quality and concern for existing conditions and/or proposed changes in the landscape. (A.C.E. 1984.)

Visual Sensitivity Level(s) (Sensitivity level):
(a) U.S. Forest Service, Visual Management System usage. A three-level rating system used to delineate areas receiving different amounts of exposure (present or potential) to user groups with differing attitudes towards changes in scenic quality (such as might occur as a result of management activities). The system initially classifies all travel routes, special interest areas, and water bodies into areas of primary and secondary aesthetic management importance on the basis of their national importance, number of users, duration of use, and area size. The system next uses the assumption that aesthetic users and minor concern to functional users of forest areas (such as daily commuters and loggers) as the other basis for classifying the entire planning area into the three sensitivity levels. (After U.S. For. Serv. 1974.)

(b) An index of the relative degree of user interest in scenic quality and concern for existing or proposed changes in the landscape features of that area in relation to other areas in the planning unit. (U.S. Bur. of Land Manage. 1977.)

Visual Vulnerability: An evaluation of a landscape's ability to accept change without diminishing visual quality. (A.C.E. 1984.)

(a) Measure of the degree to which a given landscape is capable of absorbing man's impacts without significant modification of its positive visual qualities. High vulnerability indicates that natural conditions are easily disturbed, and that such disturbances would be highly visible in the event of development; low vulnerability conditions permit development to be absorbed with less evident alteration to the landscape. (Tetlow et al. 1977.)

(b) The degree to which man-made changes might be seen in the landscape and their potential for degradation (of scenic quality); in essence, the landscape's resistance or susceptibility to visual changes. (Litton 1974.)

(c) The susceptibility of an object or changed condition to critical evaluation as a consequence of its location in a position where it can be readily seen by the public. As applied to landscapes, it means their susceptibility to criticism (pro or con) as a consequence of their availability to public observation. (Schwarz et al. 1976.)

AESTHETIC ZONING:

Zoning which regulates property in the interest of protecting aesthetic values. The U.S. Supreme Court, in the 1954 Berman vs. Parker case, upheld this extension of the original legal justification for zoning powers with its finding that "It is within the power of the legislature to determine that the community should be beautiful as well as healthy." (After Abrams 1971.)

Mitigation: A method or procedure designed to reduce or lessen the impacts caused by development in visual activities on the environment.

Rehabilitation: A short-term management alternative which returns existing adverse visual impacts, through modification or elimination, to a desired scenic quality. (U.S. Bur. of Land Manage. 1977).

Visual Resource Management Class (VRMC): The degree of visual change acceptable within a designated portion of the characteristic landscape; based upon the physical and sociological characteristics of any given homogeneous area and serving as a management objective.

CARDINAL VALUE (Cardinal unit):
The numerical values assigned to a variable which relate directly with some physical property (height, weight, and so forth). Each number has some meaning by itself about the measured property. Also see Ordinal Values. (Schwarz et al. 1976.)

Interval Scale: A type of scale which does not have an absolute zero point but possesses equal intervals and differences. (Rubin and Elder 1980.)

Ordinal Value: Numerical values assigned to a variable which represents a ranking only. The numerical values have meaning only when compared to one another. Because of this, mathematical operations performed on the value (means, modes, differences, and so forth) will not necessarily be valid, and the results of such operations must be carefully interpreted. Also see Cardinal Value. (Schwarz et al. 1976.)

Ratio Scale: A type of scale consisting of magnitudes with an absolute zero point, for which both intervals (differences) and ratios can be calculated. All statements of ratio must be based on this scale. (Rubin and Elder 1980.)

Weighting:
(a) Assigning numbers to express the relative importance of items in a group or series under consideration. (After Webster 1963.)
(b) The assignment of numerical values to resource yields when their values cannot be directly compared by existing techniques for quantification on some measurement scale. The assigned numerical values are usually referred to as "weights" or "multipliers." As a technique, weighting is usually done according to some more or less objective sense of the relative importance of the different types of resource yields. While weightings are usually added (that is, additive weighting) to obtain a measure of the total social value of resource uses or resource yield mixes for planning areas, they may also be multiplied or divided (or some combination of these processes) to facilitate decision making. (Schwarz et al. 1976.)

SIMULATION:
The realistic visual portrayal which demonstrates the perceivable changes in the landscape features of a proposed management activity through the use of photography, artwork, computer graphics, and other such techniques.

Accuracy: To be in exact conformity to a truth, standard, rule, or model.

Photomontage:
(a) A combination of several distinct photographic pictures so they often blend with or into each other to produce a composite picture which may or may not appear to be made up of separate pictures. (Webster 1963.)
(b) A composite picture or edited film in which contrasting shots or sequences are juxtaposed or blended for the purpose of suggesting a total idea or impression, or developing a theme. (After Webster 1963.)
(c) A composite picture or edited film in which contrasting shots or sequences are placed side by side or blended for the purpose of suggesting a total idea or impression. (U.S. Bur. of Land Manage. 1977.)

Representativeness: The depiction or description of something as having a particular character.

REFERENCES

Abbey, E. 1968. *Desert solitaire.* New York: Ballantine.

Acking, C-A. and G.J. Sorte. 1972. Methods for presenting planned environment. (In Swedish). Lund, Sweden: School of Architecture, Lund Institute of Technology.

Acking, C-A. and R. Küller. 1973. Presentation and judgment of planned environment and the hypothesis of arousal. In *Environmental design research*, edited by W.F.E. Preiser, Stroudsburg, PA.: Dowden, Hutchinson and Ross. 1:72–83.

Acking, C-A., C. Ohlsson, and U. Sjogren. 1976. Environmental simulating methods and public communication. Document 8. Stockholm: Swedish Council for Building Research.

Adrian, T. 1972. Oblix-computer program. Cambridge: Center for Computer Graphics, Harvard University.

Ady, J., B.A. Gray, and G.R. Jones. 1979. A visual resource management study of alternative dams, reservoirs, highway and transmission line corridors near Copper Creek, Washington. In *Our National Landscape*, compiled by G. Elsner and R. Smardon, 590–97.

Aguilo, M. 1981. Metodologia para la evaluacion de la fragilidad visual del paisaje. Ph.D. dissertation. E.T.S. de Ingenieros de Caminos. Madrid: Universidad Politecnica.

Aguilo, M., et al. 1982. *Guia para la elaboracion de estudios del medio fisico.* Contenido y Metodologia. Madrid: CEOTMA.

Allen, M. 1970. *Vision and highway safety.* Philadelphia: Chilton.

Allentuck, M. 1974. Sir Uvedale Price and the picturesque garden: the evidence of the Colerton Papers. In *The Picturesque Garden and its Influence Outside the British Isles,* edited by N. Pevsner, Washington, DC: Dumbarton Oaks, 57–76.

Alonso, S.G., M. Aguilo, and A. Ramos. 1983. *Directrices y Tecnicas Para la Estimacion de Impactos.* Madrid: Trabajos de la Catedra de Planificacion, Universidad Politecnica.

Anderson, J., et al. 1976. Land use and land cover classification system for use with remote sensor data. G.S. Prof. Paper No. 964, U.S.G.S. Washington, DC: U.S.D.I.

Anderson, J.M. 1970. A television aid to design presentation. *Architectural Research and Training* 1:20–24.

Anderson, L., J. Mosier, and G. Chandler. 1979. Visual absorption capability. In *Our National Landscape*, compiled by G. Elsner and R. Smardon, 164–71.

Anderson, L.M. 1981. Land use designations affect perception of scenic beauty in forest landscapes. *Forest Science* 27:392–400.

Anderson, T.W., E.H. Zube, and W.P. MacConnell. 1976. Predicting scenic resource value. In *Studies in Landscape Perception,* edited by E.H. Zube Publ. No. R-76-1. Amherst, MA: Institute for Man and Environment, University of Massachusetts, 6–70.

Andersson, S. 1973. Structure, identity and scale. Proceedings of the Symposium on Landscape Planning. Ljubljana, Yugoslavia.

Andrews, R.N.L. 1979. Landscape values in public decisions. In *Our National Landscape,* compiled by G. Elsner and R. Smardon, 686–92.

Andrews, R.N.L. and M.J. Waits. 1978. *Environmental values in public decisions: a research agenda.* Ann Arbor, MI: School of Natural Resources, University of Michigan.

Angelo, M. 1979. The use of computer graphics in the visual analysis of the proposed Sunshine ski area expansion. In *Our National Landscape,* compiled by G. Elsner and R. Smardon, 439–46.

Appleyard, D. 1969. Why buildings are known. *Environment and Behavior* 1(2):131–56.

Appleyard, D. 1970. Styles and methods of structuring a city. *Environment and Behavior* 11: 100–17.

Appleyard, D. 1977. Understanding professional media: issues, theory and a research agenda. In *Human Behavior and Environment,* edited by I. Altman and J.F. Wohlwill, New York: Plenum 1:43–88.

Appleyard, D. and K.H. Craik. 1978. The Berkeley environmental simulation laboratory and its research program. *International Review of Applied Psychology* 27 (1):53–55.

Appleyard, D., K.H. Craik, M. Klapp and A. Kreimer. 1973. The Berkeley environmental simulation laboratory: its use in environment impact assessment. Working Paper No. 206. Institute of Urban and Regional Development, University of California, Berkeley, California.

Appleyard, D. and L. Fishman. 1977. High-rise building versus San Francisco: measuring visual and symbolic impacts. In *Human Responses to Tall Buildings,* edited by P.J.Conway, Stroudsburg, PA: Dowden, Hutchinson and Ross, 81–100.

Appleyard, D., K. Lynch and J.R. Meyer. 1964. *The view from the road.* Cambridge: MIT Press.

Appleton, J., ed. 1976. *The aesthetics of landscape.* Didcot, Oxon, England: Rural Planning Services, Ltd., Publication No. 7.

Appleton, J. 1975. *The experience of landscape.* New York: Wiley.

Architects Design Group. 1978. Visual impact analysis for a proposed compressor station near Arbroath. Prepared by Architects Design Group for British Gas Corp.

Arnheim, R. 1954. *Art and visual perception.* Berkeley: University of California Press.

Arthur, L.M. 1977. Predicting scenic beauty of forest environment: some empirical tests. *Forest Science* 23(2):151–60.

Arthur, L.M., T.C. Daniel, and R.S. Boster. 1977. Scenic assessment: an overview. *Landscape Planning* 4: 109–129.

Ashihara, Y. 1983. *The aesthetic townscape.* Cambridge: MIT Press.

Atkins, J.T. and W.G.E. Blair. 1983. Visual impacts of highway alternatives. *Garten und Landschaft* 8(83): 632–35.

Babbie, E.R. 1979. *The practice of social research.* Belmont, CA.: Wadsworth.

Bacon, W. and A.D. Twombly. 1979. Visual management system and timber management application. In *Our National Landscape,* compiled by G. Elsner and R. Smardon, 539–547.

Baird, B.E., S.R.J. Sheppard, and R.C. Smardon. 1979. Visual simulation of offshore liquified natural gas (LNG) terminals in a decision-making context. In *Our National Landscape,* compiled by G. Elsner and R. Smardon, 636–644.

Baird, J.C. and E. Noma. 1978. *Fundamentals of scaling and psychophysics.* New York: Wiley.

Baldwin, M.F. 1970. The Santa Barbara oil spill. *University of Colorado Law Review* 42(1): 33–75.

Barker, R.G. 1968. *Ecological psychology.* Stanford, CA: Stanford University Press.

Beauty for America Proceedings of the White House Conference on Natural Beauty. 1965. Washington, DC: U.S. Government Printing Office.

Belasco, W.J. 1981. *Americans on the road.* Cambridge: MIT Press.

Bell, P.A., J.D. Fisher, and R.J. Loomis. 1978. *Environmental psychology.* Philadelphia: W.B. Saunders.

Beveridge, C.E. and D. Schuyler, eds. 1983. *The papers of Frederick Law Olmsted, Vol. III, creating Central Park.* Baltimore, MD: Johns Hopkins University Press, 140–148.

Blair, W.G. E. 1980a. Visual resource management. *Environmental Comment* (June 1980): 6–15.

———. 1980b. Visual success story at a new interchange. *Environmental Comment* (July 1980): 16–19.

Blair, W.G.E., L. Isaacson, and G.R. Jones. 1979. A comprehensive approach to visual resource management for highway agencies. In *Our National Landscape,* compiled by G. Elsner and R. Smardon, 365–372.

Blair, W.G.E., I. Robertson, and D. Dingfield. 1982. The visual effect of port redevelopment alternatives. *Coastal Zone Management Journal* 9(3/4): 323–50.

Blair, W.G.E., D.H. Walters, and E.W.S. Mah. 1982. Substation visual simulation techniques. Prepared by Jones and Jones for Bonneville Power Administration, Portland, Oregon.

Blake, P. 1964. *God's own junkyard*. New York: Holt, Rinehart and Winston.

Blanco, A. and M. Aguilo. 1981. La valoracion del paisaje. In *Enciclopedia del Medio Ambiente*. Madrid: CEOTMA y UPM.

Blau, D.H., M.C. Bowie, and F. Hunsaker. 1979. Visual resources inventory and Imnaha Valley study: Hells Canyon National Recreation Area. In *Our National Landscape*, compiled by G. Elsner and R. Smardon, 428–38.

Boar, J., ed. 1970. *Architectural graphics standards*. New York: Wiley.

Bock, R.D. and L.V. Jones. 1968. *The measurement and prediction of judgment and choice*. San Francisco: Holden-Day.

Bosselman, P. 1983a. Simulating the visual impacts of urban development. *Garten und Landschaft* 8(83): 636–640.

———. 1983b. Visual impact assessment at Berkeley. *Urban Design International* 4:(3)35–7.

Boyle, K.J. and R.C. Bishop. 1984. Lower Wisconsin River recreation: economic impacts and scenic values. Madison, WI: Dept. of Agricultural Economics, University of Wisconsin.

Brace, P. 1980. Urban aesthetics and the courts. *Environmental Comment* (June 1980): 16–19.

Brockman, F. and L.C. Merriam, Jr. 1979. *Recreational use of wildlands*. New York: McGraw-Hill.

Brogden, H.E. 1972. Some observations on two methods in psychology. *Psychological Bulletin* 77:431–437.

Brolin, B. 1980. *Architecture in context*. New York: Van Nostrand Reinhold.

Brookshire, D.S. and T.D. Crocker. 1981. The advantages of contingent valuation methods for benefit-cost analysis. *Public Choice* 36: 235–252.

Brookshire, D.S., B.C. Ives, and W.D. Schulze. 1976. The valuation of aesthetic preferences. *Journal of Environmental Economics and Management*, 3:325–46.

Brush, R.O. 1976. Perceived quality of scenic and recreational environments: some methodological issues. In *Perceiving Environmental Quality: Research and Application*, edited by K.H. Craik and E.H. Zube. New York: Plenum, 47–58.

———. 1980. Landform and scenic preference: a research note. *Landscape Planning* 8:301–306.

———. 1984. Branching out: opportunities and techniques for designing the productive forest. *Landscape Architecture* 75 (3): 54–9.

Brush, R.O. and J.F. Palmer. 1979. Measuring the impact of urbanization on scenic quality: land use change in the Northeast. In *Our National Landscape*, compiled by G. Elsner and R. Smardon, 358–64.

Buhyoff, G.H., W.A. Lueschner, and L.K. Arndt. 1980. Replication of a scenic preference function. *Forest Science* 26 (2):227–30.

Buhyoff, G.H. and J.D. Wellman. 1979. Environmental preferences: a critical analysis of a critical analysis. *Journal of Leisure Research* 11:215–18.

Buhyoff, G.H., J.D. Wellman, and T.C. Daniel. 1982. Predicting scenic quality for mountain pine beetle and western spruce budworm vistas. *Forest Science* 28:827–38.

Buhyoff, G.H., J.D. Wellman, H. Harvey, and R.A. Fraser. 1978. Landscape architects' interpretation of people's landscape preferences. *Journal of Environmental Management* 6:255–62.

Burke, H.D., G.H. Lewis, and H.R. Orr. 1968. A method for classifying scenery from a roadway. *Park Practice Guideline Development* 3–68: 125–41.

Burnham, J.B., et al. 1974. A technique for environmental decision-making using quantified social and aesthetic values. BNWL-1787. Richland, WA.: Battelle Northwest Laboratories.

Buttell, F.H. and W.L. Flinn. 1977. Conceptions of rural life and environmental concerns. *Rural Sociology* 42:544–55.

California, University of, Wildland Research Center. 1959. Conserving wildland resources through research. Introductory Report. Berkeley: Univ. of California Agricultural Experiment Station, Wildland Research Center.

Carlson, A.A. 1977. On the possibility of quantifying scenic beauty. *Landscape Planning* 4 (2): 131–172.

Carp, F., R. Zawadski, and H. Shorham. 1976. Dimensions of urban environment and quality. *Environment and Behavior* 8 (2): 239–264.

Carr, S. and P. Schissler. 1969. The city as a trip: perceptual selection and memory in the view from the road. *Environment and Behavior* 1:7–35.

Catlin, G. 1968. An artist proposes a national park. In *The American Environment*, edited by R. Nash, Reading, MA: Addison-Wesley, 5–9.

Cerney, J.W. 1974. Scenic analysis and assessment. CRC Critical Reviews. *Environmental Control* 4(2): 221–50.

Chenoweth, R.E. 1983. A multidimensional scaling analysis of aesthetic preferences. In D. Amadeo, J.B. Griffin and J.J. Potter, eds., EDRA 1983 Proceedings of the 14th International Conference of the Environmental Design Research Assn., University of Nebraska, Lincoln, Nebraska, 145.

———. 1984. Visitor employed photography: a potential tool for landscape architecture. *Landscape Journal* 3(2): 136–43.

Chenoweth, R.E. and B.J. Niemann. 1983. *Scenic beauty evaluation of the Alpine Lakes Wilderness area.* Madison, WI: Landmark Resarch.

———. 1984. Lower Wisconsin River boaters survey. Madison, WI.: Dept. of Landscape Architecture, University of Wisconsin.

Cherem, G.J. 1973. Looking through the eyes of the public, or public images as social indicators of aesthetic opportunity. In Aesthetics Opportunity Colloquium Proceedings. Logan, UT: Utah State University.

———. 1977. Visitor employed photography: a tool for interpretive planning on river environments. In *Proceedings River Recreation Management and Research Symposium.* Minneapolis, MN: U.S.D.A. For. Serv. Gen. Tech. Rep. NC-28, North central For. Exp. Stn.

Chisholm, C., R. Holzheimer, and J. Robinson. 1974. *Nantucket Island: an analysis of the natural and visual resources.* Cambridge: Harvard Graduate School of Design, Dept. of Landscape Architecture.

Ciccetti, C. and V.K. Smith. 1973. Congestion, quality deterioration, and optimal use: wilderness recreation in the Spanish Peaks Primitive Area. *Social Science Research* 2:18–30.

Clark, D.B., et al. 1976. Assessment of major industrial applications: a manual. London: Dept. of the Environment, Research Report No. 13.

Clark, K. 1961. *Landscape into art.* Boston: Beaver Press.

Clawson, M. 1959. *Methods for estimating demand for and value of outdoor recreation.* Washington, D.C.: Resources for the Future. Reprint No. 10.

Cohen, H., T. McLaren, S. Moss, R. Petyk, and E. Zube. 1977. *Pedestrians and wind in the urban environment.* Institute for Man and Environment Report R-77/13. Amherst, MA: University of Massachusetts.

Cole, B. *Sienese painting.* New York: Harper and Row.

Colorado Department of Highways. 1978. *I-70 in a mountain environment, Vail Pass, Colorado.* FHWA-TS-78-208. Washington, DC: Dept. of Highways for the Federal Highway Administration in cooperation with U.S. For. Serv.

Conner, J.R., K.C. Gibbs, and J.E. Reynolds. 1973. The effects of water frontage on recreational property values. *Journal of Leisure Research* 5(2): 26–36.

Cook, T.D. and D.T. Campbell. 1979. *Quasi-experimentation: design and analysis issues for field settings.* Boston: Houghton Mifflin.

Coomber, N.H. and A.K. Biswas. 1973. *Evaluation of environmental intangibles.* Bronxville, NY: Geneva.

Cordell, H.K. and J.C. Hendee. 1982. *Renewable resources recreation in the United States: supply, demand and critical policy issues.* Washington, DC: American Forestry Assn.

Costonis, J.J. 1982. Law and aesthetics: a critique and a reformulation of the dilemmas. *Michigan Law Review* 80:355–461.

Coughlin, R.E., R.E. Dunlap, R. Kaplan, W.R. Sims, C. Steinitz, and H. Vaux. 1982. Assessing aesthetic attributes in planning water resource projects. *Environmental Impact Assessment Review.* 3 (4):406–417.

Council on Environmental Quality. 1979. *Environmental quality—1979: the tenth annual report of the Council of Environmental Quality.* U.S. Government Printing Office, Washington, DC.

Countryside Commission for Scotland. 1978. *Scotland's scenic heritage.* Perth, Scotland.

Cox, G.C. and C.F. Wilkinson. 1981. *Federal public land and resources law.* New York: Foundation.

Craik, K.H. 1968. The comprehension of the everyday physical environment. *Journal of the American Institute of Planners* 34:29–37.

———. 1971. The assessment of places. In *Advances in Psychological Assessment*, edited by P. McReynolds. Palo Alto, CA: Science and Behavior Books.

———. 1972. Appraising the objectivity of landscape dimensions. In *Natural Environments: Studies in Theoretical and Applied Analysis,* edited by J.V. Krutilla, Baltimore, MD: Johns Hopkins University Press, 292–346.

———. 1975. Individual variations in landscape description. In *Landscape Assessment: Values, Perceptions and Resources,* edited by E.H. Zube, R.O. Brush and J. Gy. Fabos, Stroudsburg, PA: Dowden, Hutchinson and Ross, 130–150.

Craik, K.H. and D. Appleyard. 1980. Streets of San Francisco: Brunswiks lens model applied to urban inference and assessment. *Journal of Social Issues* 36:72–85.

Craik, K.H., D. Appleyard, and G.E. McKechnie. 1980. Impressions of a place: effects of media and familiarity among environmental professionals. Research Technical Report. Institute of Personality Assessment and Research, University of California, Berkeley, California.

Craik, K.H. and N.R. Feimer. 1979. Setting technical standards for visual assessment procedures. In *Our National Landscape,* compiled by G. Elsner and R. Smardon, 93–100.

Craik, K.H. and E.H. Zube, eds. 1976. *Perceiving environmental quality: research and application.* New York: Plenum.

Cronbach, L.J. 1957. The two disciplines of scientific psychology. *The American Psychologist* 12:671–84.

Crystal, J.H. and R.O. Brush. 1978. Measuring scenic quality at the urban fringe. *Landscape Research* 3 (3):9–11, 14.

Cuff, D. 1979. Graphic and mental representation of environments. In *Environmental Design: Research, Theory and Application*, edited by A.D. Seidel and S. Danford, Washington, DC: Environmental Design Research Assn., 10–17.

Cullen, G. 1971. *The concise townscape.* New York:Van Nostrand Reinhold.

Cunningham, M.C., J.A. Carter, C.P. Reese, and B.C. Webb. 1973. Toward a perceptual tool in urban design: a street simulation pilot study. In *Environmental Design Research*, edited by F.E. Presier, Stroudsburg, PA.: Dowden, Hutchinson and Ross. 1:62–71.

Cutler, M.R. 1972. A study of litigation related to management of Forest Service administered lands and its effect on policy decisions, part 2: a comparison of four cases. Thesis submitted to Dept. of Resource Development, Michigan State University, Lansing, Michigan.

Dana. S.T. and S.K. Fairfax. 1980. *Forest and range policy.* New York: McGraw-Hill.

Daniel, T.C., L.M. Anderson, H.W. Schroeder, and L.W. Wheeler III. 1977. Mapping the scenic beauty of forested landscapes. *Leisure Sciences* 1:35–53.

Daniel, T.C. and R.S. Boster. 1976. *Measuring landscape aesthetics: the scenic beauty estimation method.* U.S.D.A. For. Serv. Research Paper RM-167, Rocky Mountain For. and Range Exp. Stn., Fort Collins, Colorado.

Daniel, T.C. and W.H. Ittelson. 1981. Conditions for environmental perception research: comment on "the psychological and representation of molar physical environments" by Ward and Russell. *Journal of Experimental Psychology: General* 110:153–57.

Daniel, T.C. and H.W. Schroeder. 1979. Scenic beauty estimation model: predicting perceived beauty of forest landscapes. In *Our National Landscape*, compiled by G. Elsner and R. Smardon, 514–23.

Daniel, T.C. and J. Vining. 1983. Methodological issues in the assessment of landscape quality. In *Behavior and the Natural Environment*, edited by I. Altman and J.F. Wohlwill, New York: Plenum, 39–84.

Davis, K.C. 1971. *Administrative law treatise.* 1970. Supplement. St. Paul, MN: West.

Dearden, P. 1980. Landscape assessment: the last decade. *Canadian Geographer*, 24(3):316–325.

Diamond, H.L. et al. 1983. *Outdoor recreation for America—1983: an assessment twenty years after the report of the Outdoor Recreation Resources Review Commission.* Washington, DC: Resources for the Future.

Dick, B. 1981. Generic visual impact checklist. Syracuse, NY: School of Landscape Architecture, C.E.S. & F., S.U.N.Y.

Dillman, D.A. 1978. *Mail and telephone surveys: the total design method.* New York: Wiley.

Dougal, M.D., et al. 1973. Summary report—Ames Reservoir environmental study. Iowa State Water Resources Research Institute, Iowa State University, Ames, Iowa.

Downing, A.J. 1869. *Rural essays.* New York: Geo. A. Leavitt.

Downs, R.M. 1970. The cognitive structure of an urban shopping center. *Environment and Behavior* 2:13–39.

Draper, J.B. 1974. The Rainbow Bridge Case and reclamation projects in reserved areas. *Natural Resources Journal* 14(3): 431–445.

Dunn, M.C. 1974a. Landscape evaluation: a further perspective. *The Planner*, 10:935–36.

———. 1974b. Landscape evaluation technique: an appraisal and review of the literature. Birmingham, England: Centre for Urban and Regional Studies, University of Birmingham.

Dutton, C.E. 1882. *Tertiary history of the Grand Canyon District.* Monographs of the U.S. Geological Survey, Vol. II. Washington, DC: U.S. Government Printing Office.

Echelberger, H.E. 1979. The semantic differential in landscape research. In *Our National Landscape*, compiled by G. Elsner and R. Smardon, 524–31.

Economic Research Service. 1981. U.S. population grew faster in non-metro areas. In *Rural Development Perspectives*. Washington, DC: U.S. Dept. of Agriculture.

EDAW, Inc. 1978a. Platte River Power Authority Rawhide Energy Project visual analysis. Prepared by EDAW, Inc., Environmental Planning for Platte River Power Authority.

———. 1978b. Visual sensitivity of river recreation to power plants. Prepared by EDAW, Inc. for Power Plant Siting Staff, Minnesota Environmental Quality Board, St. Paul, Minnesota.

EDAW, Inc., A. Lind, and S.R.J. Sheppard. 1981. Aesthetic resource evaluation of the California coastline. In POCS Technical Paper 81-5, U.S.D.I., Bureau of Land Management, 114–47.

Ekbo, G. 1969. *The landscape we see.* New York: McGraw-Hill.

Ellsworth, J. 1982. Visual assessment of rivers and marshes: an examination of the relationship of visual units, perceptual variables and preference. Unpublished Masters thesis, Dept. of Landscape Architecture, Utah State University, Logan, Utah.

Elsner, G.E. 1979. Computers and the landscape. In *Our National Landscape*, compiled by G. Elsner and R. Smardon, 88–92.

Elsner, G.E. and R.C. Smardon, tech. compilers. 1979. *Proceedings of Our National Landscape, a conference on applied techniques for analysis and management of the visual resource.* Gen. Tech. Rpt. PSW-35, U.S.D.A., Forest Service, Pacific Southwest Forest and Range Exp. Stn., Berkeley, California.

Engen, T. 1971. Psychophysics: scaling methods. In *Experimental Psychology*, edited by J.W. Kling and L.A. Riggs. New York: Holt, Rinehart and Winston, 47–86.

Environmental Studies Board, Panel on Aesthetic Attributes. 1982. Assessing aesthetic attributes in planning water resource projects. Washington, DC: Environmental Studies Board, National Research Council.

Erickson, D. 1980. Seattle—coping with visual impact. *Environmental Comment* (July 1980): 8–15.

Evans, G.W. and K.W. Wood. 1980. Assessment of environmental aesthetics in scenic highway corridors. *Environment and Behavior* 12 (2):255–273.

Ewald, W.R., Jr. and D.R. Mandelker. 1977. *Street graphics* (2nd printing). Washington, DC: The Landscape Architecture Foundation.

Expert Panel on Project 8. 1973. *Conservation of natural areas and of the genetic material they contain.* Paris:UNESCO.

Fabos, J.G. 1971. An analysis of environmental quality rating systems. In *Recreation Symposium*, edited by E. Larson, 4 ed., Upper Darby, PA: U.S.D.A. Forest Service, Northeastern For. Exp. Stn., 40–55.

Falk, W.W. and T.K. Pinhey. 1978. Making sense of the concept rural and doing rural sociology: an interpretive perspective. *Rural Sociology* 43:547–558.

Feimer, N.R. 1984. Environmental perception: the effects of media, evaluative context and observer sample. *Journal of Environmental Psychology* 4 (1): 61–80.

Feimer, N.R., K.H. Craik, R.C. Smardon, and S.R.J. Sheppard. 1979. Appraising the reliability of visual impact assessment methods. In *Our National Landscape*, edited by G. Elsner and R. Smardon, 286–95.

Feimer, N.R., R.C. Smardon, and K.H. Craik. 1981. Evaluating the effectiveness of observer-based visual resource and impact assessment methods. *Landscape Research* 6:12–16.

Felleman, J.P. 1979. *Landscape visibility—theory and practice.* Syracuse, NY: School of Landscape Architecture, C.E.S.&F., S.U.N.Y.

———. 1982. Visibility mapping in New York's Coastal Zone: a case study of alternative methods. *Coastal Zone Management Journal* 9:249–270.

———. 1983. Simulation methods. *Urban Design International* 4 (3): 32–3.

Felleman, J.P., R.S. Hawks, R.A. Lambe, J.F. Palmer, and R.C. Smardon. 1983. Aesthetic resources: inventory, analysis and evaluation. A short course offered by the U.S. Corps of Engineers, July 18–22, Fort Belvoir, VA. by the School of Landscape Architecture, C.E.S. & F., S.U.N.Y., Syracuse. Multisectional manual.

Fenneman, N.M. 1931. *Physiography of the Western United States.* New York: McGraw-Hill.

Ferguson, A.B., Jr. and W.P. Brysan. 1972. Comment—Mineral King: a case study in Forest Service decision-making. *Ecology Law Quarterly* 2:480–531.

Ferguson, F.E., Jr. and J.L. Haggard. 1973. Regulation of mining land activities in the national forests. *Land and Water Law Review* 8:391–427.

Fines, K.D. 1968. Landscape evaluations: a research project in East Sussex. *Regional Studies* 2:41–55.

Fleming, L. and A. Gore. 1979. *The English garden.* London: Michael Joseph Ltd.

Flinn, W.L. and D.E. Johnson. 1974. Agrarianism among Wisconsin farmers. *Rural Sociology* 39:187–204.

Ford-Robertson, F.C., ed. 1971. *Terminology of forest science, technology, practice and products.* Washington, DC: Society of American Foresters.

Fraser, B. 1982. *Public involvement handbook.* British Columbia: Ministry of Forests.

French, J. 1975. Barreling through the notch. *Sierra Club Bulletin*, 60:8.

Frey, C. 1978. The old man is smiling. *Conservation News*, 43 (4).

Frey, J.E. 1981. Preferences, satisfactions and the physical environments of urban neighborhoods. Ph.D. dissertation, The University of Michigan and University Microfilms International, Ann Arbor, Michigan.

Garling, T. 1976. The structural analysis of environmental perception and cognition: a multi-dimensional scaling approach. *Environment and Behavior*, 8(3): 385–415.

Gerdes, H. and P. Bosselmann. 1980. You ought to be in pictures. *Planning* (December 1980): 12–14.

Gerner Sanderson Faggetter Cheesman and Centre for Environmental Studies. 1979. *Landscape principles study for Upper Yarma Valley and Dandemong Ranges: summary and landscape manage-*

ment. Parville, Australia: Centre for Environmental Studies, University of Melbourne, 1.

Gibson, J.J. 1950. *The perception of visual world.* Boston: Houghton Mifflin.

———. 1960. Pictures, perspective and perception. *Daedalus* 89:216–27.

———. 1966. *The senses considered as perceptual systems.* Boston: Houghton Mifflin.

———. 1971. The information available in pictures. *Leonardo* 4:27–35.

———. 1979. *The ecological approach to visual perception.* Boston: Houghton Mifflin.

Gilg, A.W. 1975. The objectivity of Linton-type methods of assessing scenery as a natural resource. *Regional Studies,* 9:181–190.

Giorgio, J.W. 1972. Parklands and federally funded highway projects; the impact of Conservation, Society v. Texas. *Environmental Affairs,* 1(4): 882–901.

Goodman, W.M. 1972. Scenic Hudson revisited; the substantial evidence test and judicial review of agency environmental findings. *Ecology Law Quarterly* 2:801–865.

Gordon, R.J. and B.A. Shaine. 1978. Alaska natural landscapes. Joint Federal-State Land Use Planning Commission for Alaska.

Gray, B.A., J. Ady, and G.R. Jones. 1979. Evolution of a visual impact model to evaluate nuclear plant siting and design option. In *Our National Landscape,* compiled by G. Elsner and R. Smardon, 491–498.

Grdén, B.G. 1979. Evaluations and recommendations concerning the visual resource inventory and evaluation systems used within the Forest Service and Bureau of Land Management. In *Our National Landscape,* compiled by G. Elsner and R. Smardon, 296–304.

Green, D.M. and J.A. Swets. 1966. *Signal detection theory and psychophysics.* New York: Wiley.

Greenbie, B. 1976. *Design for diversity.* Amsterdam: Elsevier.

Gregory, R.L. 1978. *Eye and brain: the psychology of seeing,* 3rd ed. New York: McGraw-Hill.

Groat, L. 1982. Meaning in post-modern architecture: an examination using the multiple sorting task. *Journal of Environmental Psychology* 2:3–22.

Guarding the World's Heritage. 1980. *Development Forum* 7(8): 46–48.

Hack, G., A. Gerstenberger, D. Graziano, and K. Ovetz. 1974. Improving city streets for use at night: the Norfolk experiment. Prepared for the Norfolk Redevelopment and Housing Authority and William M. C. Lam Associates, Urban Planning Dept. Cambridge: MIT Press.

Haggard, J.L. 1975. Regulation of mining law activities on Federal lands. *Rocky Mountain Mineral Law Institute* 21:349–391.

Hake, H.W. and A.S. Rodwan. 1966. Perception and recognition. In *Experimental Methods and Instrumentation in Psychology,* edited by J.B. Sidowski. New York: McGraw-Hill.

Hampe, G.D. and F.P. Noe. 1979. Highway attitudes and levels of roadside maintenance. In *Our National Landscape,* compiled by G. Elsner and R. Smardon, 373–377.

Hamson, D. and T. Ristau. 1979. A case study: Death Valley National Monument California-Nevada. In *Our National Landscape,* compiled by G. Elsner and R. Smardon, 340–347.

Hanamoto, A. and L. Biesbroeck. 1979. Combining computer and manual overlays—Williamette River Greenway study. In *Our National Landscape,* compiled by G. Elsner and R. Smardon, 610–617.

Harper, D.B. and J.D. Warbach, eds. Visual quality and the coastal zone. Syracuse, NY: College of Environmental Science and Forestry, S.U.N.Y.

Harrison, J.D. and W.A. Howard. 1972. The role and meaning in the urban image. *Environment and Behavior* 4:399–411.

Hart, J.S. 1975. *The look of the land.* Englewood Cliffs, NJ: Prentice-Hall.

Hart, W.J. and W.W. Graham. 1967. How to rate and rank landscapes. *Landscape Architecture* 57:121–22.

Hebblethwaite, R.L. 1973. Landscape assessment and classification techniques. In *Land Use and Landscape Planning,* edited by D. Lovejoy. Aylesbury: Leonard Hill Books, 2:19–50.

Herzog, T.R. 1984. A cognitive analysis of preference for field and forest environments. *Landscape Research* 9(1):10–16.

Herzog, T.R., S. Kaplan, and R. Kaplan. 1976. The prediction of preference for familiar urban places. *Environment and Behavior* 8(4): 627–645.

Hochberg, J.E. 1962. The psychophysics of pictoral perception. *Audio-Visual Communication Review* 10:22–54.

Hochberg, J.E. and V. Brooks. 1962. Pictoral recognition as an unlearned ability. *American Journal of Psychology* 75:624–628.

Hochberg, J. and V. Brooks. 1978. The perception of motion pictures. *In Handbook of Perception, Volume X: Perceptual Ecology,* edited by E.C. Carterette and M.P. Friedman. New York: Academic, 259–306.

Hoffman, H. and W. Kuehnemann. 1979. Comparison of the results of two measuring methods determining the horizontal standard visibility within the visual range. *Atmospheric Environment* 13:1629–1634.

Holland, S.S. 1964. Landforms of British Columbia—a physiographic outline. Bulletin #48, Columbia Dept. of Mines and Petroleum Resources.

Hornbeck, P.L. and G.A. Okerlund, Jr. 1973. *Visual values for the highway user: an engineer's workbook.* For U.S. Dept. of Transportation. Washington, DC: U.S. Government Printing Office.

Hubbard, H. and T. Kimball. 1917. *An introduction to the study of landscape design.* New York: MacMillan.

Hudspeth, T.R. 1982. Citizen participation in revitalization of the Burlington, Vermont waterfront. Burlington: Environmental Program, University of Vermont.

Impact Consultants. 1980. Draft environmental impact statement—MCI telecommunications facility, Pompey, N.Y. Syracuse, NY: Impact Consultants.

Institute of Ecology: 1971. Optimum pathway matrix analysis approach to the environmental decision-making process—test case relative impact of proposed highway alternatives. Athens, GA:University of Georgia.

International Joint Commission. 1975. Preservation and enhancement of the American Falls. International Joint Commission Canada and United States.

Jackson, P., L. Velasqueres, and D.B. Harper. 1977. Scenic and visual resources of the Hudson River Basin, Parts A and B. Syracuse, NY: School of Landscape Architecture, C.E.S. & F., S.U.N.Y.

Jacobs, P. and D. Way. 1969a. How much development can landscape absorb? *Landscape Architecture* 58:70–72.

———. 1969b. *Visual analysis of landscape development.* Cambridge, MA: Dept. of Landscape Architecture, Harvard University.

Jacques, D. 1980. Landscape appraisal: the case for a subjective theory. *Journal of Environmental Management* 10:107–113.

Janke, R. 1978. *Architectural models.* New York: Architectural Press.

Janssens, J. 1984. Looking at buildings: Individual variations in the perception of building exteriors. Lund, Sweden: School of Architecture, Lund Institute of Technology.

Jefferson, T. 1955. *Notes on the State of Virginia.* W. Peden, ed. Chapel Hill, NC: University of North Carolina Press.

Johns, E. 1976. Art, environment and education. In *The Aesthetics of Landscape*, edited by J. Appleton, 90–93.

Johnson, C.G. 1974. Mineral King visual analysis. San Francisco: Landscape Architecture Group, U.S. Forest Service, Region 5.

Johnson, F.R. and A.E. Haspel. 1983. Economic valuation of potential scenic degradation at Bryce Canyon National Park. In *Managing Air Quality and Scenic Resources at National Parks and Wilderness Areas*, edited by R. Rowe and L. Chestnut, Boulder, CO: Westview Press, 235–245.

Johnson, Johnson and Roy, Inc. 1980. Visual improvement plan: downriver industry. Prepared by Johnson, Johnson & Roy, Inc. for Downriver Community Conference, Wyandotte, Michigan.

Jones, G.R., B. Gray, and J. Ady. 1975. Visual impact study: statement of findings alternative closed cycle cooling systems, Indian Point Nuclear Generating Plant. Prepared by Jones & Jones through Battelle Northwest for U.S. Nuclear Regulatory Commission.

Jones and Jones. 1973. A plan for the Nooksack. Prepared for Jones and Jones for Whatcom County Park Board, Bellingham, Washington.

———. 1975. Environmental, ecological and aesthetic resources of the Upper Susitna River, Alaska. Report to the U.S. Army Corps of Engineers, Jones and Jones, Seattle, Washington. Final Report DOD-ACE, Alaska District Contract Number DACW85-C-0057.

———. 1976. Visual impact of high voltage transmission facilities in Northern Idaho and Northeastern Montana. Portland, OR: Bonneville Power Authority.

———. 1977. Aesthetics and resource management for highways. Sponsored by U.S. Dept. of Transportation, Washington, DC.

———. 1980. Visual assessment of alternative uses for Terminal 91. Appendix to Draft Environmental Impact Statement on Alternative Uses for Terminal 91. Prepared for Port of Seattle.

Kansas City, Missouri City Planning Department. 1967. Measuring the visual environment. Community Renewal Program Tech. Rpt. No. 11, Kansas City, Missouri.

Kanter, J. 1980. The Adirondack Park Agency: aesthetic considerations in project review. Unpublished thesis, School of Landscape Architecture, C.E.S. & F., S.U.N.Y., Syracuse, NY.

Kaplan, R. 1973. Predictors of environmental preference: designers and clients. In *Environmental Design Research*, edited by W.F.E. Prieser. Stroudsburg, PA: Dowden, Hutchinson and Ross, 265–274.

———. 1979. A methodology for simultaneously obtaining and sharing information. In *Assessing Amenity Resource Values*, edited by T.C. Daniel, E.H. Zube and B.L. Driver. U.S. Forest Service Gen. Tech. Rpt. RM-68, Rocky Mountain For. and Range Exp. Stn., Fort Collins, Colorado.

Kaplan, S. 1975. Some methods and strategies in the prediction of preference. In *Landscape Assessment: Values, Perceptions and Resources*, edited by E.H. Zube, R.O. Brush, and J.A. Fabos, Stroudsburg, PA.: Dowden, Hutchinson and Ross, 118–119.

———. 1977. Participation in the design process: a cognitive approach. In *Perspectives on Environment and Behavior*, edited by D. Stokols. New York: Plenum, 221–223.

Kaplan, S. and R. Kaplan. 1982. *Cognition and environment: functioning in an uncertain world.* New York: Praeger.

Kaplan, S., R. Kaplan, and J.S. Wendt. 1972. Rated preference and complexity for natural and urban visual material. *Perception and Psychophysics* 12(4): 354–356.

Kates, R. 1966–67. The pursuit of beauty in the environment. *Landscape* 2(16):21–25.

Kaufman, L. 1974. *Sight and mind: an introduction to visual perception.* New York: Oxford University Press.

Kell, G.W. 1979. Project visual analysis for the Allegheny National Forest. In *Our National Landscape*, compiled by G. Elsner and R. Smardon, 565–571.

Kennedy, J.M. 1974. *A psychology of picture perception.* San Francisco: Jossey-Bass.

Kerlinger, F.N. 1973. *Foundations of behavioral research.* New York: Holt, Rinehart and Winston.

Kopka, S.J. 1979. People, planners and policy: is there an interface? In *Our National Landscape*, compiled by G. Elsner and R. Smardon, 730–737.

Kreimer, A. 1977. Environmental preferences: a critical analysis. *Journal of Leisure Research* 9:88–97.

Krutilla, J.V. and A.C. Fisher. 1975. *The economics of natural environments: studies in the valuation of commodity and amenity resources.* Baltimore, MD: Johns Hopkins University Press.

Küller, R. 1972. A semantic model for describing perceived environments. Document 12. Stockholm: National Swedish Institute for Building Research.

———. 1976. The use of space—some physiological and philosophical aspects. In *Appropriation of Space*, edited by P. Korosec-Serfaty, Proceedings of the Strasbourg Conference, CIACO, Louvain-la-Neuve.

———. 1979. A semantic test for use in cross-cultural studies. *Man-Environment Systems* 9(4/5): 253–56.

———. 1980. Architecture and emotions. In *Architecture for People*, edited by B. Mikellides. London: Studio Vista, 87–100.

———. 1986. Environmental psychology in a Swedish perspective. In *Handbook of environmental psychology* edited by I. Altman and D. Stokols. New York: Wiley.

Kunit, E.R. and K.S. Calhoun. 1973. Smith River Highway visual analysis study. Prepared by Royston, Hanamoto, Beck, and Abey, Inc. for U.S. Forest Service Contract 39-4402. U.S.D.A., Forest Service EM-7700-3, Washington, DC.

Kusler, J. 1980. *Regulating sensitive lands: a guidebook.* Cambridge, MA: Ballinger.

Lam, T.C.M. and A.J. Klockars. 1982. Anchor point effects on the equivalence of questionnaire items. *Journal of Educational Measurement* 19:317–322.

Lam, W. and T. Miagni. 1980. Perception and lighting as formgivers for architecture—course manual. Cambridge, MA: W. Lamm Associates.

Lambe, R.A. and P.L. Phillips. 1981. Main Street: a reflection of Lancaster, New Hampshire. In *Community Explorations: A Design and Planning Portfolio*, edited by R. Lambe. Syracuse: School of Landscape Architecture, C.E.S. & F., S.U.N.Y., 29–39.

Landmark Research, Inc. 1981. Final report on valuation of pack river lands in the Alpine Lakes Wilderness area. Madison, WI: Landmark Research.

Langer, S.K. 1951. *Philosophy in a new key.* Cambridge: Harvard University Press.

Latimer, D.A., H. Hogo, and T.C. Daniel. 1981. The effects of atmospheric optical conditions on perceived scenic beauty. *Atmospheric Environment* 15:1865–1874.

Laurie, M. 1975. *An introduction to landscape architecture.* New York: Elsevier.

Leopold, A. 1921. The wilderness and its place in forest recreation policy. *Journal of Forestry* 19(7): 718–721.

———. 1949/1970. *A sand country almanac with essays on conservation from Round River.* New York: Sierra Club, Ballantine.

Leopold, L.B. 1969. *Quantitative comparison of some aesthetic factors among rivers.* U.S.G.S. Circular No. 620, Washington, DC.

Levitt, R.A. 1981. *Physiological psychology.* New York: Holt, Rinehart and Winston.

Lewis, P.H., Jr. 1963. Landscape analysis: Lake Superior South Shore Area. Wisconsin Dept. of Resource Development, Madison, Wisconsin.

———. 1968. The outdoor recreation plan. Wisconsin Development Series, Wisconsin Dept. of Resource Development, Madison, Wisconsin.

Linton, D.L. 1968. The assessment of scenery as a natural resource. *Scottish Geograpical Journal* 84:219–238.

Litton, R.B., Jr. 1968. Forest landscape description and inventories—a basis for land planning and design. U.S. For. Service Research Paper PSW-49. Pacific

S.W. For. and Range Exp. Stn., Berkeley, California.

———. 1972. Aesthetic dimensions of the landscape. In *Natural Environments Studies in Theoretical and Applied Analysis*, edited by J.V. Krutilla. Baltimore and London: Johns Hopkins University Press, 252–291.

———. 1973. *Landscape control points: a procedure for predicting and monitoring visual impacts.* U.S.D.A. Research Paper PSW-91. Pacific S.W. For. and Range Exp. Stn., Berkeley, California.

———. 1974. Visual vulnerability of forest landscapes. *Journal of Forestry* 72 (7):392–397.

———. 1979. Descriptive approaches to landscape analysis. In *Our National Landscape*, compiled by G. Elsner and R. Smardon, 428–438.

———. 1982. Visual assessment of natural landscapes. In *Environmental Aesthetics: Essays in Interpretation*, edited by B. Sadler and A. Carlson, Western Geographical Series. Victoria, B.C.: Dept. of Geography, University of Victoria, 20:97–115.

Litton, R.B., Jr. and R.J. Tetlow. 1978. *A landscape inventory framework: scenic analysis of the Northern Great Plains.* U.S.D.A. For. Serv. Resarch Paper PSW-135. Pacific S.W. For. and Range Exp. Stn., Berkeley, California.

Litton, R.B., Jr., R.J. Tetlow, J. Sorenson, and R.A. Beatty. 1971. *Water and landscape: an aesthetic overview of the role of water in the landscape.* Port Washington, NY: Water Information Center.

Lockard, W.K. 1977. *Drawing as a means to architecture.* Tucson, AZ: Pepper Publishing.

Lynch, K. 1960. *The image of the city.* Cambridge, MA: MIT Press.

———. 1976. *Managing the sense of a region.* Cambridge, MA: MIT Press.

———. 1981. *A theory of good city form.* Cambridge, MA: MIT Press.

Malm, W. 1979. *Visibility and physical perspective: proceedings of the workshop in visibility values.* U.S.D.A., GTR, WO-18, Ft. Collins, Colorado.

Malm, W., K. Kelley, J. Molenar, and T. Daniel. 1981. Human perception of visual air quality (uniform haze). *Atmospheric Environment* 15:1875–1890.

Mann, R. 1979. A technique for the assessment of the visual impact of nearshore confined dredged materials and other built islands. In *Our National Landscape*, compiled by G. Elsner and R. Smardon, 654–659.

Mann, R. and Associates. 1975. *Aesthetic resources of the coastal zone.* Prepared for the Office of Coastal Zone Management/NOAA. Cambridge, MA: Roy Mann Associates.

Marshall, R. 1930. The problem of the wilderness. *Science Monographs* 30:141–148.

Martin, C.L. 1968. *Design Graphics*, 2nd edition. New York: MacMillan.

Marx, L. 1968. Pastoral ideals and city troubles. In *The Fitness of Man's Environment*. Smithsonian Annual II. Washington, DC: Smithsonian Institution Press, 119–144.

MacAdam, D. 1981. Perceptual significance of colormetric data for colors of plumes and haze. *Atmospheric Environment* 15(10/11): 1797–1803.

McCarthy, M. 1979. Complexity and valued landscapes. In *Our National Landscape*, compiled by G. Elsner and R. Smardon, 235–240.

McCloskey, M. 1967. A landscape policy for public lands. *Denver Law Journal* 45(2): 149–166.

McCullagh, M. 1981. The prediction of visibility by optical techniques—an amenity study. *Computer Applications in Geology* 7(389):1008–1031.

McHarg, I. 1969. *Design with nature.* Garden City, NY: Natural History Press.

McKechnie, G.E. 1976. Simulation techniques in environmental psychology. In *Psychological Perspectives in Environment and Behavior*, edited by D. Stokols. New York: Plenum, 169–189.

McPhee, J. 1979. *Coming into the country.* New York: Bantam Books.

Mertes, J.D. and R.C. Smardon. 1984. Application of video (VTR) technology in landscape planning, design and management. In Proceedings of Annual Council of Educators in Landscape Architecture Conference, July 24–27, Guelph, Canada.

Michelsen, W. 1966. An empirical analysis of urban environmental preferences. *Journal of the American Institute of Planners* 32:355–360.

Middleton, W. 1952. *Vision through the atmosphere.* Toronto: University of Toronto Press.

Milgram, S. 1972. Psychological map of New York City. *American Scientist* 60:181–194.

Miller, R.J. 1973. Cross-cultural research in the perception of pictoral materials. *Psychological Bulletin* 80(2): 135–150.

Mills, L.V. 1979. Visual resource management of the sea. In *Our National Landscape*, compiled by G. Elsner and R. Smardon, 717–723.

Ministry of Environment, British Columbia. 1981. *Visual resources.* APD Catalogue 81, Assessment and Planning Division.

Ministry of Environment, British Columbia, Terrestrial Studies Branch. 1981. APD Bulletin 28. Biophysical resources of the Slocan Valley, O.R. Travers, Coordinator.

Ministry of Energy, Mines and Petroleum Resources, British Columbia. 1982. Guide to the energy review process.

Ministry of Environment, British Columbia, Surveys and Resource Mapping Branch. 1982. Terrain classification system.

Ministry of Forests, British Columbia. 1981. *Forest landscape handbook.* W.H. Van Heek, Coordinator.

Moeller, G.H., R. MacLachlin, and D.A. Morrison. 1974. *Measuring perception of elements in outdoor environments.* U.S. For. Serv. Research Paper NE-289, N.E. For. Exp. Stn., Upper Darby, Pennsylvania.

Murray, A.C., ed. 1967. *Methods of landscape analysis.* London: Landscape Research Group.

Murray, B.H. and B.J. Neiman, Jr. 1979. Visual quality testimony in an adversary setting. In *Our National Landscape,* compiled by G. Elsner and R. Smardon, 693–699.

Myklestad, E. and J.A. Wager. 1976. *Preview: computer assistance for visual management of forested landscape.* U.S.D.A. Forest Service Research Paper NE-355.

Nairn, I. 1965. *The American landscape, a critical review.* New York: Random House.

Nassauer, J.I. 1979a. Managing for naturalness in wildland and agricultural landscapes. In *Our National Landscape,* compiled by G. Elsner and R. Smardon, 447–453.

———. 1979b. Visual quality criteria for Illinois. Unpublished Masters thesis, Dept. of Landscape Architecture, University of Illinois, Urbana, Illinois.

———. 1983. Framing the landscape in photographic simulations. *Journal of Environmental Management* 17:1–16.

National Agricultural Lands Study. 1981. *National agricultural land study final report.* Washington, DC: U.S. Government Printing Office.

Nevius, B. 1976. *Cooper's landscapes: an essay on the picturesque vision.* Berkeley: University of California Press.

New York State, Dept. of Env. Conservation. 1982. Visual resources. In *SEQR Handbook.* Albany, NY: N.Y.S., D.E.C.

Nickerson, D.B. 1980. Perspective plot: an interactive analytical technique for the visual modeling of land management activities. In-service report, U.S. For. Serv., Pacific N.W. For. Research Stn., Portland, Oregon.

Niels, D., et al. 1980. *Humanscale: a project of Henry Dreyfuss Associates.* Cambridge, MA: MIT Press.

Nieman, T.J. and J.L. Futrell. 1979. Projecting the visual carrying capacity of recreation areas. In *Our National Landscape,* compiled by G. Elsner and R. Smardon, 420–427.

Note. 1970. Mineral King Valley: who shall watch the watchmen? *Rutgers Law Review* 25(1):103–114.

Note. 1975. Preserving scenic areas: the Adirondack land use program. *The Yale Law Journal* 84:1705–1721.

Oakland, City of. 1982. Draft environmental impact report for Trans Pacific Center phase II. Prepared by Environmental Impact Planning for City of Oakland Planning Dept., Oakland, California.

O'Brien, R.J. *American sublime.* New York: Columbia University Press.

Oles, P.S. 1979. *Architectural illustration: the value delineation process.* New York: Van Nostrand Reinhold.

Olmsted, F.L. 1870. *Public parks and the enlargement of towns.* Cambridge, MA: Riverside Press. Reprinted in *Civilizing American Cities,* edited by S.B. Sutton, Cambridge: MIT Press, 52–99.

Osgood, C.E., G.J. Suci and P.H. Tannenbaum. 1957. *The measurement of meaning.* Urbana, IL: University of Illinois Press.

Outdoor Recreation Resources Review Commission. 1962. *Outdoor recreation for America.* Washington, DC: U.S. Government Printing Office.

Palmer, J.F. 1979a. Conducting a wildland visual resources inventory. In *Our National Landscape,* compiled by G. Elsner and R. Smardon, 109–116.

———. 1979b. The conceptual typing of trail environments: a tool for recreation research and management. In *Assessing Amenity Resource Values,* edited by T.C. Daniel, E.H. Zube, and B.L. Driver, U.S. For. Serv. Gen. Tech. Rpt. RM-68. Fort Collins, Colo.: Rocky Mountain For. and Range Exp. Stn., 14–22.

———. 1980. Approaches for assessing visual quality and visual impacts. Syracuse, NY: School of Landscape Architecture, C.E.S. & F., S.U.N.Y.

———. 1983. Assessment of coastal wetlands in Dennis, Massachusetts. In *The Future of Wetlands: Assessing Visual-Cultural Values,* edited by R.C. Smardon. Totowa, NJ: Allenheld-Osmun Publishers, 65–80.

———. 1983a. A visual character approach to the classification of backcountry environments. *Landscape Journal* 2:3–12.

———. 1983b. Visual quality and visual impact assessment. In *Social Impact Assessment Methods* edited by K. Finsterbusch, L.G. Llewellyn and C.P. Wolf, Beverly Hills: Sage, 263–283.

———. 1984. Neighborhoods as stands in the urban forest. *Urban Ecology* 8:223–236.

Palmer, J.F. and E.H. Zube. 1976. Numerical and perceptual landscape classification. In *Studies in Landscape Perception,* edited by E.H. Zube. Amherst, MA: Institute for Man and Environment, University of Massachusetts, 73–146.

Palmer, T.T. 1973. Scenic resources of Lycoming County. Lycoming County Planning Commission, Williamsport, Pennsylvania.

Parke, M. 1966. *View protection regulations.* P.A.S. Report 213. Chicago: American Society of Planning Officials.

Paullson, M.J. 1979. The visual information system. In *Our National Landscape,* compiled by G. Elsner and C. Smardon, 182–188.

Pearce, S.R. and N.M. Waters. 1983. Quantitative methods for investigating the variables that underly preference for landscape scenes. *Canadian Geographer* 27(4):328–344.

Pedhazur, E.J. 1982. *Multiple regression in behavioral research.* New York: Holt, Rinehart and Winston.

Penning-Rowsell, E. 1974. Landscape evaluation for development plans. *The Planner* 10:930–934.

———. 1981a. Assessing the validity of landscape evaluations. *Landscape Research* 6(2):22–24.

———. 1981b. Fluctuating fortunes of gauging landscape values. *Progress in Human Geography* 5:25–41.

Peterson, G.L. 1967. A model of preference: quantitative analysis of the perception of the visual appearance of residential neighborhoods. *Journal of Regional Science* 7(1): 19–31.

Petrich, C.H. 1979. Aesthetic impact of a proposed power plant on an historic wilderness landscape. In *Our National Landscape,* compiled by G. Elsner and R. Smardon, 474–84.

Pick, A.D. and H.L. Pick, Jr. 1978. Culture and perception. In *Handbook of Perception, Volume X: Perceptual Ecology,* edited by E.C. Carterette and M.P. Friedman. New York: Academic, 19–42.

Pitt, D.G. 1976. Physical dimensions of scenic quality in streams. In *Studies in Landscape Perception,* edited by E.H. Zube, Institute for Man and Environment, Pub. No. R-76-1. Amherst, MA: Univ. of Massachusetts, 143–161.

Pitt, D.G. and E.H. Zube. 1979. The Q-sort method: use in landscape assessment research and landscape planning. In *Our National Landscape,* compiled by G. Elsner and R. Smardon, 227–234.

Planning Environment International. 1975. Visual quality. In *Interim Guide for Environmental Assessment,* HUD Field Office Edition. Washington, DC: HUD and U.S. Government Printing Office, 13-1–13-12.

Pogačnik, A. 1977. Spatial information system for design of visual environment. Ljubljana, Yugoslavia: Geodetic Survey of Slovenia.

———. 1979a. A visual information system and its use in urban planning. *Urban Ecology* 4:29–43.

———. 1979b. Environmental public preferences as obtained by the method of photo interpretation in the Ljubljana Region. *Urban Ecology* 4:45–59.

Poland, S.S. 1969. Development of recreational and related resources at hydroelectric projects licensed by the Federal Power Commission. *Land and Water Law Review* 4(2):375–398.

Porteous, J.D. 1982a. Approaches to environmental aesthetics. *Journal of Environmental Psychology* 2:53–66.

———. 1982b. Urban environmental aesthetics. In *Environmental Aesthetics: Essays in Interpretation,* edited by B. Sadler and A. Carlson, Western Geographical Series. Victoria. BC: Dept. of Geography, University of Victoria, 20:67–89.

Powell, M. 1981. Landscape evaluation and the quest for objectivity. *Landscape Research* 6(2):16–18.

Prak, M.L. 1977. *The visual perception of the built environment.* Deft, Netherlands: Deft University Press.

Proshansky, H.M. 1976. Environmental psychology and the real world. *American Psychologist* 31:303–310.

Proshansky, H. and W. Ittelson. 1970. *Environmental psychology.* New York: Holt, Rinehart and Winston.

Prown, J.D. 1980. *American painting; from its beginnings to the Armoury Show.* New York: Rizzoli International.

Public Land Law Review Commission. 1970. *One third the nation's land.* Washington, DC: U.S. Government Printing Office.

Punter, J.V. 1982. Landscape aesthetics, a synthesis and critique. In *Valued Environments,* edited by J.R. Gold and J. Burgess. London: George Allen and Unwin, 100–123.

Ramati, R. 1981. *How to save your own street.* Garden City, NY: Doubleday.

Rapoport, A. and R. Hawks, 1970. The perception of urban complexity. *American Institute of Planners Journal* 36:106–111.

Rapoport, A. and R.E. Kanter. 1967. Compexity and ambiguity in environmental design. *American Institute of Planners Journal* 33:210–221.

Ray, S. 1976. *The lens in action.* New York: Hastings House.

Repton, H. 1907. *The art of landscape gardening.* J. Nolen, ed. Boston: Houghton Mifflin.

Reynolds, I.K. 1978. The relationship of land values to site characteristics: some implications for scenic quality management. *Journal of Environmental Management* 66:99–106.

Ribe, R. 1982. On the possibility of quantifying scenic beauty—a response. *Landscape Planning* 9:61–75.

Robinson, J.W. 1980. Images of housing, Minneapolis: a limited study of urban residents attitudes and values. Unpublished Masters thesis, University of Minnesota.

Rosenburg, N. 1974. *Microclimate—the biological environment*. New York: Wiley.

Ross, M.G. and S.J. Kopka. 1983. An elementary linkage analysis of variables in the communication of landscape simulations: implications for visual resource management. *Landscape Research* 8:13–21.

Roy Mann Associates, Inc. 1975a. Peer review of the evaluation of Hart and Miller Islands and alternatives for dredged materials disposal. Prepared by Roy Mann Associates for Maryland Dept. of Natural Resources, Annapolis.

———. 1975b. *People and the Sound, shoreline appearance and design: a planning handbook*. New England River Basins Commission and National Park Service, North Atlantic Region, Boston, Massachusetts.

Runte, A. 1979. *National parks: the American experience*. Lincoln, NE: University of Nebraska Press.

Sauer, C.O. 1925. The morphology of landscape. *Publications in Geography*. Berkeley, CA: University of California, 2(2):19–53.

Sax, J.L. 1973. Standing to sue: a critical review of the Mineral King decision. *Natural Resources Journal* 13(1): 76–88.

Scharf, B. 1975. *Experimental sensory psychology*. Glenview, IL: Scott, Foresman.

Schauman, S. 1982. On a clear day in Ogunquit, Maine. In *Coastal Zone Management Journal* 9(3/4):313–322.

Schauman, S. and M. Pfender. 1982. An assessment procedure for countryside landscapes. Seattle: Dept. of Landscape Architecture, University of Washington.

Scheele, R.F. and G.W. Johnson. 1979. The Mt. Mitchell scenery assessment. In *Our National Landscape*, compiled by G. Elsner and R. Smardon, 129–135.

Scherer, S.D. and R.C. Embree. 1983. Photomontage technique for siting electrical transmission lines. *Garten und Landschaft* 8/83:629–631.

Schiffman, H.R. 1976. *Sensation and perception*. New York: Wiley.

Schomaker, J.H. 1979. Measurement of preferences for proposed landscape modifications. *Landscape Research* 3 (3):5–8.

Schroeder, H.W. and T.C. Daniel. 1980. Predicting the scenic quality of forest road corridors. *Environment and Behavior* 12:349–66.

———.1981. Progress in predicting the perceived scenic beauty of forest landscapes. *Forest Science* 27 (1):71–80.

Schultze, W.D., R.C. d'Arge, and D. Brookshire. 1980. Valuing environmental commodities: some recent experiments. *Land Economics* 57(2):151–169.

Schwarz, C.F. 1976. Definition of wildlands. In *Wildland Planning Glossary*, edited by C.F. Schwarz, E.C. Thor and G.H. Elsner,. U.S. For. Serv. Gen. Tech. Rpt. PSW-13. Pacific S.W. For. and Range Exp. Stn., Berkeley, California, 232–233.

———. 1977. Pansy Basin landscape management evaluation. In Pansy Basin Advanced Logging Studies 1973–1977, 1–71. Final Report, U.S.D.A., For. Serv., Pacific N.W. Region, Portland, Oregon.

Seaton, R. and J. Collins. 1972. Validity and reliability of ratings of simulated buildings. In *Environmental Design: Research and Practice*, edited by W. Mitchell. Stroudsburg, PA.: Dowden, Hutchinson and Ross. 1, EDRA 3.

Seattle, City of, Dept. of Community Development. 1971. Seattle urban design report: determinants of city form, 1. City of Seattle, Dept. of Community Development.

Senate Committee on Interior and Insular Affairs. 1972. Hearings on Senate 3354: National land use policy, part 1, part 2. Washington, DC: U.S. Government Printing Office.

Shafer, E.L., Jr. 1967. Forest aesthetics—a focal point in multiple use management and research. 14th IUFRO Congress, Paper 7, Section 26, Munich, Germany.

Shafer, E.L., Jr., J.F. Hamilton, and E. A. Schmidt. 1969. Natural landscape preferences: a predictive model. *Journal of Leisure Research* 1(1):1–19.

Shafer, E.L., Jr. and T.A. Richards. 1974. *Comparison of viewer reactions to outdoor scenes and photographs of those scenes*. U.S. For. Serv. Research Paper NE-302. N.E. For. Exp. Stn., Upper Darby, Pennsylvania.

Shafer, E.L., Jr. and M. Tooby. 1973. Landscape preference: an international replication. *Journal of Leisure Research* 5(3):60–65.

Shankland, R. 1970. *Steve Mather of the national parks*. New York: Knopf, 145–146.

Sheppard, S.R.J. 1982a. Landscape portrayals: their use, accuracy and validity in simulating proposed landscape changes. Unpublished dissertation, University of California, Berkeley, California.

———. 1982b. Predictive landscape portrayals: a selective research review. *Landscape Journal* 1 (1):9–14.

———. 1983. How credible are visual simulations? *Landscape Architecture* 73(1): 83–84.

Sheppard, S.R.J. and T. Tetherow. 1983. Visual assessment of surface mining in the Alton Coal Field. *Garten und Landschaft* 8/83: 624–628.

Shirvani, H. 1981. *Urban design review: a guide for planners*. Washington, DC: Planners Press, American Planning Assn.

Shuttleworth, S. 1980. The use of photographs as an environment presentation medium in landscape studies. *Journal of Environmental Management* 11:61–76.

Simonds, J. 1961. *Landscape architecture: the shaping of man's natural environment*. New York:McGraw-Hill.

Sims, W.R. 1974. Iconic simulations: an evaluation of their effectiveness as techniques for simulating environmental experience along cognitive, affective, and behavioral dimensions. Unpublished Ph.D. dissertation. Massachusetts Institute of Technology, Cambridge, Massachusetts.

Sive, D. 1970a. Securing, examining and cross-examining expert witnesses in environmental cases. *Michigan Law Review* 68:1175–1198.

———. 1970b. Some thoughts of an environmental lawyer in the wilderness of administrative law. *Yale Law Review* 70 (4):612–651.

Smardon, R.C. 1979. The interface of legal and aesthetic considerations. In *Our National Landscape*, compiled by G. Elsner and R. Smardon, 676–685.

———. 1982. An organizational analysis of Federal agency visual resource management systems. Ph.D. dissertation, Univ. of California, Berkeley and University Microfilms International, Ann Arbor, Michigan.

———. 1984. Assessing community image: tools for perception and consensus building. In *Symposium Proceedings: Environmental Preference and Landscape Management*, edited by A. Devin and S. Taylor, New London, CT: Connecticut College, 12–18.

———. 1983. Urban visual impact assessment and design evaluation through simulation. *Urban Design Review* 6 (2/3):12–15.

———. 1984. When is the pig in the parlor; the interface of aesthetic and legal considerations. *Environmental Review* 8(2):146–161.

Smardon, R.C., N.R. Feimer, K.H. Craik, and S.R.J. Sheppard. 1983. Assessing the reliability, validity and generalizability of observer-based visual impact assessment methods for the Western United States. In *Managing Air Quality and Scenic Resources at National Parks and Wilderness Areas*, edited by R. Rowe and L. Chestnut. Boulder, CO: Westview Press, 84–102.

Smardon, R.C. and J.P Felleman. 1982. The quiet revolution in visual resource management: a view from the coast. In Visual resource management in the coastal zone: The move from procedure to substance, edited by R.S. Smardon and J.P. Felleman. *Coastal Zone Management Journal* 9 (3/4):211–214.

Smardon, R.C. and M. Goukas. 1984. Village of North Syracuse main street assessment study. School of Landscape Architecture Occasional Paper No. ESF-84-010, C.E.S. & F., S.U.N.Y., Syracuse, New York.

Smardon, R.C. with M. Hunter. 1983. Procedures and methods for wetland and coastal area visual impact assessment. In *The Future of Wetlands: Assessing Visual-Cultural Values*, edited by R. Smardon. Totowa, NJ: Allenheld-Osmun, 171–206.

Smardon, R.C., M. Hunter, J. Resue, M. Zoelling, and R. Standiford. 1982. *Our National landscape: annotated bibliography and expertise index*. Berkeley: Agricultural Sciences Publications, Division of Agricultural Sciences, University of California.

Smardon, R.C., W. Price, and M.R. Volpe. 1984. St. Lawrence River scenic access study. School of Landscape Architecture Occasional Paper No. ESF-84-004, C.E.S. & F., S.U.N.Y., Syracuse, New York.

Smardon, R.C., S.R.J. Sheppard, and S. Newman. 1984. Visual impact assessment manual. School of Landscape Architecture Occasional Paper No. ESF-009, C.E.S. & F., S.U.N.Y., Syracuse, New York.

Smardon, R.C., D. Sundquist, M.J. Hunter, and V. Bouchard. 1980. Visual impact assessment of the Manteo (Shallow bag) Bay Project on the Oregon Inlet area in Dane County, North Carolina. Atlanta, GA:, National Park Service, Southeast Region.

Smith, H.N. 1970. *Virgin land—the American West as symbol and myth*. Cambridge, MA: Harvard University Press.

Southworth, M.S. 1969. The sonic environment of cities. *Environment and Behavior* 1(1):49–70.

———. 1977. *Environmental quality in cities and regions*. London: Environmental Design.

Starkey, O.P. and J.L. Robinson. 1969. *The Anglo-American realm*. New York: McGraw-Hill.

Stebbins, T.E., Jr. 1980. Luminism in context: a new view. In *American Light: The Luminist Movement 1850–75*, edited by J. Wilmerding. Washington, DC: National Gallery of Art, 211–234.

Steinitz, C. et al. 1974. The interaction between urbanization and land: quality and quantity in environmental planning and design. Cambridge, MA: Harvard University Graduate School of Design.

Steinitz, C. et al. 1978. Simulating alternative policies for implementing the Massachusetts Scenic and Recreational Rivers Act: the North River demonstration project. Graduate School of Design, Dept. of Landscape Arch., Harvard University, Cambridge, Mass.

Steinitz, C. and M. Paulson. 1976. A visual quality analysis model applied to the coastal zone. In *Visual Quality in the Coastal Zone Proceedings*, edited by D.B. Harper and J.D. Warback. Syracuse, NY: School of Landscape Architecture, C.E.S. & F., S.U.N.Y., 174–88.

Steinitz, C. and P. Rogers. 1970. *A system model of urbanization and change.* Cambridge, MA: Colonial Press.

Stevenson, A.E., J.A. Conley, and J.B. Carey. 1979. A computerized system for portrayal of a landscape alteration. In *Our National Landscape*, compiled by G. Elsner and R. Smardon, 151–56.

Stewart, N.H. 1980. Rosslyn: a monumental intrusion? *Environmental Comment* (July 1980): 4–7.

Stewart, T.R., P. Middleton, and D. Ely. 1983. Urban visual air quality judgments: reliability and validity. *Journal of Environmental Psychology* 3(2): 129–146.

Stilgoe, J. 1982. *Common landscapes of America 1580 to 1845.* New Haven, CT: Yale University Prss.

Stone, E.H. II. 1978. *Visual resource management.* Washington, DC: American Society of Landscape Architects.

Sunwoo, P., J. Penzien, F.J. Bundschuh, Jr., and P.R. Los. 1977. *Highway photomontage manual.* U.S. Dept. of Transportation, Demonstration Projects Div., Arlington, Virginia.

Swets, J.A. 1973. The relative operating characteristics in psychology. *Science* 182:990–1000.

Tabachnick, B.S. and L.S. Fidell. 1983. *Using multivariate statistics.* New York: Harper and Row.

Tetlow, R.J. and S.R.J. Sheppard. 1977. *Visual resources of the Northeast Coal Study Area 1976–1977.* Prepared for the Environment and Land Use Sub-Committee on Northeast Coal Development by the Analysis/Interpretation Division Resource Analysis Branch, Ministry of the Environment, Province of British Columbia, Victoria.

———. 1979. Visual unit analysis: a descriptive approach to landscape assessment. In *Our National Landscape*, compiled by G. Elsner and R. Smardon, 117–124.

Thayer, R.L. and B.G. Atwood. 1978. Plants, complexity and pleasure in urban and suburban environments. *Environmental Psychology and Non-Verbal Behavior* 3(2): 67–75.

The Architects' Journal. 1968. Natural lighting: use of models. *The Architects' Journal* (October 23, 1968).

Thiel, P. 1961. A sequence-experience relation for architecture and urban spaces. *Town Planning Review* 32(1):33–52.

Thompson, R.H. 1973. Decision at Rainbow Bridge. *Sierra Club Bulletin* 58:8–9, 30–31.

Thoreau, H.D. 1854/1960. *Walden or life in the woods; On the duty of civil disobedience.* New York: Signet.

Tlusty, W. 1979. The use of VIEWIT and Perspective Plot to assist in determining the landscape's visual absorption capability. In *Our National Landscape*, compiled by G. Elsner and R. Smardon, 201–208.

Torgerson, W.S. 1958. *Theory and methods of scaling.* New York: Wiley.

Travis, M.R., G. Elsner, W. Iverson, and C.G. Johnson. 1975. *VIEWIT's computation of seen areas, slope and aspect for land use planning.* U.S.D.A. For. Serv. Gen. Tech. Rpt. PSW-11.

Treimen, E.F., D.B. Champion, M.J. Wecksung, G.H. Moore, A. Ford, and M.D. Williams. 1979. Simulation of the visual effects of power plant plumes. In *Our National Landscape*, compiled by G. Elsner and R. Smardon, 485–490.

Tunnard, C. and B. Pushkarev. 1965. *Man-made America: chaos or control?* New Haven, CT: Yale University Press.

Turner, A.R. 1966. *The vision of landscape in Renaissance Italy.* Princeton, NJ: Princeton University Press.

Twiss, R.H. and R.B. Litton, Jr. 1966. Resource use in the regional landscape. *Natural Resources Journal* 6(1): 76–81.

Twito, R.H. 1978. *Plotting landscape perspectives of clearcut units.* U.S. For. Serv. Gen. Tech. Rpt. PNW-71. Portland, Ore.: Pacific N.W. For. and Range Exp. Stn.

Tzeng, O.C.S. 1983. A comparative evaluation of four response formats in personality ratings. *Educational and Psychological Measurement* 43:935–950.

Udall, S. 1979. The energy crisis and the American landscape. In *Our National Landscape*, compiled by G. Elsner and R. Smardon, 748–752.

Ullrich, J.R. and M.F. Ullrich. 1976. A multidimensional scaling analysis of perceived similarities of rivers in Western Montana. *Perceptual and Motor Skills* 43:575–584.

Ulrich, R.S. 1974. Scenery and the shopping trip: the roadside environment as a factor in route choice. Michigan Geographical Publication No. 12. Ann Arbor: Dept. of Geography, University of Michigan.

———. 1977. Visual landscape preference: a model and application. *Man-Environment Systems* 7:279–293.

———. 1984. View through a window may influence recovery from surgery. *Science* 223:420–421.

U.S.D.A., Forest Service. 1972. U.S. Forest Service handbook. Washington, DC: U.S. Government Printing Office.

———. 1977. Landscape management visual display techniques handbook. In-service manual FSH 2309.17. U.S. Dept. of Agriculture, Washington, DC.

U.S.D.A., Forest Service. 1974. *National forest landscape management, Vol. 2., Chapter 1: The visual management system.* U.S.D.A. Handbook 462. Washington, DC: U.S. Government Printing Office.

U.S.D.A., Soil Conservation Service. 1978. *Procedure to establish priorities in landscape architecture.* U.S.D.A., S.C.S. Tech. Release 65, Washington, DC.

———. 1979. *Landscape resource glossary.* Preliminary edition, Engineering Division, Soil Conservation Service, Washington, DC: U.S. Dept. of Agriculture.

U.S. Dept. of Energy/Wirth Associates. 1983. Fort Peck-Havre transmission line project, Montana, final environmental impact statement. DOE/EIS-0090-F. Western Area Power Administration.

U.S.D.I., Bureau of Land Management. 1980a. *Visual resource management program.* Div. of Recreation and Cultural Resource. Stock No. 0024-011-000116-6. Washington, D.C: U.S. Government Printing Office.

———. 1980b. *Visual simulation techniques.* Washington, DC: U.S. Government Printing Office.

U.S.D.I., Bureau of Land Management, and the State of North Dakota. 1978. Draft West-Central North Dakota regional environmental impact study on energy development. Bismark, ND: BLM State Office.

U.S.D.O.T., Federal Highway Administration. 1981. *Visual impact assessment for highway projects.* U.S.D.O.T., F.H.W.A., Washington, DC: Office of Environmental Policy.

U.S.E.P.A. 1979. *Protecting visibility research.* EPA 450/5-79, 008. Research Triangle, N.C.

U.S. Nuclear Regulatory Commission. 1979. Final environmental statement for the Greene County Nuclear Power Plant. Proposed by the Power Authority of the State of New York. U.S. Nuclear Regulatory Commission Docket No. 50-549, NUREG-0512.

U.S. Water Resources Council. 1970. Standards for planning water and land resources. Washington, DC: Water Resources Council.

———. 1983. Economic and environmental principles and guidelines for water and related land resources: implementation studies. Washington, DC: U.S. Government Printing Office.

U.S. Laws, Statutes, etc.
1850. Swampland Act. Ch. 84, 9 Stat. 519.
1897. Organic Act. Ch. 2, 30 Stat. 34–36.
1916. National Park Act. Ch. 408, 39 Stat. 535.
1918. Migratory Bird Act. Ch. 128, 40 Stat. 755.
1929. Migratory Bird Conservation Act. 257 45 Stat. 1222.
1960. Multiple Use-Sustained Yield Act. PL 86-517, 74 Stat. 215.
1964. Wilderness Act. PL 88-517, 78 Stat. 890.
1966. Watershed Protection & Flood Protection Act. 16 U.S.C. s. 1000–1009.
1968. Wild and Scenic Rivers Act. PL 90-542, 82 Stat. 852.
1969. National Environmental Policy Act. PL 91-190, 83 Stat. 852.
1974. Forest and Rangeland Renewable Resources Planning Act. 16 U.S.C. s. 1601–1610.
1976. Federal Land Policy and Management Act. PL 94-579, 90 Stat. 2743.
1976. National Forest Management Act. PL 94-588, 90 Stat. 2949.
1977. Clean Air Act Amendments. 16 U.S.C. ss. 7401 et seq. (P.L. 95-95).

University of California, Santa Cruz. undated. Issue twelve: visual. In Draft Environment Impact Report for Proposed Junipero Serra Peak Observatory. Prepared by the University of California, Santa Cruz, 137–189.

Unwin, K.I. 1975. The relationship of observer in landscape evaluation. *Transactions of Institute of British Geographers* 66:130–134.

Uttal, W.R. 1981. A taxonomy of visual processes. Hillsdale, NJ: Erlbaum.

van Leeuwen, H. and W. van Ingen. 1968. Ontvikkeling en gebruik van de entheskoop. Wageningen: Landbouwhogeschool.

Vance, J.E., Jr. 1972. The search for the ideal. *Annals of the Association of the American Geographers* 62:185–210.

Velasques, I.L. 1979. The visual environment of cities: a method of analysis. Unpublished Masters thesis, School of Landscape Architecture, C.E.S. & F., S.U.N.Y., Syracuse, New York.

Vermont Transportation Board. 1979. Designating scenic roads—a Vermont field guide. Montpelier: Vermont Scenery Preservation Council.

Vineyard Open Land Foundation. 1973. Looking at the vineyard: a visual study of a changing island. West Tisbury, MA: Vineyard Open Land Foundation.

Vining, J. 1983. Emotionality in environmental decisions: the interaction of problem and decider characteristics. Unpublished doctoral dissertation. University of Arizona, Tucson, Arizona.

Vining, J., H. W. Schroeder, and T.C. Daniel. (1984). Predicting scenic values in forested residential landscapes. *Journal of Leisure Research* 16:124–135.

Wagar, J.A. 1964. *The carrying capacity of wildlands for recreation.* Forest Science Monograph 7. Washington, DC: Society of American Foresters.

Wagar, J.A. and E. Mykelstad. 1976. *Preview: computer assistance for visual management of forest landscapes.* Research Paper NE-355. Upper Darby, PA.: U.S. Forest Service.

Wagstaff and Brady and Robert Odland Associates. 1982. San Gorgonio wind resource study, draft environmental impact report/environmental impact statement #158. Prepared by Wagstaff and Brady for the County of Riverside, California and U.S.D.I., Bureau of Land Management, Berkeley, California.

Ward, L.M. 1977. Multidimensional scaling of the molar physical environment. *The Journal of Multivariate Behavioral Research* 12:23–42.

Watzke, J.R. and R. Küller. 1984. A new environmental attention technique. Architectural Psychology Newsletter 14(1-2): 24–35.

Waugh, F. 1918. Landscape engineering in the national forests. U.S.D.A., For. Serv. Washington, DC: U.S. Government Printing Office.

Weisberg, H.I. 1979. Statistical adjustments and uncontrolled studies. *Psychological Bulletin* 86:1149–1164.

White, M. and L. White. 1962. *The intellectual versus the city.* Cambridge, MA: Harvard University Press.

Willmott, G., R.C. Smardon, and R. McNeil. 1983. Waterfront revitalization in Clayton, New York. *Small Town* 14(3): 12–19.

Winkel, G.H., R. Malek, and P. Thiel. 1969. The role of personality differences in judgments of roadside quality. *Environment and Behavior* 1:199–223.

Wirth, C.L. 1980. *Park, politics and people.* Norman, OK: University of Oklahoma Press.

Wohlwill, J.F. 1976. Environmental aesthetics: the environment as a source of effect. In *Human Behavior and Environment: Advances in Theory and Research*, edited by I. Altman and J.F. Wohlwill. New York: Plenum, 1:37–66.

———. 1977. Visual assessment of an urban riverfront. Dept. of Man-Environment Relations, Pennsylvania State University, University Park, Pennsylvania.

Wohlwill, J.F. and G. Harris. 1980. Response to congruity or contrast for man-made features in natural recreation settings. *Leisure Science* 3(4):349–365.

Wood, M. 1972. An analysis of simulation media. Unpublished Masters thesis, School of Architecture, University of British Columbia, Vancouver.

Wright, G. 1974. Appraisal of visual landscape qualities in a region selected for accelerated growth. *Landscape Planning* 1:307–327.

Yeomans, W.C. 1976. Spallumcheen: the visual environment. Burnaby: British Columbia Land Commission.

———. 1979. A proposed biophysical approach to visual absorption capability. In *Our National Landscape*, compiled by G. Elsner and R. Smardon, 172–182.

———. 1983. *Visual resource assessment: a user guide.* B.C. Ministry of Environment, British Columbia.

Yeomans, W.C., ed. 1978. Adams River: a resource analysis (with supplement). Surveys and Resource Mapping Branch, Ministry of Environment, British Columbia.

Yuill, C.G. and S.A. Joyner, Jr. 1979. Assessing the visual resource and visual development suitability values in metropolizing landscapes. In *Our National Landscape*, compiled by G. Elsner and R. Smardon, 318–357.

Zoelling, M.M. 1981. Urban high-rise dwellers' visual perceptions of form and space in the Central Business District of Syracuse, New York. Unpublished Masters thesis, School of Landscape Architecture, C.E.S. & F., S.U.N.Y., Syracuse, New York.

Zube, E.H. 1970. Evaluating the visual and cultural landscape. *Journal of Soil and Water Conservation* 24 (4): 137–41.

———. 1973a. Rating everyday landscapes of the Northeastern United States. *Landscape Architecture* 63(3):370–375.

———. 1973b. Scenery as a natural resource: implications of public policy and problems of definition, description, and evaluation. *Landscape Architecture* 63(2):126–132.

———. 1974. Cross-disciplinary and intermode agreement in the description and evaluation of landscape resources. *Environment and Behavior* 6(1):68–69.

———. 1980. *Environmental evaluation: perception and public policy.* Monterey, CA: Brooks/Cole.

———. 1981. An exploration of southwestern landscape images. *Landscape Journal* 2(1):31–40.

———. 1984. Landscape meaning, assessment and theory. *Landscape Journal* 3(2):104–110.

Zube, E.H., R.O. Brush, and J. G. Fabos, eds. 1975. *Landscape assessment: values, perceptions and resources.* Stroudsburg, PA.: Dowden, Hutchinson and Ross.

Zube, E.H. and H.A. Dega. 1964. Wisconsin's Lake Superior shoreline. Wisconsin Dept. of Resource Development, Lake Superior South Shore Area Report Number 3.

Zube, E.H. and C. Law. 1984. Perceptions of the sky in five metropolitan areas. *Urban Ecology* 8:193–202.

Zube, E.H. and L.V. Mills. 1976. Cross-cultural explorations in landscape perception. In *Studies in Landscape Perception*, edited by E.H. Zube. Amherst: Institute of Man and Environment, Univ. of Massachusetts, 162–169.

Zube, E.H., D.G. Pitt, and T.W. Anderson. 1974. Perception and measurement of scenic resources values in the Southern Connecticut River Valley. IME Publication No. R-74-1. Amherst: Institute for Man and Environment, University of Massachusetts.

Zube, E.H., J.L. Sell, and J.G. Taylor. 1982. Landscape perception, research, application and theory. *Landscape Planning* 9:1–35.

GLOSSARY REFERENCES

Abrams, C. 1971. *The language of cities: A glossary of terms.* New York: Avon Books.

Army Corps of Engineers. 1984. Visual impact assessment procedures for U.S. Army Corps of Engineers. Prepared by the State University of New York, College of Environmental Science and Forestry, Syracuse, New York.

Arnheim, R. 1954. *Art and visual perception.* Berkeley, CA: Univ. of Calif. Press.

———.1969. *Visual thinking.* Berkeley, CA: Univ. of Calif. Press.

Baldinger, W.S. 1960. *The visual arts.* New York: Holt, Rhinehart and Winston.

Barron, J.C. 1972. Economics of environmental management. Environmental Education Series Publ. EM 3654, Washington State Univ., Coll. of Agric., Coop. Ext. Service, Pullman, WA.

Blair, W.G.E. 1980. Visual resource management. *Environmental Comment* (June 1980): 6–15.

Burnhart, C.L., Ed. 1963. *American college dictionary.* New York: Random House.

California Council of Intergovernmental Relations. 1973. General plan Guidelines. State of California, Governor's Office, Sacramento.

Craik, K.H. and N.R. Feimer. 1979. Setting technical standards for visual assessment procedures. In G.H. Elsner and R.C. Smardon (tech. coord.), *Proceedings of Our National Landscape: A Conference on Applied Techniques for Analysis and Management of the Visual Resource,* Gen. Tech. Rpt. PSW-35, U.S.D.A., Forest Service, Pacific Southwest Forest and Range Experiment Station, Berkeley, California.

Cullen, G. 1961. *Townscape.* London: The Architectural Press.

Daniel, T.C. 1976 and R.S. Boster. 1976. *Measuring landscape aesthetics: the scenic beauty estimation method.* U.S.D.A., For. Serv. Research Paper RM-167, Rocky Mountain For. and Range Exp. Stn., Fort Collins, Colorado.

Durrenberger, R.W. 1973. *Dictionary of environmental sciences.* Palo Alto, CA: National Press Books.

Felleman, J.P. 1979. *Landscape visibility mapping-theory and practice.* Syracuse, NY: School of Landscape Architecture, C.E.S. & F., S.U.N.Y.

Heyman, I.M. and R.H. Twiss. 1971. Environmental management of the public lands. *Ecology Law Quarterly* (1):94–141.

Holland, W.D. 1971. Soil-habitat information for forest land. In *Proceedings of Symposium on Forest Land Inventory for Management* (Edmonton, Alberta, 1970), p. 12–24. C.L. Kirby and C.F. Nolasco, eds., Canada Forest Service, Forest Research Laboratory, Edmonton.

Hornbeck, P.L. and G.A. Okerlund, Jr. 1975. *Visual values for the highway user: an engineer's workbook.* U.S. Department of Transportation, Federal Highway Administration. Washington, D.C.: U.S. Gov. Print. Off.

Hubbard, H.V. and T. Kimball. 1917. *An introduction to the study of landscape architecture.* New York: Macmillan.

Jackson, J.B. 1984. *Discovering the vernacular landscape.* New Haven and London: Yale University Press.

Jones and Jones. 1977. Esthetics and visual resource management for highways. Prepared by Jones and Jones for the U.S. Department of Transportation, Federal Highway Administration, National Highway Institute and Office of Environmental Policy.

Kepes, G. 1944. *The language of vision.* Chicago: Paul Theobald and Company.

Litton, R.B., Jr. 1972. Aesthetic dimensions of the landscape. In *Natural Environments; Studies in Theoretical and Applied Analysis,* edited by J.V. Krutilla. Baltimore and London: Johns Hopkins University Press, 252–291.

———.1974. Visual vulnerability of forest landscapes. *Journal of Forestry* 72(7):392–397.

Litton, R.B., Jr., R.J. Tetlow, J. Soresen, and R.A. Beatty. 1971. *Water and landscape: an aesthetic overview of the role of water in the landscape.* Port Washington, NY: Water Information Center.

Lynch, K. 1960. *The image of the city.* Cambridge, MA: MIT Press.

———.1961. The pattern of metropolis. *Daedulus,* (Winter 1961): 81.

———.1976. *Managing the sense of a region.* Cambridge, MA: MIT Press.

Monkhouse, F.J. 1970. *A dictionary of geography: definitions and explanations of terms used in physical geography,* 5th edition. Baltimore, MD: Penguin Books.

O'Connell, P.J., ed. 1974. *Encyclopedia of sociology.* Guilford, CT: The Dushkin Publishing Group.

Rasmussen, S.E. 1959. *Experiencing architecture.* Cambridge, MA: MIT Press.

Robinson, D.G., I.C. Laurie, J.F. Wagar, A.L. Traill, eds. 1976. *Landscape evaluation.* Report of the Landscape Evaluation Research Project to the Countryside Commission for England and Wales. Manchester, England: University of Manchester.

Rubin, A.I. and J. Elder. 1980. *Building for people: behavioral research approaches and directions.* National Bureau of Standards Secial Publication 474. Washington, D.C.: U.S. Gov. Print. Off.

Runes, D.D. and H.G. Sehrickel. 1946. *Encyclopedia of the arts.* New York: Philosophical Library.

Sandpoint Zone Planning Team. 1974. Land use planning. U.S. Forest Service, Idaho Panhandle National Forest, Sandpoint, Idaho.

Santayana, G. 1955. *The sense of beauty.* New York: Modern Library (1st ed., 1896).

Savigear, R.A.G. 1965. A technique of morphological mapping. *Annals of the American Asso. of American Geographers* 55(3):514–538.

Schauman, S. and M. Pfender. 1982. An assessment procedure for countryside landscapes. Dept. of Landscape Architecture, University of Washington, Seattle.

Schwarz, C.F., E.C. Thor and G.H. Elsner. 1976. *Wildland planning glossary.* Gen. Tech. Rpt. PSW-13, USDA Forest Service, Pacific Southwest Forest and Range Experiment Station, Berkeley, CA.

Simonds, J.O. 1961. *Landscape architecture: the shaping of man's environment.* New York: McGraw-Hill.

Stamp, L.D., ed. 1961. *A glossary of geographical terms.* New York: Wiley.

Tetlow, R.J. and S.R.J. Sheppard. 1977. *Visual resources of the Northeast Coal Study Area 1976–1977.* Prepared for the Environment and Land use Sub-Committee on Northeast Coal Development by the Analysis/Interpretation Division Resource Analysis Branch, Ministry of Environment, Province of British Columbia, Victoria.

Tunnard, C. and B. Pushkarev. 1963. The paved ribbon: the aesthetics of freeway design. In *Man-made America: Chaos or Control.* New Haven and London: Yale University Press, 159–276.

U.S. Department of Agriculture. 1974. USDA procedures for planning water and related land resources. Washington, D.C.

U.S.D.A., Forest Service. 1973. *National Forest landscape management, volume 1.* U.S. Gov. Print. Off., Washington, D.C.

———.1974. *The visual management system, Volume 2, Chapter 1.* USDA Handbook No. 462, U.S. Gov. Print. Off., Washington, D.C.

———.1975. *Forest Service manual;* 2300–2399 Recreation Management. U.S. Forest Service, Washington, D.C.

U.S. Department of the Interior, Bureau of Land Management. 1977. BLM manual; sections 6300, 6310 and 6320, visual resource management. Bureau of Land Management, Washington, D.C.

———.1980. *Visual resource management programs.* U.S. Gov. Print. Off., Washington, D.C.

U.S.D.I., Bureau of Outdoor Recreation. 1974. Land protection techniques: selected terms and definitions (draft). Bureau of Outdoor recreation, Washington, D.C.

U.S. General Accounting Office. 1969. Glossary for systems analysis and planning, programming, budgeting. U.S. General Accounting Office, Washington, D.C.

Vaughn, A. 1974. A background paper prepared for the Workshop on Visual Impact. Forestry Department, Ontario, Canada.

Webster. 1960. *Webster's new twentieth century dictionary of the English language,* 2nd edition. Cleveland, Ohio: World Publishing Company.

———.1963. *Webster's third new international dictionary of the English language,* unabridged. Springfield, MA: G. and C., Merriam Company.

Wohwill, J. Environmental aesthetics: the environment as source of affect. In *Human Behavior and Environment: Advances in Theory and Research,* edited by I. Altman and J.F. Wohwill New York: Plenum, 1:37–66.

Wolf, M.L. 1951. *Dictionary of the arts.* New York: Philosphical Library.

AUTHOR INDEX

Abbey, E., 90
Abrams, 310, 332
Acking, C., 189, 193, 194, 217, 272
Adrian, T., 260
Ady, J., 27
Aguilo, M., 278, 287, 290, 291, 292, 295, 300
Allen, M., 54
Allentuck, M., 7
Alonso, S., 278, 290
Anderson, J., 108
Anderson, J.M., 194
Anderson, L., 89, 111, 135, 164, 171, 179, 180, 205, 214
Anderson, T., 26, 27, 89, 93, 107, 111, 179
Andersson, S., 248
Andrews, R., 29
Angelo, M., 192
Appleton, J., 15, 112, 293
Appleyard, D., 26, 27, 100, 117, 121, 122, 123, 124, 126, 130, 135, 189, 190, 193, 199, 224, 239, 248, 261, 266
Architects Design Group, 27
Arndt, L., 92
Arnheim, R., 71, 318, 323, 324, 325
Arthur, L., 88, 89, 93, 94, 168, 182
Ashihara, Y., 116, 118
Atkins, J., 24, 241
Atwood, B., 130, 135

Babbie, E., 179
Bacon, W., 204
Bagley, M., 88, 100
Baird, B., 26, 27, 190
Baird, J., 171, 174, 176
Baldinger, W., 315, 316, 317, 321, 328, 331
Baldwing, M., 24
Barker, R., 64
Barron, J., 311
Beatty, R., 113, 208, 220, 328
Belasco, W., 11
Bell, P., 173
Beveridge, C., 8
Bishop, R., 89, 94
Biswas, A., 89, 94
Blair, W., 24, 112, 190, 205, 213, 220, 224, 229, 233, 238, 240, 241, 310
Blake, P., 4, 12
Blanco, A., 295
Blau, D., 213, 214
Boar, J., 50
Bock, R., 177
Bosselman, P., 27, 117, 129, 135, 190
Boster, R., 91, 92, 93, 99, 168, 172, 174, 176, 177, 205, 210
Bowie, M., 213, 214
Boyle, K., 89, 94
Brace, P., 226
Brockman, F., 83
Brogden, F., 183

Brolin, B., 239
Brooks, V., 71, 72, 73, 76
Brookshire, D., 94
Brown, T., 111
Brush, R., 15, 86, 88, 89, 135, 205, 224
Bryson, W., 23
Buhyoff, G., 89, 91, 92, 93, 176, 182
Bundschuh, F., 190, 192
Burke, H., 292
Burnham, J., 113
Buttell, F., 106

Cairns, W.J. & Associates, 27
Calhoun, K., 27, 205
California Council on Intergovernment Relations, 313
California, University of, Wildland Research Center, 83
Campbell, D., 179, 183
Carey, J., 190
Carlson, A., 91, 93, 142
Carp, F., 130, 135
Carr, S., 117, 123, 130, 135
Catlin, G., 7, 83
Cerney, J., 91
Chandler, G., 89, 111, 164, 205, 214
Chenoweth, R., 87, 89, 93, 94, 123
Cherem, G., 89, 94
Chisholm, C., 26, 27
Ciccetti, C., 89
Clark, D., 4, 284, 289

AUTHOR INDEX

Clawson, M., 89, 94
Cohen, H., 135
Cole, B., 4
Collins, J., 131, 175
Colorado Department of Highways, 27, 30
Conley, J., 190
Conner, J., 89, 94
Cook, T., 179, 183
Coomber, N., 89, 94
Cordell, H., 85
Costonis, J., 240
Coughlin, R., 30
Countryside Commission for Scotland, 26, 27
Cox, G., 83
Craik, K., 16, 18, 89, 92, 93, 100, 117, 123, 130, 135, 189, 190, 194, 205, 210, 212, 266, 326
Crocker, T., 94
Cronbach, L., 183
Crystal, J., 135
Cuff, D., 72
Cullen, G., 120, 121, 133, 135, 325
Cunningham, M., 189
Cutler, M., 23

Dana, S., 10, 13
Daniel, T., 17, 88, 89, 91, 92, 93, 94, 99, 100, 168, 172, 174, 176, 177, 179, 180, 182, 205, 210, 326
Davis, K., 23
Dearden, P., 88
Dega, H., 89, 93
Deregowski, J., 71, 72
Diamond, H., 85
Dillman, M., 170
Dingfield, D., 233, 238
Dougal, M., 27
Downing, A., 8
Downs, R., 135
Draper, J., 23
Dumap, R., 30
Dunn, M., 295
Durrenberger, R., 319
Dutton, C., 90

Echelberger, H., 89
Economic Research Service, 104
EDAW, Inc., 27, 192, 204, 208, 213
Ekbo, G., 248
Elder, J., 325, 326, 331, 333
Ellsworth, J., 112
Elsner, G., 16, 205, 211, 224, 310, 311, 319, 323, 331, 332, 333
Embree, R., 27, 192
Engen, T., 171
Environmental Protection Agency, 53
Environmental Studies Board, Panel on Aesthetic Attributes, 30
Erickson, D., 27, 117, 123, 126, 135, 237
Evans, G., 89

Ewald, W., Jr., 117
Expert Panel on Project, 8
Ely, D., 135

Fabos, J., 15, 88, 205, 224
Fairfax, S., 10, 13
Falk, W., 106
Feimer, N., 18, 91, 100, 112, 131, 135, 205, 212, 326
Felleman, J., 30, 49, 54, 61, 114, 135, 229
Fenneman, N., 206
Ferguson, A., 23
Fidell, L., 182
Fines, K., 26, 27, 89, 93
Fisher, A., 89, 94
Fisher, J., 173
Fishman, L., 117, 239, 261
Fitzgerald, R., 27
Fleming, L., 6
Flinn, W., 105, 106
Ford-Robertson, F., 83
Fraser, B., 176, 210
French, J., 23
Frey, C., 23, 117, 133, 135
Futrell, J., 205

Garling, T., 130, 135
Gaya, S., 292
Gerdes, H., 190
Gerne Sanderson Faggetter Cheesman and the Center for Environmental Studies, 26, 27
Gerstenberger, A., 126, 129, 135
Gibbs, K., 89, 94
Gibson, J., 64, 65, 66, 67, 71, 72, 73, 74, 293
Gilg, A., 91
Giorgio, W., 23
Goodman, W., 23
Gordon, R., 27
Gore, A., 6
Goukas, M., 117, 123, 124, 132, 133, 135
Graham, W., 89
Grant, 133
Gray, B., 112
Graziano, D., 126, 129, 135
Grden, B., 206, 210, 212, 218
Green, D., 174
Greenbie, B., 112
Grinde, K., 310, 314, 317, 319, 322, 323, 327, 329, 330, 331, 332, 333
Groat, L., 135

Hack, G., 126, 129, 135
Haggard, J., 23
Hake, H., 171
Halprin, L., 121
Hamill, L., 91
Hamilton, J., 94
Hampe, G., 27, 30
Hamson, D., 23
Harper, D., 15, 26, 27

Harris, G., 89, 93
Harrison, J., 130, 135
Hart, J., 106
Hart, W., 89
Harvey, H., 176
Haspel, A., 89
Hawks, R., 116, 130
Hawks, R.S., 30
Hebblethwaite, R., 289, 291
Hendee, J., 85
Herzog, T., 89, 130, 135
Heyman, I., 311
Hochberg, J., 71, 72, 73, 76
Hoffman, H., 53
Hogo, H., 182
Holland, S., 208, 311
Hornbeck, P., 55, 324
Howard, W., 130, 135
Hubbard, H., 111, 310, 312, 316, 318, 323, 327, 328, 329, 331
Hudspeth, T., 117, 133, 135
Hunsaker, F., 213, 214
Hunter, M., 205, 206, 208, 210, 213, 216, 218

Impact Consultants, 56
International Joint Commission, 27, 30
Isaacson, L., 205
Itami, R., 111
Ittelson, W., 175

Jackson, J., 311
Jackson, P., 26, 27
Jacobs, P., 111, 117, 135
Jacques, D., 91
Janke, R., 190
Janssens, J., 268, 274
Jefferson, T., 8
Johns, E., 15, 18
Johnson, C., 23
Johnson, D., 105
Johnson, F., 89
Johnson, G., 89
Johnson, Johnson & Roy, 27
Jones, G., 27, 205
Jones, L., 177
Jones & Jones, 26, 27, 54, 89, 192, 204, 209, 212, 310, 311, 314, 315, 319, 320, 321, 322, 323, 327, 328, 330, 331, 332
Joyner, S., 117, 135

Kansas City, Missouri, City Planning Department, 135
Kanter, J., 24, 56, 116
Kanter, R., 130
Kaplan, R., 30, 91, 104, 112, 116, 130, 135, 182
Kaplan, S., 111, 112, 116, 130, 135, 182, 193
Kates, R., 12
Kaufman, L., 44
Kell, G., 27

Kelley, K., 182
Kennedy, J., 71, 72, 73, 74
Kepes, G., 315, 318, 324
Kerlinger, F., 179
Kimball, T., 111, 310, 312, 316, 318, 323, 327, 328, 329, 331
King, R., 111
Klapp, M., 266
Klockars, A., 172
Kopf, A., 310, 314, 317, 319, 322, 323, 327, 329, 330, 331, 332, 333
Kopka, S., 18, 135
Kreimer, A., 93, 266
Krutilla, J., 89, 94
Kuller, R., 189, 193, 194, 268, 270, 271, 275
Kunit, E., 27, 205
Kusler, J., 25

Lam, T., 51
Lam, W., 172
Lambe, R., 30, 117, 132, 135
Landmark Research, Inc., 87, 89
Langer, S., 71
Lattimer, D., 182
Laurie, M., 111
Leopold, A., 82, 90
Leopold, L., 24, 89, 93, 99
Levitt, R., 40, 43
Lewis, P., 89, 93, 142
Linton, D., 89
Litton, R., 26, 27, 61, 89, 93, 107, 111, 113, 123, 205, 208, 211, 212, 220, 283, 289, 292, 320, 328, 330, 331
Lockard, K., 190
Loomis, R., 173
Los, P., 190, 192
Lueschner, W., 92
Lynch, K., 26, 27, 94, 112, 117, 118, 120, 121, 122, 123, 124, 126, 135, 163, 224, 248, 317, 323

MacAdam, D., 53
MacConnell, W., 89, 94, 111
Mah, E., 229
Malek, R., 117, 135
Malm, W., 182
Mandelker, D., 117
Mann, R., 205, 206, 208, 211, 212
Marshall, R., 82
Martin, C., 190
Marx, L., 106
McCarthy, M., 112
McCloskey, M., 24
McCullagh, M., 57
McHarg, I., 209, 220
McKechnie, G., 190
Merriam, L., Jr., 83
Mertes, J., 135
Meyer, J., 26, 27, 117, 121, 123, 124, 126, 135, 248
Miagni, T., 51
Middleton, P., 135

Middleton, W., 53
Milgram, S., 123
Miller, R., 72
Mills, L., 92, 208
Ministry of Environment, British Columbia, 214, 218
Ministry of Forests, British Columbia, 204
Molenar, J., 182
Monkhouse, F., 311
Mosier, J., 89, 111, 164, 205, 214
Murray, A., 15
Murray, B., 23
Myklestad, E., 190, 211

Nairn, I., 4, 12
Naussauer, J., 94, 108, 111, 203, 204
Neiman, B., Jr., 23, 204
Nevius, B., 7
Newman, S., 204, 205, 206, 211, 218, 291, 296, 297
Nickerson, D., 190, 211
Nieman, T., 87, 93
Noe, F., 27, 30
Noma, E., 171, 174, 176

Oakland, City of, 192
O'Brien, R., 6, 7
O'Connell, P., 313
Ohlsson, C., 272
Okerlund, G., Jr., 55
Oles, P., 190
Olmsted, F., 8
Osgood, C., 268, 269
Outdoor Recreation Resources Review Commission, 11, 85, 142
Ovetz, K., 126, 129, 135

Palmer, J., 26, 27, 30, 88, 89, 93, 94, 117, 130, 135, 213, 310, 314, 317, 319, 322, 323, 327, 329, 330, 331, 332, 333
Parke, M., 238
Paullson, M., 58, 190
Pearce, S., 89
Pedhazur, E., 182
Penning-Rowsell, E., 17, 104
Penzien, J., 190, 192
Peterson, G., 117, 130, 135
Petrich, C., 27, 170, 174, 175, 178, 179, 180, 181
Pfender, M., 103, 104, 112
Phillips, P., 117, 132, 135
Pick, A., 72
Pick, H., Jr., 72
Pinkey, T., 106
Pitt, D., 26, 27, 89, 104, 107, 111, 172, 176, 179, 205
Pogacnik, A., 117
Poland, S., 24
Pope, A., 6
Porteous, J., 17, 119
Powell, M., 92

Prak, M., 118
Pratt, 89
Proshansky, H., 64
Public Land Law Review Commission, 142
Punter, J., 5, 17
Pushkarev, B., 4, 12, 331

Ramati, R., 117, 135
Ramos, A., 278
Rapoport, A., 116, 130
Ray, S., 41
Repton, H., 6
Reynolds, I., 89, 94
Ribe, R., 91, 93
Richards, T., 94
Ristau, T., 23
Robertson, I., 233, 238
Robinson, J., 117, 133, 135
Rodwan, A., 171
Rosenburg, N., 50
Ross, M., 18
Roy Mann Associates, 26, 27, 89
Rubin, A., 325, 326, 330, 333
Runes, D., 315, 316, 318, 320, 321, 327
Runte, A., 10

Santayana, G., 310, 311, 315
Sauer, C., 106
Savigear, R., 316
Sax, J., 23
Scharf, B., 43, 44, 45
Schauman, S., 24, 103, 104, 112, 114, 310, 330
Scheele, R., 89
Scherer, S., 27, 192
Schiffman, H., 41, 42, 45, 46
Schissler, P., 117, 123, 130, 135
Schmidt, E., 94
Schomaker, J., 189, 190, 193, 194
Schroeder, H., 94, 135, 179, 180, 182, 205, 210
Schultze, W., 94
Schuyler, D., 8
Schwartz, C., 27, 83, 310, 311, 319, 323, 331, 332, 333
Seaton, R., 131, 175
Seattle, City of, 135
Sehrickel, H., 315, 316, 318, 320, 321, 327
Sell, J., 17, 91, 133, 168, 182
Serpell, R., 71, 72
Shafer, E., Jr., 11, 94
Shaine, B., 27
Shankland, R., 11
Sheppard, S., 26, 27, 89, 114, 189, 190, 192, 193, 194, 195, 199, 204, 205, 206, 211, 212, 213, 218, 291, 296, 297, 323, 332
Shirvani, H., 118
Shuttleworth, S., 94
Simonds, J., 111, 112, 327, 330
Sims, W., 30, 189, 190, 193, 194, 199

Sive, D., 23
Sjogren, U., 272
Smardon, R., 16, 26, 27, 30, 49, 104, 111, 112, 117, 123, 124, 132, 133, 135, 142, 190, 202, 204, 205, 206, 208, 209, 210, 211, 216, 218, 224, 291, 296, 297, 310, 314, 317, 319, 322, 323, 327, 329, 330, 331, 332, 333
Smith, H., 89
Sorenson, J., 113, 208, 220, 328
Sorte, G., 271
Southworth, M., 135, 261
Stamp, D., 311
Standiford, R., 205
Starkey, O., 205
Stebbins, T., 8
Steinitz, C., 26, 27, 30, 58, 248, 287, 290, 300
Stevenson, A., 190
Stewart, N., 27
Stewart, T., 135
Stilgoe, J., 5, 7
Stone, E., 224
Suci, G., 268, 269
Sunwoo, P., 190, 192
Swetz, J., 174

Tabachnick, B., 182
Tannenbaum, P., 268, 269
Taylor, J., 17, 89, 133, 168, 182
Tetherow, T., 192
Tetlow, R., 27, 89, 93, 111, 113, 205, 208, 213, 220, 313, 323, 328, 332
Thayer, R., 130, 135
The Architects' Journal, 236
Theil, P., 117, 121, 124, 135
Thompson, R., 23
Thor, E., 310, 311, 319, 323, 331, 332, 333
Thoreau, H., 90
Tlusty, W., 192
Torgerson, W., 171, 172, 174, 176, 177
Travis, M., 58, 211, 286, 290
Treimen, E., 190

Tunnard, C., 4, 12, 331
Turner, A., 5
Twist, R., 311
Twito, R., 190, 211
Tzeng, O., 172

Udall, S., 142
Ullrich, R., 89, 117, 130, 133, 135, 182
UNESCO, 11
U.S.D.A. Forest Service, 25, 56, 89, 93, 94, 99, 113, 147, 190, 204, 212, 213, 220, 311, 312, 313, 314, 315, 316, 318, 321, 322, 323, 327, 329, 330, 331, 332
U.S.D.A. Soil Conservation Service, 114
U.S. Department of Energy, 192
U.S.D.I. Bureau of Land Management, 89, 93, 104, 112, 145, 147, 190, 204, 212, 213, 220, 295, 310, 312, 313, 314, 315, 316, 318, 319, 320, 321, 322, 323, 328, 330, 331, 332, 333
U.S.D.I. Bureau of Outdoor Recreation, 313
U.S.D.O.T. Federal Highway Administration, 164, 238
U.S.E.P.A., 53
U.S. General Accounting Office, 321
U.S. Nuclear Regulatory Commission, 24
U.S. Water Resources Council, 30, 114, 142
University of California, Santa Cruz, 27
University of Michigan, 220
Uttal, W., 38, 64

Vance, J., Jr., 106
van Ingen, W., 266
van Leeuwen, H., 266
Vaughn, A., 313, 331
Vaux, H., 30
Velasques, I., 26, 27, 123
Vermont Natural Resources Council, 112

Vermont Transportation Board, 111, 112
Vineyard Open Land Foundation, 26, 27
Vining, J., 17, 100, 168, 171, 182

Wagar, J., 83, 190, 211
Wagstaff and Brady and Robert Odland Associates, 27, 192, 195
Waits, M., 29
Walters, D., 229
Warbach, J., 15
Washington State, Department of Ecology, 24
Waters, N., 89
Watzke, J., 275
Waugh, F., 142
Way, D., 111, 117, 135
Weisberg, H., 183
Wellman, J., 93, 176, 182
Wendtt, J., 116, 130
Wheeler, L., 180
White, M. and L., 8
Wilkinson, C., 83
Willmott, G., 117, 131, 132, 133, 135
Winkel, G., 117, 135
Wirth, C., 11
Wirth Associates, 27, 192
Wohlwill, J., 88, 89, 92, 93, 116, 130, 326
Wolf, M., 310
Wood, K., 89
Wood, M., 189, 193, 195
Wright, G., 117, 135

Yeomans, W., 111, 202, 204, 205, 206, 208, 209, 212, 213, 214, 218
Yuill, C., 117, 135

Zoelling, M., 117, 130, 132, 133, 135, 205
Zube, E., 8, 15, 16, 17, 18, 19, 26, 27, 89, 91, 92, 93, 104, 107, 111, 133, 135, 142, 168, 172, 176, 179, 189, 205, 224

SUBJECT INDEX

Accessibility:
  intrinsic fragility, 282
  proximity, 283
  visual exposure, 283
Accuracy ranges, 49, 56, 61
Acton, Massachusetts, visual easements, 104
Acuity, of vision, 41
Acuity threshold, 53
Acuity types:
  detection, 45
  recognition, 45
  resolution, 45
Adirondack Park Agency, 25, 56
Aesthetic impacts, types of:
  adverse aesthetic impact, 29
  aesthetic enhancement, 29
Aesthetic quality, 168
Aesthetic value, 168
Affordances, theory of, 69
Agrarian attitude:
  corporate agricultural landscapes, 105
  utilitarian values, 105
Algorithm, computer, 57
Algorithm logic, 57
Alpine Lakes Wilderness area:
  land appraisal techniques, 87
  market-comparable approach, 87
  U.S. Forest Service, 87
  wilderness values, 87
Ambient optic array, 65, 69, 72

Ambiguity, 116, 130
Ameliorating scenic ills:
  anti-ugly movement, 12
  Appalachian Regional Development Act, 12
  Clean Air Act Amendments of 1977, 12
  Highway Beautification Act of 1965, 12
  President Johnson, 12
  Surface Mining and Control and Reclamation Act of 1977, 12
  White House Conference on Natural Beauty, 12
American West:
  despoiled nature, 8
  garden, 8
  wilderness, 8
Analog simulations:
  energy transmission, 57
  optical transforms, 57
Anatomy, 40
  acuity and contrast, 45
  retina, 42
  retinal processing, 44
  visual system, 40
Anthos, 245
Anti-urbanism, 8
Apparent access, 163
Apparent color, 53
Appleyard, Donald:
  dynamic perceptions, 121

  in motion, 121
  moving through it, 121
  notation systems, 121
  The View from the Road, 121, 124
Application scales:
  neighborhood/district, 117, 133
  streetscape/place, 117, 133
  transportation corridor/roadside view, 117, 133
  urbanizing region, 117, 133
Applied techniques:
  computer and quantitative approaches, 16
  descriptive approaches, 16
  psychometric and social science approaches, 16
Appraise aesthetic effects:
  appraise significant effects, 34
  judge overall effects, 34
Appropriate context for project review:
  geotemporal scales, 26
  project planning context, 26
Architecture and perception, review of, 118
Area and structure coherence, 161
Area visibility, classes of:
  ambiguous, 61
  hidden, 61
  visible, 61
Areawide assessments, 26

359

Army Corps of Engineers, 19, 30
Artificial light:
  detailed lighting analysis, 237
  fluorescent, 51
  high intensity discharge, 51
  incandescent, 51
  nighttime lighting, 237
  offsite impacts, 237
Artificial light impact factors, 237
Artistic landscape description:
  abstract properties, 97
  design professionals, 97
  landscape architects, 97
Assess aesthetic effects:
  describe effects, 34
  determine significant effects, 34
  identify effects, 34
Assessing countryside, process for:
  assessment context, 104
  client/user, 105
  evaluation, 109
  landscape, 106
  overall process, 113
Assessment context, ultimate use, 104
Assessment design:
  case study, 179
  criteria:
    assessment and design, 179
    degree of control, 179
    difficulty of interpretation, 179
    formal requirements, 179
    utility, 179
  correlation methods, 182
  experimental design, 180
  quasi-experimental design, 183
Assessment methods:
  behavioral measures, 178
  criteria for evaluating:
    reliability, 184
    sampling, 185
    validity, 184
  perceptual preference assessment, 174
  surveys and questionnaires, 170
Atmospheric effects:
  brightness contrast, 51
  color contrast, 51
Atmospheric extinction, 53
Atmospheric particles:
  particle size, 53
  particle shape, 53
Attention, act of, scanning the visual field, 70
Authority spectrum, 48
Average eye height, 40
Axonometrics, 188

Balance system, semicircular canals, 40
Barker, Rodger, social psychology, 64
Basic visual elements:
  color, 297
  line, 297
  scale, 297
  shape, 297
  space, 297
  texture, 297
Behavioral measures:
  behavioral observation, 178
  behavior of nonusers nonparticipant, 178
  face validity, 178
  indirect indices, 178
  links between:
    actual behavior, 178
    attitudes, 178
    preference, and opinions, 178
  observing or measuring behavior, 178
Behavioral paradigm:
  predictive landscape dimensions, 18
  statistical analysis, 18
Bill of Rights:
  freedom of expression, 22
  just compensation for property taken, 22
Binocular field, 41
Blind spot, 43
Boccaccio, 5
Boulding, Kenneth, imageability, 119
Brennon, Justice William:
  aesthetic importance, 118
  general welfare, 118
  just compensation, 118
  reasonable beneficial use, 118
  taking of property, 118
British Columbia, Canada:
  Forest Landscape Handbook, 204
  government agencies, 204
Broad legislative policies, 22
Brown, Lancelot "Capability", 6
Bryant, William Cullen, 7
Bureau of Indian Affairs (BIA), 85
Bureau of Land Management (BLM):
  contrast rating procedure, 164, 204
  descriptors:
    sparsley vegetated and semi-arid basin and range, 148
    grass lands, 148
    Great Plains, 148
    Southwest, 148
  distance zones, 150
  physical attributes, 148
  sensitivity:
    changes in scenic quality, 150
    user attitude toward landscape, 149
    visual resource management (VRM), 16, 19, 85, 142
  contrast rating levels, 164, 204
  degrees of modification/change, 151
  Desert Conservation Plan Area, California, 145
  management classes, 150, 204
  North Dakota energy development, 145
  regional assessments:
    special uses, 145
    special areas, 145
    scenic quality, 148
    sensitivity levels, 148
    user attitudes and volumes, 148
  Visual Simulation Techniques, 190
  VRM uses:
    federal lands, 146
    permit processing, 146
Burham, Chicago Plan, 116

Calibration, calibrate, 61
Case study:
  advantages:
    exploratory, 180
    pilot studies, 180
  Arizona Desert, 179
  assessments:
    cognitive characteristics, 179
    cultural characteristics, 179
    physical characteristics, 179
  Connecticut River valley, 179
  description:
    cultural values, 179
    historic values, 179
    land use diversity, 179
    visibility, 179
  disadvantages:
    lack of control, extraneous variables, 180
    limited inference, 180
    restricted comparisons, 179
    restricted generalizations, 179
    single geographic area, 179
    standard of comparison, 180
  preference data, 179
  road corridors, 179
Catalysts for community action:
  dialogue for visual assessment, 104
  increased awareness, 104
Categorical rating scales, 171
Cathedra for Urban Planning, University of Ljubljana, 248
Catlin, George, 7
Central New York, 54
Central park concept, 116
Chicago World's Fair, 116
Citizen participation, 56
City Beautiful Movement:
  Chicago, 116
  Philadelphia, 116
  Washington, D.C., 116
Citywide scale studies, 26
Clarity of vision, 43
Claude, 5
Clayton, New York study, waterfront revitalization, 131
Clean Air Act Amendments of 1977:
  National Parks, 142
  Wilderness areas, 142
Coefficient of reflectivity:
  porous surface, 128
  smooth specular surfaces, 128
Cognitive processes, 64, 76
Color(s):
  perception of, 43, 53
  blue-violet, 44

green, 44
yellow-red, 44
sensitivity, highest, yellow-green, 44
spectrum of, 44
Commercial strips:
cognitive confusion, 117
visual disorder, 117
way-finding problems, 117
Community planning, 116
Comparative sketches, Olmsted and Vaux, 8
Complexity, 116, 130
Comprehensive planning, 116
Computer computations:
algorithm logic, 57
data texture, 57
Computer data texture:
cell format, 57
shape, 57
size, 57
Computer graphics, simulation
advantages, 195
analysis tool, 195
limitations, 195
Computer graphics, simulation accuracy:
resolution, 195
software options, 190
terrain information, 195
Computer program examples:
cell-by-cell search, 302
predetermination of cells, 300
sectorial search, 304
Computer, role of in Yugoslavian Study programs:
interactive, 252
problem-oriented, 252
search routines, 252
retrieval, 252
storage, 252
Concentric grid, 60
Conceptual framework, 19
Cone of vision, 41
Conglomerate drawing, 72
Contrast:
color, 51
maximum, 45
threshold, 45
Conventions:
advocates of:
art critics, 71
art historians, 71
artists, 71
symbols arranged by rules, 71
Cooper, James Fenimore, 7
Correlation methods:
advantages:
degree of causal relationship, 183
systematic association, 183
variance in preference ratings, multiple-R statistic, 183
dependent/criterion variables, 182
goals:
description, 182

explanation, 182
prediction, 182
independent/candidate variables, 182
objective measures:
on site, 182
photographs, 182
perceptual preference techniques, 182
prediction model-objective measures:
beta coefficients, 182
curvilinear function, 182
regression equation, 182
statistical control:
multivariate techniques, 182
regression techniques, 182
subjective measures:
ratings of photographs, 182
subjective measures, disadvantages:
reliability, 182
validity, 183
subjective measures, review of, 182
Council on Environmental Quality (CEQ):
CEQ guidelines, 29
CEQ regulations:
categorical exclusions, 151
environmental assessment, 151
environmental impact statements (EIS), 151
EIS preparation, 151
finding of no significant impact (FONSI), 151
significant environmental effects, 151
Countryside, 104
assessment guidelines, 114
evaluation criteria:
character/congruence/contrast, 111
fitness, 112
fragility or visual absorption capabilities (VAC), 111
information, 112
preference, 112
structures or spatial definition, 112
uniqueness, 112
vividness/intactness/unity, 112
human activity:
ambiguous, 108
animals and structures, 107
landscape:
change:
population shift, 104
elements:
human activity, 107
land use/cover, 108
sky, 107
topography, 106
vegetation, 107
water, 107
typical, 105
land use/cover:
indicator of meaning, 108
interaction of landscape elements, 108
stereotypes:
agrarianism, 105
pastoralism, 106

ruralism, 106
Countryside/rural landscape quality, 108
Courts, outdoor advertising, 117
Craik, Kenneth:
environmental displays, 130
media of presentation, 130
observers, 130
response formats, 130
Critical Areas of Environmental Concern, 153
Critiques and reviews, 17
Cross-cultural perception, 71, 73
interpretation of perspective picture, 73
Cross-section, vertical exaggeration, 56
Cullen, Gordon:
aesthetic principles, 120
art of relationship, 121
content/fabric of towns, 121
optics/serial vision, 121
perceptions of urban building and spaces, 120
place, 121
quality of graphic analysis, 120
Townscape, 120
urbanscape analysis, 120
Cultural values, 22

Dante, 5
Dark adaption, 44
Dark adaption curve, 44
Data errors, in simulation, 195, 199
Data model:
areal and temporal sampling, 61
data type, 61
decision concept, 61
Data types:
pentenary data, 59
primary data, 59
quarternary data, 59
secondary data, 59
tertiary data, 59
Deceptive landscape descriptions:
human-made, 106
natural, 106
Decisions/actions, scales of:
district/neighborhood, 117
land use/street, 117
region, 117
street/structure, 117
transportation corridors, 117
Decision framework:
accuracy requirements, 49
authority base, 48
output format, 49
scenario probability, 49
Decisionmaking-framework, 30
Define aesthetic resources:
develop evaluation criteria, 33
identify aesthetic resources, 33
Degree of reflectivity, high:
light colors, 128
metal surfaces, 128
Demographic trends, 104, 202, 282

Department of Defense (DOD), 85
Department of Transportation (DOT), 19
Depth perception, 41
Designer(s), 116
Design guidelines:
  enhance, 220
  mitigate, 220
  rehabilitate, 220
  sources, 220
Digital simulation:
  aspect, 58
  multiple times seen, 58
  perspectives, 58
  terrain slope, 58
  visibility maps, 58
  weighting distances, 58
Digital spatial formating:
  decision rules, 59
  shape, 59
  texture, 59
Direct glare, determinants of:
  brightness of surroundings, 128
  intensity of source, 128
Disparity in management, 85
Distance zones:
  background, 54
  factors:
    atmospheric optics, 54
    local shapes and textures, 54
    perception, 54
    physiology, 54
  foreground, 54
  midground, 54
District/neighborhood:
  citizen values and attitudes, 117
  downtown revitalization, 117
  historic district preservation, 117
  studies, 133
  waterfront revitalization, 117
Documentation, existing, types of information, 235
Downing, Andrew Jackson, 8

Early wilderness advocates, 82
Ecological meaning, types of:
  affordances, 65
  events, 65
  layout, 65
Ecological optics, 69
Ecological perception, 72
Economic approaches, expert:
  cost-benefit analysis, 94
  real estate appraisal techniques, 94
  travel cost method, 94
Economic and Environmental Principals and Guidelines for Water and Related Land Resource Implementation Studies, 30
Economic value, 84
Electromagnetic spectrum, 40
Enclosure, 68
Energy source parameters, 50
Energy waves, 65

English landscape park, 8
Environmental data, four dimensional, 60
Environmental decisionmaking, stages of:
  environmental inventory, 30
  policy formation, 30
  post-impact evaluation, 30
  program planning or project design, 30
Environmental display, purpose of:
  descriptive assessment, 133
  evaluative assessment, 133
  preconstruction predictive assessment, 133
Environmental impact statement (EIS), 29
Environmental litigation, 49
Environmental meaning:
  affordances, 68
  events, 68
  perception, 70
Environmental planning:
  Coastal Zone Management Act (CZM), 13
  Federal Land Policy and Management Act (FLPMA), 13
  Forest and Rangeland Renewable Resource Planning Act (RPA), 13
  National Environmental Policy Act (NEPA), 13
Environmental preference:
  Ljubljana sample, marking photographs:
    ambient preferences, 262
    landscape details, 262
    panoramic photographs, 262
    representative scenes, 262
  Ljubljana, Slovenia, Yugoslavia:
    questions, 261
    representative citizens, 261
  participatory photo-interview:
    abilities of graphic expression, 263
    Adriatic coast, 262
    advantages, 263
    citizen sample, 262
    disadvantages, 263
    photographic copies, 263
    photoposters, 262
    respondents, 263
    transparent overlays, 263
  passive photo-interview:
    evaluation of scenic beauty, 263
    photographic posters, 263
    public preferences, 263
    representative views, 263
    Slovenian regions, 263
  visual presentation media, 262, 263
  written questionnaire(s) without visual stimuli:
    Great Britain, 261
    Sweden, 261
    United States, 261
    Yugoslavia, 261
    Ljubljana region, 261
    Sarajevo, 261
Environmental psychologist, 64, 98
Environmental review, 143

Environmental simulation:
  analog, 57
  digital/numeric, 57
  field testing, 56
  hybrid, 58
  three-dimensional iconic, 57
  two-dimensional iconic, 56
Environmental structure:
  medium, 65
  substances, 66
  surfaces, 66
Error:
  acceptable limits, 61
  relative contribution, 61
Error, types of:
  blunders, 61
  random, 61
  systematic, 61
Euclidean zoning, 117
Evaluate, who will:
  assessment context
    community planning, 111
    litigation, 111
  public surrogates, 111
  trained observers, 111
Evaluation criteria, 111, 241
  ability to absorb change, 111
  inherent visual qualities, 111
  people's preference, 111
Event change:
  mechanics, 68
  space, 68
  time, 68
Events, types of:
  change in color/texture, 68
  change in state of matter, 68
  reshaping/repositioning of surfaces, 68
  reversible, 68
Executive branch, implementing laws, 23
Experimental control:
  control group, 180
  control of assignment:
    matching, 180
    random, 180
  control of experimental setting:
    field environment, 181
    natural setting, 181
  experimental group, 180
Experimental design:
  advantages:
    experimental control, 180
    dependent variable, 180
  disadvantages:
    cost, 181
    difficult to conduct, 181
    difficult to generalize, 181
    extraneous variables, 180
  identifying characteristics:
    explanation/causal inference, 181
    experimental control, 180
    specification of methods, operationalization, 181
  independent variable, 180

treatment, 180
Expert approach, 90, 118, 122
  advantages:
    data collected in field, 91
    flexible, 91
    in-house, 91
    strong traditional grounding, 91
    versatility, 91
  basic vocabulary, 122
  commonalities, 122
  disadvantages:
    arbitrary:
      combining of landscape
        components, 91
      reliability, 91
      selection of variables, 91
      weighting of variables, 91
    differ from public values, 91
    elitist, 91
    fine arts tradition, 91
  graphic exploration, 122
  juxtaposition, 122
  relationships, 122
  sequences, 122
  summary:
    composite map, 129
    evaluative assessments, 129
Expert paradigm, 91
Expert quantitative approaches, overall
    landscape evaluation, 93
Expert recording and analysis techniques:
  analysis, 123
  establishing visual control points, 122
  light, 125
  process, 122
  summary, 129
  visibility, 124
  visual elements, 123
Eye muscle functions:
  accommodation, 41
  pupil movement, 41

Farsighted, 42
Federal government:
  national defense, 22
  own and management property, 22
  regulate interstate commerce, 22
Federal Highway Administration (FHWA):
  sample scoping questionnaire, freeway
    spur, 156
  scoping questionnaire:
    project characteristics, 155
    significant viewer response issues, 156
    significant visual resource issues, 156
    visual environment of project, 155
    visual impacts and impact
      management, 156
  visual environment of project:
    affected environment, 155
    human environment, 155
  visual impact guidance, 164
  visual impacts and impact mitigation:
    major visual impacts, 156

visual mitigation measures:
  avoiding, 156
  compensating, 156
  minimizing, 156
  rectifying, 156
  reducing, 156
Field observations:
  photographic record, 235
  walking, 235
Field of vision, 40
Figure-ground perception:
  lateral inhibition, 46
  saccide eye movements, 46
Film cutting rate:
  information arousal, 76
Fish and Wildlife Service (FWS), 85
Focal accommodation, 54
Focal length, 40
Forest Service (FS), 16, 19, 85, 99, 142
  characteristic landscape, 147
  visual quality objectives (VQO), 150, 203
  visual management system (VMS), 23
  descriptors:
    vegetated mountain landscapes:
      Pacific Northwest, 148
      Rocky Mountains, 148
  distance zones, 54
  sensitivity, intensity of usage of:
    recreation areas, 149
    water bodies, 149
  sensitivity levels, 149, 204
  variety classes, 148, 203
  visual absorption capability (VAC), 164,
    204
  visual management system (VMS):
    degrees of modification/change, 151
    regional guides, 145
    Forest and Rangeland Renewable
      Resource Planning Act (RPA) of
      1974, 145
  uses:
    land use planning, 145
    national forests, 145
    timber management plans, 145
    visual absorption capability, 146
    visual corridor analysis, 146
    visual management objectives (VQO),
      25, 150, 203
Forest Service and Bureau of Land
    Management (BLM):
  distance zones:
    convenient viewpoints, 150
    viewing corridors, 150
  federal lands, management
    responsibilities, 147
  importance or intensity of use, 148
  landscape interpretations, 148
  modifying descriptors, 147
  physical attributes, 147, 148
  sensitivity level of landscape to the
    viewer, 149
  volume criteria
    frequency of travel, 149

visibility, 150
Forest Service, BLM and Soil Conservation
    Service:
  common elements:
    mapped data, 150
    three-way matrices, 150
Formal aesthetic model, trained
    expert standards, 168
Fovea, 43, 45
Foveal detail, 70
Foveal (macular) field, 41
Foveal vision, 45
Fragility, 278
Framework, 33
French military, defilade problem, 56

Garden(s), 5
  design, 5
Garten und Landschaft, 245
General visual impact assessment
    guidelines, 220
Generic impact assessments, 26
Generic process:
  appraise effects, 34
  assess effects, 34
  define resources, 33
  inventory resources, 34
Geographers, 14, 97
  cultural, 106
Geological Survey (USGS), remote sensing
    data, 108
Geotemperal scales:
  large/areawide, 26
  linear/scenic corridor, 26
  management decisions, 30
  regional, 26
  site/project, 26
  town/citywide, 26
Glare:
  adverse effects of:
    visual disability, weakening of
      vision, 127
    visual discomfort:
      squinting, 127
      visual avoidance, 127
  primary, direct light source, 126
  secondary, reflected light, 126
Gibson, J.J., 64, 65, 69, 74
  ecological:
    laws of surface, 66
    perception, 69
    theory, 69
    theory of optics, 69
  The Ecology of Visual Perception, 65
  perceptual psychology, 64
  visual perception, 64, 65, 69, 74
Gilpin, Reverend William, 6
Grand Central Terminal, historic
    landmark, 118, 226
Gravity, polarity, 65
Guidelines:
  color, 220
  contrast, 221

Guidelines (Continued)
  diversity in the landscape, 221
  edges, 221
  enhancement, 222
  form, 221
  line, 221
  mitigation, 222
  rehabilitation, 222
  roadside details, 220
  texture, 220
  water, 220

Halprin, Lawrence:
  RSVP Cycles, scores, 121
Health, safety, morals and general welfare, 22
Hidden areas, 56
Highway Beautification Act, 142
Highway test:
  final land use map, 257
  optimize development, 257
  proposed highway, 256
  views from the highway, 256
  views to the highway, 256
Historian, 18, 97
Historic and cultural factors:
  landscape global character, 282
  special-value areas/sites:
    aesthetics, 282
    history, 282
    tradition, 282
    uniqueness, 282
  testimonial role, 282
Historic Preservation Act of 1966:
  criteria for adverse effect:
    alteration of setting, 225
    out of character, 225
    National Register, 225
    Section 106, 225
Homunculus, 69
Horizon, 40, 53
Housing and Urban Development Administration (HUD), 701
  planning assistance program, 26
  threshold approach:
    apparent access, 163
    area and structure coherence, 161
    perception of visual quality:
      existing residents, 158
      project residents, 158
    visual content, 158
Hudson River Valley, 7, 9
Hudson River Valley School of Painting:
  Bierstadt, Albert, 8
  Church, Frederick, 8
  Cole, Thomas, 8
  Cropsey, Jasper F., 8
  Durand, Asher, 8
  Heade, Martin Johnson, 8
  Kensett, John F., 8
Humanistic paradigm, qualitative, 18, 19

Idaho-Montana, 54

Ideal conditions, for vision, 45
Identifying landscape values, 14
Illustrative example, nuclear power plant, 179
Image assessment, 124
Image of the City:
  district, 119
  edge, 119
  landmark, 119
  node, 119
  path, 119
Incident light:
  foot-candles, 44
  illuminance, 44
Index of uniqueness value, 99
Indiana, 105
Industrial development, 278
Industrial installation, visual impact, 278
Influence zone, 45
Information description:
  planning goals, 250
  reserved space, 250
  visual-aesthetic data, 250
Information sources:
  black-and-white panoramic photography, simulate visual experience, 248
Interdisciplinary environmental planning, 13
Internal data consistency, 49
Interposition, landscape, 54, 57
Intrinsic meaning:
  affordances, 68
  changes in layout or events, 68
  layout of surfaces, 68
Invariants:
  line drawing:
    corner, 74
    edge, 74
    fiber, 74
    fissure, 75
    occluding edge, 74
    skyline, 75
  non-line:
    cast shadows, 75
    change in reflectance, 75
    change in texture, 75
    shading on a curved surface, 75
Inventory:
  (aesthetic) resources:
    forecast conditions without plans, 34
    forecast with alternate plans, 34
    survey existing conditions, 34
  rural landscape, 208
  wildland landscapes, 208
Iris, 41
Irving, Washington, 8

Jefferson, Thomas:
  agrarian society, 8, 105
  values of rural landscape, 8
Johns, Ewart, 15
Johnson, Mrs. Lyndon B., 14

Joint International Commission, 30
Judicial branch/courts:
  standing, 25
  test of law's legitimacy, 23
Judicial review:
  procedural, 25
  substantive, 25
Jurisdiction:
  Constitution of the United States divides powers, 22
Just noticeable difference (jnd), 45

Key view selection:
  expert analysis example criteria, 232
  public involvement example:
    candidate views, 233
    key views, 233
    viewer groups, 233
    view types, 233
    visual importance, 233
Knowing:
  environmental information:
    abstracting, 71
    extracting, 71
Kozarje, Yugoslavia, 254

Land management, 143
Landmark protection laws, 118
Landscape(s), 5
  aesthetics assessment:
    descriptive inventory, 168
    public preference models, 168
  analysis methods and procedures, 14
  as physical and cultural concept, 106
  assessment quality:
    design and planning assessment, 170
    drawing inferences, 170
    measurement procedures, 170
  assessment reviews, 88
  components:
    human performance, 296
    industrial installation construction, 297
    intrinsic value, 296
    landscape composition, 296
    structures, 296
    vegetation, 296
    water and land, 296
  continuum, 82
  disposal:
    Desert Land Sales Act, 10
    General Ordinance of 1785, 10
    Homestead Act, 10
    land grants to railroads, 10
    Morrill Act, 10
    Timber Culture Act, 10
  homogeneous appearing larger units, 106
  inventory:
    Canada provincial, 208
    coastal, 208
    Northern Great Plains, 208
    rural, 208

water and wetlands, 208
management, purposes for:
  intangible commodities:
    aesthetic, 168
    symbolic, 168
  tangible commodities, 168
modern concept of, 5
policy:
  amelioration of visual blight, 12
  development of recreation landscapes, 11
  disposal of public lands, 10
  environmental planning, 13
  preservation of unique landscapes, 10
preservation:
  Adirondack Forest preserve, 10
  Antiquities Act of 1906, 10
  UNESCO Biosphere Reserve, 11
  United Nations World Heritage List, 11
  Wilderness Act of 1964, 10
  World Heritage Sites, 10
  Yellowstone National Park, 10
  Yosemite State Park, 10
  Yosemite Valley, 10
quality:
  human perception, 168
  judgment process, 168
simulation, 4, 188
symbolism, 104
unit, 106
unit judgment:
  landscape diversity, 106
  visibility, 106
units for scenic easements:
  local viewsheds, 106
  political boundaries, 106
values, 7
  application of:
    atmospheric envelope, 142
    corridor, 142
    landscape continuum, 142
    site, 142
visibility, 48–51, 283
Landscape architect, 8, 91, 93, 97, 104, 146, 164, 220
Landscape Australia, 245
Landscape painting(s), 5, 8
Landscape Planning, 245
Landscape Research, 245
Landschap, 5
Landskip, 5
Land use planning, 26
Land use/street scale:
  commercial strips, 117
  preserving streetscapes, 117
  redesign, 117
  rehabilitation, 117
Layout, theory of:
  continuity of surface, 68
  ground, 68
  horizontal axis, passage of the sun, 68
  surfaces, texture and color, 68

vertical axis, gravity, 68
Legal context, 22
Legal controls:
  consideration, 25
  performance, 25
  specification, 25
Legal developments:
  providing compensation, 118
  restricting use of property, 118
  use of police power, 118
Legal progressions and trends:
  courts' ability, aesthetic injury, 25
  shift in emphasis:
    common nuisance, 25
    common trust, 25
    eminent domain, 25
    federal and state legislation, 25
    zoning and architectural controls, 25
Legislative branch, creating laws, 22
Lewis, Phil:
  environmental corridors, 142
  State of Wisconsin, 142
Light:
  ambient level of illumination, 65
  artificial, 51, 126
  direct, 40
  natural, 126
  quality of, 125
  radiant, 65
  reflected incident, 40, 41
  wave phenomenon, 40
Light adaption, 44
Lighting, adverse effects, 126
Light scattering, blue-red spectrum, 53
Light sensitive receptors:
  cones, 43
  rods, 43
Light sensory systems:
  daytime, 42
  night, 42
Light wavelengths:
  absorbed, 49, 53
  reflected, 49, 53
Light wave propogation:
  absorption, 51
  diffraction, 51
  reflection, 51
  refraction, 51
Linear sequential experience, 142
Litigation, context of:
  cost of documentation, 105
  field notes, 105
  photographic specifications, 105
  process design, 105
  scrutiny, 105
Litton, R. Burton, Jr.:
  guidelines, 220
  landscape control points, 123
Ljubljana, Slovenia, Yugoslavia, 248
Local government control:
  design review ordinances, 225
  zoning, 225

Location criteria:
  aesthetic gestalt, 261
  city centers, 260
  computer graphics simulation, 260
  energy development/infrastructure, 260
  housing development, 260
  industrial land use, 260
  meaning of, visual messages, 261
  public opinion, 261
  recreation land use, 260
  transit ways, 260
  visual absorption, 261
Lorenzetti, Ambrogio:
  Effects of Good Government in the Town and City, 4
  Sala della Pace of the Palazzo Publico, 4
  Siena, Italy, 4
Loss of sharpness at distance, distance zones:
  background, 292
  foreground, 292
  middleground, 292
Lowell, Massachusetts, 116
Lund Institute of Technology, School of Architecture, 266
Lund simulator:
  development of:
    evaluate, 266
    exteriors, 267
    eye movements, 267
    eye movement behavior, 268
    interiors, 267
    landscapes, 267
    movement, axional directions, 267
    relatoscope, 267
    scales, 267
    semantic lever, 267
    simulate, 267
    Swedish Council of Building Research, 267
    television camera, 267
    three-dimensional scale model, 267
    videotape, black and white, 268
  studies:
    attention, 274
    attentional performance, 275
    building exteriors, 274
    cognition, 274
    differences in perception, 274
    eye movement behavior, 274
    motoric reaction time, 275
    perceived qualities, 274
    perception, 274
    project/dissolve grey rings, 275
    simulator applications, 275
Lynch, Kevin:
  analytical techniques, 120, 248
  city resident interviews, 120
  field reconnaisance, 120
  public sample, 120
  trained observers, 120
  comprehensive approach:
    mapping systems, 119

Lynch, Kevin (*Continued*)
  notational, 119
  imageability, 119, 120
  Image of the City, 118
  legibility, 120
  Managing the Sense of the Region, 117
  visibility, 120

Macular vision, 43
Magnitude estimation, method of, 172
Managers, 116
Martini, Simone, Siena, Italy, 4
Marx, pastoralism, 106
Measures to minimize harm, 29
Media, comparison:
  effects on observers, 131
  viewer sequences, 131
Media of presentation:
  architectural elevations and plans, 130
  color slide simulations, 130
  direct exploration, 130
  video with modelscope, 130
  viewing a model, 130
  viewing photographs, 130
Medium of the terrestrial environment, 65
Mississippi, 105
Mississippi River, Great River Road, 84
Mitigation measures, specific measures:
  artificial lighting, 243
  existing visual resources, 243
  shadow, 243
  solar glare, 243
  view obstruction, 244
  visual contrast, 244
  visual quality, 244
Modelscope:
  photography, 57
  video recording, 57
Modifiers:
  local level, 109
  regional scale, 108
Monochrome, 44
Monocular field, 41, 75
Montana, big sky country, 107
Monte Carlo simulation, 61
Motion parallax:
  binocular perspective, 75
  motion perspective, 76
  shift in the rate of motion, 76
Motion pictures, use of:
  juxtaposing views of objects, 76
  movement-dependent information, 76
  permits change, 76
  series of events reduced, 76
  special experience, 76
  successive views, 76
Motion recording:
  panning action, 75
  zoom shot, 75
Movement:
  interpretations, 121
  notation systems, 121
  perceptions, 121

  sequence of events, 121
  views, 121
Movies, three-dimensional, 75
Multidisciplinary, 16
Multilayered context, 116
Multiple resource planning, 26
Multisensory experience:
  air quality, 135
  daytime glare, 135
  night time light intrusion, 135
  pedestrian wind effects, 135
  shadow effects, 135
  sound, 135
Mutuality, 69

National Environmental Policy Act of 1969 (NEPA), 19, 22, 23, 225
  guidelines, 29, 114
National Land Use Act Hearings, 142
National park, 7
National Park Service (NPS), 19, 30, 142
National Register of Historic Places, 152
National Research Council (NRC), 30
Naturalistic bias, 142
Naturalness, meaning of, 202
Nearsighted, 42
New towns:
  Columbia, 116
  Radisson, 116
  Reston, 116
New York State Environmental Quality Review Act (SEQRA):
  suggested inventory process:
    community visual resource values, 152
    Critical Areas of Environmental Concern, 153
    public participation, 152
    visual scoping process, 152
New York State Public Service Commission, 25
Niagara Falls, 30
Niche, 69
Night blindness, 44
Night illumination studies, 129
Night lighting applications:
  directional spread, 51
  horizontal source, 51
  vertical source, 51
Nitrogen dioxide, brownish coloration, 53
Nonquantitative landscape description terms, 93
Nonquantitative public approaches:
  landscape taxonomy, 93
  use defined landscape components, 93
Nonquantitative techniques:
  classification of landscape types, 93
  inventory of features, 93
Nonreflective glass, angle of incidence, 128
Normative public values, 9
Northern District, of Syracuse:
  camera light meter, 129
  note problem areas, 128

Northern Wisconsin, tax incentives, 84
North Syracuse, New York:
  notation system, 124
  visual districts, 124
Nostalgic image, 105

Object brightness, 53
Object steropsis, 54
Observation conditions:
  illumination, 290
  seasonality, 290
  single or repeated views, 290
  spatial composition, 290
  view duration, 290
  visual basin parameters, 290
Observation points, selection of, example:
  computerized methods, 291
  key observation points, 290
  number of observations, 290
  observation conditions, 290
  previsible attitudes, 290
  representative landscape views, 291
  simulation accuracy, 291
  viewpoint selection, 291
  visual attractions, 291
  visual control points, 291
Observer-based measures, 168
Observers:
  comparing groups, 131
  designer/planner preferences, 131
  group representation, 131
  public reactions, 131
Observer's response:
  analyzing the analysis of observer responses, 177
  categorical ratings:
    judgmental criteria, 177
    true perceived scenic beauty, 177
  categorical rating scale:
    cumulative frequency, 178
    cumulative probability, 178
    frequency, 178
    z values, 178
  distributions of ratings, 178
  Scenic Beauty Estimation Model (SBE), 178
  measurement of:
    landscape-centered scaling, 175
    process of separation, statistical standardization, 175
    process of standardization, 176
    scaling methods, 175
    scaling of objectives, 175
    scaling of observers, 175
    scaling of observers and stimuli, 175
    stimulus-centered scaling, 175
    translate ratings, 176
Olmsted, Frederick Law, Sr.:
  Boston, 116
  Central Park, Manhattan, 116
  Hartford, 116
  Prospect Park, Brooklyn, 116
  St. Louis, 116

San Francisco, 116
Trenton, 116
Operative process, Spanish study:
   evaluate possible impact, 299
   industrial plant location, 299
   mitigate, 299
   steps:
      area visually affected, 299
      evaluation, 299
      new viewsheds, 299
      observation point selection, 299
      probable impact, 299
      project information, 299
      simulation, 299
      surrounding landscape description, 299
Optical simulation:
   Forest Service, 190
   multiple projection, 190
Organic city planning:
   housing conditions, 116
   living conditions, 116
Orientation:
   observation with backlighting, 281
   illumination, 281
   landform configuration, 281
   southern orientation, 281
Orthagonal geodetical network:
   macroregional scale, 248
   regional planning scale, 248
   urban planning scale, 248
Orthagonal locations, 60
Our National Landscape, 16, 205
Outdoor landscape stimuli, 40
Outdoor recreation classification system:
   Bureau of Land Management, 142
   Forest Service, 142
   National Park Service, 142
   Outdoor Recreation Resources Review Commission (ORRRC), 142
Output format, 49

Pacific Northwest, Cascade Peaks, 109
Paired comparisons, method of, 171
Palm Springs, city of:
   aesthetic guidelines, 118
   performance based, 118
Panoramic views, 41
Paradigms:
   behavioral, 18
   humanistic, 18
   of landscape assessment:
      cognitive, 133
      experiential, 133
      expert, 133
      psychophysical, 133
   professional, 18
   strengths and weaknesses, 18
Partial enclosure, 68
Pastoralism:
   romantic notion, 106
   visual expectation, 106
Perceived landscape quality, 168

Perception, macrotheory of, 64, 72
Perceptual preference assessment:
   environmental representation:
      drawings, 175
      models, 175
   landscape quality assessment, 174
   perceptual responses, 175
   pictorial representation, 175
   ratings, 176
   response measurement:
      magnitude estimation, 176
      paired comparisons, 176
      Q-sort procedures, 176
      rank order, 176
   stereotypical reactions, 175
   symbolic environment, 175
   validity, 175
Perceptual psychology, 64
Perceptual unit, 106
Performance prediction model:
   analysis, 48
   input, 48
   output, 48
Performance predictions, scenarios, 49
Peripheral vision, 41, 43
Perspective, clues of, 73
Perspective construction, 190
Perspective images, credibility of, 72
Perspective views:
   computer graphic animations, 49
   video modeling, 49
Photographic:
   representation, 94
   sampling, 94
   specifications, 105
Photomanipulation, 190, 195
   massing studies, view blockage, 190
   multiple projection, 190
   photomontage, 190
   photosimulation, 190
Photon, 44
Photoreceptors, 43, 45
Physical attributes, typology of:
   activity pattern, 123
   architectural pattern/distribution/land use, 123
   degree of enclosure, 123
   paths, 123
   street trees, 123
Physical effects, unintended, 117
Physical landscape descriptions:
   physical elements, 98
   physical scientists, 98
Physiology of vision, 40
Pictorial depiction, principles of, 73
   line drawings, 74
   motion picture, 75
   non-line invariants, 75
   stationary monocular perspective, 73
Picture perception, 71
   theories of:
      conventions, 71
      elements of light, 71

      optic information, 71
      similarity, 71
Picture plane, 40
Picture representation, 71
Pictures, visual representations, 71
Picture similarity, common qualities, 71
Picturesque, 6
Picturesque landscape, 7, 9, 10, 18
Place:
   locomotion, 68
   nested, 68
   order of adjacency, 68
Planners, manager/orchestrator, 116
Point light source, cone of vision, 57
Point of observation:
   envelope:
      aperture, 69
      face, 69
      facet, 69
      spherical angle, 69
Pope, Alexander, *Essay on Criticism,* 6
Position of the horizon, 40
Post construction evaluation, 194
Post management evaluation, landscape quality, 169
Post occupancy evaluation, in architecture, 169
Poussin, 5
Powers:
   explicit, 22
   implicit, 22
Preference, landscape:
   conscious notions, 112
   unconscious notions, 112
Preference tests, 112
Preservation phase, 14
Preliminary analysis:
   viewer, 114
   visibility, 114
   visual resource, 114
Presentation methods, conventional, 266
Price, Sir Uvedale, 7
Private development, control of:
   architectural controls, 117
   general zoning, 117
Professional approach, physical phenomena, 133
Professional media, review of, Appleyard, Donald:
   communications model, 189
   conceptual simulations, 189
   experiential simulations, 189
Project information:
   dynamic simulations, 234
   key views, 229
   simulations, 234
   static simulations, 234
   viewers, 229
   visibility, 229
Projective geometry, 92
Proshansky, environmental psychology, 64
Proximity:
   average traffic intensity, 283

Proximity (Continued)
  number of visitors/observers, 283
  to villages and roads, 283
Psychological landscape descriptions:
  environmental psychologists, 98
  feelings, 98
Psychophysics/representation of observer's response:
  cognition and perception, 174
  cognitive or mental processes, 173
  isomorphic sensory system, 174
  perceived landscape quality, 173
  perceived value, 174
  perceptual/judgmental process, 173
  theoretical psychophysics, 173
  Theory of Signal Detection (TSD), 174
Public approach, criticism:
  generic public, 92
  judgmental variability, 92
Public assessments:
  citizen input, 92
  empirical social sciences:
    reliability, 92
    validity, 92
  representation/response format:
    verbal, 92
    visual, 92
Public assessment approach, planners and designers, 169
Public assessment method choices, 92
Public hearings:
  transportation planning, 116
  urban renewal, 116
Public Land Law Review Commission, 142
Public participation, 14
Public policy, 4
Public preference approach, reasons for:
  ethical, 169
  feedback system, 168
  improve design and planning process, 169
  legal, 169
  public viewpoint, 168
Public values, 18
Public values nonmarket economic approaches, contingent valuation methods, 94
Pupil, 41
Pupil size, 41
Pupillary movements:
  large movements, 42
  saccide movements, 42

Qualitative information, 18, 19
Quantification argument, 142
Quantitative public approaches:
  number of scales:
    affective qualities, 93
    physical dimensions, 93
  photographic stimuli, 93
  single response measure, 93
  statistical correlation techniques, 93
Quasi-experimental design:
  advantages, utility, 183
  disadvantages:
    lack of control:
      composition of experimental groups, 184
      experimental setting, 184
      measurement of extraneous variables, sources of variation, 184
  goals:
    explanation, 183
    prediction, 183

Recognition acuity, 45
Recreation landscapes:
  Civilian Conservation Corps (CCC), 11
  Land and Water Conservation Fund Act of 1965, 12
  Multiple Use and Sustained Yield Act, 11
  National Recreation and Scenic Trails Act, 11
  Outdoor Recreation Resources Review Commission (ORRRC), 11
  state parks, 11
  Wild and Scenic Rivers Act, 11
Recreation phase, 14
Red flag criteria, 30
Referent axis, 65
Reflected light intensity:
  foot-lambert, 45
  lamberts, 45
  luminance, 45
Reflective glare:
  scattered glare, nonparallel light, 126
  spot glare, parallel light rays, 126
Reflective glare, determinants, light source:
  brightness, 128
  reflectivity, 128
Reflective surfaces, highly, 128
Regional land use planning, 26
Regions:
  increased density, 117
  suitability for urban development, 117
  urbanization, 117
Regulations:
  procedural components, 23
  substantive components, 23
Regulatory process, branches of government:
  executive, 22
  judicial, 22
  legislative, 22
Regulatory situations, types of:
  public land management, 30
  public projects involving private lands, 30
  public regulation of private lands, 30
Reliability:
  between-observer agreement, 184
  consistency, 184
  inter-observer reliability, 184
  stability of measurement, 184
  test-retest reliability, 184
Renderings:
  accuracy/bias, 194
  credibility, 194
  flexibility, 194
Rennaisance, drawings, 56
Representation, comparing modes:
  analysis of variance, 271
  difficult dimensions, 271
  faulty information, 271
  housing areas-Malmo, Sweden:
    color movie, 270
    pictures, 270
    surveys, 270
  naturalistic model, 271
  semantic rating scales, 271
Reproduction quality, of simulation, 199
Repton, Humphrey, 6
Resolution acuity, 45
Resort concept, 83
Response formats:
  cognitive mapping, 133
  open-ended responses, 133
  photoquestionnaires, 133
  questionnaires, 133
  rating scales, 133
Response measurement, methods and procedures of:
  categorical rating scales, 171
  interpretability, 171
  magnitude estimation, 172
  paired comparisons, 171
  response methods, review, 171
  scale of measurement:
    direct psychological scale, 171
    direct response scales, 171
    indirect scale, 171
  sorting methods, 172
  utility, 171
Retina, 40, 69
Retina sensitivity, 50
River basin planning, 26
Rosa, 5
Rural and natural environments:
  Canada, 202
  United States, 202
  visual values, 202
Rural and wildland environments:
  management activities:
    agricultural development, 202
    commercial and cultural development, 202
    energy exploration and extraction, 202
    flood control development, 202
    forest product utilization, 202
    industrial development, 202
    outdoor recreation complexes, 202
    transportation, 202
    utility developments, 202
  VIA procedure:
    Canada, 203
    Europe, 203
    United States, 203
Rural and wildland environments, unique qualities, special land use problems, 203
Ruralism values:
  ambivalent, 106

nonurban, 106
Rural landscape, 8

Sampling:
   intuitive procedures, 185
   objective choice of units, 185
   probability procedures:
      random, 185
         stratified sampling, 185
   sampling of observers/judges, 185
   sampling of other units, 185
   units chosen for measurement, 185
   unit domain specification, 185
San Francisco, California, 117
Santa Barbara, Calif., City of:
   guidelines, 118
   performance-based, 118
   prescriptive, 118
Scale models, 57, 190
   principles of similitude, 57
   problems:
      extraction of data, 57
      simulation of phenomena, 57
   simulation:
      Appleyard and Craik:
         Environmental Simulation
            Laboratory, 190
         University of California, Berkeley,
            190
      model photography, 190
   scale consistency, 57
Scenarios, 49
Scenery classification:
   Bureau of Land Management, 148
   Forest Service, 148
Scenery composition, 55
Scenic beauty, 96
Scenic Beauty Estimation Method (SBE), 99, 176, 177
Scenic corridor, 26, 142
Scenic resources, 22
Scientific landscape description criteria:
   appropriateness, 100
   comprehensiveness, 100
   generalizability, 100
   reliability, 100
   sensitivity, 100
   utility, 100
   validity, 100
Scoping, visual impact assessment:
   CEQ regulations and scoping, 151
   Federal Highway Administration,
      scoping questionnaire, 155
   HUD threshold approach, 158
   New York State Environmental Quality
      Review Act (SEQRA), visual
      scoping process, 152
Seattle, Washington:
   disclosure and mitigation, 225
   ordinance, 126
Sequential spatial experience, 142
Shadow:
   offsite shadow impacts, 236
   offsite shadows, 129, 236

shadow pattern, winter solstice, 236
shadow projections, techniques for:
   The Architect's Journal, 236
   Graphic Standards, 236
   simulate shadows and patterns, 236
Shirvani, Hamid, *Urban Design Review: A Guide for Planners*, 118
Shoreline and coastal planning, 26
Short-term memory, 41
Sight, coming into, accretion, 70
Sight, going out of:
   darkness, 70
   distance, 70
   occlusion:
      accretion, 70
      decretion, 70
Sightline delineation methods, 62
Sightlines, 56
Significance:
   institutional recognition, 33
   public recognition, 33
   technical recognition, 33
Significance, levels of:
   acceptable, 243
   acceptable with mitigation, 243
   beneficial, 243
   indeterminate, 243
   unacceptable, 243
Significant viewer response issues:
   cultural significance, 156
   scenic values, 156
   test of visual compatibility, 156
   values and goals of local viewer groups, 156
Simulation:
   bias-free:
      response equivalence, 189, 193, 194
      response bias, 194
      simulation bias, 193
   credible, Appleyard, Donald:
      apparent realism, 193
   effective motion picture, 76
   predicting responses prior to construction, 189
   principles of:
      accuracy, 192
      bias-free, 193
      comprehension, 193
      credibility, 193
      representativeness, 192
   representative:
      range of views and conditions, 192
      typical views, 192
      typical worst case situation, 192
   response differences, 189
Simulation accuracy, 190, 192
   abstraction, 190
   aesthetic response equivalence, 190
Simulation comprehension:
   audience suitability, 193
   understood by users, 193
Simulation computer programs, 190
Simulation effectiveness and validity:
   Craik, K.H.:

environmental displays, 189
   process model, 189
   response equivalence, 189
Simulation examples, 192
   in practice:
      accuracy, 192
      assumptions, 190
      environmental impact documents, 190
      public meetings, 190
Simulation media:
   bias, 189
   relative equivalence, 190
Simulation methods:
   data model, 59
   critique of:
      general simulation techniques:
         data errors, 195, 198
         presentation, 199
         reproduction quality, 199
         use of illustration skills, 199
   media:
      computer graphics, 195
      photomanipulation, 195
      renderings, 194
      scale models, 194
   physics model, 59
Simulation rendering techniques, distortion avoidance, 190
Simulation research and information sources:
   examples in practice, 190
   research, 189
   technical guides, 190
Simulations for project visual analysis, 188
Simulation skill:
   artistic prowess, 199
   illustrator training, 199
Simulation techniques, 4, 194
Simulator in practice:
   black and white, 272
   color intensity, 272
   depth of field, 272
   environmental simulation:
      highway, 272
      town square, 273
   eye level relatoscope, 272
   grey tones, 272
   lighting conditions, 272, 273
   Lund simulator:
      difficulties, 273
      Swedish municipalities, 273
   optical quality, 272
   realistic facades, 272
   scales, 272
   stage-set models, 272
   sufficient model detail, 271
   three-dimensional model, 271
Simulator prototypes:
   Landbouwhogeschool:
      urbanoscope, 266
      Wageningen, Holland, 266
   University of California, California, 266
Site design and specific structures, 226

Site improvements, 227
Site review processes:
  San Francisco, 117
  Seattle, 117
Skull position (of eyes), 40
Socially oriented planning, professional neutrality, 116
Social need for outdoor recreation, 142
Sociologist, 105, 129
Social scientist, 116, 129
Soil Conservation Service (SCS), 16, 19, 104, 108
  advises groups and individuals, 113, 147
  descriptors, range of localities, 148
  hierarchical landscape taxonomic classification:
    landuse/cover, 108
    modifiers:
      regional scale, 108
      local level, 109
  Landscape Management System (LMS):
    landscape use, 150
    priority of landscape architecture treatment, 150
    uses:
      conservation districts, 146
      high priority areas, 146
      landscape architect, 146
      Small Watershed Development Projects Act of 1966, 146
      water resource planning, 146
    visibility, 150
  no single approach:
    diversity of project scales and landscapes, 113
    paucity of research, 113
Solar glare:
  Environmental Comment, 237
  offsite solar glare, 236
  solar glare impacts, 236
Solar movements, 50
Solar position:
  illumination, 50, 126
  shadow configurations, 50, 126
Sorting methods, 172
Spatial arrangement, tri-dimensional, 76
Spatial sampling:
  areal, 60
  random, 60
  regular, 60
  selected, 60
  stratified, 60
Spectral distribution, 50
Specular surface, 128
Spot glare:
  angle of incidence, 127
  horizon, 127
Standard design height, 40
Standard horizontal visibility, 53
State-of-the-art conferences and symposia:
  Incline Village, Nevada (1979), applied techniques, 16

Landscape Research Group:
  Methods of Landscape Analysis (1967), 15
  The Aesthetics of Landscape (1976), 15
State University of New York at Syracuse (1975), coastal zone, 15
University of Massachusetts (1973), values, perceptions, resources, 15
State environmental policy acts (SEPAs), 225
State government:
  management of critical resource areas, 22
  own and manage property, 22
  police powers, 22
State and local wildlands, 85
State parks and forest systems:
  condemnation, 84
  fee simple acquisition, 84
  recreation access, 84
  Swampland Act of 1850, 84
  wildland aesthetics, 84
State register of historic places, 152
Statewide recreation planning, landscape inventories, 142
Stationary monocular clues:
  aerial perspective, 74
  continuity of outline, 74
  linear perspective, 74
  size perspective, 73
  texture density, 74
  texture perspective, 73
  transitions between light and shade, 74
  upward location, 74
Stereoscopic depiction, stereoscopic landscape scenes, 75
Stern, Paul, apparency, 119
Stewardship, 112
Stratified random sample, 69, 185
Streetscape/place, 117
Structures, 226
Sublime, 7
Sublime landscape, 7, 9, 18
Substances:
  aggregates, 66
  heterogeneous, 66
  impenetrable, 66
  opaque, 66
  permanent in shape, 66
  resistant to deformation, 66
  rigid, 66
  solid, 66
Sullivan, Louis, 8
Sunlight:
  electromagnetic energy, 50
  incandescent source, 50
Supreme Court:
  Fifth Amendment, 118
  historic preservation, 118
  New York City, 118
  Penn Central Transportation Company, 118

Surface layout, 73, 74
Surfaces, heated, 56
  principles of:
    absorbance, 67
    cohesion, 67
    color, 67
    illumination, 67
    layout, 67
    reflectance, 67
    shape, 67
    texture, 67
    viscosity, 66
Surveys and questionnaires:
  attitudes, 170
  closed-ended questions, 173
  distinction between:
    attitudes, 173
    behavior, 173
  interviews:
    interviewer probe, 170
    personal contact, 170
  open-ended questions, 173
  opinions, 170
  perceptions, 170
  question wording, 170
  sampling:
    appropriate population, 170
    bias, 170
    sampling procedure, 170
    survey administration, 170
  survey question bias:
    emphasis of problem issues, 171
    labeling stimulus scenes, 171
Susceptability:
  number of observers, frequency of use, 295
  observer's attitude, 295
Symbolic goals, existence values, 168
Symbolic meanings, 105
Symbolic values, 106, 168
Systematic evaluation, need for:
  architect, subjective evaluation, 268
  environmental psychology, 270
  evaluation, 268
  perceptual dimensions, 269
  semantic analysis, 270
  semantic description model, 269
  validation studies:
    neuropsychological responses, 269
    perceptual responses, 269

Techniques and technology, visual impact assessment:
  modelscopes, 135
  scale models, 135
  video, 135
Thiel, Philip, sequence-experience notation, 121, 124
Temporal phenomena, types of:
  periodic, 61
  random, 61
  trend, 61
  uniform, 61

Textural qualities, 46
Thoreau, Henry David, 7, 8
Topographic map, 56
Transformation, pictorial recording, 72
Transitways:
  highways, 117
  siting and design, 117
Transportation corridor/roadside view, 117, 133
Twentieth-century planning:
  city and town extensions, 116
  metropolitan and regional planning, 116
  new towns, 116
  suburbs, 116
  urban renewal, 116
Twiss, Robert and R. Burton Litton, regional landscape, 142
Two-dimensional formats, 49, 56
True pictures, problems:
  caricature, 72
  faithfulness of color, 72
  light intensity, 72
  projective perspective, 72
Typological framework, 22

Udall, Stewart:
  atmospheric envelope, 142
  Johnson Administration, 142
  insidious threats, 142
Uniqueness, 112
United Kingdom, 28
United States, 28, 117
  belt line highways, 117
  early settlements, 116
  new towns, 117
  planned industrial towns, 116
US Department of Transportation guidance, 164
US Housing Act of 1937, community planning, 116
US wildland resource distribution:
  accessibility disparity, 84
  Alaska, 84
  effective acreage, 84
  per capita distribution, 84
  West, 84
Unit size, choosing a:
  assessment objectives, 106
  homoheterogeneity, 106
University of Washington:
  children's books, 105
  farm scenes, 105
  pictorial descriptions, 105
Urban, 116
Urban aesthetics:
  environmental impact statement (EIS), 226
  government decisions, 226
  personal and property rights, 226
  ease law:
    bill boards, 117, 225
    junkyards, 225
    US Supreme Court:
      Berman vs. Parker, 225
      Grand Central Terminal, 118, 226
      urban renewal, 225
      Washington State Supreme Court, Seattle, 226
      zoning, 226
Urban design, 26
Urban design review:
  design components, 118
  performance based, 118
  prescriptive, 118
  prototypes, 118
  standards, 118
Urban environmental aesthetics, review of, 118
Urban environmental situations:
  highrise buildings/residents, 130
  role of urban vegetation, 130
Urban landscape, 17, 19
Urban landscape visibility:
  changes in viewable area, 125
  observer, 125
  vantage points, 125
  viewshed, 125
Urban non-environment relationships:
  correlations of physical attributes, 130
  familiarity, 130
  preference for urban environment, 130
  role of:
    meaning, 130
    memory, 130
    perception, 130
    personality, 130
    symbols, 130
Urban planning, European, Paris:
  Hausmann, 116
  Napolean III, 116
Urban renewal, 26
Urbanscape at night, 126
Urban visual analysis, 116, 118
  combining expert and social science, 133
  decisions/actions, 117
  development of expert approach, 118
  new techniques, 135
  procedural guidance, 133
  professional/expert recording and analysis, 122
  social science approach, 129
Urban visual characteristics:
  site improvements, 227
  structures, 226
  users, 229
Urban visual impact(s):
  artistic elite:
    architecture, 224
    urban design, 224
  community appearance, 224
  cultural meaning, 224
  determining:
    site and environs:
      existing visual resources, 238
      view obstruction, 238
      visual contrast, 239
      visual quality, 239
      viewing conditions:
        artificial light, 237
        shadow, 236
        solar glare, 236
  environmental review process:
    design tradition, 224
    effects of alternatives, 224
    offsite visual impacts, 224
  evaluation of:
    criteria:
      artificial light, 242
      existing visual resources, 242
      shadow, 242
      solar glare, 242
      view obstruction, 242
      visual contrast, 242
      visual quality, 242
    significance:
      accurate visual simulations, 243
      degree of effect, 243
      number of viewers, 243
      types of viewer, 243
      visual setting, 243
  positive visual impacts, 224
  psychological well-being, 224
  research, 224
  visual character, 224
Urban visual impact assessment, major issues:
  illustrations of actual views:
    representative views, 225
    viewpoint selection, 225
  viewer constituencies:
    land use, 225
    view sensitivity, 225
  visual criteria:
    special review districts, 225
    visual vocabularies, 225
  visual resources:
    basic viewing conditions, 225
    displace resources, 225
    increase/decrease visual quality, 225
    modify visual character, 225
    replace, 225
  visually affected environment:
    mapping techniques, 225
    visibility analysis, 225
Urban visual studies, procedural guidance for, 133
uses, 229
Utilitarian values, 105

Validity:
  accuracy of measurement, 184
  content validity, 184
  cross-validation/conjoint validity, 184
  face validity, 184
  sensitivity, 185
  utility, 185
Validity and reliability, 18, 19

372 SUBJECT INDEX

Value judgments:
  nostalgic, 105
  real interpretations, 105
Vegetation, chromatic contrast within, camouflage, 281
Vegetation, seasonal changes, opacity, 281
Verbal landscape description, 96
  art history, 97
  cross disciplinary, 97
  geography, 97
  geomorphology, 97
  landscape architecture, 97
  philosophical aesthetics, 97
  psychology, 97
Vermont, scenic roads, 114
Vernacular design, 22
Vertical angle, 57
Vibrations, 65
Viewer positions, 55
Viewing analysis:
  moving viewers, 55
  stationary viewers, 55
View obstruction:
  field observations, 239
  lateral view extent, 238
  middleground, 238
  visual features, 238
Views to the project, target object, 56
Viewshed:
  angle of visual incidence, 292
  boundaries, 289
  consequences:
    alteration of view, 289
    modifying visual conditions, 289
  drawing methods, 289
  loss of sharpness at distance, 292
Viewshed, properties of:
  amount of area viewed, 292
  basin edges, 293
  basin holes, 293
  calculating the visual basin:
    contour lines, 293
    grid division, 293
    survey graph, 293
  compact visual basins, 293
  edge configuration, 293
  index of roughness, 294
  intervisibility, 294
  land shape, 293
  shadow zones, 293
  silhouette, 293
  visibility, 292
  visual basin:
    circular shaped, 293
    elongated shape, 293
    semi-circular, 293
  visibility conditions, 283
  visible area, 291
  visual basin, 283
Viewshed determination examples:
  automatic:
    cell-by-cell search, 288
    predetermination, 287
    sectorial search, 287

VIEWIT, 287
direct in-situ, 283
Hebblewaite method, 284
profiles, 284
selection of observation points, 290
Viewshed map, 57
Visibility, 45, 49, 62, 124, 283
  accuracy standards, 61
  analysis, 48
    data types, 59
    decision framework, 48
    phenomenon physics, 48
    simulation, 56
  criteria:
    background, 125
    foreground, 125
    middleground, 125
  effects of installation, 283
  future viewshed installation, 283
  influence zone, 283
  recognition threshold, 283
  visibility distance, 283
Visible area:
  flat area:
    earth's curvature, 291
    height reduction, 291
    light refraction, 291
    object height, 291
  visibility average conditions, 292
Vision, 69
  with cones, photopic, 43
  with rods, scotopic, 43
Visitor employed photography:
  respondent samples, 94
  self-selected landscape features, 94
Visual absorption capability (VAC), VAC factors:
  biophysical, 214
  perceptual, 214
  proposed activity, 214
Visual analysis, 16
Visual angle, 45, 53
Visual assessment, bias, 189
Visual assessment techniques, 104
Visual basin parameters, 293
Visual content, 158
Visual contrast:
  accurate simulations, 239
  Architecture in Context, 239
  public involvement, sampling, 239
  representative viewpoint, 239
  visual character, 239
Visual control points:
  directed photographs, 122
    map position and direction, 123
  motion photography:
    movie, 123
    video, 123
  random photographs, 123
  user-employed photography, 123
Visual criteria, 153
Visual data base, 135, 248
Visual description/representation criteria:
  accuracy and realism, 100

  comprehensibility and evaluatability, 100
  cost effectiveness, 100
  engagement, 100
  flexibility, 100
Visual descriptive approaches:
  photographs, 94
  sketches, 94
Visual detection, 45
Visual EAF Addendum, 154
Visual elements, characterize, data sheet, 123
Visual elements, typology of:
  type of view, 123
  viewer distance, 123
  viewer elevation, 123
Visual environment, affected:
  existing documentation, 229
  field observations, 229
  project information, 229
Visual exposure, viewsheds:
  nuclei, 283
  roads, 283
Visual field, 70
Visual fragility:
  biophysical factors, 280
    chromatic contrast:
      soil and vegetation, 280
      within vegetation, 281
    orientation, 281
    slope, 281
    soil and land cover, 280
    vegetative:
      density, 280
      height, 280
      seasonal changes of, 281
      strata diversity, 280
  historic and cultural factors, 282
  industrial installations, 278
  perceptual factors, 282
    area viewed, 282
    hollows/shadow zones, 282
    position in altitude, mean angle of incidence, 282
    viewshed shape, 282
  potential accessibility:
    distance, 278
    visibility, 278
    visual accessibility, 278
  visual absorption, 278
  visual fragility analysis, evaluation, 280
  visual quality, 278
  visual vulnerability, 278
Visual impact, scoping, 151
Visual impact analysis (VIA):
  controversy, 146
  environmental assessment, 146
  environmental impact assessment, 146
  significant environmental impact, 146
  visual mitigation, 146
Visual impact assessment (VIA):
  area or lineal studies, 202
  scenic corridors, 202
  point, or view specific, 202

SUBJECT INDEX 373

VIA, impacting activity/land use characteristics:
  project aesthetics:
    environmental, 214
    internal, 213
    relational, 213
  visual absorption capability (VAC), 214
VIA, role of simulations:
  analytical tool, 188
  design tool, 188
  documentary evidence, 188
  information device, 188
  response eliciting stimulus, 188
VIA, sensorial measurement:
  visual contrast, 297
  visual elements, 297
  visual dominance:
    median distances, 298
    position in space, 297
    scale, 297
    surrounding landscape, 296
  visual intrusion:
    dominant landscape components, 298
    industrial plant situation, 298
    maximum intrusion, 298
    visibility conditions, 298
  weights, 297
VIA, testimonial role:
  compatibility, 298
  cuestas, 298
  landscape content, 298
VIA, visual impact assessment and mitigation:
  contrast, 216
  generalizability, 218
  multiple evaluations, 218
  national visual management system, 218
  photographic documentation, 218
  rating sheet, 216
  reliability, 218
  sensitivity, 218
  validity, 218
  written documentation, 218
VIA applications framework:
  agency, 204
  model VIA format, 206
  private practitioner, 204
  research activity, 203
  VIA criteria, 205
VIA criteria summary, 205–206
VIA key viewpoints:
  simulation techniques, 190, 212
    Bureau of Land Management, 190
  Visual Simulation Techniques, 190
VIA key viewpoints analysis:
  scenic assessment, 212
  sensitivity analysis, 212
  simulation techniques, 212
VIA line-of-sight determinations, landscape control points, 211
VIA methodology research, 205
VIA model format:
  assessing impacting activity/land use characteristics, 213

key viewpoint analysis, 212
landscape description, 206
line-of-sight determination, 210
observer characteristics, 209
procedural guidance, 206
visual impact and mitigation summary, 216
VIA private practitioners, 204
VIA process:
  assessment process, 224
  perceptions, 224
  resources, 224
VIA systems application/research activity:
  British Columbia, 204
  private practitioners, 204
  research in VIA methodology, 205
  US Bureau of Land Management, 204
  US Forest Service, 203
Visual impacts, determination of, public involvement example:
  courtroom testimony, 240
  public response, 240
  sampling program, 240
  Shreveport, Louisiana, 240
Visual information, 70, 72, 250
  decisionmaking, 250
  distance, 251
  edges of visibility, 251
  evaluate information, 250
  factual information, 251
  invarients, 70, 72
    discontinuities, 70
    gradients, 70
    ratios, 70
  meaning:
    ambient, 250
    compositional interpretation, 250
    distance, 250
    manmade scenes, 250
    meaningful scenes, 250
    natural scenes, 250
    planning categories, 250
    semantic interpretation, 250
  observation point, 250
  viewing heights, 250
  viewing position, 250
  visual-aesthetic quality, 250
  visual topology:
    direct visibility, 250
    indirect visibility, 250
    invisibility, 250
Visual information system:
  general use:
    comprehensive planning, 252
    optimize conditions, 252
    optimize land use, 252
    viewing points, 252
  technical aspects:
    computers, 251
    decisionmaking, 251
    Fortran IV, 251
    information priorities, 251
    mathematical operations, 251
    observing point coordinates, 251

value interpretations, 251
view location, 251
visual sensitivity, 251
Visual management system (VMS), 14, 23
Visual model:
  testing of, future land use optimization:
    Kozarje, Yugoslavia, 254
    land use map, 256
    location optimization, 254
    synthesize thematic map, 256
    urban development optimization, 254
  use of:
    changes:
      visual data bank, 254
      visual message content, 254
    comparisons:
      computer processing, 254
      visual simulation, 254
    compositional qualities, 254
  Ljubljana Master Plan:
    location criteria, 257
    photographic material, 257
    public questionnaire, 257
    visual absorption, 257
    visual inventory, 257
    visual performance criteria, 257
    visual structure, changes in, 257
  panoramic photographs, 248
  photographic simulation, 259
  scenic values, 250
  Slovenian landscape:
    Ljubljana, 258
    new land use location, 258
    social values, 258
  tests:
    interactions between land uses, 259
    new/isolated land development, 259
    successive visual changes, 259
    visual absorption, 259
Visual notation system:
  The Image of the City, 94
  scenic notation, 94
Visual perception, 70, 76
Visual physiology:
  analysis implications, 46
  anatomy, 40
Visual public description:
  descriptive features, 92
  public consensus, 92
  user-defined record, 92
Visual quality:
  alternatives, 29
  decreasing, 12
  developed visual quality, underutilized areas, 240
  evaluation:
    aggregation, 296
    basic visual elements, 297
    capacity models, 295
    global evaluation, 296
    industrial plant, 297
    land classification, 295
    landscape components, 296
    subjective, 295

Visual quality (*Continued*)
   trained professionals, 296
   visual impact assessment, 297
   expert appraisal:
      delegation, 240
      well-defined criteria, 240
   recognized settings, 239
Visual range, 53
Visual resource(s), 106
   existing:
      official recognition, 238
      recognition:
         historic meaning, 238
         rarity, 238
         scientific value, 238
Visual resource management (VRM), 142
   classes of problems:
      detailed visual impact assessment, 164
      scoping potential visual impact, 151
      visual inventory/analysis for landscape planning, 145
   common elements:
      assessing people's attitude, 150
      use of landscape, 149
      visibility of landscape, 150
      geographic mapping of:
         priorities for professional attention, 150
         management objectives, 150
         visual quality maintenance levels, 150
      physically based landscape:
         inventory, 148
         visual quality evaluation, 148
   decisionmaking, 146
   decisionmaking process, 143
   federal agency activities, 146
   integration of scenic/visual values, 143
   interdisciplinary land use planning term, 146
   management of federal lands, 143
   need for development:
      environmental legislation, 144
      federal court cases, 143
      public concern, 143
   sensitivity analyses, 149
   in United States:
      historiographs, 144
      key agency administrators, 144
   visual impact assessment, 164
   visual inventory/evaluations, 148
   visual management objectives, 150
   VRM practitioner, 146
Visual simulation(s):
   defensibility, 199
   ease of understanding, 199
   future or proposed environment, 188
   images, 188
   models, 188
   objectivity, 199
   pictures, 188
   principles of, 188
Visual structure, pattern of nested solid angles, 69

Visual system, 70
Visual values, 13, 14

Washington, North Central Cascades, Alpine Lakes Wilderness Area, 87
Water Resources Council:
   scenic values, 142
   landscape continuum, 142
Water resources planning:
   Germany, 142
   Great Britain, 142
   United States, 142
Waugh, Frank:
   landscape engineering, 142
   National Forests, 142
Wave characteristics of light:
   amplitude, 44
   wave length, 44
Western United States, 54
White House Conference on Natural Beauty, 4, 14, 16
Wilderness Act of 1964, 82
Wilderness areas, 82
Wilderness definition, 82, 83
   absence of human habitation/improvements, 83
   experiential qualities, 83
   minimum size, 83
   naturalness, 83
Wilderness landscapes, 7
Wildland(s), 82, 84
   definition, 83
Wildland artistic renderings:
   Bierstadt, Alfred, 90
   Cole, Thomas, 90
   Holmes, William, Grand Canyon, 90
   Moran, Thomas, 90
Wildland contemporary photography:
   stereo aerial photography, 90
   video, 90
Wildland description:
   choice of methods:
      branching tree diagram, 88
      framework, 88
   historical and popular perspectives, 88
      artistic renderings, 90
      contemporary photography, 90
      verbal descriptions, 90
   professional vs. publically based methods, 90
   purposes, 86
   quantitative vs. non-quantitative approaches, 93
   selecting a procedure, 100
   sets of available criteria, 100
   verbal vs. visual approaches, 94
Wildland edge, 82
Wildland legislation:
   Migratory Bird Conservation Act of 1929, 83
   Migratory Bird Treaty Act of 1918, 83
   National Park Act of 1916, 83
   Organic Act of 1897, 83
   Swampland Act of 1850, 83

Wild and Scenic Rivers Act of 1968, 83
Wilderness Act of 1964, 83
Wildland management legislation:
   Federal Land Policy and Management Act of 1976, 84
   Multiple Use Sustained Yield Act of 1960, 83
   National Environmental Policy Act of 1969, 83
   National Forest Management Act of 1974, 84
Wildland ownership:
   federal government, 84
   private land owners, 85
   state and local governments, 84
Wildland planning, 84
Wildland protection, Wisconsin:
   scenic easements, 84
   state and county zoning, 84
Wild landscapes, 9, 82
Wildlands in the United States, 83:
   distribution, 85
   legislation, 83
   management, 85
   ownership, 84
Wildland values:
   economic values, 84
   recreation values, 84
   wildland aesthetic, 84
Wildland verbal descriptions:
   Abbey, Edward, 90
   Dutton, Clarence, Kanob desert, 90
   Leopold, Aldo, Wisconsin marsh, 90
   McPhee, John, 90
   Thoreau, Henry David, *Walden Pond*, 90
Wildland visual analysis division:
   professional/expert based, 90
   publically based, 90
Wright, Frank Lloyd, 8

Yellowstone National Park, 83
Yosemite National Park, 83
Yugoslavian study:
   automation system, 251, 264
   coded information, 251
   comprehensive planning, 248
   data bank, 248
   historic background:
      after the second World War, 248
      before the first World War, 248
      between the two wars, 248
   planning categories, 250
   research, 264
   urban and regional planning, 248
   visual-aesthetic analysis, 248
   visual-aesthetic relations:
      classical heuristic approach, 248
      solution spaces, 248
   visual data banks, 248
   visual evaluation, 263
Zube, E.H.:
   landscape continuum, 142
   paradigms, 18, 133